The Multi-Cultural Family

The Family, Law & Society
Series Editor: Michael D Freeman

Titles in the Series:

Parents and Children
Andrew Bainham

Marriage and Cohabitation
Alison Diduck

The Multi-Cultural Family
Ann Laquer Estin

Domestic Violence
Michael Freeman

Resolving Family Conflicts
Jana Singer and Jane Murphy

The Multi-Cultural Family

Edited by

Ann Laquer Estin

University of Iowa, USA

ASHGATE

© Ann Laquer Estin 2008. For copyright of individual articles please refer to the Acknowledgements.

All rights reserved. No part of this publication may be reproduced, stored in a retrieval system or transmitted in any form or by any means, electronic, mechanical, photocopying, recording or otherwise without the prior permission of the publisher.

Wherever possible, these reprints are made from a copy of the original printing, but these can themselves be of very variable quality. Whilst the publisher has made every effort to ensure the quality of the reprint, some variability may inevitably remain.

Published by
Ashgate Publishing Limited
Gower House
Croft Road
Aldershot
Hampshire GU11 3HR
England

Ashgate Publishing Company
Suite 420
101 Cherry Street
Burlington, VT 05401-4405
USA

Ashgate website: http://www.ashgate.com

British Library Cataloguing in Publication Data
The multi-cultural family. – (The family, law & society)
1. Minority families – Legal status, laws, etc. 2. Minority families – Legal status, laws, etc. – Western countries 3. Domestic relations 4. Muslim families – Legal status, laws, etc. – Western countries

Library of Congress Control Number: 2007941117

ISBN 978–0–7546–2648–0

Printed and bound in Great Britain by
TJ International Ltd, Padstow, Cornwall

Contents

Acknowledgements

The editor and publishers wish to thank the following for permission to use copyright material.

Arizona Journal of Internationa and Comparative Law for the essay: Antoinette Sedillo Lopez (2000), 'Evolving Indigenous Law: Navajo Marriage–Cultural Traditions and Modern Challenges', *Arizona Journal of International and Comparative Law*, **17**, pp. 283–307.

Azizah Y. al-Hibri (2003), 'An Islamic Perspective on Domestic Violence', *Fordham International Law Journal*, **27**, pp. 195–224. Copyright © 2003 Azizah Y. al-Hibri.

Blackwell Publishing Limited for the essays: Barbara Yngvesson (2002), 'Placing the "Gift Child" in Transnational Adoption', *Law and Society Review*, **36**, pp. 227–56. Copyright © 2002 Blackwell Publishing; James R. Coben (2002), 'Building a Bridge: Lessons Learned from Family Mediation Training for the Hmong Community of Minnesota', *Family Court Review*, **40**, pp. 338–49.

Copyright Clearance Center for the essays: Ann Laquer Estin (2004), 'Toward a Multicultural Family Law', *Family Law Quarterly*, **38**, pp. 501–27; Syed Mumtaz Ali and Enab Whitehouse (1992), 'The Reconstruction of the Constitution and the Case for Muslim Personal Law in Canada', *Journal of the Institute of Muslim Minority Affairs*, **13**, pp. 156–72. Copyright © 1992 Taylor & Francis Ltd; Lucy Carroll (1997), 'Muslim Women and "Islamic Divorce" in England', *Journal of Muslim Minority Affairs*, **17**, pp. 97–115. Copyright © 1997 Taylor & Francis Ltd.

Intersentia for the essay: Marie-Claire Foblets (2000), 'Migrant Women Caught Between Islamic Family Law and Women's Rights. The Search for the Appropriate "Connecting Factor" in International Family Law', *Maastricht Journal of European and Comparative Law*, **7**, pp. 11–34.

Johns Hopkins University Press for the essay: Carla Makhlouf Obermeyer (1995), 'A Cross-Cultural Perspective on Reproductive Rights', *Human Rights Quarterly*, **17**, pp. 366–81. Copyright © 1995 Johns Hopkins University Press.

Journal of Law and Family Studies for the essay: Jini L. Roby (2004), 'Understanding Sending Country's Traditions and Policies in International Adoptions: Avoiding Legal and Cultural Pitfalls', *Journal of Law and Family Studies*, **6**, pp. 303–22. Copyright © 2004 Journal of Law and Family Studies.

Loyola of Los Angeles International and Comparative Law Review for the essay: Marie Egan Provins (2005), 'Constructing an Islamic Institute of Civil Justice that Encourages Women's Rights', *Loyola of Los Angeles International and Comparative Law Review*, **27**, pp. 515–40.

David Novak (2000), 'Jewish Marriage and Civil Law: A Two-Way Street?', *George Washington Law Review*, **68**, pp. 1059–78. Copyright © 2000 David Novak.

Oxford University Press for the essays: Edwige Rude-Antoine (1991), 'Muslim Maghrebian Marriage in France: A Problem for Legal Pluralism', *International Journal of Law and the Family*, **5**, pp. 93–103. Copyright © 1991 Oxford University Press; John Murphy (2000), 'Rationality and Cultural Pluralism in the Non-Recognition of Foreign Marriages', *International and Comparative Law Quarterly*, **49**, pp. 643–59. Copyright © 2000 Oxford University Press; Jacinta Ruru (2005), 'Indigenous Peoples and Family Law: Issues in Aotearoa/New Zealand', *International Journal of Law, Policy and the Family*, **19**, pp. 327–45. Copyright © 2005 Oxford University Press; John Eekelaar (2004), 'Children Between Cultures', *International Journal of Law, Policy and the Family*, **18**, pp. 178–94. Copyright © 2004 Oxford University Press.

Russell Sage Foundation for the essay: Unni Wikan (2000), 'Citizenship on Trial: Nadia's Case', *Daedalus*, **129**, pp. 55–76. Copyright © 2000 Russell Sage Foundation.

Sydney Law Review for the essay: Patrick Parkinson (1994), 'Taking Multiculturalism Seriously: Marriage Law and the Rights of Minorities', *Sydney Law Review*, **16**, pp. 473–505. Copyright © 1994 Sydney Law Review.

University of California for the essay: Pratibha Jain (2005), 'Balancing Minority Rights and Gender Justice: The Impact of Protecting Multiculturalism on Women's Rights in India', *Berkeley Journal of International* Law, **23**, pp. 201–22. Copyright © 2005 Regents of the University of California.

UCLA Journal of International Law and Foreign Affairs for the essay: Ruth Halperin-Kaddari (2000–2001), 'Women, Religion and Muticulturalism in Israel', *UCLA Journal of International Law and Foreign Affairs*, **5**, pp. 339–66.

University of Toronto Press Incorporated for the essay: Annie Bunting (2004), 'Complicating Culture in Child Placement Decisions', *Canadian Journal of Women and Law*, **16**, pp. 137–64.

Leti Volpp (2000), 'Blaming Culture for Bad Behavior', *Yale Journal of Law & the Humanities*, **12**, pp. 89–116. Copyright © 2000 Leti Volpp.

Willamette Journal of International Law and Dispute Resolution for the essay: Alison Dundes Renteln (2002), 'Cross-Cultural Dispute Resolution: The Consequences of Conflicting Interpretations of Norms', *Willamette Journal of International Law and Dispute Resolution*, **10**, pp. 103–15. Copyright © 2002 Willamette Journal of International Law and Dispute Resolution.

Every effort has been made to trace all the copyright holders, but if any have been inadvertently overlooked the publishers will be pleased to make the necessary arrangement at the first opportunity.

Series Preface

The family is a central, even an iconic, institution of society. It is the quintessentially private space said, by Christopher Lasch, to be a 'haven in a heartless world'. The meanings of 'family' are not constant, but contingent and often ambiguous. The role of the law in relation to the family also shifts; there is increasing emphasis on alternative dispute mechanisms and on finding new ways of regulation. Shifts have been detected (by Simon Roberts among others) from 'command' to 'inducement', but it is not a one-way process and 'command' may once again be in the ascendancy as the state grapples with family recalcitrance on such issues as child support and contact (visitation) arrangements. Family law once meant little more than divorce and its (largely) economic consequences. The scope of the subject has now broadened to embrace a complex of relationships. The 'family of law' now extends to the gay, the transgendered, 'beyond conjugality', perhaps towards friendship. It meets new challenges with domestic violence and child abuse. It has had to respond to new demands – from women for more equal norms, from the gay community for the right to marry, from children (or their advocates) for rights unheard of when children were conveniently parcelled as items of property. The reproduction revolution has forced family law to confront the meaning of parentage; no longer can we cling to seeing 'mother' and 'father' in unproblematic terms. Nor is family law any longer a 'discrete entity', but it now interfaces with medical law, criminal law, housing law etc.

This series, containing volumes on marriage and other relationships (and not just cohabitation), on the parent–child relationship, on domestic violence, on methods of resolving family conflict and on pluralism within family law, reflects these tensions, conflicts and interfaces.

Each volume in the series contains leading and more out-of-the-way articles culled from a variety of sources. It is my belief, as also of the editors of individual volumes, that an understanding of family law requires us to go beyond conventional, orthodox legal literature – not that it is not relevant, and use is made of it. But to understand the context and the issues, it is necessary to reach beyond to specialist journals and to literature found in sociology, social administration, politics, philosophy, economics, psychology, history etc. The value of these volumes lies in their coverage as they offer access to materials in a convenient form which will not necessarily be available to students of family law.

They also offer learned and insightful introductions, essays of value in their own right and focused bibliographies to assist the pursuit of further study and research. Together they constitute a library of the best contemporary family law scholarship and an opportunity to explore the highways and byways of the subject. The volumes will be valuable to scholars (and students) of a range of disciplines, not just those who confront family law within a law curriculum, and it is hoped they will stimulate further family law scholarship.

MICHAEL D. FREEMAN
University College London

Introduction

Around the world, in an age of migration and globalization, families stretch across and between social, cultural and legal frameworks. Beyond the work that all families carry out, the multi-cultural family navigates a complicated balance of tradition and change, home and diaspora, community and autonomy. These families absorb many tensions born of transformation, and pose in turn new challenges for legal orders premised on more stable community membership and identity. This volume collects some of the literature on multi-cultural questions in family law, considering different manifestations of these issues in places from North America, Europe, Australia and New Zealand to Israel, India and South Africa.

The problems addressed here have their origins in the process of conquest and colonization of the Americas, Africa and Asia by Western European nations over several centuries. Colonizers spread their legal systems along with other aspects of their cultures, imposing their norms at different levels on the peoples they encountered. More recently, as waves of immigration have brought many people from the former colonies to live and work in the centres of economic power, the flow of cultural and legal practices has reversed. On both sides, our societies have been fundamentally changed by these processes, just as individual families have been.

A 'multi-cultural' family is one shaped by multiple cultural and legal frameworks. These frameworks often overlap with ethnic, racial, religious or national identities. In the law, issues of multi-cultural accommodation come to the forefront most readily and most often in the context of marriage and divorce, which mark the primary spot where the law intersects with families and thus with the broad range of social and cultural systems that families inhabit. The essays collected here address marriage and divorce conflicts, but also consider other friction points, including reproductive rights, domestic violence, adoption, child custody and family violence. Because working with multi-cultural families raises particular challenges for practitioners, a number of these pieces focus on dispute resolution in a multi-cultural context.

Multiculturalism has generated a large and interesting literature in philosophy and political theory which lies beyond the scope of this collection. In international law, the attempt to mediate and transcend cultural and political differences is reflected in human rights principles that apply to many questions of family law (see generally Estin, 2002). These norms have become part of the substantive or constitutional law of many countries and are referenced in various essays included here, but the larger subject of international human rights is also beyond the scope of this project. When legal decision-makers face the challenge of reconciling the claims of pluralism and individual rights in family law, their decisions are made within the parameters of a given legal system, which provide a far narrower range of options than might be available in the universe of theory. Some of the most interesting and important questions, however, concern the extent to which multi-cultural approaches can and should be permitted to shift or expand the normative boundaries of particular legal traditions.

Marriage and Divorce

Multi-cultural challenges and conflicts take a unique form in every nation, as a result of distinct historical, political, and social circumstances. Broadly conceived, however, there are several distinct patterns of multiculturalism. One pattern, familiar in Europe as well as in North America, Australia and New Zealand, emerges when a liberal democracy, with a largely secular and unitary family law system, faces claims by religious minority groups for accommodation of their distinct legal traditions. A second pattern, typical in the former European colonies in Asia, Africa and the Middle East, involves a pluralistic legal system in which personal status matters including family law are assigned to separate legal authorities based on the religious or cultural background or identity of the individuals concerned. A third pattern, which may overlap with either of the first two, arises from the tension between the law of a dominant society and the indigenous or customary law of non-immigrant minority groups.

Religious Minority Groups and the Secular State

The law of marriage and divorce in Europe and those countries with laws based on the European tradition is formally secular today, but it maintains a shape established by Christian tradition and ecclesiastical law. This is particularly evident in the qualifications for marriage and the restrictive approach to divorce of these legal systems. During the centuries when Jews were not allowed citizenship in these countries, Jewish communities retained autonomy to follow their own marriage and divorce practices, but the modern rule in the West extends national citizenship regardless of religion, and subjects all members of the national polity to the same system of family law.

For members of religious minority groups, whose traditional law is based on different principles, the ostensibly secular provisions of European marriage and divorce law present significant conflicts. The primary challenge for these broader societies is to establish and define the space within which members of different groups can maintain their religious and legal traditions. For group members, the challenge is to build institutions that work within the larger framework of a unitary legal system. In terms of constitutional or human rights, the central questions involve non-discrimination and the freedom of religion. Essays included in this volume address aspects of this problem in Australia, Canada, England, the United States, Belgium and France, considering a range of issues that arise for members of the Islamic and Jewish communities within these nations.

Part I begins with an overview of these issues in the United States. In 'Toward a Multicultural Family Law' (Chapter 1), Ann Laquer Estin assesses the treatment of distinct cultural or religious traditions in marriage, divorce and custody disputes, describing various accommodations of this diversity by the US courts and framing a set of limiting principles for this process. Estin observes that the argument for pluralism is supported by constitutional norms of religious freedom and the prohibition on racial or religious discrimination, while at the same time constrained by legal and constitutional norms of due process and gender equality.[1]

Patrick Parkinson reviews the Australian Law Reform Commission's work on multiculturalism and family law in 'Taking Multiculturalism Seriously: Marriage Law and the Rights of Minorities' (Chapter 2). The Commission's project represents a much more systematic and comprehensive approach to multiculturalism issues than the more ad hoc common law approach, and while Parkinson finds reasons to applaud the Commission's work, he also criticizes its hesitation to look beyond Western cultural values in its recommendations concerning the minimum age for marriage and the recognition of polygamous relationships. Ultimately, Parkinson believes that the normative boundaries for accommodation should not remain as narrowly drawn as the Commission proposes.

Edwige Rude-Antoine analyses issues faced by immigrants who have come to France from its former colonies in North Africa in 'Muslim Maghrebian Marriage in France: A Problem for Legal Pluralism' (Chapter 3). Based on the results of interviews conducted in two cities, Rude-Antoine describes the continuing importance within these communities of practices such as the father's role in approving his child's choice of a spouse, payment of dowry by the husband to the wife at the time of a marriage and traditional wedding rituals, and she juxtaposes this with the French commitment to civil regulation of marriage and a clear separation of the secular and the religious. In arguing for greater flexibility in the French system to resolve some of these cultural conflicts, Rude-Antoine acknowledges limits to pluralism which 'derive from the basic values and evolution of French society' (p. 75), but also identifies fundamental continuities between the Islamic and French approaches to these questions that should make it possible to find a basis on which the traditions can co-exist.

Writing about conflict of laws questions, Marie-Claire Foblets expands on these issues in 'Migrant Women Caught Between Islamic Family Law and Women's Rights: The Search for the Appropriate "Connecting Factor" in International Family Law' (Chapter 4). Reviewing the question of what law courts should apply in cross-border family law disputes, particularly where the parties have dual or mixed domicile or citizenship, Foblets puts the choice of law question at 'the very core of cross-cultural conflict management in contemporary multicultural society in Europe' (p. 94).[2] She looks closely at the case of Moroccan women claiming protection under the secular law in Belgium, based on reviewing case files and conducting interviews. Ultimately, Foblets recommends a rule that would let the parties determine what law should govern their relationship, subject to constraints based on principles such as the non-discrimination law of the host country.

John Murphy considers the invocation of public policy in English case law in 'Rationality and Cultural Pluralism in the Non-Recognition of Foreign Marriages' (Chapter 5).[3] Suggesting that broad assertions of 'public policy' may be seen as reflecting judicial cultural imperialism, Murphy argues that a clearer delineation of the particular concerns in any given context

---

1 One topic discussed here is the enforcement of religious marital agreements. Other articles addressing this question in the United States and Canada include Blenkhorn (2002), Fournier (2001) and Qaisi (2000).

2 There is a significant literature on the private international law questions triggered by different marriage rules and practices, such as unilateral divorce. See, for example, Reed (1996).

3 Other sources addressing these issues in England and Wales include Bainham (1996) and Poulter (1986). For Ireland, see Shúilleabháin (2002).

would be preferable. Murphy illustrates his broader argument, that clear identification of the competing cultural values at stake is important to the process of rational decision-making, with an analysis of the policy concerns in the area of child marriages. In Murphy's approach, 'where incommensurable cultural values exist and the courts (rightly or wrongly) are precommitted to the domestic cultural value' (p. 119), the competing values should be acknowledged even if they are ultimately excluded from the decision. As Murphy notes, the same approach could be taken to other conflicts that have developed around proxy marriages, forced or arranged marriages, or polygamy.

Forced marriages present a particularly difficult clash of values, and Unni Wikan's 'Citizenship on Trial: Nadia's Case' (Chapter 6) addresses a Norwegian case involving a young woman kidnapped by her parents and brought to Morocco, apparently with the goal of forcing her marriage.[4] In describing the subsequent efforts in Norway to procure her release and the prosecution of the parents that followed, Wikan places citizenship at the centre of her analysis, noting that the Norwegian citizenship of the family allowed the diplomatic intervention that returned Nadia to Norway. Citizenship also formed the basis for the court's verdict. Since the parents had chosen to become Norwegian citizens, the court insisted that they could maintain the customs of their country of birth only so long as those customs did not come into conflict with Norwegian law. In Wikan's account, rights of citizenship and laws providing for family reunification are a double-edged sword, since they expose the children of immigrants 'to immense pressure to comply with arranged marriages' (p. 139) giving rise to serious conflicts between 'cultural rights' and the human rights of individual citizens.

Taking a different perspective on what appear as forced marriage cases, Leti Volpp in 'Blaming Culture for Bad Behavior' (Chapter 7) compares narratives in which two groups of young women marry older men. She argues that when the actors involved are white, the behaviour is treated as an individual aberrance, but that when they are immigrants of colour the dominant narrative attributes the problematic behaviour to their culture.[5] She maintains that when this occurs, ethnic difference is equated with moral difference and is used to suggest that there are irreconcilable tensions between cultures. Volpp suggests that these are misreadings of culture, which 'prevent us from seeing, understanding, and struggling against specific relations of power – both within "other" cultures and our own' (pp. 144–45).

With their discussion paper on 'The Reconstruction of the Constitution and the Case for Muslim Personal Law in Canada' (Chapter 8), Syed Mumtaz Ali and Enab Whitehouse present a more muscular claim for multiculturalism. Linking the circumstances of Muslims in Canada to the sovereignty demands of Native peoples and French Canadians, Ali and Whitehouse argue that Canada's Muslims are denied true religious freedom by the lack of public funding for Islamic educational institutions and the obstacles to the creation of a system of Muslim personal and family law. They envision a separate legal regime for Muslims governing marriage, divorce, separation, maintenance, child support and inheritance, which would be available on a voluntary basis and in cooperation with the existing judicial system in Canada.[6]

4 Questions concerning forced marriage or the marriage of children are also addressed in international human rights law. See generally Bunting (2000) and Symington (2001).

5 While Volpp's focus here is on youthful marriages, she has made related arguments in the context of family violence: see, for example, Volpp (1994).

6 The proposal for Shari'a arbitration in Canada, discussed by Provins in Chapter 24, was made by Ali and the Islamic Institute for Civil Justice.

Ali and Whitehouse argue that neither the secular judicial system nor the informal efforts of the Muslim community have been 'adequate to the task of resolving these problems in a manner that really serves the needs of the Muslim community, as a community' (p. 186). This argument points to the dual nature of their argument for multiculturalism, which includes both a claim about the religious freedom of individuals and a claim about the rights of their religious community to autonomy and self-government in a sphere that would otherwise belong to the government.

Scholars have noted that Muslim personal law may operate even in the absence of official recognition of the type that Ali and Whitehouse advocate. Pearl and Menski describe the English Muslim law (or *angrezi shariat*) developed by institutions such as the Islamic Shari'a Council, which has become 'a dominant legal force within the various Muslim communities in Britain' (1998, p. 58).[7] Even within a voluntary system, however, there are important concerns about fairness and the treatment of women. Lucy Carroll's essay on 'Muslim Women and "Islamic Divorce" in England' (Chapter 9) suggests some of the complexities of the interaction between official and unofficial law as well as important reasons for caution in implementing a pluralist approach. With careful comparison to the Islamic law applied in Pakistan, Carroll identifies rulings of the Islamic Shari'a Council that have imposed unnecessarily harsh interpretations of Islamic law on South Asian women in divorce cases in England. Carroll argues that moderate and educated Muslims need to interest themselves in the question of Muslim law in a non-Muslim environment, and she observes that 'individual Muslim women who possess the strength of personal character and religious faith to take their own individual stands may push the community in more liberal and humane directions' (p. 203) (see also Ali, 2003). Both the Ali–Whitehouse essay and Carroll's chapter were written well before the recent controversy in Ontario over a proposal to allow Shari'a divorce arbitration, described by Provins in Chapter 24.

There are both parallels and distinctions between Islamic and Jewish religious law in their interactions with secular Western family law systems. In the Jewish community, concern has centred on a religious bill of divorce known as a *get*. A divorced woman cannot remarry within the tradition unless she has obtained a *get* from her husband in a proceeding supervised by a religious tribunal. The *get* requirement causes considerable hardship to observant Jewish women whose husbands are uncooperative and has generated a range of responses from secular courts and legislatures attempting to moderate these hardships in some manner.[8]

In 'Jewish Marriage and Civil Law: A Two-Way Street?' (Chapter 10), David Novak addresses the *get* problem and examines the question of accommodation between secular and religious law from a Jewish perspective. Novak sets out the traditional Jewish teachings on the interaction between religious and civil authority, including the principle that marriage as a sacrament is a subject exclusively within the jurisdiction of the Jewish community. For this reason, he rejects the view put forward by some scholars that Jewish marriage can be treated as a kind of civil contract, and expresses larger concerns with the attempt to create secular remedies for the *get* problem.[9] Novak concedes that resolving these dilemmas from within the

[7] For discussion of this issue in England, see also Poulter (1990).

[8] There is a large literature on the *get* problem; see, for example, Bleich (1984), Breitowitz (1993), Broyde (2001), Freeman (1996) and Zornberg (1995).

[9] For an attempt to address the *get* problem though prenuptial agreements that would be enforceable in civil court, see Herring and Auman (1996); also Greenberg-Kobrin (1999).

tradition 'requires a degree of unanimity in the Jewish community at large that is sadly absent at present' (p. 226), but argues that invoking an internal remedy would help in 'restoring the confidence of both Jewish women and men in the moral power of their own religious authorities' (p. 227).

Legal Pluralism and Women's Rights

Those countries that take a pluralist approach to the law of marriage and divorce are explicitly multi-cultural. Their legal systems incorporate multiple laws, each applicable to different segments of society, with jurisdiction defined on the basis of religion. Individual members of these constituent groups are subject to the regulation of the group in most matters concerning the family. The characteristic challenge for these societies lies in the tension between respect for the authority and autonomy of the group and the protection of the rights of individuals as citizens. Often, these questions are debated within the framework of international human rights, and particularly with reference to norms of gender equality. In these materials, India, South Africa and Israel stand as examples of pluralist systems, and several essays consider women's rights within Muslim tradition in the context of reproductive rights and spousal violence.

In 'Balancing Minority Rights and Gender Justice: The Impact of Protecting Multiculturalism on Women's Rights in India' (Chapter 11), Pratibha Jain considers the impact of granting group rights to religious and cultural minorities. After reviewing constitutional and statutory provisions that attempt to balance the rights of women and the rights of cultural minorities in India, Jain addresses efforts by the judiciary to confront these conflicts. She writes that 'while the Indian model of cultural pluralism aimed to provide minority groups with protection from the imposition of a dominant majority culture while simultaneously bridging gaps between various communities, the model has instead achieved the exact opposite result' (p. 249). Jain argues that the existence of parallel legal systems has reinforced separatist tendencies within India and reinforced patriarchal and traditional practices that have denied women their constitutional right to equal treatment.[10]

As in India, debates over the pluralist legal system in South Africa have centred on the conflict between customary norms and values of gender equality. In 'A Critical Analysis of Customary Marriages, *Bohali* and the South African Constitution' (Chapter 12), R. Songca notes the coexistence of both customary marriage, which permits polygamy, and civil monogamous marriage on the Western model. Songca discusses the arguments for abolishing polygamy and the practice of paying *bohali*, or bridewealth, which occurs with both types of marriage. The essay argues that both practices can be regulated to avoid abuses and protect women's interests.[11]

Ruth Halperin-Kaddari's essay, 'Women, Religion and Multiculturalism in Israel' (Chapter 13), extends the debate with an inquiry into women's status in the state of Israel. Noting that Israeli law places family law within the scope of religious authority, Halperin-Kadari argues

[10] On Hindu marriage and divorce law, see generally Basu (2001) and Duncan, Derrett and Krishnamurthy (1983). On the development of Muslim family law in South Asia, including Pakistan, see Haider (2000).

[11] Many writers have addressed these and related questions in South Africa, including Bennett (2000), Bonthuys and Erlank (2004), Fishbayn (1999) and Nhlapo (1995).

that this rule 'renders full equality for women impossible' (p. 272). She points out that both in constitutional terms and in its reservations to international human rights conventions, Israel has subordinated women's equality to religious cultural norms. Looking beyond family law, Halperin-Kaddari carefully charts the formal and informal ways in which the integration of religion with the state has served to limit women's full participation in civic or public life.[12]

Focusing on women's status in Islam, Carla Makhlouf Obermeyer provides 'A Cross-Cultural Perspective on Reproductive Rights' (Chapter 14). Obermeyer reviews the debate over universalism and relativism in the context of women's status and international human rights, and then suggests that the dichotomy between Western societies and those in the Middle East has been overdrawn. She goes on to describe commonalities and points of convergence and urges greater attention to the issues in their particular social and cultural contexts, observing that '[o]nly when we can comprehend local notions of rights can we begin the two-way process of translation and develop culturally relevant definitions and policies' (p. 309).[13]

Azizah Y. al-Hibri provides 'An Islamic Perspective on Domestic Violence' (Chapter 15). Challenging the view that Islamic tradition permits a husband to abuse his wife, al-Hibri works closely with the Qur'anic text to demonstrate that the tradition should be read as rejecting hierarchy and promoting harmonious marital relations. She argues that '[i]t is intolerable that any kind of violence, including domestic violence, be given religious cover and justification' (p. 312) and closes with the observation that early Muslim jurists agreed that wife abuse was a crime and that '[i]t is now time for the rest of the Muslim community to catch up with this vision' (p. 340).[14]

Indigenous and Customary Law

A third setting for multiculturalism questions involves indigenous or customary law and the norms of non-immigrant minority groups that exist in tension with a dominant legal system. Indigenous communities may be accorded a measure of self-government that includes regulation of marriage; in the United States, for example, Native American tribes continue to exercise governmental authority over family law questions. Alternatively, questions of customary or informal marriage and other traditions may surface in legal proceedings within the mainstream society or another more formal or westernized legal context. The issues are discussed in esseys here based on New Zealand and the United States and in a essay on the more general conflict of laws problems raised by customary law.

Jacinta Ruru discusses the recognition and use of Maori customary law in 'Indigenous Peoples and Family Law: Issues in Aotearoa/New Zealand' (Chapter 16).[15] Using marriage and property law and children and parenthood as case studies, Ruru asserts that the New

---

[12] The situation in Israel is also addressed in Cornaldi (1996) and Raday (1992). On the conflict between feminism and multiculturalism, see generally Okin (1999) and Volpp (2001).

[13] Other sources exploring the question of gender equality under Islamic law include al-Hibri (1997), Mashhour (2005) and Mayer (1991).

[14] For other cross-cultural analyses of family violence issues, including spousal abuse and child maltreatment, see Abu-Odeh (1997), Horsburgh (1995), Maguigan (1995), Renteln (2004), Terhune (1997) and Zion and Zion (1993).

[15] Maori family law issues are also discussed by Atkin and Austin (1996) and Swain (1995).

Zealand legislation and judicial decisions demonstrate an awareness that the Maori people have a culture-specific approach to these questions, and reflect an attempt to recognize and provide for Maori custom. She also argues, however, that the present law and policy papers fail to address the issue comprehensively.

In 'Evolving Indigenous Law: Navajo Marriage-Cultural Traditions and Modern Challenges' (Chapter 17), Antoinette Sedillo Lopez focuses on the largest Native American nation within the United States. She describes the work of Navajo tribal courts in reclaiming traditional values within a legal framework largely imposed by the dominant society. Based on these values, the Navajo courts have upheld marriages celebrated under tribal custom as 'common law' marriages. Lopez also discusses legislation by the Navajo Tribal Council expanding the range of circumstances in which the tribe will recognize marriages. Under federal law, the United States also recognizes Native American marriages that comply with tribal law or custom, and Lopez notes that historically this extended even to polygamous marriages.[16]

Recognition of marriages under informal or customary law is an issue that crosses national borders. Lona N. Laymon reviews the question in 'Valid-Where-Consummated: The Intersection of Customary Law Marriages and Formal Adjudication' (Chapter 18), considering the situation of both indigenous minority group members in a colonial setting and immigrant individuals who bring with them customary marriages from other nations. As she notes, these are issues that arise in many legal contexts, including divorce, property and financial rights, inheritance, insurance, public benefits, custody, adoption and immigration cases. Laymon considers both evidentiary difficulties involved in the proof of an unregistered customary marriage or divorce and public policy standards that may operate to deny recognition to some marriages. In addition, she discusses a variety of equitable doctrines and policies that may allow for accommodation of different practices but may also distort the meaning of those traditions in the process of fitting them into familiar legal categories.

Children

Across the globe, the broad consensus holds that legal decisions concerning a child should be based on the child's welfare or 'best interests'. In different cultural and legal systems, however, this standard is differently understood (see Alston, 1994 and An-Na'im, 1994). Resolving these differences is another multi-cultural challenge which has seen significant debate in the context of child marriage or practices that may cause physical harm to children. The essays included in Part II focus on questions concerning children and their own cultural identity, as well as the formation of parent–child relationships.

John Eekelaar's 'Children Between Cultures' (Chapter 19) begins with the premise that the basis for protection of cultural rights and practices is the obligation of the liberal state to treat all its members with respect, rather than an obligation owed to the communities themselves, and he asserts that the state must respect the interests of children in determining their own futures. Eekelaar discusses the fluidity of cultural identifications of people from mixed cultural and racial backgrounds, suggesting that in cases involving children it is often impossible to predict the child's long-term interests. He argues that while the state should respect the right

[16] On the family law jurisdiction of Native American groups, see Atwood (2000) and Zion and Zion (1993); also Goldberg-Ambrose (1994).

of parents to pass their religion or culture to their children, the state should intervene if the parents' actions would result in clear harm to the children or if one parent's attitudes would alienate the child from the other parent, that parent's culture or religion, or if the parent would 'close the children's mind entirely to the community around them' (p. 436).[17]

In 'Complicating Culture in Child Placement Decisions' (Chapter 20) Annie Bunting suggests that any consideration of culture and community in the placement of children must be attentive to the social contexts in which a child lives his or her life, and informed by fluid understandings of culture rather than essentialist conceptions of identity. Reviewing the Canadian cases and commentary on race and culture as factors in assessing a child's best interests, Bunting argues that race and culture are factors that ought to be weighed in these decisions, but that they should not be given critical or determinative weight at the risk of perpetuating racism rather than undermining it.

With international adoption, individual families may become multi-cultural in the sense of crossing and blending different racial, ethnic, national or religious affiliations. Jini Roby considers adoption practices in different cultural and legal contexts in 'Understanding Sending Country's Traditions and Policies in International Adoptions: Avoiding Legal and Cultural Pitfalls' (Chapter 21). Roby argues that understanding of factors such as the cultural traditions, religious beliefs and national child and family welfare policies of sending countries is critically important to a mutually respectful and dignified adoption process (see also Hearst, 2002).

In her challenging article, 'Placing the "Gift Child" in Transnational Adoption' (Chapter 22), Barbara Yngvesson examines the emphasis on consent and voluntarism in the practices of adoption, arguing that this emphasis can 'obscure the dependencies and inequalities that compel some of us to give birth to and give up our children, while constituting others as "free" to adopt them' (p. 492). In transnational adoptions, the state plays an important role in producing identity rights that move with the child, and also in establishing reproductive and other policies that produce physically abandoned children and in regulating the process by which these children may be moved across borders. Yngvesson explores both identity and enchainment, noting that these adoptions 'forge the most intimate international ties' (p. 507) and that they remain inherently incomplete, 'leaving open the possibility that a life story might connect the adoptee to *two* names, *two* nationalities (or more) and to multiple parents' (p. 509).

Multi-cultural Dispute Resolution

Lawyers and judges face the daily challenge of bringing distinct cultural traditions into a sort of dialogue as they work to resolve disputes within the multiple frameworks of particular families. All of the essays in this volume address this type of multi-cultural practice, but those in Part III focus on the process of dispute resolution. Another important consideration,

---

[17] Other sources on the treatment of religion in child custody disputes include Ahdar (1996), Mumford (1998) and Vahed (1999). These problems are particularly complex when they also involve an international law dimension; see, for example, Bruch (2000), Henderson (1997) and Starr (1998).

addressed only indirectly here, is the 'cultural competence' required of lawyers and judges who must translate norms of fairness and respect across linguistic and other boundaries.[18]

In 'Cross-Cultural Dispute Resolution: The Consequences of Conflicting Interpretations of Norms' (Chapter 23), Alison Dundes Renteln advocates broader consideration of traditional law, folkways and beliefs that may affect litigants' behaviour in legal disputes involving cultural differences (see also Renteln and Evans-Pritchard, 1994 and Renteln, 2004). Renteln describes her research into the 'cultural defence' as a form of applied legal pluralism, and her essay argues that 'general principles of law and human rights law require that national legal systems take into account the standards of the ethnic minority group' (p. 522). Renteln offers several examples of the kinds of disputes in which cultural evidence is important and raises the important question of how the specifics of a 'tradition' can be determined, particularly when there are divergent practices within the same ethnic or religious group.

In Canada, proposals to allow Muslims to settle family disputes under Shari'a law are explored by Marie Egan Provins in 'Constructing an Islamic Institute of Civil Justice that Encourages Women's Rights' (Chapter 24). Provins locates the issue in the context of Canadian and international laws and describes the recommendations to allow arbitration by religious tribunals made in 2004 by Marion Boyd after she was appointed to study the issue in Ontario (see Boyd, 2004). Provins describes the advantages and disadvantages of arbitration according to religious principles and reviews a number of controversial questions that might be subject to Shari'a arbitration. She notes that arbitration of various types of disputes also occurs in Jewish tribunals in Canada and while she supports allowing arbitration by religious courts as a matter of religious freedom, she argues at the same time for 'stricter guidelines to guard against inequality of women' (p. 537).[19]

Finally, James R. Coben discusses the incorporation of one ethnic minority group into a statewide mediation programme in 'Building a Bridge: Lessons Learned from Family Mediation Training for the Hmong Community of Minnesota' (Chapter 25). Cohen's essay discusses a 40-hour training programme in the Hmong language designed to allow participants to become certified as mediators for divorce and child custody matters.[20] The programme included opportunities for dialogue about those areas where Hmong tradition and Minnesota family law diverged, as well as presentations that emphasized subjects that 'were not open to cultural relativity' (p. 567). Coben identifies four such areas: 'domestic violence cannot be tolerated or negotiated, "self-help" to seize property or enforce judicial decisions is prohibited, bigamy is illegal, and underage marriages are voidable' (p. 567.) Beyond the introduction to family mediation, Coben notes that the Minnesota programme provided a forum for discussion of the painful challenges of assimilation and translation across cultural boundaries.

---

18 Regarding lawyering in cross-cultural contexts, see Bryant (2001), Razack (1998) and Tremblay (2002).

19 Provins's essay notes that Boyd's recommendations were rejected in Ontario in September 2005 (see also Blackstone, 2005). Note, however, that amendments in 2006 to the Ontario Arbitration Act and Family Law Act adopted many of Marion Boyd's recommendations, and would permit religious tribunals to arbitrate family disputes provided that all arbitration be conducted exclusively in accordance with the law of Ontario or another Canadian jurisdiction.

20 On mediation across cultures and in particular cultural contexts, see also Klock (2001) and Shah-Kazemi (2000).

Conclusion

Taken collectively, these essays suggest both the potential for multi-cultural dialogue and accommodation and important reasons for caution. Our globalized economic and social networks, and the ease with which we now cross geographic and national borders, permit an intensity of communication and interaction among peoples that is unparalleled in human history. But the acceleration of cultural exchange has heightened many deep and important differences between cultures, religions and world views. With these changes, the need for careful attention to difference and thoughtful translation between, across and within groups is every day more urgent.

References

Abu-Odeh, Lama (1997), 'Comparatively Speaking: The "Honor" of the "East" and the "Passion" of the "West"', *Utah Law Review*, **2**, pp. 287–307.

Ahdar, Rex (1996), 'Religion as a Factor in Custody and Access Disputes', *International Journal of Law, Policy and the Family*, **10**, pp. 177–204.

al-Hibri, Azizah Y. (1992), 'Marriage Laws in Muslim Countries: A Comparative Study of Certain Egyptian, Moroccan and Tunisian Marriage Laws', *International Review of Comparative Public Policy*, **4**, pp. 227–44.

al-Hibri, Azizah (1997), 'Islam, Law and Custom: Redefining Muslim Women's Rights', *American University Journal of International Law and Policy*, **12**, pp. 1–44.

Ali, Kecia (2003), 'Progressive Muslims and Islamic Jurisprudence: The Necessity for Critical Engagement with Marriage and Divorce Law', in Omid Safi (ed.), *Progressive Muslims: On Justice, Gender and Pluralism*, Oxford: Oneworld, pp. 163–89.

Alston, Philip (1994), 'The Best Interests Principle: Towards a Reconciliation of Culture and Human Rights', *International Journal of Law and the Family*, **8**, pp. 1–25.

An-Na'im, Abdullahi (1994), 'Cultural Transformation and Normative Consensus on the Best Interests of the Child', *International Journal of Law and the Family*, **8**, pp. 62–81.

Atkin, Bill and Austin, Graeme (1996), 'Cross-Cultural Challenges to Family Law in Aoteroa/New Zealand', in Nigel Lowe and Gillian Douglas (eds), *Families Across Frontiers*, The Hague: Kluwer Law International, pp. 327–45.

Atwood, Barbara Ann (2000), 'Tribal Jurisprudence and Cultural Meanings of the Family', *Nebraska Law Review*, **79**, pp. 577–655.

Bainham, Andrew (1996), 'Family Law in a Pluralistic Society: A View from England and Wales', in Nigel Lowe and Gillian Douglas (eds), *Families Across Frontiers*, The Hague: Kluwer Law International, pp. 295–307.

Basu, Monmayee (2001), *Hindu Women and Marriage Law: From Sacrament to Contract*, New Delhi: Oxford University Press.

Bennett, T.W. (2000), 'The Reform of Customary Marriage Law in South Africa', *Recht in Afrika*, pp. 1–24.

Blackstone, Laureve (2005), 'Courting Islam: Practical Alternatives to a Muslim Family Court in Ontario', *Brooklyn Journal of International Law*, **31**, pp. 207–51.

Bleich, J. David (1984), 'Jewish Divorce: Judicial Misconceptions and Possible Means of Civil Enforcement', *Connecticut Law Review*, **16**, pp. 201–89.

Blenkhorn, Lindsey (2002), 'Note: Islamic Marriage Contracts in American Courts: Interpreting Mahr Agreements as Prenuptials and Their Effect on Muslim Women', *Southern California Law Review*, **76**, pp. 189–234.

Bonthuys, Elsje and Erlank, Natasha (2004), 'The Interaction Between Civil and Customary Family Law Rules: Implications for African Women', *Journal of South African Law*, pp. 59–77.

Boyd, Marion (2004), 'Dispute Resolution in Family Law: Protecting Choice, Promoting Inclusion', available online at: http://www.attorneygeneral.jus.gov.on.ca/english/about/pubs/boyd/fullreport.pdf.

Breitowitz, Irving (1993), *Between Civil and Religious Law: The Plight of the Agunah in American Society*, Westport, CT: Greenwood Press.

Broyde, Michael J. (2001), *Marriage, Divorce and the Abandoned Wife in Jewish Law: A Conceptual Understanding of the Agunah Problem in America*, Hoboken, NJ: KTAV.

Bruch, Carol S. (2000), 'Religious Law, Secular Practices, and Children's Human Rights in Child Abduction Cases Under the Hague Child Abduction Convention', *New York University Journal of International Law and Policy*, **33**, pp. 49–58.

Bryant, Susan (2001), 'The Five Habits: Building Cross-Cultural Competence in Lawyers', *Clinical Law Review*, **8**, pp. 33–107.

Bunting, Annie (2000), 'Child Marriage', in Kelly D. Askin and Dorean M. Koenig (eds), *Women and International Human Rights Law*, vol. 2, Ardsley, NY: Transnational Publishers, pp. 669–96.

Cornaldi, Michael (1996), 'Protecting Minority Cultures and Religions in Matters of Personal Status Both Within State Boundaries and Beyond State Frontiers – The Israeli System', in Nigel Lowe and Gillian Douglas (eds), *Families Across Frontiers*, The Hague: Kluwer Law International, pp. 385–94.

Duncan, J., Derrett, M. and Krishnamurthy, T.K. (1983), 'Hindu Family Law', in Mary Ann Glendon (ed.), *International Encyclopedia of Comparative Law*, vol. 4 (ch. 11), Tübingen: Moore Siebeck, p. 80.

Estin, Ann Laquer (2002), 'Families and Children in International Law: An Introduction', *Transnational Law and Contemporary Problems*, **12**, pp. 271–306.

Fishbayn, Lisa (1999), 'Litigating the Right to Culture: Family Law in the New South Africa', *International Journal of Law, Policy and the Family*, **13**, pp. 147–73.

Fournier, Pascale (2001), 'The Erasure of Islamic Difference in Canadian and American Family Law Adjudication', *Journal of Law and Policy*, **10**, pp. 51–95.

Freeman, Michael (1996), 'Law, Religion and the State: The *Get* Revisited', in Nigel Lowe and Gillian Douglas (eds), *Families Across Frontiers*, The Hague: Kluwer Academic Publishers, pp. 361–83.

Haider, Nadya (2000), 'Islamic Legal Reform: The Case of Pakistan and Family Law', *Yale Journal of Law and Feminism*, **12** pp. 287–341.

Hearst, Alice (2002), 'Review Essay: Multiculturalism, Group Rights, and the Adoption Conundrum', *Law and Society Review*, **36**, pp. 489–506.

Henderson, Monica (1997), 'Note: U.S. State Court Review of Islamic Custody Decrees – When are Islamic Custody Decrees in the Child's Best Interests?', *Brandeis Journal of Family Law*, **36**, pp. 423–44.

Herring, Basil and Auman, Kenneth (1996), *The Prenuptial Agreement: Halakhic and Pastoral Considerations*, Northvale, NJ: Jason Aronson.

Horsburgh, Beverly (1995), 'Lifting the Veil of Secrecy: Domestic Violence in the Jewish Community', *Harvard Women's Law Journal*, **18**, pp. 171–217.

Klock, Kimberly A. (2001), 'Resolution of Domestic Disputes Through Extrajudicial Mechanisms in the United States and Asia: Neighborhood Justice Centers, the Panchayat, and the Mahalla', *Temple International and Comparative Law Journal*, **15**, pp. 275–77.

Maguigan, Holly (1995), 'Cultural Evidence and Male Violence: Are Feminist and Multiculturalist Reformers on a Collision Course in Criminal Courts?', *New York University Law Review*, **70**, pp. 36–99.

Mashhour, Amira (2005), 'Islamic Law and Gender Equality – Could There be a Common Ground? A Study of Divorce and Polygamy in Sharia Law and Contemporary Legislation in Tunisia and Egypt', *Human Rights Quarterly*, **27**, pp. 562–96.

Mayer, Ann Elizabeth (1991), 'Religious Law and Legal Pluralism: Islam and the State', *Cardozo Law Review*, **12**, pp. 1015–56.

Mumford, S.E. (1998), 'The Judicial Resolution of Disputes Involving Children and Religion', *International and Comparative Law Quarterly*, **47**, pp. 117–48.

Nhlapo, Thandabantu (1995), 'Cultural Diversity, Human Rights and the Family in Contemporary Africa: Lessons from the South African Constitutional Debate', *International Journal of Law and the Family*, **9**, pp. 208–25.

Okin, Susan Moller (1999), *Is Multi-culturalism Bad for Women?*, Princeton, NJ: Princeton University Press.

Pearl, David and Menski, Werner (1998), *Muslim Family Law* (3rd edn), London: Sweet and Maxwell.

Poulter, Sebastian (1986), *English Law and Ethnic Minority Customs*, London: Butterworth.

Poulter, Sebastian (1990), 'The Claim to a Separate System of Personal Law for British Muslims', in Chibli Mallat and Jane Connors (eds), *Islamic Family Law*, London: Graham and Trotman, pp. 147–66.

Qaisi, Ghada G. (2000), 'Note: Religious Marriage Contracts: Judicial Enforcement of Mahr Agreements in American Courts', *Journal of Law and Religion*, **15**, pp. 67–81.

Raday, Frances (1992), 'Israel – The Incorporation of a Religious Patriarchy in a Modern State', *International Review of Comparative Public Policy*, **4**, pp. 209–25.

Razack, Sherene (1998), *Looking White People in the Eye: Gender, Race and Culture in Courtrooms and Classrooms*, Toronto: University of Toronto Press.

Reed, Alan (1996), 'Transnational Non-Judicial Divorces: A Comparative Analysis of Recognition under English and U.S. Divorce Jurisprudence', *Loyola Los Angeles International and Comparative Law Journal*, **18**, pp. 311–37.

Renteln, Alison Dundes (2004), *The Cultural Defense*, Oxford: Oxford University Press.

Renteln, Alison Dundes and Evans-Pritchard, Deirdre (1994), 'The Interpretation and Distortion of Culture: A Hmong "Marriage by Capture" Case in Fresno, California', *Southern California Interdisciplinary Law Journal*, **4**, pp. 1–15.

Shah-Kazemi, Sonia Nourin (2000), 'Cross-cultural Mediation: A Critical View of the Dynamics of Culture in Family Disputes', *International Journal of Law, Policy and the Family*, **14**, pp. 302–25.

Shúilleabháin, Máire Ní (2002), 'Accommodating Cultural Diversity under Irish Family Law', *Dublin University Law Journal*, **24**, pp. 175–98.

Starr, June (1998), 'The Global Battlefield: Culture and International Child Custody Disputes at Century's End', *Arizona Journal of International and Comparative Law*, **15**, pp. 791–832.

Swain, David (1995), 'Family Group Conferences in Child Care and Protection in Youth Justice in Aotearoa/New Zealand', *International Journal of Law and the Family*, **9**, pp. 155–207.

Symington, Alison (2001), 'Dual Citizenship and Forced Marriages', *Dalhousie Journal of Legal Studies*, **10**, pp. 1–35.

Tremblay, Paul R. (2002), 'Interviewing and Counseling Across Cultures: Heuristics and Biases', *Clinical Law Review*, **9**, pp. 373–416.

Vahed, M.A. (1999), 'Should the Question: "What is in a Child's Best Interest?" be Judged According to the Child's Own Cultural and Religious Perspectives? The Case of the Muslim Child', *Comparative and International Law Journal of Southern Africa*, **32**, pp. 364–75.

Volpp, Leti (1994), '(Mis)identifying Culture: Asian Women and the "Cultural Defense"', *Harvard Women's Law Journal*, **17**, pp. 57–101.

Volpp, Leti (2001), 'Feminism Versus Multiculturalism', *Columbia Law Review*, **101**, pp. 1181–218.

Zornberg, Lisa (1995), 'Beyond the Constitution: Is the New York Get Legislation Good Law?', *Pace Law Review*, **15**, pp. 703–84.

Bibliography

Anderson, Sir Norman (1983), 'Islamic Family Law', in Mary Ann Glendon (ed.), *International Encyclopedia of Comparative Law*, vol. 4 (ch. 11), Tübingen: Moore Siebeck, p. 55.

Armstrong, Alice, Beyani, Chaloka, Himonga, Chuma, Kabeberi-Macharia, Janet, Molokomme, Athaliah, Ncube, Welshman, Nhlapo, Thandabantu; Rwezaura, Bart and Stewart, Julie (1993), 'Uncovering Reality: Excavating Women's Rights in African Family Law', *International Journal of Law and the Family*, **7**, pp. 314–69.

Berkovits, Bernhard (1990), 'Get and Talaq in English Law: Reflections on Law and Policy', in Chibli Mallat and Jane Connors (eds), *Islamic Family Law*, London: Graham and Trotman, pp. 119–46.

Breitowitz, Irving (1992), 'The Plight of the Agunah: A Study in Halacha, Contract, and the First Amendment', *Maryland Law Review*, **51**, pp. 312–421.

Browning, Don S., Green, M. Christian and Witte, John Jr (2006), *Sex, Marriage and Family in World Religions*, New York: Columbia University Press.

Broyde, Michael J. and Ausubel, Michael (eds) (2005), *Marriage, Sex and Family in Judaism*, Lanham, MD: Rowman & Littlefield.

Carroll, Lucy (1982), 'Talaq-Tafwid and Stipulations in a Muslim Marriage Contract: Important Means of Protecting the Position of the South Asian Muslim Wife', *Modern Asian Studies*, **16**, pp. 277–309.

Chanock, Martin (1989), 'Neither Customary nor Legal: African Customary Law in an Era of Family Law Reform', *International Journal of Law and the Family*, **3**, pp. 72–88.

Cherry, Kristen (2001), 'Marriage and Divorce Law in Pakistan and Iran: The Problem of Recognition', *Tulsa Journal of Comparative and International Law*, **9**(1), pp. 319–54.

Coomaraswamy, Radhika (2002), 'Identity Within: Cultural Relativism, Minority Rights and the Empowerment of Women', *George Washington International Law Review*, **34**, pp. 483–??.

Edge, Peter (2001), *Legal Responses to Religious Difference*, The Hague: Kluwer Law International.

Estin, Ann Laquer (2004), 'Embracing Tradition: Pluralism in American Family Law', *Maryland Law Review*, **63**, pp. 540–604.

Falk, Ze'ev W. (1983), 'Jewish Family Law', in Mary Ann Glendon (ed.), *International Encyclopedia of Comparative Law*, vol. 4 (ch. 11), Tübingen: Moore Siebeck, p. 28.

Foblets, Marie-Claire (1994), 'Community Justice Among Immigrant Family Members in France and Belgium', in René Kuppe and Richard Potz (eds), *Law and Anthropology: International Yearbook for Legal Anthropology*, vol. 7, Dordrecht: Martinus Nijhoff Publishers, pp. 371–85.

Fontes, Lisa Aronson (2005), *Child Abuse and Culture: Working with Diverse Families*, New York: Guilford Press.

Garg, Sampak P. (1998), 'Law and Religion: The Divorce Systems of India', *Tulsa Journal of Comparative and International Law*, **6**, pp. 1–20.

Ghanea, Nazila (2004), 'Human Rights of Religious Minorities and of Women in the Middle East', *Human Rights Quarterly*, **26**, pp. 705–29.

Glenn, H. Patrick (2000), *Legal Traditions of the World: Sustainable Diversity in Law*, New York: Oxford University Press.

Goldberg-Ambrose, Carole (1994), 'Heeding the "Voice" of Tribal Law in Indian Child Welfare Proceedings', in René Kuppe and Richard Potz (eds), *Law and Anthropology: International Yearbook for Legal Anthropology*, vol. 7, Dordrecht: Martinus Nijhoff Publishers, pp. 1–26.

Greenberg-Kobrin, Michelle (1999), 'Civil Enforceability of Religious Prenuptial Agreements', *Columbia Journal of Law and Social Problems*, **32**, pp. 359–400.
Griffiths, Anne (1997), *In the Shadow of Marriage: Gender and Justice in an African Community*, Chicago: University of Chicago Press.
Guthartz, Stacey A. (2004), 'Domestic Violence and the Jewish Community', *Michigan Journal of Gender and Law*, **11**, pp. 27–??.
Hamilton, Carolyn (1995), *Family, Law and Religion*, London: Sweet and Maxwell.
Hellum, Anne (2000), 'Review Essay: Human Rights and Gender Relations in Postcolonial Africa: Options and Limits for the Subjects of Legal Pluralism', *Law and Social Inquiry*, **25**, pp. 635–55.
Hing, Bill Ong (1993), 'Beyond the Rhetoric of Assimilation and Cultural Pluralism: Addressing the Tension of Separatism and Conflict in Immigration-Driven Multiracial Society', *California Law Review*, **81**, pp. 863–925.
Hooker, M.B. (1975), *Legal Pluralism: An Introduction to Colonial and Neo-Colonial Laws*, Oxford: Clarendon Press.
Jansen, Y.O. (2006), 'Unifying Babylon: Can Post-Colonial States Successfully Unify a Plural (Legal) Society?', *Widener Law Journal*, **16**, pp. 71–110.
Jessup, Owen (1992), 'Village Courts in Papua New Guinea: Constitutional and Gender Issues', *International Journal of Law and the Family*, **6**, pp. 401–16.
Kabeberi-Macharia, Janet (1992), 'Family Law and Gender in Kenya', *International Review of Comparative Public Policy*, **4**, pp. 193–207.
Karst, Kenneth (1986), 'Paths to Belonging: The Constitution and Cultural Identity', *North Carolina Law Review*, **64**, pp. 303–77.
Kearney, Pauline and McKenzie, Robin (1991), *Multiculturalism: Family Law*, Sydney, NSW: Law Reform Commission (Australia).
Kuenyehia, Akua (2006), 'Women, Marriage, and Intestate Succession in the Context of Legal Pluralism in Africa', *UC Davis Law Review*, **40**, pp. 385–404.
McGlynn, Clare (2006), *Families and the European Union: Law, Politics, and Pluralism*, Cambridge: Cambridge University Press.
Merin, Yuval (2005), 'The Right to Family Life and Civil Marriage under International Law and its Implementation in the State of Israel', *Boston College International and Comparative Law Review*, **28**, pp. 79–148.
Minow, Martha (1995), 'The Constitution and the Subgroup Question', *Indiana Law Journal*, **71**, pp. 1–26.
Motilla, Augustin (2004), 'Religious Pluralism in Spain: Striking the Balance Between Religious Freedom and Constitutional Rights', *Brigham Young University Law Review*, pp. 575–606.
Murphy, John (2000), *Ethnic Minorities, Their Families, and the Law*, Oxford: Hart Publishing.
Narayan, Uma (1997), *Dislocating Cultures: Identities, Traditions, and Third-World Feminism*, New York: Routledge.
Ncube, Welshman (1991), 'Dealing with Inequities in Customary Law: Action, Reaction and Social Change in Zimbabwe', *International Journal of Law and the Family*, **5**, pp. 58–79.
Nichols, Joel A. (2007), 'Multi-tiered Marriage: Ideas and Influences from New York and Louisiana to the International Community', *Vanderbilt Journal of Transnational Law*, **40**, pp. 135–96.
Ocran, Modibo (2006), 'The Clash of Legal Cultures: The Treatment of Indigenous Law in Colonial and Post-colonial Africa', *Akron Law Review*, **39**, pp. 465–82.
Opperman, Brenda (2006), 'The Impact of Legal Pluralism on Women's Status: An Examination of Marriage Laws in Egypt, South Africa, and the United States', *Hastings Women's Law Journal*, **17**, pp. 65–92.

Parkinson, Patrick (1996), 'Multiculturalism and the Regulation of Marital Status in Australia', in Nigel Lowe and Gillian Douglas (eds), *Families Across Frontiers*, The Hague: Kluwer Law International, pp. 309–26.

Perry, Twila L. (1998), 'Transracial Adoption: Mothers, Hierarchy, Race and Feminist Legal Theory', *Yale Journal of Law and Feminism*, **10**, pp. 101–64.

Poulter, Sebastian (1988), 'Review Essay: Cultural Pluralism in Australia', *International Journal of Law and the Family*, **2**, pp. 127–33.

Quick, Abdul Hakim (1998), 'Al-Mu'allaqa: The Muslim Woman Between Divorce and Real Marriage', *The Journal of Islamic Law*, **3**, pp. 27–40.

Quraishi, Asifa and Syeed-Miller, Najeeba (2004), 'No Altars: A Survey of Islamic Family Law in the United States', in Lynn Welchman (ed.), *Women's Rights and Islamic Family Law*, London: Zed Books, pp. 177–229.

Rahmatian, Andreas (1996), 'Termination of Marriage in Nigerian Family Laws: The Need for Reform and the Relevance of the Tanzanian Experience', *International Journal of Law, Policy and the Family*, **10**, pp. 281–316.

Rajan, Rajeswari Sunder (2003), *The Scandal of the State: Women, Law, and Citizenship in Postcolonial India*, Durham, NC: Duke University Press.

Rosettenstein, David S. (1995), 'Transracial Adoption in the United States and the Impact of Considerations Relating to Minority Population Groups on International Adoptions in the United States', *International Journal of Law and the Family*, **9**, pp. 131–54.

Sarat, Austin and Berkowitz, Roger (1994), 'Disorderly Differences: Recognition, Accommodation, and American Law', *Yale Journal of Law and the Humanities*, **6**, pp. 285–316.

Shachar, Ayelet (2001), *Multicultural Jurisdictions: Cultural Differences and Women's Rights*, Cambridge: Cambridge University Press.

Shachar, Ayelet (2005), 'Religion, State, and the Problem of Gender: New Modes of Citizenship and Governance in Diverse Societies', *McGill Law Journal*, **50**, pp. 49–88.

Shah, Prakash A. (2003), 'Attitudes to Polygamy in English Law,' *International and Comparative Law Quarterly*, **52**, pp. 369–400.

Shenje-Peyton, Angeline (1996), 'Balancing Gender, Equality, and Cultural Identity: Marriage Payments in Post-Colonial Zimbabwe', *Harvard Human Rights Journal*, **9**, pp. 105–44.

Shweder, Richard A., Minow, Martha and Markus, Hazel Rose (eds) (2002), *Engaging Cultural Differences: The Multicultural Challenge in Liberal Democracies*, New York: Russell Sage Foundation.

Stolzenberg, Nomi Maya and Myers, David N. (1992), 'Community, Constitution and Culture: The Case of the Jewish Kehilah', *University of Michigan Journal of Law Reform*, **25**, pp. 633–70.

Sullivan, Donna J. (1992), 'Gender Equality and Religious Freedom: Toward a Framework for Conflict Resolution', *International Law and Politics*, **24**, pp. 795–856.

Sunder, Madhavi (2001), 'Cultural Dissent', *Stanford Law Review*, **54**, pp. 495–567.

Terhune, Cassandra (1997), 'Comment: Cultural and Religious Defenses to Child Abuse and Neglect', *Journal of the American Academy of Matrimonial Lawyers*, **14**, pp. 152–92.

Uzoma, Rose C. (2004), 'Religious Pluralism, Cultural Differences, and Social Stability in Nigeria', *Brigham Young University Law Review*, pp. 651–64.

Volpp, Leti (1996), 'Talking "Culture": Gender, Race, Nation and the Politics of Multiculturalism', *Columbia Law Review*, **96**, pp. 1573–617.

Wegner, Judith Romney (1982), 'The Status of Women in Jewish and Islamic Marriage and Divorce Law', *Harvard Women's Law Journal*, **5**, pp. 1–33.

Weisbrod, Carol (1999), 'Universals and Particulars: A Comment on Women's Human Rights and Religious Marriage Contracts', *Southern California Review of Law and Women's Studies*, **9**, pp. 77–97.

Wing, Adrien Katherine (2001), 'Polygamy for Southern Africa to Black Britannia to Black America: Global Critical Race Feminism as Legal Reform for the Twenty-first Century', *Journal of Contemporary Legal Issues*, **11**, pp. 811–80.

Witte, John Jr (1997), *From Sacrament to Contract: Marriage, Religion and the Law in the Western Tradition*, Louisville, KY: Westminster John Knox Press.

Yilmaz, Ihsan (2005), *Muslim Laws, Politics and Society in Modern Nation States*, Aldershot: Ashgate.

Zahraa, Mahdi and Malek, Normi A. (1998), 'The Concept of Custody in Islamic Law', *Arab Law Quarterly*, pp. 155–77.

Zion, James W. and Zion, Elise B. (1993), 'Hozho' Sokee' – Stay Together Nicely: Domestic Violence under Navajo Common Law', *Arizona State Law Journal*, **25**, pp. 407–26.

Part I
Marriage and Divorce

Religious Minority Groups and the Secular State

[1]

Toward a Multicultural Family Law

ANN LAQUER ESTIN*

I. Introduction

As the United States becomes a more diverse and multicultural society, law and legal institutions face new challenges. In the criminal law, there is the complicated question of when a defendant's conduct may be excused on the basis of a "cultural defense."[1] For family law, there are issues posed for courts when disputes involve unfamiliar ethnic, religious, and legal traditions. Over the past two decades, courts around the country have encountered Islamic and Hindu wedding celebrations, Muslim and Jewish premarital agreements, and divorce arbitration in rabbinic tribunals. In these cases, courts have struggled to understand and accommodate the tremendous cultural and religious diversity of America today within a legal framework established long ago.[2]

The project of building a multicultural family law is complicated by the fact that American family law is based on specifically Christian norms. In England, before the colonization of North America, family law was ecclesiastical law, and it remained within the jurisdiction of the church until the mid-nineteenth century.[3] Although jurisdiction over family matters in the American colonies was in secular courts, the content of our early family

---

* Professor of Law, University of Iowa. A longer version of this paper was published as *Embracing Tradition: Pluralism in American Family Law*, 63 MD. L. REV. 540 (2004).

1. *See generally* JAMES G. CONNELL, CULTURAL ISSUES IN CRIMINAL DEFENSE (2000). These are controversial and difficult problems, particularly in the context of family violence. *See, e.g.*, Holly Maguigan, *Cultural Evidence and Male Violence: Are Feminist and Multiculturalist Reformers on a Collision Course in Criminal Courts?*, 70 N.Y.U. L. REV. 36 (1995); Cassandra Terhune, *Comment, Cultural and Religious Defenses to Child Abuse and Neglect*, 14 J. AM. ACAD. MATRIM. LAW. 152 (1997). *See also* Alison Dundes Renteln, THE CULTURAL DEFENSE (2004).

2. Courts in England, France, Canada and other western, industrialized nations face similar questions. *See, e.g.*, SEBASTIAN POULTER, ENGLISH LAW AND ETHNIC MINORITY CUSTOMS (1986).

3. *See* HOMER H. CLARK, JR., THE LAW OF DOMESTIC RELATIONS IN THE UNITED STATES (2d ed. 1988) 22-23 (marriage requirements), 125 (annulment), 406-07 (divorce).

law was firmly rooted in English ecclesiastical law.[4] Beyond the specific legal rules governing marriage, annulment, and divorce, American marriage policies grew from a set of religious and political ideas that were directly enforced through governmental policies over more than a century.[5] Family law rules appear to be secular and neutral to the contemporary observer, but they still reflect this religious heritage. As a result, our rules do not always fit well with practices drawn from different traditions, and it can be difficult to determine to what extent accommodation is appropriate.

This article reviews a number of areas in which cultural and religious accommodation has become an issue in private family law disputes. Part I considers the circumstances in which courts extend recognition and respect to marriages, divorces, and custody decrees which originate within a particular tradition and which differ in significant respects from the model that is more familiar in our legal culture. Part II describes courts' responses to cases that raise questions of religious law or practice in the context of marriage and divorce. Part III offers some reflections on the process of accommodation, arguing that the courts' decisions in these cases demonstrate the importance of incorporating this diversity within a larger framework of fundamental values established in American and international law.

I. Recognition and Respect: Marriage, Divorce, and Custody

As people and families move across geographic and cultural boundaries, their legal circumstances become complicated by the variation in laws and customs governing marriage, divorce, and parental status.[6] Over generations, the principles of conflict of laws or "private international law" have evolved to help coordinate this diversity. As patterns of movement around the globe have shifted, however, individuals are more likely to maintain their connections within multiple social and legal frames.

A. Marriage

Traditional conflict of laws principles applied in the United States hold that a marriage valid in the place of celebration is valid everywhere.[7] This

4. *Id. See also* MICHAEL GROSSBERG, GOVERNING THE HEARTH: LAW AND THE FAMILY IN NINETEENTH-CENTURY AMERICA 34, 65-66, 103-13, 197-98 (1985).

5. *See generally* NANCY F. COTT, PUBLIC VOWS: A HISTORY OF MARRIAGE AND THE NATION (2001).

6. *See generally* Ann Laquer Estin, *Families and Children in International Law: An Introduction*, 12 TRANSNAT'L L. & CONTEMP. PROBS. 271 (2002).

7. EUGENE F. SCOLES ET AL., CONFLICT OF LAWS §13.5 (3d ed. 2000). This rule is incorporated into state marriage statutes in some jurisdictions, including those based on the UNIFORM MARRIAGE & DIVORCE ACT § 210, 9A U.L.A. 194 (1998). A few state statutes, based on the Uniform Marriage Evasion Act, provide that a marriage of domiciliaries formalized in another state will not be recognized if it is void under the law of the parties' domicile. *See* CLARK, *supra* note 3, at 42; SCOLES, *Id.*, at § 13.13.

rule is based on a policy judgment that the state where a marriage is solemnized is best able to guarantee that it was based on the free consent of the parties, and on a broader policy in favor of sustaining the validity of marriages.[8] Marriage validation policies apply most strongly when parties have relied on the validity of their marriage over time, when the challenge to the marriage is made by a third party, or when the defects relate to formalization rather than substantive marriage restrictions.[9] The policy is traditionally subject to narrow exceptions, "when a claimed incident of the marriage is sought to be enjoyed in a state where such enjoyment violates strong public policy," such as the policies against incestuous or polygamous marriages.[10] Private international law principles on marriage recognition are similar to the ones established in the United States. The Convention on Celebration and Recognition of the Validity of Marriages,[11] adopted by the Hague Conference on Private International Law in 1977, reflects a strong marriage validation policy with a provision permitting states to refuse recognition to marriages on grounds of public policy.

1. SOLEMNIZATION AND CONSENT

Laws in the United States permit marriages to be formalized by either civil or religious authorities, after the parties have obtained a marriage license.[12] State laws vary in terms of requirements for marriage ceremonies, with some listing specific clergy who may officiate and others providing broadly for solemnization in accordance with the traditions of "any religious denomination, Indian Nation or Tribe, or Native Group."[13] Statutes that appear to deny to some religious groups the right to celebrate marriages within their own traditions present an obvious constitutional problem, and a court may choose to interpret such a statute broadly to avoid this result.[14]

8. SCOLES, *supra* note 7, at 543-44; CLARK, *supra* note 3, at 41-44. Because of the strong marriage validation policy, a marriage is sometimes upheld under the law of the parties' domicile even if the marriage was not valid under the law of the place of celebration.

9. *Id.* at 544-45. *See also* RESTATEMENT (SECOND) OF CONFLICT OF LAWS § 283 (1971) ("validity of a marriage will be determined by the local law of the state which, with respect to the particular issue, has the most significant relationship to the spouses and the marriage").

10. SCOLES ET AL., *supra* note 7, at § 13.5. Historically, state laws prohibiting racial intermarriage were also considered to state a "strong public policy," which was the basis for denying recognition to an out-of-state interracial marriage. *See id.* §13.10.

11. Opened to signature Oct. 1, 1977, Misc. 11 (1977) command paper 6930, reprinted in 16 I.L.M. 18 (1977). *See* http://www.hcch.e-vision.ni/index—Hague Conference on International Law. *See generally* Willis L.M. Reese, *The Hague Convention on Celebration and Recognition of the Validity of Marriages*, 20 VA. J. INT'L L. 25 (1979).

12. *See generally* CLARK, *supra* note 3, § 2.3. A small group of states also recognize informal or "common law" marriages, which generally involve neither a license nor a ceremony; *see id.* § 2.4.

13. UNIF. MARRIAGE & DIVORCE ACT § 206, 9A U.L.A. 182 (1998).

14. *See* Persad v. Balram, 724 N.Y.S.2d 560 (Sup. Ct. 2001).

Case law in many states sustains the validity of marriages even when the statutory formalities were not properly followed. A marriage may be upheld despite a failure to obtain or properly record a license, or despite the fact that the official or clergy member who celebrated the marriage was not legally qualified to perform marriages.[15] This approach is easily extended to marriages celebrated with different customs or traditions. Thus, in *Aghili v. Saadatnejadi*,[16] the parties obtained a marriage license in Tennessee and had an Islamic wedding blessing performed by an *imam*. Several weeks later, they had a formal wedding reception and began living together as husband and wife. Although the husband later disputed the validity of the marriage, arguing that the license had not been properly returned after the ceremony and that the *imam* was not authorized to perform marriages, the court upheld the validity of the marriage. In *Persad v. Balram*,[17] the wedding celebration was a two-hour "Hindu marriage or 'prayer' ceremony" conducted by a Hindu priest, or *pandit*, before 100 to 150 guests at the bride's home. When the husband challenged the validity of the marriage seven years later, the court rejected his arguments despite evidence that the parties had not complied with the New York marriage statutes.

Sometimes, however, the gap between traditions is harder to bridge. In *Farah v. Farah*,[18] the court had a more difficult time assimilating unfamiliar marriage customs within the traditional conflict of laws norms. After the couple signed a marriage contract described as a "proxy marriage form," or *nikah*, in Virginia, their marriage was concluded by their representatives in an Islamic ceremony in England. A month later, the couple traveled briefly from Virginia to Pakistan for a formal wedding reception, or *rukhsati*, which "symbolizes the sending away of the bride with her husband." When the husband challenged the validity of the marriage a year later, the appellate court looked to the law of England, and concluded that the marriage was not valid because the proxy ceremony did not conform with the requirements of English law.[19] Although this analysis was based on the traditional conflict of laws rule, the court's ruling contradicts the marriage validation policy and was not a necessary result. In other cases American courts have extended the presumption favoring marriage to religious or traditional marriages solemnized in other countries,

15. *E.g.*, Carabetta v. Carabetta, 438 A.2d 109 (Conn. 1980); *but see, e.g.*, Moran v. Moran, 933 P.2d 1207 (Ariz. Ct. App. 1996). *See generally* CLARK, *supra* note 3, at 40-41.

16. Aghili v. Saadatnejadi, 958 S.W.2d 784 (Tenn. Ct. App. 1997).

17. Persad v. Balram, 724 N.Y.S.2d 560 (Sup. Ct. 2001).

18. Farah v. Farah, 429 S.E.2d 626 (Va. Ct. App. 1993).

19. The court rejected the possibility that the marriage could be held valid by application of Islamic law, since the marriage was not "performed" in Pakistan.

despite evidence of defects in the formalization process. For example, in *Xiong v. Xiong*,[20] the court sustained the validity of a marriage celebrated in a traditional Hmong ceremony in Laos in 1975 by a couple about to flee from the country. Acknowledging that the couple had not complied with the formalities required by the Laotian government, the court determined that the marriage should be upheld as a putative marriage, based on their good faith belief in its validity.

Beyond the question of formalities, the question of marital consent may arise in different cultural contexts. In some traditions, marriages may be arranged by relatives, a practice that does not present difficulties so long as both the bride and groom give their consent. Traditions in which a father or guardian has the authority and the right to consent to marriage on behalf of his child or ward are more problematic. Norms of both domestic and international law mandate that marriage be based on the free and full consent of the parties,[21] and in this context the court's obligation is to support an individual's right to make this decision in the face of pressures to conform to traditional roles. When consent has not been freely given, courts have the power to grant an annulment. In *Singh v. Singh*,[22] a New York court inquired carefully into the circumstances of a Hindu marriage celebrated in India, and granted an annulment because the bride had refused to perform an essential part of the ritual known as the "seven steps" or *saptapadi*. This type of careful determination of consent is particularly important in cases involving youthful marriages, notwithstanding the fact that some states permit the marriage of young teenagers with their parents' approval.[23]

Expanded marriage recognition rules, which uphold the validity of marriages celebrated in diverse cultural settings, are an easy first step toward a multicultural family law. This approach honors the choices and expectations of individuals and their communities, and frequently serves

20. Xiong *ex rel.*, Edmondson v. Xiong, 648 N.W.2d 900 (Wis. Ct. App. 2002). *See also* Amsellem v. Amsellem, 730 N.Y.S.2d 212 (Sup. Ct. 2001) (extending recognition to religious marriage concluded in France without civil ceremony).

21. *See* Article 16 of the Universal Declaration of Human Rights, G.A. Res. 217A, U.N. GAOR, 3rd Sess., pt.1, Resolutions, at 71, U.N. Doc. A/810 (1948) ("[m]arriage shall be entered into only with the free and full consent of the intending spouses") and United Nations Convention on Consent to Marriage, Minimum Age for Marriage, and Registration of Marriages, art. 1(1) 521 U.N.T.S. 231, *available at* http://www.unhchr.ch/html/menu3/b/63.htm, (U.N. Marriage Convention) (1962). *See also* Convention on the Elimination of all Forms of Discrimination Against Women [hereinafter CEDAW], art. 16 (1)(b) and (2), 19 I.L.M. 33 (1980) (CEDAW).

22. Singh v. Singh, 325 N.Y.S.2d 590 (Sup. Ct. 1971). *See also* In the Marriage of S, 5 Fam. LR 831 (Family Court 1980) (Australia); Hirani v. Hirani, (1983) 4 FLR 232 (Court of Appeal – Civil Division) (England).

23. *See infra* notes 29-34 and accompanying text.

506 *Family Law Quarterly, Volume 38, Number 3, Fall 2004*

to protect a financially vulnerable spouse who might otherwise be left without the legal remedies available to a legal spouse.

2. Marital Capacity

Questions of marital capacity present a more difficult case for accommodation. In conflict of laws, substantive marriage prohibitions have been a basis for denying recognition to marriages as a matter of public policy, particularly if a marriage is one that violates the law of the state in which the parties are domiciled.[24] Historically, these conflicts have sometimes concerned the variations in degree of family relationship permitted between spouses.[25] These differences, many of which trace to ecclesiastical law, seem relatively minor until our field of vision widens to include a broader range of religious and cultural traditions. Enforcement of the stricter limitations may have a significant impact on individuals and families from within these traditions.[26] Recognizing this possibility, some marriage statutes include exceptions that acknowledge these differences.[27] In addition, courts may have discretion to uphold such a marriage if it was valid where celebrated, particularly when the parties have relied on its validity for a significant period of time.[28]

Another set of questions concerns the minimum age for marriage. In international law, the betrothal or marriage of children is discouraged.[29] Most

24. Scoles et al., *supra* note 7, § 13.8. Most legal systems outside the U.S. assess the formal validity of a marriage based on the law of the place of celebration, and its substantive validity based on the personal law of the parties, which may be either the law of their domicile or nationality. *Id.* at 547-48.

25. State laws vary as to whether first cousins marriage or uncle-niece and aunt-nephew marriages are allowed. *See* Clark, *supra* note 3, § 2.9. *See also* Martin Ottenheimer, Forbidden Relatives: The American Myth of Cousin Marriage (1996); Denise Grady, *No Genetic Reason to Discourage Cousin Marriage, Study Finds*, N.Y. Times, Apr. 3, 2002.

26. *See id.* at 82-84; *see generally* Poulter, *supra* note 2, at 8-16.

27. *E.g.*, R.I. Gen. Laws (2003) § 15-1-4 (exception for marriages "solemnized among the Jewish people within the degrees of affinity or consanguinity allowed by their religion"); Unif. Marriage and Divorce Act § 207(a)(3), 9A U.L.A. pt. 1 183 (1998) (uncle-niece marriage and aunt-nephew marriage allowed if "permitted by the established customs of aboriginal cultures").

28. *E.g.*, *In re* May's Estate, 114 N.E.2d 4 (N.Y. 1953) (extending recognition to uncle-niece marriage concluded in Rhode Island; although marriage would not have been permitted in NY, where parties were domiciled, it was not "within the prohibition of natural law"); Leszinske v. Poole, 798 P.2d 1049 (N.M. 1990). *Cf.* Catalano v. Catalano, 170 A.2d 726 (Conn. 1961) (holding that uncle-niece marriage in Italy was invalid where uncle was domiciled in Connecticut). *See generally* Scoles et al., *supra* note 7, § 13.11.

29. *See* U.N. Marriage Convention, *supra* note 21, art. 2 (states "shall take legislative action to specify a minimum age for marriage. No marriage shall be legally entered into by any person under this age, except where a competent authority has granted a dispensation as to age, for serious reasons, in the interests of the intending spouses"); and CEDAW, *supra* note 21, art. 16(2) ("The betrothal and marriage of a child shall have no legal effect, and all necessary action, including legislation, shall be taken to specify a minimum age for marriage and to make the registration of marriages in an official registry compulsory.").

state statutes today set eighteen as the age of consent for marriage, and provide that somewhat younger individuals may be married with parental consent or court approval.[30] Some states allow older teenagers to marry without parental consent, and a few permit marriages of children as young as twelve or thirteen.[31] Within this legal framework, there is room for substantial cultural variation, although there are also reported cases in which attempted marriages of young teenagers have been held to violate the criminal law.[32] These differences generate significant conflict of laws questions, but marriages of minors who travel across state lines to avoid the limitations of local laws have generally been upheld, unless challenged in an annulment proceeding brought by one of the parties or their parents.[33] Questions of marital age are closely related to the question of marital consent, and when there are indications that a youthful spouse has not freely agreed to a marriage it can and should be annulled.[34]

Prohibitions against polygamous marriage have been more strenuously enforced, most notably in the national conflict over Mormon polygamy that reached the Supreme Court in 1879 in *Reynolds v. United States*.[35] Rules barring polygamous marriages reflect a cultural and religious tradition, discussed in the Court's opinion in *Reynolds*, which justified monogamy in civil and political terms but also noted that it had been an offense under the ecclesiastical law in England. Challenges to polygamy laws might be easier to frame under the contemporary First Amendment doctrine,[36] but courts continue to understand these statutes in secular terms.[37] Even in this setting, marriage validation principles have considerable force, and American courts have been willing to recognize polygamous foreign or Native American marriages for purposes such as determining legitimacy or inheritance rights.[38]

30. *See* CLARK, *supra* note 3, § 2.10.

31. *See* Chris Burritt, *N.C. May Raise Minimum Age for Marriages*, ATLANTA CONSTITUTION, Apr. 26, 2001 (reporting that more than 200 thirteen year olds were married in North Carolina in 1998); Amy Argetsinger, *Assembly Votes to Ban Some Teen Marriages*, WASH. POST, Apr. 11, 1999, at C04 (debating new minimum age for marriage in Maryland).

32. *E.g.*, State v. Moua, 573 N.W.2d 202 (Wis. Ct. App. 1997) (statutory rape conviction following traditional Hmong marriage to thirteen or sixteen-year-old girl); People v. Benu, 385 N.Y.S.2d 222 (Crim. Ct. 1976) (sustaining child endangerment conviction where defendant arranged marriage of thirteen-year-old daughter).

33. *See* CLARK, *supra* note 3, § 2.10; SCOLES ET AL., *supra* note 7, § 13.12.

34. *E.g.*, B v. L, 168 A.2d 90 (N.J. Super. Ct. 1961) (granting annulment to sixteen-year-old girl who was taken to Italy to be married; marriage was not consummated and plaintiff-bride returned to the U.S. five weeks later). This is supported by the Marriage Convention, *see supra* note 29; *see generally* Egon Schwelb, *Marriage and Human Rights*, 12 AM. J. COMP. L. 337 (1963).

35. Reynolds v. United States, 98 U.S. 145 (1878). *See generally* COTT, *supra* note 5, at 105-31.

36. *See infra* note 84 and accompanying text.

37. Potter v. Murray City, 760 F.2d 1065, 1070 (10th Cir. 1985) (describing monogamy as "inextricably woven into the fabric of our society . . . the bedrock upon which our culture is built").

38. SCOLES ET AL., *supra* note 7, § 13.16, 13.17, 13.18. *See In re* Dalip Singh Bir's Estate,

Because marriage restrictions are culturally based and widely variable, it is difficult to find a sufficiently neutral perspective from which to evaluate them. There is a broad international consensus to support a minimum age for marriage, but no agreement on what that age should be. Proscriptions against the marriage of siblings or parents and children are widely shared across cultures, but marriages between cousins are favored in some traditions and discouraged in others. Polygamy, although generally in decline around the world, is subject to different constraints in different cultural settings. Courts and legislatures, responding to this diversity, should carefully consider whether particular marriage restrictions are still based on a strong and secular policy foundation. Norms of international law may be useful to this inquiry, along with constitutional principles of equal protection and religious liberty.

B. Divorce

In contrast to the marriage validation policy, which reflects a widely shared agreement about the importance of marriage, public policy concerning divorce has been more divided. Divorce was impossible under the English ecclesiastical law, and this legacy had an influence on American law.[39] Grounds for divorce have varied widely among the states, with some taking more liberal approaches and others narrowly limiting access or refusing to authorize divorce until recent years. In comparison to this restrictive approach based on Christian tradition, Jewish and Islamic law have permitted divorce for millennia.

Historically, the varying grounds for divorce in different states and the strong public policy interests behind these grounds have complicated interstate recognition of divorce decrees. Since the 1940s, however, courts in the United States have been obligated to extend full faith and credit to a divorce decree entered in a state in which either spouse was domiciled.[40] Since the 1970s, with the shift toward no-fault divorce grounds across the country and around the world, the older public policy concerns have

188 P.2d 499 (Cal. Ct. App. 1948) (dividing estate between two surviving wives). *See also* Royal v. Cudahy Packing Co., 190 N.W.2d 427 (Iowa 1922) (widow entitled to worker's compensation recovery despite fact of potentially polygamous marriage). This practice reflects a trend in the case law and conflict-of-laws literature toward considering issues of marriage validity differently depending on the context in which these issues arise. A marriage may be extended recognition for purposes of some incidents of marriage—such as inheritance law or tort recovery—even though it would not be recognized for other purposes. SCOLES *et al., supra* note 7, at 545-47.

39. *See* CLARK, *supra* note 3, § 12.1; NELSON MANFRED BLAKE, THE ROAD TO RENO: A HISTORY OF DIVORCE IN THE UNITED STATES (1962).

40. Williams v. North Carolina, 317 U.S. 287 (1942) and Williams v. North Carolina, 325 U.S. 226 (1945) *reh'g denied* (1945). *See generally* CLARK, *supra* note 3, at 423-26; *see also* RESTATEMENT (SECOND) OF CONFLICTS OF LAW § 71 (1971).

almost entirely disappeared. In place of the concern to restrict divorce, conflict and recognition rules are now driven primarily by concerns for procedural fairness and the protective policies embodied in statutes governing the incidents of divorce.[41] Similar developments have broadened the grounds for international recognition of divorce decrees, reflected in the Hague Convention on the Recognition of Divorces and Legal Separations ("Divorce Recognition Convention").[42]

1. COMITY

Although full faith and credit rules do not apply in the international context, American courts may give effect to foreign court judgments on grounds of comity. The classic statement of the doctrine of international comity comes from the Supreme Court's opinion in *Hilton v. Guyot*,[43] which included a list of factors federal courts were to apply in determining whether to extend respect to a foreign court judgment. For the most part, these are procedural, including the requirements that there be a "full and fair trial . . . before a court of competent jurisdiction, conducting the trial upon regular proceedings, after due citation or voluntary appearance of the defendant."[44] The *Hilton* factors have been applied in international divorce cases, such as the Michigan decision in *Dart v. Dart*,[45] which concluded that an English divorce judgment should be enforced on grounds of comity and *res judicata* despite the substantive differences between the law applied and Michigan law.[46] Until the era of divorce reform, some foreign divorces were procured by American citizens or domiciliaries seeking to avoid the stringent divorce laws of their home states. States varied in their willingness to recognize these decrees, even when based on personal jurisdiction over

41. *See* SCOLES, *supra* note 7, § 15.3 ("[W]hen the propriety of a dissolution is at issue in a state other than the state of rendition, the case will often be viewed in due process terms, very much similar to those obtaining with respect to all civil litigation"). *See generally* RESTATEMENT (SECOND) OF CONFLICTS OF LAW § 98 (1971) ("A valid judgment rendered in a foreign nation after a fair trial in a contested proceeding will be recognized in the United States so far as the immediate parties and the underlying cause of action are concerned").

42. The Hague Conference on Private International Law, Convention on the Recognition of Divorces and Legal Separations, June 1, 1970, 1975 U.K.T.S. 123 (Cmnd. 6248), reprinted at 8 I.L.M. 31 (1969) ("Divorce Recognition Convention"). *See* hcch.e-vision.nl/index_en.php. *See generally* Friedrich Juenger, *Recognition of Foreign Divorces—British and American Perspectives*, 20 AM. J. COMP. L. 1 (1972).

43. Hilton v. Guyot, 159 U.S. 113 (1895).

44. *Id.* at 202-03.

45. Dart v. Dart, 597 N.W.2d 82 (Mich. 1999).

46. In the *Dart* case, the husband had renounced his U.S. citizenship in order to inherit from a large family trust, and the parties had resided together in England with their children for more than a year at the time he began divorce proceedings in England. The wife filed a action in Michigan several days after she was served with process in the English proceeding. The dispute in *Dart* was not over the granting of the divorce, but on the substantive difference between the property division rules applied in England and Michigan.

both parties, but with the advent of no-fault divorce there is no longer much reason to object to a foreign divorce.[47] From a due process perspective, applying the test from *Hilton*, consensual foreign divorces do not present serious concerns. From this perspective, an *ex parte* foreign divorce is far more problematic, particularly if it affects the property, support, or custody rights of a party not present before the court.[48]

Although many other countries base jurisdiction for divorce on nationality or citizenship, American courts have generally refused to recognize foreign divorce decrees obtained by parties domiciled in the United States, even when that divorce might be valid under the law of the foreign country.[49] By contrast, under the Divorce Recognition Convention, member states are required to recognize divorce decrees obtained in "judicial or other proceedings" in another contracting state that are legally effective there, when there is jurisdiction based on one of a variety of grounds, including both nationality and habitual residence.[50] The convention includes a procedural dimension: contracting states may refuse to recognize a divorce if, "in light of all the circumstances, adequate steps were not taken to give notice of the proceedings . . . to the respondent, or if he was not afforded a sufficient opportunity to present his case."[51]

Applying these principles, American courts can readily extend recognition to divorce decrees entered by foreign courts in proceedings that look similar to our own. As with recognition of divorce decrees across state lines, the primary concern is with familiar questions of procedural fairness. Courts have a more difficult time applying principles of comity to foreign divorces that come from different cultural and legal frameworks, such as Jewish and Islamic personal law.

47. *See* Rosenstiel v. Rosenstiel, 262 N.Y.S.2d 86 (1965) *cert. denied*, 384 U.S. 971 (1966)(extending recognition to a consensual Mexican divorce despite lack of domicile). *See* CLARK, *supra* note 3, at 431-33; SCOLES, *supra* note 7, at 15.20-15.22.

48. In U.S. domestic law, a divorce decree entered without personal jurisdiction over both spouses is generally not effective to resolve these questions. *See* Vanderbilt v. Vanderbilt, 354 U.S. 416 (1957); Estin v. Estin, 334 U.S. 541 (1948).

49. *See, e.g.*, Atassi v. Atassi, 451 S.E.2d 371 (N.C. Ct. App. 1995) (denying recognition to Syrian divorce obtained by U.S. citizen domiciled in North Carolina); Ahmad v. Ahmad, 2001 WL 1518116 (Ohio Ct. App. 2001) (denying recognition to Jordanian divorce where parties were domiciled in Ohio); Tal v. Tal, 601 N.Y.S.2d 530 (Sup. Ct. 1993) (denying recognition to Israeli religious divorce where parties were Israeli citizens but had not lived in Israel for more than five years). *Cf.* Sherif v. Sherif, 352 N.Y.S.2d 781 (Fam. Ct. 1974) (extending recognition to Egyptian divorce where both parties were domiciled in Egypt "at all crucial points in their marital history").

50. Divorce Recognition Convention, *supra* note 42, art. 2. According to the treaty, the expression "habitual residence" is deemed to include domicile where that concept is used as a basis for divorce jurisdiction. *Id.* at art. 3. Note that the convention does not apply to findings of fault or "ancillary orders" including specifically orders relating to pecuniary obligations or to the custody of children." *Id.* at art. 1.

51. *Id.* at art. 8. Contracting states are also permitted to refuse recognition to a divorce or legal separation if recognition is "manifestly incompatible with their public policy." *Id.* at art. 10.

2. Talaq and Get

Divorce in the Jewish tradition is effected through a process in which the husband delivers a document known as a *get* to his wife.[52] The process is conducted with rabbinic supervision, before a religious tribunal or *bet din* because the rules for writing and delivering the *get* are quite complicated. In Islam, divorce is effected by a pronouncement made by the husband known as a *talaq*. Within the United States, a divorce concluded by *get* or *talaq* has no secular legal effect, but in those countries in which marriage and divorce are matters of personal law, subject to the jurisdiction of religious authorities, a divorce by *get* or *talaq* may be given full legal effect with no additional court proceeding.

American courts have extended comity to divorces by *get* or *talaq* in foreign countries, but only when certain procedural requirements are satisfied. The case law suggests that the most important of these are that the court have jurisdiction based on the domicile of at least one of the parties,[53] and that the respondent have notice and some opportunity for a hearing before the divorce is granted.[54] In practice, this approach has meant that courts in the U.S. have not recognized nonjudicial divorces unless there are subsequent judicial proceedings.[55]

Historically, the suspicion of divorce by *get* or *talaq* in our legal tradition seems tied to our highly restrictive attitudes toward divorce based on different religious values. In an era of unilateral no-fault divorce, the more important questions concern substantive and procedural fairness, particularly when a unilateral foreign divorce might deprive a spouse or children of the various protections extended by U.S. divorce and custody laws. This issue is particularly sharp when foreign laws discriminate on the basis of gender, or deny remedies such as spousal support or property division that would be available in proceedings here. Thus, in *Chaudry v. Chaudry*,[56] the

52. *See generally* Irving Breitowitz, *The Plight of the Agunah: A Study in Halacha, Contract and the First Amendment*, 51 Md. L. Rev. 312 (1992). Disputes over delivery of a *get* are discussed *infra* at notes 95-107.

53. *Compare* Aranoff v. Aranoff, 642 N.Y.S.2d 49 (App. Div. 1996) (denying recognition to Israeli divorce where rabbinic court had no personal jurisdiction over the wife) *with* Tal v. Tal, 601 N.Y.S.2d 530 (Sup. Ct. 1993) *with* Shapiro v. Shapiro, 442 N.Y.S.2d 928 (Sup. Ct. 1981) (enforcing terms of Israeli religious divorce based on parties' domicile). *See generally* Comment, *United States Recognition of Foreign, Nonjudicial Divorces*, 53 Minn. L. Rev. 612 (1969).

54. Cases refusing to give effect to *ex parte* divorces by *talaq* include Shikoh v. Murff, 257 F.2d 306 (2d Cir. 1958); Seth v. Seth, 694 S.W.2d 459 (Tex. Ct. App. 1985).

55. *See* Chaudry v. Chaudry, 388 A.2d 1000 (N.J. Super. Ct. 1978) (upholding divorce by *talaq* at the Pakistani consulate in New York, which was later confirmed by trial and appellate courts in Pakistan).

56. *E.g.*, Atassi v. Atassi, 451 S.E.2d 371 (N.C. Ct. App. 1995). The more serious concern today lies with the financial incidents of divorce and issues of custody and child support. Courts sometimes give effect to a foreign divorce but allow a spouse to raise these issues in the new forum.

court determined that husband's divorce by *talaq*, made at the Pakistani consulate in New York, could be given respect as a matter of comity because it was later confirmed by trial and appellate courts in Pakistan in a proceeding for which the wife had notice and an opportunity to be heard. In *Chaudry*, the husband was domiciled in New Jersey and the wife in Pakistan. The court also decided, however, that wife should have the opportunity to relitigate issues of custody and child support in the court in New Jersey.[57]

For courts, it may prove difficult to address the question of comity in purely procedural terms. Substantive differences in the divorce laws of different countries, particularly where these differences suggest important problems of gender equality, may also factor into this decision. These questions are less important where the issue is whether to recognize a change in the parties' marital status, which could be readily achieved in a no-fault *ex parte* divorce proceeding in the United States, and more important where the issue involves property, support, and other consequences of a divorce decree.

C. International Custody Disputes

Questions of cultural and religious tradition also play a role in child custody disputes, and courts have regularly struggled with the dilemma presented when two parents with different religious practices have different ideas about how their children should be raised.[58] In some international custody disputes, cultural issues overlay questions of recognition and comity. As with divorce decrees, courts begin by considering jurisdictional and procedural matters. With custody disputes, this is followed by an inquiry into the substantive problem of determining the "best interests of the child" in a cross-cultural context.

1. Jurisdiction and Procedure

With the advent of the Uniform Child Custody Jurisdiction and Enforcement Act (UCCJEA),[59] now in effect in thirty-nine states and the District of Columbia, international custody cases are addressed within the same jurisdictional framework that applies to interstate cases. Under the

57. *Chaudry*, 388 A.2d at 1006-07. The court did not permit the wife to reopen issues of spousal support and property division.

58. *E.g.*, Sagar v. Sagar, 781 N.E.2d 54 (Mass. App. Ct. 2003) (dispute between Hindu parents over performance of ritual of Chudakarana); Kendall v. Kendall, 687 N.E.2d 1228 (Mass. 1997) (dispute between fundamentalist Christian father and Orthodox Jewish mother). *See generally Annot. Religion as a Factor in Child Custody and Visitation Cases,* 22 A.L.R. 4th 971 (1983).

59. Unif. Child Custody Jurisdiction and Enforcement Act, 9 U.L.A. pt. 1 649 (1999). *See generally* http://www.nccusl.org.

UCCJEA, a foreign country may be the "home state" of a child for jurisdictional purposes, and custody orders entered in another country under circumstances that satisfy the requirements of the statute are entitled to recognition and enforcement.[60] The statue provides, however, that these principles need not be applied "if the child custody law of a foreign country violates fundamental principles of human rights."[61] Beyond the UCCJEA, courts may also enforce foreign custody orders on the basis of comity.[62]

In international law, the Hague Conference has approved two important conventions addressing international custody disputes. The Convention on the Civil Aspects of International Child Abduction (Child Abduction Convention),[63] which applies in the United States and seventy-four other contracting states,[64] is designed to remedy the wrongful removal or retention of a child outside the child's habitual residence with a summary return mechanism that can be invoked by a person with rights of custody. The Convention on Jurisdiction, Applicable Law, Recognition, Enforcement and Cooperation in Respect of Parental Responsibility and Measures for the Protection of Children (Child Protection Convention),[65] which has been signed, ratified, or acceded to by twenty-eight countries,[66] addresses more traditional conflict of laws issues. The Child Protection Convention supports and extends the Child Abduction Convention, placing primary

60. UCCJEA § 105. *E.g., In re* Marriage of Medill, 40 P.3d 1087, 1095-96 (Or. Ct. App. 2002). Under the previous uniform statute, this approach was optional. Some courts recognized foreign countries as a child's home state; *e.g.,* Dincer v. Dincer, 701 A.2d 210 (Pa. 1997) (Belgium), but others did not; *e.g., In re* Marriage of Horiba, 950 P.2d 340, 344-46 (Ore. Ct. App. 1997) (Japan). *See generally* Ivaldi v. Ivaldi, 685 A.2d 1319, 1323-25 (N.J. 1996).

61. UCCJEA § 105(c). Although the statute does not elaborate what is meant by this provision, there are a variety of human rights norms applicable to family law matters, including the child's right to a hearing, the child's right to have decisions based on the child's best interests, and rights against discrimination based on gender in matters relating to marriage and family relations. *See infra* notes 69-80 and accompanying text; *see generally* Estin, *supra* note 6, at 287-95.

62. *E.g.,* Bliss v. Bliss, 733 A.2d 954, 958-60 (D.C. Ct. App. 1999) (Russian custody order).

63. Hague Conference on Private International Law, Convention on the Civil Aspects of International Child Abduction, Oct. 25, 1980, T.I.A.S. 11670, 1343 U.N.T.S. 89, reprinted in 19 I.L.M. 1501 (1980).

64. The Child Abduction Convention was implemented in the United States with the International Child Abduction Remedies Act (ICARA), Pub. L. No. 100-300, § 2, 102 STAT. 437 1988, codified as amended at 42 U.S.C. §§ 11601-11610 (2004). A list of participants in the Child Abduction Convention is *available at* hcch.e-vision.nl/index_en.php. The convention is not in effect in most countries in which religious courts exercise jurisdiction over child custody matters. *See* Carol S. Bruch, *Religious Law, Secular Practices, and Children's Human Rights in Child Abduction Cases Under the Hague Child Abduction Convention*, 33 N.Y.U. J. INT'L L. & POL. 49 (2000).

65. Hague Conference on Private International Law, Convention on Jurisdiction, Applicable Law, Recognition, Enforcement and Co-operation in Respect of Parental Responsibility and Measures for the Protection of Children, reprinted in 35 I.L.M. 1391 (1996).

66. *See* http://www.hcch.e-vision.nl/index_en.php.

jurisdiction for matters such as custody and visitation with the authorities of the child's habitual residence. Both conventions provide a system for cooperative efforts between the governments of contracting states. The Child Abduction Convention allows a state to refuse to return a child to his or her habitual residence if "this would not be permitted by fundamental principles of the requested State relating to the protection of human rights and fundamental freedoms."[67] Similarly, the Child Protection Convention allows a state to refuse to recognize custody or visitation orders if a child or parent was not given an opportunity to be heard or if recognition "is manifestly contrary to public policy of the requested State, taking into account the best interests of the child."[68]

In making a determination whether to enforce a foreign custody decree under the UCCJEA or on the basis of comity, and in applying the Child Abduction Convention, courts look beyond the grounds for jurisdiction and whether the respondent had notice and an opportunity for a hearing. The references to principles of human rights in both the UCCJEA and the Child Abduction Convention authorize courts to inquire into whether the foreign decree was based on a consideration of the best interests of the child. This determination presents some difficulty, however, when a decree was issued by a court working in a different religious or cultural context.

2. Custody and Human Rights

The United Nations Convention on the Rights of the Child provides that: "In all actions concerning children, whether undertaken by public or private social welfare institutions, courts of law, administrative authorities or legislative bodies, the best interests of the child shall be a primary consideration."[69] As this language suggests, there is broad international agreement that a "best interests" standard is appropriate. Unfortunately, there is no international consensus on what this standard means or how it should be applied in custody cases.[70] This means that individual courts face the responsibility of translating between cultures in particular cases.

American courts are prepared to recognize that religious and cultural

67. Child Abduction Convention, *supra* note 63, art. 20.

68. Child Protection Convention, *supra* note 65, art. 23. The Child Protection Convention has not been ratified by the United States, but it provides a useful reference point for the emerging international practice. *See generally* Linda Silberman, *The 1996 Hague Convention on the Protection of Children: Should the United States Join?*, 34 Fam. L.Q. 239 (2000).

69. United Nations Convention on the Rights of the Child, art. 3(1), G.A. Res. 44/25 (Annex), U.N. GAOR, 44th Sess., Supp. No. 49, at 166, U.N. Doc. A/RES/44/49 (1990); 30 I.L.M. 1448 (1989) [hereinafter CDC).

70. Philip Alston, *The Best Interests Principle: Toward a Reconciliation of Culture and Human Rights*, 8 Int'l J.L. & Fam. 1, 5 (1994). Alston also notes the famous indeterminacy of the best interests standard as applied in domestic law. *Id.* at 4, 18-19.

factors are a legitimate part of a best interests analysis. For example, in *In re the Marriage of Malak*, the California Court of Appeal required enforcement of a decree entered by an Islamic court in Lebanon awarding custody to the father.[71] The decree recited that the court had considered the children's environmental, traditional, moral and cultural links to Lebanon, the fact that Arabic was their native language and that they had been raised in the Islamic religion, the difficulties of moving to a place with radically different customs and traditions, and their father's material prospects in Lebanon as compared to their mother's uncertain situation in the United States.[72] Courts are more wary, however, where a foreign custody decree appears to be based solely on religious principle. In *Ali v. Ali*, the New Jersey Superior Court refused to enforce a custody decree of the Sharia Court of Gaza based on due process concerns and evidence that under the law applicable in that court, "a father is automatically entitled to custody when a boy is seven . . . the mother can apply to prolong custody until the boy is nine . . . however, at that time, the father or the paternal grandfather are irrebuttably entitled to custody."[73] In a sharply divided opinion, the Maryland Court of Special Appeals extended recognition to a Pakistani custody order in *Hosain v. Malik*.[74] Experts testifying for both the mother and the father agreed that the applicable statute—a British colonial enactment known as the Guardians and Wards Act of 1890—required the Pakistani court to consider the welfare of the minor child. They disagreed on whether the court had in fact applied a

71. *In re* Marriage of Malak, 227 Cal. Rptr. 841 (Ct. App. 1986). Both parties were Lebanese nationals and they maintained a home there; the wife was notified of the proceeding in Lebanon and did not appear. The parties had lived together for five years in the United Arab Emirates before the wife removed the children to California. The husband unsuccessfully attempted to have the California courts enforce a custody decree entered by the Abu Dhabi Sharia Court in the United Arab Emirates (UAE); there was evidence forwarded from the American Embassy in Abu Dhabi that in a Sharia divorce in the UAE, "custody of minor children would almost always be given to their Muslim father." *Id.* at 848 n.2.

72. *Id.* (noting that mother was unemployed, constantly moving from one place to another, and that she might not be able to remain legally in the U.S.).

73. Ali v. Ali, 652 A.2d 253, 259 (N.J. Super Ct. 1994). The New Jersey court ruled that such presumptions "cannot be said by any stretch of the imagination" to comport with a best interests of the child analysis, and that because the decree was "diametrically opposed" to the law of New Jersey, the court would not recognize it on the basis of comity. *Id.* at 260. *See also* Amin v. Bakhaty, 798 So. 2d 75 (La. 2001) (court need not defer to Egyptian court that would not apply a best interests test); Tataragasi v. Tataragasi, 477 S.E.2d 239, 246 (N.C. Ct. App. 1996) (Turkish decree did not address best interests); Tazziz v. Tazziz, 533 N.E.2d 202 (Mass. Ct. App. 1988) (remanding for consideration of law applied in custody proceeding before Sharia court in Israel).

74. Hosain v. Malik, 671 A.2d 988 (Md. Ct. Spec. App. 1996). *Malik* is criticized in June Starr, *The Global Battlefield: Culture and International Child Custody Disputes at Century's End*, 15 ARIZ. J. INT'L & COMP. L. 791, 819-11 (1998), and Monica E. Henderson, Note, *U.S. State Court Review of Islamic Law Custody Decrees—When Are Islamic Custody Decrees in the Child's Best Interest?*, 36 U. LOUISVILLE J. FAM. L. 423, 436-440 (1998).

best-interests test, or if instead it had based its decision on the Islamic doctrine of *hazanit*, applicable under the statute as part of the personal law of the parties.[75] The court noted that *hazanit* was in some respects similar to "the traditional maternal preference" once applicable in Maryland. Acknowledging that such preferences "are based on very old notions and assumptions (which are widely considered outdated, discriminatory, and outright false in today's modern society)," the court nevertheless sustained enforcement of the Pakistani decree, writing:

> we are simply unprepared to hold that this longstanding doctrine of one of the world's oldest and largest religions practiced by hundreds of millions of people around the world and in this country, as applied as one factor in the best interest of the child test, is repugnant to Maryland public policy.[76]

Another human rights question in these custody cases concerns gender equality. Laws that do not give men and women "the same rights and responsibilities as parents" violate the United Nations Convention on the Elimination of All Forms of Discrimination Against Women (CEDAW)[77] and other human rights treaties that prohibit discrimination on the basis of sex. *Hosain*, like many other difficult international custody cases, involved a mother who fled to the U.S. and invoked the jurisdiction of its courts in order to avoid litigating custody under laws likely to favor the father.[78]

75. *Id.* at 991-92, 1003 (describing expert testimony); *Id.* at 1001, 1004-05 (describing right of *hazanit*). The court described *hazanit* as a system of "complex Islamic rules of maternal and paternal preference depending on the age and sex of the child." *Id.* at 1004.

76. *Id.* at 1004-05. A dissenting opinion disagreed that the Pakistani order was in fact based on a best interests analysis; *See id.* at 1016-22.

77. CEDAW, *supra* note 21. Article 16 requires that States Parties ensure, on a basis of equality of men and women:

(a) The same right to enter into marriage;
(b) The same right to freely choose a spouse and to enter into marriage only with their free and full consent;
(c) The same rights and responsibilities during marriage and at its dissolution;
(d) The same rights and responsibilities as parents, irrespective of their marital status, in matters relating to their children. In all cases, the interests of the children shall be paramount;
(e) The same rights to decide freely and responsibly on the number and spacing of their children, and to have access to the information, education, and means to enable them to exercise these rights;
(f) The same rights and responsibilities with regard to guardianship, wardship, trusteeship and adoption of children, or similar institutions where these concepts exist in national legislation. In all cases the interests of the children shall be paramount;
(g) The same personal rights as husband and wife, including the right to choose a family name, a profession and an occupation;
(h) The same rights for both spouses in respect of the ownership, acquisition, management, administration, enjoyment and disposition of property, whether free of charge or for a valuable consideration.

78. Litigation in Pakistan was complicated for the mother by the facts that she began living with another man shortly after leaving her husband, and that she appeared in the Pakistani proceeding only through counsel. Hosain argued that she would have been considered an apostate

The argument can be made that requiring mothers and children to litigate custody under such laws would violate fundamental principles of human rights.[79] By making explicit reference to principles of human rights, both the UCCJEA and the Child Abduction Convention allow courts to consider this problem. This is uncharted territory, however, with few landmarks to assist courts in setting a course.[80]

Taken collectively, the marriage, divorce and custody cases discussed here suggest both policies that support multicultural accommodation and several important constraints on that process. There is the policy of supporting and validating marriages in a wide range of cultural contexts, subject to the requirement that the spouses give their free consent to the marriage. There is the policy of extending recognition to foreign divorce or custody decrees, subject to norms of procedural fairness. The cases also suggest the importance of additional constraints on the process of accommodation, arising from norms of gender equality and from the protective policies embedded in our family law, such as the commitment to furthering the best interests of a child.

II. Religion and Neutral Principles

Principles of religious law, important to marriage and divorce practices in Judaism and Islam, create serious complications in some secular divorce disputes. Courts and legislatures have made attempts to accommodate these practices, but the tangle of religious and legal principles has been difficult to resolve. In this context, the principal dilemma for courts is not how to understand and apply foreign law, but whether and to what extent these disputes can be addressed within the secular jurisdiction of state courts.

A. First Amendment Issues

With its 1879 decision in *Reynolds*, the Supreme Court concluded that the First Amendment protection for free exercise of religion extended to

---

and disqualified for custody on that basis, *id.* at 1004, and that she could have been arrested for adultery if she had returned to Pakistan to participate in the hearing, *id.* at 1006. *See also* Amin v. Bakhaty, 798 So.2d 75 (La. 2001). In *Amin*, an Egyptian woman married to U.S. citizen domiciled in New Jersey brought their child to visit her family in the U.S. Her husband returned to Egypt, secured an *ex parte* divorce, filed for a "declaratory judgment of permanent custody," and had his wife prosecuted and convicted for removing the child from Egypt without his permission. Under the circumstances, the court in *Amin* declined to defer to the jurisdiction of the Egyptian courts.

79. *See* Bruch, *supra* note 64.

80. The human rights principle articulated in the UCCJEA is very recent, and litigants have not yet had much success in using this provision of the Child Abduction Convention. For courts' treatment of analogous language in the Child Abduction Convention, *See* PAUL R. BEAUMONT & PETER E. MCELEAVY, THE HAGUE CONVENTION ON INTERNATIONAL CHILD ABDUCTION 174-75 (1999).

matters of religious belief or opinion but not to religious practices.[81] In its opinion, the Court described marriage legislation including the rule of monogamy, as serving an important secular purpose, and rejected defendant's claim to constitutional protection for religious polygamy.[82] Although the distinction was eventually discarded,[83] it is still difficult to argue under contemporary doctrine that a law appearing to be neutral and generally applicable is a violation of the right to free exercise of religion because of its effects on some religious practice.[84] This suggests that while it may be good policy to broaden the range of religious practices and family traditions recognized and accommodated in state law, courts are not likely to conclude that such accommodation is constitutionally required.

With notable exceptions, such as polygamy and child marriage, accommodation of diverse religious and cultural traditions in the family setting is relatively easy when it is clear that individual family members have chosen to participate in a particular institution or practice. Typically, there will be no occasion for the law to intervene. Accommodation becomes much more difficult when family members disagree about religious matters. This is sometimes a problem in custody cases, when one parent's claim for free exercise and accommodation of religious practices is met by the other parent's argument against government endorsement of religion.[85] Courts cannot decide these cases on religious grounds, and therefore search for a neutral basis on which they may be resolved. There are analogues of this problem in court cases concerning internal church disputes. The Supreme Court has concluded that civil courts may resolve church disputes using "neutral prin-

81. *Reynolds*, 98 U.S. 145 at 166; *See id.* at 164 ("Congress was deprived of all legislative power over mere opinion, but was left free to reach actions which were in violation of social duties or subversive of good order").

82. *Id.* at 165. ("Marriage, while from its very nature a sacred obligation, is nevertheless, in most civilized nations, a civil contract, and usually regulated by law. Upon it society may be said to be built, and out of its fruits spring social relations and social obligations and duties, with which government is necessarily required to deal").

83. Wisconsin v. Yoder, 406 U.S. 205 (1972) (allowing religious exception to compulsory school attendance law for Old Order Amish children).

84. *See* Church of the Lukumi Babalu Aye v. City of Hialeah, 508 U.S. 520 (1993); Employment Div., Dep't of Human Resources v. Smith, 494 U.S. 872 (1990). *But see* Keith E. Sealing, *Polygamists Out of the Closet: Statutory and State Constitutional Prohibitions Against Polygamy Are Unconstitutional Under the Free Exercise Clause*, 17 GA. ST. U. L. REV. 691, 747-52 (2001); Todd M. Gillett, Note, *The Absolution of Reynolds: The Constitutionality of Religious Polygamy*, 8 WM. & MARY BILL RTS. J. 497, 526-28 (2000). *See also* State v. Green, 99 P.3d 820 (Utah 2004).

85. *E.g.*, Kendall v. Kendall, 687 N.E.2d 1228 (Mass. 1997) (dispute between fundamentalist Christian father and Orthodox Jewish mother); Sagar v. Sagar, 781 N.E.2d 54 (Mass. Ct. App. 2003) (dispute between Hindu parents over performance of ritual known as Chudakarana). *See generally* James G. Dwyer, *Parents' Religion and Children's Welfare: Debunking the Doctrine of Parent's Rights*, 82 CAL. L. REV. 1371 (1994).

ciples" of contract, property, or trust law, but may not make decisions "on the basis of religious doctrine and practice."[86] When possible, courts faced with religious family disputes may take the same approach. Therefore, to the extent that family members have used the tools of contract, property and trust law, their marriage and divorce issues may come before the courts as private law disputes.

B. Religious Marriage Law

Issues of marriage and marital status are important in a number of systems of religious law. For Roman Catholics, marriages within the church can be dissolved only by an annulment, available either to husband or wife, which must be granted by ecclesiastical authorities. In Judaism, marriages are terminated by the husband's delivery of a *get* document to the wife in a proceeding before a rabbinic tribunal. Within Islam, a husband may terminate a marriage by a repudiation or *talaq* for any reason. Within each of these traditions, the grounds for terminating a marriage and the consequences of a divorce or annulment are legal questions with important implications for individuals. While religious law is not within the expertise of most divorce practitioners, aspects of these questions may have an important influence on civil divorce litigation.

In Judaism and in Islam, the legal rights of husbands and wives are distinct. Historically, in both traditions, men were permitted to take multiple wives and to divorce their wives freely. For wives, the primary legal protection was in the form of an agreement, signed at the time of the marriage, imposing obligations on the husband in the event he exercised his right to divorce. This agreement is known as a *ketuba* in Jewish tradition, and a *nikahnama* in Islam. In the Islamic tradition, this payment owed by the husband to the wife is known as a *mahr* or *sadaqa,* and sometimes described as a marriage gift. In the Jewish tradition, there is some additional protection for the wife from the fact that a rabbinic tribunal supervises the *get* process.[87]

Although clearly understood to be binding as a matter of religious law, it is not always apparent in contemporary circumstances whether these marriage agreements should be enforceable in secular courts. Disputes over Jewish and Islamic marriage agreements litigated in civil courts have drawn on two sets of neutral principles. In one group of cases, these contracts are tested for enforceability under the rules applied to civil contracts

86. R.W. Jones v. Wolf, 443 U.S. 595 (1979). *See generally* Kent Greenawalt, *Hands Off! Civil Court Involvement in Conflicts Over Religious Property*, 98 COLUM. L. REV. 1843 (1998).

87. *See generally* POULTER, supra note 2; DAVID PEARL & WERNER MENSKI, MUSLIM FAMILY LAW (3d ed. 1998); Breitowitz, *supra* note 52.

or prenuptial agreements. In another group of cases, which result from the *get* requirement in Jewish law, courts apply both contract principles and the law governing arbitration agreements. These neutral principles have provided a framework that allows for some recognition of religious marriage commitments in the context of secular divorce proceedings.

1. Premarital Agreements

Historically, agreements contemplating divorce were not enforceable in the United States as a matter of public policy. Since 1970, courts and legislatures have articulated principles that permit enforcement of premarital agreements, but impose requirements on the process that are not found in ordinary commercial cases. When confronted with Jewish or Islamic marital agreements, courts begin with the general principles governing prenuptial agreements. In a number of cases, courts have ordered a husband to make the promised payments, finding that the secular terms of the agreement gave rise to an enforceable contract.[88] In others, however, courts have struggled with problems of cultural and legal context, eventually concluding that agreements should not be enforced.[89]

Three published California decisions have addressed this question, illustrating some of the difficulties of this process. In the first, *In re the Marriage of Noghrey*,[90] a wife sought enforcement of a written promise made by her husband immediately before their marriage, to settle on her in the event of a divorce, his house in Sunnyvale and "$500,000 or one-half my assets, whichever is greater." The wife filed for divorce after seven and a half months of marriage. The court refused to enforce the agreement, based on the principle that an agreement that encourages divorce violates public policy. Noting the wife's testimony that neither she nor her parents possessed great wealth, the court concluded that "[t]he prospect of receiving a house and a minimum of $500,000 by obtaining the no-fault divorce available in California would menace the marriage of the best intentioned spouse."

In a second case, *In re the Marriage of Dajani*,[91] the court considered

88. *E.g.*, Odatalla v. Odatalla, 810 A.2d 93 (N.J. Super. Ct. 2002); Akileh v. Elchahal, 666 So. 2d 246 (Fla. Dist. Ct. App. 1996) ($50,000 *sadaq*); Aziz v. Aziz, 488 N.Y.S.2d 123 (Sup. Ct. 1985) ($5,000 *mahr*).

89. In addition to the cases discussed here, *see* Kaddoura v. Hammoud, (1998) O.J. No. 5054; (1999) 44 R.F.L. (4th) 228 [168 D.L.R. (4th 503] (Ont. Gen. Div.) (Canada) (denying enforcement of *mahr* on the basis that it was "fundamentally an Islamic religious matter"), discussed in Pascale Fournier, *The Erasure of Islamic Difference in Canadian and American Family Law Adjudication*, 10 J.L. & Pol'y 51 (2001).

90. *In re* Marriage of Noghrey, 215 Cal. Rptr. 153, 155-56 (Ct. App. 1985).

91. *In re* Marriage of Dajani, 251 Cal. Rptr. 871 (Ct. App. 1988). *But see In re* Marriage of Bellio, 129 Cal. Rptr. 2d 556 (Ct. App. 2003), which enforced a provision in a premarital agreement providing for payment to wife of $100,000 in the event of a divorce. The court in *Bellio*

a contract providing for payment to the wife of a deferred dower with a value of 5,000 Jordanian dinars, equivalent to about $1,700. The husband offered testimony of an expert in Islam, who testified that a wife who initiated divorce proceedings forfeited the right to her dower. The court accepted this view, concluding that the wife was not entitled to enforce the agreement in this situation, and noting in dicta that such an agreement was unenforceable under *Noghrey* as an inducement to divorce.

In a third case, *In re the Marriage of Shaban*,[92] the court considered a *mahr* agreement entered into at the time of the parties' marriage in Egypt in 1974. When the parties divorced in California in 1998, the husband argued that the wife's remedies were limited by the agreement to a recovery of her dowry payment of 500 Egyptian pounds, worth about $30. Under California community property law, the wife was otherwise entitled to share community property worth $3 million. The opinion in the case included an English translation of the *mahr* agreement, which recited the dower amount but had no substantive terms addressing other remedies or community property rights. The court rejected the husband's argument that the agreement reflected the parties' intention to have their marriage and property relations governed by Islamic law.[93]

Taken out of their original cultural and legal context, these agreements present a dilemma. These agreements are grounded in a context in which husband and wife have vastly different rights than what is specified in the New Jersey or California divorce laws, and they may not be written in terms that are familiar to American courts. Courts evaluate them using the principles that govern more familiar premarital agreements. Understandably, civil courts hesitate to interpret or apply religious law, and in our system there is no authoritative source of guidance on provisions of religious law. Responding to these circumstances, some advocates have begun to develop marital agreements that adapt their traditions to the American legal environment.[94]

The most important issues for the courts concern the specific intentions of the parties rather than the general provisions of religious law, because these cases turn on the law of contract. Expert testimony about the cultural context or meaning of a practice may be useful, but it serves in this setting

noted its agreement with the result in *Noghrey*, and disagreed with *Dajani* on the basis that "[a] dowry worth only $1,700, payable upon dissolution, is insufficient to seriously jeopardize a viable marriage."

92. *In re* Marriage of Shaban, 105 Cal. Rptr. 2d 863 (Ct. App. 2001).

93. *Id.* ("An agreement whose only substantive term is that the marriage has been made in accordance with 'Islamic law' is hopelessly uncertain as to its terms and conditions"). The court noted that the term "Islamic law" is uncertain given the different Islamic nations.

94. *See, e.g.*, Azizah al-Hibri, *Muslim Marriage Contract in American Courts*, lecture presented May 20, 2000; text *available at* http://www.karamah.org/sp/azizah_20000520.php.

522 Family Law Quarterly, Volume 38, Number 3, Fall 2004

only as an aid to interpretation of the parties' meaning. Because these cases must be decided on the basis of secular contract law, individuals who intend that their religious marital agreements be enforceable in civil courts should consider utilizing contract law principles to make this result more certain.

2. Divorce Jurisdiction

Similar problems of context and interpretation arise in the cases involving the Jewish *get*. A centuries-old tradition requires a husband seeking divorce to appear before a rabbinic court or *bet din* to deliver the *get* to his wife.[95] Jewish law requires that the *get* be given and received freely, and when either spouse refuses to cooperate, there are few sanctions the *bet din* can impose. Without completion of this process, neither party is free to marry under Jewish law, although the practical and religious consequences of this are significantly more serious for women.[96]

In countries like the United States, where divorce lies within the jurisdiction of the civil courts, rabbinic tribunals play at most a secondary role. For observant Jews, divorce requires both a civil proceeding and an appearance before the *bet din*. In one common scenario, however, a husband refuses to provide a *get* in order to coerce his wife into making significant financial concessions in the civil divorce proceeding.[97] This presents a dilemma for civil divorce courts, which cannot take jurisdiction over the religious dimension of the proceeding.

Civil divorce courts sometimes rely on contract theories as a basis for ordering a recalcitrant spouse to appear before the *bet din*. Where there is an express promise in a separation agreement to deliver a *get*, courts have ordered specific performance of the agreement.[98] Alternatively, several courts have concluded that the execution at the time of the marriage of a *ketuba* which included the words "according to the law of Moses and Israel" gave rise to an implied promise to grant or receive a *get* in the

95. *See generally* Breitowitz *supra* note 52. Breitowitz writes that this procedure was initiated in the tenth century at the same time that polygamy was abolished among Jews, effectively converting divorce from a unilateral privilege of the husband to a process requiring the mutual consent of both spouses.

96. *See* Breitowitz *supra* note 52; *see also* Lisa Zornberg, *Beyond the Constitution: Is the New York Get Legislation Good Law?*, 15 Pace L. Rev. 703 (1995).

97. *E.g.*, Perl v. Perl, 512 N.Y.S.2d 372 (App. Div. 1987). Occasionally, it is the wife who refuses to cooperate. *E.g.*, Rubin v. Rubin, 348 N.Y.S.2d 61 (Fam. Ct. 1973) (enforcing promise in separation agreement making wife's alimony payments conditional on her cooperation in obtaining a *get*). *See also* Michael Freeman, *Law, Religion and the State: The Get Revisited, in* Families Across Frontiers 361, 365-72 (Nigel Lowe & Gillian Douglas, eds. 1996) (describing *get* disputes in England, Australia, Germany, France and the Netherlands).

98. *See* Breitowitz, *supra* note 52, at 340-42. *See also* Andrea G. Nadel, Annotation, *Enforceability of Agreement Requiring Spouse's Co-operation in Obtaining Religious Bill of Divorce*, 29 A.L.R. 4th 746 (1984).

event of a civil divorce.[99] But there are troubling First Amendment issues with this approach, and other courts have refused to grant this sort of relief.[100] Moreover, because of the rule in religious law that the *get* must not be coerced, civil sanctions designed to enforce a premarital or separation agreement may be counterproductive.[101]

Given these difficulties, some of the *ketubot* now signed by Jewish couples take a different approach. In *Avitzur v. Avitzur*, after the husband refused to provide the wife with a *get*, she sought specific performance of his agreement in their *ketuba* to submit marital disputes to the jurisdiction of the *bet din*.[102] While the husband objected to enforcement of this provision, on the ground that it would "violate the constitutional prohibition against excessive entanglement between church and State," the New York Court of Appeals disagreed. Concluding that the case could be decided "solely upon the application of neutral principles of contract law, without any reference to religious principle,"[103] the court drew an analogy between enforcing this provision and enforcing an agreement to arbitrate a dispute in any other nonjudicial forum.

Since *Avitzur*, observant Jews have begun to utilize arbitration agreements to shift jurisdiction over their divorce proceedings from civil to rabbinic court.[104] Once proceedings before the *bet din* are concluded, the parties present the tribunal's orders to the civil court for confirmation as an arbitration award and incorporation into the civil divorce decree. Civil courts retain some control of these cases: proceedings are subject to the require-

99. *E.g.*, *In re* the Marriage of Goldman, 554 N.E.2d 1016 (Ill. App. Ct. 1990); Minkin v. Minkin, 434 A.2d 665 (N.J. Super. Ct. 1981), *but see* Mayer-Kolker v. Kolker, 819 A.2d 17 (N.J. Super. Ct. App. Div. 2003).

100. *E.g*, *Mayer-Kolker*, *supra* at note 99; Aflalo v. Aflalo, 685 A.2d 523 (N.J. Super. Ct. 1996) (holding that order compelling *get* would violate husband's right to the free exercise of religion); *In re* Marriage of Victor, 866 P.2d 899 (Ariz. Ct. App. 1993) ("If this court were to rule on whether the ketubah, given its indefinite language, includes an unwritten mandate that a husband under these circumstances is required to grant his wife a *get*, we would be overstepping our authority and assuming the role of a religious court"). *See also Goldman*, 554 N.E.2d at 1025 (Johnson, J., dissenting).

101. *See* Breitowitz, *supra* note 52, at 61 ("The key problem in the prenuptial agreement, therefore, is halachic rather than secular in nature, and there is little the current legal system can do to resolve it"). The preferred solution within the Orthodox community is legislation that requires an individual married in a religious ceremony must take steps to remove any religious barriers to the other party's remarriage before being granted a divorce. *E.g.*, N.Y. Dom. Rel. L. § 253 (1999). The New York "get law" is only a partial solution, however, and raises a different set of First Amendment concerns. *See* Breitowitz, *supra* note 52, at 385-93, and Zornberg, *supra* note 96, at 749-52.

102. Avitzur v. Avitzur, 446 N.E.2d 136 (N.Y. 1983).

103. *Id.* at 138.

104. *See* Basil Herring & Kenneth Auman, The Prenuptial Agreement: Halakhic and Pastoral Considerations (1996).

ments of state arbitration laws, and to certain minimum requirements of due process and fairness.[105] In addition, courts generally will not confirm arbitration awards concerning child support or custody without an independent consideration of the best interests of the children.[106]

Shifting proceedings to the *bet din* may help wives to procure a *get* from an unwilling husband, but there are also cases suggesting that wives may face significant procedural or substantive disadvantages in the religious forum. It is very important within the Jewish community that divorced women receive a *get*, and because the *bet din* cannot force the husband to provide one, a wife may be pressured to agree to her husband's terms. Traditional gender roles and expectations undoubtedly play a powerful role in this setting as well. Courts have noted the problem of duress in this context, refusing to enforce arbitration or separation agreements signed under various types of pressure.[107]

In comparison with the questions of recognition and respect for marriages and divorces discussed in Part I, disputes at the boundary of religion and law present a different set of challenges. This is reflected by the divergent approaches taken by courts and by an ongoing debate within different religious communities over these questions.[108] While the tools of contract and arbitration law may prove to be some help in defining and mediating these conflicts, there are significant limits to how far such "neutral principles" will go.[109]

105. *See* Kovacs v. Kovacs, 633 A.2d 425 (Md. Ct. Spec. App. 1994); Stein v. Stein, 707 N.Y.S.2d 754 (Sup. Ct. 1999). The same issues are considered when a *bet din* arbitrates other types of civil disputes, *e.g.*, Ghertner v. Solaimani, 563 S.E.2d 878 (Ga. Ct. App. 2002).

106. *E.g.*, *Kovacs*, *supra; In re* Marriage of Popack, 998 P.2d 464 (Colo. Ct. App. 2000); *see also* Hirsch v. Hirsch, 774 N.Y.S.2d 48 (Sup. Ct. App. Div. 2004).

107. *See, e.g.*, Stein v. Stein, 707 N.Y.S.2d 754 (Sup. Ct. 1999); Segal v. Segal, 650 A.2d 996 (N.J. Super. Ct. 1994); Golding v. Golding, 581 N.Y.S.2d 4 (App. Div. 1992); Perl v. Perl, 512 N.Y.S.2d 372 (App. Div. 1987); *but see* Greenberg v. Greenberg, 656 N.Y.S.2d 369 (App. Div. 1997) (agreement not extracted under duress where failure to agree would have led *bet din* to order a *siruv*, a type of communal ostracism).

108. On the attempt to develop contemporary Islamic marriage contracts see *supra* note 94. Scholars looking for ways to resolve the problem of the *agunah* from within Jewish tradition include Breitowitz, *supra* note 52, and David Novak, *Jewish Marriage and Civil Law: A Two-Way Street?*, 68 GEO. WASH. L. REV. 1059, 1075 (2000) ("Traditional Jews . . . should be even more concerned with this non-Jewish, secular remedy to a Jewish moral problem when they . . . could largely solve the problem by the exercise of their own authority within their community").

109. However these issues are resolved, women who seek to remain within their tradition and exercise the rights available in the larger society will sometimes face difficult choices beyond the ability of courts to address. A married Jewish woman who believes she needs a *get* may not be able to secure a divorce and remarry within her tradition. A Muslim wife may not be able to collect her *mahr* if she institutes no-fault divorce proceedings in circumstances in which she would not be entitled to divorce under Islamic law.

III. Accommodation and Change

The growing body of multicultural family law in the United States demonstrates that our legal tradition is capacious enough to embrace greater cultural and religious diversity, and defines some of the principles that constrain the process of multicultural accommodation. For courts and legislators, the challenge of pluralism lies in getting this balance right: making space for a broader range of legal principles, social relationships, and groups, without discarding our most important values. Within the United States, the argument for cultural and religious pluralism can be grounded in the constitutional protections for religious freedom under the First Amendment[110] and the prohibitions on racial or religious discrimination under the Fifth and Fourteenth Amendments.[111] At the same time, family law is also surrounded by important legal and constitutional norms of due process, and protections against gender discrimination in state and federal law.[112]

Courts encountering unfamiliar practices and traditions today respond pragmatically, in the best common law tradition. Judges evaluate the parties' dispute, attempting to understand the place and importance of unfamiliar cultural and religious practices. They reevaluate familiar legal principles in order to determine whether they may be extended to or harmonized with a different set of traditions. When the correspondence is relatively close, courts have not hesitated to make accommodations. When the claims of pluralism come into conflict with the core values of our own legal tradition, however, accommodation requires a more cautious approach.

International human rights laws reflect some of the same conflicting norms that characterize these family law cases. International treaties protect individual rights, including rights of women and children that may not be recognized in particular countries or cultures.[113] These agreements also protect cultural rights, including specifically, the right of members of ethnic, religious and linguistic minority groups, "in community with other members of their group, to enjoy their own culture, to profess and practice their own religion, or to use their own language."[114] In addition, international conventions prohibit discrimination on grounds such as "race, colour, sex, language, religion, political or other opinion, national or social origin, property, birth or other status,"[115] and protect the freedom of "thought,

110. *E.g.*, Wisconsin v. Yoder, 406 U.S. 205 (1972).

111. *E.g.*, Loving v. Virginia, 388 U.S. 1 (1967).

112. In constitutional terms, this is expressed in Orr v. Orr, 440 U.S. 268 (1979).

113. *E.g.*, CEDAW, *supra* note 21, and CRC, *supra* note 69.

114. Art. 27, International Covenant on Civil and Political Rights 6 I.L.M. 368 (1967) [hereinafter ICCPR].

115. Art. 2, Universal Declaration of Human Rights, *supra* note 21; art. 2(2); ICCPR, *supra*

conscience and religion."[116]

Human rights laws may provide a useful reference point for courts struggling with issues of pluralism and family law. Where there is a conflict between claims for cultural and religious diversity and claims for individual rights or gender equality, human rights norms affirm the importance of both of these goods. For domestic courts, this normative framework suggests the importance of opening a space in which traditions may be accommodated, and, at the same time, attending to other important values.

The requirement that marriages be based on the full and free consent of the parties is repeated in numerous United Nations declarations and conventions, including the Universal Declaration of Human Rights,[117] the International Covenant on Civil and Political Rights (ICCPR),[118] and the International Covenant on Economic, Social and Cultural Rights (ICESCR).[119] The obligation to extend equal rights to women and men "as to marriage, during marriage, and at its dissolution" is included in the Universal Declaration as well as the ICCPR and ICESCR, and elaborated in the Convention on the Elimination of all forms of Discrimination Against Women (CEDAW).[120] The child's right to have determinations based on his or her best interests is similarly rooted in international law, including the Declaration on the Rights of the Child[121] and the Convention on the Rights of the Child (CRC).[122] These conventions have been very widely ratified around the world, establishing a broad international consensus that could be characterized as customary international law.[123]

As each case is decided, judges are developing what one scholar has described as internal choice of law principles that are necessary when traditions co-exist.[124] As they determine how far to assimilate distinct cultural

---

note 114. The list as formulated in the CRC includes: "race, colour, sex, language, religion, political or other opinion, national, ethnic or social origin, property, disability, birth or other status. Art. 2(1), CRC, *supra* note 69.

116. Art. 18, Universal Declaration of Human Rights, *supra* note 21; art. 2(2), art. 18, ICCPR, *supra* note 114; art. 14, CRC, *supra* note 69.

117. Universal Declaration of Human Rights, art. 16, *supra* note 21.

118. ICCPR, art. 23, *supra* note 114.

119. International Covenant on Economic, Social and Cultural Rights, art. 10(1), 6 I.L.M. 360 (1967). *See also* the U.N. Marriage Convention, *supra* note 29.

120. CEDAW, art. 16, *supra* note 21.

121. United Nations Declaration on the Rights of the Child, G.A. Res. 1386 U.N. GAOR, 14th Sess., U.N. Doc. A/4354 (1959).

122. Convention on the Rights of the Child, *supra* note 69.

123. The United States ratified the ICCPR in 1992, and has signed CEDAW and the CRC. This agreement is broad but not universal. The tensions between norms of international human rights and norms prevalent in other systems have been particularly notable with respect to Islamic law and tradition; *see e.g.*, Alison Dundes Renteln, *Cultural Bias in International Law*, 92 AM. SOC'Y INT'L L. PROC. 232, 238-39 (1998).

124. H. PATRICK GLENN, LEGAL TRADITIONS OF THE WORLD: SUSTAINABLE DIVERSITY IN LAW 30-39 (2000).

practices into the mainstream legal tradition, the courts operate within a larger political and social context, defined by fundamental values including principles of due process, nondiscrimination, gender equality, and religious freedom. Part of this context is an understanding of the courts' role in family law matters that includes what Carl Schneider has called a "protective function."[125]

In the working out of this process, courts face particularly important questions in relation to traditional practices that are heavily gendered. For reasons described by Ayelet Shachar, women have been particularly vulnerable to oppression within traditional family law systems.[126] Courts also face difficult questions concerning individual religious freedom and the claims of religious groups. Legal rules that prohibited divorce for Catholics or Hindus, or restricted Jewish or Islamic women to the traditional divorce practices of their religion, would clearly violate nondiscrimination and religious freedom principles. It is less clear whether a private agreement to the same effect could be enforced, particularly in light of the possibility that an individual's religious beliefs may change over time. In addition, since cultures and tradition are complex, variable, and changing, courts should be especially alert to the ongoing debate within many communities about adapting traditions to new circumstances and defining the appropriate boundaries between civil and religious law.

125. Carl E. Schneider, *The Channelling Function in Family Law*, 20 HOFSTRA L. REV. 495, 497 (1992). Schneider writes: "One of law's most basic duties is to protect citizens against harms done them by other citizens. This means protecting people from physical harm, as the law of spouse and child abuse attempts to do, and from non-physical harms, especially economic wrongs and psychological injuries."

126. AYELET SHACHAR, MULTICULTURAL JURISDICTIONS: CULTURAL DIFFERENCES AND WOMEN'S RIGHTS, 36, 55-56 (2001). To the extent that jurisdiction over family law matters is assumed by religious authorities, there is a risk that women will remain particularly vulnerable, and secular courts need to be sensitive to these circumstances.

[2]

Taking Multiculturalism Seriously: Marriage Law and the Rights of Minorities

PATRICK PARKINSON*

1. *Law in a Multicultural Society*

Australia is one of the few countries in the world in which almost the entire population consists either of migrants or descendants from migrants. Its indigenous peoples who have lived in Australia for some 40,000 years, now represent only about 1 per cent of the population.[1] The majority of the people are classified as Anglo-Celtic, that is, people of English, Irish, Scottish and Welsh descent. In 1988, they represented 75 per cent of the population.[2] However, the composition of Australia is changing rapidly. Having maintained a "white Australia" policy until after World War II,[3] Australia has gradually opened up to migrants from all over the world. In 1986, over 20 per cent of the Australian population had been born overseas, and of these, 56 per cent were born in a non-English speaking country.[4] In 1989–90, 42 per cent of the settler arrivals had been born in Asia[5] (of which the majority came from South-East Asia) and only 32 per cent were born in Europe.[6] The Australian population of 16.5 million people continues to increase at a rapid pace. Approximately one million people arrived as settlers between 1982 and 1992.[7]

---

* Senior Lecturer, Faculty of Law, University of Sydney. The author is grateful for the research assistance of Lici Inge and Ann Moubarak, and to the NSW Law Foundation Legal Scholarship Support Fund for its financial assistance.

1 Price, C, *Ethnic Groups in Australia* (1989) Australian Immigration Research Centre at 2.

2 Ibid.

3 The "white Australia" policy was put in place through the *Immigration Restriction Act* 1901 (Cth). Section 3 required prospective migrants to take a dictation test of fifty words in a European language. By an amending Act in 1905, the word "European" was replaced by the words "a prescribed language" to avoid giving offence to Japan and India. The "white Australia" policy was also carried into effect by the *Pacific Island Labourers Act* 1901 (Cth) which provided for the deportation of all such labourers by 1905. A few were later allowed to remain on compassionate grounds. See further, Clark, M, *A Short History of Australia* (3rd edn, 1986) at 196–199.

4 Australian Bureau of Statistics, *Overseas Born Australians 1988: A Statistical Profile* (1989) ABS, Canberra at 47.

5 Price, above n1 at 2. Asians represented only 4.5 per cent of the Australian population in 1988 but the Asian community is growing especially rapidly.

6 Bureau of Immigration Research, *Settler Arrivals 1989–90* (1991) Australian Government Publishing Service, Canberra.

7 Bureau of Immigration Research, *Settler Arrivals by State of Intended Residence, 1990-91: Statistical Report No 5* (1992) Australian Government Publishing Service, Canberra at 3, 65. In the same period, over 500,000 people left Australia to go overseas for the long-term. Cited in Cronin, K, "Immigration Problems in Family Law", *World Congress on Family Law and Children's Rights*, Sydney, July 1993.

A. *Multiculturalism and International Law*

The rapid changes in the ethnic origin of the Australian population have led to consideration of how Australia should adapt its institutions and traditions, largely derived from England, to reflect the cultural diversity of the population. The rights of minorities to be able to practise their religion and maintain their culture are protected by various conventions in international law. For example, article 27 of the International Covenant on Civil and Political Rights (1966) provides that in states which have ethnic, religious or linguistic minorities, persons belonging to such minorities shall not be denied the right, in community with other members of their group, to enjoy their own culture, to profess and practise their own religion, and to use their own language.[8] This is subject to the qualification, contained in article 18(3), that states are entitled to impose such limitations on the exercise of people's freedom to manifest their religion or beliefs as are necessary in the interests of public safety, order, health or morals, or for the protection of the fundamental rights and freedoms of others. Other instruments of international law also provide limitations on the exercise of cultural and religious freedom. Australia is a signatory to the Convention on the Elimination of All Forms of Discrimination Against Women and the Convention on the Rights of the Child. The protection of the rights of women and children may at times conflict with particular cultural practices which would otherwise have a claim to recognition.

The competing rights contained within these various international covenants and conventions create a difficult balancing operation for governments in a multicultural society such as Australia. On the one hand, they must respect the cultural practices of minority groups within the society. On the other hand, they must protect "minorities within minorities", that is, the vulnerable members of ethnic minorities, from cultural practices which are oppressive.[9]

B. *Dimensions of Multiculturalism in the Legal System*

Recognition of the cultural diversity of the Australian population (and indeed the diversity of lifestyles and beliefs among Australians of Anglo-Celtic descent) has led for calls to adapt the legal system so that it is better suited to the demands of a multicultural society.[10] The Australian Government's official policy on multiculturalism, the National Agenda for a Multicultural Australia(1989)[11] (hereinafter cited as "National Agenda") stated that one of the government's objectives for its multicultural policy was "to promote equality before the law by systematically examining the implicit cultural assumptions of the law and the legal system to identify the manner in which they may unintentionally act to disadvantage certain groups of Australians".[12]

---

8 See also Article 30 of the Convention on the Rights of the Child.

9 Sadurski, W, "Last Among Equals: Minorities and Australian Judge-Made Law" (1989) 63 *ALJ* 474 at 481.

10 See, eg, Bird, G (ed), *Law in a Multicultural Australia* (1991); Bird, G, *The Process of Law in Australia: Intercultural Perspectives* (2nd edn, 1993).

11 Office of Multicultural Affairs, *National Agenda for a Multicultural Australia* (1989) Australian Government Publishing Service, Canberra (hereinafter cited as "National Agenda").

12 Id at 17.

As a means of fulfilling this objective, the Australian Law Reform Commission was given a reference on multiculturalism and the law which focused upon the areas of family law, criminal law and contract law which are within the legislative competence of the federal government. The Commission reported in 1992.[13]

Multiculturalism means different things to different people however.[14] In terms of the legal system, the claim to respect for the rights of minorities may take five different forms. First, an acceptance of cultural diversity means that the freedom of particular groups to enjoy their culture or religion should not be restricted unless this is necessary to protect the human rights of others. This is the fundamental obligation imposed by article 27 of the International Covenant on Civil and Political Rights. The government should not prohibit minorities from practising their religion, using their own language or enjoying their own culture. In western democracies, these rights are primarily protected by the principles of freedom of speech, religion and assembly.[15] Laws which single out particular ethnic minorities or religious groups by prohibiting cultural or religious practices which are particular to them violate the principle of equality before the law.[16] Nonetheless, laws which are neutral on their face and apparently of universal application may in practice have a discriminatory impact upon particular groups by inhibiting the enjoyment of their culture or exercise of their religion, and it was the elimination of this form of discriminatory impact which was expressed as an objective of the National Agenda.

The second dimension of multiculturalism which is expressed in international conventions and covenants is that governments should act to prevent discrimination based upon religion or ethnicity. Article 26 of the International Covenant on Civil and Political Rights prohibits discrimination on the grounds of race and national origin, as does the International Convention on the Elimination of All Forms of Racial Discrimination. These international obligations are given effect in domestic law by legislation such as the *Racial Discrimination Act* 1975 (Cth). State anti-discrimination laws are also consistent with the aims of the international conventions.

The third dimension is that the legal system should be accessible to people irrespective of their cultural background and first language. If people from a non-English speaking background are to be able to understand court cases in which they are involved, this means that they will need interpreter services

---

13 *ALRC* Report No 57, *Multiculturalism and the Law* (1992) Australian Government Publishing Service, Canberra.

14 See eg Bullivant, B, "Australia's Pluralist Dilemma: An Age-old Problem in a New Guise", (1983) 55 *Aust Q* 136; Jupp, J, "Multiculturalism: Friends and Enemies, Patrons and Clients" (1983) 55 *Aust Q* 149; Jayasuriya, L, "Rethinking Australian Multiculturalism: Towards a New Paradigm" (1990) 62 *Aust Q* 50.

15 This protection may be provided by constitutional law, as in the United States, but it may also be protected sufficiently by political tradition where the values are so deeply embedded in the culture that they are vigorously defended by those with access to power and influence within the society.

16 In the constitutional law of the United States, this fundamental principle was expressed by Stone J in his famous footnote 4 in *United States v Carolene Products Co* 304 US 144 (1938) at 152–3. He stated that one of the grounds on which legislation could be subjected to "more exacting judicial scrutiny" was if it was directed at particular religious, national or racial minorities, or expressed prejudice against "discrete and insular minorities".

both in court and in the earlier stages of the legal process, such as interviews with police and legal representatives.[17] They may also need other assistance, such as explanation of basic aspects of the legal process with which Anglo-Celtic people could expect to be familiar, for example, the role of juries. Education about the law is also an aspect of overcoming the cultural gulf which inhibits members of ethnic minorities from having greater access to the legal system. Education is necessary not only to convey basic information to people about their rights and obligations under Australian law, but also to overcome misconceptions people may have about the requirements of Australian law, based upon their experiences in their countries of origin.[18]

A fourth possible dimension of multiculturalism in relation to the law is that government officials and courts should take account of particular cultural factors in the application of the general laws of the land to individuals. Thus, in child custody and access cases involving children of mixed race, account might be taken of such factors as the importance for the child's cultural development and sense of identity of maintaining links with his or her extended family. The willingness or unwillingness of one parent seeking custody to allow contact with the family of the other parent might be an important factor in the ultimate decision.[19] In criminal cases, officials or courts might take account of the cultural context in which the offence occurred in deciding whether to prosecute, whether to convict, or how to sentence.[20] Specific exemptions, whether de facto or de jure, might be given to particular ethnic groups where the interference with their religious freedom outweighs any public benefit of the application of the law to them. For example, in a multicultural society, it would be consistent with good policy both to require the wearing of safety helmets by motorcyclists generally, and to take account of the objections of the Sikh community, who wear turbans for religious reasons, either by exempting them from the helmet requirement or by exercising a discretion not to prosecute them.[21]

A fifth potential dimension for multiculturalism is that the law should be sufficiently pluralistic to allow different communities to be governed by their

---

17 D'Argaville, M, "Serving a Multicultural Clientele: Communication Between Lawyers and Non-English-speaking Background Clients" in *Law in a Multicultural Australia*, above n10 at 83.

18 See eg, Australian Law Reform Commission, *Multiculturalism and the Law*, Research Paper no 1, "Family Law: Issues in the Vietnamese Community" (1991) at 24–30.

19 Above n13 at ch 8. See also *Goudge and Goudge* (1984) FLC 91–534 (Evatt CJ dissenting); *DKI and OBI* [1979] FLC 90–661; *In the Marriage of McL; Minister for Health and Community Services (NT) (Intervener)* [1991] FLC 92–238.

20 For example, in *R v Isobel Phillips* (NT Court of Summary Jurisdiction, 19 September 1983, unreported) the defence of duress was allowed to an aboriginal woman from the Warumungu tribe because the evidence demonstrated that she was required by tribal law to fight in public with any woman involved with her husband, and was under a threat of death or serious injury if she did not respond. Australian Law Reform Commission, *Recognition of Aboriginal Customary Law* (1986) Report No 31, Australian Government Publishing Service, Canberra, at para 430, in fn 82. See also the recommendations of the Australian Law Reform Commission on the need to take account of cultural factors in the application of the criminal law: Above n13 at ch 8.

21 There is a specific legislative exemption for Sikhs in England: *Motor-Cycle Crash Helmets (Religious Exemption) Act* 1976. For the position in Australia, see ALRC Report No 57, above n13 at 175–176.

own laws on matters where cultural values differ significantly between different groups. If this claim were accepted, then it might mean that tribal aboriginal communities would be exempted from the application of the general laws of the land to the extent that these laws conflict with aboriginal customary laws, and that where there was a breach of customary law, it should be dealt with by the elders of the community rather than by the ordinary courts.[22] Divorce, property division and disputes concerning child custody might similarly be dealt with by the civil courts in accordance with the cultural norms of a particular religion or ethnic group where both the parties to the marriage were, at the time of the marriage, and at the time of the hearing, members of that ethnic or religious community. Thus talaq divorces could be recognised where both husband and wife were adherents to the Islamic faith, and child custody determinations would conform to the cultural and religious rules of their ethnic community.

This fifth claim for multiculturalism is the most controversial of all. Sensitivity to cultural practices conflicts with the principle, which is a fundamental premise of western legal systems, that all members of society should be governed by the same laws. Apart from adherence to the fundamental precepts of the western legal tradition, there are other reasons for not allowing different communities to be governed by different legal norms. The recognition and enforcement of certain cultural norms and rules by the law of the country could, in certain instances, violate the principle that the government should protect the rights of vulnerable members of minority groups from practices which are regarded by the dominant culture as oppressive. The Australian Law Reform Commission gave as its reasons for rejecting the possibility of separate laws that:

> Imposing special laws on people because they belong to a particular ethnic group could introduce unjustified discriminations into the law, lead to unnecessary and divisive labelling of people, and possibly be oppressive of individual members of that group.[23]

C. *The National Agenda for a Multicultural Australia*

The first four dimensions of multiculturalism have gained support from government policy. The extent and limits of the government's commitment to multiculturalism is expressed in the National Agenda. There, multiculturalism is defined as having three aspects, cultural identity, social justice and economic efficiency. The right to cultural identity means that all Australians have the right to express and share their individual cultural heritage, including their language and religion. This right is subject to carefully defined limits. Australians must accept the basic structure and principles of Australian society, defined as comprising the Constitution and the rule of law, tolerance and equality, parliamentary democracy, freedom of speech and religion, English as the national language and equality of the sexes. Social justice in the context of a multicultural policy means the right of all Australians to equality

---

22 This approach was rejected by the Australian Law Reform Commission in its report on Aboriginal customary law, in favour of the limited recognition of customary laws for specific purposes. ALRC Report no 31, above n20. For comment, see Poulter, S, "Cultural Pluralism in Australia" (1988) 2 *Int'l J Law & Fam* 127.

23 Above n13 at 11–12.

of treatment and opportunity, and the removal of barriers of race, ethnicity, culture, religion, language, gender or place of birth. The third aspect, economic efficiency, means the need to maintain, develop and utilise effectively the skills and talents of all Australians, regardless of background.[24]

Australia's multicultural policy thus seeks to allow linguistic and cultural diversity within a framework of commitment to values which are seen to be fundamental to Australian society. The notion of the rule of law is a protected principle, but individual rules are not. Indeed, the National Agenda indicated that all members of society should be able to enjoy the basic right of freedom from discrimination, which includes not only overt discrimination but "that unwitting systemic discrimination which occurs when cultural assumptions become embodied in society's established institutions and processes".[25] The institutions and processes of the law are a particular locus for western cultural assumptions.

2. *Multiculturalism and Australian Family Law*

Acceptance of cultural diversity, and recognition of cultural issues in the application of the law, are especially important in relation to family law, for as the Australian Law Reform Commission observed: "Families play a central role in the development of a person's cultural identity and the transmission of culture, language and social values".[26] Yet it is also in the realm of family life that there is the greatest clash between the values and cultural assumptions of the dominant Anglo-Celtic majority, and the values of various ethnic minorities. Australian family law neither defines the "family" nor gives the family a special legal status. The focus of the law is on the individual members of the family, and their respective rights and obligations.[27] Furthermore, as entrance into a marriage is voluntary, so exit from it may be the unilateral decision of one person who is unwilling to remain in the marriage, subject to a separation period of twelve months before making an application for dissolution. Australian family law exalts the values of individual freedom over obligations to family or community, and despite its lack of definition of the word "family" the law largely assumes the nuclear family as the focus of its attention.[28]

By contrast, the values of many ethnic minorities within Australian society emphasise the importance of collective values. Marriages are not merely alliances of individuals. They may also be alliances of families. The notion of "family" extends beyond the nuclear family to embrace a wide range of relatives and the organisation of the family, along with its hierarchies and power structures, includes this extended network of kinship. The husband and wife owe obligations not only to each other and to their children, but also to this extended family.[29]

---

24 *National Agenda* above n11 at vii.

25 Id at 15.

26 Australian Law Reform Commission, *Multiculturalism: Family Law* (1991) Discussion Paper No 46 at 8.

27 Id at 7.

28 *Mehmet and Mehmet (No 2)* (1987) FLC 91–801; Dickey, A, "The Notion of 'Family' in Law" (1982) 14 *U WA LR* 416.

29 See eg, the accounts of the traditions of Turkish, Lebanese and Sri Lankan families in

While the National Agenda set as a goal the elimination of that "unwitting systemic discrimination which occurs when cultural assumptions become embodied in society's established institutions and processes",[30] it is questionable whether it is possible to eliminate this form of discrimination in the realm of family law without abandoning those cultural assumptions which represent cherished values of political and social life in Australia. Indeed, the National Agenda betrays its own western cultural assumptions when it says: "Fundamentally, multiculturalism is about the rights of the individual".[31] The very language of human rights, in which the multicultural policy is couched, owes its origins to the western legal tradition, and in particular, the enlightment precepts of the French and American Revolutions. And although the notion of human rights has now been encapsulated in universal declarations and conventions under the auspices of the United Nations, "rights" in Australia still carry with them the connotations of individual liberties and freedoms which reflect western understandings of the nature of a political democracy. A multicultural policy which is "fundamentally about the rights of the individual", may involve little more than a western legal and political system which employs interpreters.

Given the strength of the philosophy of individualism and the recent commitment to gender equality within Australian society, cultural values will necessarily be excluded which emphasise the cohesiveness of the family as more important than individual freedoms, the importance of parental authority over children as more important than adolescent autonomy, or the patriarchal authority of male heads of the household rather than gender equality. There is thus only a limited room for multiculturalism in family law. If certain premises are accepted as given, that Australian family law should uphold the freedom of individuals both in the entry into and exit from marriage, that there should be one law governing all Australians in terms of divorce, property division, maintenance and the law concerning children, and that the law should maintain its commitment to the equality of the sexes and the protection of children's rights, then there is little scope for the law to adjust its cultural assumptions to be more inclusive of the cultural values of ethnic minorities.

3. *Multiculturalism and Marital Status*

A. *Marital Status and the Right of Cultural Expression*

In one area of family law, there ought to be greater scope for the recognition of cultural diversity. This is in the law concerning the recognition of marital status. One application of article 27 of the International Covenant on Civil and Political Rights and of other similar international human rights provisions, is that allowing minority groups to enjoy their own culture and to practise their own religion means recognising as marriages in Australian law those marriages which are recognised by the customs of the ethnic community, and

---

Storer, D, *Ethnic Family Values in Australia* (1985).

30 See n25 above.

31 *National Agenda* above n11 at 15.

placing only those restrictions on entry into marriage which are necessary to protect the rights and interests of the parties to the proposed marriage.

It was recognised by the Australian Law Reform Commission in its report on Aboriginal customary laws, that in the case of tribal Aboriginal communities, respect for the indigenous culture can best be achieved by not recognising Aboriginal customary marriages as legal marriages at all.[32] It has been estimated that at least 90 per cent of marriages among traditional aborigines are not contracted under the *Marriage Act* 1961.[33] Traditional aboriginal marriages are recognisable as marriages in the western sense inasmuch as they are socially ratified arrangements which involve an expectation of relative permanency. However, to recognise them as marriages with all the legal consequences of this in Australian law would be to reconstruct them within a western legal and cultural framework. The application to customary marriages of the laws on divorce and its consequences contained in the *Family Law Act* would mean foisting on the parties to traditional marriages consequences which have no traditional equivalent and which may be disruptive to Aboriginal culture.[34] A further reason for not giving effect to existing aboriginal customary laws concerning marriage is that codification of customary law would involve the State in enforcing promises to marry which would run counter to contemporary western ideas concerning consent to marriage.[35] For these reasons, the Australian Law Reform Commission recommended in 1986 that traditional Aboriginal marriages should receive functional recognition for specific purposes only.[36]

While Aboriginal marriages constitute an exception, in most cases the goal of multiculturalism would be advanced by the recognition as legal marriages of all those unions which are regarded as marriages by the ethnic or religious community, and allowing marriages to take place in accordance with the traditions and practices of that community. To a large extent, the legal requirements for the ceremony of marriage law do this. There are few practical constraints

---

32 ALRC, Report No 31, above n20 at pars 233–257. A similar view has been taken by the Queensland Law Reform Commission Report No 44, *De Facto Relationships*, (1993). Its tentative proposal in a working paper was that traditional Aboriginal marriages should be recognised specifically in the definition of de facto relationships, giving rise to property and maintenance rights under the proposed legislation. It reversed its view in the report, although it noted that traditional marriages would be likely to come within its general definition of a de facto relationship (see Report at 13–16 hereinafter QLRC Report No 44).

33 Dagmar, H, *Aborigines and Poverty: A Study of Interethnic Relations and Culture Conflict in a WA Town*, (1978) Katholicke Universiteit, Nijmegen, at 101. The Department of Family Services and Aboriginal and Islander Affairs (Qld) estimated on the basis of 1986 data that between 40 per cent and 60 per cent of Aboriginal and Torres Strait Islander couples did not identify as married under Australian law: QLRC, Report No 44, above n32 at 14.

34 ALRC Report No 31, above n20 at par 256.

35 Id at pars 248–251.

36 Id at par 265. Traditional marriages are recognised for a number of purposes in the Northern Territory, for example, the *Status of Children Act* 1978, the *Family Provision Act* 1979, the *Administration and Probate Act* 1979, the *Workmen's Compensation Act* 1979, and the *Motor Accidents (Compensation) Act* 1979. Victoria recognises aboriginal marriages for the purposes of allowing a couple to adopt: *Adoption Act* 1984. The *Compensation (Commonwealth Government Employees) Act* 1971 (Cth) also recognises aboriginal marriages in allowing compensation to a spouse for the death of a government employee.

upon people marrying in accordance with their own traditions and culture. The only requirement is that the priest or other religious leader is a registered minister of religion or otherwise an authorised marriage celebrant.[37]

B. *The Limitations on Recognition of Marital Status*

There must be an irreducible minimum of legal regulation of marriage if the law is to protect the human rights of individuals[38] and to uphold important social values. In western societies, that irreducible minimum has been that the law should ensure that the consent of each party to the marriage is freely given, which means that the courts must be prepared to declare as a nullity those marriages which have been procured by fraud or duress. The law must also ensure that children too young to give a valid consent to marriage are prohibited from doing so. Finally, there has been seen to be a compelling social interest in the prohibition of incestuous relationships which is sufficient to override the wishes of the parties to a prospective marriage. These minimal requirements of the law have remained relatively constant over the centuries; what has varied has been the manner of their interpretation. In particular, the laws concerning minimum marriage age and the prohibited degrees of consanguinity and affinity have changed considerably in the last one hundred years.[39]

The protection of the fundamental human rights of individuals may at times conflict with the cultural practices of certain ethnic minorities. An illustration of this is the problem of arranged marriages. Arranged marriages in western societies involve a potential clash between the values of individualism which predominate in western societies and the importance placed upon family, kinship and parental authority by other cultural groups.[40] The question which has arisen in Australia and elsewhere, is whether the laws of duress as a ground for nullity[41] should apply to cases in which a young person succumbs

---

37 *Marriage Act* 1961 (Cth) ss25–39. For a declaration of nullity in relation to a Hindu marriage for failure to comply with these requirements see *Rewal and Rewal* (1991) FLC 92–225.

38 See generally, Poulter, S, "Ethnic Minority Customs, English Law and Human Rights" (1987) 36 *Int'l Comp LQ* 589. Poulter argues that limitations on the recognition of the cultural practices of ethnic minorities are justifiable if they derive from the human rights provisions of international law, and furthermore, that where a refusal to recognise or uphold a custom would amount to the denial of a person's human rights, then a strong case exists for the recognition of that custom.

39 Glendon, M, *The Transformation of Family Law: State, Law and Family in the United States and Western Europe* (1989).

40 For discussion of the cultural background to arranged marriage, see Poulter, S, *English Law and Ethnic Minority Customs* (1986) at 22–26; Bradley, D, "Duress and Arranged Marriages" (1983) 46 *Mod LR* 499. For discussion of arranged marriages in traditional aboriginal communities, see ALRC Report No 31, above n20 at pars 224–229.

41 The *Marriage Act* 1961, s23B provides that a marriage is void where:
"(a) either of the parties is, at the time of the marriage, lawfully married to some other person;
(b) the parties are within a prohibited relationship;
(c) by reason of section 48 the marriage is not a valid marriage;
(d) the consent of either of the parties is not a real consent because:
(i) it was obtained by duress or fraud;
(ii) that party is mistaken as to the identity of the other party or as to the nature of the ceremony performed; or
(iii) that party is mentally incapable of understanding the nature and effect of the

to strong parental pressure to enter into an arranged marriage and later seeks to have the marriage annulled.

The issue of consent to marriage is governed by the Convention on Consent to Marriage, Minimum Age for Marriage and Registration of Marriage to which Australia is a signatory. Article 1(1) provides:

> No marriage shall be legally entered into without the full and free consent of both parties, such consent to be expressed by them in person after due publicity and in the presence of the authority competent to solemnise the marriage and of witnesses, as prescribed by law.[42]

Article 23 of the International Covenant on Civil and Political Rights provides similarly that: "No marriage shall be entered into without the free and full consent of the intending spouses".[43]

There have been variations over the years in the approach taken by the courts to the level of coercion necessary to vitiate consent to a marriage. In *Scott (falsely called Sebright) v Sebright*,[44] it was held that there can be no consent to marry if a person is in such a state of mental incompetence that he or she is unable to resist pressure improperly brought to bear. The relevant "mental incompetence" might arise from "natural weakness of intellect" or from fear.[45] A stricter test was adopted in *Szechter v Szechter*.[46] Sir Jocelyn Simon P held that the coercion had to be the product of an immediate danger to life, limb or liberty, and this was the position in England and Australia before the 1980s. This test precluded the possibility that an arranged marriage might constitute duress. Indeed, in certain English cases in the 1970s and early 1980s, applications to declare arranged marriages a nullity on the grounds of duress were rejected.[47]

However, in the Australian case of *In the Marriage of S*[48] the *Szechter* test was expanded to take account of psychological pressure, and the arranged marriage of a sixteen year old girl was annulled.[49] It was clear from the evidence that the young woman was utterly unhappy with the arrangement. Whatever argu-

---

marriage ceremony; or
(e) either of the parties is not of marriageable age,
and not otherwise."

42 (1964) 521 UNTS 231. There were 36 signatories as at 1991.

43 (1966) UKTS 6 (1977).

44 (1886) 12 PD 21.

45 This test was not lightly satisfied in subsequent cases. In *Cooper (falsely called Crane) v Crane* [1891] P 369, a man arranged for a marriage ceremony to take place in a church at a particular time, and by deception, brought the woman to that place. He then threatened that unless she went through a ceremony of marriage with him, he would shoot himself. She knew that he was in the habit of carrying a revolver. It was held that the coercion was not sufficient in this case to constitute duress.

46 [1971] P 286.

47 *Singh v Singh* [1971] P 226, and *Singh v Kaur* (1981) 11 Fam Law 152.

48 (1980) FLC 90–820.

49 In this case, the applicant was married according to the rites of the Egyptian Coptic Orthodox Church. The marriage had been arranged for her by her parents. Her husband-to-be was living in Egypt at the time, and they became engaged while on a visit to Egypt. The girl was very resistant to the marriage, but came under strong pressure from her parents to go through with it. She only stayed with her husband for four days after the ceremony, and the marriage was not consummated.

ments might have been made concerning respect for minority cultural values was displaced by the primary concern of respect for the individual freedom of the young person.[50] As Watson S J stated:

> The applicant is still a child and ... is entitled to the court's protection of her rights. She, and not her parents, has the right to choose whom she shall marry. That is a right to self-sovereignty to which culture, religion and family must bow.[51]

C. *The Australian Law Reform Commission's Approach*

In approaching the issue of multiculturalism in the recognition of marital status, the Australian Law Reform Commission stated its approach as follows:

> The approach adopted by the Commission to reform of family law in a multicultural society is that, generally speaking, the law should not inhibit the formation of family relationships and should recognise as valid the relationships people choose for themselves. Further, the law should support and protect these relationships. However, the law should restrict a person's choice to the extent that it is necessary to protect the fundamental rights and freedoms of others and should not support relationships in which the fundamental rights and freedoms of individuals are violated. Instead, it should intervene to protect them.[52]

The first aspect of the Law Reform Commission's position (that the law should restrict a person's choice concerning marriage to the extent that it is necessary to protect the fundamental rights and freedoms of others) is consistent with the traditional liberal view expounded in the nineteenth century by John Stuart Mill and in the twentieth century by writers such as H L A Hart, that the law has no place in restricting individual freedom except to the extent that this is necessary to prevent harm to others.[53] If marriage is predicated upon a full and free consent given by the parties, it is difficult to see why recognition of any relationships as marriages should contravene this principle, unless the marriage was bigamous and harm would be caused either to the first spouse or to the new spouse as a result of the bigamous relationship.

However, the Commission went beyond the "harm principle" in stating that the law should not "support relationships in which the fundamental rights and freedoms of individuals are violated". It was not clear from either the Discussion Paper or the Report what the Commission might have had in mind by this.[54]

---

50 The English Court of Appeal has taken a very similar view to the one in *In the Marriage of S. Hirani v Hirani* (1982) 4 Fam LR (Eng) 232 was a case involving an arranged marriage of a 19 year-old Indian Hindu woman, to a man whom she (and her parents) had never met prior to the engagement. The Court of Appeal held that a threat to life, limb or liberty was not necessary. What mattered was that the pressure which was brought to bear destroyed the reality of the consent. See Ingman, T and Grant, B "Duress in the Law of Nullity" (1984) 14 *Fam L* 92. For Canadian authority see *AS v AS* (1988) 15 RFL (3d) 443.

51 Above n48 at 75, 178.

52 Above n26 at par 3.28. The Law Reform Commission's basic approach was strongly endorsed by Professor R Bailey-Harris in her inaugural lecture as Dean of Law at Flinders University in 1992. See the extract in Parker, S, Parkinson, P and Behrens, J, *Australian Family Law in Context*, (1994) at 109–111, and Professor Chipman's response, at 112–13.

53 For a more recent defence of this position see Sadurski, W, *Moral Pluralism and Legal Neutrality* (1990).

54 The President of the Commission, the Hon Justice Elizabeth Evatt, summarising the discussion paper, gave as examples of the application of this principle, people who are in

The principle perhaps draws attention to the fact that in certain situations the law's insistence that there is a valid and continuing marriage may involve supporting relationships in which the human rights of one of the parties have been, or are being, violated. This would be the case if the law were to uphold the validity of marriages which were entered into as a result of fraud or duress since this would be to violate the rights of the person who was tricked or coerced into the relationship. The Commission may also have intended to offer a principled basis for a liberal law of divorce.

In setting out the philosophical approach which was to guide them, it was inevitable that the Law Reform Commission should uphold certain values which are fundamental to the western legal tradition and which are recognised in international guarantees of human rights. It could not do otherwise. Multiculturalism may involve compromises of many kinds, but no host culture can be expected to compromise its most fundamental values in order to accomodate the cultural practices of ethnic or religious minorities. In the words of Watson SJ (above), there are certain individual human rights "to which culture, religion and family must bow".[55]

What was surprising about the work of the Australian Law Reform Commission with respect to marriage was not its basic philosophical approach but its failure to carry this through in most of its key recommendations. As will be seen, the effect of the recommendations which the Commission made, combined with the issues which are important to ethnic minorities which it chose to ignore, meant that its work reinforced the hegemony of western values, and reasserted the monocultural character of the law. There was not a single recommendation which can be seen as leading to a greater degree of cultural pluralism in Australian marriage law, nor anything which indicated a greater tolerance for values which lie outside of those held in mainstream Australian culture. On the contrary, the Report recommended changes which reduced the level of acceptance of minority cultural practices. If this was merely the failure of one law reform report to fulfil its mandate, it might be dismissed as unfortunate but of little long-term significance. However, the importance of the Law Commission's work is that in all probability it did correctly judge the mood of the nation on the issues which it was asked to address. On some issues, its provisional recommendations were supported by a great majority of those who made submissions. Furthermore, one of its provisional recommendations was enacted by Federal Parliament within a short time after the release of the Discussion Paper.

This raises a number of questions. First, it must be asked whether Law Reform Commissions, which engage in community consultations with a view to making recommendations which are supported by a majority, are an appropriate way of reforming the law in order to protect the interests of minorities. Secondly, questions must be asked about the degree to which Australian society is willing to embrace cultural diversity and to demonstrate respect for values which are either alien to, or contrary to, those values which predominate in

positions of relative powerlessness, such as children and victims of violence. Evatt, E, "Multiculturalism and Family Law" (1991) 5 *Aust J Fam L* 86.

55 Above n48 at 75, 178.

the mainstream. Respect for the human rights of minorities may in some circumstances mean that the majority must allow individuals within ethnic minorities to make choices, and to follow cultural norms and traditions, which in the view of many in the majority, are not in the best interests of the individuals who form part of the minority ethnic group. Thirdly, it must be asked whether in fact there are any legitimate grounds upon which the majority may insist upon the preservation of its values through law in circumstances which go beyond the "harm principle" and a commitment to equality and individual freedom. It is a feature of modern political discourse that so much contemporary public debate is conducted in terms of the language of discrimination and gender equality. The principle that all discrimination is wrong has emerged amongst the liberal intelligentsia in Australian society as the new public morality, and this has led to an implicit rejection of all other bases for moral judgment. The Australian Law Reform Commission's discussion of marriage law was no exception. Yet its recommendations could not be justified using the reasons it advanced without resort to paternalistic arguments. It will be argued that ultimately there are reasons why society may enforce its morality which go beyond the "harm principle" and the maintenance of values of equality and freedom. Society is entitled to protect its traditional morality even if this hinders the cultural expression of minorities, although the circumstances in which this will be justified are very rare.

4. *The Law Reform Commission's Recommendations*

The Commission made numerous recommendations concerning family law, and certain of their recommendations may be seen as consistent with their basic approach.

A. Customary Marriages and De Facto Relationships

Two of the issues which the Commission considered were the problem of customary marriages, and the recognition of de facto relationships. In its discussion paper, the Commission recommended that customary marriages, that is, marriages contracted overseas which conform to the customs of the particular community but for which no marriage certificate exists, should be recognised for some purposes, in particular, maintenance and property applications.[56] However, in its final report the Commission concluded that the existing law was adequate, since an absence of documentation could be overcome by other evidence and customary marriages could be treated as void marriages, thereby giving access to various forms of ancillary relief under the *Family Law Act*, if they involved a recognisable marriage ceremony.[57]

On the recognition of de facto relationships, the Commission took the view in its Discussion Paper, that established de facto relationships should give rise to property and maintenance rights as they do in New South Wales under the *De Facto Relationships Act* 1984.[58] The Commission's recommendations

---

56 Above n26 at par 3.38.

57 Above n13 at par 5.2.1. *Lengyel v Rasad (No 2)* (1990) 100 FLR 1.

58 Above n26 at par 3.49.

presupposed that the Federal Government does not have the constitutional power to legislate concerning the property rights of people in de facto relationships unless they live in the Territories or are amenable to Commonwealth jurisdiction on some other basis.[59] Consequently, the recommendation in the Discussion Paper was limited. In its Report, however, the Commission recommended that the Attorneys-General of the various States meet with the federal government to consider uniform national legislation concerning de facto relationships.

The Commission's recommendations on de facto relationships were justified as consistent with its philosophy that the law should recognise as valid the relationships people choose for themselves,[60] although the Commission did not consider in any depth what it is that couples choose for themselves in entering a de facto relationship.[61] Yet if there was any impetus to increase the legal recognition of de facto relationships, it would have come from within the mainstream of European culture, not from ethnic minorities. Extending the degree to which de facto relationships are given legal recognition will do nothing to make the existing law more sensitive to the cultural values of most ethnic minority groups in Australia. Indeed, it would reinforce modern western cultural assumptions in the law rather than diminishing them. Certainly, the submissions from the Islamic community made it clear that de facto relationships were quite unacceptable to Muslims and that they were concerned by the way in which the existing laws undermined the sanctity of marriage.[62]

B. Dissolution of Marriage

The Commission also considered certain issues in relation to dissolution of marriage. One question was whether a divorce which was recognised as such by the religious faith to which the parties belong should be treated as a valid form of divorce in Australian law. As the Commission noted, to recognise religious and customary divorce in this way, subject to proper registration requirements, would be consistent both with the way in which marriage ceremonies are treated, and with the Commission's own philosophy on the regulation of marital status. Despite this, it recommended in the Discussion Paper that customary divorces should not be recognised, and affirmed this recommendation in the Report.[63] This is justifiable if it is accepted that while there may be many recognised forms of marriage ceremony, there is a public interest in ensuring that divorce should be allowed only after a period of

59 In the view of some commentators, the federal government does have the legislative power to make laws concerning the property rights of de factos: See Joint Select Committee on Certain Aspects of the Operation and Implementation of the *Family Law Act*, *The Family Law Act: Aspects of its Operation and Interpretation* (1992) Australian Government Publishing Service, Canberra at 269.

60 Above n13 at par 5.26.

61 The issue is mentioned in passing in the Discussion Paper at par 3.48. The assumption that creating statutory powers for the courts to alter parties' interests in property and to award maintenance to a former de facto partner is supportive of the parties' own choice in choosing a non-married relationship is highly questionable (above n26).

62 For example, the submissions to the ALRC from S Ahmed and the Australian Federation of Islamic Councils Inc.

63 Above n26 at par 3.60; above n13 at par 5.29.

separation which is sufficient to allow time for consideration and attempted reconciliation.[64] The existing law also requires consideration of the welfare of the children in the process of dissolution.[65] Nonetheless, it would be possible to allow a party to seek a declaration, after twelve months' separation, that a customary divorce was valid, and subject to consideration of the welfare of the children, thereby maintaining the substance of the existing requirements of the law. This could be an alternative to filing for dissolution in the usual manner. While some forms of customary divorce are more open to husbands than to wives, gender equality would be assured by the fact that both spouses would have the same possibility of filing for divorce, and on the same terms. They might choose an action for a declaration of the validity of the earlier divorce, or a civil application for dissolution.

The other issue concerning dissolution of marriage which the Commission considered was whether the civil law should be used to compel a party within whose power it is to grant a religious divorce to do so when the marriage has been dissolved under civil law. The problem arises particularly in relation to Jewish law where divorce may only be accomplished by one of the parties, the husband. Similar problems may arise in Muslim communities in relation to talaq divorces. Under Jewish law, the husband must make a formal delivery to the wife of a Bill of Divorcement, the gett, and the wife must then accept it for the divorce to be valid. In the past, the Family Court has both received an undertaking from a husband to do everything necessary to give the wife a gett[66] and ordered a wife to appear before the Rabbinical Court to accept a gett.[67] It has also made the level of maintenance orders conditional on the granting of a gett.[68]

In response to this problem, a majority of the Commission recommended that the Court should have the power to postpone making a decree absolute, and may adjourn other proceedings (unless they relate to a child) until satisfied that an impediment to the other party's remarriage has been removed which it is solely within the power of the first party to remove, or that there are extenuating circumstances which justify the making of the decree absolute or the hearing of the application despite the failure to remove the impediment.[69] This was the only recommendation on the question of marital status in which the Law Reform Commission responded positively to the concerns raised by members of certain ethnic minorities; perhaps this is because, on this issue, there is a coincidence between contemporary western values and the concerns raised by women denied the freedom to remarry by the refusal of their husbands to grant a religious divorce.

64 *Family Law Act* 1975 (Cth) ss48–50.

65 *Family Law Act* 1975 (Cth) s55A.

66 *Shulsinger and Shulsinger* (1977) FLC 90–207.

67 *In the Marriage of Guriazda*, unreported, 23 Feb 1983 (cited in ALRC Report No 57 above n13 at 105).

68 *Steinmetz and Steinmetz* (1980) FLC 90–801.

69 One specific circumstance given is that the party has genuine grounds of a religious or conscientious nature for not removing the impediment.

C. *The Immigration Fraud Problem*

As significant as the recommendations which the Australian Law Reform Commission did make are the matters of importance from a multicultural perspective which were not even raised as issues. The Commission made no mention of the issue of arranged marriages, although it may be assumed that it saw no reason to amend the law as it was laid down in the *Marriage of S*, since the present law is consistent with the Commission 's basic approach. The other issue of particular concern to ethnic minorities which has arisen on numerous occasions in the Family Court is the problem of cases in which one party's consent to the marriage was procured by fraudulent misrepresentations.

In a number of cases, known as the immigration fraud cases, the law of nullity has been invoked where one person was induced to marry another by fraudulent protestations of love in circumstances where the primary motive for entering into the relationship was to gain permanent residency in Australia. The complaint of the applicant for nullity was that the respondent had either indicated the real motive for the marriage shortly after the wedding, or had abandoned the marriage as soon as possible after the wedding, once the permanent residence was believed to be sufficiently secure.

Historically, courts have been very reluctant to annul a marriage because of fraud. In particular, courts have refused to accept the notion that fraudulent misrepresentations which induce consent, should be sufficient to be a ground for nullity. Sir Francis Jeune, in *Moss v Moss (otherwise Archer)* said: "[W]hen there is consent no fraud inducing that consent is material".[70] However, in *In the Marriage of Deniz*,[71] it was held that a marriage was void where the man involved had no intention of remaining in a marital relationship with a young woman, but was motivated only by immigration concerns.[72] Frederico J said that for the relevant fraud to be sufficient as a ground of nullity it must go "to the root of the marriage contract". It did so in this case, since the respondent did not have the slightest intention of fulfilling in any respect the obligations of marriage. The marriage was annulled.

This decision was formally distinguished in *Otway and Otway*,[73] but McCall J affirmed in that case the principle that fraudulent misrepresentations inducing consent did not constitute fraud within the meaning of the *Marriage Act*. Subsequently, the cases of *Al Soukmani and El Soukmani*,[74] and *Osman and Mourrali*,[75] followed the views in *Otway* and did not follow *Deniz*.[76]

---

70 [1897] P 263 at 269.

71 (1977) 31 Fed LR 114.

72 The female applicant was an Australian citizen in her fourth year of high school. Her family was Lebanese. The male respondent was a Turkish national who, at the time of his purported marriage to the respondent was seeking permanent residence in Australia. The respondent sought and was given the permission of the applicant's parents to marry the applicant. He convinced the applicant that he loved her and she agreed to leave school and marry him. The parties went through a ceremony of marriage. After the wedding, he told her that the only reason he was marrying her was to obtain permanent residence in Australia. On learning this, she suffered a nervous breakdown and attempted to commit suicide.

73 (1987) FLC 91–807.

74 (1990) FLC 92–107.

75 (1990) FLC 92–111.

76 The rejection of Deniz was confirmed again in *Najjarin v Houlayce* (1991) FLC 92–246.

The current approach of the Family Court may be illustrated by *Osman and Mourrali*. In this case, the parties met in Lebanon in 1987. Shortly afterwards, the applicant came to Australia where she gained resident status. She sponsored the respondent to migrate to Australia as her fiancé. In March 1988, the parties went through an Islamic betrothal ceremony, the kitab. Although this constituted a legal marriage ceremony in Australian law, according to Lebanese Muslim custom the marriage is not complete until another ceremony, the erais, occurs some time later. No cohabitation or consummation takes place until after this ceremony. Within a month of the kitab ceremony, the respondent made it clear that he did not wish to marry the applicant. Nygh J found, on the balance of probabilities, that the principal motive of the respondent in getting married was to facilitate his migration to Australia. Nonetheless, the application for an annulment was rejected. The applicant knew that the kitab ceremony was a valid marriage under Australian law, and therefore this case was one of fraudulent misrepresentation only. Nygh J rejected the view that fraudulent misrepresentation could found a decree of nullity. In conclusion, he stated:

> Annulment had some attractions in the past when divorce was difficult and seen as socially shameful. The ground for divorce of one year separation requires no investigation of guilt and cannot produce any stigma. It is easily established and indeed the wife in this case, as I can now call her, would have been relieved far more expeditiously and cheaply from her bonds some time ago, if she had proceeded for dissolution.[77]

This comment ignores the very great social stigma associated with divorce in some ethnic communities. In *Deniz*, it was reported that the applicant had tried to commit suicide and said that she would rather die than be divorced. It would have been possible for the Law Reform Commission to recommend changes in the law of nullity which would have acknowledged the importance of nullity as an alternative to divorce for some people, in a way which was consistent with the principle of international law that marriages should only be recognised where the parties to it have given a free and full consent. The silence of the Law Reform Commission on this issue leaves the law of nullity locked in nineteenth century rigidity at a time when the law of divorce has been transformed by the modern "no-fault" approach.[78]

The problem of immigration fraud may now have been diminished in practice by changes to the *Migration Act* 1958. Whereas hitherto permanent residence was granted as an immediate consequence of marrying an Australian citizen, the position now is that where the prospective marriage partner was

---

For discussion of the legal issues see Davis, B, "Fraud and Annulment of Marriage" (1988) 2 *Aust J Fam L* 138; Jessep, O, "Fraud and Nullity of Marriage in Australia", (1989) 3 *Aust J Fam L* 93; Davis, B, "Logic Fraud and Sham Marriages" (1989) 3 *Aust J Fam L* 191.

77 Above n75 at 77, 743–744.

78 In *Scott v Sebright*, above n44, Butt J emphasised as a reason for great caution in granting a decree of nullity, that "public policy requires that marriage should not be lightly set aside, and there is in some cases the strongest temptation to the parties more immediately interested to act in collusion in obtaining a dissolution of the marriage tie". Now that the law does little to restrict the availability of divorce, and collusion is not a major issue, there is no reason to adhere to a restrictive interpretation of the grounds for a decree of nullity.

sponsored to enter Australia for the purposes of marrying an Australian citizen or permanent resident, the sponsored partner's permanent residence will not be confirmed until after two years have elapsed.[79] Separation or dissolution within the two-year period is not a bar to being granted permanent residence, but the applicant has to show such circumstances as that injunctions have been granted as a result of domestic violence, or a conviction of the nominating spouse for violence against the applicant has been recorded, or the nominating spouse has an access order or a formal child maintenance obligation.[80] This makes it very difficult to succeed in marrying an Australian with the secret motive only of attaining permanent residence.

D. *Other Recommendations*

Two other recommendations which the Commission made deserve more detailed consideration, for they raise particular questions about the willingness of the majority to compromise western cultural values for the sake of cultural pluralism. These issues are the age of marriage, and the question of polygamous marriages.

5. *The Minimum Age for Legal Marriage*

In its Discussion Paper the Law Reform Commission considered the question of restricting the entry into marriage, and recommended that the law be changed to increase the minimum age of marriage for females to 18 years. As the law stood at the time of the Discussion Paper, females could marry at 16 and males at 18. However, the *Marriage Act* allowed the court to authorise marriage of a young person up to two years below the minimum age, in "exceptional and unusual" circumstances.[81] This meant that girls could get married at 14 with the permission of the court, and boys at 16. Parental consent, or the permission of the court in lieu of consent, was also necessary for the marriage of a minor. The Commission considered that this difference in the minimum age for marriage was probably inconsistent with the *Sex Discrimination Act* 1984.[82] Rather than adopting the least restrictive approach for both males and females, and reducing the minimum age of marriage for males to 16 years, the Commission recommended that the minimum age for both sexes be 18 years. Other reasons given for choosing 18 as the minimum age were that there "must sometimes be doubt whether the consent of a person under 18 is freely given", and that "there must be serious doubt that a person so young is capable of discharging the obligations that marriage involves".[83]

This issue was taken up soon afterwards by the Federal Parliament which passed the *Sex Discrimination Amendment Act* 1991, raising the minimum marriage age to 18 for both sexes.[84] It remains possible for a court to authorise the

79 Migration Regulations 1993 (Cth) (Sch2) Part 801.

80 Id at 801.732.

81 *Marriage Act* 1961 s12.

82 Above n26 at pars 3.52 and 3.54.

83 Id at par 3.52.

84 In the Second Reading Speech, it was noted that 38 countries, as at 1990, had a minimum age for marriage which was common for males and females. Of these, 24 prescribed a

marriage of a person under 18, but no change was made to the test that authorisation be permitted only in "exceptional and unusual" circumstances. The present law thus makes no reference either to an assessment of the capacity of the minor to make up his or her own mind, nor to the relevance of the cultural practices of the community to which the minor belongs. Parental consent to the marriage of a minor continues to be necessary, although the court may override a parent's refusal to consent.[85]

The question of the minimum age of marriage is one which is of considerable importance for certain ethnic minorities in Australia. In many cultures, including Aboriginal communities,[86] it is quite common for young women to marry in their mid-teenage years, and at a much earlier age than is traditional in modern Anglo-Celtic culture. Teenage marriages were once very common in Western European societies as well. In Roman law, the common law and canon law the minimum age for marriage was 14 for boys and 12 for girls. The reasons for restrictions on marriage prior to the twentieth century were not to ensure that the minor was sufficiently mature to enter marriage but rather to ensure that the young person married someone of whom the parents approved.[87] This was accomplished by parental consent laws (which were particularly strict in European countries) and requirements that the banns of marriage be read in church, as was required by English law.[88]

However, in recent years, there has been a trend away from teenage marriage in western countries. In the Australian population generally, the age of both men and women at first marriage is steadily on the increase. In 1966, the median age at first marriage for men was 23.8, while in 1976 it was 23.6. By 1987 it had risen to 25.9, and by 1992 it was 26.9. The median age for women at first marriage in both 1966 and 1976 was 21.2. By 1987 it was 23.8 and by 1992, 24.7.[89] There has been an especially sharp decline in the numbers of teenage brides. 31.3 per cent of women who turned 20 in 1971 were married. In 1986, the figure had dropped to 8.5 per cent.[90] There are many reasons for this. Pre-marital sex is no longer frowned upon in the way it was in previous generations, and with the decline in adherence to religious teachings on chastity before marriage, a wedding ceremony is not seen by many as a precondition for

---

minimum age of 18 years. Most of these were in Europe. Ten countries had a minimum age of 16 years: Second Reading Speech, *Sex Discrimination Amendment Act* 1991, Hansard, House of Representatives, 6 March 1991, 1416.

85 *Marriage Act* 1961 (Cth) ss14 and 15. It is not always necessary under the present law for both parents to consent. The Schedule to the *Marriage Act* 1961 (Cth) provides for the operation of the requirement of parental consent in a various circumstances. For example, where the parents are separated or divorced, the only consent necessary is that of the parent with whom the minor has been living.

86 See ALRC Report No 31, above n20 at par 261. Marriages may take place from the onset of puberty.

87 Goode, W, *World Revolution and Family Patterns* (1963) at 41.

88 *Lord Hardwicke's Act* 1753. See also Stone, L, *Road to Divorce*, (1990) at 123–24; Parker, S, *Informal Marriage, Cohabitation and the Law, 1750–1989* (1990).

89 Australian Bureau of Statistics, *1992 Marriages Australia*, (1993) Australian Government Publishing Service, Canberra at 11. The same trend may be seen by examining the marital status of women aged 20–24 in 1971 and 1986. In 1971, nearly two thirds of women in this age group had married. In 1986, nearly two thirds remained unmarried. McDonald, P, "Families in the Future: The Pursuit of Family Autonomy", (1988) 22 *Fam Matters* 40–47.

90 McDonald, ibid.

being sexually active. The widespread practice of abortion and the increasing acceptance of single parenthood without marriage has significantly reduced the number of marriages for which an unintended pregnancy is the direct catalyst. With the high level of participation in higher education, it has become common for people to postpone marriage until after they have completed tertiary studies. In many cultural groups, including the Anglo-Celtic majority, people enter de facto relationships as a stage of courtship before making the commitment of marriage. The increase in women's participation in the workforce may also have had an effect on the age at which women enter marriage.

The reasons why people may be postponing marriage are thus many and various. For some people, the postponement of marriage is a possibility because their internalised values allow them to make choices (for example concerning pre-marital sex, de facto relationships and abortion) which others would not wish to make as a result of religious or other objections. A multicultural policy which gives recognition to the relationships which people choose for themselves would take account of those cultures in which teenage marriage is culturally accepted, and the reasons why some people may want to marry at an age when others are entering de facto relationships or engaging in sexual intercourse without living together.

The law as it stood before 1991 represented a reasonable accommodation of the different cultural views within the Australian community. The normal minimum age for marriage for young women was set at the age when they may give a legally valid consent to sexual intercourse. In exceptional and unusual circumstances, consent could be given by a court to the marriage of a female under 16 or a male under 18.[91] The requirement that the circumstances should be exceptional and unusual was justifiable in relation to females given that sexual intercourse with a girl under 16 would otherwise be a criminal offence. The result of the legal changes brought about by the *Sex Discrimination Amendment Act* 1991 (Cth) is that the law is now less accommodating to cultural differences concerning the minimum age for marriage than it was before. A couple may lawfully form a de facto relationship at the age when a woman's

91 Two reported decisions on the question of consent to the marriage of a person beneath the normal minimum age indicate the approach the courts have taken in the past. In *Re K (An Infant)* [1964] NSWLR 746, a 15 year old applicant who was pregnant was given permission to marry. The applicant wished to marry in Holland, but since her domicile was in Australia, the Dutch authorities sought the permission of the Australian authorities before permitting the wedding. Pregnancy was not regarded as a sufficient reason. Additional reasons which justified the order included that the parents had consented, that the fiance was in steady employment and that the girl was "unusually mature". Disapproval of unmarried mothers in the part of Holland where the young person lived was also a factor. By contrast, in *Re S G* (1968) 11 FLR 326, the court refused permission to a 15 year old girl of Greek background who wished to marry a 23 year old man. The marriage was supported by the parents and a Greek Orthodox priest. The priest testified that the marriage was perfectly normal and usual by Greek standards. Nonetheless, the court held that these cultural factors were insufficient. Such a teenage marriage, viewed in the light of Australian law and custom, was certainly unusual, but to qualify under the Act the circumstances had to relate to the particular parties concerned, and not merely to a class or kind of persons to which those parties belong. See also *Re Z* (1970) 15 FLR 420. In 1989, 13 females were permitted to marry under the age of 16; above n84 at 1416.

consent to sexual intercourse is valid, but not a marriage, unless they have the permission of the court and parental consent.[92]

The Australian Federation of Islamic Councils criticised the ALRC recommendation on the basis that it is inequitable to prevent people entering into marriage at the same age at which they can lawfully enter a de facto relationship. The Federation commented:

> Issues of genuine consent and capability of discharging the "obligations" of marriage should be the same whether the young couple are married or living in a de facto relationship .... There is no advantage from the viewpoint of public policy in preventing people marrying under the age of 18 if they wish to do so and have their parents' consent. To oblige them to wait to 18 increases the likelihood that they will enter into a de facto relationship, which from the Islamic point of view, is to encourage them to commit a serious sin.

Could the ALRC 's approach nonetheless be justified? The two reasons given for increasing the minimum age to eighteen years rather than having the minimum age being sixteen for both males and females, require critical examination. The first reason given in the Discussion Paper was that there "must sometimes be doubt whether the consent of a person under 18 is freely given".[93] Clearly, the Commission was concerned about parental pressure to marry, and this concern was no doubt strongest in regard to arranged marriages in certain ethnic minority households. Given the decision concerning the law of duress in *the Marriage of S*, that arranged marriages entered into under parental pressure may be declared void, it is surprising that the Commission should have deemed it necessary to put special impediments in the way of young people who wish to marry when there are no legal impediments of any kind upon people entering into de facto marriages.

Is such a paternalistic approach justified? Its implication is that the cultural practice of teenage marriages should be discouraged so that young people will have a greater chance of making decisions free from the cultural influences and traditions of the ethnic group to which they belong. Seen in this light, the Commission's recommendation was not in the least consistent with allowing for cultural diversity. Interestingly, its approach was in direct contrast to its report on the recognition of Aboriginal customary law some six years earlier.[94] It is also quite inconsistent with the current emphasis in the law on children's rights to autonomy commensurate with their maturity and level of understanding.[95]

---

92 Forty-six females aged 16, and 180 females aged 17, married in 1992, compared with 1052 females under 18 in 1989. There has thus been a significant reduction in the number of young women marrying below the age of 18 since the Act came into force. Sources: ABS *Marriages Australia* 1992 (above n89); above n84 at 1416.

93 Above n26 at par 3.52.

94 The majority of the Commission recommended in this report that customary marriages should be recognised irrespective of the age of the parties. One Commissioner considered that marriage should not be recognised where a partner was below marriageable age (which was 16 at the time). ALRC Report No 31, above n20 at par 261.

95 In *Secretary, Department of Health and Community Services v JMB and SMB* (1992) 175 CLR 218 the High Court adopted the reasoning of Lord Scarman in *Gillick v West Norfolk and Wisbech Area Health Authority* [1986] AC 112 that a child (or adolescent) should have the right to decide a matter when he or she has sufficient understanding and intelligence to be capable of making a decision on the issue in question. For criticism, see

The second argument of the Commission given in the Discussion Paper was that "there must be serious doubt that a person so young is capable of discharging the obligations that marriage involves". Certainly, teenage marriages in the past have had higher divorce rates than marriages which are contracted later. However, this needs to be interpreted in the light of factors which might explain the greater incidence of unstable marriages in this age group. Many teenage marriages in the Anglo-Celtic community in the past were contracted in rebellion against parents, in order to get away from home, or as a result of a pregnancy. Such marriages began in inauspicious circumstances, and may well have been based upon weak foundations. While teenagers belonging to ethnic minority groups may at times want to marry at a young age for similar reasons,[96] the more common situation is that teenage marriages are encouraged by parents, are not "forced" by pregnancy, and the young couple begin their married life supported by an extended family.

Of course, it may seem better to a modern and secular mind for young people to postpone marriage until they are more mature. They may lawfully be sexually active from the age of sixteen years onwards, and live in a de facto relationship from that age. It is a popular belief that living together as a form of "trial marriage" enhances the prospects for the stability of the marriage, although there is strong research evidence to the contrary.[97] Indeed, one submission from a state government department even appeared to extol the virtues of living together before marriage. In suggesting the factors which should be taken into account by a court in granting permission to marry below the age of 18, the Ethnic Affairs Commission of New South Wales recommended that the court should look favourably on situations where the parties "demonstrate adequate maturity and understanding of the personal and legal implications of marriage and have lived in a similar relationship with each other for a reasonable period, or there is a pregnancy or children". On this approach, in order to gain the consent of the court to the marriage, the couple might have to violate their own personal values and/or the cultural and religious rules of their community. A chaste couple, seeking to live by the precepts of their faith concerning sexual relations, and opposed to living together before marriage, would be less likely to be allowed to marry than a couple who had abandoned the restraints on sexual behaviour which only a generation ago were part of the accepted morality of the Australian community.

The minimum age recommendations of the Australian Law Reform Commission, and the submissions which supported them,[98] indicate how difficult

---

Parkinson, P, "Children's Rights and Doctors' Immunities: The Implications of the High Court's Decision in *Re Marion*" (1992) 6 *Aust J Fam L* 101.

96 See the case study of an application to marry by a 14 year old girl in a Lebanese family in Humphrey, M, "Religion, Law and Family Disputes in a Lebanese Muslim Community in Sydney" in Bottomley, G and de Lepervanche, M (eds), *Ethnicity, Class and Gender in Australia* (1984) at 183. She was supported in her desire to marry by her mother but opposed by her older brother who was the male head of the family. One of her motives for marriage was to escape the brother's control.

97 Parker, et al, above n52 at 52.

98 Submissions supporting the ALRC 's proposal referred to the importance of encouraging young people to continue in education until 18, and emphasised the need to discourage premature marriage decisions.

it is for those imbued with the values of a secular western culture to let go of those values in the name of respect for cultural diversity. To allow young people to marry at 16 without needing to demonstrate "exceptional and unusual circumstances" to a court would mean to allow them to make choices for themselves which might not seem, to paternalistic observers, to be in their best interests.

In stark contrast to the ALRC 's approach, was the decision of the Supreme Court of the United States in *Wisconsin v Yoder*.[99] This case was not about the minimum age for marriage but about the rights of Amish parents to withdraw their children from compulsory school education after the eighth grade.[100] The reasons they gave were that they did not want their children to be exposed to corrupting social influences at an age which was vital for the development of their religious values,[101] and that they wished instead to give their young people a practical education in the traditional agrarian lifestyle of the community. The State of Wisconsin argued that the public interest in the education of its young people until the age of sixteen overrode any objections that the parents had of a religious nature. It was also argued that compulsory education was needed to protect the interests of young people who might, at a later stage, wish to leave the Amish community. Both these contentions were rejected by the Supreme Court. The objections of the Amish to a high school education were deeply held and grounded in their religious beliefs and practices. In the light of this, the state was not entitled to say that its beliefs about what is best for young people should override the views of the parents. The practical agricultural education of the Amish would prepare young people for the future even if they chose to leave the Amish community, and the state interest in high school education was not otherwise sufficiently compelling to justify the interference in the freedom of religion of this minority group. Douglas J dissented in part since there was no evidence concerning the wishes of some of the young people involved in the case about whether they would have preferred to remain in school.

Although the issues in *Wisconsin v Yoder* were different from those concerning the minimum age for marriage, the broader questions of policy are the same. The Supreme Court required the State of Wisconsin to recognise and respect the right of minority groups to hold onto a different vision of the "good life" from that of the mainstream culture and to allow for cultural diversity even in the face of mainstream values about the importance of high school (and tertiary) education. While Douglas J's partial dissent clearly had merit in its insistence that the young person's own voice be heard on the issue, the evidence of at least one of the young people was that she adhered to the precepts of the Amish faith.[102] The principle that the state should recognise that different communities, and the individuals within them, may have different values on issues such as high school education and the minimum age for marriage is an important one.

---

99 406 US 205 (1972).

100 The children concerned were fourteen and fifteen years old.

101 The Amish live in rural comunities separated from the mainstream of American life, and largely without recourse to twentieth century technology.

102 Above n99 at 237.

It is sufficient to protect young people's rights that the law continue to insist that the young person gives a free and full consent to the marriage as specified by the Convention on Consent to Marriage and article 23 of the International Covenant on Civil and Political Rights. If there are concerns about the reality of a young person's consent this might be addressed by requiring counselling prior to marriage as a minor, and such counselling could involve an exploration of the life options available to the young person other than entering marriage at that stage.

6. *The Recognition of Polygamous Relationships*

The Discussion Paper also recommended that polygamous marriages should not be recognised in Australia,[103] and this recommendation was affirmed in the Report. The reasons given in the Report were that to recognise the legal status of polygamy would "offend the principles of gender equality that underlie Australian laws", and that there was very little support for the recognition of polygamy in the Australian community.[104] The Commission did however, suggest that bigamy might be abolished as a criminal offence, since entering a bigamous marriage would involve making a false declaration contrary to other provisions of the *Marriage Act*, and thus the monogamous nature of marriage is sufficiently protected by the law.[105]

A significant minority of Australians belong to religious or cultural groups in which polygamy has traditionally been practised or accepted. Certain tribal Aborigines practice polygamy,[106] as do people in the Highlands of Papua New Guinea.[107] Polygamy is also known in other cultures in Africa, Asia and the Middle East. Polygamy is accepted within Islam, although the extent of its practice varies significantly between countries. Australia has a sizeable Muslim community; in 1986 it represented 0.7 per cent of the population.[108]

In Islam, the circumstances in which polygamy is accepted are limited. One Muslim commentator noted that "polygamous" marriage is not an unlimited right enjoyed by a Muslim husband. It should be exercised only under exceptional circumstances, after obtaining permission from the existing wife.[109] A submission from the Australian Federation of Islamic Councils pointed out that the historical context for the recognition of polygamy was the shortage of eligible men in the aftermath of a war, when many women were left as widows and their children left fatherless.[110] The Federation described the present cultural practice as follows:

> Nowadays, as a general rule, a second wife should not be married unless the first wife is suffering from a serious disease or is disabled, unable to have

---

103 Above n26 at par 3.44.

104 Above n13 at par 5.10.

105 Id at par 5.11. *Marriage Act* 1961 (Cth) s96(1).

106 Storer, above n29 at 306–308.

107 See Jessep, O, "The Governor-General's Wives: Polygamy and the Recognition of Customary Marriage in Papua New Guinea" (1993) 7 *Aust J Fam L* 29.

108 *National Agenda* above n11 at 6.

109 Ahmed, S, Submission to the ALRC. See also Storer, above n29 at 208.

110 Australian Federation of Islamic Councils Inc, Submission to the ALRC.

> children, of unsound mind or suffering from some similar problem which makes her unable to look after the home and children and to be a proper wife and mother.
>
> The second requirement is that a man who marries more than one wife must treat his wives equally in all matters. If he cannot do this, he should restrict himself to one wife, and in fact, in Muslim countries the vast majority of marriages are monogamous.

Polygamy is a practice which is completely alien to western traditions and culture. The concept of marriage which is embodied in Australian law owes its origins to Christian beliefs concerning marriage as a monogamous and life-long commitment.[111] The classic definition of marriage at common law is the one given by Sir James Wilde in *Hyde v Hyde and Woodmansee*[112] that "marriage, as understood in Christendom, may for this purpose be defined as the voluntary union for life of one man and one woman to the exclusion of all others". A very similar definition, without the reference to Christendom, is to be found in the *Marriage Act* 1961[113] and the *Family Law Act* 1975.[114] The monogamous nature of marriage in Australian law is reinforced by the criminal law, which makes bigamy a criminal offence punishable by up to five years imprisonment.[115]

Polygamous relationships are recognised by Australian family law in one respect. Section 6 of the *Family Law Act* 1975 provides that a marriage that is, or has at any time been, polygamous and was validly contracted overseas is deemed to be a marriage for the purposes of proceedings under the Act. The effect of section 6 is to recognise a polygamous marriage as having all the consequences under the *Family Law Act* of a valid marriage without being a valid marriage. Thus, according to this section, a party to a polygamous marriage could apply under the *Family Law Act* for such relief as maintenance, property alteration, and adjudication of disputes concerning children.

That polygamous relationships are not recognised as marriages for any other purposes than the application of the *Family Law Act* is clear from the *Marriage Act* section 88D(2)(a). This prevents the recognition in Australian law of polygamous relationships contracted overseas. The section provides that a marriage shall not be recognised as valid if "either of the parties was, at the time of the marriage, a party to a marriage with some other person and the

111 This understanding of the meaning of "marriage" is also reflected in the interpretation of the word in s51(xxi) of the Federal Constitution. In *A-G for Victoria v The Commonwealth* (1962) 107 CLR 529 at 577, Windeyer J stated that the meaning of marriage constitutionally was wider than its common law meaning, but that meaning provided its central type. He declined to express a view on whether the Parliament could make polygamy lawful in Australia under the marriage power since he thought "that question has absolutely no reality".

112 (1866) LRIP & D 130. Sir James Wilde is better known by his later title, Lord Penzance. The case concerned whether a potentially polygamous marriage contracted in Utah should be recognised in English law. It was held that it should not be. On potentially polygamous marriages see also *Khan* [1963] VR 203. Amendments to the *Marriage Act* 1961 (Cth) in 1985 had the effect of making a potentially polygamous marriage contracted overseas a valid marriage for all purposes.

113 *Marriage Act* 1961 (Cth) s46.

114 *Family Law Act* 1975 (Cth) s43(a).

115 *Marriage Act* 1961 (Cth) s94.

last-mentioned marriage was, at that time, recognised in Australia as valid". Thus, since Australian law would recognise as valid a first marriage,[116] even though by the law of its place of celebration it was potentially polygamous, it would not recognise as valid the second marriage. There is a possibility that a polygamous marriage might be recognised under section 88E despite the provisions of section 88D(2). This preserves the common law rules of private international law and a marriage might be recognised under these rules which is not recognised under the previous sections. Sykes and Pryles argue that a polygynous or polyandrous marriage could be recognised under section 88E(1) if the marriage were formally valid by the law of the country of solemnisation and if each party had the capacity to enter into an actually polygynous or polyandrous union either by their antenuptial laws of domicile, or the law of their intended matrimonial home.[117]

Whatever theoretical possibilities are raised by section 88E, they are nullified in practice by the immigration rules. Under the *Migration Act* 1958, a migrant to Australia may sponsor a spouse. However, this excludes marriages which are recognised solely because of the operation of section 88E of the *Marriage Act* 1961.[118] It is not possible to sponsor more than one spouse. Subsequent spouses could be considered as de facto spouses, since the *Migration Act* allows the sponsorship of de facto partners.[119] However, a "de facto" spouse would only be allowed to migrate to Australia if it could be shown that the first marriage had ended.[120]

The effect of these provisions, taken together, is that there is no possibility of an actually polygamous relationship existing in Australia, since it would not be possible for more than one legal spouse to gain entry to Australia. The only possible application of section 6 of the *Family Law Act* is to the case of a man who married two wives in another country, legally divorced the first, and then migrated to Australia with the second. This second "marriage" would be treated by the immigration authorities as a de facto relationship since it would not be recognised in Australian law as a valid marriage as a result of section 88D(2)(a) of the *Marriage Act* 1961. It would, nonetheless, be treated as a relationship which was, at one time polygamous, within section 6 of the *Family Law Act.*

The existence of the crime of bigamy and the non-recognition of polygamous relationships as marriages is not problematic for all ethnic minorities in which polygamy is accepted. While bigamy is a crime, it is not an offence to live together with more than one partner. Thus de facto polygamy is lawful, and indeed, the continuance of polygamous practices in Aboriginal communities is facilitated by not recognising traditional Aboriginal marriages as legal

116 *Marriage Act* 1961 (Cth) s88C.

117 Sykes, E and Pryles, M, *Australian Private International Law* (3rd edn, 1991) at 448. See also Neave, M, "The New Rules on Recognition of Foreign Marriages — Insomnia for Lawyers" (1990) 4 *Aust J Fam L* 190.

118 *Migration Act* 1958 (Cth) s12.

119 Migration Regulations 1993, reg 1.3 (definition of spouse), reg 1.6 (definition of de facto spouse). Normally, the couple must have been living together for six months in order to qualify as de facto spouses (reg 1.6(1)).

120 *Chen v Minister for Immigration, Local Government and Ethnic Affairs* (1992) 110 ALR 192.

marriages at all. The non-recognition means that polygamous relationships cannot constitute the offence of bigamy. However, the recognition of de facto polygamy by the law is not a sufficient accomodation of the practices of all minority groups since there are some, such as the Islamic community, which do not believe it is morally right to live in de facto relationships, and which regard it as morally important to obtain the legal recognition of the marriage.

The basic philosophy of the Australian Law Reform Commission — that the law should recognise and support the relationships which people choose for themselves — would suggest that polygamous relationships should be recognised as marriages in Australian law unless to do so would violate the rights of the individuals concerned or the rights of others. One reason given by the Commission for rejecting the recognition of polygamous marriages was that the great majority of submissions opposed such recognition. This raises issues about the role of law reform agencies in developing policies concerning multiculturalism. If the role of a law reform commission is seen to be to engage in public consultations and to seek a consensus in favour of particular proposals then the views of powerless or unpopular minorities are unlikely to be accepted. The opinion of a majority is not a sufficient reason for denying the human rights of a minority to cultural and religious expression. It is for the protection of such minorities that human rights instruments such as the International Covenant on Civil and Political Rights exist.

The major argument which the Commission gave against recognising polygamy was that it would compromise Australia's commitment to gender equality.[121] The Discussion Paper stated:

> There is no doubt that polygamy is alien to mainstream Australian culture and to the western European culture from which it derives. Nor is it consistent with a concept of marriage that focuses on the one to one relationship of the parties. In most societies where it is allowed, men, but not women, have the right to take more than one spouse. Unless the right to take more than one spouse applied equally to men and women, polygamy would clearly offend the principles of sexual equality which underlie Australian law.[122]

However, it would be possible to frame a law recognising polygamy which took account of the need for gender equality. To conform with the basic principles of Australian family law, the law would need to be gender-neutral, recognising both polygynous and polyandrous relationships, and would require the full and free consent of the first marriage partner. One approach would be to require the consent of the Family Court to a polygamous marriage, after an enquiry, assisted by the Family Court Counselling Service, to ensure that the parties to the initial marriage and to the new marriage gave a full and free consent, and that the marriage was justified by the cultural practices of the ethnic group to which one or more of the parties belonged.

It should be recognised that in practice, the very small number of polygamous marriages which might be contracted under such a provision would be likely to be polygynous marriages since, in most ethnic groups represented in Australia in which marriage to more than one person simultaneously is traditionally accepted,

---

121 Above n13 at par 5.10.
122 Above n26 at par 3.43.

it is the male who takes a second wife. However, it is difficult to argue that Australian law should refuse to recognise polygamous marriages on the grounds of gender equality if the law is formally equal and all the parties (including the first wife) want the marriage to be recognised.

A further objection to polygamy on the grounds of gender equality is that the practice of polygamy is oppressive to women. This may be so. In certain cultures, having more than one wife is a sign of high social status, and this may have the implication that wives are a form of chattel and a symbol of wealth and power. However, even accepting that this is true in some cultures, it is not universally the case where polygamy is practiced. It has also been argued that polygamy is discriminatory because the male has a claim to have exclusive sexual relations with each wife whereas by definition, wives in a polygynous relationship do not have an exclusive sexual relationship with the husband.[123] It could be argued, although the Australian Law Reform Commission did not do so explicitly, that polygamy should be prohibited on the basis of the Commission's philosophy that it should not support relationships in which the rights of individuals are being violated. To be consistent with this approach the law would also need to state explicitly that de facto relationships will only be accepted where they are entirely monogamous.[124]

The difficulty with this line of argument is that it is open to the criticisms of cultural imperialism and of being paternalistic in its approach. It is one thing to pass laws against discrimination and to provide women with legal remedies which empower them in cases where they are being treated unequally. It is another thing entirely to justify laws on the basis that they are for women's own good even though the women themselves want to enter into such a relationship, especially if safeguards against forced acceptance of the second marriage are put in place, such as requiring the consent of a court after due inquiry. The argument concerning gender equality may also be double-edged.[125] If the law only recognises the claims of a first wife in cases where there is another de facto wife in the household, then this may leave second

---

123 Above n107 at 38. Modern Australian law does not, however, enforce the moral claim to sexual fidelity in marriage, either by criminalising adultery or by making it a relevant issue in divorce proceedings or property and maintenance applications.

124 For an illustration of a form of de facto polygamy in which one de facto wife received property by means of a constructive trust, see *Green v Green* (1989) 17 NSWLR 343. In this case, each "wife" (two were de facto and one was de jure) lived in separated houses, and were not known to each other until shortly before the husband's death. See also *In re Fagan (Deceased)* (1980) FLC 90–821 in which a woman who lived with the deceased was treated as a putative spouse under the *Family Relationships Act* 1975 (SA), s11, even though for part of the relevant period (a minimum of five years' cohabitation) he was also living with his wife. Jacobs J held that the definition of putative spouse did not imply that the relationship should be monogamous and exclusive. It is uncertain whether a polygamous relationship could come within the meaning of de facto spouse under the *De Facto Relationships Act* 1984 (NSW). The definition (s3) requires that the couple "live together" as husband and wife on a bona fide domestic basis although not married to each other. This might imply that the relationship should be exclusive and monogamous. The same definition exists in other legislation.

125 For example, in Papua New Guinea, where the Governor-General elected one of his wives to be the "Lady", and to share in the Vice-Regal life, there were arguments from women's groups which had hitherto opposed polygamy, that the Governor-General should treat all his wives equally. Above n107 at 29–30.

"wives" without the benefit of certain legal rights associated with being a de jure or de facto spouse.[126]

If polygamy is to remain unrecognised by Australian law, it must be on other grounds entirely. The argument of gender equality can only be sustained as a form of paternalistic reasoning, and not within the liberal principles adopted by the ALRC. Another reason for prohibiting polygamy might be proffered. It could be argued that it is justifiable for Australian law to legislate in order to preserve its traditions and fundamental values even when the behaviour which is proscribed occurs between consenting adults and is in accordance with the beliefs and practices of a minority group. This is consistent with the view of Patrick Devlin who argued in *The Enforcement of Morals*[127] that every society has a "public morality", a moral structure which forms part of its community of ideas, and that the law may be utilised to preserve a society's morality in the same way as it uses the law to safeguard anything else which is essential to its existence.[128] Indeed, he gave as an example society's ideas about the institution of marriage. In reference to English law, he wrote:

> Whether a man should be allowed to take more than one wife is something about which every society has to make up its mind one way or the other. In England we believe in the Christian idea of marriage and therefore adopt monogamy as a moral principle. Consequently the Christian institution of marriage has become the basis of family life and so part of the structure of our society. It is there not because it is Christian. It has got there because it is Christian, but it remains there because it is built into the house in which we live and could not be removed without bringing it down. The great majority of those who live in this country accept it because it is the Christian idea of marriage and for them the only true one. But a non-Christian is bound by it, not because it is part of Christianity but because, rightly or wrongly, it has been adopted by the society in which he lives. It would be useless for him to stage a debate designed to prove that polygamy was theologically more correct and socially preferable; if he wants to live in the house, he must accept it as built in the way in which it is.[129]

Most controversial of Lord Devlin's ideas was his notion that it would be sufficient to prohibit a consensual practice that it aroused intolerance, indignation and disgust in the person in the street.[130] In stating this, he was not proposing intolerance and indignation as virtues, but rather indicating one of a number of practical limitations on the right of the state to enforce the morals of the majority. Criminalisation would only be justified where the disapproval of the relevant conduct by the majority was so intense as to amount to disgust at the practice. Devlin's views were strongly contested by H L A Hart, who

---

126 A second "wife" in a polygamous relationship might be treated as a de facto spouse for certain purposes (see n124 above), but not for all purposes. For example, under the *Wills, Probate and Administration Act* 1898 (NSW) s61B(3A), a de facto spouse may only claim on an intestacy where the deceased had not been living with his or her de jure spouse in the two years prior to death. This therefore excludes a de facto living polygamously with the male and first wife from claiming a share of the estate on an intestacy.

127 Devlin, P, *The Enforcement of Morals* (1965).

128 Id at 9–11.

129 Id at 9. See also id ch 4 and Rostow, E, "The Enforcement of Morals" [1960] *Camb LJ* 174 at 190–191.

130 Above n127 at 16–18.

adopted the traditional liberal position advanced by J S Mill, that the freedom of the individual should be curtailed only to the extent that is necessary to protect the interests of others.[131]

The issue of polygamy is a particularly interesting test of the strength of the relative positions in the Hart-Devlin debate, although the particular context for the debate was, of course, the legalisation of homosexuality between consenting adults. Hart did respond to the question of allowing polygamy but his argument was an unconvincing one. He suggested that a law punishing bigamy was defensible on the basis of the "harm" principle because, in a country where deep religious significance is attached to monogamous marriage and to the act of solemnising it, the law against bigamy protects religious feelings from offence by a public act desecrating the ceremony. He went on to argue that this was different from enforcing morals:

> It is important to see that if, in the case of bigamy, the law intervenes in order to protect religious sensibilities from outrage by a public act, the bigamist is punished neither as irreligious nor as immoral but as a nuisance. For the law is then concerned with the offensiveness to others of his public conduct, not with the immorality of his private conduct, which, in most countries, it leaves altogether unpunished.[132]

Hart's recognition that offence to the strongly held beliefs and sensibilities of the majority concerning the monogamous nature of marriage might be a sufficient justification for laws prohibiting polygamy meant that, on this issue, he was in substantial agreement with Devlin. For Devlin, also, the offensiveness to others of a person's conduct was an indication that the state ought to be entitled to legislate to prohibit that conduct even though it occurred between consenting adults. Nonetheless, it is questionable whether the public objection to polygamy has anything at all to do with the desecration of the ceremony of marriage. In an age when living together outside marriage is so widespread, to go through a marriage ceremony with a second wife is not to desecrate the marriage ceremony but to pay it a double honour. There is no greater reason to suppose that those who would wish their polygamous relationships to have the full recognition of the law as marriages show any more disrespect for the marriage ceremony than those who remarry after a divorce. Furthermore, it is not the fact of going through a second marriage ceremony without divorcing the first spouse which is so offensive to public sensibilities, but the fact of simultaneous cohabitation with more than one wife. Although the law does not criminalise such behaviour to the fullest extent by making de facto polygamy a punishable offence, it indicates its disapproval in many other respects, not only through the law of bigamy but by non-recognition of polygamous relationships as marriages for the purposes of social security entitlements, superannuation payments, and other benefits which are dependent on the recognition of de facto or de jure marriage.

If the idea is accepted that in the ultimate analysis, a majority may assert a right to preserve its moral values,[133] the question remains as to how those values

131 Hart, H L A, *Law, Liberty and Morality* (1963).

132 Id at 41.

133 It should be noted that Article 18(3) of the International Covenant on Civil and Political Rights specifically allows limitations on the exercise of religious freedom to protect pub-

should be ascertained, and how the decision should be made that they require preserving by law. Devlin's appeal to the intolerance, indignation and disgust of the person in the street, while intended as a means of limiting the enforcement of morals to cases where the clash between majority and minority values is extreme, has rightly attracted criticism as justifying intolerance. Rednecked instinct is not an adequate basis for a coherent and moral policy concerning the rights of minorities. As Ronald Dworkin said of Lord Devlin: "What is shocking and wrong is not his idea that the community's morality counts, but his idea of what counts as the community's morality".[134]

Perhaps a better way of assessing whether consensual behaviour should be proscribed is to ask whether allowing it would contravene the most basic traditions of the community. The test of tradition is a means of establishing both the public character and the importance of the moral principle which it is claimed should be upheld. In most cases, the traditions of western democracies will point in the direction of not proscribing the consensual behaviour of individuals, since the commitment to individual liberty is deeply entrenched as an important value in western societies. If the importance of the tradition is such that its preservation overrides the commitment to individual liberty and privacy, then it may be assumed that it forms a fundamental precept of the society. In Devlin's words, it is a principle "built into the house in which we live".[135]

How then might the balance be found between the rights of a minority and the preservation of fundamental moral and cultural values which are part of a society's community of ideas? In each case, the importance of preserving the inherited cultural values of the majority must be balanced against the effects of such a law on the minority's capacity for cultural expression. Perhaps the preservation of marriage as a monogamous institution is an example of where the preservation of traditional values might override the claims of the minority group to recognition of polygamous unions as marriages.

In Australia, an insistence upon preserving marriage as a monogamous institution would be more compelling if the Christian understanding of marriage were preserved by the law in other respects, and other marriage-like relationships were not given legal recognition. However, the widespread acceptance of de facto relationships which involve no promises of lifelong commitment, and their recognition by law for a multitude of purposes,[136] undermines any claim that the law seeks to uphold Christian values. While de facto relationships are not defined as "marriages" in law, to the extent that they attract the same benefits as marriages, and are recognised in the same way as marriages for specific purposes, the law treats them as equivalent to marriages. Homosexual relationships are also recognised for a small number of purposes in Australian law.[137] For example, a homosexual may sponsor

---

lic order, health or morals.

134 Dworkin R, "Lord Devlin and the Enforcement of Morals" in Wasserstrom, R (ed), *Morality and the Law* (1971) at 69.

135 Above n126 at 9.

136 See Wade, J, *Australian De Facto Relationships Law* (CCH looseleaf service); Parker, et al, above n52 at chs 9 and 21.

137 On the law in New South Wales, see Lesbian and Gay Legal Rights Service, *The Bride*

his or her partner for immigration to Australia as an interdependent person.[138]

Given the extent to which the law already recognises marriage-like relationships and equates them with marriages for many purposes, it requires strong justification for the law to refuse to recognise the particular practices of a minority ethnic group. If polygamy were fundamental to the cultural expression of an ethnic minority, and, as in the case of Islam, recognition of a second marriage as a de facto relationship would not be acceptable, then the case for allowing polygamy in Australia would be very strong. Within the Islamic community in Australia however, there were divisions of opinion. On the one hand, it was argued that since polygamy is recognised in the Qur'an, and is recognised by Muslims even if it is uncommonly practised, it should be recognised in Australian law.[139] On the other hand, the Australian Federation of Islamic Councils did not call for the recognition of polygamy, stating that it was not a major issue for the Islamic community in Australia. In other parts of the world, the incidence and acceptance of polygamy has declined with women's increasing assertion of their rights.[140] Polygamy may thus be a fading institution in many parts of the world, fighting a losing battle with modernity. In the case of polygamy, the case for recognition is not strong enough at the present time, to justify a further undermining of society's commitment to the preservation of the institution of monogamous marriage.

7. *Conclusion*

Taking multiculturalism seriously means that every effort should be made to demonstrate respect for the beliefs, values and cultural practices of minority ethnic groups, and to allow them the right to practice their religion, to use their language and to enjoy their culture without interference from the State. Such a position does not imply a belief in cultural relativism, but rather a respect for the human rights of ethnic minorities. While generally this is accomplished in western democracies by ensuring that ethnic minorities enjoy the same freedoms as the rest of the population, and are protected from discrimination, there are many situations where the law consciously enshrines majority values at the expense of the rights of ethnic minorities.

Where fundamental human rights are not at issue, and there is room for recognition of different cultural values within a system in which one set of rules applies in principle to all members of the community, then laws which

---

Wore Pink (2nd edn, 1994); Winters, S, "Gay and Lesbian Relationships and the Law of New South Wales" (1992) *1 Aust Gay & Lesb LJ* 71. The QLRC Report No 44, above n33 at 11, recommends that the proposed de facto relationships legislation should include homosexual relationships within the definition of a de facto relationship.

138 Under the Migration Regulations 1993, (Sch2), Part 814, gay and lesbian partners may be recognised in the category of interdependency (class 814 permit). The criteria are that the applicant has a relationship with the nominator which is acknowledged by both and which involves living together, being closely interdependent, and having a continuing commitment to mutual emotional and financial support.

139 Ahmed, S, submission to the ALRC.

140 See Storer, above n29 at 156 (disappearance of polygamy in Turkey due largely to women's awareness of their legal rights in marriage) and 208 (polygyny rare in Pakistan and confined to the landlord class). See also Jessep, above n107.

enshrine western cultural assumptions to the prejudice of minorities need to be subjected to strict scrutiny. Every effort should be made to accomodate minority cultural practices to the greatest extent which is compatible with the traditions of the dominant culture.

The Australian Law Reform Commission's report on multiculturalism as far as it concerned marital status failed to take multiculturalism sufficiently seriously. It examined the issues of marital status by reference only to western cultural assumptions, and it made its recommendations by applying western cultural values. The question which arises for Australia's legal system is whether it can or should embrace a wider concept of cultural diversity than is involved in passing anti-discrimination laws and providing interpreters in courts. Can a society with deep roots in European traditions of law and life embrace the cultural identity of other societies without losing its own? Is it possible for there to be one set of laws which applies to all irrespective of race or religion, which is at the same time "multicultural"? The law might be multicultural to the extent that most cultural practices are not prohibited, freedom of religion is assured, and state and federal anti-discrimination laws provide certain remedies for those who are discriminated against on the grounds of race or ethnicity. However, this reflects only some of the possible meanings of "multiculturalism" discussed earlier. Significantly, both the protection of fundamental freedoms and the prohibition of discrimination represent cherished values of the dominant culture, and laws of this kind would be in place irrespective of the Australian government's endorsement of a multicultural agenda.

Is there a willingness in the Australian political community to make the compromises in the law necessary for multicultural policies to be translated into legal reforms? The ALRC 's report on Aboriginal customary law provided a model for how to do this in relation to the Aboriginal community. More thought needs to go into ways in which the cultural practices of other ethnic minorities could be better respected.

[3]

MUSLIM MAGHREBIAN MARRIAGE IN FRANCE: A PROBLEM FOR LEGAL PLURALISM

EDWIGE RUDE-ANTOINE*

ABSTRACT

The recent immigration of Maghrebian families to France has led to a rise in the number of cases of marriages contracted under Islamic law which have resulted in issues for the French legal system. This article examines the effect on the private lives of Muslim Maghrebians of this confrontation between two different cultural and legal systems. It discusses the extent to which the French response can be seen as a restrictive demand for acculturation by the society of residence and whether this functions to integrate or exclude the new immigrants. This serves as a case study in the ways in which a pluralist society may seek to resolve conflicts of culture and norms.

INTRODUCTION

When we try to analyze the problems posed by the marriages of Muslim Maghrebian[1] immigrants for law and social control in France, it is notable how little evidence is available about the real character of these relationships, beyond the constant formal statements of Islamic law.[2] This is true as far as it affects both the actual opinions and attitudes of Maghrebians and the workings of their own institutions. As sociologists of law recognize, the effect of law derives from such sources as much as from codes or statutes.

In crossing the Mediterranean, the Maghrebian populations have found themselves in situations which are on the margins of their own legal codes and encountered a state which is more interested in controlling the flow of migrants than solving problems of cultural pluralism. French law has traditionally been based on a monistic conception of social order, although the possibility of a more pluralist alternative was recognized by Gurvitch (1937) and Ehrlich (1913) and developed by legal anthropologists like Gluckman (1958) and Griffiths (1986).

Maghrebian immigration is often perceived as irrelevant to the cultural identity of France. These groups encounter the great historic separation of church and state in Western Europe while retaining for

*Centre de Recherche Interdisciplinaire de Vaucresson, 54 rue de Garches, 92420 Vaucresson, France.

themselves what is sometimes seen as a pre-modern elision of this boundary, a stance which has been encouraged by the recent revival of Islamic fundamentalism. While the principle of secular systems is that no one moral code may be imposed rather than another, the Islamic world sees the law as an expression of religious principles, 'Thus Muslim law establishes models of behaviour with respect to the moral code and social usefulness' (David 1974).

This view of social organization may, however, remind us of the significant religious elements which remain in the character of Western law and institutions. Both Weber (1921) and Durkheim (1915) underlined the significant role of religion in creating the ideological and cultural conditions for social life, a theme which has been pursued by more recent writers like Adler (1963) (1977), Hocart (1973) and Gauchet (1977) (1985). The analysis of Muslim Maghrebian marriage reasserts the relevance of religion as a moving force in social relations and raises the questions of reconciling a diversity of beliefs within the unitary legal institutions of modern states.

METHODOLOGY

This research is based on a comparative study of legal texts and on the analysis of sixty informal interviews conducted with Maghrebian immigrants in the Goutte d'Or district in the 18th Arrondissement in Paris and in Amiens in 1984 and 1985. These interviews were intended to elicit both the factual aspects of the respondents' situation and their perceptions of this experience. The sample is not claimed to be representative: it seeks to document the qualitative aspects of marriage which can be identified without commenting on their distribution.

The main series of interviews was preceded by a preliminary survey of ten informants, which was used to develop a list of themes to be explored systematically in subsequent interviews. If these topics did not arise spontaneously they were introduced by the interviewer using a list of standardized questions. A scheme of thematic analysis was tested on a random selection of five interviews and then used to analyze the data generated by the main series. The analysis sought to distinguish those attitudes and opinions which recurred with some frequency and could be considered typical of the sample from those which seemed to be idiosyncratic, requiring further analysis in the light of the particular situation of their author.

MAGHREBIAN MARRIAGE: LEGAL FORMS AND PRACTICAL VARIATIONS

How have Maghrebians responded to the contrast between the legal systems of their country of residence and their countries of origin? The answer to this question requires us to consider a number of different dimensions of marriage law.

Choice of Spouse

In pre-Islamic society, fathers, under the authority of the clan, had absolute control of their children's choice of a spouse. This right, known as *jabr*, persisted into modern times but has recently been abolished by Maghrebian civil codes.[3] However, these retain some restrictions on the freedom of a woman, even when she has reached the age of majority, to agree to a marriage without the presence of a parent or a *walî*.[4] The practice of *jabr* survives among some families resident in France and others invariably attach importance to parental approval of the choice of a spouse. The approval of brothers, grandparents or uncles may also be sought. While the father's role is given greatest weight, mothers can carry out relevant transactions and organize meetings between the future spouses. Although economic and patrimonial influences are still important considerations in the selection of a spouse, and a dowry would normally be paid, there are indications that emotional attachments are becoming more significant.

The Maghrebian Dowry

The dowry was originally adopted by Muslim societies as a device for achieving economic equilibrium between different groups. In France, the dowry remains important and is normally paid on marriage within Maghrebian groups. While it has a simple utilitarian function of providing capital for the purchase of household goods and a symbolic or protective value for the woman and for the potential loss to her husband from misconduct, it is also seen as critical to validating the marriage under Islamic law. The traditional law of Islam places a husband under an obligation to settle property on his future wife at the time of marriage. Pre-nuptial agreements, whether between the families involved, the bride's father and her fiancé, or the parties themselves, are treated very seriously by Islamic commentators. Whichever form the agreement takes, the dowry, or the goods bought with it, become the woman's exclusive property. These principles continue into modern Maghrebian codes, which define the payment of the dowry as essential to the validity of the marriage. Under French social and economic conditions, the traditional dowry seems to be giving way to other forms of exchange such as continuing financial support after marriage or for a period of advanced education. This development may reflect the growing employment of women outside the home and the status afforded to this.

These two forms of dowry are associated with two different types of marriage. The traditional form of capital transfer establishes the woman as someone whose identity is created only through her domestic life. Her father is likely to remain the principal actor in discussions about the dowry and its subsequent management. The newer form marks a cultural change where the payment is translated into marketable skills or resources so that a woman becomes an agent on her own behalf. She has an independent identity in relation to the outside world, with inevitable implications for the dynamics of the marriage.

Polygamy

Restraints on marriage also manifest the values of a culture. The antithesis between the Muslim and Western worlds is rooted in the religious division between Christianity and Islam. The Christian Church banned polygamy and endogamy from early times (Goody 1985). Islam has always allowed a man to marry up to four wives, provided that they are treated equally, although it is acknowledged that this injunction is difficult to respect in practice. Before this, the husband could have as many wives as he wished, so the Koranic measure was intended to establish a certain degree of social justice.

Tunisia is the only Maghreb country to have abolished polygamy, which is, of course, prohibited by the French Civil Code.[5] The change in Tunisia was justified by reference to the impossibility of achieving the ideal of perfect equality between polygamous wives and to the evolution of customs and mores within the country. Polygamy is still permitted in Algeria and Morocco. While the rule about equal treatment remains, its definition and enforcement is left to the husband's conscience, although existing and prospective wives must be informed about this expectation. A Moroccan woman can, however, opt, at the time of marriage, for a monogamous union. This is justified by a reluctance to impose a polygamous regime on minority social or religious groups with other beliefs and practices. Although the Algerian code does not contain any similar provisions, the courts do have some discretion in its application, reflecting changing social values in this area.

Maghrebians living in France are critical of the system of polygamy, largely as a result of the material and emotional difficulties of accommodating several wives and their children under the same roof. Some informants, while generally rejecting polygamy, thought it might be tolerable during wartime to compensate for the reduction of the male population. For others, though, polygamy was still an important aspect of the legitimacy of family life under Islamic law. It symbolized an attachment to traditional values and defined the place of each individual within the hierarchy and social solidarity of the clan.

Endogamy

Endogamy is another feature of Maghreb societies whose practice varies with the social status of the people involved. All the Maghrebian codes prohibit marriage between certain groups of kin and those related by wet-nursing.[6] However, the levirate, where a widow marries her brother-in-law, and cousin marriage, remain important aspects of Maghrebian life.

The levirate may be seen as a way of preserving a relationship between a woman and her children. When her husband dies, she traditionally has the choice of returning to her own kin, in which case her children remain with her husband's family, since they are members of his clan rather than hers, or of perpetuating her relationship with his family by marrying another male, normally a brother. Marriage between cousins is a way of preventing the dispersal of family assets, since the dowry remains within the extended kinship group. However, this practice is more controversial and some clearly reject it for family or medical reasons, although others believe that the prior acquaintance of the parties will contribute to the success of the marriage.

Marriage rules are important markers of social boundaries. A rule of exogamy, which requires someone to marry outside a specified group, may also act as a rule of endogamy, defining the limits of those who are considered members of the society, which among many traditional peoples may be identified with the community of humans. Islamic marriage rules prohibit union with a polytheistic partner.[7] A Muslim man may marry a woman who is a member of a revealed religion, such as Christianity or Judaism, but a Muslim woman may not marry a non-Muslim.[8] This particular prohibition is based on the belief that a non-Muslim husband will not respect his wife's faith and that the children will not receive an Islamic religious education. It can still be found in the modern legal codes of the Maghreb countries and is widely respected among the immigrant community in France.[9]

Matrimonial Capacity

Islamic rules sanction marriage at a precise age. The Maghreb countries have tried to discourage such early marriages by raising the age of capacity.[10] However, a few informants in France confirmed that very young children could still be contracted to marry either to serve the economic interests of their families or as a means of assuring their virginity and preserving family honour. In practice, though, most people seem to marry at a much later age and the preservation of the possibility of marrying so young seems to have more to do with the desire to increase birth rates than any belief in its intrinsic merits.

The Wedding Ceremony

Marriage rituals are an important way of symbolizing and expressing the meaning of the relationship to a society. They combine features which derive both from the specific preferences of the parties and their families and from the general framework of law and social values. Islamic law does not require any specific form of words to consecrate a marriage. This relationship is established by a simple exchange of consent in the presence of two witnesses. In practice, publicity is a prominent feature of the contract. The Koran enjoins the parties to 'Announce the wedding to the beat of drums' so that the community shares in the foundation of a new home. Such an emphasis on the public proclamation of contracts is typical of preliterate societies where collective memory rather than written records is the basis of the legitimacy of a relationship. Modern legislation, however, places greater weight on the generation of a written record of the marriage, although the requirement for witnesses has been retained.[11]

Maghrebians living in France have a choice of means for contracting a marriage; the Koranic rite, the secular intervention of their country's consul, the civil authorities according to the French code or some combination of lay and religious ceremonies. The selection in any particular case reflects the degree to which the parties retain traditional Islamic values or have become integrated into the host community. A Koranic wedding alone has no legal recognition in France, although it can provide a religious validation for a civil or consular wedding. The only way to have Maghrebian law apply is for a couple to be married by a consular officer of their own country. If the parties are not citizens of the same state, however, the consul can only *record* their union. The cost of traditional Koranic weddings has led many immigrants to adopt the civil forms, but there is still a strong emotional attachment to the historic ritual.

From this review, it is clear that Maghrebian society in France is far from homogeneous. The variety of backgrounds from which the population originated and the conflicting interests involved make it impossible to formulate a single definition of Maghrebian marriage in France. To what extent have French matrimonial legal proceedings been able to find ways of reconciling these factors and of developing an accommodation between this immigrant group and the host society?

INSTITUTIONAL RESPONSES TO MAGHREBIAN MARRIAGES

Interviews with the civil authorities in Paris and Amiens, together with information from Maghrebian consulates and a representative of the Paris Mosque, revealed a variety of responses to marriage issues. These find their expression in increasingly diverse interpretations of the applicable rules.

The Town Hall

It is often only when a marriage file is being compiled, in order to establish that a valid civil marriage can be conducted, that gaps emerge between the French legal code and the realities of the situations in which it must be applied. There are, for example, frequent administrative difficulties for officials trying to establish the identities and dates of birth of parties to a proposed marriage from countries with different systems of civil registration. Bureaucratic rationality may also encounter cultural problems. Maghrebians are often puzzled by the need for both parents' consent to the marriage of a minor, when their own customs treat this purely as a matter for the father's concern.

The town hall sees its role as the application of French law, disregarding as irrelevant matters like the payment of a dowry and overriding differences, such as those in the definitions of prohibited kin, between domestic and Maghrebian codes. It is not clear to what extent this response derives from ignorance of the foreign laws and mores or from a deliberate attempt to conserve French culture in the face of changing social realities.

The Consulate

The choice of a consular wedding reflects a desire of the parties to acknowledge the ethical force of Islam and their ties with their home country. The consulate will apply Maghrebian law, recognizing the role of the dowry and accepting the degrees of prohibited kin laid down by the home country's code.

PROSPECTS FOR THE SOLUTION OF CULTURAL AND LEGAL CONFLICTS

In purely formal terms, French legal responses to international variations in marriage law may seem rational. In practice, however, this image is often out of step with the realities of institutional behaviour. Reactions to the marriage of Maghrebian immigrants show that the issues involved are neither merely matters of private concern nor confined to the law alone but extend to the historical attitudes of French society towards cultural pluralism and the place of the sacred in civil life.

The Cultural Choices of French Society

Historically, France has a tradition of assimilating immigrants, such as the Italians who arrived at the end of the nineteenth century or the Poles who settled in the North during the 1920s. Immigration has only been seen as a social problem with the coincidence of the growth in migration from North Africa and the economic crisis of the 1970s. This change is reflected in the shifting balance of immigration law between encouraging the inclusion or exclusion of migrants from French society and institutions. In this particular case, attention needs to be given to the legacy of republican secularism and the great conflicts of French history: Church and State, monarchists and republicans, doctrinaire Catholicism and religious toleration. The secular state is part of the French solution to social diversity, providing a common basis of integration for all citizens.

The presence of Maghrebian Muslims, especially their familial attitudes, may be seen as a threat to this settlement. In particular, the place afforded to civil marriage constantly brings the identity between religion and social behaviour expressed in Islam against the separation established in France between these dimensions of human experience. The problems may, however, be exaggerated by emphasizing the contrast between Islamic dogma and the actual practice of Muslim societies.

Nevertheless, the challenge posed by the role of religion in Muslim life alerts us to the pretence of French society that the sacred has been relegated to history. Sacredness has often been confused with religion. In fact, it remains a key source of legitimation. It is simply that the secular has become sacred. A differentiated society finds its source of integration in a split between religion and civil life, whose foundation is no less mystical than faith itself. French marriage finds its public meaning in a civil code which is dissociated from the private meanings of the parties but provides an ultimate source of regulation out of the acceptance by all citizens that their faith in the secular institutions of liberal democracy takes priority for most purposes over their personal religious principles. Maghrebian marriage expresses a continuity of belief between religion and civil society, where there is no distinction between national law and private sentiment and each derives from the same sacred source. When transported to a different environment, as with migration to France, this identity is weakened. While religious faith survives, it cannot rely on the support of other social institutions to sustain its influence on everyday life. It becomes one among a number of forces competing to affect marriage. In the face of this diversity of legitimations, the incipient heterogeneity of marriage in the Maghreb finds a greater opportunity to express itself.

Legal Responses to Cultural Conflict

The problem for law-makers is that, in such a dynamic situation, their responses risk becoming static forces which are irrelevant to the real issues. The rules of positive law fix certain cultural messages. French marriage law gives priority to individual freedom, as, for example, in its requirements about consent. The theory of independent will and the desirability of agreement dominate every aspect of the matrimonial union. The role of the state is to guarantee these basic principles. In Islam, the law revealed by the prophet overrides everything, even the political order. The state merely seeks to ensure that it is respected. Maghrebian law is not legitimated by appeals to state power or to some principle of rationality but by divine authority. In France, the law is sacred: in the Maghreb the sacred is law.

The marriage of Maghrebian immigrants in France is a point at which these conflicting principles must be reconciled. The compromise appears in the legal standards adopted. If, as Lévi-Strauss (1971) writes, 'ritual corresponds to man's view of the world', does the attachment of these immigrants to their matrimonial rites demonstrate a deep attachment to their country of origin, which may be insufficiently recognized by the application of French civil law, or is it merely nostalgia?

The debate over nationality has been very animated in the last few years. The Islamic countries, whose law of nationality is based on *jus sanguinis* and religious affiliation, have claimed a perpetual relationship with their nationals who live in France. Given the way in which Islam is established as not solely a private faith but as a set of rules for public conduct, this relationship may be seen as a barrier to integration. As other research (Marceau-Long 1988) has shown, the acquisition of French nationality does not necessarily affect the status of immigrants in the face of such claims. The Maghreb countries do not, for example, recognize the marriages of Muslim women to non-Muslims, while French law has difficulty accommodating the role of the *walî* or the position of those claiming kinship on bases other than those recognized in France.

Rouland (1988) has suggested that the appropriate response lies 'in the confirmation that each culture has the right to relative autonomy with respect to others whose limits should be fixed in a spirit of reciprocity'. France is already confronting this problem by negotiation with other European countries which share similar cultural, religious and economic traditions. Perhaps the same approach might be adopted in responding to Maghrebian immigration rather than simply trying to impose a solution. If complete agreement is not possible, then a convention might at least define the areas of difference and the possibilities of choice. As Carbonnier (1978, 1988) has pointed out, French law already recognizes the possibility of using a variety of procedures to achieve a similar objective, as in the case of divorce.

Naturally, public policy will set some limits to this kind of pluralism. There are wider interests involved. But public policy is not a static concept.

> The requirements of public policy are not fixed. Public policy is only a reflection of the requirements of a social milieu at any given time. But the laws in each country change. What, at a given moment, can run counter to public policy will perhaps no longer do so in the future and vice versa. Development can be cyclic. The whole question . . . is one of constant instability. (Niboyet 1949:492)

The limits to pluralism derive from the basic values and evolution of French society. In the case of marriage, the courts rely on these considerations when dismissing practices such as polygamy on the grounds of public policy, in the sense that they are contrary to the principles on which the law is founded, nor simply to the law itself.

The solutions to cultural conflicts are not to be found exclusively in immediate experience but demand an appreciation of the role of the sacred. We must look for fundamental continuities which underlie the particular institutional forms taken in different societies. Rituals of separating parties from previous statuses and relationships, holding them in social suspense and then readmitting them to the everyday world in newly-defined roles are as much a part of French civil ceremonies as they are of the observances of Islam. At this level, it may be possible to find a basis for co-existence without denying the validity of each other's culture. Our society should not be afraid to confirm the authenticity of its own culture and beliefs. The present task is to reshape the law and distinguish more clearly between its ritual and its sacred elements. The ritual aspects of marriage can then be left to express the preferences of different social groups, while the sacred aspects of law seek to express a more fundamental ethical order of human rights.

NOTES

[1] The Maghreb is a generic term for the former French colonies in North Africa.

[2] — Tunisian Code of Civil Status *(La Magalla)* 1955: Roussier, *Le Code tunisien du statut personnel, Revue juridique et politique de l'union francaise*, Paris 1957, 213–30; Andre Colomer, *Le code de status personnel tunisien, Revue algerienne, tunisienne et marocaine de legislation et jurisprudence*, Algiers, 1957, 115–227.
— Moroccan Code of Civil Status (*La Mouolawwana*) 1958: Colomer, *Le Code de statut personnel marocain*, Algiers, 1961, 79–201.
— Code of Algerian Family Law 1984, Law of 9 June 1984, No 84.11, JORA, 12 June 1984. Boormans, *Statut personnel et Famille au Maghreb de 1940 a nos jours*, explains the difficulties involved in publishing the Algerian code.

[3] 'Tunisian Code of Civil Status, Art 3; Moroccan Code of Civil Status, Art 12; Algerian Family Code, Arts 9–13.

[4] The *walî* is the person who either proposes or accepts the marriage on behalf of the young girl or woman: Moroccan Code of Civil Status, Arts 5, 12 & 13; Algerian Family Code, arts 11 & 12; in Tunisia the *walî* is used only in the case of minors.

[5] Tunisian Code of Civil Status, Art 18; French Civil Code, Art 147.

[6] The Koran forbids a man from marrying his wet-nurse or any of her daughters, called foster-sisters: Kasimirski, *Le Coran*, Suran IV, verse 23. This has been extended so that a breastfed child may not marry the wet-nurse or her ascendants ad infinitum, a foster daughter or her descendants ad infinitum, foster sisters or their descendants ad infinitum, and paternal or maternal aunts of the wet-nurse: Algerian Family Code, Arts 27–9; Moroccan Code of Civil Status, Art 28; Tunisian Code of Civil Status, Art 17.

[7] Kasimirski, *Le Coran*, Surah 2, verses 221–2.

[8] Kasimirski, *Le Coran*, Surah 60, verse 10.

[9] Moroccan Code of Civil Status, Art 29, al 5; Algerian Family Code, Art 31; Tunisian Code of Civil Status, Art 5.

[10] The Moroccan Code of Civil Status specifies eighteen for men and fifteen for women; in Tunisia, the Law of 20 February 1964 sets twenty for men and seventeen for women. Algeria specifies twenty-one for men and eighteen for women.

[11] Tunisian Code of Civil Status, Art 3, al 2; Algerian Family Code, Arts 9 and 18; Moroccan Code of Civil Status, Arts 41, al 2. The Moroccan Code treats marriage as a private bilateral contract.

REFERENCES

Adler, A. (1963), *Le sens de la vie*, Paris, Payot.
Adler, A. (1977) 'Faiseurs de pluie, faiseurs d'ordre', *libre*, 2. 45, Paris, Payot (Petite bibliothèque Payot).
Carbonnier, J. (1978), *Sociologic juridique*, Paris, Puf.
Carbonnier, J. (1988), *Flexible droit*, Paris, LGDG.
David, Jauffret-Spinosi, (1988), *Les grands systèmes de droit contemporains*, Paris, Jurisprudence générale, Dalloz, (Précis Dalloz) 9e. ed.
Durkheim, E. (1912), *Les formes élémentaires de la vie religieuse*, Paris.
Ehrlich, E. (1913), *Fondements de la sociologie du droit* (Gpundlegunf der Soziologie des Rechts).
Gauchet, M. (1977), 'La dette du sens et les racines de l'Etat', *Libre*, 2, 5, Paris, Payot, (Petite bibliothèque Payot).
Gauchet, M. (1985), *Le désenchantement du monde: une histoire politique de la religion*, Paris, Gallimard.
Gluckman, M. (1955), *The Judicial Process among the Barotse*.
Goody, J. (1985), *L'évolution de la famille et du mariage en Europe*, Préface G. Duby, Paris, Ed A. Colin.
Griffiths, J. (1986), 'What is Legal Pluralism?', *Journal of Legal Pluralism*, 24, 1.
Gurvitch, G. (1937), *Morale théorique et Science des moeurs*.
Hocart, A. M. (1973), *Le mythe sorcier et autres essais*, Paris, Payot, (Petite Bibliothèque Payot).
Levi-Strauss, C. (1971), *L'homme nu*, Paris, Plon.
Marceau-Long (1988). *Etre français aujourd'hui et demain*, vols I et II, Union générale d'Editions, La documentation française, Paris.
Niboyet, J. H. (1949), *Cours de droit international privé français*, 2e. édition.
Rouland (1988), *Anthropologie juridique*, Paris, Puf.

[4]

Migrant Women caught between Islamic Family Law and Women's Rights. The Search for the Appropriate 'Connecting Factor' in International Family Law

Marie-Claire Foblets

Summary

In recent decades 'conflicts justice' in the realm of international family law has undoubtedly gained momentum in most European immigration countries. This is largely due to an increase in the number of cases relating to family disputes among migrants submitted to the courts. In the first part of this contribution (§ 2: 'The legal techniques at hand. The dramatic lack of adaptation of century-old techniques') I briefly describe how 'conflicts justice,' in the domain of cross-cultural family relations, is facing the impact of an unprecedented cross-boundary mobility of people from all over the world. This cross-border mobility has engendered a new type of social and cultural pluralism in most European host countries. In the second part (§ 3: 'The case of Moroccan women claiming protection under Belgian secular law') I illustrate the discussion on possible legal solutions for handling the 'conflicts justice' consequence of this cross-border mobility by referring to the very problematic position of Moroccan women who have immigrated to Belgium.

§ 1. Introduction

My paper builds upon one particular aspect of a vast issue that is very much at the core of the debate in Europe today: how to conceive the future of our (multicultural) societies in terms of peaceful cohabitation with the many newly-immigrated communities from

* M.-Cl. Foblets, LL.M., Lic. Phil., Dr. Anthropology, Professor of Law and Anthropology at the Universities of Leuven, Brussels and Antwerp in Belgium, Associate Professor at the Université Paris I/Sorbonne, Honorary Advocate of the Bar of Brussels, and Head of the Department of Social and Cultural Anthropology at the University of Leuven.

all over the world. I will focus on the position of Muslim (migrant) women in that debate.

Conflicts of civilization(s) are a fascinating topic of research. However, in practice, these conflicts are probably among the most difficult to settle. It is one thing to speak of clashing cultures as a subject of academic interest; it is yet another to deal with them on a day-to-day basis.

The subject which I propose to discuss here is of necessity but a very small part of a vast field, namely the question which arises when the judge in a family court in Europe today is obliged to consider what degree of recognition he - or she [1] - will give to family laws that apply to migrant communities of foreign origin but that clash with the domestic legal culture. As a consequence of the massive migration movements from the former colonies of the Western powers, the question is becoming increasingly important in almost all European countries, particularly in the realm of family law. In barely twenty years (i.e. since the sixties and the seventies) these migration movements have caused major changes in the area of international family law.

On average, up to 10% of the population in most of what have until recently been called 'Western-European' countries today are of non-Western, i.e. non-European, origin. Many people immigrated from the former colonies in the sixties and seventies primarily because of labour immigration facilities. Since the late eighties, mainly people seeking asylum under the 1951 UN Convention Relating to the Status of Refugees have been drawn to Europe. [2]

Post World-War II immigration to Europe is characterized by two main features that are very much a challenge, and often an obstacle, to those lawyers who are looking for appropriate techniques to allow for the peaceful management of clashes between the basic values of the host-society (expressed, for example, by the 1950 European Convention on Human Rights [3]) and those cultural values imported by newly immigrated populations. The first feature is the cultural and demographic diversity of the many groups who have immigrated from all over the world: statistics demonstrate

1. For purposes of facility, in this contribution I will henceforth use only the masculine gender of nouns that may equally refer to male and female judges.

2. J.-Y. Carlier, D. Vanheule (eds.), *Europe and Refugees: A Challenge?*, (Kluwer Law International, 1997); H. Crawley, *Women as Asylum Seekers. A Legal Handbook*, (ILPA, 1997); E. Guild, *The Developing Immigration and Asylum Policies of the European Union. Adopted Conventions, Resolutions, Recommendations, Decisions and Conclusions*, (Kluwer Law International, 1996).

3. *European Treaty Series* [ETS], N° 5. Text amended according to the provisions of Protocol N° 3 (ETS N°45), which entered into force on 21 September 1971, of Protocol N° 5 (ETS N° 55) which entered into force on 20 December 1971, and of Protocol N° 8 ETS N° 118), which entered into force on 1 January 1990 and comprising also the text of Protocol N° 2 (ETS N° 44) which, in accordance with article 5, par. 3 thereof, has been an integral part of the Convention since its entry into force on 21 September 1970.

their extremely heterogeneous origins. The second feature is the very resistance shown by a growing number of migrants to various attempts at assimilating them into the host society, primarily by having them adopt the values of the majority society. Some groups show more resistance than others. So far, Muslim groups have proved to be among the most resistant.

The reasons why these two features constitute an impediment - a challenge, to say the least - to lawyers today are basically linked to the legal history of Europe, and of continental Europe in particular. The techniques inherited from the past to cope with conflicts of legal issues have not been conceived with a view to the present-day situation (*cf. infra*, § 2). My intention in this presentation is basically twofold. In the first part, I will briefly explain the main reasons for the present lack of adaptation of legal techniques in continental Europe, which are largely an inheritance from the past, to enable the handling of issues related to the recognition accorded to non-Western legal cultures claiming the protection of the law. These claims may be particularly provocative when it comes to granting recognition to discriminatory legal traditions and systems. In § 3 of my paper ['The case of Moroccan women claiming protection under Belgian (secular) law'], I will illustrate the discussion of possible solutions to this vast problem by referring to one concrete study we published in 1998 in Belgium,[4] at the request of the Belgian authorities. That study illustrates the way lawyers cope with one particular case: the protection of immigrant Muslim (more particularly Moroccan) women (and their daughters) within the realm of family law.

§ 2. The legal techniques at hand. The dramatic lack of adaptation of century-old techniques

A. Unprecedented cross-boundary mobility: the internationalization of family law in Europe today

The issue of the recognition to be given to non-Western legal cultures that claim legal protection in Europe touches on a highly sensitive, socially and politically, problem area. It forces an open discussion on the question of the degree of cultural tolerance to be shown by the courts in the host country and the role of judges when handling disputes involving migrants from non-Western countries. Problems related to marital property law, descendance, the mutual rights and obligations of spouses, adultery and cohabitation, inheritance and transfer of property, child custody, conflicts of nationalities within one family, and so on, sharply manifest how difficult it has become for family judges in Europe to achieve justice in conflicts involving disputants of non-Western origin. So far, most disputants, for the mere reason that they have kept their

4. *Cf. infra* §3.: M.-Cl. Foblets, *Femmes marocaines et conflicts familiaux en immigration: quelles solutions juridiques appropriées*? [Migrant women from Morocco involved in family disputes. What are appropriate legal solutions?], (Maklu, 1998).

foreign nationality, continue to resort - at least partially - to the principles of the legal system in their country of origin.

Two questions then arise:

1. Does the European judge acknowledge the 'foreign' family rules as law?, and
2. Does he acknowledge these rules to be on equal terms with his (own) legal system?

In order to answer these questions and to understand the underlying issue at stake, one must find out whether the legal techniques at hand offer the appropriate facilities to enable the judges properly to resolve the increasing number of ever more complex international family disputes that occur within their jurisdiction. I will here address, firstly, the question what these techniques might be, and secondly, whether they are sufficiently attuned to the social and demographic developments that have occurred in Europe since the sixties and the seventies.

B. 'Conflicts justice': the choice-of-law rules

The techniques that are used by the courts to resolve international family disputes are called 'choice-of-law techniques', 'choice-of-law rules', or even 'conflicts rules'. These techniques deal with a series of questions that can be grouped together under the following headings:

1. Jurisdiction (will a court of a particular state accept the case?);
2. Choice-of-law (what law will the court apply if it does accept the case?);
3. Recognition and enforcement of foreign judgments (can other states and nations be expected to honour the judicial findings of the court handling the case?). Analytically, these three series of questions are distinct. Functionally, however, they are intertwined.

A lack of consensus on the way to deal with these three questions explains a great deal of the complexities related to contemporary choice-of-law techniques. I will not attempt to describe these complexities here: the subject is far too difficult and the literature built up over the years too voluminous to be 'manageable' in a brief contribution like this.[5]

5. See for general writings on the choice-of-law problem, *i.a.*: A.P. Vonken, 'Balancing Processes in International Private law. On the determination and weighing of interests in the conflict of laws and the "openness" of the choice of law system', in Centre of Foreign Law and Private International Law (ed.), *Forty Years on: The Evolution of Postwar Private International Law in Europe*, Centre for Foreign Law and Private International Law, (Kluwer, 1990), 171-194; S.E. Cox, 'Razing Conflicts Facades to Build Better Jurisdiction Theory: The Foundation - There is no Law but Forum Law', 28 *Valparaiso University Law Review* 1 (1993), 1-82; W. Singer, 'Real Conflicts', 69 *Boston University Law Review* 1 (1989), 3-129. Two examples of introductory comments on the choice-of-law problem (continued...)

I will therefore focus on the second question, the question as to what law the court should apply to cross-boundary disputes. More particularly, I will look briefly at the kind of issues that this question raises in dealing with conflicts between Western and non-Western laws (*cf. infra* § 2 E).

Before I develop my exposé on the choice-of-law model(s) in contemporary Europe, it may be useful very briefly to recall the origins of our choice-of-law techniques in Europe (*cf. infra* § 2 C) and emphasize the role played by the judges in applying these techniques (*cf. infra* § 2 D).

C. The origins of conflicts law

Cross-boundary relationships between individuals pre-date, by many centuries, post-colonial migration to Europe. They occurred as soon as members of different human societies began to deal with each other. But the true beginning of conflict-of-law techniques, as we know these techniques today, had to await the revival of Roman law in the twelfth century when *glossators* began to link the choice-of-law problem to a passage in the first title of the Justinian Codex. [6] Medieval scholars began to debate whether local *statuta* could be applied extraterritorially to citizens abroad, and whether foreign citizens within a forum's territory were bound by its laws. By viewing the problem in this fashion, the *glossators* hit upon what has since been called 'choice-of-law rules,' a term suggesting that choice-of-law problems are caused by the clash of sovereign commands and that the ultimate solution could only be found in the reconciliation of sovereignty and the exigencies of interstate relationships [7].

The search for criteria that would determine the spatial dimension of laws preoccupied scholars for centuries. In Medieval European society there were good reasons to ponder conflict-of-law questions. In sixteenth-century France, for example, even after the Kings had established the crown's supremacy, the law varied from province to province and there was a fundamental divergence between the Germanic *'coutumes'* (customs) of Northern France and the *'droit écrit'* (written law) that prevailed south of the Loire Valley.

5.(...continued)
in relation to post-war migration to Europe, and in particular to the question of contemporary cross-cultural family issues, are: J. Deprez, 'Les évolutions actuelles du droit international privé français dans le domaine du droit familial en relation avec les convictions religieuses' [French private international law: recent developments in the domain of family relations with respect to religious convictions], 45 *Revue de droit canonique* (1995), 7-40; M. Verwilghen, R. de Valkeneer, *Relations Familiales Internationales* [International Family Relations], (Bruylant, 1993); E. Jayme, 'Identité culturelle et intégration: le droit international privé postmoderne', *Recueil des Cours* (1995), 9-268; J. Meeusen, *Nationalisme en internationalisme in het internationaal privaatrecht*, (Intersentia, 1997).

6. Even if this title is concerned with religion, rather than with conflicts problems.

7. See, *i.a.*: A. Ehrenzweig, *A Treatise on the Conflict of Laws*, (West Publishing Co., 1962), 312-313.

The idea that it is possible to reconcile the territorial limits of sovereignty and the free play of relationships between individuals[8] across national borders reappears in later centuries. In fact, it has become a central preoccupation of modern conflict-of-law analysis.[9] Among lawyers there is much discussion on the choice of the appropriate law to be applied to familial relations that are designated as 'mixed,' 'cross-cultural,' 'multipatrial,' or just 'international,' meaning either that the family members are of different cultural backgrounds or that the family group has settled in a country that is not that of their common origin.[10]

D. 'Conflict-of-Law Justice': The Role of Judges in International Family Disputes

In practice, questions concerning the choice of the law applicable to multi-state family cases present themselves to a variety of decision-makers: not only to the parties themselves, but also to their legal counsellor, the courts, administrative agencies and legislatures. They take on an aspect of particular urgency in the context of cross-cultural litigation involving not just different, but clashing, i.e. more or less incommensurate, family laws: African, Asiatic or Islamic family laws on the one hand, European family law on the other hand.

The rough and tumble of a lawsuit in this type of case puts into even sharper focus the consequences of choosing one rather than another law to determine the fate of spouses and their common children. Cross-cultural conflicts of law leave the judge who has to deal with family disputes in an awkward position: he is compelled to act as a multi-state decision-maker and his judgment will affect relationships among family members who, by definition, are not confined to his own culture. Cross-cultural family conflicts require the judge to consult 'unfamiliar' foreign law which, he may find out, is as unsatisfactory as his own law (the *lex fori*) because both were framed with reference to local circumstances with scant regard for transnational realities.

The earliest attitude of many European judges to this question, an attitude which is not yet wholly extinct, was to regard the rules of social intercourse among family members in non-Western communities as not really constituting law in any true sense of the

8. In practice, choice-of-law problems only arose when the *ius commune* had to give way to local statutes and many conflicts issues were controlled by superior law that eliminated the need for choice.

9. The choice-of-law rules determine the law that is the 'most suitable' to be applied to a particular relationship (the so-called choice-of-law-process) by tracing the interests of the parties involved and the connecting factors (*cf. infra*) that determine whether one national law or another is to resolve a concrete dispute. Choice-of-law techniques thus ultimately raise a highly political question, namely the question which 'connecting' factor is most suitable to express the nexus between a given legal relationship and a particular state jurisdiction.

10. In the latter case, the internationalization of the family relation is not a matter of cultural diversity among family members, but it results from the minority position of the family group within the country of (temporary or definite) residence.

word.[11] At present, however, it is hardly, if at all, doubted that non-Western family laws are indeed valid law, at least for the people concerned. The question then arises as to what law is to be applied when these people settle in Europe.

That last question, arising from the fact that many non-Europeans have settled in Europe over the last thirty years, is perhaps of the greatest practical importance for the European societies today. At the moment there are hundreds of thousands of Muslims living in Europe.[12] The number of Algerians married to French women has increased sharply over the last thirty years.[13] I know of no recent statistics concerning immigration to Britain from the Asiatic and African parts of the Commonwealth, but I believe the rate there must be comparable to that found in France. These numbers make clear that the conflicts between Western and non-Western family laws in Europe today have become a key issue in the area of international family law.

I shall first present a general sketch of the four main factors that, either independently or in combination, form the basis of the contemporary choice-of-law debate among law practitioners in most European host countries: (1) nationality; (2) domicile; (3) the choice of the 'better law'; and (4) party autonomy. Against that outline, I will risk a glimpse into the future and consider the issue for Muslim women of migrant origin in a number of concrete situations.

E. In Search of the Appropriate 'Connecting Factor'

The policies of the courts and other authorities regarding the choice of the law to be applied to migrant family issues vary considerably, both historically and geographically, from one country to another and from one domain of family law to the other. Case law, on the whole, has often been guided by rather incompatible goals. In some cases, courts primarily aim at the integration of migrants. The first concern then is to apply a uniform set of rules to all, regardless of their origin, race or creed. This is the way private international disputes are settled by American and Canadian courts.[14] In the U.S. and in Canada, traditionally and up to the present, the choice of the applicable law is determined by the parties' domicile. In continental Europe, on the contrary, courts have traditionally favoured preservation of the cultural distinctiveness of foreigners and newcomers: conflict-of-law rules have therefore led to a preference for a person's national law.

11. With the result, *i.a.*, that if anyone to whom domestic law (the law of the host country) was applicable entered into a personal relation with another who was subject to another national law, the relationship automatically was considered to be governed by the domestic law.
12. G. Nonneman, T. Niblock, B. Szajkowski (eds.), *Muslim Communities in the New Europe*, (Ithaca Press, 1996).
13. See *i.a.*: E. Todd., *Le destin des immigrés. Assimilation et ségrégation dans les démocraties occidentales*, (Seuil, 1994), esp. 280 sq..
14. Fr. K. Juenger, *Choice of Law and Multistate Justice*, (Martinus Nijhoff Publishers, 1993), 88 sq.

However, these incongruities between choice-of-law rules are not just the product of differences among the countries involving choice-of-law traditions, nor of the tacit incompatibilities between conflicts policy objectives underlying these different traditions. Today in Europe, the choice-of-law problem itself in its very essence has changed. The change relates to the historical changes in the position of migrants in the countries of residence. Much of the present-day unease with the choice-of-law techniques in the face of conflicts issues is directly linked to the growing self-awareness (identity awareness) of sedentary migrant communities in most European countries. This has been accompanied by a gradual strengthening of their legal position and by the emergence of their ever more pressing claim to a separate system of personal law. [15]

To explore this fundamental change in the very nature of the choice-of-law problem, I will here address the problem in the light of each of the above-mentioned 'connecting factors': nationality, domicile, 'better law' and party autonomy. I will briefly demonstrate the extent to which the strengthening of the legal position - in the wake of stabilization, mainly due to naturalization - of migrants in most European host countries over the years has introduced both immense complexity and much artificiality into the choice-of-law problem when it comes to selecting the most appropriate family law for the resolution of individual disputes.

1. Nationality

It was not until the middle of the nineteenth century in continental Europe that the civil law definition of nationality as a personal quality [16] was incorporated into what were for most countries the very first rules developed with regard to conflict-of-law issues. It was provided that the national law of a person best resolves questions concerning the family relations and all matters linked - directly or indirectly - with someone's personal status. The first meaning of such rules holds that the national law best responds to the expectations of a person who relies on the law in organizing his or her family relations,

15. On the emerging claims of Muslim communities in matters of family law in Europe, and particularly in the United Kingdom, see *i.a.*: J. Nielsen., 'Das islamische Recht und seine Bedeutung für die Lage der muslimischen Minderheiten in Europa' [Islamic law and its significance for the situation of Muslim minorities in Europe], *EPD-Dokumentation*, 34/87 (3 August 1987), and more recently, from the same author: *Muslims in Western Europe*, (Edinburgh University Press, 1992); S. Poulter, 'Cultural Pluralism and it's Limits: A Legal Perspective', in Commission for Racial Equality (ed.), *Britain: A Plural Society*, (1990); Union of Muslim Organisations (UMO), *Why Muslim Family Law for British Muslims?*, (UMO, 1983). For an overview of the situation in French speaking Europe, in relation to Muslims: M. Verwilghen, J.-Y. Carlier (eds.), *Le statut personnel des musulmans. Droit comparé et droit international privé* [The Personal Status of Muslims. Comparative law and private international law], (Bruylant, 1992).

16. The concept of nationality as a person-bound quality was first introduced with the Napoleonic civil code.

even if conduct takes place wholly within another state's jurisdiction. In this perspective, nationality is a constitutive element of one's identity. [17]

The repercussions of this position, when interpreted in present-day context, may be odd. In present-day Europe most migrants have definitively settled in the host country (i.e. that of residence). Except for the first generation of these groups, the vast majority have given up the hope of returning to the country of their forebears. The Dutch sociologist H. Entzinger characterizes their stay in the host countries as 'life-long temporariness.' [18] They raise their families in the country of residence, hence the community of language, culture and affiliation becomes largely divorced from the concept of nationality as a personal quality and applies, rather, to what social scientists call ethnicity.

European civil courts, however, are still bound by the civil law's concept of nationality. They thus may find themselves compelled to recognize conduct governed by foreign law that, in some cases, may be contrary to the basic principles of the forum's law (i.e. that of the host country), for the mere reason that the parties concerned - notwithstanding a life-long residence in the host country - have kept their nationality of origin. Up until now, conduct consisting of polygamy and wife repudiation are among the most controversial conducts that have at times been legitimated by European judges in the application of discriminatory matrimonial laws still in force in the parties' country of origin. [19]

In order to overcome this difficulty, some European countries, beginning in the seventies, have come to facilitate naturalization in the country of residence, granting nationality to migrant children *via* the place of birth (i.e. in the host country). [20] The

17. This means among other things that one's nationality regulates the claim an individual (national) can make upon others and, conversely, the claims others can place upon him or her.
18. H.B. Entzinger., P.J.J. Stijnen (eds.), *Etnische Minderheden in Nederland* [Ethnic Minorities in The Netherlands], (Boom, 1990), ch. 11, 244-264.
19. See *i.a.*: P. Lagarde, 'La théorie de l'ordre public international face à la polygamie et à la répudiation' [The theory of international public order with respect to polygamy and repudiation], in X (ed.), *Nouveaux itinéraires en droit. Hommage à François Rigaux*, (Bruylant, 1993), 262-282; B. Ancel, 'Le statut de la femme du polygame' [The status of the wife of a polygamous husband], in: Fr. Dekeuwer-Defossez (ed.), *Le droit de la famille à l'épreuve des migrations transnationales*, (L.G.D.J., 1993), 105-124.
20. Typically, the new Dutch, French and Belgian nationality laws introduced in the 1980s grant more weight to residence than in previous laws: children born in the host country whose parents (either of the parents) were themselves 'legally' (i.e. documented) born in the host country, are automatically granted the citizenship of the host country (see, *i.a.* for the Dutch Nationality Law: G.R. Groot, 'Een wetsontwerp ter wijziging van de Rijkswet op het Nederlanderschap' [A Project of Amendment of the Dutch Nationality Law], *Migrantenrecht* nrs. 5-6 (1993), 91-105; for the Belgian Law: Ch.-L. Closset, *Traité de la Nationalité en droit belge* [Treatise on the Belgian Nationality Law], (Larcier, 1993); and for France: M. Long, *Conditions juridiques et culturelles de l'intégration* (Haut Conseil à l'intégration). Rapport au Premier Ministre [Legal and cultural conditions of integration. Report to the Prime Minister], (La Documentation Française, 1992), Annex 2, 75 sq.

aim is to promote the integration of migrant families into the legal system of the country of residence. Nationality laws issued since the seventies in a growing number of European countries no longer distinguish between nationals and foreigners, but between natives and foreigners. The latter term signifies persons residing on the territory of the host country who have not (yet) acquired citizenship there. In the long term, the criterion of one's place of birth is meant to lead to a legal status (formally) that is equal for all: it is then sufficient to be born in the country of residence to become a full citizen of that country and therefore to be submitted to the totality of its legislation, including whatever laws pertain to family affairs and personal status.

2. Domicile

Yet another way to do away with uncertainty in the choice-of-law process is the solution traditionally applied in England and, as I already mentioned, also in the U.S. and in Canada.[21] In these countries the question whether a legal system is applicable to a particular situation is considered in connection with the parties' place(s) of residence (i.e. domicile) and not in reference to their nationalities.

One of the main advantages of this type of solution is that it releases the courts from being required on principle to defer migrant family disputes to the law of the nationality of origin.

However, the Anglo-Saxon choice-of-law model may also lead to surprising consequences. Take the example of a father who, conforming to English law, is obliged to maintain his legitimate children. If this rule applies to a father who is now domiciled in England but who, according to the law of his former domicile, was married lawfully to two wives at the same time, this father will be obliged to maintain the children of both his marriages. He cannot escape his duty of supporting all these children on the pretext that under English law he is only obliged to maintain his legitimate children, and that according to English law it is impossible that children, born at the same time of different women, should all be legitimate. Similarly, for the same reason - namely since English conflict-of-law rules accept as valid a family relationship which is rooted in the domiciliary law of another country - this same husband and father will be obliged to support both women. In English law, however, as enacted for the British citizen, one never thought of the possibility that a husband might have two legitimate wives. English domestic law, which becomes applicable when spouses take up residence in England, will thus have to show understanding for this sort of strange, from its perspective, yet enduring relation now subject to its authority.

Now that marriages contracted in India, between Hindus or Muslims, have in the last two decades come to be recognized in England, this type of conflicts case occurs ever

21. *Cf. supra* note 14.

more frequently. Assuming that a Muslim, according to the law of his domicile, could not deprive himself of his right to polygamy, should he be deprived of that right by reason of a marriage contracted in England during a temporary stay there? It will generally be admitted that a Muslim's right to polygamy or repudiation cannot be exercised in England in respect of a marriage celebrated in that country, since the exercise of this right will be against English law: the consequence of the English domiciliation of the spouses is that their marriage becomes a monogamous marriage. But when the young Muslim husband returns home, his English marriage - if it is still considered as a marriage at all - will not be regarded as an obstacle to the exercise of his polygamous privileges.

Likewise, conflicts rules that defer to the law of the parties' domicile allow European women to be bound by the ties of polygamous marriage through a form of marriage upheld in England. Take the example of a Muslim who has fixed his domicile in England, thereby becoming subject to English matrimonial law. While domiciled in England, he marries a British woman. If he subsequently returns with his wife to a Muslim country, the marriage will nevertheless be transformed into a Muslim marriage.

3. Nationality and domicile: the choice of the 'better law'

The lessons learnt from this sort of difficulty in the civil courts - that of determining whether a person's national law or the law of his domicile applies to cross-boundary family relations -, have induced the courts and legislatures to search for other solutions.

Historically, the controversy with regard to nationality versus domicile goes back to the notorious question of the remarriage of divorcees whose native countries did not recognize a prior divorce. This is an issue that, since the sixties in Europe, has proved troublesome in all legal systems whose conflict-of-law rules were geared to the national law principle. The fact that Spain and Italy would not permit their nationals abroad to divorce - until well after migration from these countries to Member States of the European Community had begun - called for appropriate solutions. [22] In Europe, many law practitioners still remember the bizarre situation that used to block Spaniards from marrying German divorcees and which forced many hapless fiancé(e)s to celebrate evasive marriages in Denmark. [23] The application of the personal (i.e. national) law of both fiancés ultimately resulted in the 'well-nigh absurd' [24] practice of treating German divorcees as if they still were married!

22. i.e. solutions/sentences that would not force divorcees either to abandon their new partners or to live in sin, jeopardizing the parties' and their childrens' legal status.
23. See *i.a.*: F. Juenger, 'The German Constitutional Court and Conflict of Laws', 20 *American Journal of Comparative Law* (1972), 290 sq.
24. E. Rabel *et al* (eds.), *The Conflict of Laws*, (University of Michigan Law School Ann Arbor, ed. 1958), note 307, at 558.

One of the most delicate dilemmas for the courts to solve today involves the confrontation of judges with foreign family law codes that, in spite of a near universal movement toward gender equality, still discriminate in favour of husbands and fathers. Courts in Europe are confronted with a plethora of foreign rules that do not meet forum standards of gender equality and non-discrimination. Civil judges are repeatedly required to recognize unilateral repudiations by Muslim men (of their wives). The policies of the courts in this highly delicate matter vary significantly. Courts usually do not grant divorces on more permissive grounds than those available in their own jurisdiction. However, the arguments on which the judges base their decisions vary. Some courts insist on gender equality as a basic legal principle of forum law and therefore deny validity to unilateral divorces in so far as they systematically privilege one gender (man) over the other. Other courts, on the contrary, protect gender equality less but argue against unilateral dissolution of the marriage for reasons pertaining to the proceedings (publicity, right of the wife to be properly defended before the divorce judge in the home country, and so on).

In their search for more harmonious solutions, some courts have come to mitigate the sharp distinction between nationality and domicile by the notion that, over the years, a person might have lost a 'true social connection' with his - or her - national law. Some lower courts therefore have ventured to substitute domicile for nationality whenever the law of the domicile appears to be the 'most closely connected' law. A relevant case in this respect, occurring in the Netherlands in the seventies, involved a Portuguese couple who wished to divorce before a Dutch court. Although both husband and wife had kept the Portuguese nationality, the court decided Dutch law applied since they had lived in the Netherlands for five consecutive years and were thus 'bound to the Dutch legal order'.[25]

Some legislatures have come to approve this view, among other instances for divorce, and so displaced nationality as the primary connecting factor in case either of the spouses no longer has a 'true social connection' with his or her country of citizenship. The Dutch legislature authorizes this approach for divorce in Article 1(2), in conjunction with Article 1(1b), of the *Wet Conflictenrecht Echtscheiding*[26] which states that if one of the spouses no longer has a true social connection with the country of their common nationality, the law of their common domicile will be applied, not the law of their common nationality.

After much vacillation, the same idea has gradually come to take hold in other family law issues, and in the field of succession. In France, for example, little has remained, in practice, of the principle still enshrined in Article 3(3) of the French Civil Code

25. *Hoge Raad* (Dutch Supreme Court) February 9, 1979.

26. *Wet van 25 maart 1981 houdende regeling van het conflictenrecht inzake de ontbinding van het huwelijk en scheiding van tafel en bed en de erkenning daarvan ('Wet Conflictenrecht Echtscheiding')*, *Staatsblad*, 1981, 166 sq.

(which still calls for the application of the national law of all parties involved). The French *Cour de cassation* [Supreme Court] resolves the problem of foreigners seeking divorce by adopting the domiciliary principle, a solution that very much resembles current case law in the Netherlands and in English conflicts justice (*cf. infra*).

This manipulative way of dealing with conflicts issues, also called the 'better law' (or 'proper law') approach, was first suggested by J. Morris who in 1951 published a seminal article on 'the proper law of torts' in the *Harvard Law Review*.[27] Morris proposed that judges resolve problems involving multi-state torts by selecting the law which, on policy grounds, has 'the most significant connection' with the particular tort and the specific issue at hand.

In the 'better law' approach both nationality and domicile become 'soft' connecting factors with considerably more manipulative potential. Courts may either stress the intent of the parties to stay in the country of residence or the objective links that connect the situation with the host state in order to justify their preference for the law of the domicile over the personal law of the parties. They may instead prefer to emphasize nationality over domicile in order to achieve results that appear to be more appropriate to the particular circumstances of the case.

The practical illustrations of the better law approach are numerous. The better law approach, in effect, grants courts a *carte blanche* to reconcile domicile and nationality by fashioning solutions that best fit cross-boundary family disputes. It is the civil judge who determines the territorial and personal coverage of a law: he not only defines the reach of the substantive rule that potentially applies to a given case, but also the parties' interest(s) in having this particular law applied to their relationship. In maintenance cases, for example, where discriminatory laws drastically restrict the wife's claim - as is the case under Islamic regulation -, recourse to 'better law', *in casu* the substantive law of the host country, permits the court to grant the wife the right to lay claim to reasonable financial assistance from the (ex-)husband.

Recourse to better law analysis ultimately forces reliance on the judge's policy. In effect, the better law approach benefits mainly those litigants who manage to submit their dispute to a judge who is sufficiently resourceful to exploit the conflicts issues that are submitted to his jurisdiction for the sole profit of the parties. For this reason, some international practitioners remain critical of the better law approach and consider it not to be a satisfactory choice-of-law model. While the better law approach confers broad powers on the courts, it fails to provide guidance on how to use these powers correctly. The better law approach undermines predictability without producing necessarily sound decisions.

27. J. Morris, 'The Proper Law of a Tort', 64 *Harvard Law Review* (1951), 881.

4. Party Autonomy

For several years now some scholars, *i.a.* in Belgium, have therefore advocated a greater role for party autonomy in conflicts issues involving migrant disputants.[28] Party autonomy, also called the solution of the *optio iuris*, means that the parties themselves choose the law that is applicable to their legal relationships.

Party autonomy made its entrance into the area of international family law in the second half of the seventies. The driving force behind reflections on party autonomy stems mainly from the doctrine.[29] Party autonomy was primarily seen as a remedy for the unpredictability of the application of conflict-of-law rules: the power to designate the applicable law is a means by which parties can preclude any uncertainty with respect to the result of the conflict-of-law issues that sooner or later may oppose them; at the same time they will know exactly which legal norms they are expected to comply with.

Freedom of choice appears to be eminently suitable for legal relationships that involve persons having different nationalities or where one or both have dual citizenship. Take the example of spouses who no longer share the same nationality. Which law is to be applied to their divorce? The option of making a deliberate choice in favour of one legal system thus warrants a predictable choice-of-law result. The same is true of the possibility for the recognition of illegitimate children. Some years ago two Dutch authors proposed that the principle of party autonomy should also control recognition and denial of paternity:[30] a person who is willing to recognize a child as his own should be accorded the freedom to choose the law by which the desired recognition can be achieved. This assumes, of course, that recognition is in the best interest of the child. This proposal would considerably improve the situation of Muslim children born of unmarried parents who, following Islamic law, are denied paternity. The fathers would be able, in exercising their choice of the law to be applied, to validate their paternity, thus avoiding the Islamic prohibition on illegitimate (extra-marital) fatherhood.

28. On the *optio iuris*, *i.a.*: J.-Y. Carlier, *Autonomie de la volonté et statut personnel. Etude prospective de droit international privé* [Autonomy of will and personal status: a prospective study of international private law], (Bruylant, 1992), 468 p.; and more recently, to some extent: *Voorstel van een ontwerp van Wet houdende van Internationaal Privaatrecht* [Draft Proposal of Codification of (Belgian) International Private Law], Belgische Groep Internationaal Privaatrecht/Groupe belge de droit international privé, (final report), February 1998.

29. See, *i.a.*: A.E. von Overbeck, 'L'irrésistible extension de l'autonomie de la volonté', in: X. (ed.), *Nouveaux itinéraires en droit. Hommage à François Rigaux*, (Bruylant, 1993), 620-636: R. vander Elst, 'Liberté, respect et protection de la volonté en droit international privé', in: *ibid.*, 506-516.

30. This proposal is motivated by the *favor infantis*: Th.M. de Boer, R. Otting, '"Het belang van het kind" als conflictenrechtelijk keuzemotief: ontkenning van vaderschap en erkenning van kinderen in het Nederlandse internationaal privaatrecht' ['The interest of the child' as choice-of-law principle: denial of paternity and recognition of children in Dutch private international law], in: M. de Langen, J.H. de Graaf., F.B. Kunneman, *Kinderen en recht* [Children and Law], (Kluwer, 1989), 74 sq.; 81-83.

Notwithstanding the substantive advantages of party autonomy, courts in many European countries remain relatively reluctant to apply the solution of the parties' will(s) in the field of international family relationships. In practice, only a restricted freedom of choice is permitted: the choice is generally confined to a choice from among a number of relevantly connected legal systems - either the common national or the common domiciliary law. In matrimonial property regulation, for example, only a limited choice is accepted. The spouses may, prior or during the marriage, choose the law of either party's present nationality or domicile, as well as the *lex rei sitae* (the local law where the property is located) with respect to real estate. Prior to the wedding, fiancés may also choose the law of either party's domicile. Parties will not be allowed to choose any other law. In addition to the need for certainty, there is another reason for this drastic restriction is the protection of the interests of the weaker party (or parties): the courts generally restrict the parties' freedom to select the applicable law in favour of the structurally weaker party. Party autonomy is thus subject to the restriction that the choice does not prejudice the weaker party.

§ 3. The case of Moroccan women claiming protection under Belgian (secular) law

A. Who will reorient the conflict of laws? In search of new choice-of-law maxims

It goes without saying that the evolution of post-World War II private international law in Europe deserves a more complex analysis than this succinct explanatory exposé of the most recurrent choice-of-law models that are to be found in the literature and case law of the civil courts over the last twenty years. One should devote at least a chapter to the current wave of private international law codifications in Europe and the unification and harmonization of substantive law and private international law.[31] I have not dealt with crucial components of the present-day conflicts regulations mechanisms in line with the pragmatic argument that the aim of my contribution is only to familiarize my audience with a complex, technical legal issue.

The increased significance of choice-of-law rules derives *i.a.* from the new type of legal pluralism that characterizes migrant family life today - lived at the borderline of Western and non-Western legal and family values - and that challenges the courts of host countries in their aptitude and willingness to find just and fair solutions for cross-cultural family disputes. Comparative research in different host countries suggests that issues of parental authority, the name of the child and its maintenance, the right of inheritance, matrimonial property law, and so on, involving migrant communities of

31. G.-R. de Groot, 'Op weg naar een Europees personen- en familierecht?', *Ars Aequi* (1995), 29-33; J. Erauw, 'De nood aan codificatie van het I.P.R.', J. Erauw *et al* (eds.), *Liber Memorialis François Laurent (1810-1887)*, (Story-Scientia, 1989), 745-761. *Cf. supra* footnote 27.

non-Western origin are perceived in different ways depending on the choice-of-law rule that is employed by the courts. The problem for international law practitioners today in handling family issues among communities of migrant origin in Europe is that there is no single clear-cut and exclusive technique on hand for resolving the type of choice-of-law problems these issues raise, but rather a number of possible approaches.

Since migrant communities have taken up permanent settlement in the host countries, [32] the choice of an appropriate connecting factor should no longer be shaped - as it traditionally has been - first and foremost by geographical conceptions of interstate relations (namely, temporary residence of nationals of one state in the jurisdiction of another state) but rather by a range of qualitative, functional aspects and interests that, for each choice-of-law case individually, must be weighed carefully with a view to harmonious, stable relationships between individuals and culturally dissenting - if not clashing - communities in a pluralistic society.

It is difficult, not to say impossible, to catch a glimpse of the future and evaluate, on the basis of case law at hand, the various factors that will favour, or on the contrary form an obstacle, to the future development of conflict-of-law regulation in relation to cross-boundary family issues. The success of the choice-of-law method greatly depends on the adequacy of the connecting factor. It is therefore not surprising that much contemporary conflicts writing addresses the nature of the choice-of-law problem. The choice-of-law problem touches the very core of cross-cultural conflict management in contemporary multicultural society in Europe.

B. Muslim women's choices. Religious laws and social reality

As I said in my introduction (*cf. supra*), Muslim communities are among the groups who demonstrate the most resistance to voluntary assimilation to the majority society and identification with its values and legal heritage. As a consequence of a stabilized immigration of non-Western origin, Islam has, since the late eighties, become the most important religious group in France and Belgium after Catholicism. [33] The Muslim community is steadily growing, showing a clear will to manifest itself as a religious group and claiming protection of the fundamental rights and liberties to express and freely manifest its convictions in both the private and the public area. [34]

The numeric importance of Islam in continental Europe, combined with the problematic, but until today still valid, principle that courts are to favour preservation of the cultural distinctiveness of foreigners and newcomers, and therefore give preference to the law

32. Some of them, as I mentioned above, have even started claiming protection under a separate legal status; *Cf. supra* note 15.
33. J. Nielsen, *Muslims in Western Europe*.
34. F. Dassetto, *La construction de l'Islam européen. Approche socio-anthropologique* [The construction of a European Islam. A socio-anthropological study], (L'Harmattan, 1996).

of the nationality of origin, ever more often forces upon the courts the obligation to carefully consider the way that they handle religious laws which clash with the basic principles for the protection of fundamental rights and liberties.

The problem is even more intricate (1) since Muslims originating from countries that officially adhere to Islam do not lose their nationality of origin, not even after having acquired the (new) nationality of the country of residence,[35] and (2) since most Muslims who are actually living in Europe demonstrably keep in touch with their countries of origin, investing their savings there, spending long yearly holidays with family that have remained there, choosing fiancés there, and so on.

Multiple citizenship, on the one hand, and on the other the increased risk of 'limping' situations,[36] make all the more urgent the necessity for law practitioners to find appropriate alternative solutions that solidly protect the constitutional (human rights) values prevailing in the host country, but in a way that allow Muslims (and other minorities) to conform to their religion, if that is their wish.

I recently had an occasion to deepen my reflections on this very topic as in 1997 I was offered the opportunity to collect data on the problems actually encountered by Moroccan women in Belgium[37] with regard to their role in managing family life.[38] Together with a team of young researchers,[39] and for a twelve-month period (1 January - 31 December 1997), we collected materials on family disputes involving Moroccan women domiciled in Belgium through three types of sources: inventories of the case law since 1980,[40] interviews (about 100) with law practitioners (magistrates, advocates, public officials, police officers, and so on), and, most importantly, interviews with about 80 Moroccan men and women.

35. A.K. Elgeddawy, *Relations entre systèmes confessionnel et laïque en droit international privé*, (Dalloz (coll.: Bibliothèque de droit international privé, X), 1971), 35 sq.; J. Nielsen, *Religion and Citizenship in Europe and the Arab World*, (Grey Seal Books, 1992).
36. 'Limping situations' present us with cases that are resolved differently in different countries. There appears to be no agreement among states about how to consider one and the same situation. 'Limping situations' include disagreement among states amongst other things about (1) whether to recognize the existence of a marriage, of a divorce, of paternity, and so on; (2) how to decide when a rule is discriminatory; (3) how to promote coexistence among separate normative systems, and so on. As a result, a woman may well be considered divorced (for example, via 'repudiation') in her country of origin, whereas she will be considered still married in the host country. The case is resolved differently depending on the perspective (legal system) from which it is viewed.
37. Moroccan immigrants constitute the largest group of Muslims in Belgium. Moroccan women, therefore, are the best represented group of Muslim women in the country.
38. *Cf. supra* note 4.
39. Nouhza Bensalah (sociologist & Arabist), Jinske Verhellen (lawyer & anthropologist), Annabel Belamri (lawyer), Goedele Franssens (lawyer).
40. We collected over 200 (published) court decisions.

I draw the legitimation to present here a draft outline of our findings from our informants from the women themselves - mainly from what they have made clear to me and the researchers with whom they have had long discussions over several months: the vast majority of these women, if not to say all of them, are univocally claiming protection of their position under Belgian law.

The materials show three sociological generations of Moroccan women, each of them experiencing in its own way the dilemma of religious law versus women's rights:

A first generation of women aged 60 to 70 struggle with the consequences of polygamy: their husbands most often have taken a second wife in the country of origin. These women suffer from the feeling of being solely the property of their husband. They refuse to consent to their 'repudiation' (at the initiative of the husband), as they are afraid that the husband will claim family reunification (in Belgium) for his second wife as soon as the first marriage is dissolved.

The second generation comprises women aged 20 to 40. Most of them have, at a very young age, been given away in marriage ('arranged marriages') by their parents to a relative in the country of origin. The cultural 'clash' between the two spouses is of the kind that opposes a European (Muslim) woman having completed her school education with a husband who has grown up in a Muslim country and expects his wife to submit to his authority. Ninety percent of these marriages collapse.

The third or 'intermediary' generation, finally, is made up of women of all ages who have immigrated on the basis of family reunification: they have been married to a husband who has immigrated to Belgium many years ago and who has selected a fiancé in the country of origin with the sole purpose to keep control over her and the marriage as, at the time of her marriage, the woman neither knows Belgium nor has adopted a Western lifestyle. Most women of this 'intermediary generation' feel extremely lonely in Belgium. They have no family or relatives of their own here. They are treated badly by their husband who dominates them in all aspects of life. This third category of women (nevertheless) tends to maintain high expectations by way of the protection offered under Belgian law. They find it very unfair to be 'repudiated' by their husband, for the dissolution of the marriage endangers their right to permanent residence in Belgium.

All three profiles of women show 'victims' of the anachronism that characterizes a choice-of-law rule that, until today, in principle connects them with the law of the nationality of origin.

C. The solution of the domiciliary principle

The responsibility of a researcher is, among others things, to think of concrete, alternative solutions. What, basically, do we propose?[41] We have been so radical as to propose not maintaining the still valid principle of the law of the nationality and giving reference to the application of the law of the domicile, *in casu* Belgian law: Belgian law, in our opinion, is to be applied in Belgium, except for those couples who, at the time of their marriage, have explicitly expressed the wish to remain submitted to the law of their nationality of origin (Moroccan law) for all aspects of their marital relationship. That means among others that both spouses, man and wife, fully and freely consent to that choice.

Application of the law of the domicile means a radical change in the way we in Europe have historically perceived the principle of respect due to foreigners.

The Belgian Minister of Justice has been extremely satisfied with the results of the study, mainly because it responds to the needs of law practitioners through its emphasis on application of Belgian law in as many cases as possible.[42] Critical comments are to be expected from the Moroccan representatives in Belgium; this is to be explained by the fact that their jurisdiction over Moroccan nationals in Belgium is considerably reduced by the solution(s) we suggest. We must therefore be prepared to reply to these critiques.

D. Party autonomy as a substitute for the application of Belgian law

One way to reply to these critiques is to leave some space for further application of Moroccan family law, namely in case both spouses have explicitly expressed the wish to remain submitted to the law of the country of their common origin.

Two arguments, in our view, may be advanced in support of party autonomy as a valuable substitute for the automatic application of Belgian law. The first argument is premised on the understanding that reliance on the parties' choice yields results that are superior to heteronomous adjudication by a conflicts judge. As such, party autonomy in the choice-of-law process reflects the same values and objectives as those embodied in contracts law: the parties' wills are the core of their legal relationship. Inasmuch as the courts are respectful of the parties' choices, the decision making process will be an autonomous mode of adjudication: the court establishes the facts and subjects them to the rule of law provided by the parties involved.

41. Our proposal was largely inspired by the draft proposal of Codification of Belgian International Law (*cf. supra* footnote 28), issued in early 1998.
42. These results, as I have mentioned in footnote 41, largely overlap with (some of) the solutions worked out in the draft proposal of Codification of Belgian International Private Law.

Party autonomy entails the recognition that decisions as to whether a case should be placed under one or another law cannot only be deduced from the intellectual effort of the judge.[43] Parties know better than anybody else, and *a fortiori* better than the judge, which substantive law is most effectively to govern their relationship. Take the example of a Muslim husband who sends a *talaq* (unilateral dissolution of the marriage via repudiation) by mail to his wife who is still living in Belgium. The repudiation is pronounced in Morocco, the domicile of the husband, where it is valid, but its consequences reach Belgium where the wife is still living. I speak with diffidence but I see two outcomes for this type of situation: either the Belgian judge will consider that the repudiation is in manifest contradiction with accepted Belgian principles of fair treatment and therefore denied validity in Belgium, or the validity of such a repudiation will be accepted by the judge, as it would have been if the wife had accompanied her husband to Morocco. The principle of party autonomy here would at least ensure greater certainty to the parties as to the law to be applied to their mutual rights and duties.

The second argument specifically pertains to the control by the courts over the parties' choice. By no means can the choice of the (applicable) law by the parties result in the recognition of privileges they would not enjoy under the objectively applicable law, neither can it place them - or one of them - in a better position than other citizens in the same situation (prompt divorce, relief of maintenance obligations, polygamy and so on, for example). Think of Moroccan spouses who, after twenty years of continuous residence in Europe, have both lost any true social connection with Moroccan law. The choice for Moroccan law may not prejudice the protection that the wife would enjoy under domestic matrimonial law (i.e. of the host country). Thus the choice to submit the case to Moroccan law will most probably be denied any validity in the country of residence (in Europe), for the mere reason that the discrimination of the wife in the relation to her husband under Moroccan law (*Mudawwana*) negatively affects the wife's position to the sole benefit of the husband. The spouse's choice for Moroccan matrimonial law will therefore, most probably, be considered fraudulent and therefore null and void.[44]

43. The sociological and demographic reality of the host societies today has simply become too heterogeneous. Courts are no longer in the position to determine with accuracy the full 'legal pluralism' that characterizes the many cross-boundary situations that are submitted to them: issues between family members (1) who share the same foreign nationality, (2) who possess different foreign nationalities, (3) who after a few years have acquired the citizenship of the host society but have kept one or more previous nationalities, (4) who have lost the nationality of the country of origin, but kept a true social connection with that society. The possibilities of combination are just too numerous to be listed here.

44. One may think here of slightly different situations, in which the court would determine that the chosen legal system benefits in a fraudulent way, not just the stronger party in the relationship, but even all parties involved (for example, with a view to a speedy divorce that suits the interests of both spouses). The court will then be indifferent as to the choice of law made by the parties and will employ its own choice-of-law rule(s).

E. Conditions to be respected in considering application of party autonomy

In determining the 'most appropriate' law to be applied to the relationship, both the parties' will and the content of the substantive law must be taken into account. There are two guarantees to be considered here. In the first place, the parties' choice may entail for the court an extra weighing of the interests involved. For instance, the court will necessarily exclude choices of law(s) that structurally prejudice the interests of the weaker party (most often the wife) in the relationship (as a result of discriminatory substantive laws). In the search for a 'just solution' to the choice-of-law problem, all the relevant interests - and not just the interests of the parties, but also the interests of the surrounding host society (public order arguments) - must be taken into consideration by the court. Foreign divorces, for example, may, in effect, discriminate against couples who have no power to designate a foreign more permissive divorce law as applicable to their case, for the mere reason that their relationship does not resort to conflicts law (there is no cross-boundary component in the relationship). The examples can be multiplied. Party autonomy is not to be regarded as strictly isolated.

Furthermore - and the second guarantee strengthens the first one - the parties' choice must necessarily implement the legal principles prevailing at the time of the decision and must reflect the legal convictions held by the public opinion in the host society. A choice of law by the parties should be overridden when the consequences of the choice are not justifiable in current convictions. One instance pertains to the maintenance claims between ex-spouses: under no circumstances may party autonomy entail the right for the Moroccan husband to exclude the wife from the legal principle of non-discrimination that protects her under the domestic law of the host country.

In sum, party autonomy does not entail the recognition of an unlimited freedom to choose, without restriction, the applicable law in international cases. Party autonomy in conflicts regulation does no more than reflect a similar evolution in substantive law; ultimately, it is the protective rationale and the social function of the law that keep control over the choice-of-law process. In a way, the development of the concept of party autonomy in private international law is to be viewed in connection with the popularization (as well as the individualization) under domestic law of the freedom of ordering and disposing granted to contracting parties for a growing number of issues. The solution of the *optio iuris* already applies for marital property law. In most European countries today, spouses are allowed to protect themselves with regard to the status of their common property by making an ante-nuptial contract.[45] The *optio iuris* has also been emerging in different European countries over the last few years as a response to problems regarding the choice of surnames: the extra room given to parties under domestic law to decide for themselves whether to use one partner's name, or to choose the surname for their children, offers another example of a more flexible attitude

45. Such agreement may be made either before or during the marriage and may subsequently be amended.

in respect of party autonomy under domestic law.[46] But in each of the given examples, state law ultimately maintains control over the parties' choice.

In response to the question as to how European courts today should practically cope with cross-boundary family disputes involving Muslim women of non-Western origin, party autonomy may contain part of the solution to the dilemma of women's rights versus religious law. The future will tell whether it is a well-founded solution.

F. The limits of party autonomy

Notwithstanding the above-mentioned advantages of flexibility and increased certainty, many practitioners remain extremely critical of recourse to party autonomy. One major reason is that party autonomy undermines decisional harmony, softening the traditional conflict-of-law rules by substituting 'non-rules' for fixed precepts. Party autonomy is blamed for furnishing little if any guidance in solving cross-boundary issues because the parties' will(s) most often, remain(s) undetermined, and this in turn increases the margin of error in adjudication.

It goes without saying that party autonomy, if it is to offer a valid solution to conflict-of-law issues, supposes a careful preparation of the parties agreement as to how they may achieve a harmonious experience, on a daily base, of their cross-cultural family relationships. Such preparation is part of the education needed to become full citizens in a plural surrounding. Muslim women who are offered the possibility to remain submitted to their personal status of origin (Moroccan law) are to be well-informed of the consequences of that decision, for their own benefit and the sake of their family life. Law practitioners therefore have to be trained to provide such information.

Yet another major difficulty remains: if party autonomy is to become a key concept of legal identification in contemporary society, both for men and women in their mutual relationships, it is to be offered not just to Muslims originating from foreign countries but also to converted Europeans. At this point we reach the limits of our proposals. Our suggestion to adopt new choice-of-law rules: domicile and alternatively autonomy of the parties' will is not to be generalized, for we have had no intentions of exceeding the limits of the international private law approach. Nor do we suggest that the principle of *optio iuris* is to be generalized, for that would mean a return to religious pluralism in a way that denies the secular foundation of state law and the mechanisms of protection resulting from the separation of state and religion in our countries since the late eighteenth century. We therefore restrict the solution of the *optio iuris* to categories of people of foreign origin who have kept their nationality of origin.

46. See, *i.a.*: W.E. Elzinga, G.R. de Groot, 'Naar een liberaler naamrecht' [Towards a more liberal law on names], *Hartmans Tijdschrift voor Studenten Openbaar Bestuur* (1984), 108-126.

Clearly, the role of a researcher in this type of study is limited. In my conclusion, I would like to insist on the importance of changing our Western frame of thinking inherited from the past when it comes to settling disputes among family members of foreign origin: Islamic family laws are not to be rejected *per se*, and Moroccan women may feel the need - for themselves - to continue to resort to the *Mudawwana* in managing their family life in Europe. The responsibility of the law practitioner who is to deliberate on such situations is to make sure that the woman's choice for the application of the *Mudawwana* is based upon free consent and that she is sufficiently informed on the consequences of her choice.[47] However, as to the question whether Muslim women who effectively wish to make use of the opportunity to choose the law to be applied to them, will also be able to resist - within their tradition - their husbands' privileges and the weight of 'patriarchy' (assuming they have opted for continuation of their 'submission' to Islamic family law), the answer is still unclear. This is the responsibility of the women themselves.[48]

§ 4. Conclusion

In sum, we suggest a reversed approach to the choice-of-law problem when dealing with Muslim women in particular. This approach offers, under certain conditions, the possibility for migrant women in Europe to opt for continuation of a lifestyle conforming to Islam, at least in the domain pertaining to family law. Whether migrant women will effectively make use of that possibility, once they are allowed to do so, and the way they will do it is very much a matter of their view on Muslim identity in diaspora. It is up to them to decide, for themselves, how simultaneously to advance both religious freedom and women's rights in the context of European secular society. Our hope is that the formula of the *optio,* under conditions that are of course to be clearly defined, may for them be part of the outcome as this option offers a (solid) platform for identity building in a plural context.

For the time being, we have started collecting reactions to our suggestions. Muslim women, by means of the *optio iuris*, may well be in a better position to manage their social relationships within an increasingly pluralistic society context. There is probably no more noble task for a law practitioner in contemporary Europe than to contribute to this effort through the enhancement of choice-of-law techniques. The responsibility of today's international family law practitioners in Europe, who are dealing with immigration, is not whether to refuse or validate an institution or status unknown to domestic law; rather, they must work out rules that may (help) facilitate the interplay

47. We devote a substantial part of the book to the technicalities that allow for control of the validity of the consent, and to ways for obtaining the necessary information on the effects, benefits and disadvantages of a choice.
48. On this responsibility, see also: C. Fawzi El-Sohl, J. Mabro (eds.), *Muslim Women's Choices. Religious Belief and Social Reality*, (Berg, 1994); F. Assouline, *Musulmanes. Une chance pour l'Islam*, (Flammarion, 1992).

of legal cultures in a plural context. Cultures that, through the conduct of migrant men and women, today are seeking, with variable success, to survive in cross-boundary family relationships.

[5]

RATIONALITY AND CULTURAL PLURALISM IN THE NON-RECOGNITION OF FOREIGN MARRIAGES

JOHN MURPHY*

A. *Introduction*

THIS article considers the basis on which the English courts exercise their discretion to refuse to recognise foreign marriages[1] whose *formal validity*[2] is beyond question and whose *essential validity*[3] is probably also satisfied.[4] It has been widely stated that this discretionary veto is to be wielded in accordance with the dictates of "public policy". As far back as 1945, Lord Greene MR said that such matters were to be resolved "with due regard to common sense and *some attention to reasonable policy*".[5] Nearly 40 years later, Lord Simon, similarly minded and speaking in the House of Lords, was a good deal more emphatic. He said: "[t]here is abundant authority that an English court will decline to recognise or apply what would otherwise be the appropriate foreign rule of law when to do so would be against English public policy".[6] Perhaps surprisingly, this policy-based discretionary veto has commanded virtually no academic

* Senior Lecturer in Law, Faculty of Law, University of Manchester, England.

1. I use the term "foreign marriages" to depict marriages that take place outside the United Kingdom and involve at least one foreign domiciliary. I deliberately exclude, for reasons that will become obvious, marriages abroad involving two English domiciliaries even if they are both members of ethnic minority groups.

2. Formal validity is determined unerringly by reference to the *lex loci celebrationis*: see e.g. *Berthiaume* v. *Dastous* [1930] A.C. 79; *Ogden* v. *Ogden* [1908] P 46; *Simonin* v. *Mallac* (1860) 2 Sw. & Tr. 67.

3. The essential validity of marriage concerns the capacity of each of the parties both to marry in general terms, and their capacity to marry one another.

4. Doubts as to essential validity may always be raised because the test for essential validity is uncertain and tends to fluctuate between the (most prominent) "dual domicile test"—which amounts to a presumption against recognition unless both parties had capacity according to the law of their prenuptial domicile—and the rival "intended matrimonial home test" which stipulates that a single law should govern capacity: the law of the country in which the parties intend to establish their matrimonial home. For academic discussion of these (and other less well supported tests) see R. Fentiman, "The Validity of Marriage and the Proper Law" [1985] *Cambridge Law Journal* 256; A. J. E. Jaffey, "The Essential Validity of Marriage in the English Conflict of Laws" (1978) 41 *Modern Law Review* 38. See also Law Commission Working Paper No.89, *Private International Law: Choice of Law Rules in Marriage* (London: HMSO, 1985).

5. [1946] P 122, 129 (emphasis added). Approved and re-stated by Lord Parker CJ in *Alhaji Mohamed* v. *Knott* [1969] 1 Q.B. 1, 13.

6. *Vervaeke* v. *Smith* [1983] 1 A.C. 145, 164. For other instances of judges acknowledging the role of "public policy" in this context see *Russ* v. *Russ* [1964] P 315, 327–328 (*per* Willmer LJ); *Cheni* v. *Cheni* [1965] P 65, 97g (*per* Simon P).

attention.[7] It is my intention to address that anomaly. It is wholly inadequate, as is sometimes done, both by the courts (as we have seen) and academics, simply to refer glibly to "public policy" as though its contents were somehow self-evident and its meaning plain.[8] It is also signally unenlightening merely to state, as Jaffey has done, that "[t]he premise should be that an invalidating rule of a domestic system, whether English or foreign, should only be applied to a given international marriage if there is a *good reason* for its application".[9] So doing merely recasts one nebulous term, "public policy", as another, "a good reason". Judicial synonyms have been scarcely any more illuminating. Take for example Lord Simon's famous enjoinder to have recourse to "common sense, good manners and a reasonable degree of tolerance".[10] A number of familiar criticisms can be made of the opacity of such broad terms as "common sense", "good manners" and "a reasonable degree of tolerance": they deny the common law the clarity, consistency and objectivity that are frequently (and correctly, in my view) thought to be necessary in order to legitimate and constrain the adjudicative function.[11] But beyond these objections, two further, more particular criticisms can be made in respect of the invocation of "public policy" to deny recognition to "offensive" foreign marriages.

The first of these criticisms centres on the capacity for the mask of "public policy" to be seen as judicial cultural imperialism rather than as adherence to some widely accepted social value or norm.[12] The second is that, in any event, the compendious term "public policy" conceals a series of particular concerns, only some of which are relevant to the adjudicative process, depending on context. For example, to present the denial of recognition to a bigamous marriage simply in terms of "public policy" disguises the fact that it is the preservation of the institution of monogamy within the country of recognition that is at stake in such cases.[13] Similarly, in the context of forced and arranged marriages it is the potential for the

7. It seems to have been accepted but not rigorously examined by a number of writers. See e.g. A. J. E. Jaffey, *op. cit.* n.4, at 50, S. Poulter, *English Law and Ethnic Minority Customs* (London: Butterworths, 1986) p.21, P. M. North and J. J. Fawcett, *Cheshire and North's Private International Law* (London: Butterworth's, 1992) p.626 and J. O'Brien, *Smith's Conflict of Laws* (London: Cavendish, 1999) p.462.

8. See e.g. S. Poulter, *loc. cit.* chap.3; A. J. E. Jaffey, *loc. cit.*, at 49–50.

9. A. J. E. Jaffey, *op. cit.* n.4, at 38 (emphasis added).

10. *Cheni* v. *Cheni* [1965] P 65, 99.

11. See e.g. L. Fuller, "The Forms and Limits of Adjudication" (1978) 92 *Harvard Law Review* 353, at 369; N. Duxbury, "Faith in Reason: The Process Tradition in American Jurisprudence" (1993) 15 *Cardozo Law Review* 601, at 610–632 and also the wealth of literature referenced therein.

12. The recognition of foreign marriages is an arena particularly susceptible to accusations of cultural imperialism because of the wide diversity of religious and cultural traditions discernible among Britain's ethnic communities.

13. See further on this S. Poulter, "*Hyde* v. *Hyde*: A Re-appraisal" (1976) 25 I.C.L.Q. 475.

absence of consent to the marriage that vexes the court rather than some vague, ill-defined "policy" consideration. As Cumming-Bruce J cautioned in *Radwan* v. *Radwan (No.2)*:[14]

> [I]t is an over-simplification of the common law to assume that the same test ... applies to every kind of incapacity—non-age, affinity, prohibition of monogamous contract by virtue of an existing spouse, and capacity for polygamy. Different public and social factors are relevant to each of these.[15]

In view of this, in Part D of this article I shall attempt to disinter the kinds of policy concern that arise in connection with only one type of problematic marriage: child marriage. (Similar analysis could, of course, be applied to other controversial marriage types such as non-monogamous marriages,[16] marriages involving a transfer of money or property—such as bridewealth—in consideration of a betrothal and, as we have already seen, non-consensual marriages.[17] But the point of this article is not to provide a blue-print for the resolution of all conceivable hard cases concerning the recognition of foreign marriages. The moderate amount of imagination that I possess coupled with limitations of space both preclude such an endeavour.)

Returning to my paradigm of child marriages, once I have identified the various policy concerns that the litigants may attempt to raise in seeking recognition,[18] I shall explore the weight that ought to be attached to each one. But first I should explain in greater depth the way in which the invocation of "public policy" can be perceived as culturally imperialistic.

14. [1972] 3 All E.R. 1026.

15. *Ibid.*, at 1037.

16. I use this term to avoid distinguishing between bigamous marriages, potentially polygamous marriages and actual polygamous marriages the technical differences between which are unnecessary for present purposes. But for those interested, see S. Poulter, *op. cit.* n.13.

17. In the present context, these chiefly include forced and (to a slightly lesser extent) arranged marriages.

18. Of course, underlying this whole field there are a multiplicity of broader political issues that are unlikely to be raised by the litigants. One such issue, for example, is whether recognition might be refused as part of the general failure to recognise a foreign State and all its domestic laws (see e.g. the British refusal of foreign divorce decrees obtained from Rhodesia following the Universal Declaration of Independence in 1965: *Adams* v. *Adams* [1970] 3 All E.R. 572). Another such essentially political question surrounding this area of law is whether the rules governing the recognition of foreign marriages ought to be left to Parliament rather than the courts on the basis that the political process is more likely to produce a satisfactory solution to the problem of culture clashes. This has been the Australian approach in Part VA of the Marriage Act 1961. For analysis, see M. Neave, "The New Rules on Recognition of Foreign Marriages—Insomnia for Lawyers" (1990) 4 *Australian Journal of Family Law* 190; P. E. Nygh, *Conflict of Laws in Australia* (Sydney: Butterworths, 1995) pp.375–389; E. I. Sykes & M. C. Pryles, *Australian Private International Law* (Sydney: Law Book Co. Ltd, 1991) pp.444–450.

Other examples of broad political issues that surround the recognition of foreign marriages can be found in Law Commission Working Paper No.89, *op. cit.* n.4.

B. Public Policy and Cultural Imperialism

To suggest that "public policy" can adequately resolve questions concerning the validity of foreign marriages is arguably implicitly to suggest that there is some obvious and universal, yet unstated, notion of "public policy", and further that it represents some sort of accepted, dominant ideology. This need not necessarily be the case. As Freeman has pithily pointed out elsewhere "[o]ften an examination will reveal that the so-called dominant understanding is in reality the understanding of the dominant".[19] In a pluralistic society such as Britain's—especially when confronted with a question that tests the very nature and extent of that pluralism—any assumption that there exists any such universal ideology is without foundation. Only to some of Britain's population would, say, proxy marriages[20] be unconscionable.[21] To a significant minority, such marriages would be perfectly acceptable (as would polygamous and arranged marriages). There would certainly be no universal sense of impropriety or repugnance. As Lord Merriman P recognised in *Apt* v. *Apt*,[22] there is no single problem of general unconscionability associated with proxy marriages. At a purely pragmatic level, some may be inflamed because of a suspicion that the marriage was contracted solely as a mechanism to circumvent English immigration laws.[23] Others, less concerned with the immigration implications, may instead recoil at the absence of solemnity and sense of occasion that is often absent in proxy marriages.[24] Accordingly, as Lord Merriman pointedly remarked:

> the problem should be sub-divided into categories and the test of public policy be applied, if at all, to each category separately ... I do not think it is necessary to pursue this topic further than to say that I am not satisfied that a single test of public policy can be applied to all proxy marriages indiscriminately.[25]

19. M. Freeman, "Images of Child Welfare in Abduction Appeals" in J. Murphy (Ed.), *Ethnic Minorities, Their Families and the Law* (Oxford: Hart Publishing, 2000).

20. That is, a marriage at which one or both parties was not present. See e.g. *McCabe* v. *McCabe* [1994] 1 F.L.R. 410 (discussed in J. Murphy, "The Recognition of Overseas Marriages and Divorces in the United Kingdom" (1996) 47 *Northern Ireland Legal Quarterly* 35).

21. At one point in his famous judgment in *Cheni* v. *Cheni*, Simon P recast "public policy" in terms of unconscionability. He said: "[t]he courts of this country will exceptionally refuse to recognise [a marriage] ... on the ground that to give it recognition and effect would be unconscionable in the circumstances": [1965] P 85, 98. See also Lord Parker CJ's equally crepuscular re-formulation in terms of "repugnance" occasioned to "decent-minded men or women": *Alhaji Mohamed* v. *Knott*, *supra* n.5, at 15.

22. [1947] P 127.

23. See further F. O. Shyllon, "Immigration and the Criminal Courts" (1971) 34 *Modern Law Review* 135, esp., at 136–138.

24. See e.g. *McCabe* v. *McCabe* [1994] 1 F.L.R. 410.

25. [1947] P 127, 141.

Of course, one might respond that the judges have recourse to obscurities such as "public policy" *precisely because* there would otherwise be profound disagreement over the appropriate basis for the denial of recognition. For example, Judge X may consider immigration concerns to be the crux of the case. She may also see such concerns to be a matter of public policy and, hence, be happy that "public policy" should be stated as the basis for a refusal of recognition. Judge Y may feel precisely the same way about the preservation of the institution of monogamy. Accordingly, the two judges can agree to refuse recognition on the basis of "public policy" although the particular policy concern that propels each of them towards their decision is different from the other. Sunstein has captured the point thus:

> [L]egal systems tend to adopt a special strategy for producing stability and agreement in the midst of social disagreement and pluralism: arbiters of legal controversies try to produce *incompletely theorized agreements* ... [for] [t]hey are an important source of social stability and an important way for people to demonstrate mutual respect, in law especially but also in liberal democracy as a whole.[26]

In advocating recourse to incomplete theorisation, Sunstein suggests that decision makers (including judges in multimember courts) should produce decisions on the basis of agreement over certain issues upon which consensus can be reached without supplying a grand, fully-articulated account of an over-arching background theory. As he contends, "incompletely theorised agreements are well-suited to a world—and especially a legal world—containing social dissensus on large-scale issues".[27] The decision—or agreement, to use Sunstein's word—"is incompletely theorized in the sense that it is *incompletely specified*".[28] The perceived virtue of such incompletely theorised decision-making, especially, according on Sunstein, in pluralistic societies,[29] is that "judges on multimember bodies ... [can] find commonality and thus a common way of life without producing unnecessary antagonism" because "low-level principles[30] make it unnecessary to reach areas in which disagreement is fundamental".[31] He claims further that this allows mutual respect among differently minded society members to flourish, and that "judges, perhaps even more than ordinary people, should not

26. C. Sunstein, *Legal Reasoning and Political Conflict* (New York: Oxford University Press, 1996) pp.4–5 (emphasis added).

27. *Ibid.*, at p.39.

28. *Ibid.*, at p.35 (emphasis added).

29. *Ibid.*, at p.47.

30. Sunstein states that commonality is reached at low levels of abstraction but it is more plausible that agreement is easier to reach at higher levels of abstraction: See N. Duxbury, "Ambition and Adjudication" (1997) 47 *University of Toronto Law Review* 161, at 166–167.

31. C. Sunstein, *op. cit.* n.26, p.39 (emphasis added).

challenge a litigant's or even another person's, *most defining commitments*".[32]

Yet silence on what for the litigant is a crucial and deeply held conviction can, on reflection, be perceived as insult rather than respect. To ignore the depth of the litigants' conviction on a particular matter in favour of some "low-level principle" about which each of the (English) judges on the multimember tribunal can agree may be seen by the litigants as utter disrespect for a core social or cultural value that they hold. Take as an example one of the many African societies in which polygamous marriages are not only permitted, but in fact highly valued. This high regard for such marriages often stems not only from the socio-economic advantages that they can provide for the husband concerned, but also from the fact that they help to define his community standing and prestige.[33] Now suppose that in the Court of Appeal the three Lords Justice of Appeal called upon to decide the validity of a polygamous marriage each have differing views about the morality of polygamous marriages generally. Suppose also that, on the facts, they can all agree that the marriage was, among other things, an attempt to circumvent restrictive immigration laws. They may then deny recognition to the marriage purely on the ground that it was contrary to public policy (as deduced from the relevant provisions of the immigration legislation). In eschewing any discussion of the defining qualities, or morality, of polygamous marriages, the judges may therefore expose themselves to the criticism that they treated such features of the case as "not even worth talking about". In other words, deliberate silence on the inherent values of polygamy (as they are perceived by the litigants) may appear tantamount to treating those values as "non-issues".[34] And to treat such deeply held convictions as non-issues may be argued to be culturally imperialistic. For the decision is reached only by reference to a value or norm prevalent among those in the cultural majority.

But let us be clear. The problem does *not* lie with the prioritisation of English cultural value X over foreign cultural value Y, since value Y is never even acknowledged to be a value in the first place. It is the failure to take cognisance of value Y and to acknowledge that it is a value at all that is the source of the *putative* offence. The emphasis in the last sentence is

32. *Ibid.*, at p.40 (emphasis added). The importance of highly-valued commitments to rational decision-making are discussed below.

33. See e.g. E. Hillman, *Polygamy Reconsidered* (New York: Orbis Books, 1975). For Muslims, for example, polygamy is only acceptable subject to the proviso that the man is able to provide adequately and equally for all his wives: see S. Poulter, *op. cit.* n.7, at pp.44–45.

34. Sunstein views such silence in "constructive terms". His claim is that it can "help minimize conflict, allow the present to learn from the future, and save a great deal of time and expense": C. Sunstein, *op. cit.* n.26, p.39.

warranted because I am not suggesting that there will necessarily be any such cultural imperialism. Nor am I arguing that, whatever else is at stake, foreign cultural values should always play a part in judicial decisions. I am merely saying that non-explicit references to "public policy", or references to certain (but not all) of the cultural values at stake in hard cases, can be seen as derogatory. Implicit in this is the suggestion that regardless of whether there is consensus over any particular (foreign) cultural value, there is no need to dismiss that value cursorily. Often, as I shall argue below, it may harmlessly be acknowledged without it having to play any part in the formulation of the judge's final decision. A note of caution ought, however, to be entered here: this suggestion must be distinguished from the assertion that, "in all hard cases, the worth of (supposedly) dominant cultural value X should be compared with, and weighed against, minority cultural value Y". Such comparisons may often prove to be impossible. I suggest only—no more and no less—that, as a minimum, explicit acknowledgement of (minority) cultural value Y ought to be provided if the decision is to *appear* both rational and non-ethnocentric.

But the foregoing begs the question: "why is *mere acknowledgement* of a minority cultural value any less derogatory than no acknowledgement at all?". After all, in both instances the minority cultural value plays no part in the formulation of the judge's decision. I address this issue in the next section of this article.

C. *Cultural Values: Reasons and Non-reasons*

Apart from its capacity to engender suspicions of ethnocentrism, the failure to acknowledge certain cultural values may lead to inadequate decision-making in at least three ways. First, where value Y can and ought to be weighed against value X—even if, ultimately, competing value X were to hold sway—any decision based purely on the basis of consideration of value X might legitimately be condemned as irrational. The irrationality of a decision taken without due consideration of a pertinent factor is the very stuff of a significant body of administrative law.[35] Secondly—again where values X and Y ought to be weighed against one another—any decision taken without such a comparison being made will necessarily fail to reveal the extent of the decision maker's commitment to value X (the value that we will assume prevails).[36] Such a failure means, in turn, that future hard cases are rendered unnecessarily difficult to resolve because the reasons for, and the level of commitment to, value X

35. See Taylor, "Judicial Review: Improper Purposes and Irrelevant Considerations" [1976] *Cambridge Law Journal* 272.

36. Deciding on the basis that "X is preferable to Y" compels the decision-maker to question the depth of his or her commitment to X. In cases where only X is acknowledged to be at stake, no such evaluation is necessary.

was never made clear in the initial case.[37] Thirdly, in cases where values X and Y are incommensurable, it may only be by acknowledging that Y *is* a background factor, that a decision maker may become aware of the depth of his or her commitment to value X and, hence, the problem of incommensurability. The value in identifying the level of one's commitment to value X—especially where this commitment is absolute—is again that it helps remove the prospect of unnecessary or difficult future litigation.

What I shall attempt to do in the next section is to supply an example of the way in which I consider that the adjudicative function ought to be exercised in the context of foreign marriages that might not be recognised despite their formal and essential validity. As indicated earlier, this example will involve the hypothetical case of a child marriage. The purpose of this hypothetical is to unearth the several policy considerations that would be likely to be argued by the litigants in the case. I shall also endeavour to ascribe to each the status "commitment", "reason" or "non-reason". But before doing so, I must explain what I mean by these terms.

It is often assumed (or, at least, seldom questioned) that the key to this particular branch of English conflicts law is "a proper balance" of "practicality, commonsense, individual liberty, religious tolerance and the promotion of racial harmony".[38] This list of considerations commands wide appeal, for it appears to be an enumeration of precisely the kinds of "reasons" that most libertarian lawyers would consider relevant to deciding whether to afford or deny recognition to a foreign marriage. In other words, these considerations can be invoked to form all or part of the basis for a legal decision. But what seems to go unquestioned is whether, on occasion, certain of these considerations are legally irrelevant; whether, in other words, they may sometimes be *non-reasons*. The point is this: if a consideration is, in legal terms, irrelevant to a decision, it is a non-reason. It follows that if that consideration ultimately influences the judge in reaching his or her decision, that decision must, of necessity, be an irrational one. Again, this is this stuff of much administrative law.[39]

An example perhaps illustrates the point more clearly. Take the case of arranged marriages. In Western societies the institution of marriage

37. The fact that I consider balancing exercises of this kind to be a vital part of the adjudicative process should not be seen as an attachment to Dworkian principle-based decision-making. I am as happy for the decision-maker to take account of policy considerations as principles, not least because, ultimately, Dworkin's distinction between the two is unsustainable (see e.g. S. Fish, *Doing What Comes Naturally: Change, Rhetoric and the Practice of Theory in Literary and Legal Studies* (Oxford: Clarendon Press, 1989) pp.369–370).

38. See e.g. S. Poulter, *op. cit.* n.7, at p.v.

39. For reported examples see *R.* v. *Birmingham Licensing Planning Committee, ex p. Kennedy* [1972] 2 Q.B. 140 and *Pilling* v. *Abergele UDC* [1950] 1 K.B. 636.

centres on notions of love, compatibility and individual choice. Thus, the multilateral Convention on Consent to Marriage (overwhelmingly ratified by Western States) provides that:

> No marriage shall be legally entered into without the full and free consent of both parties, such consent to be expressed by them in person after due publicity and in the presence of the authority competent to solemnise the marriage and of witnesses.[40]

Underpinning this provision is clearly a deep-seated respect both for human individuality and for the highly cherished value of autonomous choice. By contrast, according to some African and Asian traditions and religions—notably Sikhism and Islam—arranged marriages are regarded as perfectly acceptable. This is largely because they are sanctioned and affirmed by patriarchal religious doctrines. In Sikhism, for example, the subservience of women, and their inequality within a marriage, are justified by reference to the religious rewards they are due to receive for their compliance. As Sharan-Jeet Shan explains in her autobiography:

> A married woman must aspire to be a *pativarta istry* (one who worships her husband as God). In so doing she must observe *laaj* and *sharam* (chastity and honour). She must never raise her voice against her husband. His judgement in all decisions is superior ... such an irreproachable wife secures a place in heaven for herself and her husband.[41]

Even beyond religious affirmation, some South Asian cultures make family honour, *Izzat*, depend in large part on arranged marriages. That is, such marriages can be of instrumental worth in a way that could not be guaranteed by consensual marriages. As Ballard's research reveals: "*Izzat* can be increased by overshadowing other families ... [and by] contracting prestigious marriage alliances".[42] As such, simply to maintain this honour, or *Izzat*, "a family must send its daughters in marriage to families of equal status" and "[t]o enhance its *Izzat*, it must do better".[43]

On the one hand—always assuming the formal and essential validity of any particular arranged marriage—the court may be minded to afford recognition if each party's religious beliefs or cultural values accommodated such unions. On the other hand, the court may equally be "offended" if it found the marriage to be non-consensual in nature. It would be tempting to think that the judge could balance the potential offence to the court against the value of cultural tolerance that would

40. Art.1(1). Recall also that Art.12 of the European Convention on Human Rights and Fundamental Freedoms confers an equal right to "marry and found a family" upon all "men and women of marriageable age".

41. S. Shan, *In My Own Name* (London: The Women's Press Ltd, 1985) p.24.

42. C. Ballard, "Arranged Marriages in the British Context" [1978] *New Community* 181, at 184.

43. *Loc. cit.*

demand recognition of such a marriage. But in truth, it would be attempting the impossible. How, after all, does one compare the religious and cultural values that justify arranged marriages in parts of Africa and Asia with the wholly different cultural values that permeate Western thinking?[44] No judge brought up within one value-system is in a position to evaluate meaningfully the significance or centrality of doctrines and practices of another value system. It would therefore be irrational to suggest that one could reach a decision on the strength of a comparison between the two. What the judge must do in such a case, it is submitted, is identify a *commitment* to the value of personal freedom and, on this basis, exclude any evaluation of the relative merits of the foreign cultural tradition.[45]

In the context of the discretionary non-recognition of foreign marriages, many of the considerations that *might* be taken into account are, in truth, incommensurable with one another. The cultural values—both domestic and foreign—that are in binary opposition have intrinsic rather than instrumental worth and are impossible to compare.[46] As such, any decision reached on the basis of *supposed* comparison must be irrational. It would be premised upon a claim to have achieved the impossible.

What I suggest, then, is that such decisions take cognisance of the following three important things. To begin with, I reject (for the reasons given in Part B) Sunstein's notion of a "constructive use of silence" in this context, and require, as a minimum, that there be explicit *acknowledgement* of the diverse competing cultural values at stake in any particular case. Secondly, I suggest that the judges must also take note of the frequent incommensurability of these values. Finally, I consider it vital where incommensurabilities arise to decide those cases in terms of

44. As Catherine Ballard comments, "[t]here is an obvious contradiction between the South Asia view of marriage as a *contract between two families* which should be arranged by parents on their children's behalf, and the contemporary Western ideal that an intimate personal relationship should exist between a couple before *they* make a decision to marry: *ibid.*, at 181 (emphasis added).

45. I am not suggesting here that all arranged marriages should be denied recognition. They are not all *ipso facto* non-consensual. Often, *both* spouses will accept the practice (albeit with some trepidation) because of their own commitment to the religious or cultural premise for such marriages. Rather, all that I am saying is that, where one spouse contests the validity of the marriage upon entry into this country, the court may legitimately exercise its discretion to deny recognition on the basis of a commitment to consensual marriages, regardless of the protestations of the other spouse.

46. Values of instrumental worth can normally be measured in financial terms; values of intrinsic worth cannot. Neil Duxbury has captured the point well. "Whereas fungible property has a purely economic or instrumental value, personal property is property that the owner is bound up with to such a degree that its loss would cause him or her pain that could not be relieved simply by replacing the object with other goods of equal market value. Thus, a credit card is likely to be fungible, whereas many items of jewellery [such as a wedding ring] will (for their owners) have more personal significance": see N. Duxbury, "Trading in Controversy" (1997) 45 *Buffalo Law Review* 615, at 616.

commitments and non-comparative exclusions of non-reasons. It is only by making such explicit exclusion of (legal) irrelevancies that decision-making remains rational.

To be clear, what I have said so far should not be seen as the "be all and end all" of suitable decision-making in this area. Naturally, in addition to what I have so far suggested, I consider, too, a firm judicial commitment to cultural pluralism—which is necessarily guaranteed by what I have argued for[47]—to be critical. It is simply that I have not been centrally concerned with elucidating the preconditions for, and virtues of, such pluralism.[48] I have attempted *only* to make the case for the explicit acknowledgement of cultural values in all cases, and argued further, that they ought to be thought of in terms of "commitments", "reasons" (where comparison between competing values is possible) and "non-reasons" (where such comparison is impossible).

D. Cultural Values in the Non-Recognition of Child Marriages

Hitherto, I have mounted a case against both the glib use of the term "public policy" and the use of incompletely theorised judgements in order to deny recognition to foreign marriages that satisfy the usual rules concerning formal and essential validity. I have argued that in all instances specific (foreign) cultural values must at least be acknowledged even if, for reasons of pre-commitment to incommensurable (English) cultural values, they form no part of the rationale for any particular final decision. What I now want to do, in the context of child marriages, is examine the kinds of values that are actually at stake and ascertain whether they should be afforded the label "commitment", "reason" or "non-reason".

Foreign marriages involving children (especially young girls) are prevalent in a number of African, Asian and Latin American Societies.[49] English domestic law, however, imposes a minimum age for marriage of 16 years,[50] and it is generally thought (but not settled) that this minimum age applies even to foreign domiciliaries who seek to marry in this country.[51] But if foreign domiciliaries marry abroad and then seek to

47. Borrowing from, and extending the analysis of, Joseph Raz, the fact that the judges are able to acknowledge and choose between different cultural norms "inevitably upholds a pluralistic view" for "[i]t admits the value of a large number of greatly differing pursuits among which ... [the judges] are free to choose": see J. Raz, *The Morality of Freedom* (Oxford: Oxford University Press, 1986) p.399.

48. On the virtues of pluralism (and its distinctiveness from relativism) see M. Freeman, "Cultural Pluralism and the Rights of the Child" in J. Eekelaar and T. Nhalpo (Eds.), *The Changing Family: Family Forms and Family Law* (Oxford: Hart Publishing, 1998).

49. See S. Poulter, *op. cit.* n.7, at pp.16–17 and the sources there cited.

50. The Marriage Act 1949, s.2 provides: "A marriage solemnised between persons either of whom is under the age of sixteen shall be void".

51. As to the existence and extent of any doubt, see S. Poulter, *op. cit.* n.7, at p.18.

migrate to this country, will their marriage be recognised if it involves a pre-adolescent child? The answer is by no means clear. Suppose a man, A, and female, B (aged 12), who are both from country X (which allows child marriages) were to marry in country X and set up home there intending to live in X for good. Suppose further that one year later A was offered a job in the United Kingdom and decided to move there with B in order to accept it. So long as the marriage met the formal requirements for marriage in X, it would be clear that, whether the dual domicile test or the intended matrimonial home test were applied, a strong case could be made for the recognition of A and B's marriage when they subsequently came to the United Kingdom. But reported authority confirms that non-age may sometimes be a suitable basis for the courts to exercise their discretionary veto on an overseas marriage.[52] What, then, are the considerations that might justify such a veto?

Before answering this question it is important to realise that three possible situations arise out of these facts. The first is the unlikely situation in which B alone seeks recognition of the marriage.[53] The second is where A alone seeks to have the validity of the marriage confirmed and the final case is where both A and B seek to have their marriage recognised. For the sake of the present analysis, we shall deal with the second and third situations together for, in addition to the protectionist considerations that arise in connection with B (common to all three instances), the only pertinent additional factor to enter the frame is the potential offence to A in failing to grant recognition to the marriage.[54]

Let us deal with the initial situation where B alone claims recognition of the marriage. Here, four considerations would seem to obtain. First, there is the concern to protect vulnerable minors from the instability of premature marriages. As Ruth Deech, commenting on *Alhaji Mohamed* v. *Knott*,[55] put it:

> If the statistics on teenage brides are anything to go by the marriage seemed destined to break down and one can easily imagine the wife as a future deserted uneducated mother incapable of earning a living or bringing up her children.[56]

52. *Alhaji Mohamed* v. *Knott, supra* n.5. Although the marriage of the 13-year-old in this case was recognised, it is clear from Parker CJ's judgment that the court reserved the right in other cases to refuse recognition.

53. This might occur when A seeks to marry another person in this country and denies the validity of the foreign marriage. It might also occur where A has been permanently incapacitated so as not to be able to voice an opinion.

54. Of course, the broader political considerations to which I adverted earlier (at n.18) would also arise here. But for the purposes of disposing of *this* case, I am concerned only with those arguments that the litigants themselves would raise.

55. *Supra* n.5.

56. R. Deech, "Immigrants and Family Law" [1973] *New Law Journal* 110, at 111. For further recognition of the concerns associated with the instability of child-marriages, see S. Poulter, *op. cit.* n.7, at p.17 and A. J. E. Jaffey, *op. cit.* n.4, at 45.

Secondly, a concern arises as to whether young children are able to give a genuine, free and informed consent to their marriage.[57] Thirdly, in addition to the socio-economic pitfalls that can often be attributed to youths' marriages, there might also be psychological dangers for developmentally young children,[58] stemming from their involvement in sexual relationships at too early an age.[59] Finally, and counter to the first three concerns, B might argue that according to the culture in which she was brought up, there is nothing abhorrent or unnatural in a girl of her age marrying a gentleman who is considerably older and that she should be allowed to do so if she so chooses. The question with which the court would have to grapple is: "how, if at all, may the first three factors—rooted in paternalism—be weighed against the (autonomy) claim to have the culturally validated practice of child marriage recognised?". The answer would depend on whether all of these concerns can be measured along any common metric. If they can, each could then be treated as a relevant (legal) *reason* which the judge must consider in formulating a judgment. I would contend that there is a common thread linking all four of these considerations which enables them meaningfully to be compared with one another. At bottom, they are all concerns that are relevant to the assessment of where a child's best interests lie.

John Eekelaar, writing in the mid 1980s, identified three kinds of children's interests in elaborating his account of children's rights.[60] These were what he termed the basic interest,[61] the development interest[62] and the autonomy interest.[63] The concern to protect the child from an unstable marriage (with all that that may entail for the future) and prohibition against consenting to marriage at a very young age may both be seen in terms of Eekelaar's developmental interests. Equally underpinned by protectionism is the concern to protect the child from sexual exploitation which might be seen in terms of Eekelaar's basic interest. By

57. See S. Poulter, *loc. cit.*

58. There is little point in fixing an *age-based threshold* for child marriages where the avowed reason for so doing is to protect the vulnerabilities of the child that stem from immaturity. The better approach is to set a limit based upon the child's stage of development. It is implicit from his judgment in *Knott* (*supra* n.5, at 15–16) that Parker CJ was sympathetic to this approach. *Cf.* I. G. F. Karsten, "Child Marriages" (1969) 32 *Modern Law Review* 212, esp. at 215–216 (where a minimum age approach is preferred).

59. It is just such dangers that prompted Mrs Victoria Gillick into litigation in the landmark case of *Gillick* v. *West Norfolk and Wisbech AHA* [1986] A.C. 112.

60. J. Eekelaar, "The Emergence of Children's Rights" (1986) 6 *Oxford Journal of Legal Studies* 161.

61. The basic interest was seen in terms of "[g]eneral physical, emotional and intellectual care": *ibid.*, at 170.

62. The developmental interest involves allowing a child's natural capacities to develop to full advantage in such a way "as to minimize the degree to which they enter adult life affected by avoidable prejudices incurred during childhood": *loc. cit.*

63. This is "the freedom to choose his own lifestyle and to enter social relations according to his own inclinations uncontrolled by the authority of the adult world": *ibid.*, at 171.

contrast, the child's claim to have her marriage recognised, because she wishes to be treated as a married person who is capable of making such a choice for herself, can be seen in terms of her autonomy interest. Clearly, in our instance, there is a conflict between the first two kinds of interest, and the autonomy interest. But as Eekelaar and others have convincingly argued, such conflicts *can* be resolved without treating the interests at stake to be incommensurable.[64] They are all simply different aspects of the same thing—the child's interests. Since there is an element of antipathy between the various goods in issue, the optimal outcome will be achieved by some measure of trade-off between each of the competing relevant *reasons*. Furthermore, it might be noted that not only can a meaningful decision be reached according to this analytical approach, it also has the virtue of eschewing recourse to cultural relativism (which would demand that we accept the practice of child marriage simply because it is thought to represent a cultural norm in X derived from a particular custom practised there).[65]

The other problematic cases outlined earlier arise where A (either alone or together with B) claims that the marriage between A and B ought to be afforded recognition. In such instances, the key additional element to the case is the claim that A's cultural values (as evident in the practice of child marriage) ought to play a part in the judge's formulation of his or her decision. Here the judge must decide whether this contention should be rejected on the strength that it was incommensurable with B's interests (which interests, as we have seen, would ultimately underscore any decision made in the first scenario). If we value the protection of children from exploitation so highly that we will never surrender our commitment to that protection, it follows that no countervailing consideration should ever figure in the decision of a judge called upon to decide whether a marriage involving a child (with its concomitant expectation of sexual relations within the marriage) should be afforded recognition. A would-be husband might contend that, on the one hand, the English courts might well value the protection of children, but on the other hand (and in this case), this factor must be weighed against the offence caused to the husband (and others culturally sympathetic) by failing to recognise a marriage celebrated and valid in the country of the spouses' common domicile. Yet if the judge were to consider the offence to the husband (and others), he or she would at once surrender the absolute commitment

64. Though a brief account of how this is achievable is provided in "The Emergence of Children's Rights" (*op. cit.* n.60, at 171) a much fuller account is provided in J. Eekelaar, "The Interests of the Child and the Child's Wishes: The Role of Dynamic Self-Determinism" in P. Alston (Ed.), *The Best Interests of the Child* (Oxford: Clarendon Press, 1994) p.42, esp. pp.53–57. See also M. Freeman, *The Rights and Wrongs of Children* (London: Frances Pinter, 1983) p.57.

65. For an account of the problems associated with relativism, see M. Freeman, *op. cit.* n.48.

to the protection of children from exploitative marriages. The only way in which the judge could maintain that commitment would be by discounting all other cultural considerations. Put bluntly, there would be no scope for comparing the welfare of the child with the (countervailing) good of showing cultural (and perhaps also religious) tolerance towards the husband. The two "goods" not only ought not to be compared, but cannot be compared. They are incommensurable. Comparison between the two is not susceptible to measurement along a single, common metric.[66] A *commitment* to one of these goods, the protection of children, necessarily requires that the other, religious tolerance, be excluded from the decision-making process. Any attempt to evaluate the relative worth of a competing cultural value—even if this were possible—would be to abandon the absolute nature of one's commitment to the first such good. As Warner has put it:

> [t]o ignore the impossibility of comparison is to ignore the value and dignity of individual persons [in our case that of children]. Policy discourse which denies non-comparative exclusion [that is, the exclusion as *reasons* of those considerations which run-counter to an unassailable commitment that we hold] erases the value of individuals out of its policy making equations. What is at stake in the plea to recognize non-comparative exclusion is ourselves.[67]

Reaching a similar conclusion in relation to the question of whether the claims of parents to fair treatment in custody disputes should play a part in judicial decision-making, Scott Altman has voiced the opinion that:

> [C]hild welfare is so important that, even after balancing other concerns, little else matters sufficiently to be worth discussing. The strongest reason for regarding welfare as the primary aim of custody rules is that children are extremely vulnerable. Physical and psychological trauma to young people who cannot protect themselves can result in long-term disability and unhappiness. Adults have less to lose.[68]

66. As Raz explains: "A and B are incommensurate if it is neither true that one is better than the other nor true that they are of equal value": see J. Raz, *op. cit.* n.47, at p.122.

67. R. Warner, "Excluding Reasons: Impossible Comparisons and the Law" (1995) 15 *Oxford Journal of Legal Studies* 431, at 433.

68. S. Altman, "Should Child Custody Rules be Fair?" (1996–97) 35 *Journal of Family Law* 325, at 353. Of course, it might be objected that this is not really an instance of incommensurability because Altman's conclusion appears to be premised upon a comparison between parental claims to fairness and the child's interest in having his or her welfare dealt with as the paramount consideration. But the truth is that he goes no further than acknowledging that the claim to fairness to parents is an incidental issue. So much is clear from the fact that he dismisses this claim as not worth discussing. It *is*, therefore, an example of incommensurability and the parental claims play no part in the formulation of the ultimate decision on the basis of what Warner would call "non-comparative exclusion". It is an instance in which one value at stake (the claim to fair treatment for parents) is *acknowledged* but not included in the rationale for the final decision. And this is *precisely* what I am arguing for.

Importantly, the interests of the parents are *acknowledged* here, but they are ultimately excluded from the decision because of their incommensurability with the child's welfare. This is not to deny that fairness to a parent is a "good", and that it might constitute a *reason* for a decision in another context where the paramountcy of a child's welfare was not in opposition to it. It is simply that, as Raz has explained:

> The existence of more goods than can be chosen by one person [or court], which are of widely different character, speaks of the existence of more virtues than can be perfected by one person [or court]. It tells of the existence of incompatible virtues [necessitating an element of sacrifice].[69]

Certainly, a strong argument can be made that English law is committed (in the sense discussed earlier) to the protection of the children if not the active advancement of their best interests. To begin with, recall that the UK has ratified the United Nations Convention on the Rights of the Child which requires, among other things, that States "take *all* appropriate ... measures to protect the child from *all* forms of physical or mental violence, injury or abuse, neglect or negligent treatment, maltreatment or exploitation, including sexual abuse".[70] And although the provisions of the Convention do not form part of English law *directly*,[71] it nonetheless symbolises the kind of commitment to child protection I am suggesting exists. Echoing the Convention, the public law provisions of Parts III–V of the Children Act 1989 are further evidence of this commitment. And other legislative instruments (such as the Children and Young Persons Act 1933[72]) bear testimony to its existence. Against this backdrop, it would certainly be very difficult for a judge plausibly to deny the existence of a *commitment* to child protection.

E. Conclusion

In this article I have sought to expose what I consider to be two fundamental flaws in the case-law governing the discretionary non-recognition of foreign marriages: the occasional willingness to decide cases in accordance with "public policy" concerns that are left unarticulated, and the (sometimes accompanying) tendency to fail to *acknowledge* certain cultural values that (for the immigrants concerned) are perceived to be at stake. I have argued that, as a minimum, there must be cognisance of any such values. But I have also stressed that this does not mean that those values need necessarily play a part in the formulation of any

69. J. Raz, *op. cit.* n.47, at p.399.
70. Art.19 (emphasis added).
71. See G. Van Bueren, "The United Nations Convention on the Rights of the Child: The Necessity of Incorporation into United Kingdom Law" [1992] *Family Law* 373.
72. See s.1.

particular judgment. I have also suggested that where incommensurable cultural values exist and the courts (rightly or wrongly) are pre-committed to the domestic cultural value, that commitment necessitates the non-comparative exclusion of the foreign value in the ultimate formulation of their judgments.

Finally, I have been at pains to stress the need that I see for the clear articulation of reasons for decisions. Such articulation, long since thought to be central to the common law tradition[73] has, in my view, a particular significance when dealing with competing cultural values. And while silence on such prickly matters, as Sunstein correctly observes,[74] may conduce to functional, *ad hoc* decision-making, this is by no means consistent with either pluralism or rational decision-making. In the context of the recognition of foreign marriages, I would have thought that the case for both pluralistic and rational decision-making was a self-evidently overwhelming one.

73. See the text associated with n.11, *supra*, as well as the literature referenced therein.
74. See n.34, *supra*.

[6]

Citizenship on Trial: Nadia's Case

Unni Wikan

ON OCTOBER 3, 1997, Norwegians awoke to the news that Nadia, a Norwegian citizen, eighteen years old, had been kidnapped by her parents and brought to Morocco, where she was being held captive. The purpose reportedly was to have her married by force. It was Nadia herself who managed to sound an alarm by way of a phone call to a fellow employee at a store where she worked and where she had failed to show up on Monday, September 1, giving no notice. She was in a terrible state, telling how she had been drugged, beaten, and forced into a van that had transported her, in handcuffs, with her family to Morocco. Stripped of her passport, she was now being held in her father's house, and she was desperate to be set free.

Her colleague contacted their boss, who went straight to the police; when the police were slow to take action, he contacted the Ministry of Foreign Affairs.[1] They acted expeditiously. The Norwegian ambassador in Morocco was informed and a rescue plan was conceived. The ambassador would try to negotiate with Moroccan local authorities and with Nadia's father for her release.

There was every reason for Norway to engage itself, for not only was Nadia a Norwegian citizen, but her parents were too. Her father had come to Norway in 1971, at the age of twenty, and had held Norwegian citizenship since 1985—as had her

Unni Wikan is a professor in the department of social anthropology at the University of Oslo.

This essay is part of a forthcoming volume, The Free Exercise of Culture, *edited by R. Shweder, M. Minow, and H. Markus.* *© Russell Sage Foundation. All rights reserved.*

mother, who joined him in 1978. Norway does not recognize dual citizenship. Thus, from the point of view of Norway, the judicial statuses of Nadia and her parents were clear. Also, the crime, if so it was—and at this point there was much to indicate that a crime had been committed—had been perpetrated on Norwegian soil.[2] Hence, there was no question about Norway's right and duty to investigate the case and try to work out a solution.

But there was a hurdle, and it concerned citizenship. That one state does not recognize dual citizenship matters little as long as another state with which a citizen is affiliated does, and Morocco did. This had serious consequences, especially for Nadia. A Norwegian adult, she was transformed into a Moroccan child—for the legal age in Morocco is twenty, not eighteen, as in Norway. Hence, she came under her father's jurisdiction as undisputed legal head of his family. If he found it warranted to keep his daughter locked up, that was his business. All Moroccan authorities could do was to help Norway locate the family, as they did.

A week of tense negotiations, conducted by phone, followed between the ambassador and Nadia's father. Norwegians meanwhile followed the case with utmost suspense, as Nadia's case—*Nadiasaken*—had become a national issue, and the outcome was fraught with uncertainty. Three times her father promised to set her free, only to renege on his word—leading the ambassador, at one point, to call him a liar. A key problem was the father's insistence on a guarantee of "safe passage," meaning he would not be prosecuted on his return to Norway. This the ambassador could not and would not extend; it was up to the police to decide what to do after a thorough investigation. But when all hope was deemed to be lost, Nadia suddenly reappeared in the Oslo airport, her father having paid for her ticket himself. She was met by her brother, a friend of his, and a social worker who was a family friend. According to the media, Nadia was exhausted but happy to be back in Norway. All she wanted was to rest and be left in peace. A week later, she was reunited with her family when they too returned to Norway.

What was the reason for Nadia's father's turn of heart? Probably the interruption of all social welfare benefits to the family. This had been a final and drastic move on Norway's part. Though by no means poor, the family incurred a heavy loss: about 17,500 Norwegian crowns a month (U.S. $2,400 at the time) with the father's disability pension (due to a heart disease) and three child allowances. In addition, the family had a comfortable flat at subsidized rent. Stopping these payments was justified on the grounds that the family had left Norway for more than a month without informing the social welfare agencies. This constituted a breach for which it was possible to effectuate sanctions, and Norway now did—with the desired result. Nadia was set free.

But hardly had Nadia been reunited with her family before her case took a new turn: she recanted on her story. According to the media, it had all been fantasy and fabrication. Actually, she had gone to Morocco on her own accord to visit her sick grandmother. But when the family wanted to remain in Morocco longer than she wanted, she became desperate. So she pulled off the lie to marshal help. She was deeply sorry about the disturbance she had caused and the pain inflicted on her family. Now all she wanted was to be reconciled with them.

It goes without saying that this new development caused quite a stir, and many wondered what was really going on. Some Moroccan and Pakistani youths with whom I talked complained that Nadia had let them down. She had had a golden opportunity to become a rallying point for other youths who were threatened with forced marriage, and now, she had chickened out for fear of reprisals. It was perfectly understandable what she had done, but to stand brave so long and then give in . . .

There were also debates in the media—some of which I participated in myself—regarding the plight of the second generation, especially in regard to forced marriage (a common problem in Western Europe). Not that these issues had not been discussed before, but Nadia's case had been a catalyst giving them added urgency and a human face.

Following Nadia's admission of lying, her parents were reported to be preparing a lawsuit against two national newspapers and against the Ministry of Foreign Affairs for having scandalized their name. A sizable compensation would be claimed.

But it was not to be so. A year later, Nadia's parents were brought to court by the Norwegian state on a charge of "having forcibly held someone against her will" (*frihetsberøvelse*). The minimum sentence is one year in prison; the maximum is fifteen years.

Because I was called as a "cultural expert" for the court, I attended the whole proceedings.[3] I also met with Nadia's parents and her grandfather, outside court, in their home, in the company of a leader from the Moroccan community, who served as mediator. The story that follows draws on this engagement.[4]

The trial lasted for five full days, with an extra day for the verdict. Witnesses for the defense were Nadia's grandfather, her brother, the brother's friend, a social worker,[5] two Moroccan girls, a leader from the Moroccan community, and a few other family friends. Witnesses for the prosecution were Nadia, the ambassador, the police who had investigated the case, a psychologist whom Nadia had seen after her return to Norway, and a few of her Norwegian friends. In addition, the prosecution presented as evidence a tape of two telephone conversations between Nadia and her parents that Nadia had helped the police record without her parents' knowledge. The defense attorneys protested vigorously, but after a thorough consideration, the judge decided to allow the tapes.

Half of the trial (two and a half days) was spent on Nadia's parents' testimony, since proceedings were slowed down by translation. Nadia's mother said in court that she knew no Norwegian, though I know her to speak quite well, and her husband is quite fluent. But with what was at stake, it was only natural that they would seek the added assurance that translators provide.[6]

The parents' story repeated what Nadia had said on her return to Norway: she had gone to Morocco of her own accord to visit her sick grandmother. Supposedly, she had pleaded with them to let her go, against the warnings of Nadia's mother that she might lose her job if she were unable to notify her boss; they had to leave in great haste. But so much does Nadia love her grandmother that she did not care.

The parents conceded that there had been problems between Nadia and them at times. But her parents had never done anything but act in Nadia's best interests. They were trying to save her from herself and her bad Norwegian friends, they said. To that effect, they were willing to go to some lengths, naturally. But never to the point of beating her or kidnapping her or keeping her locked up. Nadia had always been free to do what she wanted. She had been a loved, even a spoiled, child. And what is more, Nadia in Morocco had been free to go where she wanted; there had been no keys, no locked doors—as Nadia admitted in court. But, as she said, where would she go (without her passport, without money, with informers all around)? "The whole country had kidnapped me!"[7]

Faced with the necessity of having to brand their daughter a liar, the parents turned to an age-old recourse: throwing the blame on others.[8] It was not Nadia's fault that she did what she did; she was under the sway of Norwegian bad influence, from both her schoolmates and some journalists who, the parents claimed, wanted to make money on her. They had tricked her into inventing these lies in order to sell her story.[9]

But according to Nadia's subsequent testimony, they also believed her to be under another kind of influence: supernatural *jinns* that had taken control over her. To her horror, she had been subjected to various cleansing rituals in Morocco (a description was given as part of the trial closed to the public). But this was not something the parents talked about in court. At no point did they present themselves as anything but modern and educated people—which indeed they were. Nor did the defense attorneys try to mount any kind of cultural defense based on the parents' supernatural beliefs, which they might not even have heard about before Nadia's testimony—although such beliefs are widespread among Moroccans in Norway. On the contrary; the defense tried to capitalize on the parents' standing as being of a prominent and cosmopolitan Moroccan family. The court was shown photos of Nadia's grandfather's palace in Morocco, and of her parents' stylish house.[10] Bringing *jinns* into the picture could only have complicated this image, though it might in fact have helped explain why Nadia was kept so long in Morocco: for the cleansing rituals to work, one most not cross the sea for a month, I am told by Moroccan-Norwegian friends.

The crown witness for the prosecution was Nadia. She made her entry from a back door, avoiding the onslaught of gazes that were sure to meet her had she come from the front. For she was a celebrity already, through no wish of her own. Indeed, she had been in hiding for over a year, living at a secret address. And when she testified in court, there were two policemen sitting guard behind her, just for security.

To bring one's parents to court—especially a mother—is considered the utmost outrage among Muslims (as among many others). It did not matter that it was not she who had done it; the charge had been brought by the Norwegian police. In the eyes of the community and her family, Nadia was a traitor. She had received threats on her life.

She entered the courtroom with a blanket over her face to avoid the gaze of the public, but also to avoid her parents' eyes. She had asked that they not be present in the courtroom proper, and they were sitting in the translator's cubicle to the very back; but it was only a few steps away and there was just a glass wall separating her and them.

She had not made it a condition of her testifying that they be absent from the courtroom proper. But she had pleaded, and her wish had been granted. No one doubted the agony she must be going through. Nor did anyone doubt the pain of her parents' hard-tested emotions. They had not seen each other for a year, parents and child, not since the day Nadia decided to tell the truth after all, having first done it in Morocco, and then having repented to cover for her parents on her return to Norway, only to be overcome by fear that they might let her down again—and then who would believe her cries for help? She was also concerned about her little sister, whom she adored and who might one day come to share her fate, as well as others, unknown, who were in the same shoes. (All this I know from her testimony in court.) So she had gone back on her cover-up story, contacted the police (whom she knew to be conducting an investigation of her parents) to tell the truth, and cooperated with them to gather evidence against her parents.

She was a fragile-looking young girl as she entered with the black blanket covering her head. But as soon as she stood up in the witness stand, the blanket removed, she appeared steadfast and strong in her demeanor. She spoke with a clear voice, and answered lucidly every question. At times she broke down. The memory was too much for her. Some time into her testimony, her attorney suggested that she be allowed to sit in front of the witness stand, the box at her back.

That must have been a relief. Standing, she had felt the full force of her parents' gaze, hitting her from the back. She had made no concession to them in the way she appeared. She was dressed in black pants and a black sweater, both tight-fitting, but not immodestly so—from a Norwegian perspective. Her parents would have felt differently. Knowing that how she dressed had been a point of contention between Nadia and her parents, I cannot help wondering if she did it on purpose. But why should she not appear her own self in court when that was what the whole battle had been about, her right to be her own person?

I never turned to look at her parents throughout Nadia's testimony. But I know others who did; one journalist reported her father shaking his head in exasperation at times as she told the court her story. Her mother reportedly cried a lot. The next day Nadia's father asked to be allowed to speak in court, out of turn. He accused his daughter of being a liar. All she had said, he said, was a lie. How could any parents do to their daughter what she accused them of? Could anyone be so callous? But Nadia had brought shame on the whole family and herself, he claimed; that was why she was desperate. She was not a virgin anymore, and in Morocco, a girl who is not a virgin before marriage has no future.

In revealing that Nadia was not a virgin, Nadia's father went public with a secret that there was no reason for him to reveal had he not wanted to. And thus he may be seen to have triggered the shame that otherwise could have remained undisclosed. Nadia had been more discreet. She had revealed to the court, as part of a closed hearing, that she had told her mother, on the way to Morocco, that she had slept with a boy.[11]

Now her father had exposed the disgrace, bringing it on himself, as it might seem, by making the matter public. But perhaps the father felt that he had already been so disgraced by his daughter's misdemeanors that there were no holds barred and nothing to lose: better to reveal the depth of her fall and be done with it.

"Here in court," he said, shaking his head, "you think it is we who have committed a wrong. But Nadia cries because her honor is destroyed. Everything she tells you is just lies and falsehood. But I know that she does not mean any of this. It is her accomplices who are making her do it. Nadia has forgotten the nine months in her mother's womb, the care and affection she received, her childhood, her upbringing until she came of age. Now we are repaid for the kindness we as parents have shown," said Nadia's father while her mother cried openly.

According to Nadia, her parents had planned to marry her to a twenty-one-year-old Moroccan (whose picture her mother had showed her) so that he could get a visa to Norway and so that she would "become Moroccan." Indeed, this was what the whole battle had been about: her wish to be Norwegian versus their insistence that she "become Moroccan" and "become Muslim."

The retraction she had produced on her return to Norway was at her parents' instruction. It was their deal for setting her free: she would ensure that they would not be prosecuted by taking the whole blame herself. Her concern for her younger siblings also contributed to her trying to pull off the lie.

That Nadia and her parents had long been at loggerheads is clear: six months before her abduction, Nadia had contacted the child welfare agency regarding her father's ostensible abuse. Her father, she said, beat her and was furious because she was "too Norwegian": she was not allowed to wear makeup, wear pants, go out to dance, have a (Pakistani) boyfriend. Her father had even gone to a café where she had worked and threatened some of the staff that he would kill them if they did not make Nadia quit. He did not want her to work in such a place. (This was confirmed by the people in question.)

As a result, Nadia was placed under child welfare custody for three months, living in a youth institution. She moved home only after her eighteenth birthday (when she became legally an adult) and with her father's assurances that he would not beat her. Apparently the move was voluntary. But as Nadia said in court, the project (her word) of the child welfare agencies was not her own. They were set on reuniting her with her family against her will.

The problems did not go away; they resumed. Her brother said in court that he did not love her anymore, not after she had said that she did not want to be a Muslim. Her parents said in court that they had nothing against Nadia being "Norwegian." She could do as she liked, even marry a Norwegian. But they did not like her drinking and smoking and staying out late at night. Would any parent, even a Norwegian parent? Two girls who served as witnesses for the defense confirmed this—that Nadia's parents had given her full freedom, even to marry the Pakistani if she wanted—but her parents were naturally upset by Nadia's disgraceful behavior. Had she not been seen drunk in the street on occasion?

But Nadia herself told a different story, about being beaten and oppressed to "become" a Muslim and Moroccan: "Did you not tell me I would have to stay in Morocco till I was married and had a baby and only then could I return to Norway?" Nadia asked her mother in a telephone conversation that was taped and presented as evidence in court. "And did you not threaten me that I would have to remain in Morocco till I rotted?"

"You have misunderstood me, my daughter, I was only joking," said the mother.

"It is not the kind of thing one jokes about," said Nadia.

A key witness for the defense was Nadia's maternal grandfather, a prominent and wealthy patriarch who wielded considerable influence in his home district in Morocco. A cordial man, he left in disgust: "I thought Norway was a democracy where there was justice before the law. But this is not democracy! The judge chose to believe a young girl over her family; they sided with her. That is injustice." He would go back to Morocco to tell the people so and to launch a court case against the ambassador who had vastly overstepped his powers. "He even offered to send a car to pick up Nadia—from her own family!"

But the worst was all the things the ambassador had said to the media, and now in court. The grandfather wanted his family's honor restored, and he was going to do it by suing the ambassador.

Had not Nadia gone to Morocco of her own free will to visit her sick grandmother? Had she not begged her parents to let her go, even though they had been concerned that she would let her employer down by not showing up for work? The grandfather's testimony on these points was in line with that of the parents. They had told the court how the decision to go to Morocco had been made impromptu on a Saturday night. The telegram (from Nadia's mother's brother) telling the family of the grandmother's serious sickness and urging them to come had arrived the day before, but there were no tickets for a flight to Morocco until two weeks later. So Nadia's father was thrilled when by sheer good luck on Saturday, he met a man who was going to drive to Morocco the next day; by chance the man had five seats free in his delivery van—just enough to accommodate Nadia's family.[12] But all this meant that the decision to go was not made until Saturday night. Nadia came home late that night and went to work early the next morning, so it was mid-Sunday before she was informed of the family's decision to travel that night. To her mother's delight she insisted on coming along. "I could not believe my ears when Nadia said she wanted to come," said her mother in court. But so much does Nadia love her grandmother that she was even willing to let her employer down and risk losing her job ("I'll get it back," her mother reported her as saying). And yet the Norwegian state prosecutes the family for having forced Nadia to go, even kidnapping her! The grandfather was outraged.

But when he was questioned about his wife's illness, he was at a loss: well, she is sick all the time. . . . How is she sick? Well, she has diabetes and she faints and such things. . . . Does she faint often? How could he know, he doesn't sit at home . . . and so on.[13] It was a sad spectacle. Watching Nadia's mother watch her father was heart-rending. Whether his exalted status had forbidden them, out of respect, to instruct him in their story, or whether he had forgotten his lines, or was just out of place in court, I cannot tell.[14] Anyway, his testimony undermined the parents' story.

Someone who might have corroborated the parents' story, the driver with whom they went to Morocco, could not be brought as a witness because he could not be identified. The parents claimed not to know anything about him save for his first name—which did not sound plausible, given that they had spent five days together. According to Nadia, they had also spent a night in his house in Morocco.

But other witnesses came out for the parents, among them the social worker. She said she could not imagine that the family would do anything bad to Nadia; she knew them to be kind and caring people. She also painted a rather dreary picture of Nadia, as did two Moroccan girls—Nadia's friends, as they said—along with her brother and a friend of his. They all declared or implied that Nadia was a rather "loose" girl, fond of drinking, smoking, and staying out late at night.

But this was not Nadia's own fault, they said. It was because of her schoolmates in high school who were such a bad influence on her. Time and again this point was stressed by witnesses of the defense. It was not Nadia herself but her schoolmates who caused her to fall.

A crown witness for the prosecution was the ambassador. Space prohibits a lengthy discussion of his testimony, but I think it safe to say that it made a strong impression on the court. He painted a most unflattering picture of Nadia's parents. Her father, he said, had even threatened to beat Nadia if Norway did not grant him "free passage." Her mother had called all Norwegian women whores.[15] Nadia had been close to a breakdown and had been cajoled and threatened by her parents in the worst possible ways—as all the staff at the Norwegian embassy in Morocco could confirm, for they had listened in on the telephone negotiations. The ambassador's testimony was entirely in line with Nadia's.

Another strong witness for the prosecution was the psychologist whom Nadia had been seeing for a year since she came back from Morocco, and who gave vivid testimonies of the traumas she had suffered.

In the end the Norwegian state chose not to include a charge of forced marriage against Nadia's parents. For though Nadia was under the clear impression that they had a marriage in mind for her, there was no firm evidence of this. The charge was simply that of forcibly holding someone against her will, with a stipulation that the offense had exceeded one month, as it had in Nadia's case.

The jury took only three days to reach a verdict. Both parents were found guilty. Nadia's father was sentenced to one year and three months on suspension, her mother to one year. Her father was also sentenced to pay a fine of 15,000 crowns (then about $2,000) and "court proceedings costs" (*saksomkostninger*) of 60,000 crowns (about $8,000) connected with bringing witnesses from abroad, the defense lawyer's journey to Morocco, and the like.

Nadia's parents thus received a sentence lighter than the legal minimum for the crime of which they were convicted. My own role may have had some significance here; the published verdict indicates as much. As a witness I was asked to answer truthfully every question but also to bring up any matter that I judged to be of significance to the case. And I did, speaking at some length on what I judged would be the cost to Nadia and her family should her parents, and especially her mother, be thrown in jail.

I was alarmed, I said, to find that whereas Nadia had had a lot of support among youths in the Moroccan community before the trial, she had lost it now. Instead, she was harshly criticized by nearly everyone; the reason I heard was that she was "throwing her parents in jail." People do not care that it is the Norwegian state that charged the parents. To them she is guilty, and of the most horrible deed: of throwing her mother in jail. Elaborating on the mother's position in Islam, I tried to make it comprehensible that the reactions would be as they were. I also gave some objective reasons why the mother should be treated more leniently. As a wife in Islam she is subject to the "law of obedience," being duty-bound to obey her husband. Hence, the benefit of the doubt should be the mother's in particular. In its published verdict, the court also noted that as there was no evidence that the mother had beaten Nadia, she should receive a milder sentence than the father.

The court granted that for the sake of the whole family, the parents must not be jailed. But it was also necessary to establish a firm precedent and underscore the seriousness of the crime. The final sentence was in accordance with the prosecutor's procedure. He had pleaded forcefully for Nadia's case, asking the court to sentence her parents while keeping the options for family reconciliation open.

In its verdict the jury noted that there had been attempts by several witnesses to present Nadia in a disreputable light (*fremstille henne i et mindre heldig lys*). However, the court had a positive impression of Nadia as a clear-headed *(ryddig)* and bright girl. In the view of the court, Nadia deserved respect for the way she managed to carry through with her testimony. The court could not see that evidence had been presented to indicate that her demeanor was any different from that of other Norwegian girls her age.

In this, the court followed the recommendation of the prosecutor, who had advocated that Nadia receive some form of redress (*oppreisning*) for the injustice she had suffered from the massive attempts by some witnesses to blacken her reputation and portray her as a liar.

In the end, Nadia stood in willful independence, a solitary figure, bereft of expressed support within the Muslim community, where she was perceived by many as a traitor. She even received threats on her life. Her parents' attempts, corroborated by others, to make her appear the dupe of bad Norwegian friends were totally against her own wish: to be perceived as a person in her own right. In time she has become a role model for others, both female and male, who gained strength and felt support from the Nadia case—without her ever trying to capitalize on her name. The only pictures that have appeared of her in the media were a snapshot published while she was in Morocco, and one of her under the black blanket on her way to court. Nor has she ever agreed to be interviewed. She lives quietly at a secret address. But I know that she has helped others who have sought her out. And by her example she has come to lend courage to others, none of whom lent her support during the trial, but who in the aftermath stand on her shoulders. To understand how that came to be, let us look at the premises and implications of the verdict.

* * *

It was the matter of citizenship that decided Nadia's fate, in more than one way. Obviously, had she not been a Norwegian citizen, the Norwegian government could not have interceded on her behalf. But it was important that her parents were also Norwegian citizens. This is clear from the writ of the verdict. It states:

> The defense attorneys have argued for acquittal on the grounds that Nadia, according to Moroccan law, becomes legally an adult (*myndig*) only at twenty years of age. Moroccan citizens are not freed from their citizenship if they acquire another. Nadia had, therefore, dual citizenship. Her parents must therefore have assumed that she was a child/minor in Morocco, and that they were in their full right to keep her there against her will.
>
> The court does not agree. When the parents have taken the step of applying for Norwegian citizenship for themselves and their children, this implies both rights and duties. An application for citizenship means that one has decided for oneself which state one wants to be most closely connected with, if not emotionally, at least judicially. That also means that one has to submit to (*innordne seg*) the rules applying in this state. The parents were well aware of what the legal age in Norway is. For a Norwegian citizen resident in Norway one cannot assume that Moroccan law should apply during short-term visits in that country, and especially not when [Nadia] has been brought there against her will. The criminal offense (*det straffbare forholdet*) was initiated in Norway. . . . Forcibly holding Nadia against her will was therefore in violation of the law.
>
> Ignorance of the law (*rettsvillfaring*), which also has been claimed as grounds for acquittal, is likewise not applicable, according to the court. Forcibly holding a person against her will is illegal in most states, if not in all. As residents of Norway, and as Norwegian citizens, [Nadia's parents] must know the rules at least in this country.

Both the subjective and objective conditions for sentencing (*domfelling*) are present, and the accused are sentenced according to the charge.

The verdict further states:

The case arises from culture conflicts. But it is the parents who have chosen to live in Norway. After many years of residence here, they are fully aware of how Norwegian society functions, for good and bad. That they wish to maintain the customs of their country of birth is unobjectionable, so long as these customs do not come into conflict with Norwegian law. Children can develop in ways that are different from what the parents hope for. But that is the risk in having children, and—not least—in letting them grow up in a different culture. The parents have made a choice as to which country their children will be molded by. That circumstance may have such consequences as resulting in the case currently before the court. Using violence and forceful deprivation of the freedom of movement as an answer is unacceptable.

The court also notes that the family continues to live in Norway and that they have two children below school age who will grow up here. Therefore, there must be aspects of Norwegian society that they, in sum, perceive as more positive than the negative ones.

The verdict was a clear statement of what the Norwegian state demands of its citizens, according to the law. And it was historic. It was the first time a Norwegian court declared—and in blunt language—what citizenship entails. Reactions varied accordingly: outrage from many members of the Muslim community; satisfaction from many others.

Mohammed Bouras, chairman of the Islamic Council, declared: "This is an insult to all Muslims. It implies that we are bushmen who do not follow Norwegian laws and rules!" It was the issue of citizenship and the judge's emphasis on the duties entailed in taking Norwegian citizenship that so caused his wrath. He was also quoted as saying, "The charges and the verdict are an offense against the family and us Muslims. The judge is requiring us to respect Norwegian laws, but does not show us any respect."[16] Mr. Bouras had been a witness for the defense.

Others were quoted as saying, "This is directed against us Muslims! The Norwegian state does not care about Nadia. They are just using her against us."[17]

It was clear that the verdict had added insult to injury. "*Justismord!*—Miscarriage of justice!" cried an editor and friend of Nadia's family.[18] "A declaration of war!" announced a prominent journalist.[19] His concern was that by not making any concession to Nadia's parents, the judge and jury had not just done injustice to them, but antagonized the Muslim community—and reactions were bound to come. There was nothing wrong with the sentence, as he saw it; it was the premises of the verdict that were unacceptable: "[Saying that] the parents ought to know how Norwegian society functions and that it is they themselves who have chosen to live here—[is] a form of paternalism (*besserwissen*) that can only be like salt in open wounds," he wrote.[20]

Nadia's parents appealed the verdict on the spot: the defense attorneys recommended it; their honor demanded it; and the monetary fine seemed an insult. I believe they would have been happy not to have to go through the whole ordeal again.[21] But such a recourse seemed precluded in the setting. I also know there were members of the Moroccan community who wished they would accept defeat on the grounds that their case seemed too weak, and the evidence against them too strong. But in the end, their efforts to appeal came to no effect.

Nadia's father died of his heart disease six months after the trial. The Norwegian state subsequently withdrew its charge against the mother. Her brother, who wanted to proceed with the case, tried to appeal to a rarely applied section of the law so as to appear in his father's stead. But he was refused, to the mother's relief. So far, an open reconciliation between Nadia and her mother and younger siblings has not been possible, due to her brother's rage. At eighteen years of age, he is holding the family in thrall, set on defending his honor. Nadia is living by herself and managing relatively well—though suffering greatly from her father's death. There are those who say that Nadia caused his death. But it may be well to remember that according to Islam, the time of one's death is written at birth. It is foreordained and cannot be changed.

Nadia's case poses a number of basic questions: what are the limits of cultural tolerance? How do we balance respect for human rights with respect for cultural difference? What of the rights of the child versus the rights of parents? And how do we enforce the law in the case of violations that were committed with the best of intentions, such as to protect one's child from harm? Religion is also an issue: should not Muslims, for example, be granted respect and the right to bring up their daughters in accordance with their religion?

These and other issues came to the fore in Nadia's case, and though the court attempted to reach a solution, as perforce it had to, I think no one who witnessed the trial felt that there were any winners. Nadia was reported by her attorney to have said that she was glad the court believed her. Beyond that, she has made no statement. Her case split a family and caused irreparable suffering. I, for one, said in court that it might have been better if it had not been tried. Mediation might have been better. But in retrospect I have my doubts, having come to realize how hard the issues were. And as the jury said in its verdict, the graveness of the crime demanded that it be tried.

The power of Nadia's case lies in the resonance of its story through time and place. One need not be Norwegian, or Muslim, or Moroccan, to be drawn in. The issues are universal, the (re)solution was particular, but anyone can take the various elements and move them around—"play" with them, if you wish. It is just that in real life, something must be done. If not, that too has consequences. Real consequences.

* * *

"Citizenship in Western liberal democracies is the modern equivalent of feudal privilege—an inherited status that greatly enhances one's life chances," wrote Joseph Carens.[22] Let me end with a story that complements Nadia's case and throws it into relief. It highlights some of what remains to be done if the thrust of Carens's dictum is to be borne out, and pertains to the plight of the child.

In 1994, three-plus years before "Nadia," another Norwegian girl, fourteen years old, was brought out of the country to

Morocco, her parents' original homeland. They too were long-time Norwegian citizens. I shall call the girl Aisha.

Like Nadia, Aisha had appealed to the child welfare agencies for help due to her father's violence. Unlike Nadia, she came from a family well known for its malfunctioning. To be brief, both Aisha's urgent appeals and those of her teachers on her behalf failed to impress the child authorities. After a brief respite with a foster family, Aisha was reunited with her family by force. Two weeks later she was taken out of the country, and not heard from again until four years later, when she reappeared in Oslo. Meanwhile, she had been married by force and had her schooling interrupted, so she is left without even an elementary-school certificate. She also is a Norwegian citizen, but all attempts on her school's and my part to make Norwegian authorities intervene for her failed.[23] As one significant document states: "Because she has gone with her family to her homeland [*sic!*], Norwegian jurisdiction does not for the time apply to the family."[24]

With the hindsight of Nadia's case, we can see why that would be. Aisha was only a child. Nadia was, after all, an adult—according to Norwegian law. Hence, it would be much more difficult for Norway to intervene on Aisha's behalf between Aisha and her parents. Also, Nadia struck an alarm: she managed to get to a telephone. Aisha never got to that point. There are other relevant contrasts, too. But the main point has been made: it takes more for a child to be heard and have her or his rights as a Norwegian citizen protected than for an adult. Therefore, the rights of the child must be strengthened, especially when dual citizenship is involved, and particularly for females.

Because of Norway's failed effort to stand by this citizen, she has been subjected to forced marriage—something Nadia was spared. When she now is back in Norway at all, it is only because she is being used as merchandise (*vare*), as she says: to bring in a husband who would not get a visa but for her. This is called "family reunification."

But Aisha defeated her family: she ran away. To her surprise, her father, who had threatened to kill her, gave up her passport and marriage certificate to the police when they came to his door requesting them. She now wonders if he has taken a lesson from the Nadia case. Is he afraid they will cancel his social welfare benefits too?

Family reunification is a double-edged sword. On the one hand, it exposes the children of immigrants in Europe, not just Norway, to immense pressure to comply with arranged marriages, and in many cases to real force. In Pakistan, for instance, marriageable girls in Norway are called *visuni*—visas. And Norwegian-Moroccan girls are spoken of as gold-edged papers. But on the other hand, family reunification is a salvation for girls like Aisha and many others who return to Norway thanks only to their quality as "visas." If not for that, many more girls might have become missing persons.

Nadia's case has a moral lesson, as I see it: human rights must take precedence over what may be termed, for lack of a better expression, cultural rights. Human rights are based in moral individualism: they are entitlements of the individual as against the state, the family, the church, or other controlling powers. And they apply across the board in liberal democracies. There can be no distinction made on the basis of ethnicity, religion, or other factors. Equality applies, as does the right of exit from the group, as Nadia and Aisha have chosen. The policy implications are these: a plural society requires a social contract to protect the rights of all members. A strong state, not a weak state, is the best guarantee of human rights, as Michael Ignatieff, among others, has argued.[25] I see the verdict in the Nadia case as an attempt by the Norwegian state to make a case for citizenship—a dissipated notion that needs to be reinvented in our times. Both Nadia's and Aisha's cases show clearly what is at stake.

Dual citizenship is often presented by academics as an asset, a resource. And so it is, for the likes of them. I hope to have made a case for the perils of dual citizenship. In this, as in many matters, the crucial question is: for whom is it an advantage? Who stands to lose and who to gain? Children, I have argued, may be the main losers, and girls most of all. Would that policymakers and other interested parties will heed the implications of Nadia's and Aisha's stories and thus reconceptualize citizenship and realize what is in jeopardy.

Telling Aisha's story to a friend in Oman recently, and dwelling on the injustices of the Norwegian state, I was struck by her comment: "She was lucky. She at least had a place to go!" My friend was right. A citizen of a European welfare state, Aisha can now call on help—now that she has lost four years of her life. Sacrificed on the altar of culture at fourteen, she is now ready, and will be helped, to get her life in order and have her human rights protected. She cannot fully appreciate how, but a girl named Nadia helped lay the foundation by changing Norwegian history.

ENDNOTES

[1]This contact was made on September 10, two days after Nadia's call. This means that the efforts by the authorities to keep the matter secret from media exposure were successful for about twenty days; the news did not break until October 3.

[2]In fact, an international arrest order had been issued against Nadia's father in case he should leave Morocco.

[3]I had been called as a witness for the defense, but when I realized that this meant that I could only be present during my own testimony (as applies to all witnesses), I asked for a redefinition of my status, and it was granted.

[4]I know more than I am able to tell, since I was also present during a part of the proceedings that was closed to the public during Nadia's testimony. In addition, I withhold information that had been given me in trust by Nadia's mother. I also do not include what I know from telephone conversations with the father's defense attorney, or from private conversation with the Moroccan leader and others. My account is a public account, based on what was revealed in the court and in the media. All translations into English of the testimony given in court, as well as any translations of quotes from other sources, are my own.

[5]This woman was a friend of Nadia's brother, having been assigned by the child welfare agencies to help him get his life in order.

[6]There were two interpreters, one in Berber for Nadia's mother, one in Arabic for her father. Since I am a fluent Arabic speaker, I could follow much of what was said by the father (not all, for there are dialect differences between his Moroccan and my Egyptian), and even a part of the mother's speech, for Berber contains a host of Arabic words and expressions. It was quite clear to me that having translators provided the defendants with a degree of flexibility, as misunderstandings and inconsistencies could be attributed to the translators, who also, in some cases, helped the defendants in their answers.

[7]The point here is one that surfaces time and again in stories of girls kidnapped to the Middle East or South Asia by their parents: they have nowhere to go, they

cannot possibly escape, even though their feet are not tied and the doors are not locked. The dangers of even attempting an escape are so dreadful that the risk cannot be run, and the dangers of succeeding are minuscule. These girls live under the threat of death, and they are observed in all and everything they do. In only two cases that I know of, among forty-odd Norwegian second-generation immigrant girls being abducted and married by force by their parents (or threatened to be married), has the girl managed to escape. See Nasim Karim, *Izzat—For ærens skyld* (Oslo: Cappelen, 1996), and Hege Storhaug, *Mashallah* (Oslo: Aschehoug, 1996) and *Hellig tvang* (Oslo: Aschehoug, 1999). For an especially harrowing case of a girl subjected to forced marriage though she was "free" to go anywhere, see Unni Wikan, *Generous Betrayal: Pluralism and Culture Politics in the New Europe* (forthcoming).

[8]For an extensive discussion of such practices in the case of Egypt, see Unni Wikan, *Life Among the Poor in Cairo* (London: Tavistock, 1980), and *Tomorrow, God Willing: Self-Made Destinies in Cairo* (Chicago: University of Chicago Press, 1996).

[9]Her father also argued in court that the Norwegian authorities and the police had pressured Nadia into keeping to her original story of falsehoods.

[10]Nadia's parents owned a house valued at about U.S. $120,000 in Morocco that they used as a holiday residence.

[11]I cannot help but wonder why she did it, and guess it might be so as to dissuade her parents from trying to marry her by force. Now the mother would know that the virginity test on the wedding night would have the whole family scandalized.

[12]This part of the parents' story rings less than true to me. From what I know (and I have many friends within the Moroccan-Norwegian community), people travelling to Morocco overland usually have their cars loaded, for there is a constant stream of people who want to go, and recruiting passengers is a way of sharing costs and company. Thus, finding a driver who is about to go with a near-empty van would take more than sheer good luck.

[13]Nadia's grandmother's illness was, of course, a key issue during the trial. As proof of their case, the parents presented a telegram they had received from Nadia's mother's brother, saying: "Your mother is ill. Come urgently." And yet Nadia's mother said she did not phone her family in Morocco during the seven days it took for them to reach home; Nadia's father said he phoned the day the telegram arrived but not after. By the time they arrived, the grandmother was quite well.

The jury found the story less than plausible. As stated in the premises of the verdict: when a close family member is gravely ill, one usually uses a phone to convey the message. The telegram appeared to be part of a cover-up operation. Moreover, if the grandmother had been so ill, one would have expected the parents to make contact during the seven days.

[14]As Nadia told the story in court, she had been forbidden to tell the family in Morocco that she had been forced to come. The appearance was to be given that she did it voluntarily.

[15]This caused quite a stir when it became known through the media. Several prominent Norwegian women, among others, were appalled to be so desig-

nated and voiced their complaints in no uncertain language. Their critique was directed not just at Nadia's mother but at other immigrants who enjoy the fruits of the Norwegian welfare society while deprecating its basic values of equality and freedom. Nadia's mother was devastated by the reaction she had triggered, and I tried to cushion the blow by telling the court and the media that to call someone "whore" in the Middle East is no big deal: it is a common swearword devoid of the literal connotations it carries in the West. This does not deny the fact (as I did not say) that Nadia's mother may well have meant that Norwegian women are whores.

[16]Cited in *Dagbladet*, 11 November 1998.

[17]Cited in *Aftenposten*, 11 November 1998.

[18]Comment made outside the court immediately after the verdict (cited in *Dagbladet*, 11 November 1998).

[19]"Declaration of War" was the headline of a commentary on the court case by Peter Normann Waage, a prominent Norwegian journalist, who covered the case for the newspaper *Dagbladet*.

[20]Ibid.

[21]I base this judgment on four sources: talks I had with the mother the evening before and her public statements that all that mattered to her was to be reconciled with Nadia; Nadia's testimony in court that her father had actually wanted to release her in Morocco once the ambassador intervened, but that it was the mother's family that was wholly against it; the father's heart disease; and reports from a close friend and trusted person in the Norwegian-Moroccan community that the father came to him shortly before his death and expressed his regret that he was forced to continue with the appeal.

Whether he wanted to or not, the father had little choice but to proceed with the appeal for the sake of the family's honor. The fact that he had married into a family far above his own family's standing complicated matters further. His marriage to Nadia's mother appears to have been a love marriage conducted against her family's wishes (which might have been why they went to Norway in the first place). To jeopardize her family's honor further by refraining from launching the appeal would have been out of the question, as I understand it.

[22]Joseph H. Carens, "Aliens and Citizens: The Case for Open Borders," *The Review of Politics* 49 (2): 1987.

[23]I was contacted by the school and asked to help after Aisha had disappeared. For further descriptions of the case, see Wikan, *Generous Betrayal*.

[24]Because the case was confidential, I cannot reveal the source of this quotation. But it stems from a superior official body (not a court) to which the case was appealed.

[25]Michael Ignatieff, "Whose Universal Values? The Crisis in Human Rights," Praemium Erasmianum Essay, The Hague, 1999.

[7]

Blaming Culture for Bad Behavior

Leti Volpp*

INTRODUCTION

When do we call behavior "cultural"? And when do we not? Why do we distinguish behavior in this way? And what are the consequences of this difference in recognition and naming? This Essay examines narratives that emerge in cases of forced and voluntary adolescent marriage. These narratives suggest that behavior that we might find troubling is more often causally attributed to a group-defined culture when the actor is perceived to "have" culture. Because we tend to perceive white Americans as "people without culture," when white people engage in certain practices we do not associate their behavior with a racialized conception of culture, but rather construct other, non-cultural explanations. The result is an exaggerated perception of ethnic difference that equates it with moral difference from "us."

In this Essay, I examine discursive representations—the narratives

* © 2000 Leti Volpp. Assistant Professor, American University, Washington College of Law. This Essay develops themes that I presented as the 1998-99 James A. Thomas Lecturer at Yale Law School. The first version of this Essay was presented at the *Journal of Gender, Race and Justice* Third Annual Symposium; subsequent versions were presented at the Law and Society 35th Annual Meeting, and at a Faculty Colloquium at the St. John's University School of Law. I received extremely helpful feedback at each of these sites, for which I am very grateful. In addition, I want to express my sincere thanks to Linda Bosniak, Pat Cain, Susan Carle, Adrienne Davis, Katherine Franke, Mitu Gulati, Serena Mayeri, Teemu Ruskola, and Sophie Volpp for their comments and suggestions. I would also like to express my appreciation to my research assistants Rose Cuison, Catherine Ng, Reiko Noda, and Wendy Wu.

that underlie public perception, legal discourse, and scholarly writings. I interrogate the way in which identity casts certain individuals outside the boundaries of our social body. Differentiation can occur through numerous identity-based distinctions—class and sexuality, for example. Here my focus is on race and immigrant status.

This Essay compares narratives in which two groups of adolescent women marry older men: girls who are white, and girls who are immigrants of color. In Part I, an examination of two cases of voluntary marriage reveals that when the actors involved are immigrants of color, we label behavior that we consider problematic as "cultural," and understand this term to mark racial or ethnic identity. Thus, we consider early marriage by a Mexican immigrant to reflect "Mexican culture." In contrast, when a white person commits a similar act, we view it as an isolated instance of aberrant behavior, and not as reflective of a racialized culture. Under this schema, white people are individual actors; people of color are members of groups. This Part examines why we equate race and culture and selectively blame culture for bad behavior.

Part II contrasts two cases of forced marriage to examine how the equation of race and culture in these cases relates to the interplay of nationalism, gender, and sexuality. This is significant because the terrain on which we articulate and understand racialized difference is frequently that of gendered treatment. The two cases of forced marriage show that prohibited behavior—parental coercion of a daughter's marriage—is conceptualized as a threat to "American" values when the perpetrator is an Iraqi immigrant, but not when the perpetrator is white. National identities, expressed here in the form of "American values," often coalesce around women's bodies and incorporate racial judgments. Thus, we project problematic behavior beyond the borders of the idealized nation by locating bad behavior on the bodies of racialized immigrant subjects.

Finally, Part III examines the consequences of selectively blaming culture by asking what we miss when we misread in this fashion. Selectively blaming culture leads to the misapprehension that certain immigrant cultures are fundamentally different from "our" culture. Ethnic difference is equated with moral difference, with which we must struggle in a multicultural state. Specifically, commentators depict the sex-subordinating practices of certain immigrants as creating an irreconcilable tension between the values of feminism and multiculturalism. The presumed existence of this conflict leads to policy proposals and theoretical conclusions that exaggerate differences between "us" and "them." Such misreadings prevent us from seeing, understanding, and struggling against specific relations of power—both within "other" cultures and our own.

I. VOLUNTARY MARRIAGE

A. Tina Akers and Wayne Compton

In September 1998, the front page of the *Washington Post* announced, "Girl, 13, Marries into Controversy."[1] Tina Akers, a thirteen-year-old, had married twenty-nine-year-old Wayne Compton in Maryland.[2] After they had dated for a few months, Tina became pregnant; she bore their son three weeks after the wedding.[3] At the time, Maryland law provided no minimum legal age of marriage: Anyone younger than sixteen with parental consent and proof of pregnancy could be legally married.[4] Critics called for Wayne Compton to be investigated for sexual assault, Tina's parents to be investigated for child abuse, and state lawmakers to outlaw such unions.[5] To date, Wayne Compton has not been prosecuted,[6] but in April 1999, Maryland legislators passed a bill raising the age of consent for minors to marry.[7] While the original bill introduced would have prohibited marriage for anyone younger than sixteen, legislators' concerns that the bill would result in more births out of wedlock led to a final version allowing fifteen-year-old girls to get married if they are both pregnant and have parental consent.[8]

Nowhere in the sound and fury over the Akers/Compton case was there any reference to their marriage as a cultural phenomenon.[9]

---

1. Amy Argetsinger, *Girl, 13, Marries Into Controversy: Arundel Says It's Legal, But Critics Say It's Child Abuse*, WASH. POST, Sept. 29, 1998, at A1.

2. *See id.*

3. *See id.* The baby subsequently died in his sleep. An autopsy gave the cause as sudden infant death syndrome, but police launched an investigation. *See* Amy Argetsinger, *Assembly Votes to Ban Some Teen Marriages*, WASH. POST, Apr. 11, 1999, at C4.

4. *See* MD. CODE ANN., FAM. LAW § 2-301 (1991).

5. *See* Argetsinger, *supra* note 1, at A10; Editorial, *Assembly's Home Stretch*, BALT. SUN, Mar. 22, 1999, at 8A (describing "shocking news" of Akers-Compton marriage and opining that it is against social norms for a 13-year-old to marry and have children).

6. Prosecutors declined, noting that Compton and her family have not filed a complaint nor shown any willingness to testify against him. *See* Argetsinger, *supra* note 3, at C4.

7. *See* H.B. 388, 413th Leg. (Md. 1999) (amending MD. CODE ANN., FAMILY LAW § 2-301 to absolutely prohibit an individual under age 15 from marrying, to require an individual between ages 15 and 16 to have parental consent and proof of pregnancy, and to require 16- and 17-year-olds to have either parental consent or proof of pregnancy); *see also Close to Home, Unhappily Ever After in Maryland*, WASH. POST, Apr. 4, 1999, at B8 (excerpted testimony on House Bill 388 of the clerk of the Anne Arundel Circuit Court before the Maryland House Judiciary Committee).

8. *See* Argetsinger, *supra* note 3, at C4. The fact that 15-year-olds can still marry puts the bill in conflict with the state's sexual offense laws. *See id.*; *see also* MD. ANN. CODE art. 27, § 464B (1999).

9. In addition to sources already cited, see Mary Allen, *Probe Goes on in Case of Married Mother, 13*, CAPITAL, Sept. 30, 1998, at A1; *Political Notes: 13-Year-Old Girl's Marriage to Be Discussed on Radio*, CAPITAL, Oct. 15, 1998, at A8.

While the two were both white, no one considered this marriage to be a moment that defined white American culture. Instead, the media, the public, law enforcement, and lawmakers understood the marriage as an example of aberrant behavior, which they variously characterized as child abuse, sexual perversion, and corruption of a minor.[10]

B. Adela Quintana and Pedro Sotelo

In contrast, when fourteen-year-old Adela Quintana and twenty-two-year-old Pedro Sotelo had a child in Texas, reporters described the case as "exposing a cultural divide,"[11] as demonstrating "a clash between two different cultures,"[12] and as engendering "public discussion about how to bridge cultural chasms."[13] In January 1996, police and child welfare officials in Houston, Texas, launched a massive search to locate Quintana, a pregnant runaway then believed to be ten years old, and her boyfriend.[14] Quintana, an undocumented immigrant, had first come to the state's attention when she attempted to apply for welfare by using a fraudulent birth certificate.[15] After Child Protective Services placed Quintana in an emergency shelter for abused children and the District Attorney charged Sotelo with aggravated sexual assault of a child, the couple fled.[16] When authorities captured them, they put Sotelo in a maximum security facility and placed Quintana in a foster home. The charges against Sotelo were dropped after a family court judge ruled that the couple had a valid common-law marriage under Texas law.[17] In Texas, children younger than fourteen cannot consent to sexual intercourse;[18] however, the statutory rape law defines a child as "a person younger than 17 years of age who is not the spouse of the actor."[19] Although for formal marriage in Texas both bride and

10. *See* Argetsinger, *supra* note 1, at A13.

11. Sandra Sanchez, *In Texas, Worlds Collide: Expectant Couple Caught in Clash of Two Cultures*, USA TODAY, Jan. 29, 1996, at 1D.

12. *Id.*

13. Syd Kearney, *Heroes and Heartaches: Putting 1996 in Perspective*, HOUS. CHRON., Jan. 2, 1997, at 5.

14. *See generally* Nina Perales, *Cultural Stereotype and the Legal Response to Pregnant Teens*, *in* MOTHER TROUBLES: RETHINKING CONTEMPORARY MATERNAL DILEMMAS 81 (Julia E. Hanigsberg & Sarah Ruddick eds., 1999). Perales's essay is an excellent and incisive critique of assumptions about pregnant Latina teenagers.

15. The birth certificate identified her as 10-year-old Cindy Garcia. *See* Jo Ann Zuniga, *Deportation Hearing for Young Couple Could Be Trying for Judge*, HOUS. CHRON., Mar. 28, 1997, at 30.

16. *See* Perales, *supra* note 14, at 82.

17. *See id.* at 85-86.

18. *See* May v. State, 903 S.W.2d 792, 794 (Tex. Ct. App. 1995).

19. TEX. PENAL CODE ANN. § 22.011(c)(1) to (2) (West 1997).

groom must be at least eighteen,[20] Quintana's age was no bar to the common-law marriage; at the time, the state had established no minimum age of consent to common-law marriage.[21]

Sotelo's civil attorney described Quintana as a physically mature "buxom lass."[22] She stated that, in rural Mexico, "once a girl hits puberty she is fair game."[23] Sotelo's criminal attorney declared that the case "was a cultural collision" and that his client was not guilty of statutory rape because he was following the customs of his rural village in Mexico.[24] The press also depicted the case as a clash of American and Mexican cultures. *Dateline NBC* sent a reporter to Mexico to interview people in Sotelo's home village about their awareness of early marriage. The program referred to Sotelo as "an innocent player in a big cultural misunderstanding."[25]

In her critique of the Quintana/Sotelo case, Nina Perales points out that it was Texas culture, embodied in statute, rather than Mexican culture, that resolved the dispute. Marriage at a young age is hardly an anomaly in Texas: Annually an average of 470 girls fourteen and younger marry there.[26] In fact, Mexican law actually provides stricter age requirements for marriage than Texas law.[27] Nevertheless, this case was understood as a definitional moment of Mexican culture.

C. Contrasting Narratives

What explains the different narratives that emerged from these

---

20. *See* TEX. FAM. CODE ANN. § 2.101 (West 1997). In Texas, one can marry at 14 with the consent of a parent, *see id.* § 2.102, or at 13 with a court order, *see id.* § 2.003.

21. *See id.* § 2.402(c). Following this case, a bill was filed to eliminate common-law marriage as a defense to statutory rape. *Bill Bars Common-Law Marriage as Rape Defense*, HOUS. CHRON., Feb. 4, 1997, at 17. The bill was enacted in 1997. *See* 1997 Tex. Sess. Law Serv. 1362 (West) (as codified at TEX. FAM. CODE ANN. § 2.401 (West 1999)) (amending the law to exclude individuals under the age of 18 from common-law marriages).

22. Perales, *supra* note 14, at 87.

23. *Id.*

24. *Id.* at 83.

25. The *Dateline NBC* program (February 1996) is described in Perales, *supra* note 14, at 84.

26. *See* Nicole Koch, *Letting Young Girls Marry Gets Another Look in Utah: Opponents Fear the Weddings Are Forced on Child Brides*, DALLAS MORNING NEWS, Sept. 27, 1998, at 10A.

27. I am indebted to Iqbal Gulati for suggesting this point. In Mexico, the age requirement for formal marriage is 18. With parental consent, or, if parents are unavailable, with the consent of grandparents, one can marry at 16 if male, 14 if female. *See* CÓDIGO CIVIL PARA EL DISTRITO FEDERAL arts. 148-49 (Mex.) (1996 WL 920101-2), *translated in* MEXICAN CIVIL AND COMMERCIAL CODES arts. 148-49 (1996 WL 915520-1) (describing the law in Mexico City). In the state of Guerrero, the home state of Pedro Sotelo, the minimum age at marriage is the same as in Mexico City. *See* CÓDIGO CIVIL GUERRERO art. 412; *see also* Navegador Juridico Internacional, *InfoJUS* (visited Oct. 5, 1999) <http://www.juridicas.unam.mx>. Many thanks to Carolina Sevilla for her assistance in researching the Mexican law.

two cases? Examining the way culture is conceptualized and linked with race provides an explanation. We sometimes assume culture to be static and insular, a fixed property of groups rather than an entity constantly created through relationships. This assumption is made much more frequently for outsider communities such as communities of color. Culture, for communities of color, is transformed into what Paul Gilroy calls a "pseudo-biological property of communal life."[28] Under such a paradigm, culture for communities of color is a fixed, monolithic essence that directs the actions of community members. Racialized culture thus becomes an essence that is transmitted in an unchanging form from one generation to the next.[29] We can contrast this racialized culture to culture that is considered to be "hegemonic"—the culture established as the norm.[30] Hegemonic culture is either experienced as invisible[31] or is characterized by hybridity, fluidity, and complexity.[32] The sophistication with which

---

28. As Gilroy writes:

> Culture is conceived along ethnically absolute lines, not as something intrinsically fluid, changing, unstable and dynamic, but as a fixed property of social groups rather than a relational field in which they encounter one another and live out social, historical relationships. When culture is brought into contact with "race" it is transformed into a pseudo-biological property of communal life.

PAUL GILROY, SMALL ACTS: THOUGHTS ON THE POLITICS OF BLACK CULTURES 24 (1993).

29. Lisa Lowe makes the helpful suggestion that we recognize "the ways in which [culture] is imagined, practiced, and continued. . . . [Culture] is worked out as much 'horizontally' among communities as it is transmitted 'vertically' in unchanging forms from one generation to the next." LISA LOWE, IMMIGRANT ACTS: ON ASIAN AMERICAN CULTURAL POLITICS 64 (1996).

30. Hegemonic culture is characterized less by what it is than by what it is not: raceless, classless culture that could not be attributed to any particular "subculture" of American society. What is considered to be hegemonic culture, the culture of the norm, is a flexible concept that constricts and expands in different contexts, depending upon who "we" are considered to be.

31. Generally, "white" culture is not marked or noted, an absence connected to the invisibility of whiteness as a race. On whiteness, see generally GEORGE LIPSITZ, THE POSSESSIVE INVESTMENT IN WHITENESS: HOW WHITE PEOPLE PROFIT FROM IDENTITY POLITICS (1998); IAN F. HANEY LÓPEZ, WHITE BY LAW: THE LEGAL CONSTRUCTION OF RACE (1996); DAVID ROEDIGER, TOWARDS THE ABOLITION OF WHITENESS: ESSAYS ON RACE, POLITICS, AND WORKING CLASS IDENTITY (1994).

32. The work of anthropologists such as James Clifford, George Marcus, and Renato Rosaldo has been foundational in developing a critical anthropology that subjects our own culture to the same level of scrutiny to which anthropologists had traditionally only subjected "other" cultures. *See generally* JAMES CLIFFORD, THE PREDICAMENT OF CULTURE: TWENTIETH-CENTURY ETHNOGRAPHY, LITERATURE, AND ART (1988); WRITING CULTURE: THE POETICS AND POLITICS OF ETHNOGRAPHY (James Clifford & George E. Marcus eds., 1986); RENATO ROSALDO, CULTURE AND TRUTH: THE REMAKING OF SOCIAL ANALYSIS (1993).

More recently, in the legal literature, norms theorists have begun to examine the way in which our society is shaped by extra-legal norms. This work could be considered a helpful step toward examining our behavior, although it is limited by its account of the development and entrenchment of norms solely in rational choice terms. For a discussion of why engaging in the insights of anthropology and sociology would be profitable for norms theory, see Mark Tushnet, *"Everything Old Is New Again": Early Reflections on the "New Chicago School,"* 1998 WIS. L. REV. 579.

we understand hegemonic culture to be complicated and contradictory—something with which we actively negotiate—is unmatched by an equally complicated understanding of outsider cultures.

These visions of culture influence our perceptions of individual acts. For communities of color, a specific individual act is assumed to be the product of a group identity and further, is used to define the group. Thus, people perceive Adela Quintana's early sexuality and marriage to be the product of Mexican identity and definitive of Mexican identity.[33] In contrast, the media does not present early sexuality and marriage by Tina Compton as the product of white identity, and thus her case does not perpetuate any perception that teen marriage is a phenomenon of "white culture."

This cultural identification may change, though, if her behavior is associated with a white identity that is differentiated from the "norm" by her class position. While narratives of the case did not explicitly highlight the couple's working-class white identity, class was a subtext in the media's description of Tina and Wayne Compton.[34] Many of the behaviors attributed to people of color are similarly ascribed to working-class whites, e.g., early marriage and excessive promiscuity.[35] Assumptions about class frequently operate to thrust working-class whites out of the presumptive normalcy of "our" culture.

However, in this case teen marriage was only implicitly presented as a phenomenon associated with class, and not explicitly named as such. Instead, Tina Akers and Wayne Compton were configured, despite their working-class identity, to be a part of "us." So long as Tina Compton belonged to "our culture," her behavior was not

33. The practices of the Orange County Social Services Agency between 1994 and 1996 demonstrated the assumption that early sexuality and marriage are part of Latino/a or Mexican culture: The agency encouraged approximately 15 pregnant adolescent girls under its protection to marry or live with the men who fathered their children. All but one of the girls were Latina. Some were as young as 13. *See* Vincent J. Schodolski, *Making a Family, But at a Cost? Pregnant Teens Pushed to Marry Adult Lovers*, CHIC. TRIB., Sept. 4, 1996, at 1. The Orange County Agency director had believed for a period that the age of consent to marriage in Mexico was 12. *See* Matt Lait, *Agency Helps Some Girls Wed Men Who Impregnated Them*, L.A. TIMES, Sept. 1, 1996, at A1. While some agency social workers said that the arrangements reflected the "cultural" mores of Mexico, others charged in internal memos that the agency's approach smacked of racism. *See* Matt Lait, *O.C. Agency Report Urges Change in Teen Wedding Policy*, L.A. TIMES, Sept. 7, 1996, at A1. *See also* Perales, *supra* note 14, at 88-89.

34. The *Washington Post* described a "pickup truck and fish tank" sitting in the front yard of her mother's house in "a dusty Annapolis suburb," and the reporter noted that she had dropped out of seventh grade the previous spring; her husband was described as an "unemployed roofer" who dropped out of school in the eleventh grade. Argetsinger, *supra* note 1, at A1.

35. For a description of how working-class whites were historically assumed to be sexually promiscuous, see Jane E. Larson, *"Even a Worm Will Turn at Last": Rape Reform in Late Nineteenth-Century America*, 9 YALE J.L. & HUMAN. 1, 30 (1997).

perceived to reflect norms associated with race. Instead, media accounts explained her behavior as reflecting trends in a national, presumptively raceless culture,[36] or ascribed her actions to a lack of rationality. In the latter construction, Tina Compton and her husband are personally dysfunctional, "perverse," and "irresponsible."[37] They are individual actors whose behavior is not the product of a group identity. Their behavior, in this view, does not reflect an ethnic or racial identity, nor is it used to define "whiteness."

We do not perceive adolescent marriage to be a property of whiteness, nor to be a classless, white cultural norm. Behavior that causes discomfort—that we consider "bad"—is conceptualized only as culturally canonical for cultures assumed to lag behind the United States. This tendency to submerge only certain groups into the forces of culture is linked to the assumption that the behavior of devalued and less powerful groups is somehow more culturally determined—that they behave in certain ways and make particular choices because they follow cultural dictates.[38]

Cultures that are thought to lag behind are often differentiated from the hegemonic culture by race. When people of color are assumed to "lag" because they are governed by cultural dictates, their cultural values stand in stark contrast to reason, supposedly a characteristic of the West. The notion that non-Western people are governed by culture suggests they have a limited capacity for agency, will, or rational thought.[39]

The assumption that people of color are governed by cultural dictates is not only dehumanizing, it is also depoliticizing because such thinking often leads us to neglect the power of "noncultural"

---

36. *See, e.g.*, Argetsinger, *supra* note 1, at A1 (describing a shift in attitudes toward teen marriage, connected to industrialization and child labor laws, that pushed young people off farms and into high schools, and noting that by 1990 only 3.7% of first-time brides were younger than 18, down from 13% in 1970).

37. *See id.* at A1, A10 (describing perspectives that marriage was sexually abusive, predatory, and pedophiliac).

38. Rosaldo describes the inverse relationship between power and possession of "cultural" traits:

> In "our" own eyes, "we" appear to be "people without culture" .... [F]ull citizenship and cultural visibility appear to be inversely related.... [A]nalysts rarely allow the ratio of class and culture to include power. Thus they conceal the ratio's darker side: the more power one has, the less culture one enjoys, and the more culture one has, the less power one wields.

ROSALDO, *supra* note 32, at 198, 202 (1993).

39. For a description of how this operates in the Western perception of China, see Teemu Ruskola, Taking Chinese Law Seriously: Towards a Critical Theory of Comparative Law 52 (unpublished manuscript, on file with author) (describing the following "ingredients" of a noxious stew that is still served today as "China": "China is changeless, the West progressive[;] the Chinese are passive, Westerners active[;] the Chinese are lemmings, Westerners individuals[;] the Chinese state is despotic, the Western state democratic[;] the Chinese are irrational, Westerners rational[;] the Chinese are ruled by morality, Westerners by law").

forces in shaping reality.[40] Cultural explanations for a particular problematic situation attribute responsibility to a static and insular "culture," and not, for example, to government policies. Take the idea that there exists in the United States a racialized underclass submerged in a "culture of poverty."[41] Suggesting that a pathological and dysfunctional "culture" is to blame for poverty obscures the role of, for example, state-sponsored segregation and private discrimination in creating poverty. Similarly, Lino Graglia has suggested that the primary explanation for lower test scores of Blacks and Hispanics is their membership in cultures that neither encourage achievement nor condemn academic failure.[42] Pointing the finger at culture in this way excludes the role of gross and systemic disparities in school funding and resources.[43]

The idea that nonwhites are more culturally determined can be traced to historical antecedents in colonialist and imperialist discourse. This discourse contrasted tradition and modernity in the service of justifying the conquest and subjugation of the colonized.[44]

---

40. For example, explaining gender subordination as "cultural" may erase linkages of this subordination with the denial of economic and political agency due to global inequalities, new articulations of patriarchies in specific regions, the legacies of colonization, or the flows of transnational capital. *See* Inderpal Grewal & Caren Kaplan, Warrior Marks: *Global Womanism's Neo-Colonial Discourse in a Multicultural Context*, 39 CAMERA OBSCURA 5, 14-15 (1996).

41. *See* DANIEL P. MOYNIHAN, THE NEGRO FAMILY: THE CASE FOR NATIONAL ACTION (1965); CHARLES MURRAY, LOSING GROUND: AMERICAN SOCIAL POLICY, 1950-1980, at 145-91 (1984) (arguing that post-1960 social welfare policies have encouraged self-destructive behavior among blacks and poor people). For a critique of the "culture of poverty" thesis, see ROBIN D.G. KELLEY, YO' MAMA'S DISFUNKTIONAL!: FIGHTING THE CULTURE WARS IN URBAN AMERICA (1997) (arguing that social scientists have contributed to a construction of the ghetto as a reservoir of pathologies and bad cultural values).

42. Professor Graglia's remarks spawned a national controversy. As the *National Law Journal* described:

> [Professor Graglia] was asked if lower test scores of blacks and Mexican-Americans are caused by genetic or cultural differences. "Blacks and Mexican-Americans are not academically competitive with whites in selective institutions," he replied. "It is the result primarily of cultural effects. They have a culture that seems not to encourage achievement. Failure is not looked upon with disgrace." He later said he didn't see any benefit in mixing white children with "lower classes" because they "perform less well in school and tend towards greater violent behavior."

Rights, Wrongs, NAT'L L.J., Sept. 29, 1997, at A20. Graglia asserted afterwards that he had misspoken, and attributed the performance gap instead to the average amount of time spent in school or doing school work. He also said that "his own cultural background—Sicilian—had similar 'cultural' deficiencies" and that he "should have kept his mouth shut." *Id.*

43. *See, e.g.*, Elvia R. Arriola, *Difference, Solidarity and Law: Building Latina/o Communities Through LatCrit Theory*, 19 CHICANO-LATINO L. REV. 1, 65 (1998) (describing research indicating that disparities in test scores between minorities and white students is dependent on the demographics of the school as a "white" or "minority" school and related policies of placing the least experienced and worst paid teachers at "minority" schools).

44. *See, e.g.*, Ruskola, *supra* note 39, at 44 (quoting GEORG WILHELM FRIEDRICH HEGEL, THE PHILOSOPHY OF HISTORY 103, 142 (J. Sibree trans., Dover Public. 1956) (1837)) ("The history of the world travels from East to West, for Europe is absolutely the end of History, Asia the beginning.... It is the necessary fate of Asiatic empires to be subjected to Europeans.").

Colonialism associated tradition with colonized peoples, ancient ritual, despotism, and barbarity, while connecting modernity to Western progress, democracy, and enlightenment.[45] According to the West, culture—not the high culture of opera, but the culture of daily activities, quotidian practices and rites—did not rule the lives of the rational thinkers of the West as it did those who were governed by tradition, folk ways, and tribal affiliations. Because the association of culture with tradition continues to linger, people tend to forget that culture undergoes constant transformation. A sophisticated and accurate understanding of culture requires us to recognize its fluidity. We are all agents who define our culture and identity, not solely marionettes positioned and directed by our culture.[46] At the same time, we must recognize that our society tends more readily to identify those who deviate from the hegemonic norm, who are perceived to inhabit outsider communities, to inherit culture that we assume to be monolithic, fixed, and dysfunctional.[47]

Of course, "our" hegemonic culture is also characterized by dysfunction. We recently came to a long-overdue realization that rates of gun-related violence are completely out of control in the United States. The spate of school shootings by white, middle-class children has led to anguished discussions about what is "wrong" with "our" culture.[48] These incidents have led to a recognition that either our culture is deeply flawed or its integrity is threatened by the

45. *See generally* CULTURES OF UNITED STATES IMPERIALISM (Amy Kaplan & Donald E. Pease eds., 1993); EDWARD W. SAID, CULTURE AND IMPERIALISM (1993); EDWARD W. SAID, ORIENTALISM (1978). The construction of this discourse, which Said described as "Orientalism," was a complex process. In presenting this simple, bifurcated description, I do not intend to suggest that this was not a hybrid, contradictory process that varied across time and space. For a study of the heterogeneity of Orientalism, see generally LISA LOWE, CRITICAL TERRAINS: FRENCH AND BRITISH ORIENTALISMS (1991).

46. *See* Stuart Hall, *Cultural Identity and Diaspora*, *in* IDENTITY, COMMUNITY, CULTURE, DIFFERENCE 222, 225 (Jonathan Rutherford ed., 1990).

47. *See* KELLEY, *supra* note 41, at 22 (critiquing the assumption that there is one identifiable ghetto culture, and asserting that this assumption can be partly attributed to ethnographers' training in the West). Kelley notes that James Clifford has observed that anthropologists studying non-Western societies are compelled to describe the communities they study not only as completely foreign to their own, but also as possessing an identifiable, homogenous culture. Kelley argues that the same holds true for interpretations of black urban America, since ethnographers can argue that inner city residents, as a "foreign" culture, do not share "mainstream" values. Their behavior is understood as shaped by unique cultural "norms," rather than reflecting individual responses to specific circumstances. *See id.* at 22-23.

48. We even have a new noun, "school shooters." The columnist Leonard Pitts noted the irony in the life of one shooting victim, Richard Peek. The first time Peek was shot, in a school shooting by Kipland Kinkel, "you heard all about it." After Peek was shot by Kinkel, Peek said that if he could, he would "make it harder for kids to get guns." The second time Peek was shot, he was killed by his 17-year-old brother in a hunting accident. Pitts asserts that we have learned to live with shootings that constitute the mundane face of American gun violence. In 1997, a mindboggling 10,369 people were murdered by firearms in the United States. *See* Leonard Pitts, *Shooting Reflects the Real Gun Crisis*, YORK DAILY REC. (Penn.), Oct. 17, 1999, at 2.

Internet, video games, access to guns, Satanic music, and irresponsible parents. Nonetheless, it is important to note that if the school shooters had not been middle-class and white, a different discourse would have emerged. Rather than hand-wringing about "our" culture, there would have been condemnation of "their" culture. Imagine, for example, that the shootings at Columbine High School had been committed by black students.[49] What narrative would have been told? There would have been less soul-searching about our nation's cultural values and what is wrong with "us." Instead, there would have been a discourse that conceptualized the violence as typifying what is wrong with "them."[50] The school shootings raise the question of why only certain groups are considered to constitute our social body, so that their achievements are our own, and their pathologies our failures.[51]

Considering some groups to be separate from our social body is a form of epistemic violence. Gayatri Spivak describes how the ideologies of colonialism and imperialism define the Other through depictions of the colonialized as exotic, primitive anthropological objects.[52] Institutional violence often accompanies this epistemic violence.[53] The experiences of Sotelo and Quintana following the conclusion of criminal proceedings reflect both forms of violence, since their "illegal" status differentiated them from "those who belong." Despite the fact that their child, Bryant, was born legally blind, in 1998 an immigration judge ordered Sotelo's deportation because he failed to establish seven years of continuous residency in the United States.[54]

49. Orlando Patterson argues that there is a disturbing double standard in how we label deviant behavior. He writes: "If the terrorist act of white, middle-class teenagers creates an orgy of national soul-searching, then surely the next time a heinous crime is committed by underclass African-American or Latino kids, we should engage in the same kind of national self-examination." Orlando Patterson, *What If the Killers Had Been Black?*, PLAIN DEALER (Cleveland), May 4, 1999, at 9B.

50. *See* Courtland Milloy, *A Look at Tragedy in Black, White*, WASH. POST, May 2, 1999, at C1. Milloy writes of hearing comments like "I'm so glad those killers weren't black. You know we'd all be in trouble if they were." He posits that if the killers in Columbine had been black, their parents would have been hauled off in handcuffs in front of television cameras, and everybody who knew them would be under suspicion. He notes that the shooters were referred to as members of a "clique," not a gang, and that one reporter referred to one of the killers as "a gentleman who drove a BMW," signifying an identification with the killers and a reluctance to demonize them as blacks would have been. *Id.* I am indebted to Mark Niles for calling my attention to this op-ed piece.

51. I borrow this phrasing from Orlando Patterson, *see supra* note 49, at 9B.

52. *See* Gayatri C. Spivak, *Can the Subaltern Speak?*, *in* MARXISM AND THE INTERPRETATION OF CULTURE 271, 281 (Cary Nelson & Lawrence Grossberg eds., 1988).

53. As Anne McClintock points out, epistemic violence is all too often supported by the planned institutional violence of armies, law courts, prisons, and state machinery. *See* ANNE MCCLINTOCK, IMPERIAL LEATHER: RACE, GENDER AND SEXUALITY IN THE COLONIAL CONTEST 16 (1993)(discussing this phenomenon in the colonial context).

54. At the time of Sotelo's application, the continuous residency requirement was seven

II. FORCED MARRIAGE

A. The Kingston Case

A second pair of contrasting cases echoes these findings and yields additional observations. In May 1998, a sixteen-year-old in Utah, forced by her father to marry her thirty-two-year-old uncle as his fifteenth wife, called 911 for help.[55] The uncle, David Kingston, was charged with incest and sexual conduct with a minor, both third-degree felonies,[56] and received a ten-year jail sentence.[57] Her father, John Daniel Kingston, the leader of a large polygamist clan, pled guilty to felony child abuse for beating her into unconsciousness when she tried to run away.[58] In Utah—as in Texas—parental consent or a court order allow marriage at an age younger than eighteen.[59] Until May 1999, marriages were only prohibited when the male or female was under fourteen years of age.[60] Since that time, the age of consent has been raised to sixteen, but fifteen-year-olds may still marry with parental consent and authorization from a judge.[61] Before the law was amended, every year about 800 girls aged fourteen through seventeen were reported to marry in Utah.[62]

Rumors of coerced arranged marriages and children sold by their parents had led to repeated attempts to enact legislation that would outlaw marriages of fourteen- and fifteen-year-olds. A bill was withdrawn in 1997 under pressure from legislators who believed child marriage prevents teen promiscuity.[63] Legislators also

---

years. This is no longer the case, thanks to the 1996 Illegal Immigration Reform and Immigrant Responsibility Act ("IIRAIRA"). *See* 8 U.S.C. § 1254, *amended by* 8 U.S.C. § 1229(b) (increasing the requirement of seven years of continuous residency for suspension of deportation to ten years under what is now called cancellation of removal, see INA § 240A(b)). IIRAIRA also amended the statute to mandate that any departure from the United States in excess of 90 days or any departure in the aggregate exceeding 180 days will preclude a finding of continuous physical presence. *See* INA § 240A(d)(2). Quintana and their child were allowed to stay pending her application for change of immigration status. *See* Jo Ann Zuniga, *Mom, Blind Child May Stay in Houston, Judge Orders Immigrant Father to Be Deported*, HOUS. CHRON., May 6, 1997, at 17.

55. *See* Stephen Hunt, *Kingston Ordered to Trial*, SALT LAKE TRIB., Dec. 11, 1998, at D1.

56. *See Utah Gets Rare Chance to Prosecute Polygamist*, COMMERCIAL APPEAL, Aug. 6, 1998, at A7.

57. *See* Julie Cart, *Incest Trial Sheds Light on Polygamy in Utah*, L.A. TIMES, June 4, 1999, at A3; Hannah Wolfson, *Alleged Polygamist Gets Up to Ten Years for Having Sex with His Niece*, AP, July 9, 1999, *available in* 1999 WL 17822686.

58. *See Wolfson, supra* note 57. He was sentenced to 28 weeks in jail, ordered to pay $2,700 in fines and an unspecified amount in restitution, and to complete an anger-management program. He had faced up to five years in prison. *See Polygamous Leader Sentenced to 28 Weeks in Jail for Whipping*, LAS VEGAS REV.-J., June 30, 1999, at 13A.

59. *See* UTAH CODE ANN. § 30-1-9 (1953 & Supp. 1999).

60. *See* UTAH CODE ANN. § 30-1-9 (1953 & Supp. 1998) (repealed in 1999).

61. *See* UTAH CODE ANN. § 30-1-9 (1953 & Supp. 1999).

62. *See* Koch, *supra* note 26, at 10A.

63. *See Outrage of the Month, Child Brides—In Utah* (visited Nov. 5, 1998)

expressed concern that such legislation would be unfairly aimed at the state's polygamists.[64] While the practice of plural marriage was renounced by the Mormon Church in 1890, it has persisted among religious splinter groups[65] and has not been prosecuted by the state for several decades.[66] The Governor of Utah, a descendent of polygamists, refused to condemn polygamy at a news conference, suggesting that it may be protected as a religious freedom.[67] His comments were quickly condemned by an organization of women who have abandoned polygamous relationships. They denounce the practice as abusive toward women and children, both inherently and as it is practiced.[68] Subsequently, the Women's Religious Liberties Union (WRLU) was founded by a woman in a polygamous relationship who asserted that polygamy appropriately channels men's sexuality. The WRLU called for a repeal of the state law banning plural marriage.[69]

The months after the sixteen-year-old's phone call led to a "raft of questions" about "Utah's dirty little secret."[70] Allegations included evidence of large-scale welfare fraud by women in plural marriages claiming to be single mothers, rampant incest and child abuse, and girls as young as ten forced into arranged marriages. The media

---

<http://www.feminist.com/outrag7.htm>.

64. *See* Mike Carter, *Legislator Struggles to Stop Utah's Pre-16 Marriages*, OREGONIAN, Feb. 8, 1998, at A24.

65. An estimated 20,000 to 100,000 people live in polygamous families, more than when plural marriage was official Mormon doctrine, and this population appears to be growing. *See* Vince Beiser, *The Perils of Polygamy*, MACLEAN'S, July 26, 1999, at 32.

66. *See* R. Michael Otto, *"Wait 'Til Your Mothers Get Home," Assessing the Rights of Polygamists as Custodial and Adoptive Parents*, 1991 UTAH L. REV. 881, 883 (noting that the last polygamy prosecution in the U.S. took place in 1965); John Hiscock, *Girl's Incest Case Evidence Set to Lift Lid on Mormon Polygamy*, DAILY TELEGRAPH (London), Aug. 6, 1998, at 14 (noting that Kingston case would be the first prosecution for polygamy in 45 years). However, Kingston was not ultimately prosecuted for polygamy.

67. *See* Mike Carter, *Child Abuse Case Raises Polygamy Questions in Utah*, STATE J.-REG. (Springfield, Ill.), Aug. 3, 1998, at 14.

68. *See id.* Tapestry of Polygamy was founded by six women who left plural marriages. They focus on allegations of sexual abuse, pedophilia, and incest. One of the founders points to the polygamous roots of many members of the state's power structure. "They all have this romantic view of how their grandfathers practiced it. But this is not grandpa's polygamy. As near as I can tell, Brigham Young was not a pedophile." Timothy Egan, *The Persistence of Polygamy*, N.Y. TIMES, Feb. 28, 1999 (Magazine), at 51-53.

69. *See* James Langton, *Mormon Women Break Silence to Praise the Joys of Polygamy*, DAILY TELEGRAPH (London), Aug. 9, 1998, at 26. The founder of the group, Mary Potter, says that "[i]n polygamy, men are properly channeled." Egan, *supra* note 68, at 54. She and other supporters of polygamy point to recent studies that maintain that men are evolutionarily wired for multiple sex partners. *See id.* An anthropologist, Janet Bennion, who has written about one of the largest polygamous clans, says she believes polygamy can offer a sense of security and a kind of sisterhood to modern women, while she concedes there have been incidents of sexual abuse, marrying of relatives, and ostracizing of older, less attractive wives within the clans. *See id.*

70. Julie Cart, *Tales of Abuse, Incest Frame "Utah's Dirty Little Secret,"* L.A. TIMES, Aug. 15, 1998, at A1.

described the polygamists as a community of people who live as "societal ciphers," with no birth certificates or driver's licenses, who do not pay taxes or vote.[71]

There has been a discourse of condemnation surrounding both the Kingston case and polygamous Mormon splinter groups more generally.[72] Historically, Mormons have been subjected to a campaign against polygamy couched in terms of national morality and even national survival,[73] rhetoric not unlike that directed against communities of color today. But the current discourse does not include accusations that Mormons, with their failure to assimilate, their failure to Americanize, threaten longstanding American values.[74] No one asserts that statewide acceptance of these diverse cultural practices is symptomatic of multiculturalism run amok. Nor does anyone characterize this as a collision between multiculturalism and feminism.[75]

71. *See id.*

72. State Senator Scott Howell, the leader of the Democratic legislative minority in Utah, who introduced legislation targeting polygamy, stated: "Here, we've got all the world coming to town for the Olympics. Do we really want to be known as the place where we let old men marry little girls?" Egan, *supra* note 68, at 55.

73. As Sarah Barringer Gordon describes, by 1890, when the church capitulated to demands that it abandon polygamy, the federal government had directed much energy toward enacting and enforcing legislation in Utah. Such legislation included the criminal punishment of polygamists, the revocation of the vote for all who could not swear they did not live in a polygamous relationship, and the forfeiture of all but $50,000 of church property. Polygamy was assumed to be based on uncontrolled male sensuality and to threaten all that was pure in monogamous domesticity. *See* Sarah Barringer Gordon, *"Our National Hearthstone": Anti-Polygamy Fiction and the Campaign Against Moral Diversity in Antebellum America*, 8 YALE J.L. & HUMAN. 295, 306-07, 327-28 (1996). *New York Times* reporter Timothy Egan notes that from the founding of the church in 1830, Mormons have been persecuted, and that their fear of outsiders is integral to their religious identity. *See* Egan, *supra* note 68, at 54.

74. *See, e.g.*, Egan, *supra* note 68, at 50; Bruce Frankel, *Lifting the Veil*, PEOPLE, June 21, 1999, at 125.

75. In writing about the Kingston case, Katha Pollitt argues that the ACLU ought to abandon its opposition to laws against polygamy. The ACLU justifies its policy on the basis of religious freedom, freedom of expression, and privacy. Pollitt, on the other hand, argues that polygamy is gender-subordinating in our current universe, whereas it might not be subordinating in a world where the age of consent were, say, 30, where teenage girls had real autonomy, where all women were well-educated and able to support themselves and their children, and where people were less isolated and less easily trapped. When Pollitt prodded the ACLU to consider how polygamy is different from "religious or cultural defenses of child abuse, domestic violence or female genital mutilation," she was told that "violence is different." Katha Pollitt, *Polymaritally Perverse*, THE NATION, Oct. 4, 1999, at 10. While Pollitt is pushing in the direction I want to go, toward recognizing that we tend to respond inconsistently to gender-subordinating behavior, I am not sure if she would endorse my assertion that our divergent responses correlate with the actor's identity. I also note that the examples she presents as the fixed practices the ACLU must really condemn—religious or cultural defenses of child abuse, domestic violence, or female genital mutilation—constitute the paradigmatic stereotype of sexism by immigrants that is thought to characterize gendered "multicultural" difference from "us."

B. The Al-Saidy Case

In contrast, when two sisters, thirteen and fourteen, were forced by their Iraqi immigrant father in 1996 to marry twenty-eight- and thirty-four-year-old men in Nebraska, critics deemed the case an illustration of "the proper limits of multiculturalism."[76] After spending two years in a refugee camp in Saudi Arabia, the Al-Saidy family resettled in Lincoln, Nebraska. Fearing that his daughters were sexually active, the father arranged their marriages to the two men, also refugees from Southern Iraq. After the older daughter ran away to the home of a male friend, the father and husband came looking for the daughters at school, and the police became involved. The girls were placed in foster care, and the parents were arrested and charged with child abuse.[77] The two husbands, Majed Al-Tamimy and Latif Al-Hussaini, were charged with first-degree sexual assault of a child, faced up to fifty-year sentences, and were eventually sentenced to four to six years in prison.[78] The elder daughter was sent to a home for girls in Omaha, the younger was placed in foster care.[79]

Attorneys for Al-Hussaini and Al-Tamimy suggested that they had married the sisters in accordance with their religion, asserted that in the "Arab world," the charges were viewed as religious persecution,[80] and called the case "a clash between cultural mores and U.S. law."[81] Predictably, the media reported this to be a case about "Muslim mores" and "Iraqi culture." However, a spokesperson from the Lincoln Islamic Foundation explained that, while Islamic law does not set a minimum age for marriage, women in contemporary Iraq typically marry at seventeen or eighteen.[82] Another observer indicated that while thirty years ago marriages of young teenage girls were not uncommon in Iraq, especially in the rural areas, today such practices are rare.[83] Nevertheless, as with the Quintana/Sotelo case, many deemed this single incident definitive of Iraqi culture.

76. Margaret Talbot, *Baghdad on the Plains*, NEW REPUBLIC, Aug. 11, 1997, at 18.

77. *See id.*

78. *See Iraqis Who Married Teens Sent to Prison*, SAN ANTONIO EXPRESS-NEWS, Sept. 24, 1997, at 12A. In Nebraska, the crime of statutory rape applies to sex between one person who is 19 years of age or more and another who is 14 years old or younger. *See* NEB. REV. STAT. § 28-320.01 (1999).

79. *See Therapy Ordered for Man Who Made Daughters Marry*, DES MOINES REG., June 14, 1997, at 10.

80. Larry Fruhling, *They Say Marriage; Law Says Rape*, DES MOINES REG., Jan. 5, 1997, at 1.

81. J.L. Schmidt, *Iraqi Father Is Jailed For "Marrying Off" 2 Young Girls*, AUSTIN AM.-STATESMAN, Nov. 20, 1996, at A16.

82. *See id.*

83. *See Iraqi Father of Child Brides Claims Culture as a Defense*, DALLAS MORNING NEWS, Dec. 4, 1996, at 39A.

Moreover, the Al-Saidy incident was almost universally depicted as threatening American values. The media described the incident as "a clash of the culture of newcomers with American mores and law. It is a conflict shrouded in issues of multiculturalism and ignorance of the ways of a strange new world."[84] One woman wrote to the *Lincoln Journal-Star*, "We cannot change our laws to suit the backward, primitive values of some immigrants, or we shall find our country in the same shape as Iraq."[85] The *Omaha World Herald* editorialized:

> [M]ulticulturalism goes too far if it insists that all cultures are equally valid. Or if it requires the dominant culture, the American culture in this case, always to yield in cultural clashes .... In a Western nation, the West's cultural traditions undergird the law. People who immigrate to this country and enjoy its opportunity and freedoms need to understand that arranged child marriages won't be tolerated.[86]

In this view, "newcomers" import primitive and backward values, threatening the Western cultural traditions that undergird America, land of freedom and opportunity.

C. Nation, Gender, and Sexuality

Why are the child marriages of nonwhite immigrants but not white Christian sects perceived as threatening Western cultural traditions? Contrasting "progressive" Western traditions to the "primitive" and "barbaric" lends credibility to the idea that Western culture is progressive.[87] Though no one depicted the Kingston case as reflecting modern and enlightened practices, the Mormon community was not condemned as a barbaric outsider culture threatening a racialized national narrative of enlightened progress. Significantly, while both the Kingston and Al-Saidy cases conjured the rhetoric of religious freedom, only the Iraqi community possessed, in the eyes of Western observers, the undesirable behavior of a racialized culture.

The contrast between the cultural traditions of the West and those of immigrants with "backward, primitive values" is somewhat ironic,

84. *Id.*

85. Rick Montgomery, *Iraqi Grooms Charged with Raping Brides; Nebraska Case Spurs Argument over Muslim Mores in the U.S.*, KANSAS CITY STAR, Dec. 15, 1996, at A1 (quoting a letter to the *Lincoln Journal-Star*).

86. Editorial, *Marriage Custom of Another Land Puts Political Correctness to Test*, OMAHA WORLD HERALD, Dec. 5, 1996, at 26.

87. As Edward Said has written, Orientalism dichotomizes the human condition into a "we" and a "they," essentializing the resulting other. When a dominant group essentializes a subordinated group by focusing on selected traits to describe the group as a whole, the dominant group defines its own characteristics—civilized, progressive—in contrast to the group that is subordinated. *See* SAID, ORIENTALISM, *supra* note 45, at 227-28.

as Western cultural traditions include child marriage and early sexuality. Ten years of age was the age of consent under English common law, as well as the age of consent in most states in 1885, when agitation to reform statutory rape law first began in the United States.[88] At that point the age of consent in Delaware was only seven years of age.[89]

Despite this, many commentators believe that cases such as the one in Nebraska threaten a long-standing Western tradition of valuing women and children. They point to cases of forced marriage,[90] Asian immigrant parent-child suicide, Hmong marriage by capture, female genital mutilation, and "wife killing" by nonwhite immigrants to assert that multiculturalism has gone too far. In their view, multiculturalism and feminism cannot coexist: Multiculturalism must give way, and feminism must triumph.[91]

Admittedly, attorneys are complicit in offering "cultural" explanations for behavior, and in cases involving immigrant defendants attorneys will frequently attempt to introduce cultural evidence to explain the social context of their clients' acts, and will thus raise the specter of culture.[92] But attorneys' "cultural defense" strategies do not seem sufficient to explain the popular assumption that only immigrant cultures originating in Asia, Latin America, Africa, and the Middle East jeopardize feminist progress. For one, any criminal defendant is entitled to raise social context evidence, including cultural factors, to explain her acts.[93] Nevertheless, when

---

88. *See* Larson, *supra* note 35, at 2.

89. *See id.* at 2 n.9. Until recently, the age of consent was 14 in South Carolina and 13 in North Carolina. *See* N.C. GEN. STAT. § 14-27.7A (1995) (raising the age of consent from 13 to 16); S.C. CODE ANN. § 16-15-140 (West 1999) (changing the age from 14 to 16 in 1996); Maryanne Lyons, *Adolescents in Jeopardy: An Analysis of Texas' Promiscuity Defense for Sexual Assault*, 29 HOUS. L. REV. 583, 609 (1992).

90. For example, Doriane Coleman has stated:

> Liberals tend to think we should embrace multiculturalism and be more lenient with these people.... [However, Iraqi marriage customs] tend to be patriarchal in nature [and] bad for women and bad for children.... The interests of our society in protecting women and children and our society's interest in having uniform laws outweigh our interest in multiculturalism.

Marriage Custom, *supra* note 86, at 26 (quoting Doriane Coleman).

91. *See, e.g.*, Doriane Lambelet Coleman, *Individualizing Justice Through Multiculturalism: The Liberals' Dilemma*, 96 COLUM. L. REV. 1093 (1996).

92. *See supra* Parts I.A, II.A (describing how attorneys representing Pedro Sotelo and the defendants in the Al-Saidy case suggested that their clients were following Mexican culture and religious tradition, respectively).

93. Our criminal justice system allows the admission of any relevant social context evidence. The issue of culture is admissible in criminal cases like any other evidence: It must be relevant, its probative value must outweigh its prejudicial effect, and it must not have the tendency to mislead the trier of fact. What is at issue in cases involving cultural evidence is the weight it is given, the responsibility of prosecutors to introduce additional evidence regarding culture so that perceptions of culture are not distorted, judicial training on cultural issues, and the question of qualifications of expert witnesses who testify about cultural practices. *See*

certain immigrant defendants present cultural factors that implicate sex-subordinating practices, we presume them to be the beneficiaries of a special treatment that is tolerated as a necessary concomitant of the pluralistic values of multiculturalism.[94] What facilitates the assumption that this is special treatment? Why presume that immigrant communities bring to the United States a deviant and demented culture that is fundamentally different from "ours"? Narratives that emerge from these "cultural defense" cases reinforce a pre-existing presumption that misogynist acts are typical of and unique to certain immigrant cultures.

What appears truly to underlie the assumption of a peculiarly misogynistic immigrant culture is the relationship between nationalism, gender, sexuality, and race. National identities, expressed here as "American values," often coalesce around women's bodies. Racializing sex-subordinating practices allows problematic behavior to be projected beyond the borders of a nation and located on the bodies of racialized immigrant subjects.

The interaction of these factors deserves scrutiny. The control of women and their sexuality is crucial to maintaining and reproducing the identity of communities and nations.[95] As Anne McClintock and others have demonstrated, images of nations are constructed in terms of familial and domestic metaphors, where women are located as the symbolic center and boundary marker of the nation.[96] In this scheme, women are mothers of the nation and guardians of its purity and honor. Purity and honor survive when women engage only in

generally Holly Maguigan, *Cultural Evidence and Male Violence: Are Feminist and Multiculturalist Reformers on a Collision Course in Criminal Courts?*, 70 N.Y.U. L. REV. 36 (1995); Leti Volpp, *Talking "Culture": Gender, Race, Nation and the Politics of Multiculturalism*, 96 COLUM. L. REV. 1573 (1996) [hereinafter Volpp, *Talking "Culture"*]. As I have argued elsewhere, I think that defense attorneys should also be cognizant of the broader ramifications, in the form of perpetuating stereotypes, that accompany presenting cultural evidence made up of crass caricatures of an immigrant's culture, although I also recognize that defense attorneys are ethically bound to represent their clients zealously. *See* Leti Volpp, *(Mis)Identifying Culture: Asian Women and the "Cultural Defense,"* 17 HARV. WOMEN'S L.J. 57, 93-100 (1994) [hereinafter Volpp, *(Mis)Identifying Culture*]. For further discussion of the risks that accompany presenting evidence that relies on group-based stereotypes, see SHERENE RAZACK, LOOKING WHITE PEOPLE IN THE EYE: GENDER, RACE, AND CULTURE IN COURTROOMS AND CLASSROOMS (1998); Leti Volpp, *Gazing Back*, 14 BERKELEY WOMEN'S L.J. 149 (1999) (review of RAZACK, *supra*).

94. Our law is already embedded with cultural norms that reflect gender subordination, such as the doctrine of provocation. The voluntary manslaughter law of most jurisdictions recognizes the sight of a wife's adultery as a valid motivation to kill. *See* Donna K. Coker, *Heat of Passion and Wife Killing: Men Who Batter/Men Who Kill*, 2 S. CAL. REV. L. & WOMEN'S STUD. 71 (1992). For the argument that access to cultural evidence is far from special treatment but is, in fact, what is required to assure equal protection, given the existence of the doctrine of provocation, see James J. Sing, Note, *Culture as Sameness: Toward a Synthetic View of Provocation and Culture in the Criminal Law*, 108 YALE L.J. 1845 (1999).

95. *See, e.g.*, JAN JINDY PETTMAN, WORLDING WOMEN: A FEMINIST INTERNATIONAL POLITICS 59 (1996).

96. *See* MCCLINTOCK, *supra* note 53, at 354-57.

sexual relations that are heteronormative and occur within the confines of state-sanctioned marriage that controls the reproduction of the state's citizenry.[97] The nation also depends on the family as a unit through which the stability of gender roles is preserved.[98] Adolescent premarital sexuality creates anxiety,[99] so the state seeks to direct this prohibited sexuality into appropriate channels, such as early marriage. Thus, we find statutes that legislate the acceptability of marriage at ages as young as thirteen with proof of pregnancy and/or parental consent, and reluctance to increase the age of consent lest the law promote promiscuity or illegitimate births.

What is the role of race in this process? Nationalist ideologies are often concerned with racial purity and subject women to reproductive and other forms of control[100] to achieve this aim. In the cases of forced and voluntary adolescent marriage discussed here, the racialized bodies and community control over the sexuality of immigrant girls appear to rupture a national fabric that is

---

97. As Jacqui Alexander points out:

> The nation has always been conceived in heterosexuality, since biology and reproduction are at the heart of its impulse. The citizenship machinery is also located here, in the sense that the prerequisites of good citizenship and loyalty to the nation are simultaneously sexualized and hierarchized into a class of good, loyal, reproducing heterosexual citizens, and a subordinated, marginalized class of non-citizens . . . .

M. Jacqui Alexander, *Erotic Autonomy as a Politics of Decolonization: An Anatomy of State Practice in the Bahamas Tourist Economy*, *in* FEMINIST GENEALOGIES, COLONIAL LEGACIES, DEMOCRATIC FUTURES 63, 84 (M. Jacqui Alexander & Chandra Mohanty eds., 1997).

98. *See* Gayatri Gopinath, *Nostalgia, Desire, Diaspora: South Asian Sexualities in Motion*, 5 POSITIONS 467, 468 (1997).

99. For discussions of anxieties caused by adolescent sexuality, see Elizabeth Hollenberg, *The Criminalization of Teenage Sex: Statutory Rape and the Politics of Teenage Motherhood*, 10 STAN. L. & POL'Y REV. 267 (1999) (describing an increase in statutory rape prosecutions and the adoption of criminal justice policies in the name of social welfare programming); Megan Weinstein, *The Teenage Pregnancy "Problem": Welfare Reform and the Personal Responsibility and Work Opportunity Reconciliation Act of 1996*, 13 BERKELEY WOMEN'S L.J. 117 (1998) (describing debates over the welfare reform act (PRWORA) and provisions of the law that attempt to discourage unwed motherhood).

100. Thus we see mass rape of women by men attempting to destroy communities and nations; for example, Serbian men raped Bosnian Muslim women as part of a policy of "ethnic cleansing." These rapes functioned both to destroy what was symbolically configured as national honor in the form of women's bodies, and to forcibly impregnate women with Serbian babies. *See* PETTMAN, *supra* note 95, at 101.

An example of other forms of control is the relationship of women and community identity post-Partition in India and Pakistan. Partition and the creation of Pakistan was accompanied by mass abduction and separation of women from their families: An estimated 50,000 Muslim women in India and 33,000 non-Muslim women in Pakistan were abducted, abandoned, or separated from their families. After Partition, both countries pursued "recovery operations" to reclaim these women. Some of these women had married and been absorbed into their new communities, so that their recovery was forced, especially when they were required to leave children behind. Ritu Menon and Kamla Bhasin interrogate why the matter of national honor was so closely bound up with women's bodies, and answer that both governments pursued communal identities—as Hindu (India) or Muslim (Pakistan), despite India's avowed secularism—that located women as boundary markers of identity. *See* Ritu Menon & Kamla Bhasin, *Recovery, Rupture, Resistance: Abduction of Women During Partition*, ECON. & POL. WKLY., Apr. 24, 1993, at WS-2.

presumptively both white and progressive. The sexuality of immigrant adolescent girls of color is marked as a racialized threat to a national cultural consensus about appropriate female sexuality and responses to that sexuality.

Women's bodies serve as "boundary markers of the nation"[101] in the context of charting societal progress. In nationalist discourse the figure of the woman acts as a primary marker of an essential communal identity or tradition.[102] Women, home, family, and nation become conflated so that women serve to signify a community's culture and tradition.[103] As a result, perceptions of the relative treatment of women have historically been used to assess the progress of a culture and to justify subjugation of different populations in the name of a racialized gender uplift. For example, British colonial rule was justified, in part, in terms of a civilizing mission that cast British colonizers as protecting oppressed native women from their victimization by native males.[104] This construction was accomplished by disregarding the agency of native women and denying the sexism endemic to Britain at the time.[105] Thus, women's bodies frequently serve as the terrain on which progress is measured.

A nation can consolidate its identity by projecting beyond its own borders the sexual practices or gender behaviors it deems abhorrent.[106] Thus, even while voluntary or forced adolescent marriages occur within white American communities, we do not conceptualize these practices as cultural phenomena characterizing white America. Rather, this undesirable behavior is projected beyond U.S. borders and characterized as an abhorrent practice imported by immigrants that undermines enlightened Western norms.[107] This projection allows the United States to maintain a self-

101. Editorial, 44 FEMINIST REV. 1, 1 (1993) ("Nationalism is gendered: women's bodies are the boundary of the nation, and the bearers of its future"), *quoted in* PETTMAN, *supra* note 95, at 59.

102. *See* Gopinath, *supra* note 98, at 468.

103. *See* PARTHA CHATTERJEE, THE NATION AND ITS FRAGMENTS: COLONIAL AND POSTCOLONIAL HISTORIES 116-57 (1993) (describing this process in the Indian context).

104. Another primary justification was the "effeminacy" of the native male that was thought to render him incapable of self-governance. *See generally* ANTOINETTE BURTON, BURDENS OF HISTORY: BRITISH FEMINISTS, INDIAN WOMEN, AND IMPERIAL CULTURE, 1865-1915 (1994).

105. As one example, British colonial officials in Egypt specifically invoked the veil and treatment of women under Islam as a justification for colonialism. The British consul general, Lord Cromer, vociferous in making these claims, was also a founding member of the Men's League for Opposing Women's Suffrage in England. *See* LEILA AHMED, WOMEN AND GENDER IN ISLAM: HISTORICAL ROOTS OF A MODERN DEBATE 152-53 (1992).

106. *See Introduction* to NATIONALISMS AND SEXUALITIES 10 (Andrew Parker et al. eds., 1992).

107. When African-Americans are the "other" accused of engaging in deviant behavior, the backdrop of normalcy shifts from "Western" values to those of white America.

image as a progressive state with a progressive culture—especially in the arena of women's rights—by naming as "other" the source of backward behavior.[108] This process occurs even when such practices are not unique to immigrants of color but in fact are legally condoned by statute, as is the case for voluntary adolescent marriage,[109] or, if illegal, appear among native-born whites as well as immigrants.

III. FEMINISM AND MULTICULTURALISM

Advocates and scholars have attempted to problematize the conflation of racialized immigrant communities and regressive sex-subordinating culture in a variety of contexts, including female genital surgeries and so-called "cultural defenses."[110] These

108. Bonnie Honig makes what I see as an important and analogous argument that we press foreigners into service on behalf of certain institutions, such as capitalism, community, and family, that seem incapable of sustaining themselves. This takes both xenophilic and xenophobic turns. An example of a xenophilic turn would be when new immigrants are symbolically mobilized to renormalize the native-born into traditional heterosexual gender roles, while "we" supposedly normalize "them" into a new national citizenship. For this Honig proffers a reading of the film *Strictly Ballroom* and an example of a trade in foreign brides—namely, the way in which immigrant women, supposedly more traditionally socialized into gender roles, properly shore up heterosexual marriages for those men seeking the way marriage is "supposed" to be. An example of a xenophobic turn would be the manner in which patriarchal immigrants are seen as threats to what Honig calls the rough gender equalities that are American liberal democracy's ambiguous achievement. *See* Bonnie Honig, *Immigrant America? How Foreignness "Solves" Democracy's Problems*, 16 SOC. TEXT 56, 63-67 (1998).

109. I recognize that an act may be legally condoned in a statute because it happened historically and rarely occurs in the contemporary moment. However, this is not the case with adolescent marriage. For example, Kentucky amended its marriage laws in March 1998 to outlaw marriage of children under 16—unless the girl is pregnant, and a district judge approves. *See* KY. REV. STAT. ANN. § 402.020 (1998). Between 1994 and 1996, 1,300 girls who were 15 or younger received marriage licenses in Kentucky; 71 of them were 12 or 13. *See* Beverly Bartlett, *Three Legislators Bungled Vows on Bill to Ban Child Brides*, COURIER-J. (Louisville, Ky.), Feb. 9, 1998, at 1F; Al Cross, *Bill Limiting Child Marriages Signed into Law by Governor*, COURIER-J., Mar. 27, 1998, at 4B. Significantly, some legislators attempted to sink the bill by tying it to a provision allowing same-sex marriage. *See Legislative Briefs*, COURIER-J., Mar. 20, 1998, at 48. Some legislators argued that the teen marriage provision would infringe on personal freedom. Others said that it should be defended by the First Amendment protection of freedom of religion. *See* Bartlett, *supra*, at 1F.

In addition, the media reports of the frequency of adolescent marriage in Maryland indicate that until the state amended the law in April 1999, *see supra* note 7, statutory approval of this practice was not solely a historical artifact. *See Close to Home, supra* note 7. Robert P. Duckworth, the clerk of the Anne Arundel Circuit Court, in his testimony to the Maryland House Judiciary Committee on House Bill 388 (the bill seeking to amend the state's marriage laws) reported:

> Two weeks ago ... a very pregnant 15-year-old bride entered our wedding room. Her partner was an immature lad of 16 years, barely able to drive.... They were escorted by both sets of consenting moms and dads.... But more troublesome than these weddings are the adolescent-adult weddings and child-adult weddings.... An expectant, 11-year-old girl arrived at a Maryland courthouse last year to wed a 21-year-old adult.... Sadly, the couple tied the knot, and their abominable union was "blessed" by the state under the approving eyes of the pubescent bride's parents.

Id. at B8.

110. *See, e.g.*, UMA NARAYAN, DISLOCATING CULTURES: IDENTITIES, TRADITIONS,

individuals have recognized that culture is neither static nor homogenous and that culture is experienced and described variously by individuals situated differently within a particular community. Further, these commentators have argued that every community is characterized by both patriarchy and resistance to patriarchy, and that women are agents, not just passive subjects of their culture.[111]

But these attempts to create a complex and accurate understanding of culture often go unheard. Susan Moller Okin recently used the Iraqi case as a launching pad to criticize multiculturalism in an essay titled, *Is Multiculturalism Bad for Women?*[112] (Her answer: "Yes."[113]) Okin asserts that there are fundamental conflicts between a commitment to gender equity and a multiculturalist respect for minority cultures, as illustrated by the Al-Saidy case, French schoolchildren wearing headscarves, African immigrant polygamous marriages, female clitoridectomy in immigrant communities, Hmong marriage by capture, parent-child suicide by Japanese and Chinese immigrants, and "wife murder by immigrants from Asian and Middle Eastern countries whose wives have either committed adultery or treated their husbands in a servile way."[114] In Okin's account, these examples reflect ethnic difference, which in turn represents moral difference. Okin then argues that we

---

THIRD-WORLD FEMINISM (1997); RAZACK, *supra* note 93; SCATTERED HEGEMONIES: POSTMODERNITY AND TRANSNATIONAL FEMINIST PRACTICES (Inderpal Grewal & Caren Kaplan eds., 1994); Lama Abu-Odeh, *Comparatively Speaking: The "Honor" of the "East" and the "Passion" of the "West,"* 1997 UTAH L. REV. 287; Isabelle R. Gunning, *Arrogant Perception, World Traveling, and Multicultural Feminism: The Case of Female Genital Surgeries*, 23 COLUM. HUM. RTS. L. REV. 189 (1991-92); Bonnie Honig, *My Culture Made Me Do It*, *in* SUSAN MOLLER OKIN, IS MULTICULTURALISM BAD FOR WOMEN? (Joshua Cohen et al. eds., 1999); Hope Lewis, *Between* Irua *and "Female Genital Mutilation": Feminist Human Rights Discourse and the Cultural Divide*, 8 HARV. HUM. RTS. L.J. 1 (1995); Hope Lewis & Isabelle R. Gunning, *Cleaning Our Own House: "Exotic" and Familiar Human Rights Violations*, 4 BUFF. HUM. RTS. L. REV. 123 (1998); Volpp, *(Mis)Identifying Culture*, *supra* note 93, at 57; Volpp, *Talking "Culture," supra* note 93, at 1573.

111. *See generally* sources cited *supra* note 110.

112. SUSAN MOLLER OKIN, *Is Multiculturalism Bad for Women?*, *in* IS MULTICULTURALISM BAD FOR WOMEN?, *supra* note 110, at 9.

113. *Id.* Margaret Talbot, writing in *The New Republic*, has similarly used the Iraqi case as a basis to criticize the undermining of the basic precept that immigrants must "respect American laws." She asserts that this case pits "respect for other cultures and sympathy for miserable refugees against a belief in a certain autonomy—personhood, really—for women and children" and writes that "the girls deserved the protection of American law, even if it embodied a notion of rights that had no place in the world of their father." *See* Talbot, *supra* note 76, at 20-22.

114. OKIN, *supra* note 112, at 18. While Okin does write that Western cultures "of course still practice many forms of sex discrimination," and notes that "virtually all of the world's cultures have distinctly patriarchal pasts," she asserts that some cultures—mostly Western liberal cultures—have departed further from patriarchal pasts than others. *Id.* at 16. Her conclusion: Female members of "a more patriarchal minority culture" may "be much better off if the culture into which they were born were either to become extinct," so its members would be integrated "into the less sexist surrounding culture," or if the culture were "encouraged to alter itself so as to reinforce the equality of women." *Id.* at 22-23.

must choose universalist values that respect women rather than succumbing to the multiculturalist or relativist disinclination to judge difference.

To assert that these cases reveal a tension between multi-culturalism and feminism is not only to rely upon a caricature of the culture of immigrant communities and communities of color, but also to posit very specific and problematic versions of feminism and of multiculturalism.[115] These discussions assume a feminism that replicates the colonialist feminism of a century ago. In the colonialist paradigm, native women were completely passive subjects of a native male subordination that grossly exceeded that experienced by women in the West.[116] Colonialist feminism emerged, in this account, in order to uplift the suffering women of the "East."[117] This brand of feminism was used to justify colonization as part of a civilizing process, along with the rule of law, education, and Christianity.[118]

The assumption of this strand of feminist theory, reflected in Okin's perspective, that immigrant women require liberation through induction into the progressive social mores and customs of the metropolitan West, has been subjected to significant criticism.[119] Critics have pointed to the manner in which feminists describe "other" women as "always/already victim,"[120] passively waiting to be rescued from cultural norms that mysteriously impose no restraints on Western feminists.

Just as these discussions perpetuate a distorted feminism, they assume a multiculturalism that resembles crude cultural relativism. Under a multicultural regime, this discourse suggests that we as a

115. *See* Volpp, *Talking "Culture," supra* note 93, at 1577-84, 1607-11.

116. For example, British suffragist Josephine Butler lamented that Indian women were:

> indeed between the upper and nether millstone, helpless, voiceless, hopeless. Their helplessness appeals to the heart, somewhat in the same way . . . in which the helplessness and suffering of a dumb animal does, under the knife of a vivisector. . . . Somewhere, half way between the Martyr Saints and the tortured "friend of man" the noble dog, stand, it seems to me, these pitiful Indian women, girls, children, as many of them are. They have not even the small power of resistance [like] the western wom[a]n [who] . . . may have some clearer knowledge of a just and pitiful God to whom she may make her mute appeal.

VRON WARE, BEYOND THE PALE: WHITE WOMEN, RACISM, AND HISTORY 156-67 (1992) (quoting Josephine Butler).

117. *See generally* BURTON, *supra* note 104; WARE, *supra* note 116; WESTERN WOMEN AND IMPERIALISM: COMPLICITY AND RESISTANCE (Nupur Chaudhuri & Margaret Strobel eds., 1992).

118. *See* sources cited *supra* note 117.

119. *See, e.g.*, NARAYAN, *supra* note 110; Hazel V. Carby, *White Woman Listen! Black Feminism and the Boundaries of Sisterhood*, *in* THE EMPIRE STRIKES BACK: RACE AND RACISM IN 70S BRITAIN 212 (CCCS eds., 1982); Chandra Mohanty, *Under Western Eyes: Feminist Scholarship and Colonial Discourses*, *in* THIRD WORLD WOMEN AND THE POLITICS OF FEMINISM 51 (Chandra T. Mohanty et al. eds., 1991).

120. *See generally* Lata Mani, *Multiple Mediations: Feminist Scholarship in the Age of Multinational Reception*, 35 FEMINIST REV. 24 (1990); Mohanty, *supra* note 119.

society would be unable to critique any culture and would be forced to accept the bizarre customs and behaviors of nonwhites at the expense of long-cherished American principles.[121] This portrayal of multiculturalism relies on problematic assumptions. First, it invents a homogenous, "American" tradition of principles, a monoculturalism of transcendent values with a "we" or "us" at an unwavering center of rationality. This assumption is historically inaccurate, relying upon distortions and marginalizations for its narrative coherence.[122] Second, this account confuses the multiculturalist valuation of ethnic particularity with a defense of cultural relativism.[123] Valuing difference does not destroy our ability to judge among differences.[124] We need not rely upon "long-cherished Western principles" that masquerade as universal values in order to make critical judgments about gender-subordinating practices.[125]

As Homi Bhabha has recently written, the construction of a conflict between feminism and multiculturalism relies on the monolithic characterizations of minority, migrant cultures.[126] Such a construction mistakenly presumes the "Western" domestic scene to be egalitarian and empowering; depicts minorities as abject

121. The meaning of multiculturalism has been the subject of enormous debate. For examples of works that examine the various meanings of multiculturalism, see MAPPING MULTICULTURALISM (Avery F. Gordon & Christopher Newfield eds., 1996); MULTICULTURALISM: EXAMINING THE POLITICS OF RECOGNITION (Amy Gutmann ed., 1994); PATRICIA J. WILLIAMS, THE ALCHEMY OF RACE AND RIGHTS (1991).

122. For a re-reading of historical experience where the social condition of people is prevailingly migratory and heterogeneous, as opposed to homogenous, see David Theo Goldberg, *Introduction: Multicultural Conditions*, *in* MULTICULTURALISM: A CRITICAL READER 1, 20-25 (David Theo Goldberg ed., 1994).

123. *See id.* at 16. As Goldberg points out, the collapsing of ethnic particularity with relativism has been facilitated by the failure of some academics to theorize the implications of a nonessentializing multicultural commitment. *See id.* at 15.

124. Note that if we were to carry the valuing of difference to an extreme, this logic—that we can both value difference and judge among difference—collapses. *See* Stanley Fish, *Boutique Multiculturalism*, *in* MULTICULTURALISM AND AMERICAN DEMOCRACY 69 (Arthur M. Melzer et al. eds., 1998). Fish argues that if one values difference as a general principle so seriously, one becomes unable to value any particular difference seriously, since this embrace of the principle of difference will inevitably involve the suppression of particularized difference. This is because the imperatives of a distinctive culture will impinge on the freedom of some other distinctive culture. If one decides, in response, that a commitment to respecting a particular culture is so strong that one stays the course no matter what, one no longer is a multiculturalist, but becomes a uni- or monoculturalist. As Fish suggests, rather than become lost in this abstracted philosophical maze, it might be more constructive to recognize multiculturalism as a demographic fact and to search for particular solutions to particular problems. *See id.* at 73-75.

125. For an example, see Joan Williams, *Rorty, Radicalism, Romanticism: The Politics of the Gaze*, 1992 WIS. L. REV. 131. In defending a nonfoundationalist ethics, Williams suggests that we are capable of making moral judgments even when we recognize that our moral certainties reflect particular cultural values, rather than perceiving them to be reflective of eternal truth.

126. *See* Homi K. Bhabha, *Liberalism's Sacred Cow*, *in* IS MULTICULTURALISM BAD FOR WOMEN?, *supra* note 110, at 79, 79.

"subjects" of their cultures of origin "huddled in the gazebo of group rights, preserving the orthodoxy of their distinctive cultures in the midst of the great storm of Western progress";[127] and assumes that Western liberal values—utterly foreign to immigrant communities—will lead to their salvation.[128]

Juxtaposing these narratives of similar stories differently perceived illustrates how distinctive interpretative lenses are applied to virtually identical behavior according to the actors' identity.[129] Our society considers the voluntary pregnancy and marriage of a young teenage girl to an older man to be the act of an aberrant individual when the girl is white, but considers it to reflect a more primitive culture when the girl is a Mexican immigrant. Under the prevailing view, a father forcing his young teenage daughters into marriage is a cultural act demonstrating the evils of multiculturalism when the actors are Iraqi immigrants, but not when they are white and Mormon. Society presumes that immigrants of color are passive victims dominated by their cultural traditions, in contrast to the rational actors of Western liberalism.

The consequences of selectively blaming culture in this way are striking: These discursive practices cause us to overlook specific relations of power, both in "other" cultures and in our own society. In hasty expressions of distaste for other cultures perceived as primitive and backward, we miss the complex ways in which power actually functions in particular communities.

A specific example may help to clarify this point. In a recent article, Katherine Franke examines how our choice to label certain practices as "sexual" eclipses important implications of behavior.[130] One of her examples is the anthropological report of ritualized practices in a community where boys must fellate older men as part of the process of becoming a man.[131] It is easy to feel disgust at the daily ingestion of semen by seven-year-old boys—to label this

127. *Id.* at 80.

128. *See id.* at 83-84.

129. The assumption that the behavior of white people reflects individual acts, while similar acts committed by immigrants of color reflect group identity, demonstrates the contours of what underlies discrimination.

130. *See* Katherine Franke, *Putting Sex to Work*, 75 DENV. U. L. REV. 1139 (1998) (examining the assault of Abner Louima by white New York City police officers, sex-related violence against civilians in the former Yugoslavia, and ritualized man/boy fellatio in Papua New Guinea).

131. *See generally id.*; *see also* GILBERT HERDT, GUARDIANS OF THE FLUTE: IDIOMS OF MASCULINITY (1981); GILBERT HERDT, SAMBIA SEXUAL CULTURE: ESSAYS FROM THE FIELD (1999). Many of these practices no longer persist. As Richard Schweder writes, these accounts have had great prominence in the lore of anthropology. Yet after a few years of contact with the West, "almost everything that was exotic about New Guinea seems to have disappeared." Richard A. Schweder, *Why Do Men Barbeque? And Other Postmodern Ironies of Growing Up in the Decade of Ethnicity*, 122 DAEDALUS 279, 285 (1993).

practice as a symptom of a horrifically bad culture, and to dehumanize those who would engage in such practices.[132] Alternatively, one could, as various commentators have, describe these practices as fundamentally homoerotic, as evidence of an exotic manifestation of homosexual behavior. Both of these responses distance the observer from the culture observed, connecting the evaluation of the "other" culture to the observer's self-image. One interpretation is condemnatory, the other laudatory; one unreflectively says "that is not me," the other says "that is me."[133] The former calls the practice culture, the latter calls it sex. Both miss the way this sexual practice signifies and enforces power relations.

As Franke describes, the fellatio is accompanied by nose-bleeding through the use of sharp grasses, as well as cane-swallowing to induce vomiting and defecation. The purpose of these rituals is to purge female body fluids that the male child inherited from the mother.[134] Boys are isolated from all women and taught that women are polluters who will deplete their masculine substance, which they must ingest in the form of semen required for boys to grow. Franke writes that, rather than considering these practices principally homoerotic and calling them "sexual," we can more appropriately understand them as part of a larger indoctrination process whereby boys learn and internalize gender norms premised upon misogyny and male superiority.[135] We could therefore argue that what is eclipsed in the selective labeling as sexual—or as cultural—is the relation of these practices to the specific manner in which gender structures social relations.[136]

---

132. In a forthcoming article, Martha Nussbaum describes the role of the emotion of disgust in different legal spheres, and notes that the male ingestion of semen is met with a greater level of disgust than the female ingestion of semen, since females are differentiated from men because they are considered receptacles for disgusting body fluids. *See* Martha C. Nussbaum, *"Secret Sewers of Vice": Disgust, Bodies and the Law*, *in* THE PASSIONS OF JUSTICE (Susan Bandes ed., forthcoming 2000).

133. Franke writes: "[Gilbert] Herdt . . . was one of the first Western observers to encounter the Sambia practices and declare: Look, homosexuality. Hallelujah, we are everywhere!" Franke, *supra* note 130, at 1146.

134. *See id.* at 1150.

135. *See id.* at 1151-52.

136. How precisely we could understand these practices as relating to the way gender structures social relations may be quite complicated. Marilyn Strathern, attempting to convey Melanesian knowledge practices as though they were a series of analyses for the way things seem from the point of view of Western anthropological and feminist preoccupations, argues that "male" and "female" might be understood not as motivating principles at work in society, but as conventional descriptions of the forms in which Melanesians make persons and things known. *See* MARILYN STRATHERN, THE GENDER OF THE GIFT: PROBLEMS WITH WOMEN AND PROBLEMS WITH SOCIETY IN MELANESIA 309-10 (1988). She writes that understanding male initiation as simply a differentiation from women looks at individuals as they are recruited into their sex as if they are individuals recruited into clan groups. *See id.* at 64. Among the drawbacks of such an approach, she suggests, is the assumption that identity consists in the possession of qualifying attributes, in whether an individual "has" the

The condemnatory reaction, which distances the observer from the practice and defines the observer as the antithesis of that practice, relies upon and perpetuates a failure to see subordinating practices in our own culture when, for example, young girls are forced to engage in non-consensual sex or are battered in the process of "becoming a woman."[137] When we gaze with condemnation at other cultures, we can miss the fact that "our" culture is also characterized by problematic, sex-subordinating behavior. The cases of adolescent marriage should make us rethink the belief that culturally-based subordination of women and girls is a phenomenon particular to immigrant communities of color. So long as we chalk up sexist behavior in other communities to their "culture," we must critically examine the fact that American culture is characterized by, for example, epidemic rates of male violence against women. Alternatively, if we say that we reject sexism as part of "our culture"—that some of us claim that domestic violence, for example, has no part of "our culture"—we should similarly recognize that segments of other communities are also engaged in a process of rejecting sexism as part of "their culture."

Extraterritorializing of problematic behavior by projecting it beyond the borders of "American values" has the effect both of equating racialized immigrant culture with sex-subordination, and denying the reality of gendered subordination prevalent in mainstream white America. The failure to interrogate these effects has real-life consequences. These assumptions about gender, race, culture, and nation do not solely raise questions of descriptive representation; they result in shifts in material reality and in distributions of power. While the sexist culture of immigrants of

characteristics that make him unambiguously masculine. *See id.* at 64-65.

Strathern argues that this is a naive correspondence between the sexed individual and the autonomy of "male" and "female" viewpoints. *See id.* at 64. For example, she points to the way in which the gender of sexual organs depends on what you do with them. *See id.* at 128, 211. The difference between male and female is created through rites, and it is a difference that turns on interaction, not attributes. Persons are not masculinized, rather persons masculinize their own organs and sexual substance. The rituals occur, not to make boys, as a special category, into men, but to ensure that they will have the internal capacity to procreate, to be fathers. And men do not in any simple way become men. They are androgynous beings composed of male and female elements, and are produced as male out of an opposite, female form. *See id.* at 211-13.

137. Many American teens learn that experiencing domestic violence is part of being a woman. Forty percent of teenage girls aged 14-17 report knowing someone their age who has been hit or beaten by a boyfriend. *See* Family Violence Prevention Fund, *Domestic Violence Is a Serious, Widespread Social Problem in America: The Facts* (visited Nov. 14, 1999), <http://www.fvpf.org/facts>. Eight percent of high-school-age girls said "yes" when asked if "a boyfriend or date has ever forced sex against your will." *Id.* The "most conservative data" available on the prevalence of father-daughter incest suggests that 1.3% of American women will experience it. At this estimate, 1.6 million American women are now or have been victims of incest. *See* Lisa Elder, *Former Miss America to Speak at Forum on Child Abuse*, DAILY OKLAHOMAN, Mar. 6, 1996, at 13.

color is used to justify calls for immigration exclusion (some race-based, some not),[138] there appears to be little headway against the shocking incidence of domestic violence in nearly one-third of intimate relationships in the United States.[139] To be perfectly clear, I am not pointing out the problematic discursive representations of racialized communities in these cases in order to assert that these cultures are not sexist.[140] Rather, I am calling for an approach to combat gendered subordination across communities, an approach that neither attacks the cultures of communities of color based on racial assumptions, nor presumes that the United States is always a site of liberation.

138. *See* Audrey Macklin, Looking at Law Through the Lens of Culture: 3 Canadian Snapshots 11 (unpublished manuscript, on file with author) (describing the demand in Canada to limit immigration from certain countries because male nationals were assumed to be "wife-beaters").

The Federation for American Immigration Reform, an organization dedicated to the principle that the "mass immigration unforeseen over the last 30 years should not continue," invokes the Iraqi case in Nebraska to demonstrate why the United States should curb immigration. Their webpage states:

> One of the most immediate effects of the overly high immigration level our country has today is the growth of groups of people who are not well assimilated into our larger national culture. This leads to worsening ethnic separatism and related problems. . . . Language aside, cultural differences alone can create problems. In November 1996, an Iraqi immigrant was jailed in Nebraska for forcing his 13- and 14-year old daughters to marry men more than twice their age, who were also jailed for statutory rape. The men explained that they were following the tradition of their country and did not understand our government's reaction. As a natural result of cultural conflict, ethnic strife and separatism grow.

FAIR, *Immigration and Ethnic Separatism* (visited Nov. 13, 1999), <http://www.fairus.org/html/04152803.htm>.

Along the same lines, but in a more explicitly racist fashion, in his national bestseller, Peter Brimelow called for an immediate moratorium on immigration from non-European countries, arguing that immigration has social consequences, among them the fact that the immigrants who enter today, compared to European immigrants of the past, are unassimilable and cause crime. *See* PETER BRIMELOW, ALIEN NATION: COMMON SENSE ABOUT AMERICA'S IMMIGRATION DISASTER 10, 19, 178-90, 202-21 (1995).

139. Thirty-one percent of American women report being physically or sexually abused by a husband or boyfriend at some point in their lives, according to a 1998 survey. Thirty percent of Americans say they know a woman who has been physically abused by her husband or boyfriend in the past year. Nearly one-fifth of women reported experiencing a completed or attempted rape at some time in their lives. This violence occurs at similar rates across communities. *See* Family Violence Prevention Fund, *supra* note 137.

140. I will reiterate here that I believe that all cultures are patriarchal. More helpful than the attempt to categorize cultures on a scale of more patriarchal to less patriarchal would be to examine how patriarchy manifests itself in ways that are similar and different across cultures or communities.

[8]

The Reconstruction of the Constitution and the Case for Muslim Personal Law in Canada

Syed Mumtaz Ali and Enab Whitehouse

Introduction

The present paper is intended for discussion. It delineates a way of looking at various facets of the current constitutional problems besetting Canada. It offers a critical analysis of a select number of themes which we believe have played a fundamental role in creating and shaping the crisis facing Canadians.

As interested observers and participants in the social/political fabric of Canadian life, we, to borrow the vernacular of sports, have tried to call things as we see them. We realize some of these judgement calls may upset some segments of Canadian society.

The intention underlying such judgement calls is neither to insult nor to vilify any group. In fact, to continue with the analogy of sports, by citing apparent infractions concerning the spirit and substance of democratic principles, we, somewhat like referees, are not making any moral judgements about the integrity of the people or groups to whom some of the remarks are addressed. Our remarks are directed at drawing attention to the inappropriateness of the behaviour involved, according to our understanding and interpretation of the rules and character of the democratic game.

As Canadians, we subscribe to the general idea of democracy. At the same time, we believe many of the political practices, institutions and processes which exist in Canada fall far short of the promise and potential that democratic theory has for meeting the social and political needs of a truly multicultural society. Radical reconstruction of the Canadian Constitution is necessary, but such reconstruction must be built upon a thoroughly democratic foundation.

Multiculturalism cannot survive in an environment that pays only lip service to the underlying principles and values of that philosophy. The principles and values of multiculturalism must be put into everyday practice.

In any democratic setup sovereignty is a structurally complex idea. Many people have different ideas about its character and scope. However, as used in the current paper, it must always be understood to be relative and not an absolute term.

The shape which sovereignty assumes in any given socio-political context must always be a function of the dialectic between the rights and duties of care of the participants in that context. Consequently, the sovereignty of the individual must be balanced against the sovereignty of other individuals. Moreover, the sovereignty of one level of government must be harmonized with the sovereignty of other levels of government. The same holds true with respect to the sovereignty association of communities and various levels of government.

However, nothing in the ensuing discussion should be construed as advocating either some form of anarchy or the breakup of Canada. Canada must remain whole and united, and it can accomplish this, we suggest, through the combination of constraints and degrees of freedom permitted by the principles and proposals set forth in this paper.

Representational Democracy

What would be required in order for Canada to be a participatory democracy? Some might wish to argue that Canada already satisfies the requirements of a participatory democracy. After all, voting is considered to be a fundamental expression of participation. Moreover, people are free to run for public office, or to help out in their association of choice, or to try to shape the policy platforms adopted by a political party. All of these count as acts of participation.

While conceding the point that there do exist a number of avenues through which Canadians can participate in the political process, nonetheless, the idea of participatory democracy need not be limited to the foregoing sorts of possibilities. For example, once elections take place, the opportunities for most Canadians to continue participating in the political process often becomes severely curtailed. This is the case because Canada operates according to the values of representational democracy. These values tend to place very determinate limits on the extent to which non-elected or non-governmental officials can participate in the political process.

There are, in general terms, two methods of putting into practice the concept of representational democracy. One approach construes the idea of representation to mean that the elected official must be faithful to the wishes, desires and interests of the electorate. Therefore, the elected official assumes the responsibility of actively seeking to convert such wishes, desires and interests into a government policy which is realized in various sorts of laws, social programmes, economic measures, environmental activity and so on.

The other general approach to the notion of representational democracy, which might be labelled the "visionary model", holds a very different picture of the role of an elected official. From the perspective of the second approach, the elected official's primary responsibility is not necessarily to serve, or actualize, or be an agent for the wishes, desires and interests of the electorate. The task of the elected official is to seek to implement what such an individual believes is in the best interests of all of the electorate, even if these beliefs run, partially or entirely, contrary to the wishes, or desires of the electorate.

Participatory Democracy and the Process of Recall

When people talk about the desire to have participation in the governing process, the discussion is often couched in terms of having direct, active, unmediated contact with the governing process. Their desire is to have more autonomy over their political lives in the sense that they do not want their point of view marginalized, shunted aside or ignored by politicians. They are seeking some way to have options to them which offer the hope of circumventing, within limits, the traditional access to power–namely, the politician. In other words, the spirit of participation is rooted in the desire to have access to a form of real power which is beyond the control of politicians and which will make politicians more responsive to the needs of the electorate than does the prospect of holding elections every four or five years.

There are a number of ways of providing the electorate with a sense of having the direct, substantive, unmediated participatory power which they seek. The power of recall is one such possibility.

Referendum Issues

Another sort of power that would enable the electorate to have direct, substantive and unmediated access to the process of governing is linked with the idea of referendum. There is almost nothing that is more conducive to a sense of helplessness than to see policies, programmes or changes being instituted over which one has no control, despite feeling very much opposed to such activities of the government.

Another possible avenue for helping the electorate to gain more direct control over the political process that affects their lives concerns the way in which election campaigns are run and financed.

There is a growing cynicism among many voters about the way campaign money plays an increasingly corrupting role in the electoral process. More and more, it seems, campaigns are about who has the most money to spend on advertising campaigns. More and more, campaigns are about which candidates can be packaged most alluringly. More and more, campaigns seem to be based on the tactics of illusion, deception, evasion and manipulation. Less and less, do campaigns seem to be directed to the needs, interests, concerns and problems of the electorate. More and more, campaigns seem to be reduced to 30 second spots, photo opportunities and repetition of names or slogans. Less and less, are campaigns about an in-depth debate and discussion of issues. More and more, campaigns are about individuals and parties winning elections. Less and less, are campaigns about ensuring that the community wins through the election of people and the promotion of issues that are most responsive to the needs and concerns of the electorate. One way of helping to eliminate such problems and thereby assist the electorate to gain some control over the electoral process, rather than be its manipulated victims, is to require that all political contributions be directed to a general election fund which serves the interests of the community as a whole. This fund would be used to underwrite the cost of such things as: debates, non-promotional campaign expenses, as well as publicizing the philosophical positions of all the candidates on various topics, issues and problems.

Sovereignty: A first Encounter

Let us examine yet another area involving the issue of personal autonomy as a basic expression of participatory democracy. Recently, the British Columbia Supreme Court handed down a decision which denied the land claims of a group of Native people. The essence of the court's decision was that the Native land claim had no merit since such claims had all been extinguished during colonial times. This act of extinguishing was accomplished by those who were acting on behalf of the authority of the sovereign power of the King or Queen of England.

The apparent ethnocentric prejudices that are ingrained in certain aspects of Canadian society which are reflected, unfortunately, in the judgement of the learned justices of the B.C Supreme Court run so deep that many people do not seem to have properly appreciated just how revealing the court's judgement is about the assumption underlying the world view of many Canadians concerning Native peoples. Other judges and governmental officials in other localities and times have made statements or rendered judgements which are similar to that of the British Columbia Supreme Court.

The Sovereignty of a people is not a function of law. It is an a *priori* given that has been recognized, appealed to, alluded to and invoked over thousands of years in virtually every society about which there exists recorded knowledge. In fact, the roots of this *a priori* principle are so fundamental and so pervasive to the human condition that no one has been able to mount a plausible, let alone convincing, argument that would justify the denial of such sovereignty in a way that would be acknowledged as a tenable philosophical position by most people.The central importance of this issue of sovereignty also is reflected in every kind of human rights document that has issued forth from the United Nations and its predecessor, the League of Nations.

Law is predicated on, and presupposes the existence of, such sovereignty. Law is derivative from sovereignty. Indeed, although one can conceive of sovereignty without law, one cannot conceive of law without presupposing the existence of a source of sovereignty to generate such law. Law does not generate itself.

Legitimate constraints and limits can be placed on the exercise of sovereignty only through mutual agreement. This sort of reciprocity is exhibited in the case of a social contract between an individual and the larger community in which both parties agree to restraining themselves in certain ways in order to preserve the autonomy and integrity of the other party to the agreement.Each party has rights in such an agreement. Each party has duties of care with respect to the other party under the reciprocal character of the agreement.

However, the willingness of a person or people to accept constraints upon one's sovereignty should not be confused with the idea of extinguishing a people's sovereignty. The latter idea is a figment of the fevered imagination of those who would shamelessly, and with an inflated sense of self-importance, try to rationalize their attempts to deny, if not usurp, the sovereignty of another people.

Neither the Supreme Court of British Columbia, nor the court system of any province, nor the Supreme Court of Canada has any jurisdiction in the matter of the sovereignty of Native peoples. In and of itself, the sovereignty of the Native people is entirely extra-legal in character. However, as indicated earlier, the trappings of legitimate legality arise in conjunction with the sovereignty of Native people only to the extent that, of their own free will and volition, Native people agree to enter into a social contract with the other peoples of Canada. This contract gives expression to the sort of constraints on sovereignty which are deemed necessary in order to protect and, where possible, enhance the integrity, autonomy and access of real power to the respective parties.

Unfortunately, historically, the non-native people of Canada tend to have misconstrued and misunderstood the nature of their relationship with Native peoples. The former have been inclined to consider themselves the superior, "civilised", divinely favoured party which has the right to impose their values, policies, programmes and will on the Native people. In short, most non native-people of Canada believe they alone had sovereignty. For the most part, there has been a dearth of any semblance of mutuality and reciprocity which has characterised the intentions and attitudes of the non-Native peoples in their dealings and interactions with Native peoples on the issue of sovereignty.

The resolution of the sovereignty problem of Native peoples is complicated immeasurably by the fact that money, natural resources and land have become inextricably caught up in the issue of sovereignty. On the one hand, vested interests — both public and private — stand to lose a considerable amount of power, property and money, both in the present as well as in the future, if the full significance and ramifications of sovereignty of Native peoples is finally acknowledged and acted upon. On the other hand , Native peoples cannot give full expression to their sovereignty as autonomous peoples unless they can exercise control over the land and resources that were taken away from them.

In fact, for Native people, the land plays a central role in their spiritual traditions, since it is a sacred responsibility that has been entrusted to them. They are the trustees of the land over which they have authority and on which they live their lives. If they are denied the capacity to nurture their relationship with the land and to fulfil their spiritual responsibilities as trustees, then they are being denied the opportunity to pursue a fundamental aspect of their religious tradition.

Presumably, Native people will be prepared, as they always have been, to enter a form of social contract with the non-Native peoples of Canada in which reciprocity, mutuality and co-operation become the central shaping forces of that contractual process. This means that the Native peoples will have to assume certain kinds of restraints upon their sovereignty and, therefore, they will not get everything they would like or to which they, morally, may be quite entitled. However, there must be a reciprocity to this constraining process. This means that all non-Native

Canadians are going to have constraints placed on their sovereignty as well with respect to the Native peoples, if we are to resolve the problem in as equitable fashion as possible under a very complicated and messy set of circumstances. This is unlikely to be a pain-free process on either side.

Nevertheless, as long as the problems surrounding the sovereignty of Native people continues to fester, then Canada will have lost its moral authority to speak out against intrusions upon the sovereignty of people which occurred in the past, are occurring now, and, very likely, will continue to occur in the future. For the Canadians to denounce the usurping or suppression of sovereignty in other places while standing neck deep in their own cess pool of usurpation and suppression, would be hypocritical in the extreme.

A Possible Solution

One possibility for resolving the sovereignty issue of Native and aboriginal people may revolve around the Yukon and Northwest Territories, together with some added incentives. More specifically, the government of Canada and the provinces could cede substantial portions of these territories to the Native and aboriginal peoples of Canada along with, say, certain areas of the northern portions of a number of provinces extending from British Columbia to Ontario. Such ceding would be done in partial exchange for all outstanding land claims in the various provinces.

From the perspective of the provincial and federal government, ceding the aforementioned land areas may be less conducive to the possibility of becoming entangled in the sort of complex legal/social problems where a spectrum of vested interests are at cross-purposes with one another. Said in another way, the above arrangement may least intrude upon, or interfere with, issues of sovereignty involving non-Native and non-aboriginal people.

To be sure, there will be some non-Natives who will be inconvenienced as a result of the proposed solution. Moreover, there undoubtedly will be economic interests which either will have to be terminated or run in accordance with the wishes of Native and aboriginal peoples. However, as is the case with some of the Native peoples who will be inconvenienced, some sort of monetary compensation may help assuage the inconvenience and difficulties suffered by non-Natives during the process of transition in which lands of sovereignty are generated for Native and aboriginal peoples.

By proposing that Native and aboriginal peoples be given custody of certain lands in the north and that these lands have provincial status, we believe that Native peoples would be in a much stronger, more tenable position through which to fulfil the spiritual responsibilities that have been entrusted to them. Furthermore, with such provincial status, we believe Native and aboriginal peoples would be in a much better position to assist the rest of us to work towards redeeming the Canadian environment as a whole and, thereby, fulfilling the sacred trust which many non-Natives also believe they have with respect to the land.

Canadian Identity:

This principle of sovereignty, and its attendant problems, actually goes to the heart of who we are as Canadians. Being a Canadian is not about CBS, Via Rail, the National Film Board, the RCMP, the Maple Leaf Flag or any other symbol one cares to choose as that which helps bind us to one another and helps define our collective identity as Canadians rather than as something else.

Wether we are talking about regions, provinces, municipalities, ministries, institutions or the federal government, we are talking about family, and we interact with the members of that family in a way that we don't interact with governments and people beyond our borders. The affection, pride or exasperation we feel toward one another has a political / cultural chemistry of its own that is not the same as the sort of chemistry that is generated by the affection, pride or exasperation one may feel towards other peoples. The straw that stirs the political / cultural chemistry of Canada and Canadians is the problem of sovereignty.

The history of French Canada or the Maritimes; the West or the Northern Territories; the provinces or the federal government; Native peoples or immigrants — all revolve around the search for asserting or claiming or fighting for their sovereignty . The story of Canada is a story of the attempts, failures and successes of a variety of people as they sought to enter into a social contract with other peoples. Such a social contract emphasized a reciprocity or mutuality of understanding and, therefore, a concomitant willingness to place constraints on their respective sovereignties in order to work out a system of rights, duties, freedoms and responsibilities which would enhance the quality of sovereignty of the parties involved in that social context.

The sense of betrayal that all peoples in Canada have experienced, at one time or another, can be traced directly to the perception, whether accurate or not, that there is an inequality in the relationship of reciprocity and mutuality that defines the social contract which links the sovereignty of one people with other people. Essentially, this means that when a people feel betrayed, they feel they have placed constraints on their own sovereignty as a people which either : (a) are not being reciprocated by others; or (b) are not leading to a sufficient level of enhancement in the quality of that aspect of their sovereignty which is not under constraint.

Sovereignty and Democracy

The issue of sovereignty involves the desire to have substantial control over, or play a fundamental role in, shaping one's destiny. Sovereignty involves the desire to have access to, and the opportunity to exercise, real power. Such power enables one to structure, orient and colour the character one's living will assume. Having access to real power in an unmediated fashion goes to the heart of the difference between representational and participatory democracy.

Representational democracy is about people giving up power to other people, i.e. the elected officials and those whom these elected officials appoint or hire. Representational democracy is mediated by, and filtered through, the understanding, likes and dislikes, weakness and strengths, ambitions and visions (if not delusions) of the people who are seeking power through elected office.

Participatory democracy is direct, responsive and focuses on sharing power with the many through a variety of channels which are specifically designed with such sharing in mind.

Once elected, governments, especially in a parliamentary system, often are not run along democratic lines but autocratic ones in which power hoarding and manipulation of power tend to become paramount. The world of 'realpolitik' is about seeking, gaining, wielding and hanging on to power. In this realm, the principles of democracy merely become watchwords that are used to clothe the naked power game in order to create an illusion of democratic modesty when, in reality, nothing of substantive value actually exists as far as democracy is concerned.

When the members of the Supreme Court make judgements, or when Parliamentary committees cast votes, or when government boards or commissions arrive at decisions, although the rule of the majority holds within the restricted confines of the court, committee, board, or commission, there is no guarantee that the respective judgements, votes and decisions reflect the wishes of the majority of the population. Consequently, all of these narrowly construed powers of majority rule constitute potential sources of encroachment upon the sovereignty of the people of the nation, province, region or municipality.

The individual often has little or no power to shape, constrain, modify or resist the aforementioned sorts of judgements, votes and decisions. Moreover, unless provisions are established that permit individuals, within certain limits, to have direct, unmediated access to the kind of power that will give them the opportunity to shape, constrain, modify or resist the process of 'realpolitik', then democracy becomes a vacuous exercise for the majority of people.

The operative principle in a democracy is not that the majority rule. Instead, what actually rules is a set of principles to which the overwhelming majority of the people agree or to which they are committed as a means of defining, establishing and regulating the social contract that underwrites a democracy. This set of principles both determines boundaries of the constraints as well as provides for a spectrum of degrees of freedom within, or through which, individuals and the collective pursue their respective sovereignties.

Representational democracy tends to spin one kind of set of constraints and degrees of freedom, while participatory democracy generates another kind of set of constraints and degrees of freedom. Naturally, there is likely to be a certain amount of overlap in the structural character of these two different approaches to implementing democracy, but in many ways, these two perceptions have quite different sorts of priorities, emphasis, interests, orientations and styles.

In effect, what rules a democracy, whether of a representational or participatory variety, is a process or procedural framework which is accepted by the majority of people. This process or framework must offer a countervailing influence against arbitrary, prejudicial or autocratic assaults upon, intrusions into, and usurpations of sovereignty. Moreover, what permits such a process or framework to rule is the degree of confidence which people have in the capacity of that process/framework to provide a means of both protecting as well as helping to actualize the sovereignty of individuals and the collective alike. Presently, the Canadian public, on both an individual and collective basis, is indicating that it has lost confidence in the capacity of the current approach to democracy in Canada to be able to resolve the problems which presently exist with respect to various aspects of the social contract– a contract that is supposed to bind us together within a common democratic framework.

Religious Freedom : Some Problems

Earlier, various aspects of the constitutional crisis concerning the Native peoples and the people of Quebec have been addressed. These sorts of issues are well known to Canadians. Indeed, much of the talk which is devoted to the current crisis usually focuses on these two peoples. However, there are others in Canada whose needs and problems must be taken into consideration if a revamped Constitution is to serve all Canadians.

For example, although many different ethnic groups and races are represented within Islam, as Muslims–as those who follow the Islamic religious tradition–all these various ethnic groups and races are one people. As a people, Muslims feel there are a number of ways in which their reality as a people is marginalized, if not denied, by the present constitutional arrangement.

To begin with, there is the question of religious freedom. While Canada prides itself as a nation in which, theoretically, individuals are free to commit themselves, if they wish, to a religion of their choice without any interference from the government, in practice this is not always the case.

Religion is not just a matter of having places of worship or having particular beliefs or values. Religion is also a matter of putting into practice what one believes, as well as acting in accordance with the values one holds in esteem. Moreover, these beliefs and values are not meant to be activated only when one enters a place of worship and switched off when one leaves that place of worship. Religious beliefs and values are meant to be put into practice in day-to-day life.

In Canada, there is said to be a separation between church and state, or temples and state, or mosque and state. This separation is intended to curtail the possibility that people in power may try to impose a certain kind of religious perspective– namely, their own– onto the citizens of the country, irrespective of the wishes of those citizens.

What, in fact, happens, however, is that government officials either: (a) use a variety of strategies, diversionary tactics and Machiavellian manipulations to camouflage their religious prejudices; or, (b) wield a set of non-religious biases in order to place a set of obstacles in the way of, as well as impose constraints upon, the way one can pursue one's religion of choice. Although, in the latter case, people in power claim that they are being neutral with respect to religious beliefs and practices, in reality there is a huge difference between being neutral and being oriented in an anti-religious manner.

No jurist or government has ventured forth with sufficient courage to delineate, in a legal opinion or government policy, just precisely what is meant or entitled or encompassed by the notion that Canada is founded "upon principles that recognize the supremacy of God"; nor have they said what it means for such principles to *recognize* the supremacy of God; nor have they said what the ramifications of such recognition and supremacy are; nor have they said what they mean by God. In fact almost every decision the courts and governments have made virtually ignore such questions, problems and issues.

Becoming a loyal citizen of Canada has nothing to do with being assimilated into some sort of pre-fabricated, monolithic, standard set of assumptions, values, beliefs, commitments and practices which public education, is among other things, intended to promote. Supposedly, such a monolithic process constitutes an allegedly unifying social and political medium. Yet, one can be taught values such as freedom, rights, democracy, social responsibility, justice and multiculturalism without going to public school and without presupposing that everyone must engage these topics in precisely the same way.

On the other hand, public education cannot teach,say, a Muslim child how to be a good Muslim. In addition, public education cannot actively assist a Muslim child to establish an Islamic identity or to adopt an Islamic way of life. Public schools cannot do this because they virtually have no expertise in, or understanding of, what Islam involves.They do not teach Arabic or the Qur'an or the Sunnah (practices) of the Prophet Muhammad (peace be upon him) ; nor do they teach Shari'ah (Islamic Law); nor do public schools have the capacity to help the individual learn how to put all of this in to practise on a day-to-day basis

Muslims are told, however, that such educational topics are not the responsibility of the public education system. Such issues are the responsibility of parents and must be done at night or on weekends or during the summer. Consequently, a supposedly neutral state has made it a matter of law, practise and convention that the public education system, despite being funded by Muslim tax money, cannot accommodate an Islamic education.

Muslims are free, of course, to begin their own educational system, but they are not permitted to have access to the taxes which they contribute to the government in order to be able to use that money for the purposes of religious education. Thus Muslims — and this is also true of Jewish, Hindu, Buddhist, Sikh, Native peoples and the Protestant Christians — must bear a special burden of paying twice if they want an education that reflects the values and practices of their religious tradition. The Catholic community, on the other hand, is permitted, more so in some places than in other places, to have access to public money to promote an educational process that does reflect the community's religious values and practices.

Such inconsistency is indefensible: morally, philosophically and logically. It is not neutral. It is discriminatory. It does not reflect the spirit of multiculturalism.

The aforementioned sort of inconsistency clearly points out that the religious freedom of a great many people in Canada, Muslims included, has been seriously circumscribed and inhibited. This is the case since the powers that be have taken something of fundamental importance to the pursuit and practice of religion — namely, education — and placed obstacle after obstacle in the path of certain peoples and communities of Canada with respect to their ability to pursue their religion of choice freely

These obstacles prevent many, if not most, religious minorities in Canada from having access to anything but a curriculum of subjugation to a preconceived master plan of assimilation. As a result, these people and communities are required to ; (a) submit to the values and practices of public education which are often antithetical to religious values and practices; or, (b) pay twice for the kind of education they want.

Equality is best served by means of offering a diversity of alternatives. Educational programmes do not have to be the same to be equal. The conditions of equality are satisfied when different educational systems meet the needs and reflect the values of the communities being served, respectively, by these different educational systems.

One may never be able to achieve a perfect fit between the diversity of educational systems which are offered and the diversity of values which exist in the community. Nevertheless, one needs to struggle in the direction of providing more flexibility and alternatives than presently exist.

Family and Personal Law

Another example of how Muslims are being prevented from being able to realize the promise of religious freedom concerns the area of Muslim family and personal law.This area covers issues such as marriage, divorce, separation, maintenance, child support and inheritance.

In Islam, Muslims are required to follow a set of constraints and degrees of freedom that have been established in Divine Law. Following Divine Law is at the heart of what being Muslim means. Muslims are not free, according to their likes and dislikes, to pick and choose what they will and will not do with respect to Divine Law. Divine Law is inherent in, and presupposed by, the practices of the Islamic religious tradition. Muslim personal/ family law is an integral part of such Islamic practices,

Muslims in Canada have no wish to impose their perspective, or way of doing things, on other Canadians. In other words, Muslims are not requesting that the non-Muslim people of Canada adhere to our practices, beliefs and values concerning Muslim personal / family law . Such an imposition would be an intrusion on the sovereignty of the non-Muslim peoples of Canada.

As indicated many times in the foregoing pages however, sovereignty is a function of reciprocity in which there is a dynamic balance between the rights and duties of care. This balance should shape our interactions with respect to one another. When such a balance is missing, then steps must be taken to re-establish reciprocity. In this regard, Muslims feel that such an imbalance does exist in Canada in a variety of areas, one of which deals with the issues surrounding the implementation of Muslim personal/ family law.

Many things in Canada are permitted as long as the people are consenting adults. Presumably, therefore, Muslim personal/ family law, which also involves the actions of consenting adults, is not at all inconsistent with some of the basic philosophical principles at work in Canadian society. Nevertheless, the likelihood of consenting Muslim adults being permitted to arrange things in accordance with the Islamic principles underlying Muslim personal/ family law is beset by a variety of problems.

Chief among the difficulties which attempts to establish Muslim personal / family law may encounter in Canada is the resistance of the legal and political community. After all, the arguments might go, there are already programmes, laws, procedures and policies in place of handling matters of marriage, divorce, separation, maintenance, child support and inheritance. These programmes, laws, and so on have evolved over a period of time and represent the way things are done in this society. Muslims who live in this society, therefore, are obliged to accommodate themselves to the existing way of handling these issues.

The problem with this sort of argument is that it totally ignores the issues of religious freedom to which Muslims are entitled. As previously indicated, for Muslims, religion is not just an abstract set of ideas that are to be taken out on special occasions and dusted off as Muslims indulge themselves in some sort of nostalgic ritual in homage to the past. Religion must be lived; it must be put into practice; it must be followed and adhered to with one's actions

Muslim personal/family law is not an arbitrary afterthought that has been tacked onto Islamic religious beliefs and practices. Such law is rooted in, and derived from, the two most basic sources of Islamic law: namely, (a) the Qur'an (the Holy Book of God's Revelation); and, (b) the practices and teachings of the Prophet Muhammad (peace be upon him) who is accepted by all Muslims as the one who was most intimate with, and had the most profound understanding of, and commitment to, God's plan for the Muslim community.

Repeatedly, the Qur'an enjoins and instructs Muslims to follow the Qur'an and the example of the holy Prophet Muhammad (p.b.u.h.). Again and again, Muslims are informed in the Qur'an that one cannot consider oneself a Muslim – one who submits to the command of God-unless one adheres to the guidelines, counsel, principles, beliefs and practices that are related to human beings through the Qur'an and the Prophet Muhammad (p.b.u.h.).

Part of the guidelines, counsel, and principles to which Muslims must adhere are the spectrum of constraints and degrees of freedom which give expression to Muslim personal/family law. Consequently, if Muslims are prevented from implementing such law, they are prevented from freely pursuing and committing themselves to the Islamic religious tradition, since adhering to the various aspects of Islamic family and personal law are all acts of worship.

If one cannot worship God as one is required to do by the tenets of one's tradition, then severe, oppressive constraints have been placed upon one's capacity to exercise religious freedom. Such constraints on, and impediments to, the exercise of religious freedom are especially oppressive in the case of those religious practices that do not require sacrifices from, or place any hardships on, people outside or within the given religious tradition.

In point of fact, the implementation of Muslim personal/family law would not entail sacrifices or hardships for anyone. This would be the case irrespective of whether one were considering Muslims or non-Muslims.

There may be people within the Muslim community who are enamoured with the Canadian way of dealing with and arranging issues of family/personal law. Those people should be left free to choose whatever they believe to be in their best interests.

There are many other people in the Muslim community, on the other hand, who feel that their sovereignty as human beings, in general, and as Muslims, in particular, has been intruded upon, undermined and marginalized through being prevented from following the requirements of their own religious tradition.

The irony of this situation is that the principles, methods, values and safeguards inherent in Islamic family/personal law are every bit as sophisticated as anything in the Canadian legal system. In fact, many aspects of Canadian law dealing with issues of personal/family law have begun, only recently, to put into practice what has long been an integral part of Islamic law. For example, the easing of restrictions with respect to divorce, which have been introduced into Canadian law just a few years ago, have been a part of Islamic law for more than 1400 years.

One also might maintain that, in many ways, Islamic personal/family law is more flexible, accessible, simple and progressive than are its Canadian counterparts. For instance, human beings have both strengths and weaknesses, and, in addition, human circumstances are quite variable and diversified. Rather than impose one system of law on everyone, Islam provides people with a variety of alternatives from which to choose the one which best meets the individual's needs and inclinations. Generally, this is not the case in the Canadian legal system, although Quebec does practice a different brand of civil law based on principles drawn from a French/Roman code of law.

Finally, many of the things for which people in the feminist movement have been fighting for many years now have been regular features of Islamic personal/family law for more than eleven hundred years. Thus, the sovereignty of women is a principle which is firmly established in Islam, and such sovereignty encompasses a great many entitlements that have surfaced only recently in North America.

For example, the right of women to be able to specify, by way of contract, precisely what arrangements are to be observed by the man during a marriage has been available to Muslim women since the early part of the ninth century. Only people's ignorance of Islam- including, unfortunately, far too many Muslims themselves - has made this truth appear otherwise.

Issues of sovereignty and religious freedom aside, there are a number of advantages that could accrue to Canada in general if official recognition concerning the right of Muslims to implement their own personal/family law were granted. To begin with, this recognition could save Canadian/provincial taxpayers money since Muslims would be underwriting the financial costs of administering and running such a system themselves. For example, tribunals for handling dispute resolution issues in areas covered by Muslim personal/family law would be set up, staffed and monitored by people from the Muslim community. All of this would be financed by user fees and contributions from the Muslim community.

Furthermore, by assuming such responsibilities, Muslims would be taking a certain burden from the shoulders of an already overwrought judicial system. This could result in a more efficient and responsive judicial process for other, non-Muslim Canadians.

The bottom line on all this is as follows. If Muslims were permitted to govern their own affairs in the realm of personal/family law, then a win-win situation would have been granted for Muslims and non-Muslims alike. Muslims would have the opportunity to realize more of their religious freedom than previously had been the case, and non-Muslims would have a more efficient, less costly, and less burdened system for dealing with their own approach to family/personal law.

In addition, by permitting alternative methods of dispute resolution in matters of family/personal law, one would be providing Muslims with a way of doing things that reflects fundamental aspects of their own sense of justice. As a result, Muslims would be shown that the promise of multiculturalism, when properly implemented, is capable of creating conditions conducive to the generation of peace of mind and happiness that come with true autonomy. Rather than feeling alienated within Canada, Muslims would become integrated, active participants in the Canadian mosaic.

Some people may have reservations about the foregoing possibilities, feeling that if such recognition were given, then one is inviting anarchy and chaos into our society. This would be the case, or so the argument might claim, because legal authorities and governments would no longer have control over what Muslims do in the areas covered by personal/family law. Moreover, what if problems arose during the administering of such a system? How would they be handled?

Although Muslims are as prone to folly, mistakes and ill-considered actions as are non-Muslims, Muslims are not children. Among them one will find intelligent, knowledgeable, insightful, wise, committed, just, compassionate, honest, sincere, hardworking, creative people. While problems undoubtedly will arise, it is rather paternalistic ethnocentrism which supposes that Muslims are not capable of resolving, within the limits of human capacity to achieve such things, their own problems in ways that utilize values, beliefs, principles and practices that exhibit integrity, responsibility, fairness and wisdom.

All kinds of organizations, institutions, administrative tribunals, universities and colleges are permitted to run their own internal affairs with little or no interference from the courts and the government. Canadian society has not disintegrated as a result of this.

Canada also will not fall apart or into an abyss of chaos if Muslims are permitted to control their own affairs in the realm of Muslim personal/family law. Canadians should look at this matter, not as if they are losing control, but as if they were broadening the mandate of sovereignty, and thereby enhancing the quality of that sovereignty. In any event, establishing such a system of law is not something which is either impossible or impractical.

The Islamic Imperative

The most fundamental reason for the plea concerning the possible implementation of Muslim personal/family law in Canada is a matter of responsibility. This is the obligation we have as Muslims, both individually and collectively, to seek to establish an environment which, as much as is feasible and practical in a non-Muslim country, is conducive to living in accordance with the way in which Allah would wish Muslims to live.

Through the principles, values and precepts which have been disclosed by means of the Qur'an as well as exemplified in the teachings and actions of the Prophet Muhammad (peace be upon him), many guidelines have been given with respect to the manner in which, among other things, matters of personal/family law should be conducted. These guidelines are not arbitrary, peripheral issues. They have been established with the structural character of human nature clearly in focus and are intended to assist us to find harmonious solutions to the problems which inevitably arise in personal and family matters.

However, solving problems is not, in and of itself, the only rule to be used in measuring the propriety of various modes of conflict resolution. For Muslims, the *sine qua non* of action is that it be undertaken with the intention of submitting oneself to Allah's will such that the action is done for the sake of Allah, as an expression of worship and love of Him.

If the governmental authorities and judicial system of a non-Muslim country have in place methods of conflict resolution that are rooted in principles and values that are governed by motives other than the intention to please God or which do not serve the best interests of the Muslim community or which contain less wisdom than do the guidelines which have been given by Allah and His Prophet, then Muslims place their spiritual and social lives in dire peril when they submit to that which is other than what Allah has ordained for those who wish to submit themselves to Him.

This struggle for an Islamic identity by means of the founding of institutions, processes and a framework that facilitates a way of life which reflects Islamic values, principles and methods is not a matter of trying to impose a Muslim perspective on non-Muslims. Furthermore, the desire for the implementation of Muslim personal/family law is not a demand that Muslims should be treated differently from other people in Canada. Rather, we are simply asking that Canada live up to: (a) the preamble of the Canadian Constitution's Charter of Rights which stipulates that Canada is a country founded on principles which recognize the supremacy of God; and, (b) the guarantee in the Charter of Rights concerning freedom of religion.

We do not believe that freedom of religion can be restricted to meaning only that one is free to think what one wants about religious issues or that one is free to perform acts of worship in one's home or place of community worship. The very nature of religion has everywhere and at all times been intended to extend into realms which fall beyond the boundaries of the home or the mosque, temple or church. Religion is a way of life, a set of values, a framework which is intended to penetrate into, shape, colour and orient all facets of an individual's life.

Naturally, due to the all–inclusive charter of religion, there is a potential for conflicts when one set of religious practices comes into antagonistic opposition to some other set of religious practices. Nevertheless, one of the beautiful, appealing aspects of the desire for seeking to implement Muslim personal/ family law in Canada on a voluntary basis and in co-operation with the existing judicial structure in this country is that no one will be affected by such a system except those who wish this to be the case. Moreover, the effort to implement Muslim/personal law is designed in a cost-effective, responsible fashion, to increase the degrees of freedom in a democratic society without, simultaneously, usurping the rights or freedoms of anyone (Muslim or non-Muslim) under the existing constitution.

Due to the present atmosphere of constitutional crisis, multicultural debates and an apparently genuine receptivity to, and preparedness for, change on the part of many Canadians, we believed that the time was right for communicating some of the concerns of Muslims to the people of Canada. While we doubt that the objectives of our campaign will be realized prior to, or in conjunction with, the resolution, for better or worse, of the present constitutional debate in Canada, nonetheless, we believe that the legitimacy and tenability of our quest will carry over into the post-crisis era of Canadian history.

Aside from the foregoing considerations, there is an element of urgency which modulates everything that has been said up to this point. More specifically, there is an increasing number of problems arising in the Muslim community in Canada involving issues of marriage, divorce, maintenance, child support, custody and inheritance.

Neither the present secular, judicial system nor the uncoordinated and largely unorganised efforts of the Muslim community is proving to be adequate to the task of resolving these problems in a manner that really serves the needs of the Muslim community, as a community, rather than as a collectivity of groups and individuals who have been woven into something of an arbitrary, social patchwork quilt whose design reflects a whole variety of influences which are often in fundamental conflict with one another. The potential for human tragedy, in general, and the undermining of spirituality, in particular, is very frightening under the present circumstances in

Canada. Consequently, the implementation of Muslim personal/ family law in Canada might go along way towards helping to lend stability and constructive direction to the Muslim community here.

[9]

Muslim Women and 'Islamic Divorce' in England

LUCY CARROLL

Three important changes in English law in the past quarter of a century have opened the doors of the English matrimonial Courts to Muslim spouses resident in England. Prior to 1973, the English Courts exercised divorce jurisdiction on the basis of domicile; spouses resident but not domiciled in England could not invoke the jurisdiction of the English Court to terminate their marriage. Until 1972 the English Courts refused jurisdiction in regard to all 'polygamous' marriages, defining this term to encompass a marriage *de facto* monogamous but 'potentially polygamous' in the sense that according to the rites by which the marriage had been solemnized, one of the parties was permitted to marry again during the subsistence of the marriage. This provision most importantly barred the English matrimonial Courts to spouses validly married according to Muslim rites in a jurisdiction where polygamy was permitted to Muslims (for instance, Pakistan or India). At the same time, if the parties (or one of them) were domiciled in England at the time of the foreign Muslim marriage, it was generally assumed that the marriage would be considered void in English law because an English domiciliary has no capacity to enter into a 'polygamous', including a 'potentially polygamous', marriage.[1]

The Domicile and Matrimonial Proceedings Act of 1973 expanded the jurisdiction of the English Courts by permitting them to entertain divorce petitions in circumstances where one of the spouses had been resident within the United Kingdom for a period of twelve months prior to the presentation of the petition, and irrespective of the domicile of the parties. The Matrimonial Proceedings (Polygamous Marriages) Act, 1972, removed the bar on matrimonial relief previously raised by the fact that the foreign marriage was either potentially or actually polygamous.[2] And the 1983 decision of the Court of Appeal in *Hussain v. Hussain*[3] held that the Muslim marriage contracted abroad by a Muslim man domiciled in England was not void because 'potentially polygamous'. The Court pointed out that the Pakistani bride, according to her personal law (Pakistani Muslim law as the law of her domicile) was not permitted another husband during the subsistence of the marriage, while the husband, according to his personal law (English law as the law of his domicile) was not permitted another wife during the subsistence of the marriage. If neither spouse were permitted to marry an additional partner, where, the Court asked, was the 'potential' for polygamy.

Although after the statutory reforms of 1972 and 1973, either of the Muslim spouses resident in England might avail themselves of the matrimonial remedies available to them through the English Courts, if the parties were domiciled in a country where Muslim law would be applicable to the marriage, the husband was more likely to choose to execute a *talaq* in preference to pursuing judicial proceedings—or permitting his wife to proceed with her divorce petition. Again, changes in English law in the past quarter of a century both restricted the husband's access to *talaq* (by making it clear that an extra-judicial event which took place within the jurisdiction of the English

Court would not effectively dissolve the marriage in English law), and considerably liberalized the rules for recognition of a 'procedural' *talaq*[4] effected abroad (by permitting such a *talaq* to take place in a country with which one of the spouses was connected by ties of nationality or habitual residence, rather than merely in the country in which the spouses were domiciled).

These developments, which were largely concessions—perhaps long over due concessions—to the multi-cultural nature of post World War II England and the presence of a significant Muslim minority, produced a disturbing reaction on the part of what might best be termed the spokesmen of Muslim male interests. It will be most convenient to examine individually the various components of the evolving situation.

I. Divorce and Muslim Law

Extra-Judicial Divorce by the Muslim Husband (talaq)

One of the features of Muslim law best known in the West concerns the facility for easy divorce which is provided to the husband. By the simple pronouncement of a verbal formula the husband can bring the marriage to an end; under the unreformed traditional law, this can be accomplished instantly and irrevocably if the husband is a Sunni. If the husband were a Hanafi (as are the overwhelming majority of South Asian Muslims; the vast majority of Muslims in England are of South Asian extraction), the fact that he uttered the fateful words while in a state of intoxication or uncontrollable rage, or the fact that he did not mean them or immediately repented having spoken them is of no legal significance—the marriage is terminated if the *talaq* were pronounced in irrevocable form.

However, the Pakistan Muslim Family Laws Ordinance, promulgated by Ayub Khan's martial law government in 1961, (*inter alia*) introduced (section 7) some minimal restrictions on the Muslim husband's rights of easy extra-judicial divorce[5] by requiring that any *talaq* pronouncement be notified to a designated local official and to the wife, and decreeing that no *talaq* would ripen into an actual divorce until ninety days after such notification had been received. During the interval, the *talaq* pronouncement remains revocable (and if revoked, will not take effect as a divorce); during this interval also the local official is enjoined to undertake attempts at reconciliation of the spouses, although whether or not he carries out, or attempts to carry out, this responsibility has no effect on the finality of the *talaq* and the effectiveness of the divorce once the ninety days have expired without a revocation of the pronouncement being issued by the husband. The most important effect of the Muslim Family Laws Ordinance, as far as *talaq* is concerned, is to convert the immediately final and irrevocable triple *talaq*—the form of *talaq* most prevalent among South Asian Hanafis in spite of its failure to conform to the pattern laid down in the Quran—into the equivalent of a single revocable *talaq*.

There are thus four procedural requirements for effecting a divorce by *talaq* valid in Pakistani law:

1. Pronouncement of the *talaq* formula.
2. Notification of the pronouncement to the requisite local official.
3. Notification of the pronouncement to the wife.
4. The passage of ninety days during which the husband refrains from revoking the pronouncement.

These 'procedures',[6] mandatory for the execution of a *talaq* effective under Pakistani law, induced the English Courts to conclude that a Pakistani *talaq* constituted a divorce "obtained by means of ... other proceedings" in the context of the Recognition of Foreign Divorces and Legal Separations Act, 1971.[7]

Recognition of talaq *Divorce in English Law*

Prior to 1971, English law in regard to dissolutions of marriage occurring under and according to a foreign legal system was clear and concise: a foreign divorce would be recognized under the common law rules as a valid divorce in English law if it were valid by the law of the spouses' domicile (which, at that time, meant the domicile of the husband). Assuming such a divorce to be valid under the law of the spouses' domicile, it appeared that a marriage could be brought to an end in English law by an extra-judicial *talaq* pronounced in England.[8] The common law rules were substantially modified by the Matrimonial Causes Act, 1973, which (i) provided (section 16(1)) that no procedure occurring within the United Kingdom could be recognized as dissolving a marriage unless instituted in a Court of law;[9] (ii) barred the recognition of a divorce obtained other than "by means of judicial or other proceedings" if both the spouses had been habitually resident in the UK for a period of twelve months prior to the divorce (section 16(2));[10] and (iii) ended the wife's domicile of dependency (section 1). Recognizing that the spouses may have separate domiciles (the wife no longer automatically acquiring her husband's domicile on marriage) meant that henceforth a divorce could only be recognized on the basis of the common law rule (foreign domicile) if it were valid according to the law of the domicile of each spouse; recognition was precluded if one of the spouses were domiciled in the UK.

Meanwhile, the Recognition of Foreign Divorces and Legal Separations Act, 1971, provided a format[11] (inspired by—but going much further than required by—the 1970 Hague Convention on the same subject) for recognition of divorces "obtained by means of judicial or other proceedings" in a country with which at least one of the parties was connected by ties of nationality, habitual residence, or domicile (including domicile as defined by the foreign country in question). The requirements for recognition of a foreign divorce under 'code' section of the 1971 Act were much more lenient[12] than those laid down by the (revised) common law rules, which were preserved by the Act of 1971, and modified by the Act of 1973.[13]

There are thus two distinct sets of criteria under which a foreign divorce might be recognized in English law. The common law rules cannot be invoked if either spouse is domiciled in England or if the spouses have (after the Act of 1986, if *one* spouse has) been habitually resident in the UK for twelve months prior to the divorce proceedings. Neither of these bars automatically prevents recognition of a foreign divorce under the legislation implementing the Hague Convention.

Extra-judicial divorces or dissolutions of marriage raise their own peculiar evidential problems, dramatically demonstrated on two occasions when the English Court held that an extra-judicial act or event had had the effect, under the relevant foreign law, of terminating the marriage, when in fact the act or event had had absolutely no effect at all on the matrimonial status of the parties according to the law of the foreign jurisdiction.[14]

The more immediately relevant problem raised by recognition of foreign divorces derived from the fact that the English Court had no jurisdiction to deal with ancillary matters unless it itself dissolved the marriage. Thus, recognizing a foreign divorce as effectively terminating the marriage, deprived the English Court of any power to make financial orders in favor of the discarded wife. Although this difficultv could arise in regard to any foreign divorce (judicial or extra-judicial), it arose predictably and cogently in regard to *talaq* divorces due to the fact that Muslim law recognizes neither any concept of division of matrimonial assets nor alimony on divorce.[15] The woman divorced by a *talaq* recognized under the regime of 1971/1973 had little redress unless a sizable *mahr* (dower) had been pledged in her favor by her bridegroom at the time of the marriage. A major incentive for a Muslim husband in England to seek to dissolve the marriage by *talaq*, rather than petitioning for divorce in the English Courts (or allowing his wife to proceed with her divorce petition) is the desire to avoid any financial responsibility for his divorced wife.

The inability of the English Court to protect the interests of the woman whose marriage was dissolved by a foreign divorce entitled to recognition in English law under the more liberal recognition rules, was addressed in Part III of the Matrimonial and Family Proceedings Act, 1984. This statute empowered the English Courts to grant financial relief to one or other spouse even in cases where the marriage had not been dissolved by the English Court.[16]

'Blackmail' of Muslim Wives in England

By no means was it a coincidence that just when it appeared clear that legislation would be passed empowering the English Courts to grant ancillary relief in cases where the marriage had been dissolved by a foreign divorce entitled to recognition under English law, spokesmen for male Muslim interests (in many circumstances this phrase is preferable to the term 'fundamentalists') began putting it about that under Muslim law a woman is not entitled to a divorce without her husband's consent, and that no Muslim marriage can be dissolved in a 'religious' sense unless the husband pronounces a *talaq*.

Although this proposition is untrue as regards Muslim law, note how closely the alleged position of the Muslim woman so postulated approximates the position of the woman in orthodox *Jewish law*. Curiously, it appears that the fallacious proposition concerning *Muslim law* was readily and uncritically accepted by English legal circles simply because of this irrelevant similarity (see also EN 17 below).

I first encountered this fallacious proposition during the course of a question period following my lectures on Muslim marriage and divorce in English law at a training session for solicitors organized by the Greater Manchester Legal Services Committee in November 1983. Having convinced my audience that Muslim law did not in all circumstances require the husband's consent to the dissolution of the marriage and did permit the Muslim wife to obtain a judicial divorce in the face of her husband's opposition, I made many (unsuccessful) attempts to locate the source of the propaganda that seemed to be being put about, particularly in the Bolton area.

The following summer, two well-meaning Members of Parliament (Leo Abse and Peter Thurnham) proposed, in quite dramatic speeches, an amendment[17] to the Matrimonial and Family Proceedings Bill which, the proposers believed, would protect Muslim women who were being 'blackmailed' by their husbands and forced to pay heavily for their spouses' consent to a 'religious' divorce.[18]

.... Under Muslim law a man may have many wives, but a woman only one husband. Thus religious divorce is essential for a Muslim woman who wishes to remarry according to her faith, but a Muslim man can be content with civil divorce alone, as he does not have religious inhibitions about remarrying as often as he wishes.

Thousands of brides face that predicament. They are vulnerable to blackmail by their husbands, who will agree to a religious divorce only for a consideration....

Cases have been brought to my attention in Bolton, of which my constituency is a part. In one case, the parties had gained British nationality but had been separated for five years with a decree absolute. The ex-husband would not, however, grant a religious divorce. He demanded £5000 and the return of the wedding jewellery as an inducement

In the second case, the husband and wife were married in India. After an unhappy relationship in Great Britain the husband sent his wife's passport to the Home Office in an attempt to get her removed, as she did not have British nationality. He eventually agreed to a religious divorce, but only if he did not have to pay maintenance and if she returned the wedding jewellery to him.

In the third case, both sides had British nationality, and the matter was settled only after violent persuasion by the wife's family ...

In the case of Mrs. Patel, her relatives fulfilled the husband's demands by paying him £4000 and returning the marriage jewellery to obtain a religious divorce. In the fifth case, the wife was not a British citizen and her relatives paid money to obtain a religious divorce after the husband threatened to arrange a deportation.[19]

Fortunately, the proposed amendment was withdrawn, the Solicitor General promising to look into the matter.

Unfortunately, the damage was done. The statements in Parliament had only served to give publicity to a grossly erroneous view of Muslim law and to place the interests of Muslim women in the United Kingdom at even greater risk.[20]

Judicial Divorce and Muslim Law

The main distinction between the rights of the Muslim spouses in obtaining a non-consensual divorce is that while the husband can effect a divorce easily without his wife's consent by pronouncement of *talaq*; the wife whose husband will not agree to a divorce (or who will agree only on terms she is unwilling to accept) has to go to Court.

All schools of Muslim law recognize that the wife has a right to approach the Court for a judicial dissolution of her marriage. Such a judicial divorce is as final, and as much a 'religious divorce', as is an extra-judicial divorce effected with the husband's consent and approval.

There is, however, considerable divergence among the schools of Islamic law concerning the precise grounds which would entitle a Muslim wife to judicial dissolution of her marriage. The classical Hanafi school is by far the most restrictive in this regard. For precisely this reason, comprehensive reform of the classical Hanafi law has been accomplished in several countries since the initial reform introduced in the Ottoman Empire in 1915. Since the majority of Muslims in the UK trace their ancestry to South Asia, the obvious statute to examine to refute the claims of the spokesmen of the interests of Muslim males is the Dissolution of Muslim Marriages Act, 1939.[21]

The statement of objects and reasons issued with the Bill which subsequently became the Dissolution of Muslim Marriages, Act, 1939, is set out below and explains the concerns behind this Act, which has now been on the statutes books of the territory presently comprising the states of Pakistan, Bangladesh, and India for more than half a century.

> There is no proviso in the Hanafi code of Muslim law enabling a married Muslim woman to obtain a decree from the Court dissolving her marriage in case the husband neglects to maintain her, makes her life miserable by deserting or persistently maltreating her, or absconds leaving her unprovided for, and under certain other circumstances. The absence of such provision has entailed unspeakable misery to innumerable Muslim women in British India. The Hanafi jurists, however, have clearly laid down that in cases in which the application of Hanafi law causes hardship, it is permissible to apply the provisions of the Maliki, Shafi'i or Hanbali law. Acting on this principle the *ulama* [i.e. religious scholars and functionaries] have issued *fatwas* [i.e. opinions concerning the religious law] to the effect that in cases enumerated in clause 3, Part A of this Bill [contained in section 2 of the resultant Act], a married woman may obtain a decree dissolving her marriage. A lucid exposition of this principle can be found in the book called *al-Hilat al-Najizah* published by Maulana Ashraf Ali Saheb who has made an exhaustive study of the provisions of Maliki law which, under the circumstances prevailing in India, may be applied to such cases. This has been approved by a large number of *ulama* who have put their seals of approval on the book.
>
> As the Courts are sure to hesitate to apply the Maliki law to the case of a [non-Maliki] woman, legislation recognising and enforcing the above mentioned principle is called for in order to relieve the sufferings of countless Muslim women.[22]

The background to this statute, enacted during the British period by rulers who had generally refrained from interference in the personal laws of its subjects is extremely interesting.

In the unique circumstances of British-India a few desperate Hanafi women had discovered that a way out of intolerable matrimonial situations existed if they were willing to apostatize, even temporarily, from Islam. In Hanafi law, apostasy on the part of a Muslim spouse dissolves a Muslim marriage; a female apostate would, however, be incarcerated until she repented of her error and then remarried on a minimal *mahr* (dower) to the man to whom she had been married at the time of her apostasy. Apostasy was not a crime in British-India; indeed, the Christian missionaries were actively seeking converts and the Evangelical lobby was strong. It is to the latter that must be credited the Caste Disabilities Removal Act, 1850, (otherwise known as the Freedom of Religion Act), which declared that the apostate lost none of his pre-existing rights (particularly rights of property and inheritance) by virtue of leaving or being expelled from caste or religious communion.

Perhaps somewhat illogically, the British-Indian Courts when confronted with the question decided that, although much of the law of apostasy was not applicable in British-India, that part of Muslim law which decreed the dissolution of the apostate's marriage was in force. A Muslim woman could thus easily shed the husband she despised by converting to Christianity. She could, and often did, then reconvert to Islam as a single woman.

Although the number of women who resorted to such desperate measures was small both numerically and statistically, the cases that did occur were widely publicized in the Urdu press and aroused considerable concern in the Muslim community. Petitions and memorials were submitted calling upon the government to overrule the Courts which were issuing declarations recognizing the dissolution of her marriage occasioned by the apostasy of the Muslim wife. The government was reluctant to take any action unless some alternative remedy were made available to the women who were using apostasy as a means of obtaining matrimonial relief otherwise unavailable to them. Meanwhile, many distinguished *ulema* issued *fatwas* proposing that Hanafi women should be allowed access to judicial divorce on grounds recognized by other Sunni schools, particularly Maliki.

The Act of 1939 was essentially a compromise: it entitled Muslim women to petition for divorce on the grounds set out below (which had been adopted from Maliki law), while at the same time laying down that apostasy on the part of a married Muslim woman would no longer have the effect of dissolving her marriage (Section 4).

Section 2 of the statute sets out the grounds on which a South Asian Muslim wife may petition the Court for divorce:

> 2. A woman married under Muslim law shall be entitled to obtain a decree for the dissolution of her marriage on any one or more of the following grounds, namely:
>
> (i) that the whereabouts of the husband have not been known for a period of four years;
>
> (ii) that the husband has neglected or has failed to provide for her maintenance for a period of two years;
>
> (iii) that the husband has been sentenced to imprisonment for a period of seven years or upwards;
>
> (iv) that the husband has failed to perform without reasonable cause, his marital obligations for a period of three years;
>
> (v) that the husband was impotent at the time of marriage and continues to be so;
>
> (vi) that the husband has been insane for a period of two years or is suffering from leprosy or a virulent venereal disease;
>
> (vii) that she, having been given in marriage by her father or other guardian before she attained the age of fifteen years, repudiated the marriage before attaining the age of eighteen years;
> provided that the marriage has not been consummated;[23]
>
> (viii) that the husband treats her with cruelty, that is to say:
>
> (a) habitually assaults her or makes her life miserable by cruelty of conduct even if such conduct does not amount to physical ill-treatment, or
>
> (b) associates with women of evil repute or leads an infamous life, or
>
> (c) attempts to force her to lead an immoral life, or
>
> (d) disposes of her property or prevents her exercising her legal rights over it, or
>
> (e) obstructs her in the observance of her religious profession or practice, or
>
> (f) if he has more wives than one, does not treat her equitably in accordance with the injunctions of the Quran;

(ix) on any other ground which is recognized as valid for the dissolution of marriages under Muslim law.

In Pakistan and Bangladesh the Dissolution of Muslim Marriages Act was amended by the Muslim Family Laws Ordinance, 1961, and a further ground on which a wife may seek a judicial divorce enumerated: "that the husband has taken an additional wife in contravention of the provisions of the Muslim Family Laws Ordinance, 1961", i.e., without the requisite prior permission of the Arbitration Council.

It is perhaps worth noting that the Act of 1939 is of general application, and applies to Muslim women in Pakistan, Bangladesh, and India, whether Hanafi or Shafi'i, Sunni or Shi'i. It should also be noted that the fact that a woman has recourse to the Dissolution of Muslim Marriages Act to secure judicial divorce does not affect her financial claims against her husband: section 5 of the Act specifically provides— "Nothing contained in this Act shall affect any right which a married woman may have under Muslim law to her dower [*mahr*] or any part thereof on the dissolution of the marriage". She would, of course, also be entitled to maintenance from her husband during the period of *iddah*. It should also be pointed out, and with some emphasis, that there is nothing to be found in the 1939 Act to the effect that the husband's consent is required for the divorce to become final, or imposing the requirement that the husband pronounce a *talaq* before the wife is free to remarry according to Muslim law and Muslim rites—nothing in fact in any way comparable to the terms proposed to be introduced into English law by the Abse-Thurnham amendment.

The grounds available under the Dissolution of Muslim Marriages Act are not really very different from those available under the English legislation. Most divorce petitions in a contested action rely on either five years' separation or unreasonable behavior to establish irretrievable breakdown of the marriage necessary to obtain a divorce under the Matrimonial Causes Act, 1973. It could be argued that the former ground is less lenient than those available under the Dissolution of Muslim Marriages Act, which entitle a wife to divorce on grounds of either failure to maintain for two years or failure to perform marital obligations for three years. The import of the English expression "has behaved in such a way that the petitioner cannot reasonably be expected to live with the respondent" is much the same as the comparable clause in the Dissolution of Muslim Marriages Act, "makes her life miserable by cruelty of conduct even if such conduct does not amount to physical ill-treatment".

A divorce granted by the Courts of India, Pakistan, or Bangladesh under the Dissolution of Muslim Marriages Act does not require the husband's consent or approval; the Muslim wife is most emphatically not in the position of the Jewish *agunah*.[24] There is absolutely no justification at all for subjecting Muslim women in England to a more fundamentalist, or less enlightened, interpretation of Muslim law than that to which their sisters in the subcontinent are subject, or for denying Muslim women in England rights which their sisters in the subcontinent have enjoyed for more than half a century.[25]

It is tragic that the well-meaning MPs were not better informed than they were, for had they been, the statements made in the House of Commons, instead of merely broadcasting an erroneous proposition concerning Muslim law and publicizing the success that Muslim men were having 'blackmailing' their ignorant and uninformed wives, could have been used to expose the error and publicize the correct state of affairs, thus achieving to some extent the goal sought by the ill-advised MPs of granting some protection to ill-used women.

Within a year or so of the discussion in Parliament concerning the Abse-Thurnham amendment, I was contacted by a solicitor representing a Muslim woman suing for divorce in the English Court. The letter indicated that both the solicitor and her client were of the opinion that the marriage would not be dissolved 'religiously' unless the husband pronounced a *talaq*; made it clear that the husband was attempting to extract a heavy price for his *talaq*; and asked for my advice. I pointed out that the client clearly had grounds for divorce under the South Asian Dissolution of Muslim Marriages Act; that the grounds available to her under the English legislation were quite comparable to those available under the Dissolution of Muslim Marriages Act; that were the marriage dissolved in South Asia under the Dissolution of Muslim Marriages Act, the husband's consent would not be necessary and the wife would not lose her rights to *mahr*; and that I saw no reason why a Muslim woman in England should be denied rights available to her sisters in Pakistan. I enclosed a copy of my article on Muslim women and judicial divorce,[26] written in response to the Abse-Thurnham debate. The solicitor replied that my letter and enclosure had been "a real eye-opener" to both her and her client. The moral is obviously that women are only vulnerable to the kind of intimidation and blackmail to which Muslim women in England are being subjected to the extent that they are ignorant of their rights under Muslim law. If they have available to them information with which they can reply to their husband's pronouncements concerning what Muslim law decrees or demands, they are able to hold their own ground and to refuse to be intimidated or blackmailed.

II. The Islamic Sharia Council and 'Islamic' Divorce

Why an 'Islamic' Divorce?

I have recently been advising a young Muslim woman who had gone through a procedure involving the Islamic Sharia Council in London and purportedly resulting in an 'Islamic divorce'. The first question which obviously arises is why, having obtained a decree absolute from the English Court before she approached the Sharia Council, the woman considered such a course necessary.

She explained to me that she thought such an 'Islamic' divorce was necessary in two respects. (i) She wanted a divorce that would be recognized in Pakistani law. Although the woman is a British national, was domiciled in England prior to her marriage, and resumed her English domicile after the parties separated some years prior to the divorce, her (ex) husband is a Pakistani national and domiciled in that country. She and her family have close friends in Pakistan and she wanted to be free to visit that country without harassment and worry. And (ii) she wanted a divorce that would be recognized in certain countries of the Middle East (e.g. Bahrain) where she is likely to travel because she has relatives living there. The fear was that in the absence of an 'Islamic' divorce, in addition to the decree absolute, her ex-husband might follow her to, or encounter her in, Pakistan or Bahrain, and there claim his conjugal rights and enforce her wifely obedience on the ground that the matrimonial bond still subsisted.

It is important to realize that in the modern world Islamic law, *as law*, does not exist as some disembodied entity floating in the stratosphere, overreaching national boundaries and superseding national law. In the modern world, Islamic law exists only within the context of a nation-state; and within the boundaries of any particular state it is only enforced and enforceable to the extent that, and subject to the reforms and modifications that, the nation-state decrees.

In regard to Pakistan, all the woman needed to do was to send a copy of the English decree (with a covering letter indicating that she was giving notice of the divorce as required by section 8 of the Muslim Family Laws Ordinance) to the local official empowered to receive notifications of divorces under the Ordinance, with a copy of the covering letter to her ex-husband. Section 7 of the Ordinance, which specifically deals with divorces effected by the husband's unilateral pronouncement of *talaq*, has been discussed above. Section 8 of the Ordinance applies the same procedural requirements (*mutatis mutandis*) to other forms of divorce,[27] including divorce by mutual consent (the extra-judicial *khul*; see below).

The wording of section 8 of the Muslim Family Laws Ordinance clearly would encompass a judicial divorce decreed on the petition of the wife. More significantly, the Pakistan Family Courts Act, 1964, specifically enacted (section 21):

> 21.(1) Nothing in this Act shall be deemed to affect any of the provisions of the Muslim Family laws Ordinance, 1961, or the rules framed thereunder; and the provisions of sections 7, 8, 9, and 10 of the said Ordinance shall be applicable to any decree for the dissolution of marriage solemnized under the Muslim Law, maintenance or dower, by a Family Court.
>
> (2) Where a Family Court passes a decree for the dissolution of a marriage solemnized under Muslim Law,[28] the Court shall send by registered post, within seven days of passing such a decree, a certified copy of the same to the appropriate Chairman [i.e. a local government official] referred to in section 7 of the Muslim Family Laws Ordinance, 1961, and upon receipt of such copy, the Chairman shall proceed as if he had received an intimidation of *Talaq* required to be given under the said Ordinance.
>
> (3) Notwithstanding anything to the contrary contained in any other law, a decree for dissolution of a marriage solemnized under Muslim Law shall—
>
> (a) not be effective until the expiration of ninety days from the day on which a copy thereof has been sent under subsection (2) to the Chairman; and
>
> (b) be of no effect if within the period specified in clause (a) a reconciliation has been effected between the parties in accordance with the provisions of the Muslim Family Laws Ordinance, 1961.

Thus a judicial decree of divorce obtained by a Muslim woman in Pakistan is, in effect, a decree *nisi*, and becomes a decree absolute ninety days after notice of the decree has been delivered to the requisite local official, unless the parties become reconciled during this period. The only way the husband can prevent the decree from becoming final is by persuading his wife to a reconciliation; he has no power of veto and cannot impose 'conditions' or require his wife to 'purchase' his acquiescence to the decree.

The Muslim Family Laws Ordinance states that its provisions apply to "all Muslim citizens of Pakistan, wherever they may be"; it thus applies to the woman's ex-husband (a Pakistani national). Notice of a divorce under section 8 of the Ordinance may be given by either spouse;[29] in the case of a judicial divorce obtained by the wife, it would primarily be her responsibility to ensure that notice was appropriately given.[30] There are no grounds for contending that a non-Pakistani woman who had been married to a Pakistani national and whose marriage had been dissolved by judicial proceedings outside of Pakistan could not give notice under section 8; and no grounds for contending that such notice (failing reconciliation of the parties within the statutory ninety days), would not lead to effective registration of the divorce in Pakistan.[31]

As far as Bahrain or any other state wherein Muslim law is applicable in matters of personal status to nationals and domiciliaries of that state, a *foreign* Muslim husband would not be permitted to invoke the *domestic law* to override a divorce obtained by his *foreign* wife in a *foreign* country. The rules of private international law would surely be held to govern the question of the matrimonial status of two foreigners who were neither nationals of or domiciled in (e.g.) Bahrain, whose marriage had not taken place in Bahrain, and who had been divorced in England. The matter would be determined by reference to the country or countries of domicile or nationality of the individuals involved. The woman is domiciled in England and a national of the United Kingdom; according to the law of her nationality and domicile, she is divorced. The ex-husband is a national of and domiciled in Pakistan; if the divorce had been notified under section 8 of the Muslim Family Laws Ordinance, by the law of his nationality and domicile, he is divorced.

The Position of the Sharia Council

The woman approached the Sharia Council in London in August 1992 (by which time she had already obtained a decree absolute), requesting that this body arrange an 'Islamic' divorce for her.

The Sharia Council is a self-constituted body, founded in 1982[32] and claiming to have branches in London, Birmingham, Manchester, Bradford, and Glasgow. It has, of course, no legal status in England; it has no legal status under Pakistani, Bangladeshi, or Indian law (the vast majority of British Muslims are of South Asian descent).

The Constitution of the Council sets forth among its objects, *inter alia*, the following:

> To advance the Islamic Religion in particular by ...Establishing a bench to operate as a court of Islamic Sharia and make decisions on matters of Muslim family law referred to it.
>
> To educate the public generally in the field of Muslim family law and to foster and disseminate information in that field.

Literature put out by the Sharia Council claims that ninety-five per cent of all the queries referred to them concern "matrimonial problems faced by Muslims in this country",[33] and the majority of these "come from women who are seeking a divorce from their husbands"; "[i]t is usually Muslim women who are seeking an Islamic divorce from their husbands who turn to us". "Even a number of cases are referred to us through the solicitors who were able to obtain civil divorces for their client but they had to turn to us to obtain an Islamic divorce".

The matter is not merely that the Sharia Council does not recognize the 'civil divorce;' the premise appears to be that a couple may be simultaneously married to each other under two sets of legal regimes, and that each marriage must be individually dissolved.

> As the Muslims normally conduct their marriages both Islamically (known as *Nikah* ceremony which is accomplished through an Imam at any Mosque or Islamic Centre), and by registering with the civil authorities,[34] this Council deals only with the Islamic *Nikah*. It has nothing to do with the civil marriage which is dissolved by the British Courts and not by us.

If the marriage ceremonies took place in the order in which they are mentioned in this extract, it might be possible to argue that from the perspective of Muslim law, it was the *nikah* ceremony which was relevant and the civil ceremony was totally superfluous. However, the ceremonies do not and cannot take place in that order, because the *nikah* (if it were to occur first) would almost certainly be in violation of the Marriage Acts—not because it was a Muslim ceremony but because it would almost certainly have taken place in an 'unregistered building'.[35] It is because the venue of the *nikah* is an unregistered building where a marriage ceremony cannot be legally performed and because the act of purporting to solemnize a marriage in an unregistered building is a criminal offense, that the civil ceremony precedes the *nikah*; the *nikah* then becomes merely a ceremony of religious celebration and blessing, legally without significance in *either* English or Muslim law as far as the status of the parties is concerned: a man can no more marry a woman to whom he is already married in Muslim law than he can in English law.

However, the civil ceremony, which routinely precedes the *nikah* ceremony, is not irrelevant in Muslim law. The legal requirements for solemnization of a marriage according to Muslim law consist merely of offer and acceptance of the contract of marriage at the same meeting and in the presence of witnesses. These requirements are fully satisfied by the civil marriage ceremony.

This very important point was underscored by the 1967 decision of the Pakistan Supreme Court in *Jatoi v. Jatoi*.[36] The question here was what law of divorce would govern the dissolution in Pakistan of a civil marriage solemnized in an English registry office between a Pakistani Muslim man and a Spanish Christian woman. Since marriage and divorce in Pakistan are governed by religious-based communal laws, a choice had to be made between the (Christian) Divorce Act, 1869, and Muslim law. The Supreme Court held that the solemnization of the marriage under the UK Marriage Act, involving as it did formal consent to the marriage on behalf of each party at the same meeting in the presence of witnesses, fully conformed to the legal requirements for solemnization of a marriage under Muslim law. The marriage having been "assimilated to the position of a Muslim marriage", the majority went on to hold that the marriage could be and had been dissolved by the husband's pronouncement of *talaq*.

Since the registry office ceremony constitutes a valid solemnization of the marriage in Muslim law, the subsequent *nikah* ceremony, rather than producing a second matrimonial tie totally separate and distinct from that created by the civil ceremony, is irrelevant in Muslim law as far as the status of the parties is concerned (note again that in Muslim law, no less than in English law, one cannot marry someone to whom one is already married).

The Muslim *nikah* is undoubtedly of social and cultural significance; it is of legal significance primarily in regard to the specification of the wife's *mahr* (dower). (The fact that the parties are already legally man and wife at the time of the *nikah* ceremony is of no significance in the context of *mahr*: the amount of dower can be set or modified by mutual agreement at any time after the marriage.)

The Islamic Sharia Council in the present case set about arranging a divorce by *khul*—an extra-judicial divorce agreed with the mutual consent of the parties. A necessary prerequisite for a *khul*—or any other form of divorce—is that the parties are at the time actually married to each other. This prerequisite fails in the present case; thus reliance on the *khul*, or upon any alleged terms of the *khul* agreement, likewise fails.

A concomitant of a divorce by *khul* is that the woman 'purchases' her freedom by making concessions in favor of her husband in order to secure his consent to the divorce.[37] Usually the Muslim wife surrenders her right to the dower (*mahr*) pledged by the husband and payable on dissolution of the marriage by death or divorce.

However, as observed by Leo Abse, M.P., in his speech to the House of Commons, children are sometimes made the currency of the barter:

> According to orthodox Jewish or Islamic law,[38] in order to remarry, the divorced parties must be in possession of a religious divorce—a *gett* as it is called within the orthodox Jewish religion, a *talaq* for the committed Moslem. The obtaining of such religious decrees requires an initiative from the husband ...
>
> Unfortunately, one partner—usually the husband—can brutally manipulate the passionate wish of the other party to be free after a civil divorce to remarry according to the religious law ....[39] Therefore *the protection that our civil law provides for maintenance and the custody of children can be subverted by a ruthless partner.*
>
> The partner—usually the husband—blackmails the wife. The price for taking the necessary initiative [for the obtaining of a 'religious' divorce] is an agreed settlement and arrangement relating to children. It might be a settlement which, if the issues were adjudicated upon openly in court, would according to the principles which this House had laid down in our civil law, be far different from that to which the hapless wife has been compelled to submit.[40]

The literature produced by the Sharia Council states that a divorce decreed by the English Court will only be recognized 'Islamically' if the husband is the petitioner or if the husband consents to the divorce in writing. In any other case the wife who wishes to be divorced 'Islamically' must apply for an 'Islamic divorce' through the Sharia Council.

> An application for divorce by the wife is known as *Khula*, a condition of which is that the wife must return to the husband any *mahr* (dower) or jewellery she received from him, if he so demands it.

The procedure for the granting of an 'Islamic' divorce to a woman applicant as set out in the Council's literature may be summarized as follows. Upon receipt of the application, the Council will attempt to correspond with the husband (or, as will most commonly be the case, ex-husband) in order to ascertain his response to his wife's (or ex-wife's) application. If no reply is received, a second letter is sent; and, if there is still no response, a third. If a reply is received and if the husband (or ex-husband) has imposed any conditions upon the granting of an 'Islamic' divorce to his wife (or ex-wife), she is required to comply with them "provided that these conditions are reasonable". Apparently the Council is the judge of the reasonableness or otherwise of the pre-conditions.

What is particularly interesting is that the Shariah Council apparently claims jurisdiction to grant a *khul* to the wife if the husband fails to reply to their communications, or in certain circumstances if the husband refuses his cooperation or consent—i.e. claims the right to impose a divorce by *khul* on the husband in *ex parte* proceedings and/or without his consent, although the 'price' of the *khul* is the woman's renouncement of claims for *mahr*, repayment of any *mahr* already paid, and return of any jewellery etc. presented to her by her husband.

The first part of this proposition reflects the Maliki view of *khul*, assuming that the Council is functioning in the role of the 'arbiters' supposedly appointed by the spouses. (The Hanafi view is that the arbiters can only attempt to reconcile the spouses and have no authority to dissolve the marriage unless the husband has specifically empowered them to pronounce *talaq* on his behalf.)

The second part of the proposition, however, departs from Maliki law to the disadvantage of the woman, for the Maliki arbiters would not automatically impose reparations upon the woman, and certainly would not automatically deprive her of her entire *mahr*. Having made a determination that the marriage should be dissolved, the Maliki arbiters would attempt to allocate blame for the discord and may award the wife all, some, or none of her *mahr*.

Particularly since women who approach the Sharia Council for a divorce have already obtained a divorce decree from the English Court, a procedure which requires that they prove grounds which are very comparable to those available to Muslim women in South Asia under the Dissolution of Muslim Marriages Act, the rather heavy handed attitude toward Muslim women urgently needs to be reconsidered.

The other problem, demonstrated by the case I have recently been involved in, is that the Sharia Council has no effective sanctions which can be invoked to ensure that the (ex) husband abides by his agreement and fulfills his responsibilities and undertakings. The *khul* in this case was granted on the (ex) wife's refund of her *mahr* and her commitment to allow her ex-husband access to the child of the marriage in accordance with prior arrangements made through the Sharia Council. The (ex) husband was also to return the jewellery given to the (ex) wife by her parents and other relatives. The (ex) wife refunded her *mahr*, but the husband did not return the wife's jewellery. And the Council was equally powerless to hold the (ex) husband to orderly arrangements concerning access to the child.

However, there is a powerful sanction available for use against the wife—the threat that without an 'Islamic' divorce, she is not free ever to marry again according to Muslim law. While remarriage may be the very last thing on the mind of a woman in the process of extricating herself from an unhappy and traumatic matrimonial situation, the fact remains that she may some years hence wish to consider remarriage. By that time she may well have lost all contact with her ex-husband and have no idea where he is or how to get in touch with him. If she believes (or is induced to believe) that her first marriage had not been effectively dissolved, she would obviously be in a difficult situation. Better, it might seem, to sever the bond 'Islamically' as well as civilly, at once, through the Sharia Council. The granting of an 'Islamic divorce.' states the Council's publication, produces "[a] great sigh of relief for the wife who feels really she is Islamically free to start a new life".

Concluding Remarks

The immediate need is for moderate and educated Muslims to interest themselves in the question of Muslim law in a non-Muslim environment. It is surely unacceptable that Muslim women in a country like England should be forced, by ignorance and social pressure, to subject themselves to an interpretation of Islamic law that is harsher than that to which women in South Asia[41] are subjected. The matter is too urgent to be left to self-appointed committees of *ulama*.

A matter to be kept prominently in mind is that, as a leading Muslim scholar in India has written, "The true Islamic law in fact stood for what is now known as the 'breakdown' theory of divorce".[42] More than a quarter of a century earlier, a distinguished Muslim jurist, Chief Justice Tyabji of Sind, explained the Dissolution of Muslim Marriages Act in the following terms:

> From the earliest times Muslim wives have been held to be entitled to a dissolution when it was clearly shown that the parties could not live 'within the limits of Allah', when (1) instead of the marriage being a reality, a suspension of the marriage had in fact occurred, or (2) when the continuance of the marriage involved injury to the wife .... The grounds stated in section 2 of Act 8 of 1939 in sub-clauses (1) to (iv) are based on the principle that a suspension of the marriage had occurred which justified dissolution, and in sub-clauses (v) to (viii) on the principle that continuance of the marriage in those cases would be injurious to the wife.[43]

In this case the learned Judge granted the petitioning wife a divorce on the ground that the husband had failed to maintain her for the statutory period of two years, although during this period the wife was living apart from her husband without legal ground (i.e. was herself in desertion and unentitled to claim maintenance from her husband unless she rejoined him in the matrimonial home) on the basis that such separate living and failure of the parties to reconcile their differences demonstrated the total breakdown of the marriage. Marriage in Islam not being a sacrament, the Judge found no merit in preserving a marriage which had broken down and equally no desecration in dissolving a marriage which had failed.

What the Muslim woman petitioning for divorce in the English Court must prove is that the marriage has "broken down irretrievably". And she must establish this breakdown by proving one of the following facts: (i) adultery coupled with the further circumstances that she finds it impossible to live with the respondent; (ii) "that the respondent has behaved in such a way that the petitioner cannot reasonably be expected to live with the respondent"; (iii) desertion for two years; (iv) separation for two years when both spouses agree to a divorce; or (v) separation for five years. This is perhaps a more limited list than that available to the Muslim wife in South Asia under the Dissolution of Muslim Marriages Act, although the entries under section 2(viii) would constitute the kind of behavior referred to by the shorthand expression 'unreasonable behavior' in the context of the English statute.

The immediate point is to emphasize how closely analogous are the grounds upon which a Muslim woman might obtain a divorce from the English Court and those upon which her sister may obtain a divorce from the Indian or Pakistani or Bangladeshi Court. A marriage that has broken down irrespective of geography.

Meanwhile, individual Muslim women who possess the strength of personal character and religious faith[44] to take their own individual stands may push the community in more liberal and humane directions—just as individual South Asian Muslim women who went to the extent of apostatizing (usually temporarily) from Islam in order to shed a husband they could not rid themselves of by less drastic means deserve credit for the passage of the Dissolution of Muslim Marriage Act of 1939.

NOTES

1. Note that before the changes under discussion, spouses domiciled in England who had been married in England (in a registry office or in a Muslim ceremony in one of the few mosques

registered as places where marriages can be solemnized) or in monogamous rites abroad (e.g. under the Indian Special Marriage Act, 1954) could approach the English Courts for matrimonial relief.

2. See Lucy Carroll, "Recognition of Polygamous Marriages in English Matrimonial Law: The Statutory Reversal of *Hyde v. Hyde* in 1972", *Journal Institute of Muslim Minority Affairs*, Vol. 5, 1984, pp. 81–98.
3. (1983) Family 26. See Lucy Carroll. "Definition of a 'Potentially Polygamous' Marriage in English Law: A Dramatic Decision from the Court of Appeal (*Hussain v. Hussain*)", *Islamic and Comparative Law Quarterly*, Vol. 4, 1984, pp. 61–71.
4. The distinction between foreign divorces "obtained by means of judicial or other proceedings" and foreign divorces obtained without the necessity of any 'proceedings' is important in English law. The Pakistani *talaq* has been held to fall in the former category, while the 'bare' or 'classical' *talaq* (such as the Indian *talaq*) has been held to fall in the latter category.
5. The Ordinance also introduced some restrictions on polygamy; required registration of Muslim marriages; raised the marriage age for girls from fourteen to sixteen years; provided an expeditious alternative to proceedings in the magistrate's court for the wife who sought maintenance from her husband; and protected the rights of succession of the 'orphaned' grandchild.
6. Or, more accurately, the actions covered by the first three entries in the list; it is difficult to characterize the waiting period of ninety days as a 'procedure.'
7. See *Quazi v. Quazi*, 1980, AC 744; *ex parte Fatima*, 1984, 2 All ER 458; *Chaudhary v. Chaudhary*, 1984, 3 All ER 1025.

   See also Lucy Carroll—(1) "The Pakistani *Talaq* in English Law: *Ex Parte Minhas* and *Quazi v. Quazi*", *Islamic and Comparative Law Quarterly*, Vol. 2, 1982, 17–37; (2) "Recognition of Foreign Divorces—*Chaudhary* and *Fatima* in the Court of Appeal: A Conflict?" *Journal of Social Welfare Law*, 1985, pp. 151–155; (3) "A 'Bare' *Talaq* is not a Divorce Obtained by 'Other Proceedings': *Chaudhary v. Chaudhary*", *Law Quarterly Review*, Vol. 101, 1985, pp. 170–175; (4) "A *Talaq* Pronounced in England is not an 'Overseas Divorce': *ex parte Fatima*", *Law Quarterly Review*, Vol. 101, 1985, pp. 175–179; (5) "*Talaq* in English Law: 'Procedural' *Talaqs*, 'Bare' *Talaqs*, and Policy Considerations in the Recognition of Extra-Judicial Divorces", *Journal of the Indian Law Institute*, Vol. 28, 1986, pp. 14–35; and (6) "The UK Family Law Act, 1986: Recognition of Extra-Judicial Divorce in England", *Journal of the Indian Law Institute*, Vol. 31, 1989, pp. 154–176.
8. See *Qureshi v. Qureshi*, 1971, 1 All ER 325. In view of the provisions of section 16(1) of the Domicile and Matrimonial Proceedings Act, 1973, this decision does not apply to extra-judicial divorces effected after 1 January 1974.
9. This provision was specifically intended to reverse by statute the decision in *Qureshi v. Qureshi*. See now section 44(2) of the Family Law Act, 1986.
10. Now see section 46(2)(c) of the Family Law Act, 1986, which raises the bar to recognition if *one* spouse (rather than *both* spouses) were habitually resident in the UK for a year prior to the institution of the divorce proceedings.

    While a Pakistani *talaq* fulfills the statutory requirement of "judicial or other proceedings," a 'bare' or 'classical' *talaq* (e.g. an Indian *talaq*) does not.
11. Sections 2 to 5 of the 1971 Act; see now section 46(1) of the Family Law Act, 1986.
12. For example, recognition was not automatically barred if one (or indeed, both) spouses were domiciled in England, or if both had been habitually resident there for a year prior to the divorce. To constitute a foreign divorce, of course, the *talaq* had to be executed abroad; no extra-judicial dissolution of marriage may take place within the jurisdiction of the English Court.
13. Section 6 of the 1971 statute; the 1973 statute (section 2) substituted a revised section 6 in the earlier Act. See now section 46(2) of the Family Law Act, 1986.
14. (1) *Viswalingam v. Viswalingam*; the case is reported in full (High Court and Court of Appeal) in *Malayan Law Journal*, 1980, p. 10. See Lucy Carroll, "A Question of Fact: Ascertainment of Asian Law by the English Court. A Critique of *Viswalingam v. Viswalingam*", *Malayan Law Review*, Vol. 22, 1980, pp. 34–65.

    (2) *Chaudhary v. Chaudhary*, 1984, 3 All ER 1025. See Lucy Carroll, "A 'Bare' *Talaq* is not a Divorce Obtained by 'Other Proceedings': *Chaudhary v. Chaudhary*", *Law Quarterly Review*, Vol. 101, 1985, pp. 170–175.
15. But note *surah* II *ayah* 214:—"For divorced women maintenance [or provision] should be provided on a reasonable scale. This is a duty on the righteous". (Yusuf Ali, trans.) The Shafi'is take this verse seriously; other Sunni schools adopt an interpretation which confers no protection on the

woman and imposes no responsibilities on the man. Note, however, the recent dramatic decision of the Dhaka High Court in *Muhammad Hefzur Rahman v. Shamsun Nahar Begum*, Vol. 47, 1995, Dhaka Law Reports 54. See Lucy Carroll, "Divorced Muslim Women in India: Shah Bano, the Muslim Women Act, and the Significance of the Bangladesh Decision", in Women Living Under Muslim Law, *Talaq-i-Tafwid: The Muslim Woman's Contractual Access to Divorce. An Information Kit*, forthcoming.

16. It needs to be noted, however, that this statute did nothing whatsoever to deal with the major evidential problem which foreign extra-judicial divorces present to the English Courts. This problem, as so vividly demonstrated in *Viswalingam*, concerns the lack of competent and informed 'expert' evidence on foreign legal systems and the consequent difficulties the Court faces in attempting to ascertain whether the alleged action or event or happening actually brought the marriage to an end under the relevant foreign law.

    Before granting an order for financial relief under the 1984 statute, the English Court will still have to reach a determination as to whether or not there has been a dissolution of the marriage by means of a 'foreign divorce' valid in the relevant foreign jurisdiction and entitled to recognition under English law.

17. According to the individual claiming credit for suggesting the amendment (the then lecturer in Muslim law at Cambridge University and subsequently dean of the faculty of law at East Anglia University), the proposed amendment was modeled on a *New York State* statute applicable to New York *Jews* (David Pearl, *Cambridge Law Journal*, 1984, pp. 249–250). This is, of course, totally irrelevant to the question of whether it should be part of *English* law applicable to *Muslims* in England. Indeed, the Muslim law of divorce and the Jewish law of divorce are so different that any proposition which assumes the two systems are analogous is *prima facie* open to serious question. For example, the only ground which Jewish law recognizes for dissolution of marriage, and the only ground on which a *gett* can be procured, is the mutual agreement of the spouses. While Muslim law recognizes divorce by mutual consent (*khul*), it also recognizes divorce at the instance of *either* spouse in the face of the opposition and resistance of the other spouse.

18. The proposed amendment read as follows (*Hansard*, 13 June 1984, col. 926):

> 9A—(1) Where a petition for divorce or nullity of marriage has been presented to the court, either party to the marriage may apply to the court at any time before decree absolute opposing the grant of the decree absolute on the ground that there exists a barrier to the religious remarriage of the applicant which is within the power of the other party to remove.
>
> (2) The Court shall not entertain an application under subsection (1) hereof unless the applicant satisfies the court of the existence of such a barrier by means of a written declaration by the religious authority which authorised or sanctioned the marriage being dissolved by the court, or which authorised or sanctioned a religious ceremony of marriage between the same parties or on proof that such authority no longer exists, by a religious authority recognised by both parties to be competent.
>
> (3) If the court is satisfied as to the existence of such a barrier then subject to the provisions of subsection (4) hereof the court shall refuse to permit the decree to be made absolute until it is satisfied by means of a written declaration by the authority referred to in subsection (2) hereof that the said barrier has been removed or that the parties have taken all such steps within their power to remove the said barrier or until the said application is withdrawn by the applicant.
>
> (4) Notwithstanding the provisions of subsection (3) hereof the court may order that the decree may be made absolute if there are exceptional circumstances making it desirable for the decree to be made absolute without delay.

Even assuming that the husband's action in securing a 'religious divorce' were necessary in order for the requirements of Muslim law to be satisfied, I entirely fail to see how the proposed clause would solve the problem it purportedly attempted to address. In the five examples proffered by Mr Thurnham, MP in his speech in the House of Commons (see extract quoted in text), it was apparently the respondent husband who was purporting to refuse the 'religious divorce.' Unless he is domiciled in England and anxious to remarry, delaying the decree absolute will not affect him adversely and may well benefit him (e.g. as long as the marriage is not dissolved, he will not become liable for payment of the deferred dower).

19. Peter Thurnham, MP, *Hansard*, 13 June 1984, cols. 928–929.
20. See Lucy Carroll, "Muslim Women and Judicial Divorce: An Apparently Misunderstood Aspect of Muslim Law", *Islamic and Comparative Law Quarterly*, Vol. 5, 1985, pp. 226–245. This article was based on a long statement which I submitted to the Solicitor General, the Lord Chancellor, and the Law Commission immediately after the discussion in Parliament on the Abse-Thurnham amendment.
21. It is extremely difficult to comprehend why this statute—so much more relevant to the situation than a New York State statute applicable to New York Jews; see EN 17 above—was not called to the attention of those advising the women so brutally exploited in the cases referred to by Peter Thurnham, MP, in the House of Commons, or to those supporting the suggested amendment.
22. *Gazette of India*, 1936, Part V, p. 154; as quoted and cited by Tahir Mahmood, *Muslim Personal Law: The Role of the State in the Subcontinent*, Nagpur, India: All India Reporter, 1983, 2nd edn, pp. 47–48.
23. See Lucy Carroll, "Muslim Family Law in South Asia: The Right to Avoid an Arranged Marriage Contracted During Minority", *Journal of the Indian Law Institute*, Vol. 23, 1981, pp. 149–180.
24. A Jewish woman who has obtained a judicial divorce from the civil Court exercising matrimonial jurisdiction in the matter of divorce, but who has been denied a *gett* by her husband and thus retains the status of 'married woman' in orthodox Jewish law.
25. See article cited in EN 20 above.
26. *Ibid.*
27. "8. Dissolution of marriage otherwise than by *talaq*. Where the right to divorce has been duly delegated to the wife [*talaq-i-tafwid*] and she wishes to exercise that right, or *where any of the parties to a marriage wishes to dissolve the marriage otherwise than by talaq*, the provisions of section 7 shall, *mutatis mutandis* and so far as applicable apply" (emphasis added.).
28. Solemnization of a marriage "under Muslim law" need not be concluded by or in the presence of a religious functionary or representative; it need not involve any religious rites or ceremonies. The legal requirements for solemnization of a marriage according to Muslim law consist merely of offer and acceptance of the contract of marriage at the same meeting and in the presence of witnesses. See further below.
29. The husband pronouncing a *talaq* must himself give notice under section 7. The corollary is that his failure to give notice conclusively evidences the fact that he retracted or revoked the pronouncement.

    The forms of divorce covered by section 8 normally occur at the initiative of the wife or through the agreement of the spouses; there is no requirement that notification of the divorce effected "otherwise than by *talaq*" be given by the husband. (A judicial divorce obtained by a Muslim husband in a jurisdiction, or under circumstances where extra-judicial divorce by *talaq* would not be recognized would also come under section 8; theoretically notice could be given by the wife no less than by the husband, once the decree were final.)
30. This is particularly the case in the province of the Punjab (where the parties to the present case resided together during the marriage; and where the ex-husband is apparently still domiciled), because in 1971 the provincial government deleted subsections (2) and (3) and part of subsection (1) of section 21 of the Family Courts Act. As applicable in the Punjab, section 21 therefore reads simply: "Nothing in this Act shall be deemed to affect any of the previsions of the Muslim Family Laws Ordinance, 1961, or the rules made thereunder".

    Interpreting the effect of the provincial amendments, the Lahore High Court in 1975 (*Muhammad Ishaque v. Ch. Ahsan Ahmad*, PLD 1975 Lahore 1118) concluded: "The Family Courts would thus continue to follow the practice of sending a copy of the decree to the Chairman concerned but at the same time it is also necessary for the wife in whose favour the decree is passed, to independently inform the Chairman about the decree as also to send a notice thereof to the husband in a formal manner".
31. I am fortified in making this statement by conversations and communications with members of the superior judiciary in Pakistan (including an individual at the time a judge of the Supreme Court) and with senior advocates in Pakistan in the period immediately after the Abse-Thurnham amendment had been proposed in the House of Commons and with specific reference to that amendment.
32. At a time when it was clear that legislation would soon be enacted (as it was two years later) which would make it impossible for a Muslim husband to absolve himself of any financial responsibility for the wife who had filed for divorce in the English Court by hastily effecting a *talaq* abroad,

thereby depriving the English Court of jurisdiction to dissolve the marriage (because, assuming the *talaq* were entitled to recognition in English law, the parties were no longer husband and wife) and, consequently, of jurisdiction to order a financial settlement in favor of the wife (because, prior to the legislation of 1984, this jurisdiction only arose if the English Court itself dissolved the marriage). See now Part III of the Matrimonial and Family Proceedings Act, 1984.

33. The Council claims to have dealt with more than 950 matters in the period (apparently) 1982–1991; a more recent (but undated) document puts the number at more than 1150.
34. The reference is to a marriage ceremony in a registry office.
35. English law requires that marriages be solemnized in a registered building. The main complication this poses for members of the Muslim and Hindu communities is that a building can only be registered for the solemnization of marriages if it is used exclusively for religious services. Many mosques and temples are used for purposes (e.g. accommodation of the religious leader and his family) other than a venue where religious services are conducted.
36. PLD 1967 Supreme Court 580.
37. The *khul* is usually concluded by the husband's pronouncement of *talaq*, although in Hanafi law such a pronouncement is not strictly required. In essence, the wife is 'buying' her husband's pronouncement of *talaq* by agreeing to the 'price' (in monetary or other terms) which he demands. The bargain necessarily fails if the alleged husband has no authority to pronounce *talaq* in reference to the woman in question—which, of course, he does not if he is no longer married to her.

    According to some Muslim jurists, the bargain cannot be enforced against the woman who, although she had grounds for judicial divorce, agreed to a divorce by *khul* and payment by her of compensation out of ignorance, as a result of pressure, or to preserve her modesty and her family's honor (by refraining from airing private matters in a public forum). That the woman in the present case had grounds for judicial divorce is proved by the fact that she had, even at the time of her approach to the Shariah Council, a decree absolute in her hands.
38. Note again the assumption that Jewish law and Muslim law are analogous and the Muslim woman whose husband has not pronounced a *talaq* is in the same position as the Jewish woman whose husband refuses her a *gett*.
39. In orthodox Jewish law, the only recognized form of divorce is the consensual *gett*; the husband has to give, and the wife has to accept, the *gett*. In the absence of a *gett*, an orthodox Jewish woman cannot remarry.

    The Muslim woman, it must be stressed, is not in a position analogous to the Jewish *agunah*. While Muslim law recognizes divorce by mutual consent (the *khul*), it also recognizes unilateral divorce by the husband (*talaq*) or by the wife (*faskh*). Of course, the woman is disadvantageously placed in that while the husband can execute his unilateral *talaq* extra-judicially, she has to claim her right of unilateral dissolution through the Courts.
40. *Hansard*, 13 June 1984, cols. 926–927; emphasis added.
41. To which geographical region the overwhelming majority of Muslims in Britain trace their origin.
42. Tahir Mahmood, *The Muslim Law of India*, Allahabad: Law Book Co., 1980, p. 95.
43. *Hajra v. Kassim*, unreported; passage in the text was quoted by the same judge in *Noor Bibi v. Pir Bux*, AIR 1950 Sind 8, p. 10.
44. The woman I most recently advised asserted with considerable feeling, after more than two years of attempting to work matters out through the good offices of the Sharia Council, "If this is Islam, then I am not a Muslim! But I know that it is not Islam; I refuse to accept that it is Islam".

[10]

Jewish Marriage and Civil Law: A Two-Way Street?

David Novak*

1. *Optimal Jurisdiction.*

The recognition of the institution of Jewish marriage by a secular polity, and the recognition of a secular polity by Jews committed to Judaism, is an issue of the overlapping of two distinct legal jurisdictions. The ramifications of this overlapping are long and complicated.

Judaism is basically constituted by its own law called the *Torah*. Judaism contains more than what is ordinarily termed "law" (*halakhah*); it also contains ideas (generally called *aggadah*, meaning "narrative"). Yet, even the exposition of ideas still requires legal justification for its valid operation in and for Judaism. Accordingly, the interpretation of ideas must be conducted within certain dogmatic limits (which are, happily, few and quite general), which are themselves legally formulated.[1] Despite the essentially legal structure of Judaism, though, the grounding of the law is not self-referential: the law does not simply present itself. The law is given by God.[2] Thus, the legal propositions of Judaism are grounded in the more elementary theological proposition that the Torah is from God (*torah min ha-shamayim*).[3]

From God *to* whom does this law come? The law is given to a community elected by God, whose members are elected either by birth or by rebirth in conversion.[4] The founding event of this community, and the subject of its tradition, is the unequivocal giving of that law by God and its unequivocal acceptance by the people.[5] That is why the law cannot be abrogated or exchanged.[6] Obedience to the law of God must always come before obedience to any human authority, Jewish or non-Jewish.[7]

The task of the Jewish community in the person of its authorized representatives, therefore, is to interpret, apply, and even augment the law of God as revealed. But the community, especially its duly empowered authorities, must never forget that the first purpose of the law is obedience to the God

---

* J. Richard and Dorothy Shiff Chair of Jewish Studies and Director of Jewish Studies Programme, University of Toronto. A.B., University of Chicago (1961); M.H.L., Jewish Theological Seminary of America (1964), rabbinical diploma (1966); Ph.D., Georgetown University (1971). The author thanks the students in his seminar on Jewish law, Faculty of Law, University of Toronto, for their valuable comments on an earlier draft of this paper.

1 *See generally* MENACHEM KELLNER, DOGMA IN MEDIEVAL JEWISH THOUGHT 1-10 (1986).

2 *See Repentance* 3.8 (Maimonides, Mishneh Torah).

3 *See Sanhedrin* 10.1 (Mishnah).

4 *See Sanhedrin* 44a (Babylonian Talmud); *Yevamot* 47b (Babylonian Talmud); *see also* DAVID NOVAK, THE ELECTION OF ISRAEL 177-99 (1995).

5 See Found*ations* 9.1 (Maimonides, Mishneh Torah).

6 *See id.* at 9.2.

7 *See Berakhot* 19b (Babylonian Talmud).

who gave it.[8] Only after this recognition can other purposes, even preconditions, *of* the law be proposed and effectively used by the human members of the covenant; indeed, that is their public responsibility. The discovery of the purposes and preconditions of the law must not detract from primary obedience to God's law but they may enhance it.[9]

The law itself is God's primordial claim on the community and all its members. The law governs, both collectively and individually, the ongoing relationship between God and the community called "the covenant" (*ha-berit*).[10] Indeed, one can see the very meaning of the word "God" as: *the One who is to be obeyed above all others.* The most universal word for *God* in the Bible is the common noun *elohim.*[11] It is also used for those human powers having justified legal authority, whose essential justification is its being subordinate to the revealed law.[12] This kind of theological constitution of authority is particularly necessary in our time, when many people, both secular and religious, take religious authority to be basically "authoritarian," that is, a projection of human power interests *onto* God. A proper theology of the law indicates how this popular impression, at least with regards to Judaism, is erroneous.

From the proper theological vantage point, it would seem to follow that Judaism's optimal polity is one where the law of God is not only supreme but has total hegemony over the life of the people.[13] The Jews ought not recognize any other law than the one God has given to them. This position comes out in the following rabbinic text, which is quite fundamental:

> Rabbi Tarfon said that even where one finds that the laws of the gentile courts [*agoriyot*] are the same as the Jewish laws, one is not permitted to attach onself to them nonetheless. That is because it is said in Scripture, 'These are the judgments [*ha-mishpatim*] (*Exodus* 21:1) which thou shalt set before them [*lifneihem*]' that is to say 'before them' and not before heathens.[14]

Interpreting the same scriptural verse, it has been said, "[y]ou may judge their cases but they are not to judge your cases."[15] In other words, the Jews are to be totally governed by their own law, despite whatever commonalities their law might have with other just systems of law. Jewish law alone must rule the Jews, although some of it may rule others if they so choose.[16] Nevertheless, others may never rule the Jews, at least in principle. What is normatively sufficient for the life of the whole people could only be lessened by the addition of any other legal authority.

This is the optimal view of Jewish law and its full polity. If not utopian, however, it seems to be ideal: something that has not yet been achieved. This

---

8 *See Bemidbar Rabbah* 19.1.

9 *See* David Novak, Natural Law in Judaism 62-82 (1998).

10 *See, e.g., Deuteronomy* 29:9-14.

11 *See* A. Marmorstein, The Old Rabbinic Doctrine of God 67-69 (1968).

12 *See, e.g., Sanhedrin* 2b, 5b, 56b, 66a (Babylonian Talmud).

13 *See Kings* 11:1 (Maimonides, Mishneh Torah).

14 *Gittin* 88b (Babylonian Talmud).

15 Mekilta de-Rabbi Ishmael 2 (Jacob Z. Lauterbach trans., 1935).

16 *See Avodah Zarah* 64b (Babylonian Talmud).

failure is because Jews have had a law and Jews have had what we now call political sovereignty, but there has never been the full convergence of both. Thus, in the days of the First Temple (from the time of Joshua to the Babylonian Exile in 586 B.C.E.), the scriptural record indicates that the nation of Israel had sovereignty—and when separated, the nations of Judah and Israel (Ephraim), respectively, were sovereign.[17] As for law at this time, though, it seems that instead of a nationally accepted written law, the people were mostly governed by ad hoc royal or prophetic decrees.[18] By the time of the return from Babylonian Captivity in the days of the Second Temple (let alone after its destruction in 70 C.E.) when the people were governed by a nationally accepted written law, their nation had already lost its political sovereignty.[19] From that point forward, Jews were governed by non-Jewish sovereign empires (Persian, Roman, etc.). As a result, the Jews have compromised the full authority of their own law due to the more politically powerful law of the governing authority.

Even now, when the Jews have regained political sovereignty in the State of Israel, that state, at least heretofore, is not governed by traditional Jewish law.[20] The State of Israel's law, like that of a Western-style democracy, is grounded in the popular sovereignty of its own people.[21] This paradigm is different, of course, from a law rooted in divine revelation and transmitted by a distinctly religious tradition (even though there might well be democratic components of this theocratic system).[22] Therefore, whatever religious law functions in the State of Israel functions as an entitlement *from* the secular state, at least as far as the secular state is concerned. Accordingly, even though the State of Israel is a Jewish state governed by a Jewish majority, Jews there who see themselves as being primarily and ultimately governed by the revealed law of Judaism still have the same problem as Jews in the diaspora: how does one live under a secular law and still maintain the supremacy of the revealed law?[23] Ironically enough, the problem is somewhat easier to deal with in the diaspora because Jewish tradition has much more experience dealing with the sovereignty of a gentile society than with the sovereignty of a Jewish society (especially a Jewish state that proclaims itself to be secular).

2. *Current Jurisdiction.*

The ancient Rabbis recognized the authority of the gentile jurisdictions within which Jews had to live. Thus, the *Mishnah* states: "All documents which are accepted in [gentile] courts, even [when] signed [by] gentiles [wit-

17 *See Joshua* 18:1; 1 *Kings* 12:20-21.

18 *See* U. CASSUTO, A COMMENTARY ON THE BOOK OF EXODUS 259-64 (Israel Abrams trans., 1967).

19 *See Ezra* 7:1-12, 10:5-8; *see also Nehemiah* 8:1-12.

20 *See* MENACHEM ELON, 4 JEWISH LAW 1520-27 (B. Auerbach & M. J. Sykes trans., 1994).

21 *See* Z.W. FALK, LAW AND RELIGION: THE JEWISH EXPERIENCE 43-57 (1981).

22 *See* DAVID NOVAK, COVENANTAL RIGHTS: A STUDY IN JEWISH POLITICAL THEORY 34-35, 209-18 (2000).

23 *See generally* Izhak Englard, *The Relationship Between Religion and State in Israel, in* JEWISH LAW IN ANCIENT AND MODERN ISRAEL 168, 168-89 (1971).

nesses], are valid [*kesherim*], except writs of divorce . . . ."[24] The later discussion of this rule in the *Talmud* bases it on the principle, "the law of the Government is law" (*dina de-malkhuta dina*).[25] The medieval commentator, Rashi, noted that this principle not only says that gentile law has authority for gentiles, but that it has authority for Jews who either choose, or even have to, partake of it.[26] Under what circumstances this involvement takes place will be examined later. Yet, this principle is not taken to be optimal but only necessary.[27] Its logic is something like that of the dictum *dura lex sed lex*, namely, a "hard" or less than perfect law is better than no law at all. As this principle applies to the situation of the Jews, matters of everyday justice are such that Jews cannot assume, in the absence of their own civil jurisdiction, that their real needs for civil justice can be suppressed.[28] Such an absence of Jewish civil jurisdiction could either be *de jure* or *de facto*. In a *de jure* situation, a Jewish civil court may not function in a host society because the non-Jewish state claims a monopoly on civil jurisdiction. In a *de facto* situation, on the other hand, a Jewish civil court might not function because Jews in a non-Jewish state do not trust its political effectiveness in rendering justice.[29]

The principle of "the law of the Government is the law" has a wider range than its application in the case of documents pertaining to inter-Jewish commercial relations certified in gentile courts. This principle also applies to Jews having to submit criminal matters to the jurisdiction of these courts, even matters that could entail the death penalty. Indeed, it is more likely that a non-Jewish host society would claim a monopoly on criminal jurisdiction than it would on civil jurisdiction. Many civil disputes can be settled by arbitration between the parties involved in the dispute themselves, whereas crimes against persons are usually considered to be offenses against society itself and thus the sole business of the state to adjudicate. In fact, in the not so distant past, Jews were frequently able to settle their own inter-Jewish civil disputes among themselves according to their own law in their own courts.

This concession to non-Jewish law is best explained by the medieval commentator Nahmanides, who wrote:

> This [power to adjudicate] is based on the power of the king to make law in his kingdom. It is something by which he and all the other kings before him conducted public business. These laws are written in the royal chronicles and law books . . . we infer this from the words *dina de-malkhuta*, namely, 'the law of the kingdom,' not the law of a particular king [*dina de-malka*]. This was even the case with the kings of Israel.[30]

---

24 *Gittin* 1.5 (Mishnah).

25 *Gittin* 10b (Babylonian Talmud).

26 *See id.* 9b.

27 *See* David Novak, The Image of the Non-Jew in Judaism: An Historical and Constructive Study of the Noahicle Laws 70 (1983).

28 *See Sanhedrin* 26.7 (Maimonides, Mishneh Torah).

29 *See id.*; *Acquisitions and Gifts* 1.15; *see also* B. M. Lewin, Otsar ha-Geonim: *Gittin* 208-10 (1941).

30 *Baba Batra* 54b (Hiddushei ha-Ramban).

In other words, a law that is simply the arbitrary whim of a sovereign does not have the moral force of law. Only a law that is part of a system of justice (what some have called a *Rechtstaat*[31]) has the moral force of law for those who live within it and under its criminal jurisdiction.[32]

The earlier medieval commentator, Rashbam, pointed out that royal authority (which could well be taken as the same for republican authority), whether Jewish or non-Jewish, is based on a voluntary contract between the government (whether sovereignty is individual as in the case of a monarchy, or collective as in the case of a republic) and the governed. Combining the views of Nahmanides and Rashbam (with whose work Nahmanides was quite familiar), one can see the most basic agreement between the government and the governed is that the governed be protected from criminal assaults against persons and their property. This agreement between the governed and government subsequently extends to the government providing the opportunity for adjudication of civil disputes that the individual parties cannot, or will not, settle between themselves. Thus, if Jews cannot always wait for their own jurisdiction to enforce their rights in civil disputes either among themselves or with others, how much more so can they never wait for their own jurisdiction to enforce their rights in criminal matters, where greater governmental power is required in order for justice to be effective.

From the primary text discussed above concerning the validity of documents, a distinction is made between non-Jewish jurisdiction for Jews in civil matters and non-Jewish jurisdiction for Jews in marital matters. The principle invoked to explain the validity of civil jurisdiction, "the law of the Government is the law," also justifies the validity of non-Jewish criminal law for Jews.[33] The whole institution of marriage is something essentially different, however, from either civil or criminal matters (even though, of course, marriage does entail civil questions pertaining to property and criminal questions pertaining to adultery). Rashi explained the difference as a result of the sacramental character of Jewish marriage (kretut), something that is fundamentally different from the private contract type character of most of civil law.[34] Another medieval commentator noted that in civil matters, the Rabbis assumed that we can rely on ordinary, rationally evident criteria (such as the reliability of public institutions like adjudication and testimony) when these institutions are constituted within a morally respectable legal order.[35]

Jewish marriage is considered to be something much deeper and more permanent than could ever be enforced by any contract, indeed the very agreement in which it originates is not considered to be contractual.[36] It is a

31 *See* Hans Kelsen, The Pure Theory of Law 312-13 (M. Knight trans., 1967).

32 *See Robbery and Loss* 5.18 (Maimonides, Mishneh Torah).

33 *See* S. Shilo, Dina de-Malkhuta Dina 269-74 (1974).

34 *See Gittin* 9b (Babylonian Talmud). Rashi also points out that because Judaism sees the establishment of a coherent system of civil and criminal justice to be a universal requirement, therefore applying to gentiles as well as to Jews, Jews can rely on any morally coherent system of justice when necessary. *See Sanhedrin* 56a-b (Babylonian Talmud).

35 *See Gittin* 9b (Babylonian Talmud).

36 *See* Novak, *supra* note 22, at 133-38.

covenant (*berit*).[37] It is entered into by the parties with no *terminus ad quem* inherent in it *ab initio*: it is meant to be "until death do us part." The termination of marriage in divorce is, therefore, not something necessary within the marriage itself; instead, it is only a possibility that requires some external factor to realize it. It is the result of an unanticipated factor (such as adultery) that comes into the marriage *post factum*.[38] Jewish divorce, from the details of Jewish marriage law and derived by inference from the negative to the positive, is itself not considered to be a matter of contract, neither in origin nor in enforcement.[39] Thus, the *Palestinian Talmud* asserts that

> the gentiles do not have anything like Jewish marriage [*kiddushin*]. Do they have anything like Jewish divorce [*gerushin*]? Rabbi Judah ben Pazi and Rabbi Hanin [said] in the name of Rabbi Honeh, senior authority of the *Sepphoris*, that they [the gentiles] either do not have divorce at all or the parties divorce each other.[40]

This exclusive view of divorce is connected to a scriptural discussion of divorce where there is an emphasis on its direct relation to the covenant with "the Lord God of Israel."[41] Thus marriage and divorce, the mandated and desired *terminus a quo* and the possible but undesired *terminus ad quem* of a uniquely Jewish relationship, are considered to be matters too far within the interior of covenantal Jewish life to be allowed any non-Jewish jurisdiction over them whatsoever.

There are, of course, some aspects of Jewish marriage that are quite similar to aspects of non-Jewish marriages, especially as regards monetary matters.[42] To assert otherwise would be fantastic. Furthermore, on the more normative level, Judaism recognizes the prohibition of adultery, the most basic violation of the marital relationship (and in some views the only justifiable ground for divorce), to be universal.[43] Adultery is a grave offense, to be punished by law, whether the adulterers are Jews or not.[44] Despite this commonality (to which I shall return at the end of this paper), Jewish marriage has such an immediately Jewish religious character that to allow any outside jurisdiction over it would be something like letting matters of Jewish worship and ritual be decided either by secular or non-Jewish religious norms.

Although it is much easier, as noted above, to justify non-Jewish jurisdiction in civil and criminal matters, despite the hope that this not be the case optimally, one can even see the absence of non-Jewish jurisdiction in Jewish

---

37 *See id.*

38 For the prohibition of initiating a marriage with the intention of subsequently terminating it, see *Yevamot* 37b (Babylonian Talmud); *Gittin* 90b (Babylonian Talmud); *Divorce* 10.21 (Maimonides, Mishneh Torah); *see also* David Novak, Law and Theology in Judaism 1-14 (1974).

39 *See Kiddushin* 5a (Babylonian Talmud).

40 *Kiddushin* 1.1/58c (Palestinian Talmud).

41 *Malachi* 2:16.

42 *See Yevamot* 122b (Babylonian Talmud). *See generally* Louis M. Epstein, The Jewish Marriage Contract (1973).

43 *See Sanhedrin* 58a (Babylonian Talmud).

44 *See id.*

marital matters as not being absolute in the past, let alone contemporaneously.

3. *Jewish Divorce and Non-Jewish Courts.*

An important exception to the general principle of excluding non-Jewish jurisdiction from Jewish marital matters is found in the following statement in the *Mishnah*: "A bill of divorce given under compulsion [*get me'usseh*] is valid if it is ordered by a Jewish court, but if by a gentile court it is invalid. If the gentiles beat a man and say to him, 'Do what the Jews tell you,' it is valid [*kasher*]."[45] It is important to explicate the fuller meaning of this rule in order to better appreciate how it relates non-Jewish jurisdiction to Jewish jurisdiction.

According to scriptural law, a man has the right to divorce his wife, but a wife has no right to divorce her husband.[46] The Rabbis assumed there need be some cause for a man to be able to exercise this right, but there are debates about what such a cause must be. The opinions on this subject range from presumption of adultery, to incompatibility, to the desire of the man to marry someone else in place of his present wife.[47] The tradition subsequently settled on incompatibility as sufficient cause for a man to divorce his wife if he so chooses.[48] Left at this level, though, it would seem that a man has almost unlimited rights in divorce, whereas a woman has no rights at all.

Even though the tradition never intended to fully equalize women and men in marriage, it did, however, limit the rights of a man and expand the rights of a woman.[49] In a variety of ways, the Rabbis removed the right to be married from some men for several reasons. One reason would be that the marriage was improperly initiated.[50] For example, when a woman had been coerced into marriage by a man, the marriage was to be subsequently annulled by a rabbinical court.[51] Thus, the right of a woman not to be married against her will was thereby recognized. As the *Talmud* later pointed out, the wording of the *Mishnah* "the woman is acquired [*niqneit*] as a wife" rather than "the man acquires [*qoneh*] a wife" is made to show that a woman is only "acquired" by a man if that is "not done under coercion [*ba'al korhah*]."[52] A coerced marriage is institutionalized rape.[53]

Moreover, the Rabbis basically gave a woman the right to sue for divorce.[54] A woman had to show that her husband had not fulfilled her scrip-

45 *Gittin* 9.8 (Mishnah).

46 *See Deuteronomy* 24:1-4.

47 *See Gittin* 9.10 (Mishnah).

48 *See Gittin* 9.10 (Maimonides Commentary on the Mishnah); *Divorce* 10.21 (Mishneh Torah); *Gittin* 90b (Babylonian Talmud).

49 *See* Novak, *supra* note 22, at 202-04.

50 *See Baba Bathra* 48b (Babylonian Talmud).

51 *See id.*

52 *Kiddushin* 2b (Babylonian Talmud).

53 Thus, the Fourteenth century commentator R. Menahem ha-Meiri noted that if there were only the biblical institution of marriage, no Jewish woman would remain a Jew. *See* Bet ha-Behirah, Kidduṣhin 8 (A. Sofer ed., 1963).

54 Maimonides noted that the court's action in forcing a man to divorce his wife is occa-

turally prescribed rights to food, clothing, and regular sexual intercourse.[55] If this could be shown, which would be quite easy in cases where the husband and wife no longer shared common domicile, then the rabbinical court should enforce the woman's right to either a proper marriage or a divorce.[56] If the husband refused to comply with the court order, the judges could even force the husband (including the use of physical coercion) to divorce his wife.[57] Thus, marriage was, in effect, defined to give a husband more duties to his wife and a wife more rights from her husband. Subsequent authorities went so far as to include the general unhappiness of a wife with her husband during the course of their marriage (when she says *ma'is alei*, literally, "he disgusts me") to be sufficient cause for a court to order him to divorce her, although others strongly disagree with ordering a divorce for a complaint so imprecise.[58] Also, a major medieval authority required the consent of a woman to accept a divorce from her husband as a condition of its being valid. Eventually, this ruling became virtually universal in Jewry.[59] Finally, with the growing acceptance of the medieval ban on polygamy (made by the same major authority who required the woman's consent to accept a divorce), it became possible to make promiscuity on the part of the husband grounds for his wife to petition the court to order him to divorce her.

The paradox of forcing a husband to do what Scripture seems to have designated to be his free option to do is ingeniously explained by the medieval jurist and theologian, Maimonides. He speculates that the coercion on the part of the court is simply a restoration of the sanity of someone who has become temporarily insane.[60] Maimonides assumes, at least at a level that might be termed the "collective unconscious," every member of the community really wants to do what is right.[61] So, the man who refuses to comply with the order of the court is truly acting out of character. The punishing action of the court, then, is in his best interest by restoring him to consciously law abiding action.[62] Accordingly, the husband's own best interest (*bonum sibi*) is seen in its being subordinate to the common good (*bonum commune*). In this case, the common good of the institution of marriage itself is not well served when marriages are allowed to continue "in name only." Conversely, the common good is well served when persons are allowed to marry whomever they truly want to marry (within the range of the community, of course).[63] All of this emphasizes the communal-covenantal nature of both marriage and divorce in Judaism.

---

sioned by a woman's petition to the court for a divorce [*she-tav'ah ha'ishah et ha-gerushin*]. *See* MAIMONIDES, COMMENTARY ON THE MISHNAH 164 (Y. Kafih ed., 1965).

55 *See Ketubot* 5.6, 6.1 (Mishnah).

56 *See id.* at 61b.

57 *See Arakhin* 5.6 (Mishnah); *Arakhin* 21a (Babylonian Talmud).

58 *See Ketubot* 63b (Babylonian Talmud).

59 *See* MENACHEM ELON, 2 JEWISH LAW 784-86 (Bernard Auerbach & Melvin J. Sykes trans., 1994).

60 *See Divorce* 2.20 (Mishneh Torah).

61 *See id.*

62 *See id.*

63 *See Kiddushin* 41a (Babylonian Talmud).

With this background in mind, one can now appreciate the force of the *Mishnah*'s authorization of the use of gentiles to coerce a Jewish man to divorce his wife. It will be recalled that this is invalid when the gentiles do this at their own initiative.[64] Only a Jewish court can have such power over Jews in a Jewish matrimonial dispute.[65] On the other hand, what justifies a Jewish court using gentiles to enforce its own decision? The cause of such action would seem to be that the Jewish court does not have the political power to enforce its own decision. The reason for permitting this recourse is that the Jewish court can, in effect, temporarily deputize gentiles to accomplish its own ends.[66] It also seems that this is not deputizing individual gentiles but, rather, deputizing a non-Jewish court. This distinction is important because to deputize individuals to commit an act of violence (which is what coercion is by definition) would surely violate the very condition of Jews being part of a larger jurisdiction, namely, "the law of the Government is law."[67]

There are few societies that have not monopolized violence for the state in the form of police power. This police power is designed to protect private persons and their property from violence, to punish violence committed against the citizens, and to protect public officials and public property from violence. As such, the fact of gentiles being deputized by Jews is justified by the primary Jewish jurisdiction requesting an ancillary non-Jewish jurisdiction to do something the Jewish jurisdiction itself cannot do in order that justice be done. This situation is the rough equivalent of one jurisdiction asking another to return a criminal to its control because this criminal has committed an act the other jurisdiction can also recognize as unjust—even by its own criteria. Without this type of justification, though, that other jurisdiction could well regard the "criminal" whose extradition is being requested to be like a political prisoner, one whose flight from his previous jurisdiction is just, and who should be granted asylum rather than their being forced to comply with the unjust orders of his or her original society.[68]

Of course, by so doing, the Jewish court has granted jurisdiction to the non-Jewish court that, in principle, it should not have. That is why this grant of jurisdiction should be considered a sort of emergency measure, something to be very rarely invoked. Nevertheless, in countries where common law pertains, if a non-Jewish court does intervene in such a Jewish matrimonial dis-

---

64 *See Gittin* 9.8 (Mishnah).

65 *See id.*

66 Thus, in their respective comments on *Gittin* 88b (Babylonian Talmud), the medieval commentators R. Solomon ibn Adret (*Hiddushei ha-Rashba*) and R. Yom Tov ben Abraham Ishbili (*Hiddushei ha-Ritva*) noted that the gentile court is only an "instrument" in the hands of the Jewish court, rather than a full agent (*shaliah*) inasmuch as a gentile could not fully effect a Jewish religious act on behalf of a Jew. *See Berahkot* 5.5 (Mishnah); *Kiddushin* 41b (Babylonian Talmud); *Baba Metsia* 71b (Babylonian Talmud). In the case of forcing a divorce, the gentile court functions like a catalyst that enables the Jewish court to complete its own enforcement of a Jewish woman's right to have her marriage terminated for just cause.

67 *See Gittin* 10b (Babylonian Talmud).

68 For example, Scripture rules that Jews are not to extradite gentile slaves back to their gentile masters when these slaves have sought asylum in a Jewish jurisdiction. *See Deuteronomy* 23:16-17. Rashi assumes that the reason for this is because such extradition would be returning a gentile slave to idolatry, something taken to be prohibited to all human beings everywhere.

pute on behalf of a Jewish court, it has created a legal precedent. So, if other cases like this come before non-Jewish courts, then by *stare decisis* what was meant to be an ad hoc measure becomes a factor relied upon by the legal system. The price the Jewish court pays for this help from the non-Jewish court is that, to a certain extent, Jewish marriage has become something not exclusively governed by Jewish criteria. This has profound ramifications for the contemporary institution of Jewish marriage in those societies where Jews have ready access to secular courts.

4. *The Modern* Agunah *Problem.*

From medieval times up to the period just before the French Revolution, European Jewish communities had a good deal of internal autonomy, especially in handling religious matters, of which marriage is a prime factor.[69] Jews were not citizens of the states in which they lived because citizenship was confined to the Christian subjects of the Christian sovereign.[70] Jews were members of a foreign nation whose particular community had a social contract with the local sovereign.[71] These Jewish communities functioned very much as *imperium in imperio*.[72] Accordingly, it was in the best interests of both the host society and the Jewish community that the Jews keep as much of their own domestic house in order as possible.[73]

Because of this political reality in pre-modern times, it was very rare for Jewish authorities to have any need of non-Jewish authorities to intervene in Jewish matrimonial matters. Thus, the problem of the *agunah* (a wife still considered, *de jure*, to be married to a *de facto* absent husband) was almost always a problem of a husband who had disappeared (either by accident or by design), not one where a husband publicly refused to follow a court order to divorce his wife.[74] Because of the political and social power of the Jewish courts at this time, such recalcitrant husbands could be subjected to very real political and social pressures to conform to the ruling of the juridical representatives of the whole community. The Jewish courts had police power over the Jews within their communal domain.[75] The *Mishnah*'s provision for the use of a non-Jewish court in such cases of willful contempt of court was largely a legal possibility, not a political and social necessity for the most part. Membership in the Jewish community was considered by neither the Jews nor their gentile hosts to be a voluntary matter. Nationhood and one's specific status in those days were considered to be matters of birth rather than volition, matters of status rather than matters of contract.[76]

---

69 *See generally* Jacob Katz, Tradition and Crisis 11-50 (1971).

70 *See id.*

71 *See id.*

72 *See id.*

73 *See id*; *see also* S.M. Nadler, Spinoza 10-15 (1999).

74 In the Talmud and post-talmudic legal literature, the attempts to find lenient solutions within the law for enabling the wives of absent husbands to remarry were almost always attempts to accept testimony from just about anyone about the death of the absent husband. *See Yevamot* 87b-88b (Babylonian Talmud).

75 *See Sanhedrin* 16b.

76 For this famous distinction, see generally Sir Henry Maine, Ancient Law (1913).

Beginning in Western Europe, all of this changed (sometimes quite abruptly) when the French Revolution and its political aftermath ended the privileges of the autonomous Jewish communities (*qehillot*). In place of these communal privileges, Jews were now entitled to become individual citizens of the secular state.[77] As individual citizens, they now had the right to form private associations, as long as these associations were not considered to be in violation of the laws of the state.[78] Accordingly, the state cannot be called upon to enforce the basically private rules of any such association.[79] Just as citizenship in the state itself is taken to be a matter of social contract, entered into voluntarily and from which one could (at least in principle) voluntarily resign, the same is true for membership in any association entitled by the state. One can simply disobey the rules of any such association or resign from it with legal impunity. Even those who did not resign from such associations could not be subjected to any police action from within such an association itself; the most the association could do is expel such recalcitrant members from membership.[80] Indeed, were this not the case, we would have the political anomaly of the state itself having less coercive power than a private association it has entitled.

Because Jewish associations usually have been local congregations, and considering the greater personal mobility of modern Jews from that of medieval Jews, it has become quite easy for Jews in contempt of the court of one congregation to simply move, with a good deal of anonymity, to another congregation. The sad fact, too, is that many traditional Jewish congregations take no action on behalf of Jewish women who have just claims to order their husbands to give them a Jewish divorce. Adding to this communal anarchy is the possibility of a modern Jew opting for no other congregation, or moving to a congregation of those modern Jewish religious movements who do not regard traditional Jewish law to be legally binding.

The issue of Jews who refuse to grant their spouses a Jewish divorce (*get*) has become a *cause célèbre* in the contemporary Jewish community.[81] Here is where the question of the interrelation of jurisdictions comes most pointedly

77 *See* KATZ, *supra* note 69, 11-60.

78 *See id.*

79 *See, e.g.*, Morris v. Morris [1973] 42 D.L.R.3d 550, 568 (Can.) (Guy, J., concurring) ("We are bound to administer the law of Canada as it is written, and the power of the civil Courts of justice should not be extended to assist rabbinical courts or, indeed, any religious sects, to enforce their orders."); *id.* at 571 (Hall, J.) ("In Canada all religious bodies are considered as voluntary associations. The law recognizes their existence and protects them in their enjoyment of property, but unless civil rights are in question it does not interfere with their organization or with questions of religious faith.") (quoting Ukranian Catholic Church v. Trustees of Ukranian Catholic Cathedral of St. Mary the Protectress [1939] 2 D.L.R. 494, 498 (Can.) (Dennistoun, J.) (citing Dunnet v. Forneri [1877] 25 Gr. 199, 206 (Can.))).

80 In his arguments for the full political emancipation of Jews in the new secular nation-states, the German Jewish philosopher, Moses Mendelssohn, stressed the point that Jewish communities should no longer exercise formal excommunication (*herem*) of deviant members because this still smacked of the communal power Jews needed to renounce in order to win citizenship for themselves. *See* MOSES MENDELSSOHN, JERUSALEM 73-75 (Allan Arkush trans., 1983).

81 There is now substantial literature on this subject. *See, e.g.*, 4 JEWISH LAW ANNUAL (Bernard S. Jackson ed., 1981); SHLOMO RISKIN, WOMEN AND JEWISH DIVORCE (1989).

into focus. Although the general problem of the recalcitrant spouse is ancient, there is the specific problem of the recalcitrant spouse in modern secular society. The point of difference is that modern spouses are also participants in the specifically modern institution of civil marriage. In ancient times, when non-Jewish authorities were infrequently (if ever) deputized by a Jewish court to force a recalcitrant spouse to do what the Jewish court itself could not get him to do, the non-Jewish elements were being imported into a purely internal Jewish matter for ad hoc assistance as it were. But now, in every modern democratic state in the West of which I know, all Jews are married in civil law, and most Jews *also* opt to be married by some form of Jewish religion.

This is a state of affairs that Jewish authorities accepted at the beginnings of the time when Jews were first being accepted as citizens in modern, secular polities. One can pinpoint it to the year 1807 when Napoleon convened what he called, with typical grandiosity, a *Sanhedrin*.[82] This body consisted of leading Rabbis in the lands under French imperial domain.[83] Napoleon wanted assurances that the Jews, who were now losing the traditional privileges of their own communal authority, would be loyal to the new state and its overall constitution.[84] The state had removed the monopoly of the Church on the legitimization of marriage by instituting civil marriage.[85] Thus, civil marriage was a necessity for anyone who wished to marry, whereas religious marriage was now only a purely voluntary matter once the required civil marriage had been performed.[86] Civil marriage, therefore, became a publicly required contract in a way that religious marriage could not be.[87] Accordingly, Napoleon wanted to know whether or not the Jews would also recognize the validity of civil marriages.[88] At the very least, this required all Jews to now become participants in civil marriage. Taken to its extreme, Napoleon's dictate seemed to require Jews to recognize civil marriages between Jews and gentiles, which is something Jewish law not only does not recognize *post factum*, but also prohibits *ab initio*.[89]

The Rabbis of the 1807 *Sanhedrin* cleverly answered the most serious challenge (that of civil marriage between Jews and gentiles) by saying that they would recognize the *civil* validity of such civil marriages.[90] In other words, they did not say they would recognize them as *Jewish* marriages (which they had no authority, of course, to do—and which I cannot imagine any one of them ever wanting to do), but that they would not interfere with the civil right of the state to recognize such marriages by its own criteria. In more traditional Jewish congregations, this hardly posed much of a problem, as most Jews civilly married to gentiles would either leave or be expelled

---

82 *See generally* S. Schwarzfuchs, Napolean, the Jews, and the *Sanhedrin* (1979).

83 *See id.*

84 *See id.*

85 *See id.*

86 *See id.*

87 *See id.*

88 *See id.*

89 *See Kiddushin* 68b (Babylonian Talmud).

90 *See* C. Touati, *Le Grand* Sanhedrin *de 1807 et le Droit Rabbinique*, *in* Le Grand Sanhedrin de Napolean 44-45 (1979).

from the congregation anyway. In more liberal Jewish congregations, though, it does pose the religious anomaly of gentiles being members of a *Jewish* congregation.

Even though the secular state has made participation in a religious marriage something *subsequent* to participation in civil marriage, traditional Jews have regarded their involvement in civil marriage as a necessity of their participation in civil society, but a necessity to which their subordination to Jewish law is *prior*. At the level of principle, this is clearly paradoxical: two separate jurisdictions, each claiming priority for itself. Nevertheless, on the practical level, there need not be troublesome confrontation because the secular state does not require one to make an ultimate commitment to its own authority. This distinguishes secular democracies from the secularism of a fascist or communist regime. All a democratic regime asks is compliance with its civil authority.[91] This policy easily enables religious people to decide whether or not such compliance is consistent with their ultimate commitment to the authority of their God as revealed and transmitted to them by their own tradition.[92]

In the case of the recalcitrant spouse, this new state of affairs actually gives the religious community a powerful new tool in its attempts to comply with the just claims of wronged spouses. This new tool is the reality that participation in a civil marriage seems to be viewed more and more as a civil contract.[93] Because in countries like Canada and the United States clergy function as the celebrants of both religious *and* civil marriages (by officiating at wedding ceremonies that combine both aspects into one event) it could be argued that one has agreed *civilly* to initiate and terminate the marriage in compliance with both civil and religious criteria. The religious criteria are assumed to have been accepted by the tacit consent of both parties in that they voluntarily consented to be married in a religious ceremony. Lawyers in both Canadian and American courts have argued for the withholding of a civil divorce decree until "religious" impediments to the remarriage of either spouse have been removed.[94] In the case of Jewish spouses, neither party can remarry, according to Jewish law, without a properly executed divorce or annulment.[95] Along these lines, many traditional Rabbis in Canada and the United States require couples before their wedding ceremony to sign a pre-

91 Anything more than that would violate the protection of religious liberty—i.e., the right to have an ultimate allegiance beyond the authority of the State—guaranteed by the First Amendment of the United States Constitution. U.S. CONST. amend. I. Thus, the Constitution recognizes religious liberty but does not create it.

92 *See* NOVAK, *supra* note 9, at 12-26.

93 *See, e.g.*, *Morris*, 42 D.L.R.3d at 553 (Freedman, C.J., dissenting) (noting that "it is important to keep in mind that we are here simply concerned with a contract between two parties and the matter of its enforcement. We are not concerned with a conflict having its genesis in an order of an ecclesiastical court and thus posing the question of the proper limits of jurisdiction between a civil Court and a religious court.").

94 For example, in Ontario the relevant law states that one petitioning for a civil divorce must have "removed all barriers that are within his or her control and that would prevent the other spouse['s] remarriage within that spouse['s] faith . . . ." Family Law Act, S.O., ch. 4, § 2 (1986) (Can.).

95 *See, e.g.*, J. David Bleich, *Modern-Day Agunot*, *in* 4 JEWISH LAW Annual, *supra* note 50, at 169-87.

nuptial agreement, stipulating that they will comply with the ruling of a Jewish court in the event of their filing for a civil divorce.[96]

How effective such arguments will actually be in the civil courts is still an open question. After all, it is rather tenuous to assume that Jewish marriage can be viewed as a kind of civil contract, for it seems that the legal equality of the parties essential to a civil contract is missing in a Jewish marital covenant.[97] The Jewish tradition seems to have no interest in equalizing the partners in a marriage.[98] Egalitarianism is not one of its desiderata.[99] Instead, one can see a series of normative decisions within the tradition that are designed to prevent or remedy the unjust exploitation of one party by another despite their essential differences, in this case the exploitation of a woman by a man.

In what might be seen as an eagerness to employ secular means to solve a basically religious problem, though, a number of scholars of Jewish law have uncritically compared Jewish marriage to a civil contract for this purpose. Despite undoubtedly noble intentions, their arguments are weak. Professor J. David Bleich states that

> [t]he [*get*] proceedings are devoid of divine reference or other religious formulae. No blessings are uttered, no credos or professions of faith are pronounced. Execution of a *get* does not require that the participants subscribe to any particular set of beliefs. Indeed, a *get* may . . . be executed even if the husband has formally renounced Judaism.[100]

Despite the correct facts mentioned by Professor Bleich, his interpretation of their implications for the view that Jewish marriage is, in effect, a civil contract is erroneous and misleading. First, the fact that blessings and other religious formulae invoking the name of God are not part of the writing or delivery of a *get* does not make it a "secular" enterprise. There are other situations in Jewish law where obviously religious acts are performed and the name of God is not invoked for a variety of very specific reasons.[101] Also, not invoking the name of God does not religiously invalidate an act *ex post facto*, even when such invocation is required *ab initio*.[102] Second, although the husband who is giving the *get* need not fulfill any religious criteria, and he could even be an apostate from Judaism, does not mean that this is a "secular" enterprise. The fact is that Judaism does not regard a nonreligious Jew, even an apostate, as being exempt from religious duties. These duties are clearly religious (*mitsvot*), irrespective of what the subjective motives of the one performing them happen to be. Whenever, wherever, and however some of them can be performed, they are to be performed.[103] Furthermore, even

---

96 *See id.*

97 *Deuteronomy* 24:1-4.

98 *See* NOVAK, *supra* note 22, at 202-04.

99 *See* DAVID NOVAK, HALAKHAH IN A THEOLOGICAL DIMENSION 61-71 (1985).

100 J. David Bleich, *Jewish Divorce: Judicial Misconceptions and Possible Means of Civil Enforcement*, 16 CONN. L. REV. 201, 257 (1984).

101 *See Blessings* 11.2 (Maimonides, Mishneh Torah).

102 *See id.* at 1.6.

103 *See* NOVAK, *supra* note 4, at 189-99.

though any Jewish husband may give the *get* to his wife, the *get* itself is to be written by someone who must be certifiable as a religiously observant Jew.[104] This requirement also pertains to those persons designated to witness the writing and delivery of the *get* to the man's wife.[105]

The problem with Bleich's statement, and others like it, is it avoids the philosophical issue at the heart of the *agunah* problem for Jews living as citizens of a democracy.[106] As distinct from ancient and medieval times, Jews are now full citizens of the regimes whose help they now seek in cases of recalcitrant spouses. Moreover, they are now participants in civil marriage, an institution in which all the citizens of the regime, Jews and gentiles alike, have equal access. As such, Jews now have more power in civil society and in civil marriage. In the short run, this seems to offer some hope of help from the state in forcing recalcitrant spouses to comply with the order of a Jewish court to either give or accept a Jewish divorce although, as we have seen, it is still too early to judge the legal effectiveness of this policy. Nevertheless, in the long run, there seem to be some important negative implications of this policy.

5. *The Price of Secularity.*

On legal grounds, most Jewish authorities have stretched the meaning of the *Mishnah*'s provision, "do what the Jews tell you," to cover the order of a secular court to a Jewish spouse to end a marriage according to Jewish religious law. The text literally says, however, "do what *Israel* tells you to do." That is, it deals with a situation where the non-Jewish authorities recognize the *communal* authority of the Jewish court in the same way the court of one national jurisdiction recognizes the national jurisdiction of another court.[107] It is like a Canadian court ordering an American citizen, who is a resident of Canada, to obey his or her American national authorities. In principle, it is a form of extradition. Where there is, however, a constitutional separation of

---

104 *See Divorce* 3.15-16 (Maimonides, Mishneh Torah); *see also Sanhedrin* 3.3 (Mishnah); *Niddah* 6.4 (Mishnah); *Sanhedrin* 27a (Babylonian Talmud) (concerning the religious qualifications for those designated to write, deliver, and witness the *get* and all other Jewish legal proceedings); *Sanhedrin* 10.1 (Maimonides, Mishneh Torah).

105 *See id.*

106 Distinguishing Jewish marriage law from the common law of England and its "conception of marriage as a sacrament" and a "sacred institution," Israeli Supreme Court Justice Haim Cohn wrote that "marriage in Jewish law is a contract, albeit a very solemn one . . . ." ELIOT N. DORFF & ARTHUR ROSSETT, A LIVING TREE 460 (1988). Unlike Bleich, whose motives are to show a particular secular aspect of Jewish religious law, Cohn, as a secularist Israeli jurist, has elsewhere stated that his intention is to show the essentially secular possibilities of Jewish law as it governs interhuman relations. *See generally* HAIM H. COHN, HUMAN RIGHTS IN JEWISH LAW (1984). If Jewish marriage (and divorce), however, is "a [civil] contract," why is marriage itself deemed a religious duty, *Yevamot* 6.6 (Mishnah), and why is divorce frequently deemed a religious duty rather than a neutral option? *See, e.g.*, *Yevamot* 10.1 (Mishnah). To use Cohn's words against his own argument: the "solemnity" of Jewish marriage (and divorce) contradicts any attempt to see it as a "contract" at all. A contract presupposes an autonomy that is always trumped by any religious obligation.

107 Accordingly, most commentators emphasize that the gentile court must recognize, either explicitly or implicitly, the authority of the Jewish jurisdiction (*dinei yisrael*) and its court (*bet din shel yisrael*). *See, e.g.*, *Gittin* 9.8 (Maimonides Commentary on the Mishnah).

church and state, a secular court could not literally say "do what Israel [the Jewish communal authorities] tells you" to any of its citizens. In the United States, as well as in Canada and other Western democracies, everyone is a citizen of the state qua *individual*; no voluntary communal association is recognized as having legal jurisdiction similar to that of the state because all Jews have been fully integrated into the secular state as citizens equal to all other citizens. That is why, as we have seen, for purposes of secular remedy to the problem of a recalcitrant spouse, marriage has to be viewed as a private contract between consenting adult individuals. A tacit part of that contract is then taken to be an agreement to fulfill certain religious requirements (both *a parte ante* and *a parte post*) when the marriage was initiated in a religious ceremony.

In terms of legal interpretation, such an elastic interpretation of a term from its original context is hardly novel in Jewish law (or in any other system of law, for that matter). This interpretation is largely the necessary function of casuistry, that is, the process whereby the law is applied to new cases, cases quite different from the situations from which the law emerged originally. When the stretching becomes quite radical, we call it a *fictio juris*.[108] Whether the new use of "do what Israel tells you" is ordinary casuistry or whether it constitutes a more radical legal fiction is debatable. Nevertheless, it is certainly a historical departure. It represents a recognition of the new, modern secularity of marriage, something the Rabbis surely did not have in mind. The price paid for this new definition of Jewish marriage is that the secular, non-Jewish state now plays a greater role in Jewish marriage than it had previously. At a time when secular definitions of marriage seem to be veering farther and farther away from traditional Jewish definitions of marriage per se (Jewish or non-Jewish), this should be a cause for concern on the part of most traditional Jewish jurists. Many traditional Jewish jurists, however, seem to be fascinated with the new possibilities of making Jewish law a matter of interest to secular legal systems.[109] A similar fascination transpires in the new field of bioethics, where Jewish ethicist-jurists have also taken a large interest.[110] Many jurists seem oblivious to the political implications of this new situation. At present, I see two specific areas of concern.

One, the principle of "do what Israel tells you" should be taken to be the ad hoc, emergency measure it undoubtedly was and was meant to be in talmudic times. The greater frequency of this problem today, especially because of the moral aspersions it casts on Judaism itself, requires a more general and a more radical solution than the rather artificial act of deputizing a non-Jewish court. The moral aspersions this general situation casts on Judaism is that it strongly implies that the Jewish tradition does not care about the exploitation of Jewish women by unscrupulous Jewish men (who are the vast majority of the recalcitrant spouses). Not only does it present Judaism in a negative moral light to the world, it also seriously tempts many Jewish women to opt out of the Jewish religious-legal system altogether. Why should modern Jew-

108 *See generally* Lon L. Fuller, Legal Fictions (1967).

109 See generally 1-2 Asher Gulak, Yesodei ha-Mishpat ha' Ivri (1922) for the pioneering work in this area.

110 *See, e.g.*, Immanuel Jakobovits, Jewish Medical Ethics (1959).

ish women remain loyal to a system that seems so helpless to protect them from exploitation by men? Doesn't the tradition itself judge these men to be acting unjustly?[111] Such resignation from a religious community, as we have seen, can be done with ease and legal impunity in any modern democracy. Jews should be very concerned if they have to *regularly* turn to non-Jewish authorities to effect justice in an internal Jewish religious matter. The non-Jewish court was never meant to be a permanent feature of the Jewish religious scene, especially in an area of Jewish life as sacramental as marriage.[112]

Traditional Jews, who know the rabbinic sources, should be even more concerned with this non-Jewish, secular remedy to a Jewish moral problem when they (that is, in the person of their religious-juridical authorities) could largely solve the problem by the exercise of their own authority within their community. The internal Jewish remedy, which does not require the importation of any secular authority, is the institution of marriage annulment. Annulment is the power of a Jewish court to invalidate a marriage in lieu of the giving of a divorce by the husband to the wife.[113] This can be done when a rabbinical court determines that there were legal irregularities in the marriage ceremony itself, irrespective of how long the couple actually lived together as husband and wife.[114] For example, the rabbinical court discovers that the Jewish couple was not married in a Jewish religious ceremony, or that the couple was married in a Jewish religious ceremony where the absence of certain acts or persons means the marriage never had been valid, or there was no public marriage ceremony at all.[115] Less easily, but still available *de jure*, is the possibility of retroactive annulment of a marriage in which, *ab initio*, nothing irregular happened in the Jewish ceremony.[116] Thus a court, by *fictio juris*, can declare the object of value which the groom is required to transfer to his bride at the outset of the marriage ceremony, to *have been* of no value (what the Talmud calls "*hefqer*").[117]

Some more conservative Jewish jurists argue that this principle of annulment is theoretical, and may only be used in the exact cases to which it was

111 In this very discussion of the divorce of a Jewish woman by a husband who has been coerced to do so, the Talmud raises the question of a woman so desperate that she would even engage an individual gentile to so coerce her husband. *See Gittin* 88b (Babylonian Talmud). Even though the Talmud concludes that there is no validity whatsoever in such a divorce, perhaps the very mention of such a possibility in this context is to emphasize the responsibility of a Jewish court to facilitate a divorce in a case where a woman's rights have been violated by her husband, and so that she not be tempted to seek such a desperate solution to her just marital complaint.

112 See *Kiddushin* 2b (Babylonian Talmud) and *Nedarim* 5.6 (Mishnah) for the sacramental character of Jewish marriage.

113 *See Gittin* 33a (Babylonian Talmud); *see also* David Novak, *Annulment in Lieu of Divorce in Jewish Law*, *in* 4 JEWISH LAW ANNUAL, *supra*, note 50, at 188-206.

114 See RABBI MOSES FEINSTEIN, IGROT MOSHEH: *Even ha'Ezer* 74-76 (1961) for the most influential decisions made in this type (*a parte ante*) of annulment.

115 See David Novak, *The Marital Status of Jews Married Under Non-Jewish Auspices*, in 1 JEWISH LAW ASSOCIATION STUDIES 61-77 (1985).

116 *See* Novak, *supra* note 113, at 188-206.

117 *See Gittin* 33a (Babylonian Talmud); *Yevamot* 89b (Babylonian Talmud).

applied in the Talmud, none of which concern a recalcitrant spouse.[118] Nevertheless, one may counter this objection with three answers. One, it is no less radical an application of the principle "the Rabbis may remove marriage from him" (what is called "*afqa'at qiddushin*") than the use of a secular court in a modern constitutional democracy is a radical application of the principle "do what Israel tells you." The logic of strict construction could equally eliminate both solutions. So, if the principle of "do what Israel tells you" is now acceptable in a uniquely modern class of cases, then the same more expansive reasoning can be used to make the principle of "the Rabbis may remove marriage from him" acceptable in a uniquely modern class of cases. Second, the use of marriage annulment also returns full legal authority in Jewish marriage to the Jews. It avoids the dangerous legal fiction—which in essence has become a much larger political fiction—that Jewish marriage is a civil contract, something it was never ever meant to be. Third, we have an important precedent where the principle of annulment was used in a case involving a large number of people, in a way not specified in the Talmud.[119]

As for the possible objection that the adoption of this rabbinic procedure would, in effect, eliminate the use of the bill of divorce (*get*) prescribed by Scripture, there are two answers. First, it is still the fact that the vast majority of traditional Jews who terminate their marriages do so with the compliance of both spouses in the giving of a bill of divorce as prescribed by Scripture and the traditional interpretation of the specifics of scriptural law. If this ceased to be the case, there would be such a crisis in traditional Jewish marriage that the likelihood of no Jewish marriage would outweigh the likelihood of no Jewish divorce. (That is because divorce always presupposes marriage, whereas marriage only sometimes entails divorce.)[120] Second, there are ways that the introduction of annulment would actually make Jewish divorce the more attractive course of action. For example, a Jewish court could rule that a couple must have been living apart, or already have been civilly divorced, for a period of a year or two or more before annulment proceedings can even be started.[121] Or, a Jewish court could rule that once the annulment took place, the recalcitrant spouse cannot be considered for remarriage in a Jewish religious ceremony again—a kind of permanent marital excommunication.

Of course, all of this requires a degree of unanimity in the Jewish religious community at large that is sadly absent at present. Indeed, the effectiveness of annulment depends on the acceptance of this procedure by the vast majority of rabbinical courts. It would require the type of Jewish unanimity that eventually made the medieval ban on polygamy, something permitted (although not mandated) in scriptural and rabbinic law, almost universally effective.

---

118 *See generally* Aaron Rakeffet-Rothkopf, *Annulment of Marriage Within the Context of Cancellation of the Get, in* 15 TRADITION 173-85 (1975).

119 *See* MOSES ISSERLES, DARKHEI MOSHEH: EVEN HA-EZER 7 n.13 (Tur).

120 That might be why it is easier to initiate a Jewish marriage than terminate it. *See, e.g.*, *Kiddushin* 9a-b (Babylonian Talmud).

121 *Cf. Yevamot* 10.2/10c (Palestinian Talmud).

The growing number of cases of recalcitrant spouses in divorce proceedings might very well be a symptom of the larger theologico-political impotence of the traditional Jewish community, which cannot or will not exercise the power it possesses. This larger problem is hardly one that can be corrected by using non-Jewish institutions as a means of remedy. In the present situation, we have what the Talmud saw as an ultimate irony, namely, the sinner is rewarded (*hote niskar*).[122] In the case of the modern *agunah*, the spouse who is faithful to Jewish law is prevented by a failed marriage from achieving a successful union with someone else, whereas the spouse in contempt of Jewish law effectively gets the law to assist him (or her) in what can only be seen as an act of unwarranted cruelty. The invocation of a totally internal Jewish remedy would go a long way of restoring the confidence of both Jewish women and men in the moral power of their own religious authorities.

The second area of concern raised by the secularization of Jewish marriage law involves the most pressing moral question facing marriage law today: the question of same-sex marriages. Jewish marriage has been able to relate to civil marriage because there has been enough commonality at the most basic level to make the relation plausible.[123] Heretofore, civil marriage precluded incestous and homosexual unions *ab initio*, and it has punished adultery *post factum*.[124] These factors are still a residue of the time when marriage was regarded as much more than a contract, even in an officially secular society.

With the virtual ignoring of adultery as a cause for penalty in divorce proceedings, and with the distinct possibility that Canadian and American courts will make their *de facto* recognition of same sex unions qua "domestic partnerships" into literal marriage *de jure*, we may fast be reaching the point when the association of traditional Jewish marriage with civil marriage will be totally detrimental to traditional Jews.[125] The most powerful arguments for granting the right to marry to same-sex couples are made on the basis of what is taken to be the contractual nature of marriage.[126] There might come a time when Jews will be forced by the state, for all intents and purposes, not only to recognize as marriages what their tradition prohibits for Jews (like a marriage between a Jew and a gentile), but to recognize a same-sex union (in such matters as hiring practices), which Judaism teaches is prohibited to any human being.[127] Indeed, there may come a time when traditional Jews will seriously doubt whether they should be civilly married at all. After all, isn't it ironic that at the same time a small homosexual minority of the population who have heretofore been barred from marrying one another are now demanding inclusion in the institution of marriage, a much larger and growing number of Canadian and American heterosexual couples involved in "long-

122 *See, e.g.*, *Hallah* 2.7 (Mishnah); *Yevamot* 92b (Babylonian Talmud).

123 *See Hullin* 92a-b (Babylonian Talmud); *cf. Vayiqra Rabbah* 23.9.

124 *See, e.g.*, Canada Divorce Act, R.S.C., ch. D-8, § 8(1) (1970) (Can.).

125 *See Sanhedrin* 39b (Babylonian Talmud).

126 See David Orgon Coolidge, *Same-Sex Marriage?* Baehr v. Miike *and the Meaning of Marriage*, 38 S. TEX. L. REV. 34-38 (1997) for a full discussion of these types of arguments.

127 *See Sanhedrin* 58a (Babylonian Talmud).

term relationships" are ignoring formal marriage, civil or religious, altogether? Clearly, both the state and religious communities have less control over spousal arrangements in our society than they had in the past.

We are also faced with the possibility that many traditional Christians and Muslims in our society will also be so opposed to sharing the institution of marriage with what they regard as a violation of natural law that they too will simply opt for religious marriage without the intrusion of what they regard as a state dedicated to undermining what they consider to be universally acceptable definitions of marriage and family. If this happens we could be faced with a legal and political battle in our society that will make the legal and political battle over abortion, for example, look mild by comparison. In the face of all of this, traditional Jews are well advised to totally reconsider the overlapping of religious and secular jurisdictions in the institution of Jewish marriage. Its liability might now have far outweighed its benefits. To employ the metaphor used in the title of this paper: What is now a two-way street might have to become a one-way street again in order for the Jewish traffic to move towards its true destination.

Legal Pluralism and Women's Rights

[11]

Balancing Minority Rights and Gender Justice: The Impact of Protecting Multiculturalism on Women's Rights in India

By
Pratibha Jain*

Introduction

Can domestic legislation honor both the rights of women and the rights of cultural minorities within liberal political systems?[1] Or are the two goals necessarily at odds? Policy makers debate the role of multiculturalism in modern liberal societies and its effect on rights of women. Determining the most constructive approach for a state seeking to accommodate these competing interests requires that policy makers be sensitive to the needs of various cultural communities as well as to the needs of women or other marginalized populations. Perhaps nowhere is this challenge as currently significant as it is in India, a majority Hindu nation that is also home to 138,000,000 Muslims—the third largest Muslim community in the world—and 24,000,000 Christians,[2] and which has seen recent and vehement upsurges in both demands for minority rights and concomitant violence against religious minorities.

This paper studies the impacts of granting group rights to religious and cultural minorities within a nation-state, recognizing that such an entity can be comprised of multiple nations,[3] and examines the methods legislators and judges

---

* B.A. (Economics), Delhi; LL.B., Delhi; B.C.L., Oxford; LL.M., Harvard. Visiting Lecturer, School of Accounting & Finance, Hong Kong Polytechnic University. I would like to thank my husband for giving me the courage to publish this paper. I would also like to thank Professors Granville Austin, Michael Davis, M.P. Singh, Henry Steiner and Mr. N. Ravi for their valuable comments on an earlier draft of this Article, and the editors of BJIL for their excellent work in editing this Article. However, all errors remain my own.

1. For the purpose of this paper, I assume legal and political equality for all citizens to be a basic tenet that defines liberal democracies. For example, India guarantees equal rights to its citizens irrespective of race, gender, ethnicity, or language through its Constitution, whereas theocratic states have legal structures that reflect the religious laws of the majority religious communities in those countries.

2. Census of India, Data on Religion 2001, *at* http://www.censusindia.net/religiondata/Religiondata_2001.xls.

3. Sarah V. Wayland explains that a nation-state requires both "common culture, broadly defined . . . [and] bounded territorial space . . . . A 'nation-state' exists when the boundaries of the nation, or people, are the same as the boundaries of the state, or political entity." Sarah V. Wayland, *Citizenship and Incorporation: How Nation States Respond to the Challenges of Migration*, 20 Fletcher F. World Aff. 35, 36 (1996).

in India have used to navigate this balancing act as an example. India is a multicultural and pluralistic democracy, which through its Constitution provides a comprehensive framework for protecting and promoting the rights of religious, cultural, and linguistic minorities. Its successes and failures in balancing multiculturalist goals against women's rights are instructive of viable and non-viable constitutional, legislative, and judicial strategies a state might adopt to protect both the rights of women and the rights of cultural minorities.[4]

Part II outlines the debate surrounding the role of multiculturalism in modern liberal societies and its effect on the rights of women. Part III briefly discusses terminology and then deconstructs certain assumptions within the above debate as to the meanings of *culture*, *multiculturalism*, and *group rights*. Part IV considers multicultural approaches to governance, with India as a case study of successes and lessons for the future. Part V explores possible solutions, including a constitutional amendment that would affirm the rights of women within a scheme that still protects group rights.

I.
The Debate

A classical liberal rights scheme bestows rights on individuals rather than groups. These rights are generally "negative" rights such as freedom from government interference in one's speech, religion, and political ideology, or the right to freedom from discrimination. Barry Brian explains that this "strategy of privatization" can only conceive of individuals, and not groups, as possessors of human rights, because providing individuals with civil and political rights against state action gives them the necessary protection to promote their cultural identities without sacrificing either their individual rights or their right to culture.[5]

Those concerned with maintaining the existence of minority cultures within a dominant national majority culture worry that such a classical scheme based on individual rights cannot adequately protect minority cultures. They seek the implementation of specific legal obligations on the state not only to abstain from interfering with the group rights of minorities but also to provide affirmative support for the enjoyment of such rights, which range from negative rights such as the right to group existence[6] and the right to equality and freedom from discrimination, to positive rights such as the right to establish autonomous regimes through their right to self-determination and fulfillment of social and economic rights.

4. *See generally* Martha C. Nussbaum, *India: Implementing Sex Equality Through Law*, 2 Chi. J. Int'l L. 35 (2001).

5. Barry Brian, *The Strategy of Privatization*, *in* Culture and Equality: An Egalitarian Critique of Multiculturalism 19-62 (2001).

6. The right to group existence is established in the Convention on the Prevention and Punishment of the Crime of Genocide, Dec. 9, 1948, art. II, G.A. Res. 2670, 3 U.N. GAOR, pt. 1, U.N. Doc. A/810, p. 174, 78 U.N.T.S. 277 (criminalizing "acts committed with intent to destroy, in whole or in part, a national, ethnical, racial or religious group as such").

Without legal protection, group-rights advocates worry that minority groups will always be at a disadvantage within the wider society.[7] In a rapidly changing world, in which cultural identity forms states, and in which mass media can penetrate even the most isolated village, minority cultures are frequently undermined by social and economic forces beyond their control and the control of their governments, no matter how sympathetic. These advocates argue that only when states recognize group rights as necessary human rights will cultural minorities be able to survive in a global environment that is often hostile to their very existence.[8]

Article 27 of the International Convention on Civil and Political Rights (ICCPR) exemplifies this conception of group rights, guaranteeing "ethnic, religious, or linguistic minorities . . . the right . . . to enjoy their culture, to profess and practice their own religion, or to use their own language."[9] Couched in both individualistic and collective terms,[10] the notion of group rights has been used to advocate for the governance of minority groups by separate and culturally specific laws. In India, such group rights include personal law regimes, the concept of which can be traced back to the colonial era wherein the early colonial states promised the various religious communities their own set of laws to govern "inheritance, marriage, caste, and other religious usages or institutions."[11] Personal laws are sometimes used as cultural defenses to criminal prosecutions and as justification for the observation of cultural practices that have a tendency to discriminate against women.[12] Such discriminatory personal or group laws govern women in various Indian communities.[13]

Feminist legal scholars worry about the impact group rights have on the rights of women.[14] Because group rights provide the leaders within a group the power to discriminate against the weaker members within the group, a legal commitment to group rights may prove detrimental to women.[15] Combined with the fact that defining culture seems to be the prerogative of the leaders

7. *See generally* BHIKHU PAREKH, RETHINKING MULTICULTURALISM: CULTURAL DIVERSITY AND POLITICAL THEORY (2000).

8. *See, e.g.*, Eric J. Mitnick, *Three Models of Group-Differentiated Rights*, 35 COLUM. HUM. RTS. L. REV. 215 (2004).

9. International Covenant on Civil and Political Rights, Dec. 16, 1966, art. 27, GA res. 2200A (XXI), 21 U.N. GAOR, Supp. No. 16, at 52, U.N. Doc. A/6316 (1966); 999 U.N.T.S. 171 [hereinafter ICCPR].

10. *See* HENRY J. STEINER & PHILIP ALSTON, *Comment on Autonomy Regimes*, *in* INTERNATIONAL HUMAN RIGHTS IN CONTEXT: LAW, POLITICS, MORALS 992-93 (Henry J. Steiner & Philip Alston eds., 1st ed. 1996).

11. Kunal Parker, *Observations on the Historical Destruction of Separate Legal Regimes*, *in* RELIGION AND PERSONAL LAW IN SECULAR INDIA—A CALL TO JUDGMENT 184 (Gerald James Larson ed., 2001).

12. *See, e.g.*, Ronald R. Garet, *Communality and Existence: The Rights of Groups*, 56 S. CAL. L. REV. 1001 (1983).

13. *See* Kirti Singh, *Obstacles to Women's Rights in India*, *in* HUMAN RIGHTS OF WOMEN—NATIONAL & INTERNATIONAL PERSPECTIVES 375-396 (Rebecca Cook ed., 1994).

14. *See generally* Leti Volpp, *Talking "Culture": Gender, Race, Nation, and the Politics of Multiculturalism*, 96 COLUM. L. REV. 1573 (1996).

15. *See generally*, Susan Moller Okin, *Justice and Gender: An Unfinished Debate*, 72 FORDHAM L. REV. 1537 (2004).

within the group, who are traditionally men, group rights appear juxtaposed against women's rights. In India for example, Muslim fundamentalist leaders historically used the personal laws as tools for denying equality to Muslim women, while "[t]he state continued to privilege group rights over the equality rights of Muslim women, rather than insisting on reform."[16] Granting group rights to preserve patriarchal traditional cultures thus sometimes appears at odds with a feminist project.

The ever-widening wealth disparity between first-world and third-world nations, increasing global poverty, international market integration, and globalization has spawned massive trans-border displacement of peoples and cultures. Multicultural populations are a reality facing most states today, forcing them to utilize political and legislative tools to balance the rights of women with the cultural rights of minority groups. Since its independence, India has relied on a two-tier system of personal laws that are specific to particular religious communities and universal civil codes that apply to all citizens. While the latter appear to protect the rights of Indian women to equal treatment and equal opportunity, the personal laws of most religious communities have historically undercut women's access to judicially enforceable civil rights.

II.
Definitions and Assumptions

Before proceeding with an exploration of the successes and failures of various Indian legislation and case law that address the balance between minority group rights and the rights of women, I would like to define a few concepts that are crucial to this paper's exploration.

A. *Culture*

None of the international conventions that purport to protect or promote group rights for minority cultures have defined what they mean by "culture," however, it is necessary to explain exactly what is being protected. J. Oloka-Onyango and Sylvia Tamale believe that the most important aspect of culture is that it is a "dynamic and evolving feature of human action," thought, and identity.[17] The United Nations Development Programme echoes this notion, asserting that "[c]ulture is not a frozen set of values and practices. It is constantly recreated as people question, adapt and redefine their values and practices to changing realities and exchanges of ideas."[18] Such a progressive understanding

16. Vrinda Narain, Gender and Community: Muslim Women's Rights in India 107 (2001).

17. J. Oloka-Onyango & Sylvia Tamale, *"The Personal is Political" or Why Women's Rights Are Indeed Human Rights: An African Perspective on International Feminism*, 17 Hum. Rts. Q. 691, 707 (1995).

18. United Nations Dev. Programme, Human Development Report 2004: Cultural Liberty in Today's Diverse World 4 (2004).

of culture as dynamic and disunited appeals to those who favor granting group rights to minorities.[19]

I would, however, contend that the term *culture*, when used to determine the rights or privileges to be given to any community, must refer to those practices that have a positive effect on the wellbeing of all group members and not just the dominant few.[20] This assertion is based on the basic goal of liberalism: ensuring the welfare of all within a community, without regard to gender, race, ethnicity, religion, or culture.

Moreover, one must take care not to essentialize culture. By describing cultural practices in homogenous terms, one ignores the relativism of these practices. Cultural relativism must be considered in any discussion on the power relationships within a culture and in determining who has the right to define what culture means. By denouncing acts practiced by certain members of a community, we help in informally institutionalizing these practices. Traces of this trend can be found in the revival of fundamentalism in some religions, which is premised on protecting the communities from outside influences alleged to desire the destruction of these groups' religious and cultural heritages. For example, after the Indian Bhartiya Janata Party (BJP) hijacked the agenda of a uniform civil code from the progressive liberals and feminists, the Indian Muslim community has more stiffly resisted a move towards formulation of a uniform civil code.

B. Multiculturalism and Gender Justice

Given that multiculturalism is a reality in almost every nation and that some traditional cultures have historically oppressed women, governments bear the burden of formulating policies that protect women's rights within a multicultural framework. Post-independence India has a strong democratic tradition and a commitment to protecting individual civil and political rights. Yet Indian society is also one of the world's most culturally diverse, with innumerable linguistic, cultural, and religious groups and influences from Dravidian, Aryan, Mughal, British, and recently U.S. traditions. Due to the sheer diversity of the Indian populace, Indian policy makers have faced a tough challenge in providing space to various minority groups to prosper while also ensuring that the individual rights of its citizens, including women, are protected.

Will Kymlicka believes that it is possible to protect multicultural ideals within a liberal democratic framework. On the importance of culture to an individual's development of self-identity, he notes: "Liberal values require both individual freedom of choice and a secure cultural context from which individuals can make their choices. Thus liberalism requires that we can identify, protect,

19. *See generally*, Adeno Addis, *Individualism, Communitarianism, and the Rights of Ethnic Minorities*, 67 NOTRE DAME L. REV. 615 (1992).

20. *See generally*, David M. Smolin, *Will International Human Rights Be Used as a Tool of Cultural Genocide? The Interaction of Human Rights Norms, Religion, Culture and Gender*, 12 J.L. & RELIGION 143 (1995-96).

and promote cultural membership, as a primary good."[21] Therefore, the importance of culture and group identity to an individual's development as a participating citizen requires leaders of multicultural liberal societies to protect both individuality and group identity.

There is merit to the argument made by "multiculturalist liberals" like Kymlicka, that membership in a group with its own language and history is important to an individual's sense of self and self-respect. But, as I argue in the beginning of this Article, within a liberal framework, no justification exists for granting group rights to minorities. Is there then any means of achieving the balance between the competing interests of multiculturalism and individual rights, including women's rights? Yes. The legitimate goal of protecting minority cultures can be accomplished by giving minority groups privileges, instead of rights, to employ necessary means aimed at preserving their group identities without infringing on the individual rights of those who constitute these groups. *Rights* differ from *privileges* in the sense that a fundamental right granted under a constitution imposes a corresponding duty on the state to protect that right. A privilege, on the other hand, does not impose any such obligation on the state. It merely gives an individual the liberty to do something without interference from the state; in other words, an individual has no legal duty to refrain from doing that privileged action.[22] Granting privileges to groups for the preservation of their religious or cultural identity, does, however, require that the limits to such privileges be defined. The limits must be in consonance with the purpose of granting these privileges in the first place, that is, to further the wellbeing of an individual. In this sense, any practice, whether cultural or religious, that hampers the growth or well-being of an individual within that minority culture *cannot* be legally protected within a rights-based framework.[23] So, in the example of India, even the personal laws would be subject to the test of fundamental rights enshrined in the Indian Constitution, including the right to equality.

An ideal strategy, then, would be for the Indian legislature to honor the Constitution by drafting a uniform *secular* civil code that meets the test of equality guaranteed under the Constitution, providing individuals with the option to be governed by their personal laws. This uniform civil code would achieve twin objectives: protecting the individual rights of citizens from being subsumed by group rights, and offering individuals the privilege to choose to be governed by their personal laws. In addition, the code would put pressure on minority groups and less powerful individuals within these groups, whether they are women or other sub-groups, to take the initiative to bring their personal laws into parity with the secular civil code with regard to the equality of rights to all members within the group.

---

21. WILL KYMLICKA, LIBERALISM, COMMUNITY AND CULTURE 169 (1989).

22. For further discussion on the difference between *rights* and *privileges*, see WESLEY NEWCOMB HOHFELD, FUNDAMENTAL LEGAL CONCEPTIONS 71 (1923).

23. For a discussion of minority rights in an Asian context, see Michael C. Davis, *Constitutionalism and Political Culture: The Debate over Human Rights and Asian Values*, 11 HARV. HUM. RTS. J. 109 (1998).

The above discussion regarding privileges underlies "reasonable pluralism,"[24] which aims to create a civic nation in which the state protects diverse religious or cultural practices so as to promote harmonious co-existence of majority and minority groups, as well as the well-being of all individuals. Reasonable pluralism incorporates the conceptions of tolerance and recognition of diversity among views. However, it restricts cultural and religious values to the private sphere, the consensus being the norm for regulating political associations. Thus, a state pursuing this model of liberalism could not authorize practices that are repugnant to the well-being of individuals—men or women.

Granting group rights in an unrestricted fashion would protect some cultural practices that have historically oppressed women. Condoning the oppression of some group members through legally protecting those cultural practices is at odds with a liberal rights agenda minded towards ensuring equal rights for all citizens. There is no doubt that globalization has profoundly influenced multiculturalism, and controversies and disagreements are bound to surround the contours of a multicultural society. In the words of Aung San Suu Kyi, "[i]t is precisely because of the cultural diversity of the world that it is necessary for different nations and peoples to agree on those basic human values which will act as a unifying factor."[25] We ought to ensure that multiculturalist notions conform to universal human rights norms, thereby ensuring women's rights within a protected culture or group.

III.
Multicultural Approaches to Law and Governance

A. *The Three Multicultural Approaches to National Governance: Assimilation, Integration, and Social or Cultural Pluralism*

1. *Assimilation*

An assimilationist approach imposes the dominant national culture on minority groups. Some feminist scholars believe that this is the best strategy that western states can follow to ensure the protection of rights of women within immigrant minority groups. Assuming that at least some forms of gender discrimination are culturally-based, Susan Moller Okin suggests that women in patriarchal minority cultures might benefit from integration intó a less patriarchal majority culture.[26] I do not believe, however, that such drastic measures would necessarily be in the interest of women within minority groups in such countries. First, any such attempt would be met with strong resistance within the community, which might result in strengthening the cultural practices, thus putting a stronger pressure on the women in these groups to observe those oppressive

24. John Rawls, Political Liberalism 36 (1993).

25. Aung San Suu Kyi, Empowerment for a Culture of Peace and Development, Address to the WCCD in Manila (Nov. 21, 1994), *at* http://www.ibiblio.org/freeburma/assk/assk3-2c.html.

26. Susan Moller Okin, *Is Multiculturalism Bad for Women?*, *in* Is Multiculturalism Bad for Women? 22-23 (Joshua Cohen et al. eds., 1999). *See also* Doriane Lambelet Coleman, *Individualizing Justice Through Multiculturalism: The Liberals' Dilemma*, 96 Colum. L. Rev. 1093 (1996).

cultural practices. A state can do very little to control the exercise of cultural practices in the private sphere; it could not, for example, realistically prevent a Muslim woman from wearing a veil inside her home. Second, even if the government can implement strong measures to control such practices and to assimilate minorities into the mainstream culture, women who have often lived in a protected environment might find themselves more vulnerable and exposed. If a state were suddenly to proscribe a particular cultural practice with gender implications, a woman might not consider herself liberated. If, however, the practice were to be weakened over a period of time through giving her tools for growth such as education and economic independence, the movement for change would come from within rather than without, increasing her ability to make a meaningful choice.

As an example, consider the interpretation of Muslim personal laws in India, where Muslims are a minority, as compared to other Muslim countries. In India, attempts to modernize Muslim personal laws, especially the laws affecting women's rights, have met with stiff resistance within the Muslim community. Courts in other Islamic countries, however, have modernized their interpretations of Muslim personal laws without any outcry from the religious clerics or the community in general.[27]

Thus, the key to reconciling the goals of multiculturalism and feminism lies not in asking women from minority cultures to assimilate, but rather recognizing that multiculturalism and feminism are neither polar opposites nor mutually detrimental. Relativism exists within the discourses of both multiculturalism and feminism. Western feminists who have branded non-western cultures as sexist and inferior to their western counterparts in assaults against multiculturalism are in no sense less relativist than those outside of western societies who use the rhetoric of culture *qua* group rights to maintain patriarchal systems.[28] Arguments on both sides harm the women's rights movement.[29]

2. *Integration*

An integrationist approach asks citizens to restrict the practice of their minority religion, language, or ethnic heritage to the private domain. Article 44 of the Indian Constitution, which directs the state to create a uniform civil code, is representative of an integrationist approach towards multiculturalism, as it aims to create a civil code that applies to all communities in India, irrespective of

27. *See, e.g.*, A.G. Noorani, *Shah Bano: Bangladesh Shows the Way*, *in* SHAH BANO AND THE MUSLIM WOMEN'S ACT A DECADE ON: THE RIGHT OF DIVORCED MUSLIM WOMEN TO *Mataa*, Readers and Compilations Series 25–26 (Women Living Under Muslim Laws, Readers and Compilations Series, 1998) (noting that the High Court Division in Bangladesh has interpreted Aiyats 240-242 of Quran to hold that a divorced woman has the right to receive a reasonable sum for maintenance for an indefinite period beyond *iddat*).

28. *See generally* Tracy E. Higgins, *Anti-Essentialism, Relativism, and Human Rights*, 19 HARV. WOMEN'S L.J. 89 (1996).

29. *See generally* Catherine Powell, *Locating Culture, Identity, and Human Rights*, 30 COLUM. HUM. RTS. L. REV. 201 (1999).

religion, while simultaneously protecting individuals' right to practice their religion privately.[30]

3. Social/Cultural Pluralism Approach

A social or cultural pluralism approach allows the existence of different religious, cultural, and ethnic principles in the public sphere. India's framework of separate personal laws for various religious communities is representative of this model and is also a good example of how a multiculturalist approach to law and governance in India has resulted in undermining women's rights. As discussed later in this Article, some people have used the rhetoric of cultural pluralism mainly for political gains without taking into account the suffering of the weaker members of the minority groups that enjoy the protection of multicultural policies.

B. Multicultural Governance in India

The task of creating a democratic system of governance after India's independence was enormous. The sheer linguistic, ethnic, religious, racial, and cultural diversity of the Indian populace posed special challenges to the constitutional framers, who understood that national unity and inter-group harmony would require protection for minority groups. While the members of the Constituent Assembly agreed on the need for a solid framework of fundamental rights, they did not agree on how to blend a scheme of civil and political rights with the concurrent challenges of forging structures for economic and social governance. It is in this context of formational dilemmas that the contemporary debate surrounding multiculturalism and its impact on women's rights in India needs to be examined.

1. The Indian Constitution

Post-independence India followed a policy of cultural pluralism by maintaining systems of separate personal laws for Hindu, Muslim, and Christian communities, while concurrently assigning itself the goal of working towards a uniform civil code. Including a Declaration of Rights was very important to the early drafters. As Granville Austin noted: "India was a land of communities, of minorities, racial, religious, linguistic social and caste. . . . Indians believed that in their 'federation of minorities' a declaration of rights was as necessary as it had been for the Americans."[31]

When addressing minority group safeguards in the Draft Constitution to the Assembly, Dr. B.R. Ambedkar, Chairman of the Drafting Committee, observed:

> I have no doubt that the Constituent Assembly has done wisely in providing such safeguards for minorities as it has done. In this country both the minorities and the majorities have followed a wrong path. It is wrong for the majority to deny the existence of minorities. It is equally wrong for the minorities to perpetuate

30. India Const. art. 44.
31. Granville Austin, The Indian Constitution: Cornerstone of a Nation 54 (1999).

themselves. A solution must be found which will serve a double purpose. It must recognize the existence of minorities to start with . . . . The moment the majority loses the habit of discriminating against the minority, the minorities can have no ground to exist. They will vanish.[32]

The group rights granted to minorities, including restricting practices that were per se discriminatory against women, were not absolute, but rather were subject to state intervention. In sub-committee meetings, some members opposed allowing the free practice of religion and thought the definition of "practice" was too wide, since this could include such anti-social practices as *devadasi*,[33] *purdah*,[34] and *sat.i*[35] Due to protest by the sub-committee members, the Advisory Committee on Fundamental Rights altered the Minorities Sub-Committee's provisions, and in its own report instructed that the right to practice religion freely should not prevent the state from making laws providing for social welfare and reforms, including laws protecting the rights of women, a provision established in Article 15 of the Constitution.[36]

Consequently, the drafters created fundamental constitutional rights with an explicit recognition of the need to protect group rights as well. Article 29, for example, protects the rights of groups to preserve their language, script, and culture and prohibits discrimination in access to public educational institutions based on religion, race, caste, or language.[37] Article 30 protects the right of religious and linguistic minority groups to establish educational institutions.[38] Other articles of the Constitution that guarantee certain fundamental rights to all citizens also operate as safeguards for groups, such as equality before the law (Article 14), freedom from discrimination on the basis of religion, race, caste, sex or place of birth (Article 15), and equal opportunity in public employment (Article 16).[39] Articles 29 and 30 bestow a positive right on groups to preserve their culture, whereas Articles 14 and 15 are couched in more individualistic terms, granting negative rights to individuals to protect them from excesses of the State.

While the negative protections from discrimination based on cultural affiliation appear in the early articles, the possibility of a uniform civil code that would ensure all citizens' equal rights to freedom from oppression appears in Part IV of the Constitution. This Part, named the "Directive Principles of State Policy," contains a range of directives to the state to seek economic, social, and

32. Constituent Assembly of India—Volume VII (Nov. 4, 1948), *available at* http://parliamentofindia.nic.in/ls/debates/vol7p1b.htm.

33. The practice of marrying a woman to a deity or temple.

34. *Purdah* literally means screen or veil. Women observing *purdah* cover themselves from head to toe and avoid the male gaze at home by remaining behind curtains and screens. *See, e.g.*, Kings College History Department, *Purdah*, *at* http://www.kings.edu/womens_history/purdah.html.

35. A widow observing *sati* immolates herself on her husband's funeral pyre.

36. INDIA CONST. art. 15 (prohibiting the state from discriminating "against any citizen on grounds only of religion, race, caste, sex, place of birth or any of them" and providing that "[n]othing in this article shall prevent the State from making any special provision for women and children.").

37. *Id.* art. 29.

38. *Id.* art. 30.

39. *Id.* arts. 14, 15, 16.

cultural protections for Indian citizens. Article 41, for example, addresses the right to work, education, and public assistance.[40] Article 38A addresses access to justice and free legal aid.[41] Article 44 establishes the goal of a uniform civil code, though its language, like the language of the other articles in Part IV, is only exhortatory: "The State shall endeavor to secure for the citizens a uniform civil code throughout the territory of India."[42]

The drafters hoped that a civil code would ensure harmony between groups and strengthen the secular fabric of the country. Instead, contemporary India suffers from internal strife and communal violence. The goal of harmonious multicultural co-existence has not yet succeeded in India where manifestations of continued inter-group tensions include the demolition of the Babri Masjid by a Hindu mob in 1993, followed by the Bombay Riots, in which over 400 persons were killed; the murder of a Christian missionary and his two sons by a Hindu mob in 1999; the Best Bakery case, in which eleven Muslims and three Hindus were burned alive in March 2002 to avenge the death of fifty-eight people on a train carrying Hindu activists in February of the same year; and the attack by Muslim terrorists on a Hindu temple in Gujarat that killed thirty persons in September 2002. Moreover, Indian leaders have failed to prioritize gender justice within the governance system, leading to a lack of protection for women whose communities operate under the personal religious laws. More recently, support for the adoption of a uniform civil code has not been based on a recognition that women's rights might otherwise suffer under the personal laws. Rather, the support, especially from the Hindu Right, stems from a desire to limit the rights of cultural minorities. Ratna Kapur and Brenda Cossman have observed:

> It was this dichotomized discourse of the debate that inadvertently allied the women's movement with the Hindu Right and its vicious attack on minority rights. Despite the efforts of some feminist activists and organizations to distinguish their position, within the broader political discourse the positions were seen as one and the same. Feminist efforts to challenge the oppression of women within the private sphere of the family were appropriated, and transformed to support the communalist discourse of the Hindu Right.[43]

2. *Legislation*

As discussed above, the Indian Constitution exhorts the state to create a uniform civil code. Indeed, the idea of a uniform civil code predates the Constitution to the time of the British rule in India. Historians have noted that the institutionalization of separate laws reinforced the boundaries between minority communities and solidified identities along religious affiliations.[44] Instead of

40. *Id.* art. 41.

41. *Id.* art. 39A.

42. *Id.* art. 44; *see also* P.M. Bakshi, The Constitution of India: with comments & subject index / selective comments (1992).

43. RATNA KAPUR & BRENDA COSSMAN, SUBVERSIVE SITES—FEMINIST ENGAGEMENTS WITH LAW IN INDIA 64 (1996).

44. *See* Maitrayee Mukhopadhyay, *Between Community And State: The Question Of Women's Rights And Personal Laws*, *in* FORGING IDENTITIES: GENDER, COMMUNITIES AND THE STATE IN INDIA 108-129 (Zoya Hasan ed., 1994).

moving toward a secular, equality-based legal system, the recognition of personal laws under the guise of protecting minorities from a dominant majority culture helped institutionalize patriarchal traditional practices that disadvantage Indian women. In particular, support for personal laws relating to polygamy, divorce, property inheritance, and maintenance, all of which directly impact the lives of women, lies at the center of the historical resistance to the implementation of a uniform civil code.

At present, India does not have a uniform civil code that would apply to all citizens irrespective of their religious or cultural identity.[45] However, all Indians can choose a civil marriage under the Special Marriage Act of 1954[46] irrespective of their religion. Should a couple register under this Act, they are bound by the Act's provisions, along with the provisions of the Indian Succession Act,[47] which relates to the succession of property, instead of their respective personal laws.[48] If a couple does not register under the Special Marriage Act, their respective personal laws apply. Thus the Special Marriage Act is an "opt out" provision for individuals who do not want to be bound to the marriage rules of their religious communities. Other examples of optional civil codes are the Guardian and Wards Act of 1890,[49] which allows civil courts to appoint a guardian for a minor. While the court is required to consider the minor's religion and governing personal laws, the minor's overall welfare is paramount. Also, the Medical Termination of Pregnancy Act of 1971[50] permits any woman in India to have an abortion irrespective of her religious or cultural identity.

Legislative reforms have followed different courses within the various religious communities. The first progressive legislation for women's rights related to restricting the practice of child marriages. Child marriage was a common practice among most Indians during the British rule, and various leaders attempted to abolish the practice. The first attempt was the Indian Christian Marriage Act of 1872, which proscribed marriage to girls under the age of twelve.[51] Due to this Act's social ineffectiveness, in 1891 the government passed the Age of Consent Act to prevent the consummation of marriages before the age of twelve.[52] Despite different practices across the various religious communities and avowed dissatisfaction amongst orthodox Hindu and Muslim classes, all political parties ultimately accepted the legislation.[53] Further, in

45. Criminal laws, on the other hand, are applicable irrespective of the caste, sex, religion or culture.

46. Special Marriage Act, No. 43 (1954) (India).

47. Indian Succession Act, No. 39 (1925) (India).

48. If two Hindus marry they may choose to be bound instead by the Hindu Succession Act No. 30 of 1956.

49. Guardian and Wards Act, No. 8 (1890) (India).

50. Medical Termination of Pregnancy Act, No. 34 (1971) (India).

51. Indian Christian Marriage Act, No. 15 (1872) (India).

52. Previous to this reform, a husband could legally cohabit with his wife if she was at least ten years old.

53. Shahida Lateef, *Defining Women through Legislation*, *in* DEFINING WOMEN THROUGH LEGISLATION IN FORGING IDENTITIES: GENDER, COMMUNITIES AND THE STATE IN INDIA 43 (Zoya Hasan ed., 1994).

1929, the Child Marriage Restraint Act raised the minimum marrying age for girls to fourteen.[54]

The Muslim Personal Law (Shariat) Application Act of 1937[55] was the first women's-rights legislation targeted at Muslim communities. The Shariat Act clarified and codified civil marriage laws to ensure the protection of divorced Muslim women's inheritance rights.[56] In support of the Bill, a Member of Parliament, Mr. Abdul Qaiyam, a Muslim himself, noted, "the *Shariat* Act [is] the result and the outcome of the great awakening that has taken place in the Muhammadan community in India . . . to restore all the rights which were granted by the Koran to Muslim women so as to put them on terms of absolute equality with men."[57] Another Member of Parliament, Mr. M.S. Aney from Berar, suggested doing away with the office of the *qazis*, which registers Muslim marriage deeds and conducts Muslim marriages, given that the Muslim community had turned to secular legislative remedies to this aspect of women's oppression. The Dissolution of Muslim Marriage Act of 1939,[58] giving Muslim women a right to unilateral divorce, was the last progressive legislation in favor of Muslim women in India. Previous to the passage of the Dissolution of Muslim Marriages Act, the Gazette of India noted:

> There is no proviso in the Hanafi Code of Muslim Law enabling a married Muslim woman to obtain a decree from the court dissolving her marriage in case the husband neglects to maintain her, makes her life miserable by deserting or persistently maltreating her or absconds leaving her unprovided for and under certain other circumstances. The absence of such a provision has entailed unspeakable misery to innumerable Muslim women in British India.[59]

The Act was compiled as an amalgamation of four different schools of jurisprudence under Islam, "picking the most liberal features from each of them."[60]

Civil legislation impacting the rights of women affected Muslim communities before addressing the rights of women under the Hindu personal laws. The second Hindu Law Committee appointed in 1944 to look into legislative reforms for a comprehensive code of marriage and succession submitted its recommendations for enacting a Hindu Code in 1947.[61] Committee reports indicate that improving women's status was the principle motivation for changes proposed to the Hindu Law in the draft code.[62] Accordingly, the Committee recommended

54. Child Marriage Restraint Act, No. 19 (1929) (India).

55. Muslim Personal Law (Shariat) Application Act, No. 26 (1937) (India).

56. *Id.*

57. 1939: I LEGISLATIVE ASSEMBLY DEBATES (OFFICIAL REPORT), 621 (1939).

58. Dissolution of Muslim Marriages Act, No. 8 (1939) (India). *See also* Lateef, *supra* note 53..

59. *Statement of Objects and Reasons Issued With the Bill Which Became the Dissolution of Muslim Marriages Act, 1939*, GAZETTE OF INDIA, 1936, Part 5:154, *reprinted in* SHAH BANO AND THE MUSLIM WOMEN ACT A DECADE ON: THE RIGHT OF DIVORCED WOMEN TO *Mataa* 33 (Women Living Under Muslim Laws, Readers and Compilations Series, 1998).

60. SHAHIDA LATEEF, MUSLIM WOMEN IN INDIA, POLITICAL AND PRIVATE REALITIES: 1890s - 1980s 71 (1990).

61. FLAVIA AGNES, LAW AND GENDER INEQUALITY: THE POLITICS OF WOMEN'S RIGHTS IN INDIA 78 (1999).

62. Robert D. Baird, *Gender Implications for a Uniform Civil Code, in* RELIGION AND PERSONAL LAW IN SECULAR INDIA: A CALL TO JUDGMENT 145 (Gerald James Larson ed., 2001).

allowing divorce and abolishing the traditional practice of polygamy. The Committee further recommended granting equal property rights to daughters and sons. Traditionalists opposed the Bill on many grounds, claiming that the grant of such rights to women impermissibly deviated from traditional Hindu practices. For example, the Shastra Dharma Prachar Sabha, a Hindu organization, distributed pamphlets during the debates on the Bill titled "Why Hindu Code Is Detestable," which proclaimed that the bill would allow inter-caste marriage, Sagotra marriage,[63] and free divorce, while criminalizing bigamy and giving married women rights to their father's property. This last consequence was especially alarming to Hindu traditionalists who saw women's property rights as a Muslim practice with no place under Hindu family law.

3. *Roleof the Judiciary*

The Indian judiciary, especially the Supreme Court, in its role as the defender of the Constitution, has been the forerunner in protecting minorities and safeguarding the multicultural ethos of the polity.[64] Though the Supreme Court has adjudicated a plethora of cases balancing the rights of minorities against more universal civil rights, I will limit my discussion here to those cases that have impacted the rights of women within minority communities.

The question of who has the power to interpret the personal laws of the various religious communities within India has plagued the judiciary from its post-independence beginnings. In *Ratilal v. State of Bombay*,[65] the Indian Supreme Court ruled that no outside authority had the right to proclaim the essential parts of a religion. The case dealt with the constitutionality of certain state Trust Acts passed with a view to regulate religious and charitable trusts. The petitioner challenged the validity of these Acts on the ground that they violated the right to freedom of religion under Articles 25 and 26 of the Constitution. The Court, allowing the appeal in part, held:

> What sub-clause (a) of clause (2) of Article 25 contemplates is not State regulation of the religious practices as such which are protected unless they run contrary to public health or morality but of activities which are really of an economic, commercial or political character though they are associated with religious practices.[66]

Further clarifying the Court's position, Justice Mukherjea wrote, "[n]o outside authority has any right to say that these [religious practices] are not essential parts of religion and it is not open to the secular authority of the state to restrict or prohibit them in any manner they like under the guise of administering the trust estate."[67] According to the Court, the state had power to regulate the trusts by a valid law, but administration of the trust in accordance with the

63. Marriage to one's relatives.

64. *See* P. Ishwara Bhat, *Constitutional Feminism: An Overview*, (2001) 2 S.C.C. (Jour) 1, *at* http://www.ebc-india.com/lawyer/articles/2001v2a1.htm.

65. A.I.R. 1954 S.C. 388.

66. *Id.* at 391.

67. *Id.* at 392.

laws was the prerogative of the religious bodies.[68] This holding demonstrated a break with prior doctrine, which considered personal views and reactions to be irrelevant even when the belief was a genuine and conscious part of the profession or the religion.

In the 1958 case *Mohammad Hanif Qureshi v. State of Bihar*, the Court reversed itself, holding that it was competent to adjudicate on the essentials of any religious practice.[69] The petitioners in this case, Muslim butchers, challenged the validity of certain state laws banning the slaughter of certain animals, including cows, on the grounds that the prohibitions violated their fundamental right to freedom of religion under Article Twenty-Five. They claimed that Islam required Muslims to sacrifice a cow on Bakr-Id-Day, a holy day in Islam.[70] Referring to interpretations of various religious books and practices of Muslims in India, the Court declined to hold that sacrificing a cow was an obligatory practice under Islam.[71]

In *Durgah Committee v. Hussan Ali*, the Court further clarified its position on adjudicating right-to-religion claims:

> In order that the practices in question should be treated as part of religion, they must be regarded by the said religion as its essential and integral part . . . unless such practices are found to constitute an essential or integral part of a religion, their claim for protection under Art. 26 may have to be carefully scrutinized.[72]

The Court went on to add that it would decide what constitutes an essential part of religion or religious practice with reference to the doctrine of that particular religion.[73] Thus, current doctrine gives courts the power to interpret the personal laws of India's religious communities. Courts had exercised this power in a number of cases,[74] but it was not until the Supreme Court's ruling in *Mohammed Ahmed Khan v. Shah Bano Begum*,[75] which granted maintenance rights to a destitute woman, did fundamentalist religious leaders create enough pressure on the Parliament to overrule the judgment and the doctrine.

Shah Bano was an aging Muslim woman whose husband unilaterally divorced her and then refused to pay her maintenance beyond the period of *iddat*, an obligatory three-month waiting period after a divorce during which remarriage is prohibited. Shah Bano sued her husband under the Criminal Procedure Code Section 125, which allows destitute wives to sue their husbands for maintenance.[76] Before *Shah Bano*, the Supreme Court had already ruled in two separate decisions that divorced Muslim women were entitled to maintenance even when they had received the customary one-time sum due to them under Muslim

68. *Id.* at 391.
69. A.I.R. 1958 S.C. 731.
70. *Id.* at 739.
71. *Id.* at 740.
72. A.I.R. 1961 S.C. 1402, 1415.
73. *Id.*
74. *E.g.*, Abdul Jalil v. Uttar Pradesh, A.I.R. 1984 S.C. 882 (holding that no text in the Holy Koran prohibits removal or shifting of graves); R.M.K Singh v. State, A.I.R. 1976 Pat. 198 (holding that the performance of particular Hindu religious ceremonies is an integral part of Hinduism).
75. (1985) 1 S.C.S. 96 [hereinafter *Shah Bano*].
76. *Id.*; INDIA CODE CRIM. PROC. § 125.

Personal Law, provided that sum was not adequate for their maintenance. In *Bai Tahira v. Ali Hussain Fidaalli Chothia*,[77] the Court ruled that Criminal Procedure Code Section 127, which provides that a woman is not entitled to maintenance if she receives sums under any customary or personal law payable to her on divorce, does not negate the social purpose underlying Section 125 and that "ill-used wives and desperate divorcees" could not be driven "to seek sanctuary on the streets."[78] The Court further held that the purpose of payment "under any customary or personal law" is to provide the divorcee with maintenance and to keep her from destitution. *Bai Tahira* proscribes a husband from hiding behind Section 127(3)(b) to shirk his Section 125 maintenance responsibilities.

Fazlunbi v. Vali reached the Supreme Court one year after *Bai Tahira*, in 1980.[79] *Fazlunbi* also involved a wife's petition for maintenance. The high court[80] sought to distinguish this case from the Supreme Court's binding judgment in *Bai Tahira*, under which the wife would be entitled to maintenance, on the ground that the husband in *Bai Tahira* had not raised a plea based on Section 127(3)(b). On appeal to the Supreme Court, that tribunal made clear in the course of overruling the lower court's decision not to grant relief to the ex-wife that "[n]either personal law nor other salvationary plea will hold against the policy of public law pervading S.127 (3)(b) as much as it does [not hold against] S.125."[81] *Bai Tahira* and *Fazlunbi*, therefore, clearly established that Muslim women have a right to continued maintenance under Section 125 if the customary amount paid at divorce is insufficient for their livelihood.

Shah Bano, issued five years later, went a step further, holding that a Muslim man has an obligation to pay maintenance to his ex-wife irrespective of the adequacy of the customary payment. It further held that in cases of conflict between the criminal code and personal laws, the criminal code would prevail. Writing for the Court, Chief Justice Chandrachud explained:

> [S]ection 125 is a part of the Code of Criminal Procedure, not of the civil laws which define and govern the rights and obligations of the parties belonging to particular religions . . . . Section 125 was enacted in order to provide a quick and summary remedy to a class of persons who are unable to maintain themselves. What difference would it make as to what is the religion professed by the neglected wife, child, or parent? Neglect by a person of sufficient means to maintain these and the inability of these persons to maintain themselves are the objective criteria which determine the applicability of Section 125.[82]

However, the Court held that Section 125 did not contradict the Muslim Personal Law. In support of this holding, the Court noted:

77. (1979) 2 S.C.R. 75 [hereinafter *Bai Tahira*].

78. *Id.* at 98.

79. (1980) 3 S.C.R. 1127 [hereinafter *Fazlunbi*].

80. High courts in India besides the Supreme Court of India are the courts which have both original and appellate jurisdiction, in addition to having writ jurisdictions.

81. *Fazlunbi*, (1980) 3 S.C.R. at 1141.

82. *Shah Bano*, (1985) 1 S.C.S. at 101.

> There can be no greater authority on this question than the holy Quran . . . . Verses (Aiyats) 241 and 242 of the Quran show that according to the Prophet, there is an obligation on Muslim husbands to provide for their divorced wives.[83]

The *Shah Bano* judgment caused agitation among Muslim religious communities, especially the portion of the Court's opinion that held the Quran itself supported the argument that continuing maintenance did not violate the tenets of Islam. Under political pressure from the leaders of the Muslim community, which resulted from the *Shah Bano* judgment, Parliament, dominated by a Congress Party majority, passed the Muslim Women's (Protection of Rights on Divorce) Act in 1986 (MWA).[84] The effect of the MWA was to reverse the right to continuing maintenance for divorced Muslims pursuant to Section 125 of the Criminal Code.[85] The MWA provides for a one-time payment within the *iddat* period. Section 3(1), "Mahr or other properties of Muslim women to be given to her at the time of divorce," states:

> Notwithstanding anything contained in any other law for the time being in force, a divorced woman shall be entitled to—(a) a reasonable and fair provision and maintenance to be made and paid to her within the *iddat* period by her former husband; (b) where she herself maintains the children born to her before or after her divorce, a reasonable and fair provision and maintenance to be made and paid by her former husband for a period of two years from the respective dates of birth of such children; (c) an amount equal to the sum of *mahr* or dower agreed to be paid to her at the time of her marriage or at any time thereafter according to Muslim law; and (d) all the properties given to her before or at the time of marriage or after her marriage by her relatives or friends or the husband or any relatives of the husband or his friends.[86]

Recently, various high courts in India have interpreted the scope of Section 3(1) to hold that a divorced Muslim woman is entitled to fair and reasonable maintenance within the *iddat* period, contemplating her future needs. For example, the Gujarat High Court's judgment in *Arab Ahmad bin Abdullah v. Arab Bail Mohamuna Sauyadbhari*, held that "in simplest language the Parliament has stated that the [MWA] is for protecting the rights of Muslim Women. It does not provide that it is enacted for taking away some rights which a Muslim Woman was having either under the Personal Law or under the general law i.e. S. 125 . . . of the [Criminal Code]."[87] The judgment relies on the Preamble to the MWA and the "reasonable and fair provision and maintenance" clause in Section 3(1)(a) of the Act in concluding that *Shah Bano* is still good law and that Section 125 of the Criminal Code still applies to divorced Muslim women.[88] Thus, although the Supreme Court has not yet ruled on the MWA, the spirit of

83. *Id.* at 105. The opinion reproduces English translations of Aiyats 241 and 242.

84. C.I.S. Part II (1986), The Muslim Women's (Protection of Rights on Divorce) Act by the Government of India, Chandigrah, May 19, 1986 [hereinafter MWA].

85. However the Act did not take away the power of the courts to interpret the personal laws.

86. MWA, § 3(1).

87. A.I.R. 1988 (Guj.) 141, 142.

88. The Preamble to the MWA states: "An Act to protect the rights of Muslim Women who have been divorced by, or have obtained divorce from, their husbands and to provide for matters connected therewith or incidental thereto." *See also* Ali v. Sufaira, (1988) 2 Kerala Law Times 94.

Section 125 is being upheld by lower courts by interpreting MWA Section 3(1) in favor of divorced Muslim women's right to adequate maintenance.

The Supreme Court's judgment in *Sarla Mudgal v. Union of India*[89] supports the adoption of a uniform civil code. Mudgal, president of Kalyani, a social welfare organization, brought a case involving three Hindu wives whose husbands had deserted them after marrying Muslim women and embracing Islam. The Supreme Court observed:

> Freedom of religion is the core of our culture . . . But religious practices, violative of human rights and dignity and sacerdotal suffocation of essentially civil and material freedoms, are not autonomy but oppression. Therefore, a uniform civil code is imperative both for protection of the oppressed and promotion of national unity and solidarity.[90]

While the question of the uniform civil code was not an issue in this case, the Court's language here indicates a judicial willingness for such a code that would protect all individuals, even within a scheme of group rights. A division bench of the Supreme Court, headed by Justice Singh, then directed the Government of India to file an affidavit detailing efforts to enact a universal civil code as urged by Article 44 of the Constitution.

In the recent case *John Vallamattom v. Union of India*,[91] the Court again made reference to a uniform civil code, which was not, however, relevant to the Court's judgment. In dictum, the Court expressed regret that Parliament had still not framed a common civil code in order to fulfill the urging of Article 44 and urged that "a common civil code will help the cause of national integration by removing the contradictions based on ideologies."[92] The government has not, however, responded to the Supreme Court's indications for a common civil code, demonstrating the inherent limitations on the judiciary's ability to pursue social and religious transformation in India. Without social and political consensus on the need for a uniform civil code among the general citizenry and the political brass, the courts will suffer from a limited ability to formulate laws and policy regulations that promote uniformity among personal laws.

Hasina Khan, a social reformer, points out that after the 1937 Shariat Act and the 1939 Dissolution of Muslim Marriages Act, Muslim women have not attained any new legislative protection against Muslim personal laws.[93] Indian courts have proved a more hospitable forum for protecting and promoting women's rights than political branches or minority institutions. The sluggishness of the latter two explains the continued Muslim practice of "triple talaq," which enables a man to divorce his wife by repeating aloud "I divorce you" three times. Even though this practice has been abolished in many Islamic nations, it still prevails in Indian Muslim communities. Recently, there were high expectations that at its annual meeting the All India Muslim Law Board would adopt a

89. A.I.R. 1995 S.C. 1531.
90. *Id.* at 1540 (internal citations omitted).
91. John Vallamattom v. Union of India, A.I.R. 2003 S.C. 2902.
92. *Id.*
93. *Help for Distressed Muslim Women*, THE HINDU, Apr. 10, 2001, *available at* http://www.hinduonnet.com/thehindu/2001/04/11/stories/14112185.htm.

model *nikahnama*, or marriage contract, with more equitable divorce laws.[94] However, the Board declared after the meeting that "law cannot ensure reforms" and that instead they would try to create more awareness among the community on the issue of divorce.[95]

In short, while the Indian model of cultural pluralism aimed to provide minority groups with protection from the imposition of a dominant majority culture while simultaneously bridging gaps between various communities, the model has instead achieved the exact opposite result. The preservation of separate personal laws has spread seeds of division among different religious communities. The continued existence of these parallel legal systems has reinforced separatist tendencies, resulting in a negative impact on the rights of Indian women in two key ways: the very creation of a system of parallel personal laws denied women their constitutional right to equal treatment, while the continued existence of this two-tier system reinforces patriarchal traditional practices, subjecting women to fixed gender roles based on pre-independence authoritarian structures.

IV.
The Way Forward: Law Reforms and Policy Changes

Democracies like India will always face challenges of providing space for discourse among different interests. India can protect its religious, cultural, and linguistic diversity only on the basis of multiculturalism. However, zealous protection of multiculturalism through the provision of group rights must not ignore the rights of women and the equally viable goal of gender justice. The present discourse on multiculturalism in India celebrates the country's diversity without sufficiently acknowledging the existence of discrimination against women based on the personal laws. Supporters of multiculturalism should also pursue feminist and gender-based alignments within cultural practices so that Indian society can realize the constitutional goals of universal equality and justice.

Some innovative legislation within the personal law systems provides hope for continuing change. The Hindu Marriage Act of 1955,[96] for example, which took its inspiration from the Special Marriage Act, is considered a piece of progressive legislation protecting Hindu women's rights. This legislation put an end to age-old practices such as polygamy. It also transformed Hindu marriage, traditionally considered to be a sacrament, into a contract, thereby providing for divorce by mutual consent.[97] However, the Hindu Succession Act of 1956[98] still allows for discrimination in the granting of rights to ancestral property. Under the Act, daughters and wives can only claim a joint share in family prop-

94. A. Faizur Rahman, Editorial, *Triple Talaq: Bad in Law and Theology*, The Hindu, July 13, 2004, *available at* http://www.thehindu.com/thehindu/op/2004/07/13/stories/2004071300491500.htm.

95. *Id.*

96. Hindu Marriage Act, No. 25 (1955) (India).

97. *Id. at* § 13.

98. Hindu Succession Act, No. 30 (1956) (India).

erty upon the death of their fathers or husbands.[99] Even when they are able to claim this share, their claim is less than that of the sons in the family.[100] Recently, the Fifteenth Law Commission, led by Justice B. P. Jeevan Reddy, proposed amending the Hindu Succession Act to provide for women's right to an equal share in ancestral property.[101] The Muslim personal laws still fail to provide equal treatment for women as well. The Muslim Personal Law in India is still uncodified. Polygamy and triple talaq are still legal. A woman desiring to divorce her husband under certain grounds, however, has recourse to a court of law under the provisions of the Dissolution of Muslim Marriage Act 1939.

Contemporary Christian personal laws also restrict the rights of women. A Christian man can divorce his wife, for example, if he finds she has committed adultery. A Christian woman, on the other hand, can seek divorce only if the charge of adultery is coupled with complaints of serious, life-endangering cruelty, or after two years of desertion without reasonable cause.[102] A Christian woman found guilty of adultery can lose her entire property to her children and husband. Interestingly, the failure of Christian personal laws to provide equal rights to women might result less from resistance within the Indian Christian community and more from the callous indifference of the government in bringing about the necessary change within Christian minority communities.[103] Any proposed change to Muslim personal laws, in contrast, generally faces stiff resistance from certain parts of the Muslim community. Most Muslim leaders maintain their right to be governed by Shariat and are in opposition to the possibility of a uniform civil code. They rely on Articles 25 and 26 of the Constitution to assert their right to practice Islam without interference by national civil laws.

The fact that religious issues have been politicized since the BJP government's ascent to power has affected the development of a meaningful discourse on the passing of uniform civil code. The growing distrust among religious communities that has resulted from sporadic instances of inter-group violence has only contributed to a fractured debate on the need for a uniform civil code. The power struggle between the fundamentalist forces within the communities, resulted in the withdrawal of the feminists from the debate. Further, the rise in communalism due to the "hindutavization" of the debate over a uniform civil code has resulted in increased pressure on women in these communities to conform to traditional practices that reinforce patriarchal structures, protected under the guise of religion or culture. Delhi recently saw attempts by the BJP govern-

---

99. See *id.* § 6, on the concept of *mitakshara* property.

100. Madhu Kishwar, *What Women Want*, THE INDIAN EXPRESS, Apr. 10, 2004, *available at* http://www.indianexpress.com/archive_frame.php.

101. Swati Chaturvedi and Rajesh Kumar, *Law Panel Proposes Equal Share In Ancestral Property For Hindu Women*, THE INDIAN EXPRESS, May 12, 2000, *available at* http://www.indianexpress.com/ie/daily/20000512/ina12053.html.

102. Sumedha Raikar-Mhatre, *Divorce & Christian Marriages in India: Till Cruelty do us Part*, THE INDIAN EXPRESS, May 20 1997, *available at* http://www.goacom.com/news/news97/may/marriages.html. Recently, however, a judgment of the Bombay high court has made it possible for Christian women to get a divorce solely on the grounds of cruelty and desertion. *Id.*

103. *See generally* Javed Anand, *Behind Demands for a Uniform Civil Code*, *in* THE SHAH BANO CONTROVERSY (Asghar Ali Engineer ed., 1987).

ment to ban girls from wearing skirts to schools. On similar footings, the fundamentalist forces in Kashmir have been exhorting women to wear *burqa*.

Policing culture is extremely controversial, and problems arise when governments start to dictate how people ought to act according to their religious faiths. It is impossible to have serious discourse regarding the formation of a uniform civil code in this hostile environment. However, there exists the possibility to develop awareness and facilitate meaningful dialogue among different communities with regard to how society can achieve equality between men and women within various religious frameworks. Since the problem has its roots in politics, the solution too has to be political. Without political will, the quest for women's rights will not be fulfilled. Though a uniform civil code based on the principle of equality between the sexes would have been an ideal solution, the hijacking of this issue by fundamentalist forces has made its adoption a difficult if not impossible tool for protecting Indian women's rights. In the highly charged political and religious atmosphere of contemporary Indian governance, with right-wing political parties and groups supporting adoption of such a code, no minority community would welcome such a measure.[104]

As an alternative to a uniform civil code, I propose a constitutional amendment to Articles 25 and 29, making the rights to practice religion and conserve culture subject to ensuring the right of equality between men and women. Consequently, this Amendment would make all personal laws subject to the test of equality. The Indian Constitution already contains precedents in this regard—Article 15, for example, carves out an exception to the right of equality, allowing the state to make special provisions for women.[105] Moreover, an amendment would further be justified by Article 5 of the Convention on the Elimination of All Forms of Discrimination Against Women (CEDAW), to which India is a signatory. Article 5requires signatories to:

> modify the social and cultural patterns of conduct of men and women, with a view of achieving the elimination of prejudices and customary and all other practices which are based on the idea of the inferiority or the superiority of either of the sexes or on stereotyped roles for men and women.[106]

My proposed amendment does not explicitly deal with the personal laws of different religious communities but arguably aims to protect them. Yet the amendment would negate claims of the right to practice gender discrimination based on religion or culture through a universal application of this proposed constitutional exception based on the individual-rights ideals of liberalism.

The paradox that protecting multiculturalism can hinder women's rights can be solved only by creating a civil society based on the separation between

104. *See* Pratap Bhanu Mehta, *Obscuring Real Issues*, THE HINDU, July 30, 2003, *available at* http://www.thehindu.com/2003/07/30/stories/2003073001431000.htm.

105. INDIA CONST. art 15(3) ("Nothing in this article shall prevent the State from making any special provision for women and children.").

106. Convention on the Elimination of All Forms of Discrimination against Women, art. 5, G.A. Res. 34/180, 34 U.N. GAOR, Supp. No. 46, at 193, U.N. Doc. A/34/46.

religion and state as envisaged in the Indian Constitution.[107] Political leaders must be sensitive to increasing demands for recognition of religious and cultural rights, but subject to the limitations imposed by the Constitution and Article 5 of the CEDAW. The Indian experience demonstrates that that there is a need to declare unambiguously the superiority of the right to gender equality over demands for preserving the sovereignty of religious or cultural groups. This Declaration should be included with other fundamental rights in the basic text or law containing these rights, whether it is the Constitution or a Declaration of Rights. Unless this is done, there are no safeguards for the protection of women's rights and the assurance of gender justice.[108]

107. *See* India Const. pmbl. Also, in a number of cases, including the case of S.R. Bommai v. Union of India, (1994) 3 S.C.C. 1, the Supreme Court held that religion is a matter of individual faith and cannot be mixed with secular activities, which only the state can regulate by enacting laws.

108. *See* Justice S. Rajendra Babu, *Third Shri Akella Satyanarayana Memorial Endowment Lecture on Gender Justice—Indian Perspective*, (2002) 5 S.C.C. (Jour) 1, *available at* http://www.ebc-india.com/lawyer/articles/2002v5a1.htm.

[12]

A Critical Analysis of Customary Marriages, *Bohali* and the South African Constitution

R. Songca

This paper discusses African customary marriages.[1] It also discusses the custom of paying *bohali* (bridewealth). Some writers have argued that customary marriages should be abolished by statute, whereas some argue that customary marriages should be modified to improve the status and rights of women who have entered into such marriages. The existence of customary marriages on one hand, and western monogamous marriages on the other hand, has not only resulted in confusion and debate in the area of family law,[2] but it is contended by some[3] that customary marriages perpetuate the inequality between women and men. For instance, under a customary marriage, a man can marry as many wives as he wishes but a woman is not allowed to marry more than one man; Polyandry is unknown is Southern Africa.[4] Supporters[5] of customary marriages have argued that these marriages are symbolic or central to the African culture and prohibiting these marriages by legislation or otherwise would be tantamount to saying

---

1 Customary marriages are marriages entered into in terms of the customary practices of a particular society. They are different from civil marriages in that they are potentially polygamous.

2 The confusion which has resulted from the existence of these two sytems of marriages will be highlighted below.

3 'Resolving the Polygamy Question' in Esther Mayambala, "Changing the Terms of the Debate to Resolve the Polygamy Question in Africa" (Graduate Paper, Spring 1994).

4 W.C.M. Maqutu, "Lesotho's African Marriage is Not a Customary Union," *CILSA* 16 (1983): 374, 380. W.C.M. Maqutu, "Current Problems and Conflicts in the Marriage Law of Lesotho," *CILSA* 12 (1979):176, 178.

5 C.R.M. Dlamini, "Should we Legalize or Abolish Polygamy?" *CILSA* 22 (1989): 330, 331.

that European culture is superior to African culture, and prohibiting these marriages by legislation would be a drastic departure from customary law.[6]

That the existence of these two systems of marriages causes confusion cannot be denied; the confusion is further exacerbated by the practice of paying *bohali* under both systems of marriage. The second part of this paper focuses on the practice of paying *bohali* under both systems of marriage. Today, the man may still give the parents of his prospective bride *bohali* although he intends to contract a monogamous civil marriage.

Although *bohali* is justified on the grounds that it 'cements' families and it ensures the proper treatment of the bride in her new home,[7] some writers argue that these justifications are no longer valid. Today, *bohali* is seen as a weapon to control women. It is the price men pay to 'buy' wives, one which entitles men to treat women as their property. The argument is that the institution of *bohali* also degrades women to the position of slaves. It is argued that because of *bohali* and polygamy, fathers sometimes force their daughters to marry against their will. It also impoverishes families.[8]

The third part of this paper looks at recommendations; ways in which women's' interests can be protected. The paper concludes that it is good that these traditional practices [i.e., *bohali* and customary marriages] have been retained;[9] nevertheless, the writer argues that they should be modified to better protect the rights of women.

Arguments for and against Polygamy

Critics of polygamy argue that polygamy degrades women to the

---

6 S. Rugege, "A Sesotho Customary Marriage is Incapable of Conversion into a Civil One?" *Lesotho Law Journal* 7 (1991): 73,78.

7 J.M. Hlophe, "The Kwazulu Act on the Code of Zulu Law, 6 of 1981 - A Guide to Intending Spouses and Some Comments on the Custom of Lobola", *CILSA* 17 (1984): 163.

8 *Id.*, at 167.

9 Section 15 (3) (a)(i)(ii) of the Constitution of the Republic of South Africa, May 1996, recognizes marriages concluded under any tradition or system of religious or personal law.

position of slaves,[10] and allowing polygamy is a return to barbarism. They also argue that it enables men to live in idleness on the excessive labour of their wives.[11]

African culture has undergone fundamental changes over the years, and so has the institution of polygamy. It cannot, therefore, be argued that men enter into polygamous marriages because they need women to work for them, as was the practice long ago. Those who allege that polygamy is uncivilized also argue that polygamy is incompatible with the christian idea of marriage.[12] The response to this assertion is that the Scriptures in the Old and New Testament do not condemn the practice, instead they are 'painfully silent'.[13] Many Africans are christians, and have reconciled the traditional way of life and the christian way of life because the Scriptures do not prohibit these institutions. Instead the Scriptures clearly prohibit divorce. When the Scriptures issued this prohibition, they were not merely stating an ideal, they were laying down a rule that had to be followed (Matthew 19.3-9).[14] It is therefore accurate to say that a civil monogamous marriage is based on society's moral views rather than on christianity, and society's moral views are influenced by some christian principles.[15] Hence, to view polygamy as uncivilized is an expression of ethnocentric bias, reflecting the traditional European morality, rather than religious teachings.[16]

Today, some women who enter into polygamous marriages are educated women who are supposedly civilized. They enter into these marriages for numerous reasons. For instance, they are disillusioned with civil marriages because of the high rate of divorce, and the fact that it is difficult for them to get out of civil marriages even when their

---

10 The Natal Native Commission Report on Native Laws and Customs 1852/1853.

11 *Supra* note 7 at 167.

12 Missionaries discouraged the practice on the basis that it was unchristian. Africans who wanted to be christians were encouraged/forced to divorce their other wives.

13 C.R.M. Dlamini, "The Christian v Customary Marriage Syndrome," *The South African Law Journal* 60 (1985): 701-704.

14 *Id.*

15 *Id.*, at 706.

16 C.R.M. Dlamini, "Should We Legalise or Abolish Polygamy?" *CILSA* 22 (1989): 330-345.

marriages have irretrievably broken down.

In some cases, women find it difficult to get men who are suitable and single. The dilemma of women is made worse by the fact that there are more women than men. These are some of the reasons some women enter into polygamous marriages. Their decision to do so does not have anything to do with either christianity or their civilization. Critics of polygamy[17] have also argued that polygamy denies women their sexual freedom and their right to equality with men in matters relating to marriage. Furthermore, polygamy discriminates against women in that it allows men to have more than one wife, whereas women cannot have more than one husband. This inequality, the argument goes, puts women in a low bargaining position in marriage and family relationships: they have been brought up to believe that their only goal in life is to marry, to satisfy their husbands' numerous needs, and bear him children.

The inferior status of women has also been attributed to polygamy. It is argued that because of polygamy, the woman is deprived of her dignity and equality as the man's partner in life. The woman is often regarded as a servant rather than a partner.[18] Inequality between men and women is not peculiar to customary (polygamous) marriages. Under Roman law, where polygamy was not practised, women were not treated as equal to men either.[19] In other western societies, the inequalities between men and women did not disappear overnight. These battles are still being fought. Giving up polygamy would be similar to giving up African culture; moreover, what will be the fate of those women and their children who have entered into those marriages? Women's advancement as will be shown, can be achieved without abolishing polygamy.

Some writers[20] respond to the argument about women's sexual freedom by stating that some women enter into these marriages fully aware that the marriages are potentially polygamous; hence, women

---

17 G.H. Joyce, *Christian Marriage: A Historical and Doctrinal Study* (1933) 18-19.

18 'Resolving the Polygamy Question' in Esther Mayambala, 'Changing the Terms of the Debate to Resolve the Polygamy Question in Africa' (Graduate Paper, Spring, 1994).

19 C.R.M. Dlamini, "Should we Legalise or Abolish Polygamy?" *CILSA* 22 (1989): 330-334.

20 *Id.*, at 336.

enter into these marriages of their own free will. Therefore, the argument that polygamy denies women their sexual freedom is open to doubt.

Secondly, in responding to the argument that polygamy puts women in a low bargaining position in marriage and family relations, supporters of polygamy counter by stating that the woman's decision to enter into a polygamous marriage is an informed one. Moreover, it is unnecessary for a man to divorce the first wife in order to marry a second one, more especially if the first wife does not object to the second marriage.[21]

It is alleged that polygamy encourages wives to compete with each other to give husbands as many male children as possible. Writers pursuing the argument that women have no control over their reproductive autonomy assert that, women cannot make their own decisions whether or not to have children, the number of children they will have, spacing of the children, whether or not to practise some form of birth control, and whether to carry a pregnancy to term. All of these issues are determined by the husband. The proponents of this argument conclude their argument by alleging that women will get some degree of reproductive autonomy if the tradition of polygamy were done away with altogether.[22] It is true that some men do not like their wives to use contraceptives because they believe that a woman should bear children as long as she is able to. Nevertheless, this notion is shared by men in both polygamous customary and monogamous civil marriages. Men, (especially blacks) aspire to have male children. This preference stems from the patrilineal nature of African society and does not have anything to do with polygamy.

Men enter into polygamous marriages for various reasons. One of the reasons is that the man sometimes decides to marry a second wife because the first cannot bear children. In this situation, the man will take another wife rather than divorce the first one. In other situations, the first wife will encourage the husband to marry another wife so that the second wife can help in performing family chores. This situation is especially true, if the first is unable to do so due to health problems.

---

21 *Id.*

22 R.J. Cook, "International Human Rights and Women's Reproductive Health", *Studies in Family Planning*, March/April, 1993, vol.24 No.2, 73 at 78.

However, these are not the only reasons men enter into polygamous marriages. This goes to show that there are various reasons why men enter into these marriages. Polygamy is part of the African culture. We should be careful not to adopt western views at the expense of our culture. Women's interest (as will be shown later) can be protected without abolishing polygamy by legislation.

It is argued that polygamous marriages lead to the man favouring one wife at the expense of the other, and consequently to mutual jealousies, rivalry and bickering.[23] Those who support the institution of polygamy concede that this argument has merit, but argue that it is an exaggeration. They assert that the argument overlooks the shortcomings in a monogamous marriage and creates the impression that if a man is married to one wife, there will always be complete attachment and compatibility. They assert that there is no evidence that there is more strife and bickering in a polygamous marriage than in a monogamous marriage. Therefore, bickering is caused by the husband's unequal treatment of his wives rather than by polygamy itself.[24]

Arguments for and against *Bohali* (Bridewealth)

Bohali is money(or other valuables) paid by the prospective husband to the parents of the bride. It symbolizes the man's gratitude to the parents of the bride for having borne him a wife. *Bohali* unites the woman and the man's family. Among Africans, marriage is not between parties only, it is a family affair. It creates a special bond between the two families. In most cases, the bride's family uses the money to pay for wedding expenses. Today, the prospective husband pays *bohali* even if the parties have decided to enter into a civil marriage. *Bohali* also signifies the husband's marital power over the wife, thereby giving the husband exclusive access to the wife. It is alleged that the institution of *bohali* is still popular today because some women do not consider themselves properly married if *bohali* has not been paid.[25] Those who support the institution of *bohali* assert that it

---

23 C.R.M. Dlamini, "Should we legalise or Abolish Polygamy?" *CILSA* 22 (1989): 330 at 334.

24 *Id.*

25 C.R.M. Dlamini, "Should *Lobola* be Abolished? A reply to Hlophe," *CILSA* 18 (1985): 361 at 363.

is a cultural institution which plays a psychological role.[26] It cannot be denied that *bohali* has been abused by many parents. There are cases where parents have demanded excessive *bohali* from their future sons-in-law. This tendency is common in cases where the woman is educated. The more educated the woman, the higher the *bohali*.[27] It is argued that some parents demand excessive amounts because they were made to pay *bohali*, or they want to repay debts they incurred when they got married.[28] Some commentators[29] concede that there is a tendency among some parents to demand exorbitant amounts from their in-laws, and that this practice may discourage or delay a marriage. They nevertheless concede that most of the money is used to pay marriage expenses, not to enrich the bride's family. The bride has to buy new clothes for herself and gifts for her in-laws.

The defenders of bohali assert that these abuses do not call for the abolition of the practice because many Southern Africans are in favour of its retention. They believe that *bohali* is a worthwhile custom, which gives them a distinctive identity.[30] Therefore *bohali* continues because of other reasons other than the need to settle debts. In any event, they argue that it is unlikely that parents would be prepared to wait for so long before settling their debts. Some academics respond[31] to the assertion that *bohali* is a means of settling debts by some parents, by arguing that, in recent years, educated blacks demand *bohali* because it is a link with their culture. For them, it indicates that despite their education and westernization, they are still blacks and are proud of retaining some of their customs.[32]

Another criticism levelled against the practice of *bohali* is that *bohali*

---

26 *Id.*

27 J.M. Hlophe, "The Kwazulu Act on the Code of Zulu Law, 6 of 1981 - A Guide to Intending Spouses and Some Comments on the Custom of Lobola," *CILSA* 17 (1984): 163 at 169.

28 *Id.*

29 *Supra* note 25 at 365.

30 *Id.*

31 *Id.*, at 366.

32 I. Sibiya -`Contemporary Trends in Marriage and its Preliminaries Among Abakwamkwanazi.' Unpublished MA Dissertation, University of Zululand (1981) 220.

is the cause and not the consequence of polygamy.[33] The problem with this view is that, a lot of people still pay *bohali* even though they intend to enter into a civil monogamous marriage. Therefore, polygamy is caused by factors other than *bohali*.[34]

Polygamy and *bohali* are an economic burden on the average person in these inflationary times. Customary marriages discriminate against women, especially in the area of the law of succession. The question, therefore, is whether these institutions should be abolished completely or reformed. The next section addresses this question.

Should we Abolish Polygamy and Bohali?

Should *bohali* and polygamy be abolished by legislation? Although this question might seem irrelevant considering the new constitutional changes, some people might still feel that it is necessary for the practices to be abolished by legislation.[35] Some writers[36] feel that abolition by legislation or to declare the practice unconstitutional would be a drastic step. They argue that legislation will either be ineffective or will lead to social problems, such as the bearing of illegitimate children. In addition, they also argue that retroactively abolishing these institutions will be prejudicial to some women, especially those who have entered into polygamous marriages.[37] Critics of legislative abolition contend that this action may encourage some men to enter into clandestine relationships and avoid commitments on the pretext that the law does not allow them to marry more than one wife.[38] They assert that polygamy should die a natural death.

Those who support the practice of *bohali* equally argue that the practice of paying *bohali* should be retained because it is a cultural institution, the practice of which involves no moral indignation among the African people.[39] This practice is respected and deeply rooted in the

---

33 *Supra*, note 27, at 170.

34 *Supra*, note 25, at 371.

35 The Practices might be challenged before the Constitutional Court as unconstitutional.

36 *Supra*, note 23, at 345.

37 *Id.*

38 See Dlamini, *supra*, note 23, at 345.

39 *Supra*, note 25, at 375.

emotions of the people.

International Conventions, the Constitution and Polygamy

Numerous international conventions indirectly proscribe polygamy because it is inherently discriminatory. For instance, Article 2(f) of the Convention on the Elimination of All Forms of Discrimination Against Women[40] requires States Parties to:

> take all appropriate measures, including legislation, to modify or abolish existing laws, regulations, customs and practices which constitute discrimination against women.

The writer submits that South Africa will still comply with its obligations if it modifies its laws regarding polygamous marriages and the practice of paying *bohali* as recommended in the last part of this article.

In addition, Article 5 (a) of the Convention requires States Parties to:

> modify the social and cultural patterns of conduct of men and women, with a view to achieving the elimination of prejudices and customary and all other practices which are based on the idea of the inferiority or the superiority of either of the sexes or on stereotyped roles for men and women.

It might be argued that South Africa, by ratifying CEDAW, and being part of a comity of civilized nations, has indicated a preparedness to rid itself of sex-based discrimination and, whenever possible, use CEDAW and other international instruments as aids to interpretation. Moreover, South Africa has a duty to comply with its obligations under CEDAW despite the fact that Parliament has not legislated its provisions into the law of the land. Another way of ensuring compliance is to make a state legally bound by the relevant principle of international human rights law. It should also have committed itself to effectively discharging its responsibility to bring domestic customary laws into conformity with the requirements of international human rights law.

Some academics[41] have highlighted the dangers of changing religious

---

[40] South Africa has ratified the Convention.

[41] Abdullahi Ahmed An-'Im, *Human Rights of Women: National & International Perspective* (Philadelphia: University of Pennsylvania Press, 1994), 176-180.

and customary laws in accordance with human rights law by stating that people should be convinced or persuaded to see the validity and utility of such a change. Abdullahi asserts that such persuasion must be grounded in a complete and realistic understanding of the rationale or authority of these laws, and the way they operate in practice.[42]

Polygamy does discriminate against women, in that men have a right that women do not have. But the response to this is that polygamy cannot be seen as discriminatory against women who favour and benefit from it.[43] This argument asserts that there is nothing wrong if a woman decides to waive her right to her dignity or autonomy by consenting to being a part of a polygamous establishment.[44]

Section 9(3) of the Interim Constitution[45] provides that: "The State may not unfairly discriminate, directly or indirectly against anyone on one or more grounds, including race, gender, sex..." and Section 15(3) and Section 15(3)(a)(1) permits legislation recognizing marriages concluded under any tradition or system of religious, personal or family law.[46]

Bennet[47] opines that any campaign to restrict the practice of polygamy will rest on Section 9(3). He nevertheless, asserts (correctly in my view) that it would be difficult to prove that polygamy is a direct cause of female subordination, especially in view of arguments that polygamy performs the valuable social functions of absorbing women into domestic units and preventing the breakdown of marriage on grounds of adultery. Bennet asserts that there is a depth of feeling about polygamy which suggests that an immediate ban would be difficult to enforce, and hence inadvisable.

The disadvantage of proscribing polygamy by legislation is that such

---

42 *Id.*

43 C.R.M. Dlamini, "Should we Legalise or Abolish Polygamy?" *CILSA* 22 (1989): 330 at 336.

44 *Id.*

45 Constitution of the Republic of South Africa, 1996, as Adopted by the Constitutional Assembly on 8 May, 1996.

46 This Section permits polygamous customary and other religious marriages.

47 T.W. Bennet, *Human Rights and African Customary Law* (Cape Town: Juta & Co., Ltd, 1995), 70.

a move will encourage cohabitation and illegitimacy; whereby the other woman will be treated as a concubine or 'second' wife without enjoying the benefits of matrimony. South Africa, unlike other first world countries is lagging behind in the area of family law. Our family law does not adequately protect the rights of women in 'live-in relationships.'

Recommendations

The people must be educated about the advantages and disadvantages inherent in polygamous marriages and the practice of paying *bohali*. This can be done through the church and by women's groups. The people have to be made aware that customary marriages can and do lead to problems.

In addition, some writers[48] argue that people who deal with these cases should have a full understanding of customary law, and the history of the law because there are viable and acceptable ways of changing customary laws and practices. For instance, this can be done by transforming popular beliefs and attitudes, thereby changing common practice. Abdullahi[49] asserts that this can be done through a comprehensive and intensive program of formal and informal education, supported by social services and other administrative measures, aimed at changing people's attitudes regarding the necessity or desirability of continuing a particular religious or customary practice. The objective of the program can be achieved not only by discrediting the religious or customary practice in question, but by also providing a viable alternative view of the matter.[50] In practice, there are options available which can be adopted.

(a) The first route is to reform customary laws with an objective of improving the situation of women. A number of alternatives can be looked into:

1. The first approach is to allow polygamy to co-exist side by side with monogamous marriages, on the premise that the parties will make the

---

[48] Abdullahi Ahmed An-Na'ni, *Human Rights of Women, National & International Perspectives* (Philadelphia: University of Pennsylvania Press, 1994), 178.

[49] *Id.*

[50] *Id.*

choice for themselves.[51]

2. The second is the approach that seeks to control polygamy, by either giving the wife a right to divorce a polygamous husband if she can prove actual or potential injury to her health, or her husband's inability to support two households, or by requiring the husband to seek permission to take another wife from a specified judicial or quasi-judicial body.

The writer will look at the above approaches and suggest ways in which they can be applied in an attempt to improve women's' rights.

Approach 1.

Under this approach, polygamy is allowed to co-exist with monogamy and the parties are expected to choose the type of marriage they want. Usually there is very little regulation by the government except to ensure that parties do not contract marriages under both systems. The constitutional bill seems to allow customary marriages. The writer is in principle not opposed to this but nevertheless, feels that some form of regulation is required. Pertinent issues which need to be decided include the following:

* whether the woman's choice was obtained, and if so, for which form of marriage.

The danger inherent in this approach is that it might be assumed that those who contract a customary marriage have endorsed polygamy as their way of life and they should be left to live according to their choice. Unfortunately this approach leaves polygamous marriages unregulated as it assumes that parties who are in polygamous marriages are in such marriages by choice, and it therefore leaves women in a very disadvantaged situation because such an assumption closes the doors for the majority of women who marry under customary law to have any legal right to seek redress for their husband's practice of polygamy.[52]

---

51 This alternative seems to have been provided for by the Constitution.

52 'Resolving the Polygamy Question' in Esther Mayambala, 'Changing the Terms of the Debate to Resolve the Polygamy Question in Africa' (Graduate Paper, Spring 1994) at 60.

Approach 2.

Polygamy is allowed to exist, but the wife is given a right to divorce her husband if she does not want the husband to take a second wife. The shortcomings inherent in this approach is that the requirement places the burden of proof on the wife to show cause why the second marriage should not take place.[53]

Under the second approach, polygamous marriages can be regulated by requiring the husband to justify his need for a second wife, either before a court or a quasi-judicial authority. Factors which might be looked into by the courts may include the following:

* whether the couple is childless and, whether the wife's health is such that she cannot permanently have sexual intercourse with the husband. Here polygamy may turn out to be the lesser evil than a divorce for a couple which has no desire to dissolve their marriage;
* whether the wife is terminally ill or crippled;
* whether the present wife freely gives him permission;
* whether his ability to support his wives and children is certain.

The most apparent benefit of this approach is the transfer of the burden of justifying the need to take an additional wife on the husband, who is not only the most interested party in the new marriage but might also have the financial ability to initiate the proceedings. Registration of customary marriages should be compulsory to assist women in proving that they were in fact married. Registration procedures should be similar to registration of civil marriages.

Conclusion

Polygamy does have its problems, but as shown above, women's interests can still be protected if this custom\practice is regulated. Few attempts have been made by people, especially western thinkers, to understand the intrinsic value of polygamy. Polygamy can provide a

---

53 *Id.*

compromise between a happy marriage and a divorce which often has drastic consequences, not only for the parties, but also for the children. Monogamy is not the ideal; the ideal is a happy and satisfying relationship in marriage.[54]

Monogamy provides the framework for the realization of a happy marriage but it does not guarantee it. It is for these reasons that we advocate for the retention of polygamy, provided that it is regulated with the aim of improving the position and rights of women who have entered into these marriages. As indicated above, there are various ways of doing this. For instance, the wife should be given a right to divorce her husband, the husband should seek her consent to enter into a second marriage, and the financial means of the husband should be examined before taking a second wife.

The writer concedes that the practice of *bohali* has in some instances been abused. Today families have abused it by requiring exorbitant amounts from their in-laws. Nevertheless, these abuses do not justify a blanket prohibition. South Africa does not experience the same problems as other countries. For instance, in some countries such as India, dowry has been associated with deaths of the parties who cannot afford it. In South Africa *bohali* plays a different role.

Women do not feel that they are properly married if *bohali* is not paid. Moreover, it helps the woman to pay her wedding expenses. There are a few people who regard *bohali* as wife purchase. In most cases, money paid as *bohali* is usually the result of negotiations between the two families. Abuses associated with this practice can be curbed. For instance, a law can be passed stipulating the maximum amount that can be demanded as *bohali*. It is for these reasons that the writer argues that polygamy and *bohali* should be retained but be modified.

---

[54] C.R.M. Dlamini, "Should we Legalise or Abolish Polygamy?" *CILSA* 22 (1989): 330 at 345.

[13]

WOMEN, RELIGION AND MULTICULTURALISM IN ISRAEL

Ruth Halperin-Kaddari[*]

Israeli society has become preoccupied with the question of multiculturalism in recent years.[1] *The issue is raised from several directions and within many contexts of cultural signifiers, including nationality, ethnicity and of course religion. It seems that the religious variable raises the most interest for the multicultural discourse, particularly in light of the definition of Israel as the State of the Jewish People in 1948 in its birth document, the Declaration of Independence, and as a Jewish and Democratic State in 1992, in the Basic Law:*

---

* Senior lecturer, Faculty of Law, Bar-Ilan University, Israel; J.S.D. Yale Law School, 1993; LL.M. Yale Law School, 1990; LL.B. Bar-Ilan University, 1989. I would like to thank my research assistants Hilla Paltiel and Hana Meidenberg, and the staff of the UCLA Journal of International Law and Foreign Affairs for inviting me to participate in the conference.

[1] To give just a few examples: MULTICULTURALISM IN A DEMOCRATIC AND JEWISH STATE (Menachem Mautner et al. eds., Ramot Publications 1998) (Hebrew); Baruch Kimerling, *The New Israelis: Many Cultures Without Multiculturalism*, 16 ALPAYIM 264, 308 (1998) (Hebrew); John Simons, *Feminism at the Border Zones*, 7 THEORY & CRITICISM 20, 30 (1995) (Hebrew); Danny Rabinovich, *Saving Brown Women*, 7 THEORY & CRITICISM 5, 19 (1995) (Hebrew).

Human Dignity and Liberty. This article will examine the feminism-multiculturalism dilemma within Israel, and map the ways in which religion affects women in Israel. After a brief introduction to the conventional dichotomy of feminism and multiculturalism, this article points to the unique situation of religion and state relations in Israel which changes the conventional construction of the dilemma, and then analyzes the various levels in which religion influences the situation of women in Israel. Only the concluding case-study of multiculturalism in Israel captures the traditional dilemma of feminism and multiculturalism.

I. THE FEMINIST-MULTICULTURAL DEBATE

Israeli society is a composition of various cultural and religious groups, the largest of which is the Jewish religion. Like many societies in the world, Israeli society has to face the question of handling its multiplicity of internal cultures: Should their existence be encouraged? Should the State stay neutral to their existence? Should they, and their members, be granted special rights? On the surface, then, it seems that this is indeed the conventional confrontation of multiculturalism. Cultures need social groups in order to survive. The traditional justification for awarding special rights to various cultural groups is that by doing so the minority group's culture and tradition is preserved. As put by Will Kymlicka, the foremost contemporary defender of cultural group rights, these are "societal cultures" which provide their "members with meaningful ways of life across the full range of human activities, including social, educational, religious, recreational, and economic life, encompassing both public and private spheres."[2] Since they carry such a significant role in their members' lives, and since they are usually in danger of extinction, the argument is that minority cultures should be protected by special rights.

At this point, the conventional multicultural discourse is faced with the following problem: the special status awarded to groups in the name of the right to culture sometimes stands in stark contradiction with the individual's status in a liberal state. Moreover, the right to culture could possibly apply to groups whose norms and values do not correspond with the liberal perception of the individual. The protection of cultures could eventually lead to a system of disrespect for individual rights in a liberal society. Thus, a central problem in protecting the right to culture, especially when the protected culture is not a liberal culture, is that the state is obliged to employ illiberal means for that purpose. The problem is complicated in light of the conventional liberal ideology that calls on the state to "stay neutral" with respect to its citizens' lifestyle. The right to culture demands that the state abandon its neutral stance and actively support cultures in need, even if those cultures' ideologies oppose the state's norms and values.[3]

As Susan Moller Okin plainly states, most cultures are suffused with practices and ideologies concerning gender. They are often preoccupied with personal (family) law, and most significantly, most religious or cultural groups "have as one of their principal aims the control of women by men."[4] Consequently, many of the cultural minorities that claim group rights are more patriarchal than the surrounding cultures. Thus, awarding group rights within liberal states

---

[2] WILL KYMLICKA, MULTICULTURAL CITIZENSHIP: A LIBERAL THEORY OF MINORITY RIGHTS 76 (Oxford Univ. Press 1995).

[3] Avishai Margalit & Moshe Halbertal, *Liberalism and the Right to Culture*, 61 SOC. RES. 491 (1994).

[4] Susan M. Okin, *Is Multiculturalism Bad for Women?*, *in* SUSAN M. OKIN WITH RESPONDANTS, IS MULTICULTURALISM BAD FOR WOMEN? 12, 13 (Joshua Cohen et al. eds., Princeton Univ. Press 1999) [hereinafter OKIN].

may actually harm women members of those groups. While there are some who hold that this presentation is too simplistic and that it ignores the women's own voices who themselves sometimes encourage and support the patriarchal practices and ideologies,[5] Okin's analysis is quite convincing. The phenomenon of the oppressed who acquiesce to the oppression is not an unfamiliar one.[6] There is a particular tension between women's rights and group rights that should be addressed separately within the general question of the state's relation to the minority groups. The question is how, if at all, this tension between commitment to gender equality and commitment to respect and encourage minority cultures can be resolved. There are various responses to this tension. Some justify awarding group rights only to liberal cultures. Others, like Avishai Margalit and Moshe Halbertal, argue that even cultures that ignore their members' rights should be accorded group rights, if they are otherwise in danger of extinction.[7] It seems that this is so even with respect to cultures that practice gender discrimination. Still others maintain that such minority groups are entitled to be "left alone" by the surrounding society. Okin herself takes a more extreme approach, arguing that since gender discrimination is prohibited, awarding rights to groups that enable discriminatory practices is unacceptable. Rather, as the middle path argues, cultures and religions should be able to develop and embrace equality within their own cultural framework.[8]

This middle path is of course not free from problems. For example, would cultures that reject egalitarianism be doomed to extinction?[9] Furthermore, there is no logical basis to stop at the equality principle and not demand the acceptance of other basic liberal values, such as autonomy and free will. The danger is clearly that such an approach would lead to respecting minority cultures only

---

[5] *See, e.g.*, Sander L. Gilman, *"Barbaric" Rituals?*, *in* OKIN, *supra* note 4, at 53; Bonnie Honig, *My Culture Made Me Do It*, *in* OKIN, *supra* note 4, at 35.

[6] False consciousness is but one expression of the phenomenon that immediately comes to mind within the feminist context.

[7] Margalit & Halbertal, *supra* note 3.

[8] *But cf.* Joseph Raz, *How Perfect Should One Be? And Whose Culture Is?*, *in* OKIN, *supra* note 4, at 95-99; Honig, *supra* note 5.

[9] Okin suggests a positive answer to that. *See* OKIN, *supra* note 4, at 22-23.

when they turn liberal.[10] It is often argued that the actual enforcement of the principle of equality entails oppression and patronizing of the minority culture.[11] Moreover, how can the surrounding liberal society, which is itself guilty of being discriminatory and patriarchal, demand anything different from the minority culture? This is the conventional feminism versus multiculturalism dilemma.

II. THE ISRAELI CASE

The Israeli context, as already mentioned, is much more complex. The conventional construction of the dilemma applies to states whose constitutional framework maintains some form of separation between religion and state, with several religious communities existing within the state. Israel is different. The State of Israel is defined as the State of the Jewish People, and as a Jewish and Democratic State. Religion in general, and the Jewish religion in particular, hold a formal and constitutional status in several areas, most significantly in the rule of religious laws over the area of family law, which means that matters concerning personal status are determined according to the religious affiliation of the parties involved in each case. The formal standing given to religion and to religious law in Israel turns the conventional multicultural dilemma on its face, from a question of awarding respect and rights to patriarchal minority culture at the expense of its own members, into a question of imposition of the patriarchal minority culture over the liberal majority, at the expense of the members of the majority.[12] The conventional feminism-multiculturalism dilemma

---

[10] Bhikhu Parekh, *A Varied Moral World*, *in* OKIN, *supra* note 4, at 72.

[11] Aziza Y. al-Hibri, *Is Western Patriarchal Feminism Good for Third World/Minority Women?*, *in* OKIN, *supra* note 4, at 41-46.

[12] *But cf.* Ruth Halperin-Kaddari, *Rethinking Legal Pluralism in Israel: The Interaction Between the High Court of Justice and Rabbinical Courts*, 20 TEL AVIV U. L. REV. 683, 744-46 (1997) (explaining Justice Barak's implied rejection of legal pluralism by revealing the

exists in the Israeli context only within those areas in which religion does not carry any formal status.

The mere granting of the formal status to religion is, in itself, a form of position-taking within the principal question that stands at the basis of the dilemma. It is a position that clearly prefers the preservation of the patriarchal culture at the expense of violation of individual rights and liberal values in general, and violation of women and of gender equality in particular. The clearest expression of this is seen in the chronology of attempts to pass a constitution in Israel. Israel did not adopt a written constitution upon its establishment. Various attempts have been made over the years to enact a bill of rights, and one of the main obstacles to that endeavor has been the issue of gender equality and equal status for women under the law. The maintenance of the rule of religious laws over the area of family law renders full equality for women impossible. Instead of a full constitution, Israel has chosen the method of enacting "Basic Laws," two of which were enacted in 1992 and address two human rights guarantees: Basic Law: Human Dignity and Liberty[13] and Basic Law: Freedom of Occupation.[14] An express right to equality is absent from both.[15] Several attempts to pass an all-encompassing Basic Law on Human and Civil Rights have failed, primarily due to the impossibility of its passage without a guarantee of the principle of religious laws in marriage and divorce.[16] A clear pattern of subordinating gender equality to religious values has been formed, one that is also seen in

false nature of legal pluralism in Israel, in light of the imposing variable within the Israeli legal framework).

[13] Basic Law: Human Dignity and Liberty, 1992, S.H. 150.

[14] Basic Law: Freedom of Occupation, 1994, S.H. 90.

[15] The common opinion, though, advanced by Chief Justice Barak, is that the scope of the basic right to human dignity is very broad and encompasses various unenumerated human rights, such as the right to equality (Barak 1994, 423-426). This interpretation was approved in a number of Supreme Court cases.

[16] Frances Raday, *Religion, Multiculturalism and Equality: The Israeli Case*, 25 Y.B. ON HUM. RTS. 193, 211 (1996) [hereinafter Raday, *Religion, Multiculturalism and Equality*]; Frances Raday, *The Concept of Gender Equality in a Jewish State, in* CALLING THE EQUALITY BLUFF: WOMEN IN ISRAEL 18-28 (Barbara Swirski & Marilyn P. Safir eds., Teachers College Press 1993) [hereinafter Raday, *The Concept of Gender Equality in a Jewish State*].

part in the present Basic Laws' provision of immunity from judicial review that is given to existing laws.[17]

The place of religion in Israel has been acknowledged, here and elsewhere, as a primary factor informing the position of women in Israel, to their detriment.[18] In terms of Israel's conformity with international standards, it has been the reason for Israel's reservations to the Convention on Elimination of all forms of Discrimination Against Women (CEDAW), as well as to the International Covenant on Civil and Political Rights (ICCPR). International law allows states to make a legal commitment to implement a convention while reserving the right not to apply some of its requirements or even principles with which they cannot comply, all this in order to enhance global acceptance of human rights obligations. However, much controversy has been created regarding reservations to the CEDAW Convention since, in many cases, they appear contrary to its very aim.[19] That is primarily so with regard to reservations on religious grounds, which mostly apply to countries applying *Shari'a* law, that submitted reservations concerning the very obligation to eliminate gender discrimination.[20] But it also applies to reservations on religious grounds that were made to CEDAW's Article 16 on equality in Marriage and Family and to CEDAW's Article 7 on equality in Political and Public life, such as the ones made by Israel.[21] These two

---

[17] For example, Basic Law: Human Dignity and Liberty states in section 10: "This Basic Law shall not derogate from the effect of any enactment, which was in effect immediately before this Basic Law came into effect."

[18] Raday, *Religion, Multiculturalism and Equality, supra* note 16, at 211; Nira Yuval-Davis, *The Bearers of the Collective: Women and Religious Legislation in Israel*, 11 FEMINIST STUD. 15, 27 (1985); Talia Einhorn, *Equality in Israeli Family Law, in* VERLAG ERNST & WERNER GIESEKING, GLIECHHEIT IM FAMILIENRECHT [Equality in Family Law—The Influence of Constitutions and International Conventions] 297, 332 (Verschraegen ed., 1997); S.I. Strong, *Law and Religion in Israel and Iran: How the Integration of Secular and Spiritual Laws Affects Human Rights and the Potential for Violence*, 19 MICH. J. INT'L L. 109, 217 (1997).

[19] KATARINA TOMASEVSKI, A PRIMER ON CEDAW FOR INTERNATIONAL DEVELOPMENT CO-OPERATION PERSONNEL 14-16 (Sida, 1998).

[20] These countries include Afghanistan, Bangladesh, Egypt, Iran, Iraq, Jordan, Libya, Maldives, Mauritania, and Pakistan. *See id.* at 15.

[21] Israel phrased its reservations in the following language:

areas present the obvious and main areas of concern for discrimination against women on religious grounds, and at the same time, it is the strongest expression possible of respect, and in fact of deference, to religious cultural norms. Officially then, as reflected by Israel's reservations and as noted in the CEDAW Committee's concluding observations to Israel's Report,[22] these are the only areas where the place of religion in Israel hampers women's advancement. The effect that the involvement of religion within Israel's polity and ethos has on women is much more vast. The following outline of the major points of reference of which the fuller picture is composed, primarily, from the perspective of the Jewish religion. It should also be noted that in discussing the effect that religion has on women in Israel, a distinction must be made between a discussion of religious women as a distinct group of women, and a discussion of the overall consequences that the religion factor has over women in Israel in general. Only the latter is our subject of interest here.

The formal integration of religion and state, particularly the rule of religious law over issues of family law and the legal consequences of this rule, makes the religion factor significant to the situation of

---

> The State of Israel hereby expresses its reservation with regard to Article 7(b) of the Convention concerning the appointment of women to serve as judges of religious courts where this is prohibited by the laws of any of the religious communities in Israel. Otherwise, the said Article is fully implemented in Israel, in view of the fact that women take a prominent part in all aspects of public life.
>
> The State of Israel hereby expresses its reservation with regard to Article 16 of the Convention, insofar as the laws of personal status binding on the several religious communities in Israel do not conform with the provisions of that Article.

Convention on the Elimination of All Forms of Discrimination against Women, K.A. 31, 180 at 195.

[22] The Committee chose to express its disapproval of Israel's reservations in the following language:

> The Committee suggested that in order to guarantee the same rights in marriage and family relations in Israel and to comply fully with the Convention, the Government should complete the secularization of the relevant legislation, place it under the jurisdiction of the civil courts and withdraw its reservations to the Convention.

Report of the Committee on the Elimination of All Forms of Discrimination Against Women, 16-17 Sessions, 1997, at 91.

women in Israel.[23] This is the strongest expression of the influence of religion over women's lives, and the impetus behind Israel's reservations to CEDAW's Articles 7 and 16. Nonetheless, apart from this formal and clear effect, religion influences women's lives in Israel by other means as well. Some means directly or indirectly result from the formal status that religion has been given in areas other than family law, and some have nothing to do with any such formal status, and are clear expressions of social-cultural norms. The latter will be called semi-formal and informal expressions of the relationship between religion and state in Israel, and will be discussed in the second part of this article. This is where the conventional feminism-multiculturalism debate will be most relevant. While critiques tend to concentrate on concrete rules of religious law regarding family lives, attention should be paid to the interrelation between them and the world outside the family. In other words, the interaction between the family on the one hand, and society and the market on the other, is deeply affected by the rule of religious law in the direction of further disadvantaging women.

III. JEWISH FAMILY LAW AND THE RIPPLE EFFECT OF FORMAL EXPRESSIONS OF RELIGION-STATE INTEGRATION

Any discussion that makes use of Jewish law as part of it, without actually going into and analyzing the law itself, is problematic, since Jewish law, perhaps more than any other religious legal system, is pluralistic.[24] It is therefore misleading to present Jewish law as one monolithic normative system, and claim a certain representation of

---

[23] Philippa Strum, *Women and the Politics of Religion in Israel*, 11 HUM. RTS. Q. 483 (1989); Radday, *The Concept of Gender Equality in a Jewish State*, *supra* note 16.

[24] ELIEZER BERKOWITZ, NOT IN HEAVEN: THE NATURE AND FUNCTION OF HALAKHA (Ktav Pub. 1983); JOEL ROTH, THE HALAKHIC PROCESS: A SYSTEMIC ANALYSIS (Ktav Pub. 1986); AVI SAGI, 'ELU VE'ELU: THE MEANING OF THE HALAKHIC DISCOURSE (Hakibutz Ha'Meuchad 1996) (Hebrew).

Jewish law on a particular issue to be an ultimate portrayal of the Jewish law on that issue. The discussion of Jewish law here pertains to a description of Jewish law as it is understood and applied by contemporary rabbinical courts in Israel. The aim of this article is to go beyond the boundaries of Jewish law "in action," to draw upon its theoretical underpinnings and value-laden messages. Since Jewish law is not a central theme of this article, space and time prevents a thorough substantive analysis, which should precede the upcoming discussion.[25] The following discussion is therefore narrowed to a specific reading of Jewish law, which, in my understanding, is sadly the conventional take on Jewish law as it is understood and practiced under Orthodox Judaism today.[26] Applicable Jewish law in Israel is in fact the Orthodox interpretation of Jewish law, and rabbinical courts are exclusively Orthodox. Therefore, the conclusions drawn below are certainly relevant to Jewish women in Israel. Once again, this discussion by no means exhausts the possibilities within Jewish law at large, nor the potential for progressive interpretation that exists within Orthodox Judaism itself.

The construction of gender in Jewish law of marriage and divorce, as it is understood and practiced in rabbinical courts in Israel, results in the unequivocal inferiority and vulnerability of women. In a nutshell, Jewish law conceives of marriage as a one-sided transaction in which the man betroths the woman and not the opposite, sanctions inequality and discrimination regarding spousal obligations and rights toward each other during the course of marriage, and sanctions harsh limitations over the process of divorce and inequalities with respect to

---

[25] Here I only rely on such an analysis that I make elsewhere, in which I also examine the possibilities of different readings and interpretations, that may lead to potentially more egalitarian directions in Jewish law. *See* Ruth Halperin-Kaddari, *Gender Construction under Halakhic Marriage and Divorce Laws*, 22 TALPIYOT 451, 464 (2000) (Hebrew).

[26] Conservative Judaism, which is also considered as adhering to *Halakha*, i.e. Jewish law, may differ on many of these issues. Examining this is obviously beyond the scope of this article, and is less relevant, since the predominant form of Judaism in Israel, certainly from the legal perspective, is Orthodoxy. On Conservative theories of Jewish law, see DAVID GOLINKIN, HALAKHAH FOR OUR TIME: A CONSERVATIVE APPROACH TO JEWISH LAW (United Synagogue of America 1991) and Elliot Dorff, *Towards a Legal Theory of the Conservative Movement*, CONSERVATIVE JUDAISM, Spring 1972, at 65.

it, all to the detriment of women. In addition to its adherence to the perception of gender roles and separate spheres in family and in public life, Jewish law also adopts a double standard with respect to the sexual behavior of men and women in general, and of married men and married women in particular. While a married man's sexual relationships with a woman other than his wife hardly carries any legal consequence, except for the very rare possibility of considering this to be grounds for divorce,[27] a married woman's sexual relations with a man other than her husband carry extremely harsh consequences: she is to be immediately divorced while losing all her monetary rights, which she had otherwise acquired according to the Jewish law. She is prohibited from later marrying either her former husband or the man with whom she had "committed adultery"; and any child that results from an adulterous relationship is considered a "bastard" (*mamzer*) who is precluded from marrying within the Jewish community, except for a convert or a *mamzer* like him/herself.[28]

These grave and unequal consequences of women's extra-marital relations profoundly implicate women's position within the divorce process, which is the main form of discrimination against women under Jewish law, and merits further explanation here. Although in principle both parties' free will is needed for the bill-of-divorce (*get*) to be valid, the wife's consent can be circumvented with no consequences on the *get*'s validity, while the husband's voluntary provision of the *get* is an absolute prerequisite, without which the divorce is invalid.[29] Invalidity of the *get* means that the wife is still a married woman, so that any sexual relations she may later conduct would still be considered adulterous, with the harsh consequences of *mamzerut* upon children who may result from those relationships as explained above. Thus, as a rule, the husband has an almost absolute

---

[27] Ruth Halperin, *Husband's Adultery as a Ground for Divorce*, 7 MEHKAREI MISHPAT (BAR-ILAN L. STUD.) 297, 329 (1989) (Hebrew).

[28] IRWIN H. HAUT, DIVORCE IN JEWISH LAW AND LIFE (Sepher-Hermon Press 1993); BENZION SHERSHEVSKY, DINE MISHPAHAH ME'ET BENTSIYON SHERESHEVSKI [FAMILY LAW IN ISRAEL] (1983) (Hebrew).

[29] HAUT, *supra* note 28; ARIEL ROSEN-ZVI, ISRAELI FAMILY LAW - THE SACRED AND THE SECULAR (Papirus 1990); Halperin-Kaddari, *supra* note 25.

control over the *get*, which the wife categorically requires in order to divorce. While rabbinical courts have the power, under certain circumstances, to coerce husbands to grant the *get*, they are apprehensive about the validity of the *get* which is dependant upon the man's "free will," and usually prefer to have only a recommendation for divorce and to send to the parties for the negotiation of terms. This leads the way for a common course of negotiation, which generally results in the woman buying her way out of the marriage by paying whatever the husband demands in terms of property rights, child support, and so on. Women who refuse to pay for their freedom to remarry, whether it is a downright payment or in the form of giving up their legal rights to the marital property, have no recourse within the Israeli legal system. They are *agunot*, i.e. women who are "chained" or "anchored" to their husbands, with no relief available to them, either in the religious system or civil system.[30]

The plight of the *agunot* is indeed the most extreme expression of women's inferiority under Jewish family law. However, a deeper reflection of the law reveals that this is but one reflection of structural inferiority that is built into the system of Jewish family law.[31] This inferiority permeates all three levels of marital life: in the entry to marriage, during marriage, and in the dissolution of marriage through

[30] Women's organizations and the rabbinical establishment (rabbinical authorities, rabbinical courts, etc.) are in sharp disagreement as to the actual number of *agunot* cases in Israel. The disagreement is over which circumstances specifically constitute that state. For instance, while women's organizations classify the conditioning of a *get* upon surrender of the woman's property rights as a refusal to grant the *get*, rabbinical courts will not recognize that woman as an *agunah*. Consequently, women's organizations maintain that there are several thousand women who are being refused a *get*, while the rabbinical establishment claims there are only several dozen of them. The problem of the *agunot*, however, is inherent to the Orthodox Jewish law of marriage and divorce, and is not unique to Israel. *See* PINHAS SHIFMAN, CIVIL MARRIAGE IN ISRAEL: THE CASE FOR REFORM (Jerusalem Inst. For Israel St. 1995); HAUT, *supra* note 28. Since it is common to all Jewish communities, and it exists wherever Jewish people wish to follow both their religious laws and the laws of the state in which they live, an international coalition of Jewish women called ICAR (both the acronym of International Coalition for Agunah Rights, and a Hebrew word meaning 'the most important thing') was formed in 1991. ICAR's goal is to advance solutions for the problem of the *agunot*. Despite the fact that their suggestions are all within the framework of Jewish law, they have mostly been met with resistance and antagonistic reactions.

[31] Halperin-Kaddari, *supra* note 25, at 464.

divorce. The point is that women's structural inferiority in family law in Israel has grave detrimental consequences on the position of women in other areas outside of family life. Thus, as explained above, the discriminatory process of divorce often leads women to give up their legal property and monetary rights so as not to get into the intolerable position of *agunah*. In other words, women's economic situation is jeopardized as a direct result of the religious law of divorce. Nonetheless, the discrimination at the dissolution of a marriage is only part of the picture. Jewish law perceives marriage as a system of mutual rights and responsibilities, clearly based on traditional separate-spheres gender ideologies.[32] The husband works outside the home and is responsible for the wife's sustenance, while the wife works inside the home and is responsible for all the housework and childcare and is also obligated to personally serve the husband. In addition, any property the wife may have had upon marriage becomes subject to her husband's management, and her earnings are put against her right to maintenance.[33] This system may have reflected gender balancing and mutuality appropriate to the social and economic conditions of the time it was designed,[34] however its application to present social norms has devastating effects upon women.

All this affects women's position far beyond the particular context of divorce and its consequences. Women's awareness of their inferiority projects on their self perception and the perception of their marital relationship. Their inferiority is internalized, and an opposite process of empowerment occurs. As the family is the basic unit of socialization, these perceptions structure the socialization process of

---

[32] Pnina N. Levinson, *Women and Sexuality: Traditions and Progress*, *in* WOMEN, RELIGION AND SEXUALITY: STUDIES ON THE IMPACT OF RELIGIOUS TEACHINGS ON WOMEN 45 (Jeanne Becher ed., 1991); Hava Lazarus-Yafeh, *Contemporary Fundamentalism--Judaism, Christianity, Islam*, 47 JERUSALEM Q. 37 (1988).

[33] MOSHE MEISELMAN, JEWISH WOMAN IN JEWISH LAW, (Ktav Pub. 1978). These specific economic rules, unlike the rules that pertain to the actual marital relationships, can be altered by the couple if they agree to do so.

[34] RACHEL BIALE, WOMEN AND JEWISH LAW: AN EXPLORATION OF WOMEN'S ISSUES IN HALAKHIC SOURCES (Schocken Books 1984); JUDITH HAUPTMAN, REREADING THE RABBIS: A WOMAN'S VOICE (Westview Press 1998); Saul Berman, *The Status of Women in Halakhic Judaism*, *in* THE JEWISH WOMAN: NEW PERSPECTIVES (Elizabeth Koltun ed., Schocken Books 1976).

children within the family.[35] The patriarchal family has long been the subject of feminist critique.[36] The summary of the law that was presented here demonstrates that in a sense, the vices of the patriarchal family, which at present are generally a reflection of strong social norms, are, in fact, normatively sanctioned under Jewish religious law and are consequently part of the Israeli legal system itself. Thus, for example, the well-known circular interaction between the women's economic dependency within the "private" family and their secondary position within the "public" market is clearly endorsed under the law itself. The difference in wage work patterns based upon gender lines can thus be seen not just as a reflection of social norms, but as an expression of the legal order.[37] In other words, the familiar social reality of separate spheres and gender roles linked to the patriarchal family structure is in fact legally endorsed and sanctioned under the Israeli legal system as a result of its incorporation of the religious law in matters of marriage and divorce.

IV. SEMI-FORMAL EXPRESSIONS OF RELIGION-STATE INTEGRATION

For the purpose of this discussion, semi-formal expressions of the interconnection between religion and state in Israel concerning women are defined as instances where women's rights, concerns, and interests are being effectively prejudiced as an indirect result of the rule of religious law in matters of marriage and divorce, or of another formal-

[35] SUSAN OKIN, GENDER, FAMILY AND THE STATE (Basic Books, Inc. 1989).

[36] *Id.*; Martha A. Fineman, *Legal Stories, Change, and Incentives--Reinforcing the Law of the Father*, 37 N.Y.L. SCH. L. REV. 227, 249 (1992); Frances Olsen, *The Family and the Market: A Study of Ideology and Legal Reform*, 96 HARV. L. REV. 1497, 1507 (1983).

[37] Statistical data reveals that, for example, even when the wife works full-time in the labor market, she still devotes twice as much time to unpaid household and family work as her husband. *See Time Use in Israel - Time Budget Survey 1991/92*, Jerusalem: Central Bureau of Statistics.

legal integration of religion and state. The clearest semi-formal expressions are reflected within the physical space where religious law governs, namely the religious courts, and relate to the actual possibility of women to participate equally with men in all levels of their operation.

Starting from the highest level of participation, namely that of judges, the various laws dealing with religious courts have been interpreted by Jewish, Muslim and Druze religious leaders to mean that only men can serve as judges in these courts. Consequently, Israel has expressed its reservation with regard to Article 7(b) of the CEDAW Convention concerning representation in public life, including in judicial posts.[38] Nonetheless, from examining recent developments within Orthodox Judaism, one could have suggested that at least with respect to Judaism, change is not impossible. The observant Jewish community is undergoing an evolution with respect to women's learning.[39] As more and more women master *halakhic* (Jewish law) knowledge and its developmental tools, and as the drive towards inclusion gains force, demands that women be included into the actual *halakhic* process as recognized by the State in the very form of rabbinical judges can be expected.[40] From the constitutional perspective, this will bring about an unprecedented entanglement of civil law in religious matters. Since rabbinical courts have formal jurisdiction within the Israeli legal system, and since they are subject to the supervision of State officials (such as within the Ministry of Religion) and their appointments are regulated by the civil law, and since they are also subject to the scrutiny of the High Court of Justice, it could be assumed that if and when such demands for inclusion are made by women, the civil legal system--through the High Court of Justice--will have to intervene. This is an unprecedented intervention

---

[38] *See supra* note 21 and accompanying text.

[39] *See, e.g.*, TAMAR EL-OR, NEXT PESSACH: LITERACY AND IDENTITY OF YOUNG RELIGIOUS ZIONIST WOMEN (Am Oved Pub. 1998) (Hebrew).

[40] We are already witnessing the beginning of this process in the form of a special program in one of the orthodox institutes for higher *torah* learning for women in Israel that trains women to be "*halakhic* advisors" on matters of family purity and reproduction. *See* Larry Derfner & Debbi Cooper, *A Step Up for Orthodox Women*, JERUSALEM POST, Oct. 8, 1999, at 6B.

because none of the conflicts involving women's demands for inclusion into the religious sphere, so far, have presented such an acute tension between women's rights to equal participation and unsettled interpretation of *halakha*,[41] in a setting that is under the overall control of the civil system, and in a matter that distinctively implicates women as a whole.

However, the normative layer on this last point has just in fact been changed, quite unexpectedly. Once again, the pattern of subordinating gender equality to religious demands has taken its toll, in the most recent amendment to the 1951 Women's Equal Rights Law.[42] This amendment passed in January, 2000, which has made some substantive and important revisions to the 1951 law, not only maintained its original qualification that excluded the law from applying to the area of marriage and divorce, but has added another qualification for religious reasons. This qualification applies to the novel affirmative action norm that was introduced in the amendment, and qualifies it from applying to religious roles, including religious judicial roles. Thus, quite ironically, the former discussion has turned moot through the act of the civil legislature, who has closed a window of opportunity that the religious community had started to open.

The case of women's certification as rabbinical advocates, which we examine next, seems similar to the previous analysis. However, notwithstanding the external resemblance, the substantive issues are quite different primarily because the case of rabbinical advocates does not raise such serious and deep *halakhic* contention and perhaps does not even raise any *halakhic* controversy. The issue of women representing clients in rabbinical courts presents a most interesting and significant development. Certified attorneys, whether male or female,

---

[41] This issue is unsettled in terms of *halakhic* interpretation. Rabbi Uziel, the first *Sepharadi* Chief Rabbi of Israel, and one of the great *Sepharadi* religious sages in the twentieth century, had in principle permitted women to serve as religious judges. *See* Ben-Zion Meir Chay Uziel, *Mishpetei Uziel*, *in* CHOSHEN MISHPAT 5 (1964). For an analysis of *halakhic* opinions regarding women religious judges, see ARIEL ROSEN-ZVI, ISRAELI FAMILY LAW: THE SACRED AND THE SECULAR 246-47 (Tel-Aviv Univ. 1990) (Hebrew); Shlomo Riskin, *Women as Canon Teachers*, *in* A GOOD EYE: DIALOGUE AND POLEMIC IN JEWISH CULTURE 698-704 (Ilan Nahem ed., Hakibbutz Hameuchad Pub. 1999) (Hebrew).

[42] Draft bill amending the Women's Equal Rights Law (no. 2), 1999 H.H., 371.

can always represent clients in rabbinical and other such religious courts in any and all matters. Both rabbinical and Moslem courts recognized the competence of rabbinical or *sharia* (Moslem) advocates, who were allowed to represent clients in the relevant religious courts, regardless of whether or not they were certified attorneys. The Rabbinical Advocates Regulations for 1967[43] originally applied to men alone, since it required graduation from a *yeshiva* (an institute of higher learning of religion and religious law, traditionally for men alone) as a primary condition for qualification as a candidate to the profession. The law was amended in 1991 to include graduates of other educational institutions of higher learning which are recognized by the Chief Rabbinical Court as eligible to train candidates for the profession. As of yet, no regulations or other directives were passed to establish the criteria for such recognition. It was not until 1994, after an institute for higher Torah learning for women petitioned the High Court of Justice, that the Chief Rabbinical Court decided upon the criteria for its recognition.[44] The High Court of Justice reviewed those criteria, and found that some of them, such as the requirement of full-time everyday studies for a full two years, were intended to make it impossible for women students to qualify for candidacy, and were thus considered discriminatory and void. Several dozen women, all of whom were religiously committed, have since passed the examinations and are now functioning as rabbinical advocates. Not surprisingly, their representation is, as of now, primarily made up of female clientele, and their performance can often be perceived to be feminist in its nature.[45] Notwithstanding the fact that this legal accomplishment had not significantly opened the doors of rabbinical courts for women, since, as we have seen, female attorneys could always represent clients there, and despite its narrow scope that does not pertain to the actual *halakhic* process, this

[43] The Rabbinical Advocates Regulations, 1967, K.T. 2119, 16.

[44] H.C. 6300/93, The Institution for Rabbinical Advocates Training v. The Minister of Religion 48(4) P.D. 441.

[45] Ronen Shamir et al., *Mission, Feminism and Professionalism: Women Rabbinic Advocates Within the Orthodox-Religious Community*, 38 MEGAMOT 313, 348 (1997) (Hebrew).

development should not be undermined. Even while recognizing the substantive differences as to the nature of the *halakhic* question involved in the two cases, the specific achievement presents a concrete accomplishment on at least two levels: one is internal, i.e. geared towards women themselves, and the other is external, i.e. geared towards the religious establishment outside of women. On the internal level, this move has led to the creation of a cadre of women committed to serve the interests of female litigants. On the external level, it has crossed the barrier against women's formal functioning within the *halakhic* world, and has even generated respect and estimation as to their capabilities. All this may have invaluable ramifications for the future struggle over women as rabbinical judges.

Within that physical space of rabbinical courts, where Jewish law governs, there is yet another expression of women's inferior position as unequal participants. Under Jewish law, women are not qualified to be witnesses in the manner in which the institute of testimony was conceived by Jewish law.[46] *Halakhic* authorities throughout the ages, however, have found various solutions and means to accept women's testimony. Hence, rabbinical courts routinely accept women's testimony and practically accord it the same evidentiary weight that is accorded to men's testimony.[47] While this is a sensible solution, it only relates on a very pragmatic level, and brings no redress on a substantive, ideological, and educational level.

Other semi-formal expressions of the integration of religion and state in Israel stem from other legal arrangements apart from the rule of religious law in the area of family law. These arrangements may include regulations of religious dietary laws (*kashrut*), supervision over the Sabbath as the official day of rest for the Jewish population, and other legal arrangements which all come under the heading of "religious legislation,"[48] and often carry particular adverse implications for women. In two instances, such arrangements have

---

[46] ROSEN-ZVI, *supra* note 29, at 243-45; Gershon Holtzer, *A Woman's Testimony in Jewish Law*, 67 SINAI 94, 112 (1970) (Hebrew); MEISELMAN, *supra* note 33.

[47] ROSEN-ZVI, *supra* note 29.

[48] CHARLES S. LIEBMAN & ELIEZER DON-YEHIYA, RELIGION AND POLITICS IN ISRAEL 24-28 (Indiana Univ. Press 1984).

resulted in litigation that confronted these detrimental effects on women. The first instance relates to the regulation of religious services in Israel, which includes the official positions of municipal rabbis[49] and the operation of religious councils in every municipality.[50] The second instance relates to the religious supervision over the Western Wall. Although the two instances relate to altogether different circumstances, they are both expressions of the effect that religious legislation may have on women, and both reflect women's attempts to challenge them. Furthermore, they indicate two different outcomes of these challenges.

With respect to the first set of circumstances, following two landmark Supreme Court decisions in 1988, women were granted the right to participate in the Committee for Selection of municipal Chief Rabbis and the right to participate in municipal religious councils. In *Poraz v. Tel Aviv Mayor,*[51] the Supreme Court allowed women to participate in the Committee for the Selection of the Tel Aviv Chief Rabbi, emphasizing that exclusion of women from serving on political committees which dealt with religious matters, constituted discrimination and was therefore void. In *Shakdiel v. Minister of Religious Affairs*,[52] the Supreme Court granted Leah Shakdiel, one of the pioneering Orthodox-feminist activists, the right to be elected to the religious council of the town of Yeruham in southern Israel. In both cases, which were decided in close proximity, the Court emphasized the secular nature of the disputed positions and functions. It should be noted that despite the landmark *Shakdiel* decision, which opened the doors for women who wished to serve on municipal religious councils, the number of women on municipal religious councils remains small. In 1996, out of 139 religious councils, only twelve councils included a woman.[53] Almost a decade after the

---

49 Regulation of Rabbis Elections, 1974, K.T. 3271, 532.

50 Jewish Religious Services Law (Combined Version), 1971, S.H. 130.

51 H.C. 953/87, Poraz v. Shlomo Lahat, Mayor of Tel Aviv, 42(2) P.D. 309.

52 H.C. 153/87, Shakdiel v. The Minister of Religious Affairs and Others, 42(2) P.D. 221.

53 This information was obtained by Ms. Atara Kenigsberg, administrator of the Forum on Women's Status at Bar-Ilan University, after going through the records of all religious councils in the country.

Supreme Court decision, women still have great difficulties in getting elected to municipal religious councils.[54]

The case of the Women of the Wall serves as an opposite illustration of the effect of religion on Jewish women. This affair began in December 1988, when a group of Israeli and foreign women, representing all religious streams in Judaism, prayed together and read from a *Torah* scroll in the women's section of the Western Wall while wearing prayer-shawls--all practices which are traditionally reserved for men alone. The group was interrupted, attacked, and dispersed by ultra-orthodox men and women who were offended by its non-traditional practices. In March 1989, the group petitioned the High Court of Justice after being violently attacked on repeated occasions when they tried to pray, even without prayer-shawls and *Torah* scrolls. They asked the court to protect their right to freedom of religion by guaranteeing their right to pray as they wished at the Western Wall. In December 1989, the Minister of Religion amended the Regulations on the Protection of Sacred Places for the Jewish People for 1981 to include a provision that prohibits the engagement in religious rituals at the Western Wall that are not in accordance with the custom of the place and that offend the feelings of those praying there.[55] The petitioners then amended their petition to include the nullification of this amendment. The Court gave its majority decision in January 1994, denying the petitions, but recommending the establishment of a governmental committee to fully investigate the subject and search for an alternative solution that would "guarantee freedom of access to the Wall while minimizing the offense to the other worshippers at the sight."[56] The group had to petition the High Court of Justice once again in 1995, to hasten the work of that committee. After many delays, deliberations of several committees, and the passage of two sets of elections in Israel, the bottom line recommendation was that

[54] It should be noted, though, that the current conflicts regarding the operation of religious councils relate to the partaking of representatives of the Conservative and the Reform streams of Judaism, and not to the question of women's participation.

[55] The Regulations on the Protection of Sacred Places for the Jewish People (Amendment), 1989, K.T. 5237, 190.

[56] H.C. 257/89, Anat Hofman v. The Commissioner of the West Wall, 48(2) P.D. 309.

the women be allowed to pray in the manner they wished, but in a secluded section of the Wall, removed from the main public area, that serves as an archeological garden. The women objected to this solution, both in principle and for practical reasons.

In May 2000, a unanimous Court finally accepted the women's position, ruling that the women's principled right to pray in their manner at the Wall had already been recognized in its 1994 decision, and that the committees' recommendation did not conform with that holding. Consequently, the Court directed the government to make, within six months, the appropriate arrangements to enable the women's group to pray at the Wall, with minimum offense to other worshippers, and with the provision of the necessary security measures.[57] The decision was met with much criticism from religious circles, adding to the growing estrangement between large parts of the religious public and the Supreme Court.[58] Within only a few days, the Knesset passed, in a preliminary reading, one of the ultra-Orthodox party's bills to issue a seven-year jail sentence to any woman who prayed at the Wall donned with *tallit* and *tefillin*, or who read from the *Torah* aloud at the Wall. The preliminary reading passed with a majority of 32-26, including several members of the Knesset from non-religious parties.[59]

Significantly, though, lack of sympathy and understanding of the women's struggle has characterized the secular public and the media as well. The press coverage included much speculation as to the women's cause and motives. It seems that from both sides, the religious and the secular, women's spiritual needs and religious interests are still hard to accept.[60] Thus, perhaps not surprisingly, the

---

[57] H.C. 3358/95, Anat Hofman v. Director General of the Prime-Minister's Office (May 20, 2000) (not yet published).

[58] Thus, for example, Chief Rabbi Bakshi-Doron was reported to condemn the Court's decision as a step in creating a schism in the nation. *See Chief Rabbi Attacks the High Court of Justice*, HA'ARETZ (visited May 22, 2000) <http://www2.haaretz.co.il/special/cotel/a/113799.asp>.

[59] *See* Editorial, *The Knesset has Shamed Itself*, HA'ARETZ (June 2, 2000) <http://www2.haaretz.co.il/special/cotel/a/182295.asp>.

[60] *But cf.* Pnina Lahav, *Up Against the Wall: The Case of Women's Struggle to Pray At the Western Wall in Jerusalem*, ISRAEL STUD. BULL. (forthcoming) (on file with author),

State's request for a rehearing of the case with an expanded panel of justices was granted, even though it is quite rare that unanimous decisions are given a rehearing.[61] This struggle, then, is not over yet.

Bearing in mind the outcome of the first Court ruling, Professor Susan Sered offers an interesting explanation for the differing results of these two conflicts--representation in religious bodies,[62] and Women of the Wall. She suggests that in the former, the conflicting parties succeeded in constructing the controversy in secular terms, thus managing to devoid it of any religious implications. In the latter, however, the women's attempt to present their struggle as a rebellion and not as revolution failed, and the religious establishment's opposition perceived it as pertaining to very theological underpinnings.[63] This thesis is relevant to the Courts' decisions as well, two of which were decided by the former Deputy Chief Justice, Professor Menachem Elon, an orthodox judge and an expert on Jewish law. In the *Shakdiel* case, Justice Elon made it a central point of his decision to stress the secular nature of the operation and the workings of religious councils, which enabled him to present the controversy as purely one of civil constitutional law that pertains to the right to equality, and not as a religious controversy at all. His decision in the *Hoffman* case, on the other hand, reads like an academic article in Jewish law, presenting a scholarly analysis of women's obligation and permission to perform *mitzvot* (religious decrees) in general, and women's permission and right to pray in prayer-groups in particular. Unlike the other two Justices, Elon constructs the controversy in religious terms, interpreting the regulations' reference to "the custom of the place" as one pertaining to the religious conventions, thus enabling him to give deference to the Chief Rabbi, who had obviously

---

suggesting that this is another expression of Israel's public general hostility to any feminist cause.

[61] H.C.R. 4128/00, Director General of the Prime-Minister's Office v. Anat Homan (July 13, 2000) (not yet published). An unusual panel of nine justices will rehear the case.

[62] Sered discusses separately the issue of participation in the body that elects municipal rabbis, and detects similar traces in this case and the case of religious councils. Since the two cases were decided in proximity, and the legal issues and their confrontation by the Court were in fact the same, I see no reason to separate the two.

[63] Susan Sered, *Women and Religious Change in Israel: Rebellion or Revolution*, 58 SOC. OF RELIGION 1, 24 (1997).

rejected altogether the women's initiative. Although he clearly sympathized with women and had demonstrated their conformity with Jewish law, he nonetheless expressed some reservations as to the motives of some of them, and on the whole, has preferred conventional religious practice and custom over the women's cause, rejecting their claim for a concrete right to pray at the Wall. Thus, by placing the controversy within the purely religious sphere, women and their rights were physically and figuratively distanced from the scene.

In light of this analysis, the second and most recent Court ruling in this affair can be seen as an attempt to relocate the controversy into the secular-constitutional sphere. Justice Maza, who wrote the decision and was joined by two women justices, had very carefully isolated the normative rights-talk from the previous case, and concluded that two of the three justices in that case had acknowledged the women's principled right to worship at the Wall. While this conclusion certainly carries a subjective interpretive component, the attempt at removing the religious contents from the scene is evident. It remains to be seen what direction this interplay will take upon the rehearing of the case.

V. INFORMAL EXPRESSIONS

For the purposes of this discussion, informal expressions of the interconnection between religion and State in Israel concerning women, include episodes where women's rights, concerns, and interests are being effectively prejudiced with no relation whatsoever to the rule of religious law over marriage and divorce or to any other formal, legal integration of religion and state. As explained above, this is the area in which the conventional feminism-multicultural debate is indeed relevant. Examples of such informal expressions of the interconnection between religion and state in Israel abound. Perhaps the most obvious one has to do with the highest form of the public sphere, namely political participation. In Israel, some of that public political space is in fact inherently closed to women, inasmuch as it is occupied by religious parties, which view politics and leadership roles as exclusively male. The current reality is that out of 120 seats in the Israeli parliament, twenty-eight are occupied by religious parties, making almost a quarter of the seats de facto closed to women. Thus, with no formal or legal sanctioning, women are partially precluded from political integration. One could, of course, argue that there is a place for formal involvement, from the exact opposite direction: the State should actively prohibit such exclusively male-represented political parties. This approach implies actual State intrusion into what is usually perceived as "internal affairs" of a community, albeit a religious community. It challenges the basic definition of the question as an internal one to community alone.[64] Moreover, it suggests that the State can legitimately impose certain values, such as gender equality, upon all its citizens.[65] These are all aspects of the intense debate on pluralism, multiculturalism, and cultural relativism, which has prevailed within the Israeli society in recent years,[66] though with not much attention devoted to explicit feminist concerns. Although this specific example of legislative and governmental representation has not yet been directly confronted, a position such as that of Frances Raday, who argues against the promotion of multiculturalism at the expense of women's rights and gender equality, could perhaps lead to legitimization of State regulation of religious political associations.[67] An opposite, more communitarian and cultural-relativist approach would obviously lead to a firm rejection of such a suggestion.

The next example perhaps demonstrates the best case study of the feminist-multicultural dilemma within the Israeli context. In July 1997, the Ministry of Traffic adopted a trial policy of sex-segregation

---

[64] Martha Minow, *Pluralisms*, 21 CONN. L. REV. 965 (1989).

[65] Yael Tamir, *Two Concepts of Multiculturalism*, *in* MULTICULTURALISM IN A DEMOCRATIC AND JEWISH STATE, *supra* note 1, at 79-92.

[66] *See supra* note 1.

[67] Raday, *Religion, Multiculturalism and Equality*, *supra* note 16. This would also be the outcome of Okin's approach, as reflected in Okin, *Is Multiculturalism Bad for Women?*, *supra* note 4.

in part of several bus lines that mainly serve the ultra-Orthodox population in Jerusalem and in Bnei-Brak. This policy was based on recommendations of a committee that the Traffic Minister had appointed to investigate ways to encourage the use of public transportation by the ultra-Orthodox communities.[68] While maintaining the personal option of each passenger for mixed sitting, the policy sanctioned the voluntary ordering of the ultra-orthodox population to direct separate embarking, debarking, and sitting in the buses. The voluntary arrangement would provide for men to enter and sit at the front of the buses, while women were to occupy only the back parts of the buses. This arrangement was to be achieved by convincing passengers to abide by the community's values and beliefs. Incidentally, the committee upon whose recommendation the policy was adopted apparently included only one woman, and among the sixteen participants of the discussion during which the policy was adopted, which included representatives of the bus companies and of the ultra-orthodox community, only one woman was present.[69] Immediately following the Ministry's decision, the Israel Women's Network appealed to the High Court of Justice, arguing that the policy was discriminatory against women because it physically and symbolically relegated them to the rear parts of society. Relying on the famous holding in the U.S. Supreme Court case *Brown v. Board of Education,*[70] the Network argued that such an arrangement of "separate but equal" violated the principle of gender equality. The State's response to the appeal clearly demonstrated the ideology of multiculturalism. In emphasizing the initiative as coming from the religious community and mostly directed at that community alone, the voluntary acceptance of the policy by the community, the overall satisfaction of the passengers, and the lack of any complaint by passengers, the State denied the network's contention of gender

[68] Recommendations of the Committee to Encourage the Use of Public Transportation within the Ultra-Orthodox Sector, May 1997 (on file with the author); Israel Women's Network appeal to the High Court of Justice in H.C. 5079/97, Israel Women's Network v. The Minister of Traffic (on file with the author).

[69] Appendix to the Israel Women's Network appeal, *supra* note 68.

[70] 347 U.S. 483 (1954).

discrimination altogether. Another line of argument in that direction that was raised in the media was the willing cooperation of the women themselves, who arguably prefer sex segregation, which enables them more freedom of movement in the back of the buses.

In a hearing three years after the appeal, following quite a few delays, the Network was practically convinced by the High Court of Justice to withdraw its appeal. In so doing, one can speculate that the Court indicated its hesitancy to confront the delicate subject of multiculturalism, and its apprehension of being once again blamed for intruding into religious affairs and circumventing religious freedoms of closed communities.[71] Nevertheless, by this move, the Court has also maintained the status quo, which, as shown by the Network's appeal, can be clearly perceived as marginalizing and in effect discriminating against women. If the former example demonstrated women's exclusion from the political sphere and encroaching upon their political space, this example demonstrates women's marginalization and encroachment upon their very physical and geographical space. The point is that both these episodes do not result in any sense from the formal, legal connection between religion and State. Thus, they demonstrate the argument that informal expressions of this integration are no less significant for the situation of women than the formal ones. Furthermore, they highlight the relationship between this subject-matter and the complex question of multiculturalism in Israel.

[71] During the 1990's, the tension between the High Court of Justice and the religious community in Israel had risen to an unprecedented peak. Menachem Hofnung, *The Unintended Consequences of Unplanned Constitutional Reform: Constitutional Politics in Israel*, 44 AM. J. COMP. L. 585, 604 (1996); Ariel Rosen-Zvi, *A Jewish and Democratic State: Spiritual Parenthood, Alienation and Symbiosis–Can We Square the Circle?*, 19 TEL AVIV U. L. REV. 479, 520 (1995) (Hebrew).

VI. Conclusion

The overall expressions of the influence of state and religious relationships on women's lives in Israel result in a combined effect of oppression of women, both in the private and in the public spheres. Unequal power within the family results in women's subordination in the private sphere, while power is all too often denied to women in the public sphere. While the formal integration of religion and State in Israel is central to this, the semi-formal and informal expressions of these relationships are no less significant. From a theoretical perspective, it is misleading to construct the formal expressions in terms of the feminist-multicultural debate since the formal imposition of the minority culture over the majority makes any claim for respect and preservation ironic. The context of the formal expressions of an integration between religion and state should be analyzed in simple human rights discourse, and the conclusion should be clear: the imposition of patriarchal religious norms over unwilling individuals cannot be justified on any legal grounds, and no multicultural arguments are relevant here. The context of the informal expressions of the integration between religion and state is the appropriate one for the multicultural discourse. In addition to the conventional arguments within the feminist-multicultural debate, the Israeli case holds another dimension. When contemplating the need to accommodate the minority culture in order for its preservation, the overall context of the integration between religion and state cannot be ignored. In light of the overall context, it is arguable that the threat of further imposing religious norms over the majority is more realistic than the threat of the cultural minority's extinction. In that case, much of the multicultural argument loses its force.

Under the current political situation, structural changes regarding the various expressions outlined in this article are rather improbable. The only venue for reform at present seems to lie within the internal mobilization of women in the religious community itself. The Orthodox feminist movement, which is slowly gaining momentum in Israel, represents the potential for social, institutional, and even normative reform of the religious community. Although this movement is still confined only to the moderate segment of the Orthodox community (and even there it faces tremendous internal opposition), it nonetheless signals the possibility of internal change even where no formal external pressure has been imposed.

[14]

A Cross-Cultural Perspective on Reproductive Rights

*Carla Makhlouf Obermeyer**

In recent months, a number of international conferences focusing on human rights and population have added a certain urgency to the search for definitions of reproductive rights that would be acceptable cross-culturally. In the last three decades, discussions of reproductive rights at each of the international conferences on population have been marked by subtle but important changes in emphasis.[1] These have come in response to evolving ideas about the rationale for reproductive rights and its implications for population policy, as well as to changes in power relations on the global scene. One key issue on the international agenda is the extent to which definitions of human rights can be transposed to non-Western cultures in ways that avoid both "homogenizing universalism" and "paralyzing relativism."[2]

The purpose of this article is to explore the commonalities that can be found between notions of reproductive rights as they developed in the Western tradition and the principles that define gender rights in Islam. This is a daunting task which requires some knowledge about several disciplinary domains and involves a comparative analysis of two philosophical and legal traditions that have often been at odds historically. In addition, the issue of women's rights in Islam is one that has brought about a polarization of viewpoints—and recent regional and international developments have

---

* This paper was presented at a symposium entitled "Family Gender and Population Policy: International Debates and Middle Eastern Realities" organized by The Population Council in Cairo, 7–9 Feb. 1994. This paper has benefited from the valuable comments of Rebecca Cook, Barbara Ibrahim, Gerald Obermeyer, Michael Reich, and Huda Zurayk. Their help is gratefully acknowledged.

1. Lynn Freedman & Stephen Isaacs, *Human Rights and Reproductive Choice*, 24 Stud. Fam. Plan. 18 (1993).
2. Rebecca Cook, *Women's International Human Rights Law: The Way Forward*, 15 Hum. Rts. Q. 230 (1993).

done little to defuse the tension between them. Clearly, this is hazardous intellectual territory where only the overly optimistic would willingly tread. I am convinced, however, that careful research will uncover more common ground than appears at first. It is this belief that motivates my pursuit.

One has to recognize at the outset that the discourse about women and their rights in the Middle East has often been dominated by the more uncompromising positions on both sides. Moreover, the exchange of these extreme views has usually excluded women, who are the group most vulnerable to abuses of reproductive rights. By contrast, woman-centered perspectives coming from both sides can provide new elements for a dialogue. More specifically, Western feminists, who have questioned traditional liberal notions of autonomy and individualism in light of the reality of women's reproductive experience, have opened the door for a redefinition of rights that is more conducive to dialogue than earlier formulations. At the same time, there are elements in Islam which can be interpreted to justify a more egalitarian approach to reproductive rights, one that is more responsive to women's needs and is espoused by a large number of Muslims. This article aims to bring to light these two tendencies and show that their shared concern for the welfare of women and men can contribute to bridging the apparent gap between them.

UNIVERSALISM AND RELATIVISM: ANTHROPOLOGICAL PERSPECTIVES

The process of translating legal and ethical concepts of rights between two different cultures is an extremely arduous task. It is useful here to pause for a moment and draw on the anthropological literature which provides many illustrations of the dilemmas that arise from encounters between different normative systems.[3] Unable to find equivalents to his or her concepts of rights and wrongs and confronted with behaviors that seem morally unacceptable, the anthropologist can adopt one of two equally undesirable stances: the first is to conclude that individuals in cultures that do not possess the same notions of rights will need to be "educated" and "enlightened" in the ways of liberal thinking—an undertaking with all the dangers of cultural imperialism; the second is to adopt the detached relativist view,[4] which holds that because any ethical principle is only

3. *See* Elvin Hatch, Culture and Morality: The Relativity of Values in Anthropology (1983); Melville Herskovits, *Statement on Human Rights*, 49 Am. Anthropologist 539 (1947); Claude Lévi-Strauss, Structural Anthropology (1963).

4. Of course, as has been repeatedly pointed out, the relativists do in the end subscribe to certain values, namely tolerance and respect for cultural integrity, and it is paradoxically, in the name of these values, that they defend cultural relativism.

applicable in a given context, the anthropologist must acquiesce even to practices that appear to violate human dignity.[5]

This dilemma has received a great deal of attention from anthropologists who have at various times had to confront value systems that were antithetical to their beliefs.[6] Recently, there have been attempts to break out of the impasse of universalism versus relativism and develop a new approach to human rights. Several researchers have examined the bases for the universality of human rights.[7] Some have questioned the strict presumption of universality upon which human rights are based, in part because it is founded on the erroneous belief that all people think in a similar fashion. These researchers have argued against developing a "single catalogue" of rights because this ignores the variability in value systems, and is not based on sufficient knowledge of how people in other cultures conceive of rights.[8] At the same time, however, the anthropological literature suggests that there is a considerable degree of flexibility in formulating notions of human dignity: moral systems based on either rights or duties can accommodate human rights, and there is no inherent contradiction between individual and group formulations of rights.[9] It is increasingly recognized that while absolute universals cannot be found, it is possible, and indeed desirable, to seek common denominators across cultures, which in turn can be used to develop contextually relevant notions of reproductive rights.

---

5. "Le Relativisme débouche sur l'éloge de la servitude," LA DÉFAITE DE LA PENSÉE (Alain Finkielkraut, La Défaite de la Pensée, 1987).
6. The first formal statement on relativism as a tenet of the anthropological *credo* was made by Herskovits in the aftermath of World War II and as the General Assembly of the United Nations was working on the Universal Declaration of Human Rights. It reflects the difficulty of reconciling a condemnation of racism and genocide with the prevalent concern of many anthropologists that Western values not be imposed on the Third World. *See* Alison Renteln, *Relativism and the Search for Human Rights,* 90 AM. ANTHROPOLOGIST 56 (1988). More recent efforts have centered on the protection of (mainly but not exclusively primitive) cultures whose survival is threatened. *See, e.g.,* 24 CULTURAL SURVIVAL REPORT: HUMAN RIGHTS AND ANTHROPOLOGY (Theodore E. Downing & Gilbert Kushner eds., 1988).
7. *See* JACK DONNELLY, UNIVERSAL HUMAN RIGHTS IN THEORY AND PRACTICE (1989); Raimundo Panikkar, *Is the Notion of Human Rights a Western Concept,* 120 DIOGENES 75–102 (1982).
8. "Les droits de l'homme impliquent une conception de l'homme en dehors de toute détermination culturelle specifique . . . un homme a-culturé, en somme." Gerald Berthoud, *Droits de l'homme et savoirs anthropologiques, in* IDENTITÄT: EVOLUTION ODER DIFFERENZ FESTGABE FÜR PROFESSOR HUGO HUBER 137 (1989). This belief is not unlike that found in Rawls' discussion of distributive justice. In the "original position," individuals stripped of all their cultural and political heritage, and placed behind the "veil of ignorance" would rationally select the same principles. JOHN RAWLS, A THEORY OF JUSTICE (1971).
9. *See* Alison Renteln, *The Concept of Human Rights,* 83 ANTHROPOS 343 (1988); Alison Renteln, *A Cross-Cultural Approach to Validating International Human Rights: The Case of Retribution Tied to Proportionality, in* HUMAN RIGHTS: THEORY AND MEASUREMENT 7 (David Cingranelli ed., 1988).

REPRODUCTIVE RIGHTS AND WOMEN'S STATUS

While reproductive rights are often formulated as elaborations of the universal human right to found a family, they also have historical roots in the West in a long tradition that emphasizes the bodily integrity of individuals and their right to protection against coercion by others.[10] In official documents drafted at each of the international conferences on population, reproductive rights are defined as the right of individuals to decide "freely and responsibly" about the number and spacing of their children (earlier formulations had emphasized couples while later ones stressed individuals). Decisions about procreation require that individuals have access to information concerning reproductive matters and have the power and resources needed to carry out their decisions—in other words, reproductive rights are dependent on individuals' ability to exercise their basic rights as human beings.[11] Therefore an examination of reproductive rights entails a consideration of the status of women in society.

It is not the purpose here, however, to undertake a general review of women's status in Islam and in the West. The social reality of women's status is complex and does not lend itself to a simplistic scoring system that would allow international comparisons—indeed, such comparisons often fail to do justice to the ambiguities that surround women's status in all cultures. One must, however, consider three important points. First, it must be noted that complete equality between the sexes is central to international human rights documents. Second, it must be recognized that complete gender equality is nowhere a reality and that even those societies that hold such equality as an ideal have by no means achieved it—hence the importance of pledges to eliminate gender based injustice, such as the Convention for the Elimination of All Forms of Discrimination Against Women (CEDAW).[12] The third point is that not all cultures subscribe to the idea of complete equality as it is spelled out in human rights documents, and the ambivalence of some countries is clearly expressed by their refusal to ratify CEDAW or by their addition of preambles and reservations to the international documents. Several countries of the Middle East have expressed such reservations, despite the fact that other Muslim countries participated in drafting the Universal Declaration of 1948 and the fact that the 1972 Charter of the Islamic Conference (the organization of Islamic

---

10. ROSALIND PETCHESKY, ABORTION AND WOMAN'S CHOICE: THE STATE, SEXUALITY, AND REPRODUCTIVE FREEDOM (1990).
11. Rebecca Cook, *International Human Rights and Women's Reproductive Health*, 24 STUD. FAM. PLAN. 73 (1993).
12. Convention on the Elimination of All Forms of Discrimination Against Women, *adopted* Dec. 18, 1979, G.A. Res. 34/100, U.N. GAOR, 34th Sess., Supp. No. 46, at 193, U.N. Doc. A/34/46 (1979).

countries) expressly endorsed international law and fundamental human rights as compatible with Islamic values.[13] Such ambivalence raises a key issue that underlies the rest of this discussion, namely whether equality as defined in international documents is indispensable to improving the welfare of women and protecting their reproductive rights.

THE MIDDLE EAST AND THE WEST: APPARENT CONTRADICTIONS

The researcher embarking on a quest for common ground is at first daunted by the polarization of opinions on the subject of women's position in societies of the Middle East. Also prevalent is the view that there is a basic incompatibility between the notions of universality and equality that are at the core of reproductive rights as human rights and the Islamic emphasis on complementarity rather than equality in gender roles.[14] It seems that, at whatever level we situate ourselves (the ethical, the legal, or the social), differences are at first more striking than commonalities, and we must face the old predicament of anthropologists: how to deal with the fact that the values that seem central to one culture, in this case the group of cultures referred to as Western, are in contradiction with those of another group of societies, that are referred to as Muslim.

Before going any further in our comparisons, it is important to mention that both these constructs—Western and Muslim—are overly general in that they ignore the diversity that exists within each broadly defined culture from the point of view of both ideology and practice.[15] In the case of Islam, several scholars have argued that one has to distinguish between what is Muslim, that is, practiced by people who are considered Muslim, and what is Islamic, that is, reflecting the essential values of the religion.[16] This distinction is most useful because it separates the ideal of the religion from

---

13. Ann Mayer, Islam and Human Rights: Tradition and Politics (1991); Abdullahi An-Na'im, *The Rights of Women and International Law in the Muslim Context*, 9 Whittier L. Rev. 491 (1987).
14. There is a wide range of views on the notion of complementarity. Some Muslims emphasize the physical, intellectual, and emotional inferiority of women; *see* Mohammed Qutb, Islam: The Misunderstood Religion (1964); while others stress that "natural" differences are not inconsistent with equality. *See, e.g.* Muhammad Abdulrauf, The Islamic View of Women and the Family (1977), *cited in* Donna Lee Bowen, *Islam and the Position of Women* (1992) (World Bank Paper); Shaykh Muhammad Mutawalli, *Issues Concerning the Muslim Woman* (1982), *cited in* Barbara Stowasser, The Islamic Impulse (1987).
15. Muslim positions regarding the status of women have been categorized into the conservatives, the activists/Islamist, and the reformers/feminists. For useful discussions of these positions, see Barbara Stowasser, *Liberated Equal or Protected Dependent? Contemporary Religious Paradigms on Women's Status in Islam*, 9 Arab Stud. Q. 260 (1987); *see also* Bowen, *supra* note 14.
16. Mohammed Arkoun, Pour une Critique de la Raison Islamique (1984).

its implementation by various sects and acknowledges diversity while protecting the central core of the religion against totalitarian claims. This is especially important at a time when militant groups are engaged in intense competition to assert their monopoly over the truth. Moreover, there is a good deal of evidence from many regions of the world suggesting that societal definitions of women's roles and reproductive rights are affected more by local and international politics than by religious doctrine as such.[17] Therefore, the prevalent polarization as discussed in this article is not inherent in the two value systems, but is a product of power relations between groups.

Such subtleties are usually ignored by those who render the fateful diagnosis of incompatibility between "Islam" and "the West." All too often, scholars from both sides have emphasized the more extreme interpretations of the situation. Thus for instance, in explaining Iran's refusal to ratify CEDAW, Sultanhussein Tabandeh argues that human rights as developed in the West are incompatible with Islam and implicitly endorses a relativist stance—i.e., "your values are not relevant to 'our' tradition."[18] Scholars examining the legal codes in countries of the region find a number of instances where such codes conflict with the universalist human rights statements endorsed by governments, and some draw the conclusion that the religion lacks "any willingness to recognize women as full, equal human beings who deserve the same rights and freedoms as men. Instead, discrimination against women is treated as something entirely natural."[19] Analyses by Middle Easterners often stress the striking differences in status between men and women and characterize Middle Eastern societies as fundamentally unjust. Typical of these views are statements such as those made by Hisham Sharabi who argues that Arab society is "neopatriarchal" and embodies much that is dysfunctional and pathological: "The dominant ideology of neopatriarchal society [is] a conservative relentless male oriented ideology, which tended to assign privilege and power to the male at the expense of the female, keeping the latter under crippling legal and social constraints."[20]

What this all means is that this whole area of research and action is burdened by a heavy baggage of conventional models and preconceived

---

17. *See, e.g,* WOMEN, ISLAM, AND THE STATE (Deniz Kandiyoti ed., 1991); Aihwa Ong, *State versus Islam: Malay Families, Women's Bodies, and the Body Politic in Malaysia*, 17 AM. ETHNOLOGIST 258 (1990); and Carla Makhlouf Obermeyer, *Reproductive Choice in Islam: Gender and State in Iran and Tunisia,* 25 STUD. FAM. PLAN. 1 (1994).

18. SULTANHUSSEIN TABANDEH, A MUSLIM COMMENTARY ON THE UNIVERSAL DECLARATION OF HUMAN RIGHTS (1970).

19. MAYER, *supra* note 13, at 136.

20. HISHAM SHARABI, NEOPATRIARCHY: A THEORY OF DISTORTED CHANGE IN ARAB SOCIETY 33 (1988).

notions. There are a number of factors that account for the power of such stereotypes and the polarization of views. Some of them have to do with the distrust that often characterizes relations between more developed nations and those that they have dominated politically and economically—in other words with a fundamental "north-south" tension, one that is vehemently expressed at the many international conferences dealing with development, population, or human rights. The emergence of groups in the Middle East claiming that they hold the key to a regeneration of society through the application of literal interpretations of the sacred texts and the threat that they have come to constitute against established governments, are additional elements that further hinder candid communication about these issues.

Another key factor is that Islam, like the other two monotheistic religions of the Middle East, emerged in a specific temporal context that can be characterized as patriarchal—a context that is to a certain extent reflected in the sacred texts.[21] Although the emergence of Islam in Arabia is widely believed to have resulted in an improvement in women's status, and although reformists and feminists have repeatedly argued that the doctrine lends itself to an egalitarian interpretation, the historically dominant tradition in Islam, as in other traditional creeds, stresses the fundamental differences between the sexes and defines different social roles and legal statuses for men and women.[22] The dominance of this interpretation is further reinforced by research that is inattentive to the discrepancy between the ideology of male dominance and the reality of women's autonomy in societies of the region. It is in fact no coincidence that, until a couple of decades ago, all analyses of Middle Eastern societies were carried out by men, who had limited access to the domestic sphere of the family and who thus ignored a significant domain of social life, one that often contradicted the monolithic message communicated in the male-dominated public sphere.

There is another set of factors that account for the prevalence of the polarization of views. These factors result from the powerful dichotomies that are often seen as embodying the Western and Islamic traditions. Philosophical comparisons and theoretical elaborations (which have also been dominated by the thinking of the establishment on both sides) have often emphasized the fundamentally different premises from which each

21. Leila Ahmed, *Women and the Advent of Islam*, 11 Signs: Journal of Women in Culture and Society 665; Leila Ahmed, Women and Gender in Islam: Historical Roots of a Modern Debate (1992).

22. Donna Lee Bowen makes the interesting point that if *shari'a* is considered broadly, then the system that it defines is equitable for the community as a whole; if, however, the "pieces" are examined separately from the point of view of individual roles, gender disparity is apparent. Bowen, *supra* note 14, at 16.

tradition starts. Thus, it is argued, whereas Western thinking about human ethical issues is seen as based on pure reason, in Islam, *aql* (reason) is considered insufficient and incapable of evaluating the divine law.[23] The reason-revelation dichotomy is further reinforced by the notion that Islam stresses not the rights of human beings, but rather their duties to obey God, and that therefore human rights cannot be defined without recourse to revealed religion.

A further tension is seen as existing between the Western idea that the individual is inherently valuable and the Islamic emphasis on the *umma* (community of believers) as the locus of moral valuations.[24] Comparative analyses of political structures in Western and non-Western societies tend to focus on the relationship between the state and traditional kinship structures as the basis of order. For instance, Max Weber's classic study defines the modern state in terms of the development of rational-legal authority, bureaucracy, liberalism, and capitalism and contrasts it with societies based on traditional familial structures or charismatic authority. Western political philosophers of the liberal tradition see the state as both a guarantor of rights and an institution against which the individual needs protection, while states in other parts of the world are seen as having a different moral status in relation to society.[25]

Such differences are seen to extend to formulations of the roles of men and women. Western liberal formulations assume the existence of the conventional nuclear family with its emphasis on the conjugal bond and its role as a retreat from the competitive world,[26] whereas the more pervasive kinship structures of Middle Eastern societies emphasize intergenerational

---

23. The primacy of revelation over reason is most dramatically illustrated by the expression "the closing of the gates of *ijtihad*," which refers to the increasing rejection of *ijtihad* (independent judgement) as a means to develop new theories of jurisprudence—a process that began in the eleventh century and was complete by the sixteenth century. Some researchers maintain that intellectuals and rationalist thinkers have for centuries been on the defensive. *See, e.g.*, ABDALLAH LAROUI, LA CRISE DES INTELLECTUELS ARABES: TRADITIONNALISME OU HISTORICISME (1978).
24. As Mernissi has repeatedly argued, the notion of equality between man and woman is thus profoundly threatening to the Muslim established order because woman is seen as embodying "uncontrolled desire, undisciplined passions, [and] is precisely the symbol of heavily suppressed individualistic trends. . . . We will not understand the resistance of Muslim society to the change in women's status and rights if we do not take into account the symbolic function of women as the embodiment of dangerous individualism." Fatema Mernissi, *Femininity as Subversion: Reflection on the Muslim Concept of Nushuz*, *in* SPEAKING OF FAITH: GLOBAL PERSPECTIVES ON WOMEN, RELIGION, AND SOCIAL CHANGE (Diana L. Eck & Devaki Jain eds., 1987); *see also* FATEMA MERNISSI, BEYOND THE VEIL: MALE-FEMALE DYNAMICS IN MODERN MUSLIM SOCIETY (1987); FATEMA MERNISSI, ISLAM AND DEMOCRACY (1992).
25. It is often suggested that, because in Islam all moral standing is invested in the *umma*, the state has little moral authority.
26. KATHARINE MCKINNON, TOWARD A FEMINIST THEORY OF THE STATE (1989); NGAIRE NAFFINE, LAW AND THE SEXES: EXPLORATIONS IN FEMINIST JURISPRUDENCE (1990).

links.[27] The legal implication of such differences is a further contrast between the civil and criminal codes of Western countries on the one hand and what has been described as a "constitutional chasm" in the Middle East: in all Middle Eastern countries, with the exception of Turkey and (to a lesser degree) Tunisia, laws derived from *shari'a* regulate personal and family status, while laws inspired by the civil codes of Western countries regulate economic transactions.

All these dichotomies can be helpful in constructing "ideal types" that are a good starting point for cross-cultural comparisons, and they may or may not stand up to empirical testing. The point is, however, that, regardless of their scientific value as tools of analysis, these dichotomies have a certain appeal because they clearly categorize the world into two sides—black and white, "us" and "them"—and thus spare us the need to get down to the reality of the many shades of grey that make up real cultures. Moreover, by linking perceived cultural differences to powerful philosophical foundations, they suggest that differences are fundamental and hence immutable.

In fact, if we critically examine these so-called fundamental differences, two major points become clear. First, the Western tradition is by no means uniformly representative of Westerners' opinions or behaviors—indeed, much of what is seen as typical of this tradition is increasingly questioned as a product of the evolution of a society that is also unequal and dominated by men, as well as by the ideology of the marketplace. In particular, critiques by Western feminists are providing new elements that mitigate this dominance and help find points of convergence with other cultures.

Second, and similarly, the dominant interpretations of Islam with their emphasis on jurisprudence are by no means a necessary development of the religion. Today, as well as in the past, Muslim feminists, mystics, and researchers concerned with human rights provide us with alternative visions that are more attentive to the needs of individuals and more open to dialogue about women's situation. In other words, while a cursory comparison of Islam and standard Western liberalism would suggest substantial incompatibilities between the two traditions, woman-centered perspectives on both sides help define a new approach to these issues, one that is situated somewhere between the two traditions.[28] In order to move towards this middle ground, we need to consider both the elements provided by Western feminists' critiques and those that exist within Islam.

---

27. William Goode, World Revolution and Family Patterns (1970).
28. Although there are in fact diverse tendencies within the feminist movement in the West (liberal, marxist, and cultural feminist tendencies are some examples of this diversity), this article does not attempt to make distinctions between these groups.

COMMONALITIES AND POINTS OF CONVERGENCE: WOMEN'S PERSPECTIVES

Western feminist approaches to the law "start with the conviction of women's unjust subordination, and they evaluate the law in terms of how it contributes to the dismantling of such injustice."[29] There are two key elements here: first, the challenge to the neutrality of the law: "In a gendered world where sexes are not equal, the application to women of seemingly neutral laws . . . does not have a gender neutral result."[30] In other words, although in the traditional liberal view the state appears to be gender-blind and impartial, some feminists argue that it is in fact far from neutral.[31] The prototype human being that is abstracted as the subject of the law is in fact an "able-bodied, autonomous, rational, educated, married, competitive and essentially self-interested" male entrepreneur.[32] Therefore, standard formulations of human rights do not really apply to human beings in a universal manner, and equal treatment that does not acknowledge both the inherent bias of the law and women's specificity is bound to perpetuate injustice.

A second important element in Western feminist critiques is the reluctance to wholeheartedly adopt male-derived notions of autonomy because they are in contradiction to the reality of women's reproductive experience and their patterns of caretaking. Although in principle a positive value, autonomy fails in practice.[33] As Nedelsky puts it, "the values we cherish [freedom and self-determination] have come to us embedded in a theory that denies the reality we know: the centrality of relationships in constituting the self."[34] It thus becomes necessary to reconceive autonomy in a way that would combine "the claim of the constitutiveness of social relations with the value of self-determination"[35] and better reflect women's involvement in relationships of nurturance and care. By modifying the two key notions of equality and autonomy, feminist theory does in fact temper the abstract universalism of human rights and provides an approach that is more relevant to the reality of women's lives. In so doing, it takes a step towards other cultural elaborations of gender that emphasize differences

---

29. Cook, *supra* note 11.
30. Naffine, *supra* note 26.
31. McKINNON, *supra* note 26.
32. Naffine, *supra* note 26.
33. Rebecca Cook, *Feminism and the Four Principles, in* PRINCIPLES OF HEALTH CARE ETHICS (R. Gillon ed., 1993).
34. Jennifer Nedelsky, *Reconceiving Autonomy: Sources, Thoughts and Possibilities,* 1 YALE J.L. & FEMINISM 7, 9 (1989).
35. *Id.*

rather than ignoring them. While cautioning about the tendency of male-dominated groups to use the argument of cultural diversity to oppose human rights, formulations of reproductive rights are increasingly respectful of the diversity of contexts in which these rights are defined and implemented.[36]

At the same time, it is also possible to find within Islam certain elements that mitigate the inequalities stemming from the legal tradition. While the legal doctrine deals with women only as wives and mothers—there are no discussions of either men or women except insofar as they belong in familial roles—the scriptures also address men and women as believers who are all to be judged according to merit.[37] A number of Koranic verses address men and women as believers and stress their equality. This clear recognition of individual believers, as equal in the sight of God, is key to the universalist ethos of Islam. Some researchers have argued that, in fact, the development of all the "schools" of Islamic jurisprudence is the result of a one-sided reading of the scriptures and that it has now become necessary to take a fresh look at the texts and restore the centrality of the more universalistic verses.[38] Moreover, the legalistic emphasis of jurisprudence is seen to have grown at the expense of other aspects of the religion. Indeed, as the Japanese Islamic scholar Murata has argued in her book, *The Tao of Islam*,[39] there is a vibrant Sufi (mystical) tradition in Islam that is unencumbered by the legalistic burden of the dominant tradition and is based on a much more egalitarian ethos when it comes to gender.[40]

Similarly, although the inegalitarian aspects of marriage, inheritance, and court testimony in Islam are well-known—a man inherits twice as much, his legal testimony is worth that of two women, he has a unilateral right to divorce his wives and can marry more than one woman—interpretations of the bases of men's position have varied greatly. The Koranic statements that God has "preferred men" who are "in charge of

---

36. Sonia Correa & Rosalind Petchesky, *Reproductive and Sexual Rights: Feminist Perspectives, in* POPULATION RECONSIDERED (G. Sen *et al.* eds., 1994).
37. In the Koran, the general term of believers *al mu'minun* is frequently used, and there are a number of statements that specifically address women as believers (*e.g.*, verses IX: 71, XXXIII: 35). THE GLORIOUS QUR'AN (Marmaduke Pickthall trans.).
38. In particular, according to An-Na'im, much of *shari'a* is based on the group of verses known as the Medinan Suras, while the earlier and more universalist Meccan Suras are deemed to have been superseded and abrogated. ABDULLAHI AN-NA'IM, TOWARDS AN ISLAMIC REFORMATION: CIVIL LIBERTIES, HUMAN RIGHTS, AND INTERNATIONAL LAW (1992).
39. SACHIKO MURATA, THE TAO OF ISLAM: A SOURCEBOOK ON GENDER RELATIONSHIPS IN ISLAMIC THOUGHT (1992).
40. Not surprisingly, the Sufis have historically been regarded with suspicion by the religious establishment.

women" (IV:34) and are "a degree higher" than women (II:228) are all somewhat ambiguous, and there has been a good deal of argument about their exact definition and implications.[41] This suggests some leeway in interpreting them in a more egalitarian fashion. In addition, Islam recognizes women's right to own property and manage their own affairs.[42] This aspect of Islamic doctrine is one that could be used to reinforce the potential for women's autonomy and equality, but it has received a great deal less attention than the unequal aspects of the doctrine.[43] Muslim feminists believe that those statements in the scriptures that stress the equality of believers before God are the authentic message of Islam, while those suggesting discrimination against women are merely reflections of the temporal conditions in which the religion developed and a distortion of its inherent egalitarianism.[44]

Another important element that is often overlooked is the emphasis in the scriptures on mutual consent rather than coercion as a basis for relations between men and women.[45] The Koran gives clear instructions about mutual consent between spouses in decisions related to child care, namely breastfeeding and weaning. "A mother should not be made to suffer because of her child, nor should he to whom the child is born (be made to suffer) because of his child. . . . If they desire to wean the child by mutual consent and (after) consultation, it is no sin for them." (II:233). There are also statements in the Hadith (compilations of the sayings of the Prophet Muhammad) concerning the use of contraceptive methods, which emphasize the need to obtain the wife's consent before practicing *azl* (withdrawal) because it may interfere with her enjoyment of sex or her desire for

---

41. In fact, different translations of the texts have not yielded the same English equivalents.

42. A right that they had long before Western countries recognized similar rights for women.

43. This is true not only of outside observers, but also of individuals in societies of the Middle East where women may sacrifice their rights to property and to their share of inheritance in favor of their male relatives. The rationale is often expressed in terms of conflict avoidance and as a tacit agreement that relatives will care for them in the future if necessary.

44. *See* Ahmed, *Women and the Advent of Islam, supra* note 21; AHMED, WOMEN AND GENDER IN ISLAM: HISTORICAL ROOTS OF A MODERN DEBATE, *supra* note 21; Mernissi, *Femininity as Subversion: Reflection on the Muslim Concept of Nushuz, supra* note 24; MERNISSI, BEYOND THE VEIL: MALE-FEMALE DYNAMICS IN MODERN MUSLIM SOCIETY, *supra* note 24; MERNISSI, ISLAM AND DEMOCRACY, *supra* note 24; AN-NA'IM, *supra* note 38.

45. The issue of consent is one that has received much attention from feminists from a variety of points of view, and it is not possible to do it justice in a broad review such as this one. How consent is determined is of course the most difficult part, whether it has to do with consent to sex (compare to the dilemmas in the West of defining the new sexual ethics), consent to marriage (how does one establish consent in Muslim marriage from a young uneducated individual), or informed consent concerning medical procedures.

children. Several scholars have in fact noted that Islam is quite open in recognizing the importance of sexual enjoyment for both partners within marriage.[46] Although little research has been carried out on this subject, there are indications that women have a sense of entitlement to sexual satisfaction in marriage.[47]

Islamic doctrine is also quite flexible when it comes to the use of contraceptive methods.[48] Concerning abortion, the general Islamic position is to allow it until ensoulment, which is believed to take place after the first trimester, and, except for the *Maliki* school of law, this results in a rather liberal policy.[49] Thus, several important components of a reproductive rights approach are encouraged in Islam.

There also exists the potential for an approach towards marriage that would be based on agreement rather than dominance and submission. This tendency however has been muted in comparison with the clear asymmetry in gender roles that is apparent in marriage practices in Muslim societies, as well as in the writings about these practices by both Muslim scholars and Western analysts. The standard view is that men have the obligation to financially provide for the family and the right to expect obedience from their wives, while women's duties are confined to companionship and the care of children, and their rights limited to financial support and equal treatment in the case of polygyny.[50] This asymmetry is built around three key concepts: the first is *wilaya* (guardianship) which means that woman needs a guardian to act on her behalf and that a father is the legal guardian of his children; the second is *nafaqa* which refers to the financial support that a man owes to his wife and children; and the third is *hadana* which summarizes the right and duty of women to care for their young children, along with the fact that these are limited by the father's legal guardianship. Analyses of *shari'a* as it has been codified in the laws of Personal Status in different Islamic countries[51] demonstrate the unequivocal way in which

46. *See* Basem Musallam, Sex and Society in Islam (1983); A. Bouhdiba, La Sexualité en Islam (1975). Indeed, in the mystical tradition sex is considered one of the ways to know God and get nearer to him.
47. Hind Khattab, The Silent Endurance (1992).
48. Donna Lee Bowen, *Islam and Family Planning* (World Bank: Europe, Middle East and North Africa Region Technical Department, 1991); Abdel Rahim Omran, Family Planning in the Legacy of Islam (1992).
49. It is worth noting, however, that in recent months there has been a hardening of this position. This change was noticeable during the International Conference on Population and Development in September 1994 where representatives of Muslim countries affirmed that abortion was unacceptable, except in extreme circumstances.
50. *See* Muhammad Abu Zahra, *Family Law, in* Law in the Middle East (Majid Khadduri & Herbert J. Liebesney eds., 1955); Fazlur Rahman, *A Survey of Modernization of Muslim Family Law,* 11 Int'l J. Middle East Stud. 451 (1980).
51. Alia Chamari, La Femme et la Loi en Tunisie (1991); Said Nouredine, Femme et Loi en Algérie (1991); Moulay Rchid, La Femme et la Loi au Maroc (1991).

man's role as the head of the household is spelled out and the resulting difficulties of defending women's rights under such a legal system. These include the potential for the coercion of girls into early marriage; a divorce legislation that is clearly disadvantageous to women; limitations that a husband can put on his wife's right to work and freedom of movement; the fact that marriage to a non-Muslim is allowed for men but not women; and the ability to grant children legal status and citizenship as the prerogative of men which is only granted to women under exceptional circumstances.

All these obstacles however are not necessarily insurmountable within the framework of Islamic jurisprudence. One major reason has to do with the fact that the texts on which marriage legislation is based, like all religious texts, contain some ambiguities and lend themselves to widely different interpretations. This makes it possible to promulgate reforms without breaking with the tradition, a strategy that was adopted in Tunisia to abolish *talaq* (repudiation at the husband's request) and replace it with an egalitarian set of divorce procedures; to outlaw polygyny as contrary to the true intent of the scriptures; and also to decrease the claim of male relatives to inheritance, thus weakening links to the extended family and strengthening the conjugal bond.

Along somewhat different lines, but with similar results, women in different parts of the Muslim world have been trying to use *shari'a* to their advantage. Thus for instance, feminists in post-revolutionary Iran have capitalized on the idea, shared among all the interpretations of Islam, that a husband has no legal right to his wife's labor or property because her only duties are to provide him with companionship and to ensure proper care of the children. They have argued that in case of divorce, the man must compensate his wife for the labor she contributed to the management of his household. Such legislation has contributed to raising the costs of divorce for men and defining the conditions for a better legal settlement for women than they had before. It has also called into question the asymmetry in the husband-wife relationship by recognizing the importance of the woman's contribution and assigning it concrete value. Another indication of the adaptability of the cultural context is that in many countries there are legal codes that have been superimposed on the Personal Status Code and clearly contradict it. Thus, for instance, most countries of the region have laws stating that all citizens are equal, labor codes emphasizing the right to work, and health laws insuring universal coverage. Although the aims behind such laws were often nationalist rather than feminist, the result has been to open the door to conflicting interpretations, and consequently to change, as these egalitarian laws can theoretically be used to support women's rights.

A further reason for the flexibility that exists concerning gender relations is that marriage in Islam is an explicit contract which can include a number of provisions. "Marriage is not a sacrament . . . still less is it a bondage. It is a civil contract between one free servant of Allah and another free servant of Allah."[52] The contractual nature of marriage makes it possible to insert provisions that protect the woman against arbitrary divorce or polygyny and guarantee her right to work or her freedom of movement. This method has been regularly used throughout history, but it has unfortunately been the privilege of those who have both the necessary knowledge of the law and the means to influence its application. Currently there are efforts by Muslim feminists and legal scholars in several countries, including Egypt and Iran, to develop a more egalitarian "model marriage contract" that would be the standard for all contracts and gradually allow for a more egalitarian definition of gender relations.

In sum, the existence of egalitarian elements in the scriptures, the ambiguity of some of the texts, the contradictions between different normative structures, and the efforts of reformists all contribute to defining a remarkably dynamic situation. Whether this potential will be directed towards dialogue that aims at improving the welfare of women, men, and families or be stifled by intolerant indictments on both sides will depend in large part on politics at the local and international levels. We must hope that enlightened scholarly exchange along with prudent policy formulation will exert some beneficial influence on these political circumstances.

CONCLUSION

The most general inference that can be drawn from this review is that, while superficial comparisons would lead us to believe that we are dealing with two incompatible systems of norms relating to gender and reproductive rights, further probing reveals a much greater potential for convergence. One implication of this is that further comparative studies of the ethical and legal bases of reproductive rights in each of these traditions are likely to uncover even greater possibilities for common themes to emerge. To do this, it will be necessary to go beyond the general legal and normative level that has been the focus of this article and attempt to understand reproductive rights in their particular contexts. How men and women perceive reproductive rights and to what extent their decisions and behavior reflect a concern over such rights, are questions that require multidisciplinary research, and they are only now starting to be addressed. Only when we can comprehend local notions of rights can we begin the two-way process of translation and develop culturally relevant definitions and policies.

At the same time, because legal reforms and ideas about rights can only provide a receptive context for changes in behavior and do not by

---

52. Marmaduke Pickthall, The Cultural Side of Islam 161 (1966).

themselves produce these changes, it is important also to devote our attention to the practical realities that would support or hinder these reforms. These range from the economic and health infrastructure, to patterns of family formation and dissolution, and the diffusion of ideas through education and exchange—in other words, to all those conditions that are a prerequisite to the exercise of human rights.

[15]

AN ISLAMIC PERSPECTIVE ON DOMESTIC VIOLENCE

*Azizah Y. al-Hibri**

INTRODUCTION

The impact of September 11, 2001, on the American Muslim community has been both severe and multi-faceted. It ranged from sadness regarding mass deaths to civil rights concerns that caused a significant number of immigrants to leave the United States altogether. The threat of sudden raids at home and at work, detentions, the use of secret evidence, profiling, and registration under the National Security Entry-Exit Registration System ("NSEERS") program, are only some of the recent developments that gave rise to these concerns.[1] In the raids, which took place in Northern Virginia in the spring of 2002, women whose homes and offices were raided suffered severe trauma, and some sought counseling to overcome the ordeal.[2]

American Muslim men suffered greater trauma because they suddenly became suspects. For example, the NSEERS program was directed at men from several Muslim countries be-

---

* The author is a professor of law at the T. C. Williams School of Law, the University of Richmond, and president and founder of KARAMAH: Muslim Women Lawyers for Human Rights ("KARAMAH"). KARAMAH is a charitable educational organization that focuses on the domestic and global issues of human rights for Muslims. It seeks to help and support Muslim communities in the United States and abroad in matters related to human rights, civil rights, and other related rights under the United States Constitution. The author is deeply grateful for the assistance of Ms. Raja' Elhabti, Director of Legal Research, KARAMAH, for her extensive assistance in completing the footnotes in this Article in a timely fashion, and to Ms. Cheryl Call, her research assistant at the law school, for her competent and fast assistance in completing the bluebooking process.

1. NSEERS is a program under which the *Immigration and Naturalization Service* ("INS") has required all non-citizen males from certain Muslim countries to register at one of its offices by a specified date.

2. On September 25, 2002, KARAMAH and the Constitution Project co-sponsored a town hall meeting for the Muslim community of Northern Virginia at George Mason University. This unique event was precipitated by the experiences of the Muslim community since September 11, 2001, which included raids and detention. For more on these events and experiences, visit http://www.karamah.org. *See Liberty, Security and the Constitution: A Town Hall Meeting for the Muslim Community, at* http://www.karamah.org/news_town_hall_meeting.htm (reporting on the town hall meeting). Video recordings of the meeting are also available.

tween the ages of sixteen and forty-five. This registration program resulted in an unexpectedly large number of arrests based usually on no more than technical violations of immigration law that rendered the registrant "out of status." These arrests led to detentions, separation of family members, and a great deal of anxiety. The freezing of Muslim charities' bank accounts and the arrest of leading, as well as obscure Muslim men around the country, only served to increase communal insecurity, especially among the male Muslim population.

These mass communal problems have trickled down to impact the American Muslim family. Generally, Muslim men and women closed ranks in these difficult times and concentrated on constructively addressing their familial and communal affairs. As a result, the American Muslim community has experienced a new awakening and a determination to become an active part of the American democratic process. In some cases, however, the cumulative effect of fear, frustration, experiences of discrimination, and job insecurity, bled into the Muslim family. Where latent problems of domestic violence already existed, the new pressures made the situation worse.[3]

Well before September 11, KARAMAH was receiving scattered calls from Muslim women around the country complaining about domestic violence. These complaints were not in themselves surprising, since it has become common knowledge that domestic violence is a problem in the United States. What was surprising about the calls, however, was that generally the women received no support from their female friends or their local religious leaders. Women in the community counseled patience, greater obedience, and stoic silence. Some *imams* blamed the wife. Underlying all these attitudes was the unspoken belief that the man had the right to "chastise" his wife. I had encountered this belief earlier when I was a member of a religious leaders' task force for the prevention of family violence. There, a Christian member of the committee stated that some Christian sects held the belief that, according to the Bible, a man had the right to "chastise" his wife.

It is intolerable that any kind of violence, including domestic violence, be given religious cover and justification. Such a

3. *See, e.g.*, Sarah Childress, *9/11's Hidden Toll*, NEWSWEEK, Aug. 4, 2003, at 37 (noting a surge in domestic violence in the American Muslim community).

belief empowers the perpetrator, giving him "divine" permission to visit harm upon others. Worse yet, it often makes a victimized spouse a willing participant in her own oppression. The result is a sado-masochistic relationship that cannot provide the family environment necessary for the welfare and happiness of its members.

In light of these facts, it is imperative that the religious perspective on domestic violence be addressed seriously and in such a scholarly fashion that individuals whose behavior is truly affected by religion would revise their behavior accordingly. In this Article, I will address the traditional Islamic view of domestic violence. But to understand the Islamic perspective on domestic violence, we need first to understand the Islamic view of gender relations, especially within the family. This view is rooted in the Qur'an, to which we turn next.

I. *THE QUR'ANIC WORLDVIEW*

The central concept in the Qur'an is that of *tawhid*, monotheism. From this concept flows the belief in only *one* God, a Supreme Being, who has no partners and whose Will supercedes those of all others. This concept defines Islam, permeates the whole Qur'an, and from it emanates the Qur'anic worldview. The Qur'anic story about the creation of Adam and the fall of Iblis [Satan] best illustrates this concept.[4]

A. *Satanic Logic*

According to the Qur'an, Iblis' fall from grace was the result of his vanity. The Qur'an provides the story in some detail. When God was about to create Adam from clay and breathe into him His divine spirit, he ordered the angels to bow to Adam once created.[5] All the angels bowed when the time came, but Iblis refused to do so.[6] God asked Iblis: "What stopped you from being among those who bowed?" Iblis responded: "I am

4. I would like to note that the significance of this story was first brought to my attention by Sheikh Hassan Khali, the late Mufti of Lebanon, may God rest his soul in peace.

5. THE HOLY QUR'AN: TEXT, TRANSLATION AND COMMENTARY 15:28-29 (a. Yusuf Ali trans., 1983) [hereinafter QUR'AN]. The cited verses of the Qur'an are often revised by the author to better reflect the subtleties of their meaning.

6. QUR'AN 15:31.

not one to bow to a man You created from clay."[7] Elsewhere in the Qur'an where the story is repeated, Iblis answers: "I am better than him; you created me from fire and created him from clay."[8]

The answer indicates that Iblis had adopted a value system based on an arbitrary hierarchical principle (i.e., fire is better than clay), which served his own arrogant and selfish purposes. Iblis was so committed to this hierarchical principle that he was willing to incur God's eternal wrath rather than violate it. In effect, Iblis deified his principle, for he permitted it to supersede Divine Will. Consequently, he violated the fundamental principle of *tawhid* and fell into *shirk* [the opposite of monotheism, that is a belief in more than one Supreme Being or will].

Iblis' arrogance was based on *jahl* [ignorance]. The Qur'an clearly tells us that "[v]erily, the most honored of you in the sight of God is the one who is most *atqakum* (righteous)."[9] Thus, the only legitimate "preference principle" in the sight of God is one based on *taqua* [piety]. Any other preferential principle is likely to be rooted in *hubris*, and hence false. False principles lead to errors or worse.

In his *Ihya' 'Ulum Al-Deen*, the medieval jurist Al-Ghazali discusses this Satanic logic and the *shirk* it leads to.[10] He notes that every time a rich man believes that he is better than a poor one, or a white man believes that he is better than a black man, then he is being arrogant. He is adopting the same hierarchical principles adopted by Iblis in his *jahl*, and is thus falling into *shirk*.

For this reason, the Islamic State, in its proper form, is not based on an oppressive hierarchy. Rather, it is based on the free consent of the people as expressed by elections [*bay'ah*], consultation, and deliberation [together, *shura*] and a constitutionalism articulated by basic Qur'anic principles.[11] The "head" of the Muslim State is not the apex of an authoritarian hierarchy, but only of a formal organizational one. Like everyone else, his or her authority is limited by the Qur'an and is based on popular

7. QUR'AN 15:33.

8. QUR'AN 7:12.

9. QUR'AN 49:13.

10. *See* 3 ABU HAMID AL-GHAZALI, 'IHYA' ULUM AL-DEEN 326-43 (Egypt: Mustafa Al-Babi Al-Halabi Press, 11th century, reprint 1939). *See id.* at 338, 342.

11. QUR'AN 60:12; 48:10; 48:18; 42:38; 3:159. *See also*, Azizah al-Hibri, *Islamic Constitutionalism and The Concept of Democracy*, 24 CASE W. RES. J. INT'L L. 1, 1, 1n.1 (1992).

will [*bay'ah*].[12] This is why in a Muslim State any citizen can hale the head of State into court.[13] There is no sovereign immunity, because there is no human sovereign. The only sovereign is God, and dominion belongs to Him alone. For this reason, Muslims have no "church hierarchy," but only *ulama*. True *ulama* are modest about their own views, recognizing that only God knows the truth with certainty.

This fact is illustrated by an early event in Islamic history. During the *khilafah* [caliphate] of 'Umar, young men complained about the large amounts of *mahr* women were demanding.[14] *Mahr* is an obligatory marital gift, sometimes monetary, that a Muslim man must give his prospective wife. The amount or type of *mahr* is usually determined by mutual agreement. Afraid that such a trend may discourage men from getting married, *Khalifah* 'Umar announced in the mosque that he was going to place an upper limit on the amount of *mahr*. An unknown old woman rose from the back of the mosque and said to 'Umar: "You will not take away from us what God has given us."[15] 'Umar asked her to explain her statement. Citing a clear Qur'anic verse, the woman established that the amount of *mahr* can be quite high.[16] 'Umar immediately responded: "A woman is right and a man is wrong."[17] He then abandoned his proposal.

Incidentally, the woman was quite on point. *Mahr* is purely the woman's right in Islamic law. She is entitled to set the amount she desires, and once she receives it, no one else may share in it.[18] She may decide to use it after marriage in starting her own business, or invest it for a later time when she may need it. It is the woman's safety net, given to her by a freely con-

12. *See* al-Hibri, *supra* note 11, at 24-26; *see also* al-Hibri, *Islamic and American Constitutional Law: Borrowing Possibilities or a History of Borrowing?* 1 U. PA. J. CONST. L. 497, 505-11 (1999).

13. Khalifah Ali, for example, was haled into court by a non-Muslim. *See* ABDUL RAZZAK AL-SANHOURI, FIQH AL-KHILAFAH WA TATAWWURUHA 213 (Egypt: Al-Hay'ah Al-Masriyah Al-'Ammah li Al-Kitab 1989) (discussing the story of *khalifah* and the absence of sovereign immunity).

14. 1 AL-GHAZALI, 'IHYA' 'ULUM AL-DEEN *supra* note 10, at 50.

15. *Id.*

16. QUR'AN 4:20.

17. *Id.*

18. MUHAMMAD ABU ZAHRAH, AL-AHWAL AL-SHAKHSIYYAH 172 (pointing out that a woman's family has the right to protect her interests by insuring that *mahr* is not too low). *See also* 7 ABD AL-KARIM ZAIDAN, AL-MUFASSAL FI AHKAM AL-MAR'AH WA AL-BAYT AL-MUSLIM 48 (Beirut: Mu'assasat Al-Risalah 1994).

senting prospective husband as a gift [*nihlah*].[19] Unfortunately, fathers sometimes appropriate their daughters' *mahr*, and husbands sometimes pressure their wives into waiving the delayed part of the *mahr*, leaving the woman financially defenseless.

Today, we are living in a world awash with Satanic logic. It is a world ordered into hierarchies based on every conceivable *jahili* criterion, i.e., criteria that are similar to those of the pre-Islamic society of *Jahilia*, the Age of Ignorance. Among these modern criteria are color, wealth, gender, ethnicity, age, technological knowledge, and so on. Given his historical era, Al-Ghazali was able to recognize many of these categories, but not all. Later historical developments helped us uncover many more. What do we do in the face of this new *Jahilia*?

Al-Ghazali noted that Muslims who are vain and arrogant, whether for individual, racial, or economic reasons, engage in Satanic logic. I agree and add to this list gender-based reasons. The Qur'an states clearly and repeatedly that we were all, male and female, created from the same *nafs* [soul].[20]

B. *The Qur'anic Diversity Principle and the Prophetic Tradition*

The very first *ayah* [verse] in *Surat Al-Nisa'* states:

> O people! Reverence God (show piety towards God) who created you from one *nafs* and created from [the *nafs*] her mate and spread from them many men and women; and reverence God, through whom you demand your mutual rights, and the wombs [that bore you], [for] God watches you.[21]

Reading this *ayah*, one wonders that if all humans are created from the same *nafs*, then why are we so different from each other. More specifically, why did God create different genders, even different races and ethnicities? The Qur'an provides us with an answer:

> O people! We created you from a [single] male and female, and made you into nations and tribes, so that you may become acquainted with each other. Verily, the most honored of you in the sight of God is the one who is most righteous (*atqakum*). . .[22]

19. QUR'AN 4:4.
20. *Id.* at 4:1; 6:98; 7:189.
21. *Id.* at 4:1.
22. *Id.* at 49:13.

I refer to this *ayah* as the Diversity Principle. It explains that we were created from two different genders and made into a multitude of different tribes and nations, so that we may enjoy each other's differences and company. Variety is the spice of life.[23]

The Prophet implemented this Qur'anic view of human relations in his own practices. He criticized the "elitism" of Quraish, his own tribe, when he said: "O kin of Quraish, God has removed from you the arrogance of *Jahiliyyah* and its patriarchal dynastic pride (*ta'ath.thumaha bi Al-aba'*). People are of Adam and Adam is of dust."[24]

The Prophet's example in relating to women is also instructive. For example, at the dawn of Islam when the Prophet was still in Makkah, seventy-three men and two women gave the Prophet their *bay'ah*.[25] The two women were Nasibah bint Ka'b and Asma' bint 'Amru. The two women's *bay'ah* were given and accepted on the same terms as those of the men.[26] The men and women then elected twelve representatives of their tribes to discuss various matters with the Prophet. Subsequently, a delegation of Arab women came to the Prophet and gave him their *bay'ah* on behalf of other Arab women. This purely women's *bay'ah* was also accepted by the Prophet, who conversed with the women to clarify the bases of their commitment.[27]

These two events and other early meetings established two important principles: (1) that *bay'ah* and *shura* are the basic principles on which the Islamic model of governance is based, and (2) that women share in that system on equal footing. The second principle flows from the Qur'anic statement that both genders were created from the same *nafs*, and that the most favored in God's sight is the one who is most pious.[28] The events also make clear that, from the first moment of revelation, women played an important role. After all, Khadijah, the wife of

23. *Id.*

24. ZAYD IBN ALI AL-WAZIR, AL-FARDIYYAH — BAHTH FI AZMAT AL-FIQH AL-FARDI AL-SIYYASI 'INDA AL-MUSLIM 62 (Virginia: Yemen Heritage and Research Center 2000).

25. *Id.* at 49 (citing 2 IBN HISHAM, AL-SIRAH AL-NABAWIYYAH 84 (Beirut: Dar Al-Qalam n.d.)).

26. Al Wazir, *supra* note 24, at 49 (noting that this *bay'ah*, incidentally, is earlier than the *bay'ah* given by a group of women to the Prophet and mentioned in the Qur'an itself).

27. QUR'AN 60:12.

28. AL-WAZIR, *supra* note 24, at 49.

the Prophet who stood by his side and supported him, was the first Muslim.

C. *The Qur'anic Harmony Principle and the Prophetic Tradition*

On the question of gender specifically, the Qur'an states in *ayah* 21 of *surat Al-Rum*:

> And among His signs is this, that he created for you mates from among yourselves, so that you may dwell in tranquility with them, and He has put love and mercy between your (hearts): Verily in that are signs for those who ponder.

I will refer to this *ayah* as the Harmony Principle.[29] The thought contained in it is repeated in various forms in the Qur'an, an indication of its significance.[30] For example, in verse 2:187, the Qur'an states: "They (your wives) are your garment and you are their garment."[31]

This is a reference to the fact that spouses are each other's sanctuary insofar as each covers the other's shortcomings and preserves his or her privacy; hence the tranquility and harmony.[32]

In another verse,[33] the Qur'an states: "O Humans revere your Guardian Lord, Who created you from a single *nafs* (soul) and created from it [the nafs] its mate, and from this scattered (like seeds) countless men and women."

In light of these and other similar verses, we may justifiably conclude that the Qur'an articulates a basic general principle about proper gender relations; namely, that they are relations between mates created from the same *nafs*, which are intended

29. An earlier version of this discussion appeared in A. al-Hibri, *Islam, Law and Custom: Redefining Muslim Women's Rights*, 12 AM. J. OF INT'L LAW & POL'Y 1, 20, 26-27 (1997).

30. *See* 1 BADR AL-DIN AL-ZARKASHI, AL-BURHAN FI ULUM AL-QUR'AN 29 (1988); *see also* 1 AL-SUYUTI, AL-ITQAN FI ULUM AL-QUR'AN 35 (1951) (describing the significance of Qur'anic repetition); FARIDA BENNANI, TAQSIM AL-'AMAL BAYN AL-ZAWJAYN 27-28 (Silsilat Manshurat Kuliyat Al-'Ulum Al-Qanuniyah wa Al-Iqtisadiyah wa Al-Ijtima'iyah, Jami'at Al-Qadhi 'Iyadh 1992). Bennani, a Moroccan Muslim who is also a law professor, argues in this award winning book that the Qur'an clearly states in several places that men and women are equal intellectually as well as physically. *Id.* She also relates *hadiths* to the same effect, and cites other evidence. *Id.*

31. QUR'AN 2:187.

32. 2 MUHAMMAD IBN AHMAD AL-ANSARI AL-QURTUBI, AL JAMI' LI AHKAM AL-QUR'AN 316 (Beirut: Dar Ihya' Al-turath Al-Arabi 1985); 2 MUHAMMAD IBN JAREER AL-TABARI, JAMI' AL-BAYAN FI TAFSEER AL-QUR'AN 94-95 (Dar al Ma'rifah 1978).

33. QUR'AN 4:1.

to provide these mates with tranquility, and are to be characterized by affection and mercy. Such relations leave no room for Satanic hierarchies, gendered or otherwise, which result only in strife, subordination, and oppression-characteristics abhorred by Islam.[34] The Prophet's example in his own household illustrates the Harmony Principle. In the absence of an oppressive family structure, his private relationships were based on open communication and mutual respect. 'A'ishah, his young wife, blossomed and felt free to think, argue, and disagree with the Prophet repeatedly. They treated each other with tender affection and kindness, and the Prophet nurtured 'A'ishah's young mind while at the same time integrating her into the life of the Muslim community where she played an important role. The Prophet told 'A'ishah that he always knew when she was annoyed with him. In those instances, she referred to God as the God of Abraham, otherwise, she referred to Him as the God of Muhammad.[35] When 'A'ishah's father found out about her behavior, he tried to strike her.[36] The Prophet intervened and admonished him for his behavior. The Prophet himself was a model "modern" husband and father, never asking anyone to wait on him and participating in household chores and childcare.[37] His great love and respect for 'A'ishah and Khadijah, even after her death, as well as his daughter Fatimah, are well-documented in history books.[38]

---

34. BENNANI, *supra* note 30, at 13-14 (noting that Muslim patriarchal societies used the concept of *qiwama* to create a hierarchical structure within the family headed by the husband). She also argues that such hierarchy contradicts the basic principle of gender equality revealed in the Qur'an. *Id.* at 27-29.

35. 3 MUHAMMAD IBN ISMA'IL AL-BUKHARI, SAHIH AL-BUKHARI BI HASHIYAT AL-SINDI 265 (Beirut: Dar al Ma'rifah n.d.).

36. 3 OMAR RIDHA KAHALAH, A'LAM AL-NISA' FI ALAMAY AL-ARAB WA AL-ISLAM 14-15 (1977); MUHAMMAD SA'ID MUBAYYID, MAWSU'AT HAYAT AL-SAHABIYAT 539 (Dar Al-Thaqafah 1990) [hereinafter MUBAYYID]; *see also* 3 AL-BUKHARI, *supra* note 35, at 268.

37. AL-GHAZALI, *supra* note 10, at 354; *see also* ABU AL-HASSAN AL-NADAWI, AL-SIRAH AL-NABAWIYA 370 (1977) [hereinafter AL HASSAN]; 2 AKRAM DIYA' AL-'UMARI, AL SIRAH AL-NABAWIYYA AL-SAHIHAH 644-45 (Maktabat Al-'Abikan 1995); *see also* al-Hibri, *supra* note 29, at 20 (citing ancient Arabic sources reporting that the Prophet used to mend his own clothes, cut meat, play with children, and perform chores around the house).

38. Indeed, all the *Sirah* [Prophet's biography] books acknowledge the Prophet's love of his family. *See, e.g.*, 2 AKRAM DIYA' AL-'UMARI, AL SIRAH AL-NABAWIYYA AL-SAHIHAH 646-47 (Maktabat Al-'Abikan 1995); SA'ID FA'IZ AL-DAKHIL, MAWSU'AT FIQH 'AI'SHAH OUM AL-MU'MININ 51-2 (dar Al-Nafa'is li Al-Tiba'ah wa Al-Nashr wa Al-Tawzi' 1993). *See also* MUBAYYID, *supra* note 36, at 531-41, 626-27, 325-28 (discussing A'ishah, Fatimah, and Khadijah respectively).

Having explained the Islamic perspective on gender relations, especially within the family, it would seem clear that domestic violence has no place within that framework. But the matter is not that easy. There is a Qur'anic verse which appears to explicitly permit husbands to chastise their wives.[39] This verse has been used by many male scholars to argue in favor of the man having the right to "hit" his wife.[40] In my view, this reading of the verse is erroneous.

There is a quick and simple argument to prove my claim: the Qur'an is internally consistent because it is a divine revelation. The Qur'an repeatedly describes the relationship between husband and wife as one of tranquility, affection, and mercy. Further, it enjoins husbands to live with their wives in kindness or leave them amicably.[41] Domestic violence is diametrically opposed to each of these Qur'anic views and ideals expressed in the various verses. Because of its internal consistency, the Qur'an could not be exhorting one ideal and enjoining the related conduct in some passages, and its opposite in another one. Consequently, an interpretation of one of the elements involved in this apparent inconsistency is wrong. For example, a verse may be interpreted too broadly when it is specific or conditional, thus distorting its true meaning. In this case, the repeated Qur'anic statements about tranquil marital relations are both unconditional and grammatically simple suggesting a general rule. On the other hand, the structure of the verse speaking about "hitting" one's wife is both conditional and structurally complex, leaving room for erroneous, culturally skewed, or subjective interpretations. Therefore, the most likely scenario is that the interpretation of this single verse is responsible for creating the apparent inconsistency, and needs to be revisited.

II. *THE "CHASTISEMENT PASSAGE"*

The so-called "Chastisement Passage" is usually translated as follows: "As to those women on whose part you fear *nushuz*, admonish them (first), (then) *wahjuruhunna fi'l madhaji'i* (abandon them in beds), (and last) *wadhrubuhunna* (hit them

39. QUR'AN 4:34.

40. *See, e.g.*, 6 AL-TABARI, *supra* note 32, at 39-44; 5 AL-QURTUBI, *supra* note 32, at 172-73.

41. QUR'AN 2:229.

(lightly); and if they obey you, seek not against them means (of annoyance or harm), for God is most high, and Great (above you all)."[42]

A. *Background, Structure, and Interpretation*

We turn first to the phrase "*wahjuruhunna fi'l madhaji'i.*" The history of the interpretation of this phrase is illustrative for later purposes. While the plain meaning of the phrase is "abandon them in bed," this meaning became subject to various interpretations. Extensive discussions were conducted on whether "abandoning them in bed" meant: "turning one's back to them in bed," abandoning sexual activity in bed, "abandoning the marital bed only," "staying in the marital bed," but abandoning sexual activity," "engaging in sexual activity, but without verbal communication," or "engaging in sexual activity and communicating, but in a tough manner."[43] The variations among these interpretations indicate that something more than a mere linguistic interpretation was at work. The reasoning of some jurists is indicative of their own cultural or personal views of gender and marital relationships.

A striking example of the intertwining of linguistic and patriarchal reasoning was provided by the respected interpreter Al-Tabari, who argued that "abandonment in bed" could not be the actual meaning of the Qur'anic phrase. He noted that if the woman is *nashiz* (which he defines as one who acts superior to her husband and dislikes and disobeys him),[44] then she would only be pleased by being abandoned in bed. Thus the word "*wahjuruhunna*" must have a different meaning. He combed the Arabic language for another meaning of the root word "*h.j.r*" and related derived forms, focusing on the noun "*hijar.*" "*Hijar*" is the rope used to tie animals. So he concluded that the better interpretation of "*wahjuruhunna fi'l madhaji*" is "tie them in bed."[45] Luckily, other jurists were scandalized by this interpretation, presumably because it contradicted the Qur'anic model of

42. QUR'AN 4:34. The translation used above is a slightly modified version of the modern translation of the Qur'an I have been using in this Article. I have preserved some of the phrases in the original Qur'anic language in order to highlight potential issues which will be considered in later discussion.

43. 5 AL-TABARI, *supra* note 32, at 41-3.

44. *Id.* at 40.

45. *Id.* at 43.

tranquility and affection. For example, Ibn Arabi exclaimed: "What an error by a scholar of Qur'an and Sunnah!"[46] Al-Zamakhshari, another respected jurist, was less circumspect. He called this interpretation, "the interpretation of the 'bores' (*Al-thuqala'*)."[47] The bores of Al-Zamakhshari are prime examples of what I call "patriarchal jurists."

Having discussed this flagrant example of a patriarchal (mis)interpretation, we now turn to the rest of the "Chastisement Passage." At first glance, this is a difficult passage to square with the Harmony Principle. For this reason, it illustrates very clearly the danger of separating an *ayah*, or part of an *ayah*, from its context to reach an isolated interpretation of its meaning. The verse has been used by some patriarchal men to justify physical violence against women.[48] Indeed, based on this passage, the respected jurist Al-Kasani stated that God *ordered* the hitting of disobedient women.[49] On the other end of the spectrum, some modernists have tried to use the Al-Tabari approach, this time to help women, by altering the settled and plain meaning of the word "*wadhrubuhunna.*"

My first comment on this verse is simple. "*Wadrubuhunna*" has its plain Arabic meaning, namely, "hit them." Now that we have gone over this hurdle, we need to ask ourselves: Does the Qur'an advocate hitting women? And, how does that square with the Harmony Principle?

1. The Qur'anic Philosophy of Social Change and Asbab Al-Nuzul (Reasons for the Revelation)

Before answering this question, we need to lay some important groundwork. First, we need to discuss the Qur'anic philoso-

46. 1 MUHAMMAD IBN ABDILLAH IBN ARABI, AHKAM AL-QUR'AN 418 (Dar Al-Ma'rifah 1987). The Sunnah is the *hadith* [sayings], deeds, and example of the Prophet. It is used by Muslim jurists as a secondary source for further clarification and guidance.

47. 5 MUHAMMAD RASHID RIDHA, TAFSIR AL-QUR'AN AL-HAKIM (known as Tafseer Al-Manar) 73.

48. In fact, the *wahjuruhunna* has met a similar, though less illustrious fate in its interpretation by some overly patriarchal males as "tie them up." Under this interpretation, women who exhibit *nushuz* and ignore advice may be tied up in the home and beaten up until they give in. 5 AL-TABARI, *supra* note 32, at 43; 9 IBN HAJAR AL-'ASQALANI, FATH AL-BARI SHARH SAHIH AL-BUKHARI 376-77 (1989). Ibn 'Arabi cast serious doubts on this interpretation. *Id.*

49. 2 'ALA' AL-DIN ABU BAKR IBN MAS'OOD AL-KASANI, BADA'I'AL-SANA'I' FI TARTIB AL-SHARA'I' 334 (1986).

phy of social change, then the reported reasons for the revelation of this verse [*asbab Al-nuzul*], and finally, the social conditions at the time of the revelation and the related prophetic interpretation.

It is a well-known fact that the Qur'an adopts a gradualist philosophy for social change. Gradualism is God's merciful recognition of the human condition and its limitations in the face of change. For this reason, the Qur'an was revealed gradually in accordance with the circumstances, needs, and capabilities of Muslims, since it would have been impossible to introduce the perfect Islamic society all at once. For example, Arabs consumed significant amounts of alcohol in pre-Islamic times. Therefore, the Qur'anic prohibition against drinking alcohol was imposed upon Muslims gradually. At first, the prohibition was only advisory, then it applied only to prayers. In the final stage, the prohibition became unconditional and comprehensive.[50]

Ancient books mention the story of the revelation [*asbab Al-nuzul*] of the "Chastisement Passage." It was revealed in a society which had barely emerged from *Jahiliyyah*. Makkan men, as opposed to Madinan men, were particularly rough with their wives, and used to hit them.[51] They carried this practice into Islam and were so violent that one night a woman complained about it to the Prophet.[52] The Prophet, a Makkan, had never raised his hand against anyone in his household.[53] When he heard about the problem, he chastised Muslim men who dared to hit their wives.[54] Acting on his own, the Prophet prohibited the practice by allowing the wife the right to *qisas* (a form of equitable retribution).[55] That very evening, the men complained loudly.[56]

50. QUR'AN, 2:219; 4:43; 5:90.

51. 5 MUHAMMD FAKHR AL-DIN AL-RAZI, TAFSIR AL-FAKHR AL-RAZI 93 (Dar Al-Fikr 1985) (quoting Al-Shafi'i noting that the society of Madinah was gentler towards women). 'Umar Ibn a'Khattab said that: "We, the kin of Quraish, our men used to possess our women. Then we came to Madinah and found their women possessing their men. Then our women mixed with their women, and our women became bold and disobedient *["tha'arat alayna Al-nisa'"]." Id. See* 1 AL-HASSAN, *supra* note 37, at 4-8, 52-61.

52. Al-'Asqalani, *supra* note 48, at 280. NASR AL-DIN AL-BAYDAWI, TAFSIR AL-BAYDAWI 111 (Dar Al-Fikr, 19th century reprint 1982) (recounting the story of a woman who came to the Prophet to complain about her abusive husband).

53. 1 IBN MAJAH, SUNAN IBN MAJAH 638 (Dar Al-Kutub Al-Ilmiyyah). *See* 2 AL-GHAZALI, *supra* note 10, at 261.

54. 10 AL-RAZI, *supra* note 51, at 93.

55. AL-BAYDAWI, *supra* note 52, at 111; 5 AL-TABARI, *supra* note 32, at 37. For more

They came to the Prophet and revisited the issue. They argued that his ruling allowed their wives to gain the upper hand.[57] At that point, the Prophet sought and received a divine revelation which reflected the Qur'anic philosophy of gradualism: the "Chastisement Passage." It appeared to reverse the Prophet's earlier ruling but, in fact, it severely limited both the act and concept of "hitting," so as to empty both from their harmful content.[58] At the same time, the rest of the Qur'an articulated a higher standard of gender communication and interaction. This is the context in which the *ayah* must be understood and interpreted.

Unfortunately, given the remaining *Jahiliyyah* blinders and despite all efforts by the Prophet to the contrary, many Muslim men unjustifiably misconstrued the Qur'anic verse as sanctioning the reprehensible practice of wife beating, and ignored the Sunnah, powerfully exemplified in the Prophet's own household.[59] This fallacious reasoning was validated by powerful social prejudices and resulted in centuries of misinterpretation and oppression. More importantly, the reasoning misconstrued the basic Qur'anic philosophy of gradualism and change as well as that of gender relations.

The gradualism reflected in the "Chastisement Passage" was not instituted to prohibit "hitting." Unlike wine drinking, there was no gradual prohibition of hitting women. The prohibition was immediate, but the approach was quite complex. For example, as we shall see later, the Qur'an radically transformed the concept of "hitting" into a non-violent symbolic act. This is why I

---

on the concept of *qisas*, see A. al-Hibri, *The Muslim Perspective on the Clergy-Penitent Privilege*, 29 LOY. L.A. L. REV. 1723-32 (1996).

56. 5 AL-TABARI, *supra* note 32, at 37; 1 IBN MAJAH, *supra* note 53, at 638.

57. 2 ABU DAWUD AL-SAJISTANI AL-AZDI, 2 SUNAN ABI DAWUD 252 (Dar Al-Jil, 9th century reprint 1988); 1 IBN MAJAH *supra* note 53, at 637.

58. QUR'AN 4:34 (describing the limitation on the act of "hitting"); 10 AL-RAZI, *supra* note 51, at 92-93 (containing a gradualist explanation of Qur'an 4:34). *See* 2 MALAKAH YUSUF ZIRAR, MAWSU'AT AL-ZAWAJ WA AL-'ALAQAH AL-ZAWJIYYAH FI AL-ISLAM WA AL-SHARA'I' AL-UKHRA AL-MUQARANAH (forthcoming) at 666-67. *See also infra* Section II.D. entitled "The Qur'anic Concept of Hitting" (explaining limitation on the concept of "hitting" in the Qur'an).

59. *See, e.g.* AL-'ASQALANI *supra* note 48, at 379 (concluding from the Prophet's statement that hitting wives is permissible "wholesale"). The Prophet's statement from which the conclusion is derived is: "The best amongst you will not hit your wives." *Id.* Al-'Asqalani does note that this position contradicts the kind relations required by the Qur'an in marriage; so he suggests utilizing threats without action. *Id.*

placed the word "hitting" in quotes. Also, the verse severely limited the "offense" for which a man may "hit" his wife.[60] It made "hitting" an act of last resort.[61] Thus, it is prohibited for the Muslim man to "hit" his wife for any reason other than the one specified in the verse. It is also prohibited for him to "hit" his wife without first going through a series of peaceful steps. In sum, the husband must first establish that the wife was *nashiz* (a concept which will also be discussed later), then the husband has to go through several steps of anger management and conflict resolution before he can even think of "hitting" his wife. If these steps do not work, then the husband is allowed to "hit" his wife *symbolically* (with a bunch of basil or a handkerchief) to express his anger and frustration. Any harm to the wife from his action is clear ground for divorce. Furthermore, this symbolic act defines the minimal standard below which no Muslim may stoop. As we shall see later, the Prophet then repeatedly articulated the higher standard in marital relations, that of tranquility and affection.

2. The Prophet's Tradition — Women and Slavery

Before discussing the Chastisement Passage in detail, I would like to make some general observations about the treatment of women and slaves in the Qur'an, two of the most downtrodden populations throughout history, including the time of the Prophet Muhammad. While the subject of slavery is now only of historical interest, the statements linking it to patriarchy and the mistreatment of women are startling in their clarity. They force us to recognize patriarchy as an institution which enslaves women, that is, an institution which is a variant of slavery.

The Qur'an and the Prophet repeatedly mentioned slaves and women in the same passages, exhorting Muslims to treat them well.[62] In the case of slavery, the Qur'an recognized it only as an undesirable, transitional, socio-political condition and

60. QUR'AN 4:34 (limiting the act of "hitting" to *nashiz* women).

61. *See, e.g.*, ZIRAR, *supra* note 58, at 666-67; *see also* 10 AL-RAZI, *supra* note 51, at 92-93.

62. *See, e.g.*, QUR'AN 49:13; 24:33; 8:70. *See also*, 2 MAJAH, *supra* note 53, at 1216-17 (quoting the Prophet as saying that slaves are "your brothers under your control, feed them of what you eat, dress them of what you wear, and do not charge them with tasks beyond their capabilities. If you do, then help them").

spelled out many ways for its elimination.[63] The Prophet repeatedly addressed slavery through action and words. For example, he made Bilal, the Ethiopian slave, the *mu'ath.thin* [the one who calls for prayers] of all Muslims, to the envy of many Arabs.[64] The Prophet encouraged his wife 'A'ishah to purchase and free Barirah, a slave woman who desired liberty.[65] On one occasion the Prophet stated that slaves are "your brothers under your control, feed them of what you eat, dress them of what you wear, and do not charge them with tasks beyond their capabilities. If you do, then help them."[66] Finally, in his famous last speech, *Khutbat Al-Wadaa'*, the Prophet emphasized that all believers, whether free or enslaved, were siblings, and that no Arab was better than a non-Arab except to the extent of one's piety.[67]

In the same speech, the Prophet analogized the status of women in his society to that of powerless slaves, and he beseeched his male audience to treat them kindly, saying: "[b]e good to women; for they are powerless captives (*awan*) in your households. You took them in God's trust, and legitimated your sexual relations with the Word of God, so come to your senses people, and hear my words."[68] He also admonished the men:

---

63. For an excellent discussion of slavery in the Qur'an see ABD AL-WAHID WAFI, HUQUQ AL-INSAN FI AL-ISLAM 156-64 (Nahdhat Misr 1999); *see also* MUHAMMAD 'AMARAH, AL-ISLAM WA HUQUQ AL-INSAN 18-22 (Dar Al-Shuruq 1989).

64. 2 IBN HISHAM, AL-SIRAH AL-NABAWIYYAH 509 (Beirut: Al-Maktabah Al-'Ilmiyyah n.d.).

65. 4 AL-BUKHARI, *supra* note 35, at 168-9.

66. *See* IBN MAJAH, *supra* note 53, at 638.

67. *See, e.g.*, 'AMARAH, *supra* note 63, at 162; WAFI, *supra* note 63, at 8.

68. 3 AL-BUKHARI, *supra* note 35, at 262 (quoting the Prophet as admonishing his male audience: "Let not one of you whip his wife like a slave, then have sexual intercourse with her at the end of the day"); 4 HISHAM, *supra* note 64, at 604 (quoting the Prophet, in his *Khutbat Al-Wadaa'*). The Prophet tells men: "Be good to women; for they are *awan* [powerless captives] in your households). You took them in God's trust, and legitimated your sexual relations with the Word of God, so come to your senses people and hear my words." *Id.*; 4 ABU JA'FAR AL-TABARI, JAMI' AL-BAYAN FI TAFSIR AL-QUR'AN 212 (Dar Al-Ma'rifa, 9th century reprint 1978) [hereinafter AL-TABARI, JAMI' AL-BAYAN] (quoting the same passage quoted by Ibn Hisham). This passage comes from *Al-Wadaa'*, and was also mentioned in 2 ABU JA'FAR AL-TABARI, TARIKH AL-TABARI 206 (Dar Al-Kutub Al-'Ilmiyya, 9th century reprint 1988) [hereinafter AL-TABARI, TARIKH AL-TABARI]. The Prophet recognized that the status of women was often no better than that of slaves, a fact which reflected his deep concern for women. Many authors have paired the two categories in their writings. *See, e.g.*, 2 'ALA' AL-DIN AL-KASANI, Kitab Bada'i' Sana'i ' fi Tartib Al-Shara'i' 334 (Dar Al-Kutub Al-'Ilmiyyah, 12th century reprint 1986) [hereinafter AL-KASANI] (stating that a husband is entitled to punish his wife as he does his slave). *See also* 5 AL-HAFIZ IBN KATHIR, AL-BIDAYA WA AL-NIHAYA 148, 170,

"[l]et not one of you whip his wife like a slave, then have sexual intercourse with her at the end of the day."[69]

It is highly significant that, even after the revelation of the "Chastisement Passage," the Prophet continued to prohibit men from hitting women.[70] In one case, he stated flatly: "Do not hit *ima' Al-lah* (female servants of God)."[71] On another occasion, he stated that those who hit their wives are not the best among the Muslims.[72] On a third occasion, echoing various Qur'anic descriptions of ideal marital relations, he told the men: "[t]he best among you, are those who are best towards their wives."[73] He added, "and I am the best among you in that respect."[74] This statement is significant given the emphasis Muslims place on emulating the Prophet. Yet many Muslim men today forget such important Prophetic examples and limit their emulation of the Prophet to the style of his dress or his grooming habits.

Al-Shawkani notes that the Prophet flatly prohibited hitting women.[75] Yet, as the perfect Muslim, the Prophet is bound by the Qur'an, including the "Chastisement Passage" that should have overruled him. So, how can we explain the Prophet's Sunnah in light of the "Chastisement Passage"?

First, it is important to note that the Prophet's sayings on the subject and his behavior are both consistent with the Qur'anic Harmony Principle. So, it seems likely that it is the reading of the "Chastisement Passage" that is problematic and overreaching. The question therefore becomes: How can we understand the "Chastisement Passage" in a way that makes it consistent with the Qur'anic view of gender relations and the Prophetic tradition? We can do this by resorting to the interpretation I briefly outlined earlier.

As stated previously, in a society where wife beating was prevalent, the Qur'an changed the meaning of "hitting," severely narrowed its justification and imposed a graduated approach to

202 (Maktabat Al-Ma'arif, 2nd printing of a 14th century reprint 1977) [hereinafter IBN KATHIR, AL-BIDAYA WA AL-NIHAYA].

69. 1 MAJAH, *supra* note 53, at 638.

70. ZIRAR, *supra* note 58, at 667.

71. 1 MAJAH, *supra* note 53, at 638.

72. *Id.*

73. AHMAD FA'EZ, DUSTUR AL-USRA FI THILAL AL-QUR'AN 161 (Beirut: Mu'assasat Al-Risala 1982) [hereinafter FA'EZ]; 1 MAJAH, *supra* note 53, at 637.

74. MAJAH, *supra* note 53, at 636.

75. ZIRAR, *supra* note 58, at 675.

anger management designed to dissipate that anger before reaching the final stage. It also upheld an ideal of spousal relations to which both genders could aspire. For these reasons, many Muslim jurists of medieval times concluded that "hitting" one's wife was "*makrouh*" [strongly disliked]. They also concluded that if the husband is unable to avoid this behavior completely, then he may only hit his wife as a last resort. The only justification for "hitting" one's wife is that of *nushuz* (which will be discussed later), and only for *nushuz*. This was considered the narrow exception that God provided in the "Chastisement Passage."

Finally, jurists educated their male contemporaries that if the husband were to "hit" his wife as a last resort, he may only do so by using a *miswak* (a soft small fibrous twig used as a toothbrush in the Arab Peninsula), a handkerchief, or some other similar object that communicates to the wife her husband's frustration without causing her physical harm. If she is harmed, she is entitled to divorce and, in some circumstances, to retribution.[76] Further evidence that the Qur'anic permission to "hit" was highly limited and only symbolic, can be found in the next verse, which states: "If you fear discord between the two [spouses], then send an arbiter from his family, and another from hers; if they wish to repair [the situation], God will reconcile them. For God has full knowledge and is expert in all things."

Domestic violence will cause more than a simple discord between spouses. It will cause fear, misery, and oppression. But, God is all-knowing, and thus domestic violence is not what is contemplated in the prior verse. Otherwise, the mediation and reconciliation recommended in this verse would be impossible to achieve.[77]

Let us now turn to the "Chastisement Passage" and examine it carefully.

---

76. This approach is not much different from one used in the United States. Some marriage counselors provide angry spouses with styrofoam sticks to hit each other as a way of releasing their frustrations.

77. QUR'AN 4:35.

B. *The Concepts of "Nushuz," "Qanitat," and "fahishah mubayyinah"*

The verse permits husbands to "hit" their wives only for "*nushuz*." So, what does this word mean? The word "*nushuz*" has many meanings in Arabic, but not all of them fit within the context of the *ayah*. The task is to determine the right scope of the meaning of the words in this context. Literally, "*nushuz*" means "to rise above, or act superior to." Hence, it is understandable that the patriarchal perspective which casts marital life into a hierarchical structure would understand "*nushuz*" in its broader linguistic meaning as disobedience by the wife; an insurrection against the husband.

A "*nashiz*" wife is the opposite of a righteous wife. We know that because the immediately preceding passage in this verse suggests it. Taking both passages together, the Qur'an makes two different rules in the same verse: one for righteous women, and one for *nashiz* women. So, to understand the meaning of "*nashiz*," we need to understand who the righteous women are.[78] The preceding passage in the verse defines them. It states (leaving critical terms in the original Arabic language):

> (vi) So, the righteous women are *qanitat* and *hafithat li' l-gaib bima* God *hafith.*

The noun "*Qunut,*" from which the adjective "*qanitat*" is derived, refers to the act of being devoutly obedient to God. So, "*qanitat*" means "women who exhibit '*qunut*,'" that is, "women who are devoutly obedient to God." The medieval Islamic scholar Al-Razi, among other jurists, concluded that since this verse was about marital relations, the obedience of righteous women included obedience to their husbands as well as to God.[79] This conclusion was simply a *non-sequitur*![80]

The word "*Al-gaib*" usually refers to the unknown; for example, the future which only God knows.[81] It also refers to that which is absent, as in "*gha'ib.*" The term "*ightiab*" is derived from this latter meaning, which refers to gossiping about an absent

78. *Id.* at 4:34.

79. 5 AL-RAZI, *supra* note 51, at 91-92; RIDHA, *supra* note 47, at 70.

80. *See, e.g.*, 10 AL-RAZI, *supra* note 51, at 92.

81. 1 MUHAMMAD MURTADHA AL-ZABIDI, TAJ AL-AROUS MIN JAWAHIRI AL-QAMUS 416 (Beirut: Manshurat Dar Maktabat Al-Hayat, 18th century reprint n.d.).

person, a serious violation of Islamic ethics.[82] So, "*Al-gaib*" in the context of this verse could be logically and linguistically interpreted to refer to the absence of certain people. For a better understanding of the identity of these people, we need to look to the rest of the phrase.

The word "*hafithat*" is a feminine plural noun from the triliteral word "h.f.th," pronounced "*hafitha.*" Like many Arabic words, the root word and its variants are rich with meanings. They have connotations of "keeping," "protecting," or "guarding." In this *ayah*, righteous women are described by the phrase "*hafithat li'l-gaib*" *bima* God *hafitha* — i.e., they are women who guard and protect in *Al-gaib* that which God guards and protects (by ordaining that we do so).

One important meaning of "*hafith,*" the derivative deverbal noun from which "*hafithat*" is derived, is the following: "*Al-muhafathah 'ala Al-'ahd*" [keeping one's covenants].[83] God and the Prophet ordered all Muslims to keep all their covenants and promises, especially their marital covenants.[84] Muslim women are equally subject to this injunction as men. The marriage contract is the contract most worthy of fulfillment, according to the Prophet, and a "solemn covenant" according to the Qur'an. In this light, one can understand the reference to righteous women as meaning those who observe their marital covenants even in the absence of those with whom the covenants were undertaken. In this case, the referent is clearly the husbands.[85] Note that there is no language of obedience to the husbands in this passage or its interpretation.[86]

Putting all these elements together within the context of the verse, which is that of marital relations, the proper interpretation appears to be the following: righteous women are those who honor their marital covenants, even in the absence of their husbands (with whom these covenants were undertaken). Consequently, *nashiz* women are those who do not honor their marital covenants, and hence disobey God. Thus, the focus of obedience here is God, not the husband.

82. AL-ZABIDI, *supra* note 81, at 417.

83. *Id.* at 250.

84. AZIZAH AL-HIBRI, THE NATURE OF THE ISLAMIC MARRIAGE: SACRAMENTAL, COVENANTAL, OR CONTRACTUAL. (forthcoming).

85. 3 AL-BUKHARI, *supra* note 35, at 252; QUR'AN 4:20.

86. ZIRAR, *supra* note 58, at 674-75.

The husband of course has the standing (as does the wife) to remind his wife; even admonish her, about keeping her marriage covenant. It is for this reason and this reason only, that the last part of the "Chastisement Passage" mentions obedience to the husband. But this obedience should not be understood as obedience to the husband's arbitrary will, but to his reminder of God's laws. To emphasize the fact that this scenario is not about the man's show of power and subjugation of the woman, the verse states that, if husbands reach the hitting stage, and their wives obey them (by obeying God's laws), then the husbands must "seek not against them means (of annoyance or harm), for God is most high, and Great (above you all)." In other words, as soon as the woman stops her *nushuz*, the husband must stop his actions. This interpretation again relies heavily on the interpretation of *nushuz*. So I turn again to this word.

In light of the interpretation of *qanitat* and *hafithat l'il gaib* provided above, the word *nushuz* is now revealed in the context of the verse as describing a woman who does not honor her marital covenant. She is in fact someone who "rises above, and acts superior" to God's law and injunctions. Again, the disagreement between my interpretation and the traditional one is one of scope and kind. Is the disobedience of the *nashiz* wife directed at God or her husband?

Some jurists have found an easy answer to this question by arguing that any woman who disobeys her husband angers God.[87] Thus, obedience to the husband is subsumed under obedience to God, an approach that borders on *shirk*. This approach is also very similar to that of later Muslim *khalifahs* who argued that obedience to the ruler is part of the obedience to God.[88] *Khalifas* even found jurists who developed the jurisprudence in support of this view. To blunt the *shirk* edge of these arguments, jurists added that "there is no duty to obey when what is required is against God's injunctions."[89] As Islamic political history shows, such addition permits an oppressive relation-

87. *See, e.g.*, AL-RAZI, *supra* note 51, at 91; AL-TABARI, *supra* note 32, at 38.

88. *See, e.g.*, 5 AL-TABARI, *supra* note 32, at 93; 5 AL-QURTUBI, *supra* note 32, at 259-60.

89. 5 AL-QURTUBI, *supra* note 32, at 259-60; *see also* WIZARAT AL-AWQAF WA AL-SHU'UN AL-ISLAMIYYAH (Kuwait 1983); 28 AL-MAWSU'AH AL-FIQHIYYAH 323-24 (Egypt: Dar Al-Sufwah 1993).

ship which is arbitrary and willful, but makes no prohibited demand.

The Qur'an states that if Muslims disagree, then they have to resolve their disagreement by resorting to the Qur'an and the Prophet.[90] So, I turn now to the Qur'an and the *hadith* for further guidance on this matter.

In his famous *Khutbat Al-Wadaa'*, the Prophet interpreted the word "*nushuz*." According to various reports, the Prophet stated in that address, "You [men] have rights against women, and they have rights against you. It is your right that they do not bring someone you dislike into your bed, or that they commit *fahishah* (an act of adultery) *mubayyinah* (which is clear and evident to all). If they do, then God has permitted you to desert them in bed, and [then] hit them lightly. If they stop, you are obliged to maintain them."[91] Thus, the Prophet appears to have interpreted the word "*nushuz*" in the Qur'anic verse to mean two things: bringing someone the husband dislikes into his bed, or committing *fahishah mubayyinah*. To understand the scope of this Prophetic statement, we need to explore further the meaning of *fahishah mubayyinah*.

As expected, many jurists interpreted the term "*fahishah mubayyinah*" broadly to include disobeying one's husband even in matters such as leaving the marital home without permission. Others, however, disagreed, stating that "*fahishah*" means simply adultery.[92] To resolve this interpretive disagreement, I follow the Qur'anic injunction to refer to the Qur'an, now that I have

---

90. QUR'AN 4:59.

91. 5 AL HAFIDH IBN KATHIR, AL-BIDAYA WA AL-NIHAYA, 202 (Beirut: Maktabat al Ma'arif 1979); 2 MUHAMMAD IBN JAREER AL-TABARI, TARIKH AL-TABARI, 206 (Beirut: Dar Al-Kutub Al-Ilmiyyah 1988). Other reports, even by Al-Tabari and Ibn Kathir themselves elsewhere, add the element of "disobedience" to the concept of *nushuz*, as presented by the Prophet in his last address. *See* 5 ABU ZAKARYYA AL-NAWAWI, RAWDAT AL-TALIBIN 177 (Beirut: Dar Al-Kutub Al-'Ilmiyya, 13th century reprint 1992) [hereinafter AL-NAWAWI] (arguing that *nushuz* includes leaving the marital home without permission, abstaining from sexual enjoyment, and refusal to cohabit, but does not include verbal abuse).

92. *See, e.g.*, 10 IBN MANTHUR, LISAN AL-'ARAB 192 (Beirut: Dar Ihya' Al-Turath Al-'Arabi, 2nd printing of a 13th century reprint 1992) (quoting Ibn Al-Athir as defining *fahisha mubayyinah*, occurring in the Prophet's last address, as adultery; also stating that others define it as extreme sin, and as leaving the marital home without permission); AL-ZABIDI, *supra* note 81, at 331 (quoting Al-Jawhari and Ibn Al-Athir as defining *fahisha mubayyinah* as adultery). It also notes that others defined it as extreme sin, and that Al-Shafi'i defined it as verbal abuse towards the wife's in-laws. *Id.*

referred to the Prophet. I would like to focus below on a couple of *ayahs* neighboring the "Chastisement Passage," which use the terms "*fahishah*" and "*fahishah mubayyinah*." This will help us better understand the Qur'anic meaning of these terms because passages of the Qur'an explain each other.[93]

In the same *surah* of the Qur'an, the expression "*fahishah mubayyinah*" is used only a few verses earlier. *Ayah* 4:19 states:

> O you who believe, you are forbidden to inherit women against their will. Nor should you *ta'dhiluhunna* (tighten your grip around them) that you may take away part of what you have given them — unless they have been guilty of *fahishah mubayyinah*; [otherwise] live with them in kindness and equity.

This is a reference to two matters: the *Jahiliyyah* practice which permitted men to inherit women as chattel, and the patriarchal practice of oppressing women until they give up their rights. The Qur'an ends the *Jahiliyyah* practice. In this *ayah*, the Qur'an also prohibits men from engaging in the *Jahilliah* practice of making life extremely difficult for women so as to force them to part with their property in return for their freedom.[94] In another passage, women are further given the right to inherit.[95]

This *ayah* permits husbands to take back part of what they have given their wives, if the wives engage in a *fahishah mubayyinah*. Otherwise, women are entitled to be treated in kindness and equity in marital life. So what is "*fahishah mubayyinah*"? As stated earlier, many jurists said that it was adultery.[96] These jurists then interpreted the verse to say that if a woman committed adultery, then the husband was permitted to cease maintaining her until she returned to him the *mahr* he gave her, and left him under the *khul'* form of divorce (initiated by the wife).[97] Some argued, however, that "*fahishah mubayyinah*" includes *nushuz*, which they defined as disobedience of the husband. But since the concept of "*nushuz*" includes that of "*fahishah mubayyinah*" (according to the Prophetic *hadith*

93. *See, e.g.*, 2 AL-ZARKASHI, *supra* note 30, at 175.
94. 4 AL-TABARI, *supra* note 32, at 209-10.
95. QUR'AN 4:7.
96. 4 AL-TABARI, *supra* note 32, at 211-12.
97. *Id.* at 212-13.

cited above), then this interpretation renders the two concepts equivalent. This result is linguistically and Qur'anically questionable.

In yet an earlier *ayah* of the same chapter, the word "*fahishah*" is used again, this time without the term "*mubayyinah*." As stated earlier, "*mubayyinah*" simply means clear and evident to all; so "*fahishah mubayyinah*" means *fahishah* which is clear and evident to all. The issue in that *ayah* is how to handle a *fahishah* that is not *mubayyinah*. The first part of *ayah* 4:15 says: "If any of your women are guilty of *fahishah*, then find four witnesses who testify against them."

This testimony would be one way to establish the *fahishah* and thus make it *mubayyinah* [evident and clear to all]. Another would be for the woman to state freely that she has committed a *fahishah*. But, as any good Muslim knows, the four witnesses requirement is a specific requirement for adultery.[98] It is levied on society to put an end to idle gossip about the chastity of women. One who accuses a woman of adultery, but cannot establish it through four witnesses (and other due process requirements articulated by jurists) will be subject to severe punishment. If the husband accuses his wife of *fahishah*, and if the wife persists in denying it, they are automatically divorced, and God will curse the aggressor between them, for God knows the truth.[99]

C. *Interpreting the Chastisement Passage*

Looking at these three *ayahs* using the word "*fahishah*" in the same *surah* of the Qur'an, each within no more than fifteen verses from the others, along with the Prophetic *hadith*, I conclude, that the meaning of *fahishah*, as enlightened by *ayah* 4:15, is simply "adultery." Given this conclusion, then, the Prophetic *hadith* which interprets *nushuz* to be in part *fahishah mubayyinah*, is referring to clear and evident adultery. This is the conclusion reached by many interpreters regarding the meaning of *fahishah mubayyinah*.[100] It also means that, while the notion of "*nushuz*" includes the concept of "*fahishah mubayyinah*," it is not

98. 1 Arabi, *supra* note 46, at 356 (stating God's wisdom is to require four witnesses for increased *sitr* [protection of privacy], even though only two are required for murder).

99. Qur'an 24:6-10.

100. 4 Al-Tabari, *supra* note 32, at 211.

equivalent to it because adultery is only one component of the two actions described by the Prophet in his speech.

Furthermore, even if the Prophet was not providing the meaning of the "Chastisement Passage" in his *hadith,* he must have been providing examples. But an instructive example must be adequately illustrative of the meaning. The examples given by the Prophet referred to two types of possible actions: (a) actions for which God has decreed *hudud* [specific punishments], and (b) actions that are a proximate cause of type (a) actions (such as bringing someone into one's husband's bed — a proximate cause for adultery). Had the *ayah* intended to cover less egregious actions, such as violations of the husband's whims and wishes, the Prophet would have indicated so and given men a more accurate idea about the scope of their rights. He did not do so.

The notion of "proximate cause" is important in the discussion. Without it, one could imagine a number of scenarios where an innocent action, such as getting a job, would ultimately lead to adultery. Indeed, some jurists have argued against women's work, even against women leaving their homes, to protect them from such attenuated and imaginative causal scenarios.[101] The logic of these jurists suffers from many shortcomings; not least among them is the fact that it is overbroad. It applies equally to men who are prohibited by the Qur'an from committing adultery. If Muslims follow this logic to its unfortunate conclusion, we will end up with an idle *ummah* [people] whose members sit at home (in isolation) to avoid temptation.

One more observation about the "Chastisement Passage": it does not appear to require the husband's actual knowledge of the actions described above, but rather a "fear" or "suspicion" of their occurrence. Jurists have puzzled over this fact, and some have concluded that actual knowledge is indeed required.[102] I disagree, but would argue for the need of a well-grounded and not a whimsical "fear" or "suspicion," so that paranoid husbands do not make their wives miserable. I believe it is unreasonable to expect that the husband may not react to well-grounded suspi-

101. *See, e.g.*, ABU AL A'LA AL-MAWDUDI, MABADI' AL-ISLAM 143 (1977); *see also* 22 SAYID QUTB, FI DHILAL AL-QUR'AN 2859 (1979); ABU BAKR JABIR AL-JAZAIRI, AL-MAR'AH AL-MUSLIMAH 84 (n.d.).

102. 5 AL-TABARI, *supra* note 32, at 39-40.

cions about his wife until he has actual proof. For one, he may save her from committing *fahishah mubayyinah*, which would ruin their family relations and her spiritual well-being. The various methods listed in the *ayah*, such as admonishment and abandonment in bed, are designed to make her reflect upon her actions. Even the ultimate stage described in the next *ayah*, but not discussed here, namely seeking reconciliation through *hakams* [arbitrators who are friends of the family], or even marriage counseling in our society, would be too late. Thus, it makes sense to start the process of communication early. The problem occurs when such communication enters the "hitting" stage, a matter which will be addressed below.

Interpretations of "*nushuz*" which force the wife to give up her independent will in favor of her husband's do not reflect the lives and example of female Islamic role models, including the wives of the Prophet who amazed Muslims by constantly arguing with him.[103] For them to have behaved otherwise would have made a mockery out of the basic concepts of *bay'ah* and *shura*. In the familial model, the bride's free consent to the marriage represents her *bay'ah* to the husband to take care of their family.[104] Disagreements and discussions are the essence of *shura* in an Islamic marriage. To corrupt this process by claiming that the wife owes her husband full obedience is no less oppressive than arguing that Muslims owe their rulers full obedience. The devastating results of such authoritarian logic continue to haunt Muslims to this day.

I conclude the analysis of the "Chastisement Passage" by focusing on the concept of "hitting" in it. Broadening the definition of *fahishah mubayyinah* broadens the scope of instances in which the husband may resort to "hitting." This is against the injunction in *ayah* 4:19, and against the letter and spirit of the Qur'an as a whole, which states that husbands should live with their wives in kindness or leave them charitably.[105] Nevertheless, scholars agree that even if we were to accept the broader definition of *fahisha mubayyina*, the man still cannot "hit" his wife as a first resort.[106] He is required to take several steps before resort-

103. 3 AL-BUKHARI, *supra* note 35, at 258-59; ZIRAR, *supra* note 58, at 664.

104. For a discussion of the meanings of the word *qawwamun*, see 5 AL-RAZI, *supra* note 51, at 37; 5 RIDHA, *supra* note 47, at 67; *see also* AL-HIBRI, *supra* note 29, at 28.

105. QUR'AN 2:229.

106. *See, e.g.*, AL-KASANI, *supra* note 49, at 334 (noting that the conjunction "and"

ing to "hitting."[107] If all these steps fail, then the husband may "hit" his wife. But what does "hitting" mean in this case?

D. *The Qur'anic Concept Of "Hitting"*

Many scholars have pondered over the Qur'anic permission to "hit," and its attendant circumstances. Given their deep belief in Islamic justice, they realized that they must look deeper into the Qur'an for a better understanding of this verse. Thus, they interpreted this passage, as they should, in light of the basic principles governing marital relations as articulated by the Qur'an and the Prophet.[108] That approach forced them to modify their common understanding of the act of marital "hitting." As a result, the jurists issued a series of limitations redefining the act of hitting itself.[109] For example, the man may not hit his wife on the face.[110] Furthermore, any "hitting" which is injurious or leaves a mark on the woman's body is actionable as a criminal offense.[111] Also, if the husband reaches that unfortunate stage

---

in the revelation requires a sequence of actions: first admonishing the wife, then deserting her in bed, and finally "hitting" her); 9 WIHBA AL-ZUHAILI, AL-FIQH AL-ISLAMI WA ADILLATUH 6855-57 [hereinafter AL-ZUHAILI]; *cf.* AL-NAWAWI, *supra* note 91, at 177 (quoting Al-Hinati, who argues that the sequential interpretation is only one of three possible ones).

107. The majority of scholars take the sequential approach. According to them, the husband must first admonish, then desert his wife's bed, and finally resort to hitting, although some argue that it is better not to reach the third stage at all. *See supra* note 106 and accompanying text (discussing the sequential approach). *See id.* at 6857 (arguing that it is better to threaten without actually "hitting"). He bases his view on the fact that the Prophet never hit a woman. *Id. See, e.g.*, SAHIH AL-BUKHARI, *supra* note 35, at 57 (quoting the Prophet as asking: "How can one of you hit his wife like an animal, then he may embrace her?"); 1 IBN MAJAH, *supra* note 53, at 638 (quoting the Prophet as asking: "How can one of you whip his wife like a slave, and sleep with her at the end of the day?").

108. Major among these is the Qur'anic verse which orders husbands to live with their wives in kindness, or leave them charitably. *See* QUR'AN 2:229.

109. Among these is the sequential interpretation of the Qur'anic verse 4:34. *See supra* note 106 and accompanying text. Other limitations are mentioned in 5 AL-TABARI, *supra* note 32, at 43-45 (noting that the man may not hit the woman *dharb ghayr mubrah wala mu'ath.thir* [in the face, or hit so as to cause pain or harm]); 5 AL-NAWAWI, *supra* note 91, at 676-77 (hitting may not cause harm or be heavy, cannot be on the face or other vulnerable areas. If it causes harm, the woman is entitled to damages). *See id.* at 7856-57 (citing medieval jurists as requiring that the "hitting" does not cause fear in the wife, is not directed against the face or abdomen, and other places that could result in serious harm).

110. *Id.*

111. 2 ABU AL-BARAKAT AHMAD AL-DARDIR, AL-SHARH AL-SAGHIR 512 (Dar Al-Ma'aref, 18th century reprint 1972) (noting that the hitting may not affect the wife's

of "hitting," he may hit the wife only with something as gentle as a *miswak* or handkerchief.[112] Finally, given the Qur'anic ideal of marital relations, the majority of Muslim scholars concluded that while the act of "hitting" is permissible in Islam, abandoning it is preferable and more graceful [*ajmal*].[113] They also concluded that a woman abused physically or verbally is entitled to divorce from her husband.[114] They lowered the bar significantly on what counts as abuse, so as to make it include verbal abuse. This interpretation is still reflected in the laws of some Muslim countries today.[115]

It is important to note that despite their strong commitment to the marriage institution, jurists did not regard marriage as an absolute right. They prohibited men who were likely to harm or oppress their prospective wives from getting married.[116] On the other hand, for those bachelors who may commit adultery, marriage was considered a duty.[117] Even if a man needed to marry to avoid adultery, but was likely to harm or oppress his prospective wife, he would be prohibited from doing so.[118] One line of reasoning notes that adultery is a matter that relates to the rights of God over us, while marriage relates to the rights of the creatures among each other (the husband and wife in this case). But God is in a better position to deal with a violation of his right than an abused woman. Thus, even if the fear of adultery ex-

---

bones or flesh. The husband may not resort to hitting his wife if he knows that it would be useless. If the husband hits his wife despite this knowledge, she is entitled to divorce and retribution). *See also* 5 AL-Nawawi, *supra* note 91, at 676-77 (stating that hitting may not cause harm or be heavy, cannot be on the face or other vulnerable areas, and if it causes harm, the woman is entitled to damages); AL-ZUHAILI, *supra* note 106, at 7856-57 (noting that the Hanafi and Shafi'i schools of thought would find the husband liable if he harmed his wife but Hanbalis would not).

112. *See* AL-TABARI, *supra* note 32, at 44; 5 AL-NAWAWI, *supra* note 91, at 676-77 (hitting may not cause harm or be heavy and cannot be on the face or other vulnerable areas and if it causes harm, the woman is entitled to damages); AL-ZUHAILI, *supra* note 106, at 7856.

113. 7 ABD AL-KARIM ZAYDAN, AL-MUFASSAL FI AHKAM AL-MAR'AH WA AL-BAYT AL-MUSLI 318 (1994); 5 AL-RAZI, *supra* note 51, at 93.

114. This view has been adopted by some personal status codes such as Jordanian Code, Personal Status Code, Provisional Law No. 61 (1976), ch. 12, art. 132; Kuwaiti Code, Personal Status, pt. 1, bk. 1, tit. 3, ch. 1, art. 126.

115. Certain Codes explicitly specify that verbal abuse is grounds for granting the wife the judicial divorce. *See* Jordanian Code, *supra* note 114, ch. 10, art. 132; Kuwaiti Code, *supra* note 114, pt. 1, bk. 2, tit. 3, art. 126.

116. AL-ZUHAILI, *supra* note 106, at 6516.

117. *Id.*

118. *Id.*

isted, some jurists argued, a man who may harm his wife is prohibited from getting married.[119]

An important Qur'anic precedent on the issue of domestic violence is found in the story of Job.[120] When Job was being tested, his wife lost her faith and blasphemed.[121] As a result, he took an oath to hit her as punishment.[122] A dilemma was thus created: a prophet should not engage in violent and unworthy behavior towards his wife. On the other hand, a prophet may not violate his oath. The divine solution to this dilemma is expressed in a Qur'anic verse, which instructs Job to satisfy his oath to hit his wife by "hitting" her with a handful of fragrant grass (or basil).[123] The intent was to satisfy the promise without harming the wife. In this way, Prophet Job resolved his dilemma.

CONCLUSION

The Qur'an offers Muslim men who are justifiably upset with their wives' conduct (as defined above), a graduated solution to deal with their frustrations and anger. At its final stage, the solution is similar to that which Job was shown to release him from his oath. However, the Qur'an also shows Muslims the way to become better Muslims and human beings by living in accordance with the ideal of marital relations, or ending the relationship amicably. The Qur'an states very clearly: "The parties should either hold together on equitable terms or separate with kindness."[124] Thus, the Qur'anic approach to the problem of husbands hitting their wives aims at eliminating such behavior altogether, but it takes into account the very nature of human beings, the complexity of their emotions, and the need for "a gestation period" for them to achieve a higher stage of develop-

119. *See, e.g.*, ABU ZAHRAH, *supra* note 18, at 24-25.

120. QUR'AN 38:44. I would like to thank Sana' Afandi, director of Karamah: Muslim Women Lawyers for Human Rights, for pointing out the significance of this story in understanding the Qur'anic verse 4:34.

121. *Id.* at 38:44.

122. *Id.*

123. The word *dighth* in Qur'anic verse 38:44 means a handful of grass or even basil. *See* 5 IBN 'ABDIN, RADD AL-MUHTAR 659 (Dar Al-Kutub Al-'Ilmiyya, 19th century reprint 1994) (explaining the meaning of *dighth* as a handful of basil, also noting that others stated that it meant "a handful of grass or thin branches"). *Cf.* Ibn 'Abdin argues that the use of basil by Job is a special case, reflecting God's mercy, and cannot be generalized to other women. Yet major medieval scholars appear to implicitly disagree. They limited the husband to the use of a *miswak* or what is similar to it.

124. *Id.* at 2:229.

ment. It also helps them reach that higher stage through a series of prescribed behavior aimed at self-control and anger management, and by describing and exhorting by words and the example of the Prophet the blissful higher stage of marital life.

The Qur'anic verses were revealed in ancient Arabia, over fourteen hundred years ago when the world viewed beating one's wife as a right. Today, our society has moved decidedly beyond that stage, and views wife abuse as the crime it really is. Earlier Muslim jurists agree. It is now time for the rest of the Muslim community to catch up with this vision, and help the troubled men within it to move to the higher stages of consciousness described in the Qur'an and implemented by the Prophet. This way, we can either achieve the Qur'anic marital ideal of tranquility, affection, and mercy, or gracefully follow God's injunction of parting ways in kindness.

Indigenous and Customary Law

[16]

INDIGENOUS PEOPLES AND FAMILY LAW: ISSUES IN AOTEAROA/NEW ZEALAND

JACINTA RURU*

ABSTRACT

This article provides a glimpse into how historical and current legislation has attempted to grapple with the practice of customary family law by the indigenous peoples of Aotearoa/New Zealand. It focuses on examining family law in two contexts: marriage and property ownership; and children and legal parenthood. The analysis provides an interesting insight into the interplay between customary law and statute law. The impact of colonization upon indigenous peoples and the practice of their law, and how governments today choose to recognize and provide for indigenous peoples is a policy issue prevalent in many of the British colonized lands. This article concludes that a comprehensive review of the nature and extent to which legislation should provide for Maori customary law is required in Aotearoa/New Zealand. The haphazard approach of current years is insufficient.

1. INTRODUCTION

The common historical and continuing experiences of colonization have hugely impacted on the role and function of families within many indigenous peoples' populations. Maori, the indigenous people of Aotearoa/New Zealand are no exception.[1] They, like many other indigenous peoples, ascribe to a unique worldview that governs their relationships with the surrounding world order. Within this belief system the role of the family unit is pivotal in maintaining cultural identity and sense of place. For hundreds of years Maori ethics determined the rights and responsibilities of Maori families. Soon after British colonization of Aotearoa/New Zealand in the nineteenth century, new laws began to displace the customary law of Maori (tikanga Maori). Today, Maori have little legal ability to pursue the application of their

* Faculty of Law, University of Otago, Dunedin, New Zealand. Email jacinta.ruru@stonebow.otago.ac.nz. My thanks to Professor Mark Henaghan and Associate Professor Nicola Peart for commenting on draft versions of this work. This article develops a paper entitled 'Maori and Family Law Post Colonization' delivered to the International Bar Association (IBA) 2004 Conference, Auckland, New Zealand, at the Family Law in Indigenous Communities session on 27 October 2004.

own law unless legislation specifically provides for it. This is despite the country's founding document, the Treaty of Waitangi, signed in 1840, stating that the British Crown guarantees to Maori the full exclusive and undisturbed possession of their properties, or, as the Maori version reads, retention of chieftainship of their own properties. This is also in spite of international law and in particular the amended 'Draft Declaration on the Rights of Indigenous Peoples'. When the New Zealand Government ratifies it, this instrument will recognize, for example, the right of Maori to practise and revitalize their cultural traditions and customs and participate fully at all levels of decision-making in matters which may affect their rights.

In 2001, the New Zealand Law Commission (NZLC) released a report entitled *Maori Custom and Values in New Zealand Law*. Its purpose was to 'examine how Maori custom and values impact on our current law' (NZLC, 2001: 1). It concluded:

> If society is truly to give effect to the promise of the Treaty of Waitangi to provide a secure place for Maori values within New Zealand society, then the commitment must be total. It must involve a real endeavour to understand what tikanga Maori is, how it is practiced and applied, and how integral it is to the social, economic, cultural and political development of Maori, still encapsulated within a dominant culture in New Zealand society (NZLC, 2001: 95).

This article takes on the challenge by examining the Maori worldview in the context of Maori customary family law and its depiction in legislation. It analyses family law in two contexts: marriage and property ownership, and children and legal parenthood.[2] These case studies aptly illustrate that there exists an inconsistent legislative history aimed at, on the one hand, restricting, and on the other, embracing Maori customary family law. In this article it is argued that even taking into account more contemporary legislative attempts to provide for tikanga Maori, the provisions remain inadequately thought through. If the NZLC's end goal of securing a place for Maori values is to transpire, a comprehensive policy review for how legislation could adequately provide for the expression of Maori customary law is required. This article tackles a small part of this much wider issue: it focuses on select family statutes to demonstrate that it is timely to pursue the NZLC's vision.

2. MAORI CUSTOMARY FAMILY LAW

The Maori world-view is described as holistic whereby it is believed that humans, and all things in the environment, descend from Ranginui (sky father) and Papatuanuku (earth mother). Maori describe themselves as tangata whenua (people of the land), and have kaitiaki (guardianship) responsibilities to look after one's own blood and bones meaning: 'One's whanaunga [relations] and tupuna [ancestors] include the plants and animals, rocks and trees. We are all descended from Papatuanuku; she is our kaitiaki and we in turn are hers' (Roberts *et al*, 1995: 7). For example, the highest mountain in Aotearoa/New Zealand, Aoraki/Mount Cook, is said to be a son of Ranginui who came down on a canoe with his brothers to meet Papatuanuku.[3] Unable to find land, they said a prayer which should have enabled them to return home, but which caused their canoe to run aground on a hidden reef, turning themselves and the boat into stone and earth. The canoe formed the South Island and the sons, who had clambered to its high side, are the lofty mountain peaks. Such traditions provide a link between the cosmological world of the gods and the present generations. The mountain's life force 'represents the essence that binds the physical and spiritual elements of all things together, generating and upholding all life'.[4]

In terms of Maori customary family law, whanaungatanga (kinship) is the underlying concept. Whanaungatanga:

> denotes the fact that in traditional Maori thinking relationships are everything – between people; between people and the physical world; and between people and the atua (spiritual entities). The glue that holds the Maori world together is whakapapa or genealogy identifying the nature of relationships between all things (NZLC SP9, 2001: para 130. See also Chadwick, 2002).

Aoraki/Mount Cook is an example of this belief system. Thus, within this paradigm, it is arbitrary to talk about owning land – just as our mother cannot be owned, land cannot be owned. Similarly, it is illogical to separate the individual from his or her relations – be it wider family or the natural environment.

The Maori family unit, whanau, includes not solely the nuclear family, but grandparents, aunts and uncles. Each whanau belongs to one or more hapu (sub-tribes) and iwi (tribe). The kinship system is rooted in the idea that people are of the land (tangata whenua). For example, the Maori word whanau means 'family', but also 'to be born'; hapu means 'sub-tribe' and 'to be pregnant', and iwi means 'tribe' and 'bone'. The kinship system is likened to a native bush:

> The rito, the centre shoot or heart of the harakeke, or flax, must be cared for to ensure new life and new shoots. It symbolizes the need of each person to be nurtured in a whanau-hapu environment. According to Maori, te whanau-hapu is the heart of life for a person. It is the ground in which kinship and social relationship obligations and duties are learned, and enabled to flourish and flower (Henare, 1994).

Children are considered taonga (treasures). The child is viewed as:

> not the child of the birth parents, but of the family, and the family was not a nuclear unit in space, but an integral part of a tribal whole, bound by reciprocal obligations to all whose future was prescribed by the past fact of common descent (Department of Social Welfare, 1996: 74–5).

Similarly, men and women are considered essential parts in the collective whole. In terms of traditional customary law, both had the capacity to hold property: 'use-rights over land and resources were "owned" or held by women as individuals as well as by men, subject only to the overriding right of the tribal community and the mana of chief over the land and people' (Ballara, 1993: 133). Marriage (which ranged from formal religious ceremonies through to mating without ceremonial observance) did not alter this reality. For example, the woman retained ownership of land that was hers prior to the marriage, and decisions regarding it were hers to make, subject to her whanau and hapu interests (Ballara, 1993: 134). If the woman's family gifted land to the man in celebration of the marriage, his right of occupancy would terminate at his wife's death if he had no blood link to the land and there were no children of the marriage. The land would revert to her family (see Ballara, 1993: 134; Ruru, 2004b: 450; Mikaere, 1994: 125).

Social control is maintained by doctrines such as tapu (sacredness). These doctrines regulate the rights and responsibilities in regard to individual behaviour and interaction with others and the environment (see Tohe, 1998). Importantly, in regard to the whanau, individual rights and responsibilities are at the whim of the collective. For instance, the whanau as a group accepts

> responsibility for each other's behaviour, checking those who show disapproved-of tendencies, mediating disputes, enjoying the public recognition accorded a member for achievement, sharing the blame when a member offends against community norms, and helping the member make reparation (Hall and Metge, 2002: 51).

While in traditional Maori society there existed no written word, or judicial court system akin to that which had developed in Britain, Maori customary law operated in a clear and comprehensible manner. The whanau-hapu-iwi kinship was at centre-stage within this values based personified world.

3. TREATY OF WAITANGI

Representatives of the British Crown and Maori chiefs signed the Treaty of Waitangi in 1840. In accordance with the English version, the Crown thought it was acquiring sovereignty in exchange for guaranteeing to Maori their full exclusive and undisturbed possession of their properties. In accordance with the Maori version, Maori thought they had given the British Crown the power to govern, but that they had retained their sovereignty over their own properties.[5] While early legislation recognized the Treaty of Waitangi,[6] by 1877 the political environment was such that there was little outcry when Chief Justice Prendergast, in *Wi Parata* v *The Bishop of Wellington*, declared the Treaty a 'simple nullity'.[7] The finding was justified on the basis that 'No body politic existed capable of making cession of sovereignty' because Maori were 'primitive barbarians'.[8]

The environment back then can be encapsulated by reference to a court system implemented to provide special rules for Maori. In the 1860s, a separate court was established, the Native Land Court, with the express jurisdiction to 'encourage the extinction' of Maori proprietary customs and to 'provide for the conversion of such modes of ownership into titles derived from the Crown'.[9] It was thought that this would 'greatly promote the peaceful settlement of the Colony and the advancement and civilization of the Natives'.[10] The Court was thus responsible for converting Maori customary land[11] into a freehold title – Maori freehold land[12] – whereupon the land could be sold, mortgaged, gifted, or confiscated.[13]

In the 1970s Maori were successful in gaining mainstream attention of their struggles for social justice, equality and self-determination.[14] In 1975 the Waitangi Tribunal was established to make recommendations on claims made by Maori that they have been prejudicially affected by Crown actions or omissions.[15] Today more than 20 statutes require decision makers to have some level of regard to 'the principles of the Treaty of Waitangi', and several statutes expressly refer to Maori customary law concepts, such as tikanga Maori, kaitiakitanga, and taonga.[16] However, strangely no family related statutes reference the Treaty.

In 1987 the Court of Appeal endorsed a 1941 Privy Council decision[17] stating that rights conferred by the Treaty cannot be enforced in the Courts except insofar as a statutory recognition of the rights can be found.[18] A decade later the High Court indicated a new interpretation rule. The High Court stated that 'all Acts dealing with the status, future and control of children are to be interpreted as *coloured by* the principles of the Treaty of Waitangi'.[19] This new direction in the family realm was justified on the basis that:

> We are of the view that since the Treaty of Waitangi was designed to have general application, that general application must colour all matters to which it has relevance, whether public or private and that for the purposes of interpretation of statutes, it will have a direct bearing *whether or not there is a reference to the Treaty in the statute.* We also take the view that the familial organization of one of the peoples a party to the Treaty, must be seen as one of the taonga, the preservation of which is contemplated.[20]

No subsequent court has adopted, much less discussed, this statement. Still, it remains an important dictum that represents the now critical place of the Treaty in today's environment. Therefore, although no family related statute expressly refers to the Treaty, it is possible to argue its relevance. If such an argument were accepted, the Family

Court would have to traverse the Treaty principles' jurisprudence and extend it to a family context.

There exists no finite list of the principles and this is appropriate, for 'What matters is the spirit... The Treaty has to be seen as an embryo rather than a fully developed and integrated set of ideas'.[21] The Courts and the Waitangi Tribunal have emphasized that Treaty principles 'require the Pakeha (New Zealanders of British origin) and Maori Treaty partners to act towards each other reasonably and with the utmost good faith'.[22] Treaty principles are commonly referred to as encapsulating partnership, mutual benefit, the Crown's obligation to protect actively Maori interests, good faith consultation, and the Crown's obligation to recognize rangatiratanga (Maori sovereignty) which could range from a tribal right to own, manage, co-manage or simply influence, or be included in some manner, in the decision-making process.[23]

This new Treaty-inclusive environment should be 'colouring' approaches to family law. This means that legislation should be according respect and value to Maori customary family laws. In practice this would mean that the Maori kinship system of whanau-hapu-iwi should be influencing decisions affecting one of their members.

4. INTERNATIONAL LAW

Another benchmark is international law. Since the 1970s, international law has been specifically providing for indigenous peoples.[24] At the United Nations level, many indigenous peoples have been involved in drafting documents for ratification. In the context of New Zealand and the immediate future, the most significant is the 'Draft Declaration on the Rights of Indigenous Peoples'. Even though this document was agreed upon by the members of the United Nations Working Group on Indigenous Populations in 1993, and adopted by the United Nations Subcommission on Prevention of Discrimination and Protection of Minorities in 1994, no country has yet ratified it. New Zealand has been a leading contender for countries to ratify an amended version.[25] Indigenous Peoples, including Maori, have not been supportive of the changes made to the original Draft Declaration.[26] But even if New Zealand ratifies the watered down amended version, New Zealand law will still have to be seen as responsive to tikanga Maori, including Maori customary family laws.

The Draft Declaration (in original and amended forms) recognizes 'the urgent need to respect and promote the inherent rights and characteristics of indigenous peoples' (preamble); states indigenous peoples have the right to maintain and develop their distinct identities (article 8); acknowledges indigenous peoples have the right to practice and revitalize their cultural traditions and customs (article 12); and accepts indigenous peoples have the right to participate fully at all levels of decision-making in matters which may affect their rights (article 19). The amended Draft admits that indigenous peoples have the right to be actively involved in devising legislative measures that may affect them (article 20). With the New Zealand Government keen to ratify the amended version,[27] the Declaration will provide a further yardstick against which to seek inclusive law.

This article now examines whether the law has and is providing for Maori involvement, and respect and value of Maori customary family laws.

5. CASE STUDY ONE: MARRIAGE AND PROPERTY

Following the signing of the Treaty of Waitangi, the British Crown assumed sovereignty of Aotearoa/New Zealand. English common law was introduced into the country. Attempts to reconcile that law with Maori customary law are evident within this case study of marriage and property. For example, an initial conflict arose in the 1860s with the establishment of the Maori Land Court. The Court was empowered to convert Maori customary land into Maori freehold land. It had two specific roles: to determine ownership of customary land by issuing a freehold title and then regulating subsequent succession to the converted freehold land. But a quandary arose: if the English intestacy law applied and the eldest son inherited land there would be no child capable of taking the land because Maori married according to custom and therefore their children were 'illegitimate' by English law standards. Early legislation recognized the dilemma and introduced a special rule for Maori: succession was to take place according to Maori custom.[28] The judiciary interpreted Maori custom to be that children succeed equally to property.[29] The interpretation led to extreme fragmentation of ownership of Maori freehold land and has been widely criticized as an inaccurate interpretation of Maori custom:

> in arriving at this rule the chief judge made no allowance for mana, for the status of members of a hapu, or for ahi ka in occupation of land.... One might have thought that if the deceased had become the sole grantee because he was the rangatira of his hapu at the time, then on his death a succession inquiry would ascertain who then became the rangatira (Williams, 1999: 180).

The equal succession rule failed to do this and thus neglected to reflect the true nature of Maori customary law. The rule viewed individual ownership as valid, thereby ignoring the Maori world-view which regarded exclusive ownership as impossible, liking it to owning one's mother (see Ruru, 2004b). This evidences an example of how legislation has attempted to cater for Maori customary law and in doing so has created an unwelcome result.

The rule is still endorsed in legislation today. If an owner of Maori freehold land passes away without a will, the Court will determine that the surviving children succeed in equal portions.[30] However, since 1993, the law has attempted to recognize and provide for an alternative to this entrenched rule; it has introduced special share-management trusts that halt individual succession. Any income derived from the land held in a whanau trust must be applied for the purposes of promoting the health, social, cultural and economic welfare, education and vocational training, and general advancement in life of the descendants of any ancestor named in the trust order.[31] This type of trust is proving popular. Significantly, it aligns more closely with Maori custom recognizing group interests in land, rather than individual ownership.

In regard to Maori customary marriages, several historical statutes provided recognition, applying similar rules as if the couple were married according to law. For example, historically a Maori woman, whether she was married according to the law or custom, could challenge an intestacy ruling on the basis that she did not have sufficient land or other property for her maintenance.[32] However, the law became somewhat more restrictive in the 1950s whereupon the general rule, mandated by legislation, became that Maori had to marry in accordance with the law.[33] Family maintenance was the sole exception to this general rule and it only applied to those customary marriages entered into before a certain date – 1 April 1952.[34] Today this remains the only explicit reference in legislation to Maori customary marriages.[35]

Instances have nonetheless arisen where Maori couples have argued before the Family Court that their customary marriage should be considered akin to a legal marriage for the purposes of the Adoption Act 1955. That Act allows 'spouses' to jointly adopt a child. In 1992, a Maori couple were successful in convincing the judge that 'spouse' should be read widely so as to enable them to jointly adopt a child without having to legally marry one another.[36] However, that case remains the sole successful case even though other couples have attempted to have that precedent applied.[37]

More recently, in 2001, matrimonial property law was radically recast with the enactment of the Property (Relationships) Amendment Act. This Amendment Act introduced entirely new rules for the division of property upon separation and death for all New Zealanders. It changed the name of the past governing statute of the Matrimonial Property Act 1976 to the Property (Relationships) Act 1976. The Property (Relationships) Act 1976 presupposes that property owned by a couple – whether married, in a civil union, or in a de facto relationship – is relationship property and it is to be equally shared. This includes the family home and family chattels as well as assets acquired by either partner during the marriage or de facto relationship. A de facto relationship is defined broadly to include partners who have lived together as a couple for three or more years.[38] Interestingly, the extension of relationship property laws to de facto couples has meant that those who have decided to marry according to Maori custom and conduct their affairs in accordance with Maori custom are caught by the new law. On separation or death, the separating or surviving partner could enforce the equal division provision and take half the couple's relationship property even if this division would be contrary to tikanga Maori. In other words, in the event of a dispute, the courts would decide property division rather than the whanau and hapu (see Ruru 2004c). There is no provision in the law to exempt the application of the regime on the basis that the couple made a conscious decision to marry according to tikanga Maori and therefore any dissolution of the relationship should be based on tikanga Maori.

This example aptly illustrates the starkness of the inconsistent legislative approaches. In summary, a couple married in accordance with tikanga Maori might be successful in jointly adopting a child even though legislation only confers that right on 'spouses'. Upon death, the surviving partner could apply for a half-share of the relationship property not because the law has done an about face and now recognizes Maori customary marriages, but because the nature of the relationship is akin to a de facto relationship.

Nonetheless, the Property (Relationships) Act 1976 affords two examples of where legislation has attempted to cater for Maori customary law. It excludes Maori land from the definition of relationship property,[39] and taonga is excluded from the family chattels' definition.[40] First, in regard to the Maori land exception, all land in New Zealand has one of six statutory statuses: Maori customary land, Maori freehold land, General land, General land owned by Maori, Crown land, and Crown land reserved for Maori.[41] Maori land incorporates Maori customary land and Maori freehold land. While Maori land was not excluded under the Matrimonial Property Act 1963 for marriages ending on death,[42] it was excluded under the Matrimonial Property Act 1976 for marriages ending inter vivos.[43] The new property relationship regime simply extends the exclusion rule to marriages ending on death and those de facto relationships ending on separation or death[44] (see Ruru 2004c). Maori land is excluded from the regime because very little land with this classification remains (it constitutes about five per cent of Aotearoa/New Zealand's landmass) and that which does is sanctioned by legislation to be recognized as a taonga tuku iho of special importance to its Maori owners which should be retained by those who have a blood link to it.[45] Hence Te Ture Whenua Maori Act 1993 (the Maori Land Act 1993) governs the rights to own and inherit Maori land in a very different manner to how other land in Aotearoa/New Zealand is governed. It creates special rules that the new relationship property regime does not disrupt.[46] A surviving spouse or de facto partner can, at most, expect a life interest in Maori freehold land.[47]

Second, in regard to the exclusion of taonga, taonga and heirlooms are excluded from the family chattels definition. This means that they generally fall outside the relationship property pool. The exclusion was an attempt to recognize that special rules should attach to certain chattels which fall more readily into a family treasure category. Signalling out taonga as property that has special cultural and ancestral significance for Maori tribes was a legislative effort to recognize that in accordance with tikanga Maori, 'individuals are not seen as owning such property...a person in possession of taonga is more of a guardian of taonga for the rest of the tribe and for future generations' (Ministry of Justice and Women's Affairs, 1988: 18). If it were a family chattel it would almost invariably be subject to the equal sharing regime and thus potentially pass into the hands of a person who had no tribal connection to it.

In the two instances where the issue of taonga has come before the courts, the judiciary has accepted that even non-Maori can argue that a chattel – in these two cases it was artwork – is a taonga even though the chattel has no Maori association: the artwork was not owned by a Maori person, made by a Maori person, or depicted any aspect of Maori culture.[48] In one of the cases, Mather J simply stated: 'Although it is a Maori word, it describes a relationship between a person or persons and property, and I see no reason why it cannot apply to a person of any ethnic or cultural background'.[49] With the Act failing to define taonga by restricting it to a Maori world-view, the precedent illustrates the vulnerability of Maori and Maori customary law (see Ruru, 2004a).

Overall, the rules relating to marriage and property are haphazard and often contrary to tikanga Maori in that they deny the whanau and hapu the responsibility to mediate and determine rights and responsibilities to property. The rules are based on an ethic that endorses individual rights and ability to own property exclusively. The recent judicial interpretation of taonga is a prime example where the court has adopted the simple literal translation of the word – 'anything highly prized'[50] – without grasping the wider implications of the Maori world being modelled on collective responsibilities.

This case study has illustrated that the legislature, both in the past, and present, is conscience that Maori have a different traditional view of marriage and property rights. But it has also illustrated the need for a comprehensive insight into the interplay between Maori customary law and statute law. Before exploring this policy issue, another case study is considered: children and parenthood.

6. CASE STUDY TWO: CHILDREN AND PARENTHOOD

This case study takes a contemporary glimpse into issues surrounding children and parenthood. Poignantly, most family related statutes, such as the Guardianship Act 1968 and the Adoption Act, are silent on tikanga Maori values and customs and are instead wholly based on the Pakeha nuclear family cultural icon.[51] However, back in 1996, the Family Court was partly successful in altering this mindset.

In *B v M*,[52] the Family Court was confronted with a case that concerned a Maori family whereby the mother wanted to formally adopt out her baby, but the grandmother argued that the baby should be nurtured within the whanau as tikanga Maori required. The customary belief is that the child is 'best placed with those in the hapu or community best able to provide, usually older persons relieved from the exigencies of daily demands, but related in blood so that contact was not denied' (Griffith, 1997: 453). However, in this instance the mother sought to depart from tikanga because she had little faith in her mother providing adequate care for the child.

While the grandmother's action for guardianship failed and the mother's right to adopt out her child succeeded, the Court accepted that when considering the best interests of a child of Maori ancestry, the Court 'must take account of Tikanga Maori'.[53] The landmark decision went on to attack the past fiction surrounding adoption stating, "The umbilical cord is not cut from the natural placenta and united to an adoptive placenta'. It held that, 'The practical effect of an adoption outside the whanau need not necessarily be to distance the adopted child from the whanau or permanently to sever significant links'.[54] This is despite the Adoption Act 1955 clearly stating:

> The adopted child shall be deemed to become the child of the adoptive parent, and the adoptive parent shall be deemed to become the parent of the child, as if the child had been born to that parent in lawful wedlock.[55]

The Court reinterpreted adoption to align more comfortably with the Maori customary practice of adoption (whangai) by stressing that 'an adoption simply adds to the child's family rather than substituting one for the other'.[56] In other words, as the Court stated:

> I did not hear the grandmother or her counsel say that if the child were adopted as the mother has planned, tikanga requires that the child would cease to exist for the whanau, for whatever the law may say the bloodlines remain.[57]

The Maori customary practice of adoption, whangai, has limited legislative recognition. The practice is not accepted under the adoption legislation – in order to become the child's legal parents, formal adoption needs to take place in accordance with the Adoption Act 1955. In fact, the Act could not be any clearer in its denial: section 19(1) states that no person is 'capable of adopting any child in accordance with Maori custom'. Moreover, in 2002, the Court of Appeal settled that a whangai child cannot bring a claim under the Family Protection Act 1955 – a whangai child is not a child within the meaning of section 3 of that Act.[58] The limited recognition relates to Te Ture Whenua Maori Act where under an owner of Maori freehold land is able to devise that land to his or her whangai child.[59]

New advances in medical technology have complicated even more the issue of parenthood.[60] In late November 2004, the Human Assisted Reproductive Technology Act was passed which makes it mandatory for those acting under the Act to consider and treat with respect 'the needs, values, and beliefs of Maori'.[61] Those persons must also gather the information from Maori persons who have donated an embryo or cell relating to their whanau, hapu, and iwi.[62] But, as illuminated in a New Zealand Law Commission (NZLC) discussion report surrounding human assisted reproduction issues, published in early 2004, the implications for Maori may need further examination.

While the NZLC was not asked to explicitly discuss current, and possible future, issues for Maori in relation to legal parenthood, several references were made. The NZLC acknowledged that Maori customary laws exist in regard to parenthood (NZLC, 2004: paras 1.10–12). It recognized that a Maori child's knowledge of his or her whakapapa (genealogy) is critical to his or her sense of identity and place in the world (NZLC, 2004: paras 1.11; 5.17; 5.18). It accepted that for Maori, genetic parents have no exclusive rights to possess their children – they hold them in trust for the whanau, and the wider hapu and iwi (NZLC, 2004: para 1.11). It appreciated from a Maori cultural viewpoint that it is quite normal for a child to have kinship carers who are no less important than the genetic parents (NZLC, 2004: para 1.12). It conceded that a regime of secrecy conflicts with customary values and child-rearing practices of Maori (NZLC, 2004: para 516). It even explicitly stated that Aotearoa/New Zealand's laws as to parental status have never reflected the customary laws and practices of Maori (NZLC, 2004: paras 1.10; 2.18).

Apart from these few observations, the NZLC went little further. Its discussion paper has nevertheless raised an urgent need for the Government to engage with Maori in this debate. For example, while it is true that for Maori it is considered the child's right to know his or her whakapapa, this principle has arisen in a Maori cultural context. This context may be significantly challenged in the new medical environment. In particular, assisted human reproduction procedures pose serious issues for Maori. The childbearing role of women is fundamental to Maori society. Reference need only be made to Maori creation stories: the idea that the earth is personified as our earth mother; the first human born was a woman; and the double and literal meanings and cultural practices associated with childbearing, identity and place in the world order (for example, the word whenua is used in reference to 'placenta/afterbirth' and 'land'). Assisted human reproduction procedures could be said to benefit Maori in that they allow a Maori couple to conceive a child in situations where natural means are impossible and thus allow that couple to gain mana (prestige) through childrearing. However, the procedures could also be said to threaten the sacredness of a woman's body via medical intervention of removing her eggs and implanting in another women, or by implanting sperm in her not of her partner's. The artificial nature of conception may conflict with the fundamentals of tikanga Maori. Additionally, it may threaten the very essence of Maori family cultural values of identity, genealogy, history and so on.

It may be premature to correlate the customary right of the child to know his or her whakapapa in this new contemporary medical era. Therefore, it is not possible to simply assume that a donor-conceived child should have the same cultural rights as a legally adopted child to know his or her genetic background. In fact it may be dangerous to over-emphasize this particular right in this new era. After all, this right to know your parentage sits alongside the cultural rights and obligations of the genetic parents and the extended family, namely that the parents hold the child in trust for the whanau. But assisted human reproduction procedures which mix genetic material via medical intervention potentially threaten these natural family relationships more so than legal adoption ever did. For example, while the genetic make-up of the adopted child is manipulated via a legal fiction after the child has been born, the genetic make-up of the assisted human reproduced child is manipulated at the time when the child was conceived. The later involves conscious individual choices to conceive the child. The former simply involves conscious individual choice(s) to allow another couple to regard the child as their own. For example, in the assisted human reproduction scenario, several competing rights and responsibilities arise between the:

— child's right to know his or her genetic identity;
— individual's right to decide if he or she wants to help another couple conceive, or give birth to, a child;
— individual's right to artificially interfere with his or her body in order to enable another couple to conceive or give birth to a child; and
— individual's extended family's right to know who that child is and take part in his or her upbringing.

At the international law level, New Zealand has ratified a number of documents which would add to this domestic debate. For example, as a party to the *Convention of the Rights of the Child*, New Zealand has recognized that children have a right to know and be cared for by their parents, and to have their identity preserved, including nationality, name and family relations.[63] While Maori customary family law is aligned to these commitments, the present-day medical environment is creating a layered world of issues which require debate. Maori need to be part of these discussions. Of particular importance is the involvement of Maori women. Interestingly, included in New Zealand's most recent four-year report to the United Nations Committee on the Elimination of Discrimination against Women are several statements made by Maori women concerned at their lack of participation in major policy initiatives.[64] It states:

> Maori women were concerned about a lack of recognition by government of their status as tangata whenua and as Treaty partners, in particular: the government using data to articulate Maori women's status from a disadvantage or deprivation perspective, which fails to recognize Maori women's innovation to pursue, develop and control their own solutions and strategies, which enable them to fully participate in an innovative New Zealand capable of sustained social and economic development (Government of New Zealand, 2002: 155).

The report lists several suggestions made by the Maori women to address their concerns, including recognition 'of the status of Maori women within the context of whanau, hapu and iwi, and of the role and value of women in communities' (Government of New Zealand, 2002: 155). It is thus imperative that the government avoids prematurely making assumptions about Maori customary family law without first seeking input from the Maori community.

This case study has focused on issues concerning children and parenthood. Like the first case study, it has highlighted an obvious awareness on behalf of the legislature that Maori have a culture-specific approach to issues relating to the family. However, the present law, and policy papers, are failing to address the issue comprehensively.

7. CONCLUSION

The two case studies have illustrated several points. First, that Maori still practice Maori customary family law. This was evidenced in the discussion of Maori customary marriage and whangai adoption. Second, current law and policy is grappling with ways in which to recognize and provide for Maori customary family law. This was evidenced in the discussion of how Maori land and taonga are excluded from the Property (Relationships) Act 1976. The policy discussions surrounding legal parenthood and assisted human reproduction is also proof of this attempt to accept and provide for Maori custom. Thirdly, while the two case studies have indicated a clear movement away from assimilation, the process is far from complete. This was evidenced in the discussion of how the Property (Relationships) Act 1976 has failed to restrict the taonga exemption to Maori, and the fact that the NZLC's legal parenthood project failed to discuss Maori issues in a thorough manner. Nonetheless, Aotearoa/New Zealand is at a turning point and it is an exciting and positive change to that which has dominated the law in this country for far too long.

The call made here is that it is time for the country to undertake a comprehensive review of how family legislation provides for tikanga Maori. The impetus created by the NZLC's 2001 report, *Maori Custom and Values in New Zealand Law*, for this type of knowledge needs to be embraced and developed. By case studying two areas within family law, this article has illustrated the need for an extensive understanding of the role and place of Maori customary law within the current legislative framework. In order to abandon past assimilationist mindsets, the attempt to provide for Maori customary law must be undertaken in a comprehensive manner. The haphazard approach of current years is not sufficient.

The Treaty of Waitangi should provide the foundation for developing a new platform against which to re-evaluate the law. Judicial dicta in support of this notion exist; the High Court has stated that statutory interpretation should be coloured by the principles of the Treaty and the Family Court has stated that certain issues require tikanga Maori to be taken into account. At the very least this would mean equal respect for both Treaty partner's world-views: Maori and Pakeha. Recent developments in international law provide extra motivation for exploring these issues. Through these starting points, we would become better equipped to answer the two pressing questions: what constitutes Maori customary law in today's society, and, how can legislation provide for it? The two case studies have revealed that there is evidence of support for this type of approach. We are in a legislative era that is attempting to recognize Maori customs and values. Instead of progressing in a piecemeal fashion it is time to come to grips with exactly what should be reflected in the legislation. The time is right to undertake such a policy review.

NOTES

[1] For a definition of indigenous peoples, see Keal P, 2003: 7 where he describes the term as those who have been subjected to colonial settlement, historical continuity with pre-invasion or pre-colonial societies, an identity that is distinct from the dominant society in which they are encased, and a concern with the preservation and replication of culture. Maori fit this definition – they are a people who have been colonized by the British, now constitute only 15 per cent of the population (Pakeha, people of British origin constitute about 75 per cent of the population), and are desperately trying to preserve their culture (for example see Maori language revival initiatives which have lead to the establishment of Maori education institutes ranging from pre-school to territory, and the commonly referred to Wai 262 Flora and Fauna Waitangi Tribunal claim – see

Solomon M, 2005). For an excellent comparison of the consequences of colonization in Australia, Canada, the United States of America, and New Zealand, see Cassidy J, 2003. For a more up-to-date picture of Maori in Aotearoa/New Zealand see Te Puni Kokiri, the Department of Maori Affairs' website at::http://www.tpk.govt.nz/maori/ (accessed 1 December 2004).

[2] For an insight into the issues discussed in this paper in regard to: the USA, see Atwood, 2000 and Estin, 2004; Canada, see Turpel, 1991, Cornet Consulting, 2002, and Women's Issues and Gender Equality Directorate, 2003; and Australia, see Law Reform Commission, 1986, Parkinson, 1994 and Behrendt, 2003. See also work in Lowe and Douglas (1996). In regard to New Zealand family legislation not discussed in this paper: see Hall, D and Metge J, 2002.

[3] The tradition is replicated in the Ngai Tahu Claims Settlement Act 1998, schedule 80. To view New Zealand legislation online: see www.legislation.govt.nz/ (accessed 1 December 2004).

[4] Ngai Tahu Claims Settlement Act 1998, schedule 80.

[5] Initially, the government of New Zealand was in the hands of the British appointed governor and his officials. Pursuant to the New Zealand Constitution Act 1852, parliamentary government was established. To cite a copy of the Treaty of Waitangi: see State Services Commission's website: http://www.treatyofwaitangi.govt.nz/ (accessed 1 December 2004); schedule one of the Treaty of Waitangi Act 1975, or Te Puni Kokiri, 2001.

[6] For example, see Native Lands Act 1862, preamble.

[7] *Wi Parata* v *The Bishop of Wellington* (1877) 3 NZ Jur (NS) 72, at 78.

[8] *Wi Parata*, idem.

[9] Native Lands Act 1865, preamble. The Maori Land Court was referred to as the Native Land Court until the 20th century.

[10] Native Lands Act 1862, preamble.

[11] Today this land is defined as land that is held by Maori in accordance with tikanga Maori: see Te Ture Whenua Maori Act 1993 (the Maori Land Act 1993), s 129(2)(a).

[12] This land is defined as land in which the beneficial ownership of which has been determined by the Maori Land Court by freehold order: see Te Ture Whenua Maori Act 1993, s 129(2)(b).

[13] See Native Land legislation including Native Lands Act 1865; Native Lands Act 1909; Maori Affairs Act 1953. See also account in Waitangi Tribunal. (2004) Tauranga Tangata. Tauranga Whenua. The Report on the Turanganui a Kiwa Claims. (Wai 814), and Williams, 1999. For examples of unfair purchasing practises and/or confiscations see: apologies contained within Crown-iwi settlement legislation: Waikato Raupatu Claims Settlement Act 1995; Ngai Tahu Claims Settlement Act 1998; Te Uri o Hau Claims Settlement Act 2002; Ngati Ruanui Claims Settlement Act 2003.

[14] For an insight into the Maori struggle to gain recognition, see any of the Waitangi Tribunal reports (reports can be accessed on line at http://www.waitangi-tribunal.govt.nz/) or Walker (1990).

[15] Treaty of Waitangi Act 1975. See Waitangi Tribunal website, ibid.

[16] For example, see Resource Management Act 1991, ss 6, 7 and 8.

[17] *Hoani Te Heuheu Tukino* v *Aotea District Maori Land Board* [1941] AC 308.

[18] *New Zealand Maori Council* v *Attorney-General* [1987] 1 NZLR 641 at 655.

[19] *BP* v *D-GSW* [1997] NZFLR 642 at 646 (emphasis added).

[20] *BP* v *D-GSW*, ibid, at 646 (emphasis added).

[21] *New Zealand Maori Council* v *Attorney-General* [1987] 1 NZLR 641 at 667.

[22] *New Zealand Maori Council* v *Attorney-General*, ibid, at 667.

[23] For example, see excellent summary discussion in *Carter Holt Harvey Ltd* v *Te Runanga o Tuwharetoa ki Kawerau* [2002] 2 NZLR 349, at paras 27–31. For a recent Waitangi Tribunal discussion see Waitangi Tribunal (2004) Te Raupatu o Tauranga Moana. Report on the Tauranga Confiscation Claims. (Wai 215). See also Hayward, 2004.

[24] For example, see Draft Declaration of Principles for the Defence of the Indigenous Nations and Peoples of the Western Hemisphere, developed and circulated by indigenous participants at the Non-Governmental Organisation Conference on Discrimination against Indigenous Populations, Geneva, 1977. See United Nations website: http://www.ohchr.org/english/issues/indigenous/ (accessed 1 April 2005), and Anaya (2004).

[25] To cite the amended version see New Zealand Ministry of Foreign Affairs and Trade website at: www.mfat.govt.nz/foreign/humanrights/indigenous/draftdec.html/ (accessed 1 April 2005).

[26] For example, see 'Maori Call for Consultation Over UN Declaration' public letter to Hon. Phil Goff, New Zealand Minister of Foreign Affairs and Trade from Aotearoa Indigenous Rights Trust, dated 6 October 2004 (can view at www.arena.org.nz/ungoff.htm/ (accessed 1 April 2005), and 'Successful Conclusion of the Indigenous Representatives' Hunger Strike and Spiritual Fast at the UN Working Group on the Draft Declaration for the Rights of Indigenous Peoples' (can be viewed at www.converge.org.nz/pma/in021204.html/ (accessed 1 April 2005)).

[27] See New Zealand Ministry of Foreign Affairs and Trade speech to the Permanent Forum on Indigenous Issues, delivered by J. Austin, 17 May 2004 (to cite see www.mfat.govt.nz/speech/past-speeches/speeches2004/17may04.html/ (accessed 1 April 2005).

[28] See Native Land Act 1865, s 30.

[29] 'Papakura: Claim of Succession' *New Zealand Gazette* 12 April 1867, 19.

[30] See Te Ture Whenua Maori Act 1993, s 109.

[31] See Te Ture Whenua Maori Act 1993, ss 214(3) and 214(6).

[32] See Native Land Act 1909, s 140(1) and Maori Affairs Act 1953, ss 121(3) and 122(2).

[33] Maori Affairs Act 1953, s 78.

[34] See Maori Affairs Act 1953, ss 79(2), 119(6).

[35] See Te Ture Whenua Maori Act 1993, s 106(4).

[36] Re Adoption of T (1992) 10 FRNZ 23; [1993] NZFLR 266.

[37] *Re R (Adoption)* (1998) 17 FRNZ 498; [1999] NZFLR 145.

[38] The Property (Relationships) Act 1976, s 2D defines a 'de facto relationship' as a relationship between two persons (whether a man and a woman, or a man and a man, or a woman and a woman) who are both aged 18 years or older, and who live together as a couple, and who are not married to one another. The section goes on to state that in interpreting whether two persons are living together as a couple a range of matters may be relevant including the nature and extent of the common residence, whether or not a sexual relationship exists, and ownership, use and acquisition of property.

[39] Property (Relationships) Act 1976, s 6.

[40] Property (Relationships) Act 1976, s 2 'family chattels'.

[41] Te Ture Whenua Maori Act 1993, s 129.

[42] The statute is silent in regard to Maori land.

[43] Matrimonial Property Act 1976, s 6.

[44] Property (Relationships) Act 1976, s 6 states 'Nothing in this Act shall apply in respect of any Maori land within the meaning of Te Ture Whenua Maori Act 1993'.

[45] Te Ture Whenua Maori Act 1993, preamble and ss 2; 17.

[46] See Te Ture Whenua Maori Act 1993, ss 99–121.

[47] Te Ture Whenua Maori Act 1993, ss 108(4); 109(2).

[48] See *Perry* v *West* 25 March 2003; DC Waitakere, FP 239/01; *Perry* v *West* 15/12/03; Laurenson J; HC Auckland CIV-2003-404-2114; *Page* v *Page* (2001) 21 FRNZ 275; Ruru, 2004a.

[49] *Perry v West* 25 March 2003, DC Waitakere, FP 239/01, at para 89.

[50] See *Perry* v *West*, ibid, at para 88.

[51] An exception is the Care of Children Act 2004. For example, it recognizes the child's potential relationship with his/her whanau, hapu or iwi. The Act came into force on 1 July 2005.

[52] *B* v *M* [1997] NZFLR 126.

[53] *B* v *M*, ibid, at 133.

[54] *B* v *M*, ibid, at 135.

[55] Adoption Act 1955, s 16(2).

[56] *B* v *M* [1997] NZFLR 126 at 135.

[57] *B* v *M* idem.

[58] *Keelan* v *Peach* [2003] 1 NZLR 589.

[59] Te Ture Whenua Maori Act 1993, s 108.

[60] For a discussion of New Zealand's current position see Parker, 2004. For a comparison with the UK see Probert, 2004.

[61] Human Assisted Reproductive Technology Act 2004, s 4.

[62] Human Assisted Reproductive Technology Act 2004, ss 47(1)(h); 63(2)(h).

[63] See articles 6 and 7. To cite a copy of the Convention see United Nation's website at: www.ohchr.org/english/bodies/crc/index.html (accessed 1 April 2005).

[64] New Zealand ratified the Convention on the Elimination of All Forms of Discrimination against Women in 1985. To cite a copy of the Convention see United Nation's website at: www.un.org/womenwatch/saw/cedaw/text/econvention.html/ (accessed 1 April 2005).

REFERENCES

Anaya, J. (2004). *Indigenous Peoples in International Law.* 2nd edn, New York: Oxford University Press.

Atwood, B. (2000) 'Tribal jurisprudence and cultural meanings of the family' 79 *Nebraska Law Review* 577.

Ballara, A. (1993) 'Wahine Rangatira: Maori women of rank and their role in the women's kotahitanga movement of the 1890s', 27 *New Zealand Journal of History* 127.

Behrendt, L. (2003) *Achieving Social Justice: Indigenous Rights and Australia's Future*, Sydney: The Federation Press.

Cassidy, J. (2003) 'The legacy of colonialism'51 *The American Journal of Comparative Law* 409.

Chadwick, J. (2002) 'Whanaungatanga and the family court' 4 *Butterworths Family Law Bulletin* 91.

Cornet Consulting and Mediation. Cornet, W. and Lendor, A. (2002) *Discussion Paper: Matrimonial Real Property on Reserve*. Prepared under contract for the Women's Issues and Gender Equality Directorate of the Department of Indian Affairs and Northern Development: report can be downloaded at www.ainc-inac.gc.ca/pr/pub/matr/int_e.html (accessed 1 December 2004).

Department of Social Welfare. (1986) *Puao-te-ata-tu: The Report of the Ministerial Advisory Committee on a Maori Perspective for the Department of Social Welfare* Wellington: Government Printer.

Estin, A. (2004) 'Embracing tradition: Pluralism in American family law' 63 *Maryland Law Review* 540.

Government of New Zealand. (2002) *Consideration of reports submitted by States parties under article 18 of the Convention on the Elimination of All Forms of Discrimination against Women. Fifth periodic report of State parties. New Zealand.* (report can be downloaded at: www.un.org/womenwatch/daw/cedaw (accessed 1 April 2005).

Griffith, K. (1997) *New Zealand Adoption: History and Practice, Social and Legal, 1840–1996*, Wellington: KC Griffith.

Hall, D. and Metge, J. (2002) 'Kua Tutu Te Puehu, Kia Mau: Maori aspirations and family law' in M. Henaghan and W. Atkin (ed), *Family Law Policy in New Zealand*, 2nd edn, Chap 2, Auckland: Oxford University Press.

Hayward, J. (2004) 'Flowing from the treaty words: The principles of the Treaty of Waitangi' in J. Hayward and N. Wheen (ed), *The Waitangi Tribunal: Te Roopu Whakamana I te Tiriti o Waitangi*, Chap 3, Wellington: Bridget Williams Books.

Henare, M. (1994) 'Te Tiriti, te tangata, te whanau: the Treaty, the human person, the family'. Paper presented at the International Year of the Family Symposium on Rights and Responsibilities of the Family held in Wellington, 14–16 October. Quoted by F. Cram and S. Pitama in 'Ko Tuku whanau, ko toku mana' in V. Adair and R. Dixon (ed) (1998) *The Family in Aotearoa New Zealand*, Chap 3, Auckland: Addison Wesley Longman NZ Ltd.

Keal, P. (2003) *European Conquest and the Rights of Indigenous Rights: The Moral Backwardness of International Society*, Cambridge: Cambridge University Press.

Law Reform Commission (Australia) (1986) *The Recognition of Aboriginal Customary Laws*. Report No. 31. Canberra: Law Reform Commission. (Report can be downloaded at: www.austlii.edu.au/au/other/IndigLRes/1986/1/index.html (accessed 1 December 2004).

Lowe, N. and Douglas, G. (ed). (1996) *Families across Frontiers*, The Hague: Kluwer Law International.

Mikaere, A, (1994) 'Maori women: Caught in the contradictions of a colonised reality' 2 *Waikato Law Review* 125.

Ministry of Justice and Women's Affairs. (1988) *Report of the Working Group on Matrimonial Property and Family Protection*. Wellington: Ministry of Justice and Women's Affairs.

New Zealand Law Commission. (2004) *Preliminary Paper 54: New Issues in Legal Parenthood. A discussion paper*. Wellington: New Zealand Law Commission.

New Zealand Law Commission. (2001) *Study Paper 9. Maori Custom and Values in New Zealand Law.* Wellington: New Zealand Law Commission.

Parker, S. (2004) 'Legal parentage of children conceived through reproductive technology: Mistaken conception and the law', *Butterworths Family Law Journal* 289.

Parkinson, P. (1994) 'Taking multiculturalism seriously: Marriage law and the rights of minorities' 16 *Sydney Law Review* 473.

Probert, R (2004) 'Families, assisted reproduction and the law' 16 *Child and Family Law Quarterly* 273.

Roberts, M., Norman W., Winhinnick N., Wihongi D., and C. Kirkwood (1995) 'Kaitiakitanga: Maori perspectives on conservation' 2 *Pacific Conservation Biology* 7.

Ruru, J. (2004a) 'Taonga and family chattels', *New Zealand Law Journal* 297.

Ruru, J. (2004b) 'Implications for Maori: Historical overview' in, Peart, N., Briggs, M., Henaghan, M., Ruru, J., Griffith, S., Beck, A. and A. Belcher *Relationship Property on Death*, Chap 16, Wellington: Brookers.

Ruru, J. (2004c) 'Implications for Maori: Contemporary overview' in, Peart, N., Briggs, M., Henaghan, M., Ruru, J., Griffith, S., Beck, A. and A. Belcher *Relationship Property on Death*, Chap 17, Wellington, Brookers.

Solomon, M. (2005) 'The Wai 262 Claim: A claim by Maori to indigenous flora and fauna: Me o Ratou Tanga Kotoa' in Belgrave, M., Kowharu, M. and D. Williams *Waitangi Revisited: Perspectives on the Treaty of Waitangi*, Chap 12, South Melbourne: Oxford University Press..

Te Puni Kokiri. (2001) *He Tirohanga Kawa ki te Tiriti o Waitangi: A Guide to the Principles of the Treaty of Waitangi as expressed by the Courts and the Waitangi Tribunal*, Wellington: Te Puni Kokiri.

Tohe, P. (1998) 'Maori jurisprudence: The neglect of Tapu' 8 *Auckland University Law Review* 884.

Turpel, M. (1991) 'Critical perspectives on family law: Race, gender, class' 10 *Canadian Journal of Family Law* 17.

Walker, R. (1990) *Ka Whawahi Tonu Matou: Struggle Without End*, Auckland: Penguin Books.

Williams, D. (1999) *Te Kooti Tango Whenua: The Native Land Court 1864–1909*, Wellington: Huia Publishers.

[17]

EVOLVING INDIGENOUS LAW: NAVAJO MARRIAGE–CULTURAL TRADITIONS AND MODERN CHALLENGES

Antoinette Sedillo Lopez*

I. INTRODUCTION

Since European contact, the Navajo Nation[1] has struggled to reclaim and continue its culture and manage its own affairs.[2] Native American[3] governments and court systems, modeled after systems in the United States, were required and established by the U.S. government as a way to assimilate native peoples.[4] However, through the creation of substantive law and dispute resolution processes that respect traditional culture, the Navajo Nation uses its legal system to continue

---

* Henry Weihofen Professor of Law, University of New Mexico; Bachelors 1979, University of New Mexico; J.D., 1982, University of California, Los Angeles. I would like to thank my colleagues Gloria Valencia-Weber and Christine Zuni Cruz for everything they have taught me about indigenous law. I also appreciate the conversations with Eric Swenson, Mary Ann Shorthair Swenson, James Zion, and my colleague Kip Bobroff. Janet Yazzie is owed my appreciation for the Navajo law she brought to my Family Law course. The summer research support provided by Dean Robert Desiderio was very much appreciated. An earlier version of this paper was presented at the International Society of Family Law, North American Regional Conference, Albuquerque, New Mexico, June 11, 1999.

1. The Navajo Nation is located on the Colorado Plateau and covers over 25,000 square miles in northeast Arizona, northwest New Mexico, and southeast Utah. It has approximately 250,000 members. Means v. District Court of the Chinle Judicial District, 26 Indian L. Rep. 6083, 6084 (Navajo Nation S. Ct. 1999).

2. For a review of the history of U.S. policy toward indigenous peoples, *see* Christine Zuni, *Strengthening What Remains*, 7 KAN. J.L. & PUB. POL'Y 17 (1997); Bethany Ruth Berger, *After Pocahontas: Indian Women and the Law: 1830 to 1934*, 21 AM. INDIAN L. REV. 1 (1997) (reviewing the history of federal policy toward Indians, particularly as it affected Indian women). For a historical perspective on the law of the native peoples of the Americas, *see* James W. Zion & Robert Yazzie, *Indigenous Law in North America in the Wake of Conquest*, 20 B.C. INT'L & COMP. L. REV. 55 (1997).

3. The author is aware that some indigenous peoples who live within the borders of the United States prefer the term Native American, some prefer the term American Indian, and most prefer to use their specific tribal affiliation. In this article the terms "Native American" and "Indian" are used interchangeably to refer to indigenous peoples who are enrolled members of a federally recognized tribe.

4. *See* AMERICANIZING THE AMERICAN INDIANS 295, 297 (Francis Paul Prucha ed., 1973). The author describes the creation of Indian courts by the Department of the Interior to criminalize traditional Indian legal practices that were inconsistent with European cultural norms. One of the "crimes and misdemeanors" punishable in the first courts was the practice of polygamy. *Id. See also*, FRANCIS PAUL PRUCHA, AMERICAN INDIAN POLICY IN CRISIS: CHRISTIAN REFORMERS AND THE INDIAN, 1865-1900, 22, 155, 208, 209 (1976).

its quest for sovereignty[5] and self-determination.[6] Thus, as is the case with most groups that have experienced imperialism and conquest,[7] the Navajo Nation uses the language and legal tools of the dominant culture[8] to recover and preserve its own culture.[9]

The Navajo Nation has been forever changed because of its experience with the Spaniards[10] and the Anglo-American United States.[11] While the Navajo Nation can never fully retrieve its pre-contact culture and way of life, it can create a space where Navajo people can manage their own affairs, plan their destiny, and evolve as a culture.[12] Tribal law and tribal courts can be a mechanism for doing

---

5. Sovereignty is a critical concept for tribes. *See, e.g.*, Rebecca Tsosie, *Separate Sovereigns, Civil Rights, and the Sacred Text: The Legacy of Justice Thurgood Marshall's Indian Law Jurisprudence*, 26 ARIZ. ST. L.J. 495 (1994); ROBERT A. WILLIAMS, JR., LINKING ARMS TOGETHER: AMERICAN INDIAN TREATY VISIONS OF LAW AND PEACE, 1600-1800 (1997).

6. *See* James M. Zion, *The Navajo Peacemaker Court: Deference to the Old and Accommodation to the New*, 11 AM. INDIAN L. REV. 89 (1983). Frank Pommersheim has written, "[t]ribal courts do not exist solely to reproduce or replicate the dominant canon appearing in state and federal courts. If they did, the process of colonization would be complete and the unique legal cultures of the tribes fully extirpated." (footnote omitted). FRANK POMMERSHEIM, BRAID OF FEATHERS, AMERICAN INDIAN LAW AND CONTEMPORARY TRIBAL LIFE 99 (1995). *See also*, Alex Tallchief Skibine, *Book Review: Braid of Feathers: Pluralism, Legitimacy, Sovereignty, and the Importance of Tribal Court Jurisprudence*, 96 COLUM. L. REV. 557, (1996); Lis Wiehl, *Indian Courts Struggling to Keep Their Identity*, N.Y. TIMES, Nov. 4, 1988, at B7.

7. *See generally* LATINOS IN THE UNITED STATES: HISTORY, LAW AND PERSPECTIVE (Antoinette Sedillo Lopez ed., 1995) (six volume anthology of articles written in English by Latino scholars regarding issues facing Latino people including the loss of their language).

8. *See, e.g.*, Antoinette Sedillo Lopez, *Colonization*, II CIRCLES: A JOURNAL OF LAW AND WOMEN STUDIES 42 (1993); Antoinette Sedillo Lopez, *Evolution*, XIX LA HERENCIA, Fall 1998, at 22.

9. *See generally* Robert Yazzie, *Law School as a Journey*, 46 ARK. L. REV. 271 (1993) (describing the process of law school acculturation and the need to use what has been learned to recover culture).

10. *See generally* Estrella Ramos Garrido, *Matrimonio de Indios y Legislacion Canonica Ante El Descubrimiento de America*, II REVISTA DE DERECHO CANONICO, UNIVERSIDAD DE SALAMANCA (Mayo 1998) (discussing Indian marital customs and the efforts of the Catholic Church to change Indian customs regarding marriage customs).

11. *See*, THE NATIVE AMERICANS, THE INDIGENOUS PEOPLES OF NORTH AMERICA, 55-61 (Richard Collins et al. eds., 1991) giving an overview of European contact with Navajo people).

12. *See* Virginia H. Murray, *A Comparative Survey of the Historic Civil, Common, and American Indian Tribal Law Responses to Domestic Violence*, 23 OKLA. CITY U. L. REV. 433, 445-46, 451-53 (1998).

so.[13] Over the last century, the Navajo Nation has developed a three-branch government structure,[14] a tribal court system,[15] and a comprehensive tribal code.[16]

Tribal regulation of marriage is an example of the tribal government and tribal court using the legal system to reclaim traditional values and to resist (at least in part) the dominant values imposed on the Navajo Nation. Identity as Diné (the Navajo's[17] term to refer to themselves) is based on clan affiliations,[18] which

---

13. *See generally* Robert Yazzie, *Indigenous Renacence: Law, Culture & Society in the 21st Century, Navajo Peacekeeping, Technology and Traditional Indian Law*, 10 ST.THOMAS L. REV. 95, 101 (1997). *See also* Frank Pommersheim, *Coyote Paradox: Some Indian Law Reflections from the Edge of the Prairie*, 31 ARIZ. ST. L.J. 439, 453-455 (1999).

14. For an overview of the Navajo Nation governmental offices and a directory of officers see the Navajo Nation's web site (visited May 30, 1999) <http://www.navajo.org/nnhomepg.html>.

15. The Navajo Nation operates a two level court system: the trial courts (including peacemaker courts) and the Navajo Nation Supreme Court. Cases are initiated in the tribal courts and appeals of trial court decisions are made to the Navajo Nation Supreme Court, which is located in Window Rock, Arizona. The Navajo courts handle over 90,000 cases a year. *See* Gloria Valencia-Weber, *Tribal Courts: Custom and Innovative Law*, 24 N.M. L. REV. 225, 232-33 (1994). For a discussion of state and federal recognition of tribal court orders and decrees *see* Gordon K. Wright, *Recognition of Tribal Decisions in State Courts*, 37 STAN. L. REV. 1397 (1985), and Gloria Valencia-Weber *Shrinking Indian Country: A State Offensive to Divest Tribal Sovereignty*, 27 CONN. L. REV. 1281 (1995).

16. The first western courts were introduced to the Navajo Nation in 1892. *See* SIXTY-FIRST ANNUAL REPORT OF THE COMMISSIONER OF INDIAN AFFAIRS TO THE SECRETARY OF THE INTERIOR 209 (1892). The contemporary Navajo Nation courts were created in 1959 and reconstituted in 1985. *See* Robert Yazzie, *"Life Comes From It": Navajo Justice Concepts*, 24 N.M. L. REV. 175, 177 (1994). As Chief Justice Yazzie points out in his article, most courts of the Navajo Nation use an adversarial model of adjudication, which is not consistent with the traditional healing approach of Navajo concepts of justice. Justice Yazzie has been a tireless advocate of using the court system to recover and preserve traditional Navajo culture.

17. The word "Navajo" comes from a Tewa word, "Navahuu," meaning cultivated field in an arroyo. *See* THE NATIVE AMERICANS: THE INDIGENOUS PEOPLE OF NORTH AMERICA 55 (Richard Collins et al. eds., 1991).

18. *See* In the Matter of the Estate of Apachee, 4 Navajo Rep. 178, 182 (Window Rock D. Ct. 1983):

> [T]he Navajo clan system is very important, with a child being of the mother's clan and "born for" the father's clan. The clan is important, and the family as an economic unit is vital. The Navajo live together in family groups which can include parents, children, grandparents, brothers and sisters, and all the members of the family group have important duties to each other. These duties are based on the need to survive and upon very important religious values which command each to support each other and the group.

are determined by blood and marriage.[19] Marriage has been an important and sacred institution in Navajo tradition.[20] The Navajo Supreme Court and the Tribal Council have attempted to find a substantive law of marriage that respects traditional Navajo culture[21] while meeting contemporary needs of Navajo people. The Navajo Nation's legal regulation of marriage has changed over time in a struggle to balance respect for sacred tradition and the needs of contemporary Navajo people.[22] Ultimately, the Navajo Supreme Court and Tribal Council developed marital tribal law in a way that resists, at least in part, dominant Anglo-American cultural values concerning marriage and meets the needs of the Navajo people.

This article first describes the role of tribal courts in recovering tribal values, and then describes the history of the Navajo legal system.[23] Although the legal system was imposed on Navajos by the federal government, the Navajos have increasingly used it to preserve and recover Navajo cultural values. Second, the article reviews the history of marital regulation on the Navajo Reservation.[24] In arriving at its current law the Navajo Nation faced two struggles in preserving

---

Id. at 182.

19. *See generally*, GARY WITHERSPOON, NAVAJO KINSHIP AND MARRIAGE (1975).

20. Hozho in a marriage is the state of affairs where everything is in its proper place and functioning in harmonious relationship to everything else. *See* Kuwanhyoima v. Kuwanhyoima, No. TC CV-334-84 (Tuba City D. Ct. 1990), *aff'd on other grounds, opinion approved*, No. A-CV-13-90 (Navajo Nation S. Ct. 1990).

21. Traditional Navajo culture is a matrilineal society. The Navajo creation story articulates that major differences between men and women justify different roles. In the story, Changing Woman explains the differences between men and women when she makes her demands on the sun:

> Remember that I willingly let you send your rays into my body. Remember that I gave birth to your son, enduring pain to bring him into the world. Remember that I gave that child growth and protected him from harm. . . . Remember, as different as we are, you and I, we are of one spirit. As dissimilar as we are, you and I, we are of equal worth. As unlike as you and I are, there must always be solidarity between the two of us.

PAUL G. ZOLBROD, DINÉ BAHANÉ: THE NAVAJO CREATION STORY 275 (1984). *See also generally* WITHERSPOON, *supra* note 19.

22. *See infra* notes 60-141 and accompanying text. This paper will look at the legal issue of marriage law in Navajo country in its legal, historical, and cultural context. *See* Antoinette Sedillo Lopez, *A Comparative Analysis of Women's Issues: Toward a Contextualized Methodology*, 10 HASTINGS W. L. J. 343 (1999) (proposing a four step approach to comparative analysis which takes cultural context, legal context, history, and perspective into account).

23. *See infra* notes 30-59 and accompanying text.

24. *See infra* notes 60-141 and accompanying text.

its values. The first struggle was with the federal government and its policy of assimilation.[25] The second struggle was with itself in trying to recover and determine its own values about the marital relationship.[26] The Navajo Nation has balanced respect for Navajo tradition with contemporary realities of the Navajo people. The Navajo Supreme Court and Tribal Council have fused Navajo traditional concepts and Anglo-American concepts to recover and preserve Navajo heritage in its marriage law.[27] Third, the article looks at state and federal marriage regulation.[28] States recognize many marriage-like relationships and "foreign" marriages including marriages under tribal law.[29] State and federal authorities must continue to respect Navajo authority over domestic matters and allow Navajo law to evolve pursuant to tribal values.

II. THE ROLE AND WORK OF TRIBAL COURTS

Scholars have evaluated and discussed the work of tribal courts.[30] Frank Pommersheim describes the work of the tribal courts as having to "transcend the

---

25. *See infra* notes 29-39 and accompanying text.

26. *See infra* notes 60-141 and accompanying text.

27. Comparative work often involves studying the impact of one legal system and culture on another legal system and culture. *See, e.g.*, DAVID J. LANGUM, LAW AND COMMUNITY ON THE MEXICAN CALIFORNIA FRONTIER: ANGLO-AMERICAN EXPATRIATES AND THE CLASH OF LEGAL TRADITIONS, 1821-1846 (1987) (comparing the Mexican legal system and the Anglo American legal system and describing their impact on each other when Anglo-Americans settled in the Mexican territory of California in the early 1800s).

28. *See infra* notes 142-158 and accompanying text.

29. *See infra* notes 159-168 and accompanying text.

30. *See, e.g.*, Michael Taylor, *Modern Practice in the Indian Courts*, 10 U. PUGET SOUND L. REV. 231 (1987) (discussing choice of law, jurisdiction, procedural and substantive issues frequently arising in tribal courts and enforcement of judgments); Frank Pommersheim & Terry Pechota, *Tribal Immunity, Tribal Courts, and the Federal System: Emerging Contours and Frontiers*, 31 S.D. L. REV. 553 (1986); Frank Pommersheim, *The Contextual Legitimacy of Adjudication in Tribal Courts and the Role of the Tribal Bar as an Interpretive Community: An Essay*, 18 N.M. L. REV. 49 (1988); FRANK POMMERSHEIM, BRAID OF FEATHERS: AMERICAN INDIAN LAW AND CONTEMPORARY TRIBAL LIFE (1995); Robert Laurence, *The Enforcement of Judgments Across Indian Reservation Boundaries: Full Faith and Credit, Comity, and the Indian Civil Rights Act*, 69 OR. L. REV. 589, 594-99 (1990) (arguing that tribal courts need not give full faith and credit to state court judgments); Gloria Valencia-Weber, *Tribal Courts: Custom and Innovative Law*, 24 N.M. L. REV. 225 (1994) (examining tribal courts role and the use of custom in tribal court cases); Christine Zuni, *The Southwest Intertribal Court of Appeals*, 24 N.M. L. REV. 309 (1994) (detailing the appellate jurisdiction of Southwest Indian Tribal Courts of Appeals; Nell Jessup Newton, *Memory and Misrepresentation: Representing Crazy Horse in Tribal Court*, 27 CONN. L. REV. 1003 (1995) (discussing the role of tribal courts in creating community identity in a dispute brought in tribal court by the Estate of Crazy Horse); Robert B. Porter, *Strengthening Tribal Sovereignty Through Peacemaking: How the Anglo-*

ravages of colonialism, while simultaneously animating traditional values in contemporary circumstances."[31] He states that some of the "tools for this work include language, narrative, and the pursuit of justice."[32] He urges tribal courts to use language carefully with an indigenous perspective, because the language and law of the colonizer is inherently suspect.[33] He believes that tribal courts should use narrative and storytelling to tell the counter-stories and save their traditions.[34] Finally, tribal courts should find their own meaning of justice that respects and cherishes their cultural identity.[35] While these suggestions are wise, tribal courts must also use the tribal legal system and its substantive law[36] to resist the

---

American Legal Tradition Destroys Indigenous Societies, 28 COLUM. HUM. RTS. L. REV. 235 (1997) (arguing that adoption of Anglo-American norms in tribal courts threatens tribal sovereignty); Nell Jessup Newton, *Praxis, A Year in the life of Tribal Courts*. 22 AM. INDIAN L. REV. 225 (1998). Finally, in 1995, the Journal of the American Judicature Society devoted an entire issue to tribal courts. *Indian Tribal Courts and Justice*, JUDICATURE, Nov.-Dec. 1995, at 110.

31. Frank Pommersheim, *Liberation, Dreams, and Hard Work: An Essay on Tribal Court Jurisprudence*, 1992 WIS. L. REV. 411, 424.

32. *Id* at 424.

33. *See id* at 425.

34. *See id.*

35. This will avoid the process of assimilation and the loss of important cultural values. *See* Kirke Kickingbird, "*In Our Image. . . After Our Likeness:" The Drive for the Assimilation of Indian Court Systems*, 13 AM. CRIM. L. REV. 675 (1976).

36. This article seeks to contribute to the growing body of scholarship examining indigenous law. *See, e.g.*, Ralph W. Johnson & James M. Madden, *Sovereign Immunity in Indian Tribal Law*, 12 AM. INDIAN L. REV. 153 (1987) (examining tribal law and court decisions concerning sovereign immunity); Michael Taylor, *Modern Practice in the Indian Courts*, 10 U. PUGET SOUND L. REV. 231 (1987) (discussing choice of law, jurisdiction, procedural and substantive issues frequently arising in tribal courts and enforcement of judgments); Frank Pommersheim & Terry Pechota, *Tribal Immunity, Tribal Courts, and the Federal System: Emerging Contours and Frontiers*, 31 S.D. L. REV. 553 (1986); Frank Pommersheim, *The Contextual Legitimacy of Adjudication in Tribal Courts and the Role of the Tribal Bar as an Interpretive Community: An Essay*, 18 N.M. L. REV. 49 (1988); FRANK POMMERSHEIM, BRAID OF FEATHERS: AMERICAN INDIAN LAW AND CONTEMPORARY TRIBAL LIFE (1995); Robert Laurence, *The Enforcement of Judgments Across Indian Reservation Boundaries: Full Faith and Credit, Comity, and the Indian Civil Rights Act*, 69 OR. L. REV. 589, 594-99 (1990) (arguing that tribal courts need not give full faith and credit to state court judgments); Michael D. Lieder, *Navajo Dispute Resolution and Promissory Obligations: Continuity and Change in the Largest Native American Nation*, 18 AM. INDIAN L. REV. 1 (1993) (examining issues decided by Navajo customary law and asserting that customary law is not used in deciding transactional matters); Vicki J. Limas, *Employment Suits Against Indian Tribes: Balancing Sovereign Rights and Civil Rights*, 70 DENV. U. L. REV. 359 (1993) (analyzing tribal court sovereign immunity decisions); Daniel L. Lowery, Comment, *Developing a Tribal Common Law Jurisprudence: The Navajo Experience*, 1969-1992, 18 AM. INDIAN L. REV. 379 (1993) (examining the use of Navajo common law in criminal law, family law, property, torts, contracts, and individual rights cases); James W. Zion & Elsie B. Zion, *Hozho' Sokee'—Stay Together Nicely: Domestic*

imposition of dominant values and law, and find solutions that come from the tribe's own values and beliefs.[37] An important purpose of the tribal courts is to meet the needs of their communities by deciding cases in a manner that creates respect for the court and acceptance by the community. The tribe must find a way to create its own solutions to contemporary problems. This may ultimately require transforming substantive laws and procedural devices that have been imposed on tribes as well as adapting traditional customs.

The English language may pose a barrier to the recovery of tribal cultural values because it may not adequately express the Navajo values sought to be applied in the court system.[38] Therefore, the court should (and does) use the appropriate Navajo term in its analysis when necessary to convey the intended

---

Violence Under Navajo Common Law, 25 ARIZ. ST. L.J. 407 (1993) (examining Navajo Courts' treatment of family violence cases); Gloria Valencia-Weber, *Tribal Courts: Custom and Innovative Law*, 24 N.M. L. REV. 225 (1994) (examining the use of custom in tribal court cases); Christine Zuni, *The Southwest Intertribal Court of Appeals*, 24 N.M. L. REV. 309 (1994) (detailing the appellate jurisdiction of SWITCA); Robert Laurence, *Dominant-Society Law and Tribal Court Adjudication*, 25 N.M. L. REV. 1 (1995) (analyzing potential and actual tribal court deviations from dominant society law rooted in formalism in the areas of double jeopardy, sovereign immunity from suit, and ex parte communications); Nell Jessup Newton, *Memory and Misrepresentation: Representing Crazy Horse in Tribal Court*, 27 CONN. L. REV. 1003 (1995) (discussing the role of tribal courts in constituting community identity in a dispute brought in tribal court by the Estate of Crazy Horse); Gloria Valencia-Weber & Christine P. Zuni, *Domestic Violence and Tribal Protection of Indigenous Women in the United States*, 69 ST. JOHN'S L. REV. 69 (1995) (describing the importance of tribal sovereignty and contrasting indigenous and Anglo legal perspectives on dispute resolution and comparing the codes and case law of fourteen tribes with regard to domestic violence); Christian M. Freitag, Note, *Putting Martinez to the Test: Tribal Court Disposition of Due Process*, 72 IND. L.J. 831 (1997) (analyzing the notion of due process in tribal courts); Robert B. Porter, *Strengthening Tribal Sovereignty Through Peacemaking: How the Anglo-American Legal Tradition Destroys Indigenous Societies* 28 COLUM. HUM. RTS. L. REV. 235 (1997) (arguing that adoption of Anglo norms in tribal courts endangers tribal sovereignty); Nell Jessup Newton, *Praxis, A Year in the Life of Tribal Courts* 22 AM. INDIAN L. REV. 285 (1998); Robert J. McCarthy, *Civil Rights in Tribal Courts: The Indian Bill of Rights at Thirty Years*, 34 IDAHO L. REV. 465 (1994) (examining the impact of the Indian Civil Rights on tribal law); Barbara Ann Atwood, *Identity and Assimilation: Changing Definitions of Tribal Power Over Children*, 4 MINN. L. REV. 927 (1999) (describing how tribes may give up cultural values and jurisdiction in child custody determinations if they adopt jurisdictional principles to accommodate the principles of the Uniform Child Custody Jurisdiction and Enforcement Act).

37. *See* EDWARD W. SAID, CULTURE AND IMPERIALISM 281-336 (1993). Professor Said has described how native writers have engaged in the process of cultural decolonization by creating works of literature which expose the mechanism of control and repression of their people. In doing so these native writers reclaim for their peoples the right of self determination. *See id.*

38. *See* Antoinette Sedillo Lopez, *Translating Legal Terms In Context*, 17(4) LEGAL REFERENCE SERVICES Q. 105 (1999) (illustrating how context is necessary in understanding meaning of legal terms).

meaning.[39] To support the work of the tribal court in preserving Navajo culture and sovereignty, state and federal courts must respect the Navajo tribal court system and its jurisdiction over internal matters on the reservation.[40]

III. IMPOSITION OF WESTERN LEGAL SYSTEM ON THE DINE

Prior to European contact, Navajo law was based on Navajo religious and cultural beliefs. Law was not created by man as a control mechanism but came from the deities as part of the Navajo way of life.[41] Navajo mechanisms for resolving disputes relied on wise elders and community involvement.[42] Traditional cultural practices did not include a formal court system.[43]

The treaty of 1868[44] established the current Navajo reservation after a disastrous attempt by the federal government to intern the Navajo people away from their homeland.[45] After setting up the reservation on the homeland of the Navajo people, the federal government set up a Court of Indian Offenses on the reservation.[46] These courts began their existence as puppets of the federal government. Anglo-American law was imposed in large part to assimilate Navajos.[47] In 1934 the Navajo Nation refused to accept the Indian Reorganization Act and did not adopt a Bureau of Indian Affairs (BIA) designed constitution.[48]

---

39. *See, e.g.*, Means v. District Court of the Chinle Judicial District, 26 Indian L. Rep. 6083, 6087 (Navajo Nation S. Ct. 1999) (describing an individual who marries or has an intimate relationship with a Navajo as a *hadane* (in law) in Navajo language and culture).

40. Of course there are other legal theories for recognizing tribal court judgments such as full faith and credit. *See, e.g.*, David S. Clark, *State Court Recognition of Tribal Court Judgements: Securing the Blessings of Civilization,* 23 OKLA. CITY U. L. REV 353 (1998). The author's position is based on a theory of inherent tribal sovereignty and the tribe's right to control its own affairs and the status of its members. *See infra* Part V.

41. *See* DAN VICENTI, ET AL., THE LAW OF THE PEOPLE—DINE BIBEE HAZ'AANII: A BICULTURAL APPROACH TO LEGAL EDUCATION FOR NAVAHO STUDENTS 116 (1972).

42. *See* MARY SHEPARDSON, NAVAJO WAYS IN GOVERNMENT: A STUDY OF POLITICAL PROCESS 47-48, 51, 78 (1963); Lieder, *supra* note 36, at 15.

43. *See* SHEPARDSON, *supra* note 42.

44. Treaty Between the United States and the Navajo Tribe, June 1, 1868, 15 Stat. 667.

45. *See, e.g.*, BRODERICK JOHNSON, NAVAJO STORIES OF THE LONG WALK PERIOD (1973) (compiling stories told by Navajos who endured the long walk); L. R. BAILEY, THE LONG WALK: A HISTORY OF THE NAVAJO WARS, 1846-68 (1964) (detailing slave raids, sheep men, careless administration of Indian and military affairs resulting in Navajo-U.S. hostilities, and the resolution of those hostilities—internment at Ft. Sumner in New Mexico).

46. *See* Laurence Davis, *Court Reform in the Navajo Nation*, 43 J. AM. JUDICATURE SOC'Y 52 (1959).

47. *See* VICENTI ET AL., *supra* note 41, at 138, 141, 155.

48. *See* Lieder, *supra* note 36, at 37.

However, the Navajo Nation created a governmental structure in response to the federal requirement to develop "modern" governments.[49] Navajo anger at a federal stock reduction program implemented on the reservation led to the Navajos beginning to take over and control the puppet governmental structure in the 1930s.[50]

In 1959 the Navajo Tribal Council created a judicial branch of its government.[51] The tribe had become concerned that if it did not have a legal system modeled on the Anglo-American system in place in the United States, states would begin to assume jurisdiction on the reservation.[52] The concern was highlighted in the case of *Williams v. Lee*[53] when a trader attempted to sue in state court to collect a debt of a Navajo couple residing on the reservation.[54] In reversing the state court case and upholding the exclusive jurisdiction of the tribal court, the United States Supreme Court emphasized the tribe's improvement in the quality of its legal system in resources and training of personnel.[55]

Currently, the Navajo court system includes seven district courts, five family courts, and a fully staffed Supreme Court.[56] The system serves over 143,000 people who live on over 25,000 square miles in Arizona, New Mexico, and Utah on the Navajo Nation.[57] Scholars have noted that the more a tribal court system looks like the Anglo-American system[58] the more it will be respected by the dominant culture.[59] However, in seeking to find respect of the dominant culture, the Navajo court system risks losing its legitimacy among Navajo people and imposing dominant values on Navajo people. This paradox is a difficult one to bridge; however, it is important that the tribal courts view their role primarily within the context of their people's needs. If the courts do not meet these needs

---

49. 25 U.S.C. § 461-79 (1994). *See also* Curtis Berkey, *Implementation of the Indian Reorganization Act*, 2 AM INDIAN J. 8 (1976).

50. *See* Lieder, *supra* note 36, at 37; *See also*, RUTH ROESSEL & BRODERICK JOHNSON, NAVAJO LIVESTOCK REDUCTIONS: A NATIONAL DISGRACE (1974).

51. *See* Navajo Tribal Code tit. 2, § 4.

52. *See* Lieder, *supra* note 36, at 37.

53. *See* Williams v. Lee, 319 P.2d 998 (1958), *rev'd*, 358 U.S. 217 (1959).

54. *See id.*

55. *See* Williams v. Lee, 358 U.S. 217, 223 (1959).

56. *See* Navajo Tribal Code tit. 7. *See also* Lowery, *supra* note 36, at 382.

57. *See* Gloria Valencia-Weber, *Tribal Courts: Custom and Innovative Law*, 24 N.M. L. REV. 225 (1994). *See also*, BUREAU OF THE CENSUS, WE THE FIRST AMERICANS 7 (1993) (report on American Indians and Alaskan natives). The Navajo Nation courts processed over 45,000 cases per year by 1987. Recently, Chief Justice Robert Yazzie of the Navajo Supreme Court reported that in 1992 the Navajo Nation's courts handled 85,000 cases including 16,000 criminal, 24,000 traffic, and 13,000 family law cases. Chief Justice Robert Yazzie, Address at the University of New Mexico School of Law (March 2, 1993) *cited* in Gloria Valencia-Weber *supra*, at 36.

58. The Anglo-American legal system is derived from the English common law. *See generally* LAWRENCE M. FRIEDMAN, A HISTORY OF AMERICAN LAW (2d ed. 1985).

59. *See* Atwood, *supra* note 36, at 929, 931.

and command the respect of the Navajo people, they do not fulfill their function either as policy makers for their communities or as deciders of disputes within the community.

IV. NAVAJO REGULATION OF MARRIAGE

Navajo regulation of marriage is complicated because the status, rights, and responsibilities of married individuals depend not only on what the Navajo Nation (and Navajo culture) extends to the married couple; but also on norms, benefits, and entitlements of federal and state governments.

Early in the history of United States/Navajo relations, one of the Navajo cultural values the federal government sought to destroy, by way of the legal system, was Navajo polygamy. One of the federal regulations first applied to the Navajo reservation outlawed polygamy.[60] Thus, the government intruded on very basic cultural values of Navajo people—their family and kinship rules.[61] On July 12, 1945, the Navajo Tribal Council enacted legislation voiding plural marriages.[62] Although Navajos by and large discontinued the cultural practice of polygamy,[63] they continued to practice the traditional religious and cultural ceremony, which required the participation of extended family members, the ceremonial consumption of cornmeal mush from a sacred basket, and other ceremonial requirements.[64] In Navajo tradition the celebration of the ceremony

60. *See* AMERICANIZING THE AMERICAN INDIANS, *supra* note 4, at 302.

61. *See generally* WITHERSPOON, *supra* note 19.

62. *See* NAVAJO TRIBAL COUNCIL RESOLUTIONS 1922-1951, 86 (1951).

63. *See* Marley Shebala, *Council Considers to Override Prez's Veto*, NAVAJO TIMES, Aug. 12, 1999, at A1. The Council passed legislation containing a provision decriminalizing polygamy but leaving unmarried status as a requirement of Navajo Marriage law. The President vetoed the legislation. *See id.*

64. *See* RUTH ROESSEL, WOMEN IN NAVAJO SOCIETY 57-60 (1981). Dr. Roessel describes the ceremony:

> The Navajo Wedding was taught to the Navajos by the Holy People, and it was the way by which the young boy and girl would begin their own life under the guidance, protection and blessing of the Holy People. The traditional Navajo Wedding Ceremony consisted of feeding all of the friends and visitors who came to see the young couple get married. Prior to the food and feast aspect came the Navajo wedding ceremony itself. This ceremony consisted of first the groom entering the hogan with his father or uncle and sitting on the westside of the hogan. After he had entered and was seated the first would enter accompanied by her father or her uncle. She would sit beside the boy and the two would be facing the east-toward the door of the hogan. The girl would sit on the right of the boy. She would pour water form a pitch-covered jug on to the boy's hands and he would wash his hands.

with family and friends was enough—the community knew that a marriage had taken place—a marriage license or other documentation was unnecessary.[65] Navajo marriage not only joined two families, but also joined four clans, so it was a unifying force in Navajo life.[66] However, in 1940 the Tribal Council passed a resolution requiring Navajo couples who wished to marry to obtain a marriage license.[67] This was probably to satisfy BIA officials who had a very heavy hand in the development of tribal law. In 1944, the Tribal Council amended the resolution to validate marriages recognized by the community but not contracted

---

> Next the boy would pour water from the same jug onto the girl's hands and she would wash her hands. This symbolized purity and cleansing.
>
> Next the medicine man would take the sacred basket in which there was corn meal mush and make a circle of corn pollen in the center of that circle. While the medicine man was doing that he would be praying quietly, and when he had finished making the decorations on the mush with the corn pollen, the basket would be placed in front of the couple, and the boy would take the first bite—by dipping two fingers in to the mush and eating from them—at the east where the basket design opens. Next, the girl would take a bite in the same way, and then they would take one bite after the other from the four directions and finally from the center. Usually the couple was instructed to eat all of the mush themselves, but at some weddings the remaining part of the mush would be passed around so that each member of the boy's family could get a bite.
>
> The traditional Navajo approach would be to have the basket remain stationary in front of the couple so that it would not be handed around and moved about as different people took bites of the mush with their fingers. After the mush has been eaten the basket is given to the mother of the boy who is instructed to keep it and preserve it at all times. . . .The traditional Navajo marriage always took place at night. . . Following the completion of eating the mush, food was passed around to all of the guests at the wedding. After this distribution and feasting had been completed, the older and happily married couples would give advice to the young married couple in terms of what to expect and how to live happily and properly with one another.

Id. *See also*, ELEANOR SCHICK, NAVAJO WEDDING DAY: A DINE MARRIAGE CEREMONY (1999).

65. Navajo culture has an oral and not a written tradition. In this tradition what is spoken is important. The written word has little meaning. Interview with Eleanor Schick, author ELEANOR SCHICK, NAVAJO WEDDING DAY: A DINE MARRIAGE CEREMONY (1999), in Albuquerque, N.M. (July 28, 1999).

66. *See* ROUSELL, *supra* note 64, at 57.

67. *See* RES. CJ-2-40, NAVAJO TRIBAL COUNCIL RESOLUTIONS 1922-1951, 78-80 (1951).

by church, state, or custom.[68] The Navajo Tribal Council directed the Tribal Council to inform the Navajo people of the change.[69]

The first case in the first published Navajo Nation reporter involved the validation of a tribal customary marriage.[70] In upholding a traditional marriage, the path was paved for the court to uphold Navajo traditions and customs in their function as mechanisms for resolving disputes.[71] Navajo courts have since taken this responsibility very seriously.[72] *In the Matter of the Marriage of Daw*,[73] a Navajo district court determined that a traditional tribal customary marriage that followed Navajo custom did not require a marriage license to be validated by a Navajo Tribal court.[74] This decision upheld traditional culture between Navajo partners[75] and gave the marriage, celebrated by a traditional marriage ceremony,

---

68. *See id.* at 84.

69. *See id.*

70. In the Matter of the Marriage of Daw, 1 Navajo Rep. 1 (Window Rock D. Ct. 1969), overruled in part, In re: Validation of Marriage of Francisco, 16 Indian L. Rep. 6113 (Navajo Nation S. Ct. 1989).

71. Navajo Tribal Code tit. 7, § 204(A) reads "In all civil cases the Court of the Navajo Tribe shall apply any laws of the United States that may be applicable and any ordinances or customs of the Tribe not prohibited by such federal laws." *See* Johnson v. Dixon, 4 Navajo Rep. 108, 109 (Navajo Ct. App. 1983) (stating that section 204 clearly expresses the intent that the Navajo Tribal Council wanted the courts to apply Navajo law, consisting of Navajo statutes, the common law (custom) and decisional law wherever possible); *See, e.g.*, Sells v. Sells, 5 Navajo Rep. 104, 108 (Navajo Nation S. Ct. 1986) (stating that the soul of the court is to apply Navajo tribal law, especially where custom and tradition are important); In the Matter of the Estate of Annie Belone, 5 Navajo Rep. 161, 164-167 (Navajo Nation S. Ct. 1987) (outlining the procedure for arguing Navajo custom in court).

72. *See, e.g.*, Davis v. Means, 21 Indian L. Rep. 6125, 6127 (1994), which is a paternity case where the court states that knowing one's point of origin (parents) is very important in Navajo culture. *See also* In the Matter of Conciliation of the Marriage of Allison, 3 Navajo Rep. 199 (Window Rock D. Ct. 1982), in which the wife petitioned for a traditional Navajo marriage conciliation and the petition was granted.

73. In the Matter of the Marriage of Daw, 1 Navajo Rep. 1 (Window Rock D. Ct. 1969).

74. The facts of the case are as follows: Helen and Jerry Daw were married by tribal custom on September 24, 1964. While they never obtained a marriage license, they registered with the Census as married, they had two children, and everyone knew them as married. Jerry Daw was killed in action in Vietnam. His widow could not obtain Veterans benefits unless her marriage was validated. (The children had prevailed in a prior paternity action so that they could qualify for social security benefits to which they were entitled). *See id.* at 1-2 (1969).

75. *See* Validating the Marriage of Garcia, 5 Navajo Rep. 30, 31 (Navajo Ct. App. 1985) (stating that the tribal court is without authority to validate a tribal customary ceremony between a Navajo and a non-Navajo—a Mexican-American male, in this case).

all of the legal recognition of a marriage formalized with a marriage license.[76] The court noted that Navajos without marriage licenses face problems in acquiring social security and military benefits for their dependents.[77] The court validated the couple's traditional marriage by stating that the Tribal Code license requirement was directory rather than mandatory.[78] The court cited Title 9, Section 61 of the Navajo Tribal Code as an enactment intended to cure defects in form and procedure.[79] The court also said that the Tribal Council did not specifically outlaw "common law marriages" after February 1, 1954.[80] Once validated by the court, the validity of the marriage would not be questioned by federal government officials.[81]

Ten years later, the Navajo Court of Appeals[82] in *The Matter of the Validation of Marriage of Ketchum* expanded on the reasoning of the *Daw* case.[83] The Navajo Court of Appeals, citing the 1877 United States Supreme Court case *Meister v. Moore,*[84] concluded that common law marriage exists unless it is repealed by statute and upheld the marriage as a common law marriage.[85] The court stated that the essential features of a common law marriage are "present consent to be husband and wife, actual cohabitation, and an actual representing of themselves to the community as married."[86] Thus, the Court of Appeals afforded the benefits of marriage to a Navajo couple who had participated in a customary

---

76. For example, a traditional tribal marriage must be terminated by a divorce. *See* In the Matter of the Validation of Marriage of Slowman, 1 Navajo Rep. 142 (Navajo Ct. App. 1977); In the Matter of Documenting the Marriage of Slim, 3 Navajo Rep. 218 (Crownpoint D. Ct. 1982).

77. In the Matter of the Marriage of Daw, 1 Navajo Rep. 1, 2 (Window Rock D. Ct. 1969).

78. *See id.*

79. *See id.* at 3.

80. *See id. See also* Navajo Tribal Council Resolution CJ-2-40, which initially required couples who were married by a traditional Navajo wedding ceremony to obtain a marriage license. However, an amendment in 1954 abolished the license requirement for weddings celebrated according to Navajo tradition.

81. *See id.*

82. The Navajo Court of Appeals later became the Navajo Supreme Court.

83. *See* In the Matter of the Validation of Marriage of Ketchum, 2 Navajo Rep. 102 (Navajo Ct. App. 1979).

84. Meister v. Moore, 96 U.S. 76 (1877). In an ejectment action that turned on the validity of an unsolemnized marriage the Court found the marriage valid under ambiguous state law.

85. *See* In the Matter of the Validation of Marriage of Ketchum, 2 Navajo Rep. 102, 104 (Navajo Ct. App. 1979). For an excellent discussion of the legal history of "common law marriage" *see* Cynthia Grant Bowman, *A Feminist Proposal to Bring Back Common Law Marriage*, 75 OR. L. REV. 709 (1996); Ariela R. Dubler, *Governing Through Contract: Common Law Marriage in the Nineteenth Century*, 107 YALE L.J. 1885 (1998).

86. In the Matter of the Validation of Marriage of Ketchum, 2 Navajo Rep. 102, 105 (Navajo Ct. App. 1979).

marriage ceremony by using the legal concept of "common law marriage" derived from Anglo-American jurisprudence.[87]

A year after *Ketchum*, in 1980 the Navajo Tribal Council eliminated the January 31, 1954 cutoff date for validation of Navajo customary marriages.[88] The Council recognized that "the Navajo people have continued to marry in tribal custom ceremonies since 1954," and "the law of validated marriages has created problems and hardships for numerous married Navajo people."[89] In an effort to encourage the move toward formalization and to ease the problem of keeping accurate records, the Council urged Navajo people to obtain a Navajo Tribal marriage license prior to marriage and to record them within three months.[90] The Council recognized the contemporary realities of the customs and behaviors of the Navajo people; eliminating the cutoff date meant that all customary marriages would be validated. This extended the federal benefits normally afforded to married couples to Navajos who were recognized by the community as being married and who considered themselves spiritually united in accordance with Navajo cultural and religious tradition.[91]

All of the Navajo cases discussed *supra* involved the tribal courts' use of the doctrine of "common law" marriage to save a marriage that had been celebrated according to Navajo tradition.[92] In a later case, the Navajo Supreme Court stated that its recognition of "common law" marriage was not derived from Anglo common law but based on its own needs and culture.[93] *Navajo Nation v. Murphy* was a criminal case in which the accused sought to use the legal doctrine of spousal privilege to prevent his partner from testifying against him.[94] He and the potential witness had never participated in a tribal or civil marriage ceremony, but he stated that he and the witness were married under "common law."[95] The Navajo Supreme Court cited *Ketchum* for the proposition that Navajo law

87. See articles cited *supra* note 85.

88. *See* Navajo Tribal Council Resolution, CAP 36-80 (Apr. 30, 1980).

89. *Id.*

90. *See id.*

91. *See* In the Matter of the Validation of Marriage of Ketchum, 2 Navajo Rep. 102 (Navajo Ct. App. 1979). Shirley and Francis Ketchum were married in a traditional marriage on June 7, 1974. They had two children. Frances died on February 8, 1979. The Social Security Administration refused to pay the claim for benefits without documentation of the marriage despite the fact that Shirley and Francis considered themselves culturally and spiritually united as a married couple under Navajo custom.

92. In the Matter of the Estate of William Al Tsosie, 5 Navajo Rep. 261 (Window Rock D. Ct. 1987). This was a probate case in which the court validated a common law marriage despite the existence of a later formalized marriage. *See also* Ration v. Robertson, 4 Navajo Rep. 15 (Navajo Ct. App. 1983), which was a dispute involving property between a man and a woman living in a common law marriage.

93. *See* Navajo Nation v. Murphy, 15 Indian L. Rep. 6035 (Navajo Nation S. Ct. 1988).

94. *See id* at 6036.

95. *See id.*

recognized common law marriage.[96] However, the court noted that it applied the spousal privilege as a matter of Navajo tradition and culture and not because of its derivation from the English common law doctrine of merger of husband and wife.[97] The court stated that medieval reasoning has no support in Navajo tradition and culture.[98] However, the court found that marriage was an important aspect of Navajo culture, and that a rule that would potentially prevent the breakup of a marriage is justified by Navajo society's interest in preserving the harmony and sanctity of marriage.[99] Despite finding that the privilege was available, the court found insufficient evidence to show that the elements of a "common law" marriage existed.[100]

However, the very next year, the Navajo Supreme Court revisited the question of whether recognizing marriages in which the parties lived together and held themselves out to the community as married without any kind of ceremony was indeed part of Navajo cultural tradition. In the case of *In re: Validation of Marriage of Francisco* the Navajo Supreme Court reviewed a case involving a couple who had lived together between October 1978 and August 1987 in Window Rock, Arizona.[101] The woman was an enrolled member of the Navajo tribe and her partner was a Hopi.[102] They combined their earnings, acquired personal property in both of their names, and accumulated debt in both of their names.[103] The man often introduced the women as his wife.[104] However, while the pair talked of marriage, they did not obtain a marriage license, marry according to Arizona state law, or participate in a traditional Navajo wedding ceremony.[105] They had no children. The man died as a result of a car accident and his heirs were entitled to the proceeds from his life insurance policy.[106] Unless her marriage was validated, the woman would not collect any part of the life insurance proceeds. Because the man was a Hopi and not a member of the Navajo tribe, the Window Rock district court ruled that under the Navajo Tribal Code (Title 9, Section 2), a Navajo member could not use the Navajo law to validate her common law marriage.[107] Under the Code she had to contract her

---

96. *See id.*
97. *See id.*
98. *See id.*
99. *See id.*
100. *See id.* The parties apparently did not reside together and the defendant presented no evidence that they held themselves out to the community as married. Further, the witness identified herself as the defendant's girlfriend. *Id.*
101. *See* In re: Validation of Marriage of Francisco, 16 Indian L. Rep. 6113 (Navajo Nation S. Ct. 1989).
102. *See id.*
103. *See id.*
104. *See id.*
105. *See id.*
106. *See id.*
107. *See id.*

marriage in accordance with applicable state or foreign law.[108] Because Arizona did not recognize common law marriage, the district court refused to validate her marriage.[109]

The Navajo Supreme Court's analysis began with a review of the history of Navajo marriage law.[110] The court recognized that it was faced with the difficult task of reconciling the Tribal Council's intent in passing the Tribal Code with the parties' expectations in recovering military and other benefits.[111] The court determined that the *Daw* case was an attempt to save traditional marriage and was probably not intended to create a new way of contracting marriage in Navajo country.[112] The court found that the court in *Daw* viewed the requirement of obtaining a marriage license as directory and not as mandatory.[113] The court determined that when read as a whole, the Tribal Council's resolution and the Tribal Code appeared to attempt to remedy the situation where there was a technical defect in a customary marriage, but did not intend to create a "common law" marriage.[114] The court cited an anthropological treatise to indicate that Navajo traditional custom did not recognize common law marriages.[115] Thus, the court said, a Navajo court could validate traditional marriages only upon evidence that a traditional ceremony occurred, but not when a traditional ceremony had not taken place.[116] The court overruled *Daw, Ketchum*, and *Murphy* to the extent they authorized a tribal court to validate a "common law" marriage.[117] The court stated that validating only Navajo traditional ceremonial marriages between Navajos would enhance Navajo sovereignty, preserve the Navajo marriage tradition, and protect those who adhere to the Navajo tradition.[118]

Next, the court discussed its view of adopting foreign legal concepts and concluded that Navajo sovereignty required that the Navajo Nation be cautious about state or foreign law infringement.[119] The court urged the Tribal Council to amend that Navajo Tribal Code so that it also regulated marriages between

---

108. *See id.* Interestingly, the well known case of *Santa Clara v. Martinez*, 436 U.S. 49 (1978) involved a Santa Clara woman who married a Navajo man. The Santa Clara Pueblo did not recognize the children of a mother of such a mixed marriage but it would have recognized the children of a father of such a marriage. The Supreme Court ultimately held that the issue of tribal membership was for the tribe to decide.

109. *See* In re: Validation of Marriage of Francisco, 16 Indian L. Rep. 6113 (Navajo Nation S. Ct. 1989).

110. *See id.* at 6113.

111. *See id.* at 6114.

112. *See id.*

113. *See id.*

114. *See id.*

115. The Court cited RAYMOND FRIDAY LOCKE, THE BOOK OF THE NAVAJO (1976). *See id.* at 6115.

116. *See id.* at 6115.

117. *See id.*

118. *See id.*

119. *See id.*

Navajos and non-Navajos because "domestic relations is the core of the tribe's internal and social relations."[120] The Tribal Code's requirement that "marriages between Navajos and non-Navajos may be validly contracted only by the parties complying with applicable state or foreign law"[121] needlessly injected foreign law to govern domestic relations within Navajo jurisdiction.[122] The court continued, "[s]uch needless relinquishment of sovereignty hurts the Navajo Nation. The Navajo people have always governed their marriage practices, whether the marriage is mixed or not, and must continue to do so to preserve sovereignty."[123] The court urged the Tribal Council to amend Title 9 of the Navajo Tribal Code so that it reflects Navajo regulation and control of domestic relations within the Navajo territorial jurisdiction.[124]

The Tribal Council responded by revising the Domestic Relations Code in 1993.[125] Interestingly, while the Council heeded the Court's suggestion to apply its domestic relations code to marriages between Navajos and non-Navajos and rescinded the provision in the Tribal Code concerning mixed marriages,[126] the Tribal Council rejected the Navajo Supreme Court's holding in *Francisco* by explicitly allowing parties to establish a common law marriage by cohabiting and holding themselves out to the community as a married couple.[127] The Tribal Council thus expanded the manner in which parties within the Navajo Nation may contract marriage.

The Tribal Code permits parties to contract marriage within the Navajo Nation as follows: by 1) signing a Navajo Nation marriage license in the presence of two witnesses,[128] 2) marrying according to the rites of any church,[129] 3) marrying before a tribal judge,[130] 4) engaging in a traditional Navajo wedding ceremony,[131] or 5) establishing a "common-law" marriage.[132] Thus, the Tribal

---

120. *Id.*
121. *Id.* (citing Navajo Tribal Code tit. 9, § 2).
122. *See id.* at 6115.
123. *Id.*
124. *Id.*
125. *See* Navajo Tribal Code tit. 9 (revised 1993) (Domestic Relations).
126. *See* Navajo Tribal Code tit. 9, § 2 (annotation).
127. Navajo Tribal Code tit. 9, § 3E.
128. Navajo Tribal Code tit. 9, § 3A.
129. Navajo Tribal Code tit. 9, § 3B.
130. Navajo Tribal Code tit. 9, § 3C.
131. Navajo Tribal Code tit. 9, § 3D provides:

> D. The contracting parties engage in a traditional Navajo wedding ceremony which shall have substantially the following features:
>
> 1. The parties to the proposed marriage shall have met and agreed to marry;
>
> 2. The parents of the man shall ask the parents of the woman for her hand in marriage;

Council responded to the contemporary needs of the community by passing legislation to remedy a social problem that is created when parties who live together and behave as a married couple do not formalize their relationship. This is much the same rationale that was used to explain the development of common law marriage in the American tradition.[133]

Common law marriage was developed to extend marital rights and responsibilities to couples who did not formalize their marriage in the days when formalization was expensive and difficult.[134] In much the same way, Navajo

---

> 3. The bride and bridegroom eat cornmeal mush out of a sacred basket;
> 4. Those assembled at the ceremony give advice for a happy marriage to the bride and groom;
> 5. Gifts may or may not be exchanged;
> 6. The person officiating or conducting the traditional wedding ceremony shall be authorized to sign the marriage license.

Id.

132. Navajo Tribal Code tit. 9, § 3E provides:

> E. The Contracting parties establish a common-law marriage having the following features:
> 1. Present intention of the parties to be husband and wife;
> 2. Present consent between the parties to be husband and wife;
> 3. Actual cohabitation;
> 4. Actual holding out of the parties within their community to be married.

Id.

133. See *infra* notes 134, 142-158.

134. Officials were not often available to solemnize the relationship and record keeping bureaucracies were not always available to record the relationship. *See* McChesney v. Johnson, 79 S.W. 2d 658, 659 (Tex. 1934). As the Texas Supreme court tells the story:

> It took root there when the conditions in Texas justified it. The sparse settlements, the long distance to places of record, bad roads, difficulties of travel, made access to officers or ministers difficult for some of our residents, lack of general education in the English language produced unfamiliarity with the laws, and, in the small settlements it was more difficult to dignify an illicit association with the name of marriage than in one of our large cities where all of us are strangers to the private life of most of its residents.

Id.

people who live in isolated and remote areas of the reservation and who may not be able to afford the costs of a traditional ceremony may choose to live as married without formalizing their union.[135] The Navajo Nation now recognizes this reality. By extending legal recognition to couples the community recognizes as married, the Navajo Nation remedies a potential social problem.

Of course, rules requiring the formalization of a marital relationship disadvantage women in disproportionate numbers.[136] Navajo women who do not have validated marriages may not have access to domestic violence protections, alimony, and property division upon separation; and inheritance, social security, veteran benefits, and insurance upon death of their partner.[137] Allowing common law marriage gives them these benefits.

In addition, there may indeed be a cultural basis for recognizing a couple who hold themselves out as married even though they do not formalize the relationship.[138] This, of course, raises questions of how tribal courts determine relevant Navajo culture. Do they look to the culture of pre-European contact? Do they look to cultural norms in the contemporary community?[139]

Cultural norms evolve over time. The cultural norms about marriage have undoubtedly evolved since pre-European contact. Indeed, "*iii nel kad*" the Navajo phrase meaning that there is going to be a wedding, literally means "bringing in the horses" referring to the exchange of traditional gifts between the uniting families.[140] However, horses did not appear on the scene until after the Spaniards arrived.[141] It is vital that the Navajo Council and the Navajo Court continue to develop their domestic law in a way that balances their traditional culture and their modern needs.

---

135. *See* ROESSEL, *supra* note 64 (describing the generous gift giving and feasting that is part of a traditional ceremony).

136. *See generally* Bowman, *supra* note 85.

137. Many of these legal protections require a legally recognized marriage. See cases cited *supra* notes 70-109 for examples of cases in which a legally recognized marriage was necessary to the parties seeking validation.

138. *See* WITHERSPOON, *supra* note 19, at 23 (stating that the basis of an affinal marital relationship is a sexual relationship). *See* Means v. District Court of the Chinle Judicial District, 26 Indian L. Rep. 6083, 6087 (Navajo Nation S. Ct. 1999) (describing an individual who marries or has an intimate relationship with a Navajo as a *hadane* (in law)).

139. For a study of the use of custom in Navajo Tribal Courts, see generally Lowery, *supra* note 36.

140. *See* ROESSEL, *supra* note 64, at 57.

141. There is evidence that horses did once exist in North America but became extinct and were then reintroduced by the Spaniards. *See* <http://www.cyberhighway.net/%7Eshirtail/new.htm> (visited Apr. 14, 2000).

V. WESTERN LEGAL REGULATION OF MARRIAGE INCLUDING COMMON LAW MARRIAGE

Western marital regulation is a statement of a society's cultural values in the ordering of its society.[142] Laws regulating marriage ensure that those who are married receive the status, rights, responsibilities, and benefits that society and their culture affords them.[143] Marriage has been described as the most fundamental of rights and the foundation of the family.[144] The history of the regulation of marriage in this country is rather complex. The definition of the marital relationship goes back to canon law.[145] The legal prohibitions of polygamous marriages were particularly vigorous.[146] Prohibitions against incest have been less so.[147]

"Common law marriage" is a marital relationship that is recognized by law, despite the fact that the couple did not formalize the relationship in accordance with legal requirements.[148] Apparently the roots of common law marriage in the common law of England are rather shallow.[149] Its rapid evolution in the United States illustrates the power of the judicial branch in the ordering of private relationships.[150] Courts used the doctrine to validate dependent

---

142. *See* Lynn D. Wardle, Loving v. Virginia *and The Constitutional Right to Marry*, 1790-1990, 41 HOW. L.J. 289, 297 (1998) (reviewing Supreme Court jurisprudence to demonstrate the importance of marriage as a social and constitutional right).

143. *See id.* at 297.

144. *See id.*

145. *See* Andrew H. Freidman, *Same-Sex Marriage and Right to Privacy: Abandoning Scriptural, Canonical, and Natural Law Based Definition of Marriage*, 35 HOW. L.J. 173 (1992) (tracing the historical evolution of the definition of marriage and arguing that the historical basis is no longer applicable to modern society).

146. *See* Jorge Martin, Note, *English Polygamy Law and the Danish Registered Partnership Act: A Case for the Consistent Treatment of Foreign Polygamous Marriages and Danish Same-Sex Marriages in England*, 27 CORNELL INT'L L.J. 419 (1994). *See also* Reynolds v. U.S., 98 U.S. 145, 164 (1878) (stating that "polygamy has always been odious among the northern and western nations of Europe; and, until the establishment of the Mormon Church, was almost exclusively a feature of the life of Asiatic and of African people. At common law, the second marriage was always void (2 Kent, Com. 79), and from the earliest history of England polygamy has been treated as an ofence[sic] against society.")

147. *See* Martin, *supra* note 146.

148. The courts will look to whether the parties agreed to live together as husband and wife, whether the parties cohabited, and whether the parties held themselves out to the community as husband and wife. *See* 52 AM. JUR. 2D *Marriage* § 45 (1970).

149. *See id.*

150. *See* Dubler, *supra* note 85 (examining the nineteenth century expansion of common law marriage in this country and arguing that judges used marriage as a vector of public policy to define the proper sexual relationship between men and women). *See also* OTTO KOEGEL, COMMON LAW MARRIAGE AND ITS DEVELOPMENT IN THE UNITED STATES (1975).

relationships so widows would receive social welfare, pension, and insurance benefits, and thus not become paupers.[151] Courts also used the doctrine to legitimize the children of long term relationships.[152] Many citizens, including the newly freed slaves, viewed the legal construct of marriage with distrust[153] especially because divorce was so difficult to obtain.[154] Some states adopted the doctrine of common law marriage,[155] while other states rejected it.[156] Courts and legislatures grappled with the dilemma of whether to legitimize marriages and give the legal benefits of marriage to individuals who behaved as if they were married or whether to discourage couples from flaunting social convention. In many cases, courts have come up with compromises—giving some rights, benefits, and responsibilities to those who have lived together, created children together, or both.[157] A major concern of the courts is preventing someone from obtaining the benefits of the marital relationship fraudulently.[158]

---

151. *See* Dubler, *supra* note 85, at 1892.

152. *See* Dubler, *supra* note 85, at 1894-1895.

153. *See* Laura F. Edwards, *"The Marriage Covenant is at the Foundation of All Our Rights": The Politics of Slave Marriages in North Carolina After Emancipation*, 14 LAW & HIST. REV. 81, 111 (1996).

154. *See* Dubler, *supra* note 85 (citing Henrik Hartog, *Marital Exits and Marital Expectations in Nineteenth Century America*, 80 GEO. L.J. 95 (1991)).

155. Nine states and the District of Columbia currently recognize common law marriage. Montana: MONT. CODE ANN. § 40-1-403 (1997); Utah: UTAH CODE ANN. § 30-1-4.5 (1998); District of Columbia: Hoage v. Murch Bos. Const. Co, 50 F.2d 983 (D.C. Cir. 1931); Alabama: Campbell's Adm'r v. Gullatt, 43 Ala. 57 (1869); Colorado: Klipfel's Estate v. Kilpfel, 92 P. 26 (Colo. 1907); Iowa: McFarland v. McFarland, 2 N.W. 269 (Iowa 1839); Kansas: Shortan v. Judd, 55 P. 286 (Kan. 1898); Pensylvannia: Knecht v. Knecht, 104 A. 676 (Pa. 1918); Rhode Island: Holgate v. United Elec. Rhys Co. 133 A. 243 (R.I. 1926); Texas: Berger v. Kirby, 153 S.W. 1130 (Texas 1930). Utah adopted common law marriage by statute specifically to get unmarried individuals who were living with a partner off the welfare rolls. *See* UTAH CODE ANN. § 30-1-4.5 (1998); *Recent Developments in Utah Law*, 1988 UTAH L. REV. 149, 280-81 (quoting from legislative history of the bill).

156. The following states abolished common law marriage: Florida (1968), Indiana (1958), Michigan (1957), Minnesota (1941), Mississippi (1956), Missouri (1921), Nebraska (1923), Nevada (1943), New Jersey (1939), New York (1933), South Dakota (1959), and Oklahoma (1994). Florida: FLA. STAT. ANN. § 741.211 (West 1986); Indiana: IND. CODE ANN. § 31-7-6-5 (Michie 1987); Michigan: MICH. COMP. LAWS ANN. § 551.2 (West 1988); Minnesota: MINN. STAT. ANN. §517.01 (West 1986); Mississippi: MISS. CODE ANN. § 93-1-15 (1994); Missouri: MO. ANN. STAT. § 451.040 (West 1986), Thomson v. Thomson, 163 S.W. 2d 792, 795 (Mo. Ct. App. 1942); Nebraska: NEB. REV. STAT. § 42-104 (1993), Collins v. Hoag & Rollins, 241 N.W. 766 (Neb. 1932); Nevada: NEV. REV. STAT. ANN. § 122.010 (Michie 1993); New Jersey: N.J. STAT. ANN. § 37:1-10 (West 1968); New York: N.Y. DOM. REL. LAW § 11 (McKinney 1988), In re Estate of Benjamin, 311 N.E.2d 495 (N.Y. 1939).

157. *See* GEERTJE ELSE WIERSMA, COHABITATION: AN ALTERNATIVE TO MARRIAGE: A CROSS-NATIONAL STUDY (1983); Katherine C. Gordon, *The Necessity and Enforcement*

VI. STATE RECOGNITION OF TRIBAL CUSTOMARY MARRIAGE

Marriages that are valid in the place they are celebrated are usually recognized in this country unless the marriage violates some strong public policy of the state.[159] As early as the nineteenth century, some jurisdictions stated that they would recognize Indian customary marriages.[160] However, it appears that courts looked for indicia of the marital relationship in ways in which it appeared that the parties satisfied the requirements of a common law marriage.[161] Although the BIA attempted to assimilate Indians by requiring them to adopt Anglo-American legal systems and substantive law, both state and federal governments have recognized marriages that complied with tribal law or custom. In 1890 Congress recognized that native communities celebrate marriage differently and passed a statute validating marriages contracted under the tribal law or tribal customs.[162]

Furthermore, in *Carney v. Chapman*, Justice Holmes noted that the passage of the statute made the issue a "federal question" and without much analysis validated a "common law" marriage of a Chickasaw couple who had celebrated a traditional Chickasaw ceremony.[163] A few years later, the Supreme Court stated in *United States v. Quiver*:

> At an early period it became the settled policy of Congress to permit the personal and domestic relations of the Indians with each other to be regulated, and offenses by one Indian against

---

of Cohabitation Agreements: When Strings will Attach and How to Prevent Them—A State Survey, 37 BRANDEIS L.J. 245.

158. *See* Bowman *supra* note 85, at 733.

159. *See* 35 AM. JUR. *Marriage* § 172; Hans W. Baade, *Marriage & Divorce in American Conflicts Law: Governmental Analysis & Restatement Second,* 72 COLUM. L. REV. 329 (1972).

160. *See* Johnson v. Johnson's Adm't, 30 Mo. 72, 84-91 (1860) (holding that children of Indian woman and white man married according to Indian custom are legitimate); McBean v. McBean, 61 P. 418, 421 (Or. 1900) (holding that marriage according to Indian custom valid where at least one Indian was involved); State v. Ta-Cha-Na-Tah, 64 N.C. 614, 616 (1870) (refusing to recognize marriage according to Cherokee custom because state does not recognize common law marriage).

161. *See* cases cited *supra* note 160.

162. *See* Carney v. Chapman, 247 U.S. 102, 38 S.Ct.449, 62 L.Ed. 1005 (1918), which was a case arising in Oklahoma in which the Supreme Court interpreted the act of Congress of May 2, 1890 c. 182 section 38, 26 Stat 81, 98 regarding validating marriages contracted under the laws or tribal custom of any Indian nation to validate a common law marriage of a Chickasaw couple.

163. *Id.*

> the person or property of another Indian to be dealt with, according to their tribal customs and laws.[164]

The courts recognized tribal marriages.[165] Even polygamous marriages in accordance with tribal custom were recognized.[166] In the 1907 Nebraska case of *Ortley v. Ross*, the Nebraska Supreme Court, in deciding a probate matter stated:

> Now, it is contended by appellants that, as the alleged marriage between the father and mother of the plaintiff was polygamous, it was neither valid in the state of Minnesota, where the parties then resided, nor in the state of Nebraska, to which they subsequently removed. This contention would be well founded if this marriage had taken place between citizens of the United States in any state of the Union. But a different rule prevails with reference to the marriages of Indians, who are members of a tribe recognized and treated with as such by the United States government; for it has always been the policy of the general government to permit the Indian tribes as such to regulate their own domestic affairs, and to control the intercourse between the sexes by their own customs and usages.[167]

The tradition of recognizing tribal marriage law is quite pronounced.[168] States, federal courts, and agencies should continue their practice of recognizing tribal marriage law. To do so is consistent with how marital law is applied generally and allows tribes to continue development of indigenous law.

---

164. United States v. Quiver, 241 U.S. 602, 603-604, 36 S.Ct. 699, 700, 60 L.Ed. 1196 (1916) (holding that a state does not have authority to prosecute Sioux Indian for adultery).

165. *See, e. g.*, Barnett v. Prairie Oil and Gas Co, 19 F 2d. 504 (1927) (holding that Creek customary marriage and divorce practices would be recognized in probate context).

166. *See* Hallowell v. Commons, 210 F. 793 (8th Cir. 1914) (holding that Omaha tribe's customs with regard to polygamy must be respected); Kobogum v. Jackson Iron Co. 76 Mich. 498, 43 N.W. 602 (1889) (holding that states have no more right to determine Chippewa tribe's marriage law than they would a foreign jurisdiction). For a 1930's view about recognizing Indian customary marriages *see* Ray Brown, *The Indian Problem and the Law*, 3 YALE L. J. 307 (1930). The author demonstrates little understanding of the cultural basis for tribal marriage customs and laws.

167. Ortley v. Ross 78 Neb. 339, 110 N.W. 982, 983 (1907).

168. *See* Thomas v. Healey, 152 Okla. 93, 3 P.2d. 1047 (1931). *See also* Ponina v. Leland, 85 Nev. 263, 454 P.2d 16 (1969) (holding that a Pauite off-reservation couple who met the requirements of Pauite tribal customs were deemed to be husband and wife under Pauite law and it would be recognized in probate of husband's estate).

VII. RELATED DOMESTIC RELATIONS ISSUES

The state deference to tribal marriage law has implications in other areas of domestic relations. A recent case decided by the Navajo Nation Supreme Court raises the related issue of tribal jurisdiction over a domestic violence criminal matter. In *Means v. District Court of Chinle* the defendant[169] was accused of threatening and committing a battery on his brother-in-law (a Navajo), and his father-in-law (a member of the Omaha Tribe).[170] The defendant filed a motion to dismiss claiming that because he is a non-Navajo (he is Oglala Sioux) he is not subject to the criminal jurisdiction of the Navajo Nation. Means argued that the Navajo Nation has no jurisdiction over him, based on the Supreme Court decision of *Duro v. Reina*.[171] In *Duro*, the Supreme Court found that for purposes of criminal jurisdiction, a tribe's inherent sovereign powers extend only to members of the tribe.[172] In response to *Duro*, Congress amended the Indian Civil Rights Act[173] to state that a tribe's criminal jurisdiction extends over all Indians.[174] Congress called the action a "recognition" of inherent rights that Indian tribes have always held.[175] Means argued that the Indian Civil Rights Act thus discriminated against him as a Native American.[176]

Apparently expecting an appeal, the Navajo Supreme Court gave detailed background about the Navajo Nation and social problems on the reservation.[177] The court did not rest only on the Navajo Nation's inherent authority to regulate domestic relation matters.[178] Because the case was a criminal case, the court relied on the Navajo Nation Treaty of 1868 as a source of Navajo Nation criminal jurisdiction over non-member Indians.[179] The court found that language in the treaty setting apart the reservation for Navajos and such other Indians as the Navajos permitted to live there gave it authority to regulate criminal matters over non-Navajo Indians.[180] Further, the court stated that the defendant's marriage to a Navajo gave him the status of a *hadane* (in-law).[181] Because of his marriage to a

169. Defendant Russel Means is a noted activist and actor.

170. Means v. District Court of the Chinle Judicial District, 26 Indian L. Rep. 6083, 6085 (Navajo Nation S. Ct. 1999).

171. *See* Duro v. Reina, 495 U.S. 676 (1990).

172. *See* Duro v. Reina, 495 U.S. 676 (1990).

173. *See* 25 U.S.C. § 1301 et seq.

174. See Helen Gaebler, Comment, *The Legislative Reversal of* Duro v. Reina*: A First Step Toward Making Rhetoric a Reality*, 1991 WIS. L. REV. 1399.

175. *Id.*

176. *See* Means v. District Court of the Chinle Judicial District, 26 Indian L. Rep. 6083, 6084 (Navajo Nation S. Ct. 1999).

177. *See id.*

178. *See, e.g.*, Begay v. Miller, 70 Ariz. 380, 222 P. 2d 624 (1950) (holding that the state court is without authority to ignore an earlier tribal divorce decree).

179. *See* Means, 26 Indian L. Rep. at 6086-6087.

180. *See id.*

181. *See id.* at 6087.

Navajo, his status as a *hadane* or in-law, his longtime residence within the Navajo Nation, and his activities on the reservation, he consented to the criminal jurisdiction of the Navajo Nation.[182] The court also pointed to the vulnerability of Navajo people if they cannot be protected from criminal activity on the reservation, and noted that criminal defendants on the Navajo Nation are treated no differently from criminal defendants in state or federal courts.[183]

The *Means* case illustrates additional consequences of Navajo marriage law and points to the need for clear definition of tribal jurisdiction in domestic matters. As is true with the tribal law of marriage the tribe should have jurisdiction over domestic matters within its borders. For the same reasons that the Navajo Nation is free to develop its law of marriage, it must enforce its domestic relations law.[184] This will allow the Navajo Nation to develop and evolve as a culture.

VIII. CONCLUSION

The Navajo people would seem to want to celebrate their marriages using traditional cultural marriage ceremonies and to live together without marital ceremonies. The Navajo Nation must determine whether and how to recognize these relationships. Because these couples function within Navajo society as married couples, the Navajo Nation may choose to give these individuals the status, rights, and responsibilities of married parties. The tribal court validation process ensures that the parties have fulfilled the tribal code requirements. The validation process also prevents parties from fraudulently obtaining benefits.

This article demonstrates the tribal court's struggle to cherish cultural traditions while addressing modern challenges in regulating Navajo marriage law. The Navajo Supreme Court's use of Anglo-American principles to preserve cultural traditions illustrates the richness, creativity, and fusion in Navajo jurisprudence. The article also demonstrates that early federal and state cases held that tribal domestic matters were well within the jurisdiction of the tribe. State and federal governments and agencies must continue to respect tribal court jurisdiction of domestic matters to allow tribes to develop their own solutions to domestic problems, and to decide their domestic disputes in a manner that is consistent with their cultural norms and values.

---

182. *See id.*

183. *See id.*

184. *See, e.g.*, In re Marriage of Limpy, 195 Mont. 314, 636 P.2d 266 (1981) (abstaining from deciding divorce between Cheyenne tribal members).

[18]

VALID-WHERE-CONSUMMATED: THE INTERSECTION OF CUSTOMARY LAW MARRIAGES AND FORMAL ADJUDICATION

LONA N. LAYMON*

"Customary law comprises unwritten longstanding rules in the areas of marriage, divorce, child custody and inheritance for each [cultural group]. Customary laws, at least theoretically, help individuals maintain their culture within a modern world."

—Adrian K. Wing[1]

I. INTRODUCTION AND GENERAL DEFINITIONS

A. INTRODUCTION

The institution of marriage is pivotal to many issues in the Western legal tradition: custody, adoption, inheritance, rights to property upon divorce, and rights to financial support are just some areas that depend upon the individual's status as "married" or "single." The marital institution involves social expectations that reflect basic tenets of Western culture. Marriage is also an important cultural expression and social construct in most non-Western cultures. The crossover between cultural meaning and legal framework is inevitable. But what happens when the legal framework comes into conflict with opposing cultural conceptions of marriage? Such a conflict is exemplified in the colonial situation, where a Western legal framework is imposed upon a non-Western culture. As will be seen in this Note, many cultures do not conceive "marriage" in the same binary terms used in the Western legal system. While this *conflict* has been a major topic

---

* B.A 1998, University of California, Irvine; J.D. Candidate 2001, University of Southern California Law School. I wish to thank Professor Alison Renteln for her helpful guidance and insight on this Note.

[1] Adrien Katherine Wing, *Communitarianism vs. Individualism: Constitutionalism in Namibia and South Africa*, 11 WIS. INT'L L.J. 295, 341 (1993).

in the field of law and anthropology generally, few have explored *accommodations* for non-Western cultures in the Western legal system.

This Note investigates the treatment of non-Western "customary" marriages in "formal" legal systems. In other words, when does the "formal" legal system recognize a non-Western, often unregistered, marriage as valid? Do legislative protections for cultural groups *really* protect customary practices in ways that preserve cultural meaning, or can this be done via common-law doctrines? This analysis draws on statutory and case law from the United States and a variety of other nations, with emphasis on case law from the African continent. I draw primarily on laws from African nations because of the large volume of new scholarship and case law dealing with issues of customary marriage on that continent.

Part II of this Note focuses on the situation of minority indigenes embedded in a colonial-based system (i.e., the "classic" colonial case study for law and anthropology). There, I examine limitations to the enforcement of customary marriages in formal courts because of evidentiary and public policy standards. Finally, the Note offers a look at the United States legal system's treatment of customary marriages that are imported from other nations. How does this formal system treat customary marriages consummated in other nations? Can the formal legal system accommodate customary law through its own equitable doctrines? I examine several United States common law constructs (the valid-where-consummated doctrine, common-law marriage, and putative marriage doctrine) that may be used to validate customary marriages. I will show , however, that the "accommodation" of customary marriages through these "equitable" doctrines is usually inconsistent with the preservation of cultural meaning or notions of group/ethnic rights.

B. Why Focus on Marriage?

In Western nations that have a non-Western, indigenous population, discord between the national legal system and a non-Western cultural practice is seemingly inevitable. Most of these nations have specifically addressed indigenous groups in statutory and case law. For example, 25 U.S.C. §371 allows for the recognition of Native American marital customs that would otherwise be legally invalid.[2] In *Osborne v. Babbitt*,[3] for example, otherwise illegitimate children sought to inherit by intestacy from a decedent whose marriage was valid only under Pawnee custom. Because federal law demanded recognition of Native American customary law, the

[2] *See* 25 U.S.C § 371 (1983) (validating the rights of heirs to a deceased Native American to be recognized even if the individual was married or born from a marriage that is only recognized in the Native American culture). *See also* 25 U.S.C. § 348 (2000).

[3] 61 F.3d 810 (10th Cir. 1995).

court accepted the heirs' arguments, recognizing that since customary law is usually unwritten, the validity of customary marriages must be judged by different standards than those used to determine non-Indian, "formal" marriages.[4] The United States is not the only country that has created a separate sphere of standards for recognizing the marital customs of its indigenous population; it seems that almost every nation with an indigenous population has attempted to accommodate their customs through legislation or case law. In fact, we will see throughout this Note that cultural evidence does not enter into U.S. courtrooms nearly as often or as fully as it does in other nations. Moreover, even when evidence of customary laws is admitted into the formal court setting, the very nature of the formal legal system changes the customary laws that it seeks to preserve.

The recognition of customary unions also plays a central role in Board of Immigration ("BIA") cases in which deference is supposedly given to the law of the "place of consummation." For example, if a valid marriage is created in Iran, the general rule holds that the marriage is valid in the United States, even if it would not have been valid if consummated in the U.S.[5] The question of whether a court should recognize a non-Western marriage also arises in cases involving divorce, custody, aid for dependant children ("AFDC"), welfare, adoption, maintenance, rape, fraud, assault, deportation, insurance, and inheritance.[6]

C. "CUSTOMARY" VERSUS "FORMAL" LAW

Before further discussion, it is necessary to define what is meant by "formal" versus "customary" law. Customary law is often discussed in terms of group or cultural rights. These are affirmative rights to cultural preservation and respect for cultural identity. South Africa and Namibia, for example, have constitutionalized group rights, thus creating positive rights to preserve culture through education and language and to have unwritten

---

[4] *See id.* at 813–14 (recognizing that an otherwise illegitimate child could be deemed legitimate since she was Pawnee, which is a tribe that recognizes marriage through mere cohabitation).

[5] *See, e.g.*, Van Voorhis v. Brintnall, 86 N.Y. 18 (1881) (finding that a marriage is recognized in New York if it is valid where consummated); People v. Ezeonu, 588 N.Y.S.2d 116, 117 (Sup. Ct. 1992) ("Generally, a marriage is recognized in New York if it is valid where consummated."). *Cf.* Spradlin v. State Comp. Comm'r, 113 S.E.2d 832, 834 (W. Va. 1960). "The rule that a marriage which is void in the jurisdiction in which it is contracted or celebrated is void everywhere is equally well established and is likewise supported by the weight of authority." *Id.*

[6] "Maintenance" claims are claims for financial support from a money-earning spouse before divorce. Such support claims are formally recognized in many African nations and are particularly embedded in nations with Roman-Dutch legal foundations. These claims may be brought alone, but they are often brought in conjunction with claims for alimony or claims for insurance benefits where a customary spouse challenges findings that he or she has an uninsurable interest in the decedent spouse. *See, e.g.*, Chawanda v. Zimnat Ins. Co., 1990 (1) SA 1019 (Zimb. High Court), *aff'd*, 1991 (2) SA 825 (discussed in detail below).

customary law treated as legally binding.[7] Formal legal systems are often (but not always) aligned with a negative rights perspective. The United States legal system, for example, tends to focus upon the rights of the individual and "negative rights." United States courts and legislatures are often hostile to the ideas of group or cultural rights since these are a form of "positive rights" outside the tradition of U.S. law.[8] Regardless of the treatment of group rights and customary law in the United States, these issues have been a focus in the international legal community and in developing nations with strong multicultural heritages.

The difference between "customary" and "formal" law is most recognizable in a colonial context. When an inflexible, written or codified form of law or precedent is imposed upon a culture that organizes itself around an oral, flexible set of social traditions, a conflict between formal and customary systems of law exists. Almost any lawyer will note, however, that the Western legal tradition is hardly inflexible or purely coded in writing; and most anthropologists will admit that most non-Western, unwritten social traditions are somewhat fixed. But, Western formal systems themselves conceive of a distance between formal and customary law through binary categories that neatly separate the "us" from the "them." As noted by Alison Renteln and Alan Dundes, westerners understand the distinction between formal and customary systems of law according to a set of binary oppositions: [9]

Customary	Formal
Oral	Written
Flexible	Fixed
Anonymous	Known Author
Old	New
Primitive	Civilized
Folk	Elite
Peasant	Aristocrat
Rural	Urban

Two things are quite remarkable in the above oppositions: first, the formal system connotes itself as superior to customary law; and second, one of the major definitive qualities of customary law is the fact that it is *unwritten*. Because of this, some authors have suggested that the phrase "customary law" is a contradiction in terms. For instance, early scholars like Emile de Laveleye suggest that the very purpose of law is to either

[7] *See* Wing, *supra* note 1, at 341, 362.

[8] *Id.* at 298. "Negative rights" are rights to noninterference from the state. "Positive rights" are the right to certain benefits and financial support from the state.

[9] *What Is Folk Law?*, *in* 1 FOLK LAW: ESSAYS IN THE THEORY AND PRACTICE OF *LEX NON SCRIPTA* 3 (Alison Dundes Renteln & Alan Dundes eds., 1994) [hereinafter FOLK LAW].

codify or alter practices that are based in nonwritten tradition.[10] Some scholars, like Renteln and Dundes, apply the term "folk law" in lieu of "customary law" because the term "custom" may have confusing connotations.[11] Regardless of the theoretical limitations to defining systems of law, courts do use the term "customary law" as distinct from mainstream Western standards of practice. Moreover, courts often assert that a customary practice may be legislated or recorded in writing, despite the idea that such lexical actions oppose the very concept of folk law in theory.

Another approach toward conceptualizing customary versus formal law focuses upon the idea of "rules" versus "processes." Competing cultural concepts of marriage provide an apt example of the distinction between rules and processes. Western culture is dependent upon binary oppositions of marital status—"married" versus "single." Authors such as John Comaroff and Simon Roberts, however, have found that the binary concept of married versus unmarried does not exist in every culture.[12] The Tswana of Africa, for instance, do not hold a theory of marriage that corresponds to the Western institution: instead, these people formalize a relationship through a long series of processes requiring years of development.[13] To an extent, much confusion in the formal legal system derives from simple mistranslation: dichotomous terms that represent married versus unmarried simply do not exist in the Tsawna language or cultural concepts of family, while the English language lacks its own words to capture the various phases of family union in Tswana culture.[14] Comaroff and Roberts point out that in Tswana custom there is no defining moment between one's status as married or single, and there are a variety of relations between Tswana men and women which may result in rights to support or "alimony" upon separation.[15] The magnitude of such rights depends mostly upon the way that each spouse's family has processed the relationship and upon the trading of goods or obligations between two families over time. Disputes over marital status and property are resolved by tribal leaders through the balancing of individual narratives and tribal or familial consensus as to what the appropriate law should be.[16] This quality of mutability in Tswana law is particularly important to members of traditional societies whose lives are often governed by nomadic movement or a subsistence that is highly conditioned on seasonal and environmental changes. Comaroff and Roberts do not suggest that Tswana custom consists of processes in the absence of

[10] EMILE DE LAVELEYE, PRIMITIVE PROPERTY (G.R.L. Marriott, trans., 1985) (1878).

[11] FOLK LAW, *supra* note 9, at 4 "All folk law is customary in the sense that it is traditional, but not all custom is law!" *Id.*

[12] *See* JOHN L. COMAROFF & SIMON ROBERTS, RULES AND PROCESSES, 133 (1981).

[13] *See id.* at 134.

[14] *See id.*

[15] *See id.* at 152.

[16] *See id.*

binding rules, but that "the value of distinguishing 'the legal' as a discrete field of inquiry" from cultural processes and narrative may be of less value in some non-Western societies.[17]

In the United States, many American Indian tribes hold concepts of familial relations similar to the African Tswana. Many tribes, like the Hopi, the Apache, the Navajo, the Zuni, or the O'odham, do not conceive of a union between two people as permanent until there is a long-term process of transferred rights and obligations.[18] Robert Cooter and Wolfgang Fikentscher explicitly note that "the married-unmarried dichotomy fits poorly when applied to Indian tribes."[19] Some tribes, like the "O'odham expect to go through several 'marriages' before settling into a permanent union."[20] Other tribes, like the Zuni, merely require cohabitation in conjunction with a family prayer delivered over the couple in the Zuni language.[21] In short, there is great cultural and social variation between tribes and between localities within tribes. In fact, each tribal court has different standards for determining whether a union between two people has been accomplished according to custom. Tribal courts attempt to apply and preserve local customary laws; however, customary marriages often frustrate the need to determine whether a couple is married or single in nontribal state courts. Native Americans often wish to maintain their cultural processes and customs, but the federal government, with its emphasis on written verification and the married-unmarried dichotomy, usually requires Native Americans to define marriage in a way that is contrary to their culture. In tribes that recognize permanent unions through cohabitation, it has been reported that:

> Tribal government officials also advise Indians to regularize marriage by having a ceremony. Navajo authorities would like a clearer criterion for marriage. The Navajo code of 1980 covered the formalities of tribal marriage. To achieve greater legal clarity, it discourages common law marriages and encourages people to have weddings before civil or religious authorities. Indeed, some Navajos say that the statute forbids courts from recognizing common law marriage. A similar policy was reported in Acoma, where [officials have] tried to discourage common law marriage.[22]

[17] *Id.* at 243.

[18] *See* Robert D. Cooter & Wolfgang Fikentscher, *Indian Common Law: The Role of Custom in American Indian Tribal Courts*, 46 AM. J. COMP. L. 509, 537–41 (1998).

[19] *Id.* at 537.

[20] *Id.* at 538.

[21] *Id.*

[22] *Id.* at 539. It should be noted that the term "common-law" marriage here is shorthand for customary marriage—courts and government officials often designate "undefinable" customary marriages as common-law marriage. This point is discussed in more detail below.

The conflict between a legal system that relies upon a dichotomy of married-unmarried and a non-Western cultural system that recognizes several variations of familial union is also exemplified in the Nigerian case *In the Matter of an Intended Marriage Between E.O. Beckley and Christiana O. Abiodun.*[23] There, an applicant requested formal legal recognition of her marriage performed according to Yoruba custom, so that her husband would be prevented from marrying another woman and foregoing support obligations.[24] According to Yoruba custom, there is more than one type of valid familial bond. Furthermore, permanent familial unions may manifest in a number of different ways: a valid bond between the couple may be created through cohabitation, payment of a dowry, a preliminary engagement ceremony (an *Idana*), payment of certain expenses, a series of manifestations from the husband and his family over an indefinite period of time, or by ceremony in a church (only used amongst Christianized sects of Yoruba). Finally, a union may be accomplished by a formalized "delivering" of the wife to the husband. The *Idana* may be performed by proxy and manifestations of consent to marriage may be made through an exchange of correspondences or messengers. The goal of these various procedures is twofold: the long-term process not only creates a familial bond between man and woman, but also creates a bond of gifts and obligations between the couple's families.

At issue in *Abiodun* was precisely when the couple became "married," if at all. Members of the Yoruba tribe could not agree to a single status of the couple at any particular point in time: some experts held that the husband's manifest consent rendered the couple married; some believed that the exchange of a dowry was more indicative of marriage; some held that the *Idana* was a *more* complete state of union between the couple; and some claimed that the *Idana* did not create *as much of a marriage* as the actual delivery of the wife to the husband.[25] Despite the apparent lack of a clear married-unmarried dichotomy, the court determined that a marriage was not completed unless there was a "delivery" of the wife to the husband.[26] The court's determination was partly based upon a book written

---

[23] Beckley v. Abiodun, 1943 (17) NIG.L.R. 59 (High Court).

[24] Customary law often only reaches courts of the national or state government and only through appeal. Usually, lower tribal courts will be in place to apply customary law directly to the people they govern. This is true in both the United States and most African nations. This does not change, however, the fact that subordinate courts have a "formalizing" effect upon customary law. Furthermore, state or national courts are often not required to take judicial notice of native court findings of a valid custom. *See* Muna Ndulo, *Ascertainment of Customary Law: Problems and Perspectives with Special Reference to Zambia*, *in* FOLK LAW, *supra* note 9, 339–46. Moreover, where judicial notice of a practice is required, native courts are still required to apply the same standards of proof and factual consistency demanded by the formal system of which they are a part.

[25] *Beckley*, (17) NIG. L.R. at 64–65.

[26] *Id.* at 65.

by a judge (a non-Yoruba expert on Yoruba custom).[27] Secondly, the court invoked Western contract law to hold that the giving of the bride was necessary to "effect a contract" by exchange of consideration.[28] In short, the court believes that contract law is surely at the heart of Yoruba custom. The imposition of Western legal principles on customary law often yields grotesque hybrids of "law" and "cultural meaning." In the *Abioudun* case, the application of contract law to Yoruba custom inserts a sense of "wife purchase" that was not within the original cultural meaning of the practice.

The idea that Western principles of contract and consideration lie at the heart of Yoruba custom seems totally misplaced. Furthermore, by holding that the Yoruba union takes place at the moment of delivery of the woman to the husband, the formal court has set a precedent that *solidifies* the customary concept of marriage: the flexibility and dynamic nature of Yoruba customary marriage is now fixed at a specific moment in the marital process. In other words, the court has made a rule out of the Yoruba marriage process. Variation and flexibility is an attribute of customary law precisely because these social groups identify themselves through their smaller, mobile communities and family groups as opposed to larger national identities. Thus, imposing formal rules upon customary processes imposes a whole new identity upon a people who previously sought their identity through community and family.[29]

Of course, the Western legal practitioner is sure to ask, "But what else is a judge to do if he wishes to resolve the case?" Since the married-unmarried dichotomy lies at the very heart of Western family law, it seems that courts are categorically unable to accommodate alternative, nondichotomous cultural constructions of family. In the end, there are several problems for the cultural minority dealing with customary marriage in court and for the legal practitioner. First, as noted in the previous discussion about Native American marriages, many cultures have been forced to construct a ceremony and implant the married-unmarried dichotomy into their cultural heritage. Second, how the formal system chooses to recognize customary marriages is often an unpredictable concoction of legal doctrine and cultural evidence because courts typically redefine non-Western practices into Western legal terms. As a general rule,

---

[27] The use of nontribal anthropologists or attorneys who practice on tribal land has been criticized because of the possibility for mistranslation and the tendency of these "experts" to fit any observed customary law into the preexisting paradigm.

[28] *Beckley*, (17) NIG. L.R. at 65. "[Delivery of the bride is] 'in effect a contract,' and no doubt . . . if one side only had given consideration, an action could be brought for the breach by the other side and the contract is not performed." *Id.*

[29] *See, e.g.*, John C. Messenger, Jr., *The Role of Proverbs in a Nigerian Judicial System*, *in* FOLK LAW, *supra* note 9, at 421, 422. "Politically preeminent is the community . . . and a hereditary leader and a council of elders direct its affairs." *Id.* Nuclear and extended families are greater sources of law and governance than any national, *or even tribal*, institution.

recognition of customary unions by Western courts is limited by evidentiary or public policy standards. Part II will show that even this general rule does not reveal a predictable pattern of adjudication.

II. DISSECTING EVIDENTIARY AND PUBLIC POLICY STANDARDS AS THEY APPLY TO CUSTOMARY MARRIAGES

Statutory and common laws impose limits on the recognition of customary unions due to either evidentiary standards or public policy. For example, under the Hindu Marriage Act of 1955, custom must be "certain and not unreasonable or opposed to public policy."[30] The purpose of this Part is to identify some trends in evidentiary and public policy standards as applied to customary marriages. Here, I refer mostly to scholarly treatment of this subject, with some application to specific cases. Furthermore, this discussion mainly draws on studies of indigenes embedded in a colonial system (e.g., the recognition of a Zulu marriage in colonial South Africa). Part III will demonstrate that the limitations imposed on customary marriages take on a more complex character when people from foreign, non-Western communities travel into the United States.

A. EVIDENTIARY STANDARDS AND THEIR LIMITS ON RECOGNITION OF CUSTOM

In countries that express a willingness to enforce and accommodate customary law, courts must choose which customs are "real" or recognizable before they enforce the practice. The recognition of customary law in common-law courts usually turns on the evidentiary character of the custom. T.O. Elias notes, "The age-old problem of customary law has been one of ensuring its certainty."[31] Even as early as *The Case of Tanistry* in 1608 there was a recognition in English common law that customs could be recognized by a court only if they were certain and of "immemorial usage."[32] The idea that a real custom only embraces the most ancient traditions of unwritten law is ironically at odds with the idea that custom is a flexible form of social control. Again the formal tendency to force a customary practice into a singular, written definition freezes the dynamic ability of customary law to change, and the idea that customary law should be ancient trumps qualities of mutability and community variation.

The use of the term "evidentiary standards" in this Note refers to the types of evidence that are considered relevant and the weight given to each

[30] The Hindu Marriage Act, 1955 (Act No. 25 of the Laws of India, 1955), *available at* http://www.sudhirlaw.com/hma55.htm.

[31] T.O. Elias, *The Problem of Reducing Customary Laws to Writing*, *in* FOLK LAW, *supra* note 9, at 319.

[32] The Case of Tanistry, 80 Eng. Rep. 516, 520 (K.B. 1608).

form of evidence. For instance, courts usually give more evidentiary weight to documents like marriage licenses, prenuptial agreements, and written acknowledgments of a marriage than they give to witnesses' narration about the ceremonial process. Of course, there are very good policies for this distinction: documents are considered to be more reliable than witnesses, and documents may provide a consistent indication of marriage in a world full of different marriage ceremonies. But, the extra weight given to written evidence in formal courts results in a burden of proof that the vast majority of cultural minorities are unable to meet since customary law is, by definition, unwritten. Regardless of the burden of proof born by a cultural minority (e.g., "more probable than not," a "preponderance," or "beyond a reasonable doubt") the recognition of customary marriages is inevitably frustrated by an evidentiary system that favors formalized evidence.

The idea that custom must be provable and certain has been translated into a requirement for "notoriety" in some formal courts. For instance, in West Africa and Ghana, nontribal courts often measure the validity of a customary practice by the number of "expert witnesses" who have heard of the practice.[33] These expert witnesses may be tribal members called by the parties, nontribal anthropologists or sociologists, or anthropological textbooks.[34] If the custom is significantly "notorious," then it is likely to be considered as real customary law and thus recognizable to the formal system.[35] The notoriety test is not in itself inconsistent with the essence of custom—clan chiefs and tribal leaders will often decide matters in the tribe by tribal consensus as supplemented by individual narration.[36] Formal notions of precedential value, however, often set a single case as the definition of customary practices for a large cultural group, thus removing all community and clan distinctions. Woodman suggests that notions of stare decisis may not only dissipate local variations, but that "once a rule has been judicially recognized, it is liable to be applied to ethnic groups other than those whose customs were in issue in the decisive cases."[37] For example, the Nigerian courts have sometimes held themselves bound by Ghanian decisions on customary law, although there is no significant ethnic group common to both countries.[38] On the other hand, lower courts do sometimes rebuff precedence and enforce or negate customary laws on the basis of their own discretion. This leads to contrary case decisions as to which customs are formally enforceable and which are not. Even worse, courts that do feel constrained by precedent may adjudicate by

---

[33] Gordon R. Woodman, *Some Realism About Customary Law—The West African Experience*, *in* FOLK LAW, *supra* note 9, at 83, 86.

[34] *Id.*

[35] Woodman, *supra* note 33, at 90.

[36] *See* COMAROFF & ROBERTS, *supra* note 12, at 26–29.

[37] Woodman, *supra* note 33, at 91.

[38] *Id.*

compromising inconsistent outcomes thus creating hybrid descriptions of customary practices that do not really exist in any culture.[39]

Another major problem with the notoriety requirement is that courts often look for consensus among nontribal experts, treatises, and judges to test the validity of a community practice.[40] Thus, the notoriety test is not really a "time immemorial" requirement but actually a proxy for the availability of experts and textbooks. Both tests reflect the formal system's need for certainty and consistency, and both pose serious consequences for the recognition of unwritten customary law.

In addition to proving ancient use or notoriety, many formal courts also require cultural minorities to show that a customary law corresponds to current practice. In other words, courts may judge the validity of customary laws by requiring the custom to be "ancient" and "notorious," or a court may emphasize the need to recognize only the most current trends in social practice. Thus, the cultural minority may be caught in the conundrum of proving that a cultural practice is both maximally ancient and maximally new at the same time. For example, in *DaBaase v. INS*, the defendant sought to show that he was divorced in Nigeria according to customs of his Ghanian tribe, and thus validly divorced for purposes of the U.S. legal system.[41] The court refused to recognize the divorce as valid since he did not provide a certified statement of "the *current* customary divorce law of that tribe."[42] Such an up-to-the-minute "certified description" of tribal customary divorce was probably unavailable to DaBaase since most customary law issues come before African tribal courts that only use oral testimony. Furthermore, and even more critical, such a certified statement would likely *not* be required in DaBaase's nation.[43] It therefore seems that in order to be recognized, a customary practice must strike a fine and often unpredictable balance between being "old" enough and being "current" enough to meet court standards.

Solidifying customary law into a singular, precedent-setting description in the name of evidentiary standards has several widely criticized effects upon custom. Many critics have noted that formal courts' emphasis on physical, verifiable manifestations of custom have drained cultural and community identity from many customs.[44] In other words, because formal courts mostly rely upon physical manifestations of a custom (as opposed to cultural meaning or narrative), they tend to treat the practice as an empty

---

[39] *Id.*
[40] *See id.* at 86–91.
[41] DaBaase v. INS, 627 F.2d 117 (8th Cir. 1980).
[42] *Id.* at 118 (emphasis added).
[43] *See* discussion *infra* Part III.A.
[44] *See, e.g.*, H. Patrick Glenn, *The Capture, Reconstruction and Marginalization of "Custom"*, 45 AM. J. COMP. L. 613 (1997).

shell. If we accept that custom is more than mere physical habit, then formal courts are perpetuating a habit that is void of cultural meaning or intent of the parties.[45] For instance, in the United States, formal courts recognized Native American marriages as manifest through mere cohabitation—if X lived with Y for so many years, the court says that they are married under tribal customary law. This is a convenient test for formal courts because it is generally easy to get an account of how long a couple cohabitates. Interviews with Zuni, Acoma, and Navajo leaders, however, suggest that each tribe requires specific prayers and public ceremony before the marriage is recognized by the tribe.[46] When the formal system asserts that the union is valid by mere cohabitation, a feeling of degradation is aroused: "If you talk of a common-law marriage in English or American common law, it's almost a denigration. Not so in Acoma."[47] Since courts are forced to recognize Native American customary marriages under federal law, they have done so by breaking down the rich variety of customs throughout the tribes into one recognizable act—cohabitation. This term conjures connotations of "living in sin," it ignores distinct tribal practices, and it de-emphasizes the cultural significance of Native American marriage practices and prayers. As mentioned in Part I of this Note, the formal system's tendency toward easily verifiable, physical manifestations of marriage also causes many government officials to request that tribes make their customs more public or more formally conspicuous through a single public ceremony. Thus, the nature of the formal system, as founded in stare decisis and verifiability, has changed both the form and cultural meaning of customary marital laws in several Native American tribes.

The use of native courts in each tribe has counteracted many of the destructive effects of the formal system upon customary law. As noted by Comaroff and Roberts, the Tswana community courts, or *kgotla*, preserve many of the mutable, customary practices through their unique processes of dispute resolution.[48] A clash between custom and formal law, however, is often greatest when a native court decision goes on appeal. Woodman observes that "superior courts have ignored native court opinions as to customary law."[49] In *Aseno v. Nkyidwuo*,[50] the state court, on review, determined that a native court had accepted customary law in a manner that was too broad. And in *Akomea v. Biei*[51] the reviewing superior state court found the custom accepted by a native court to be "ridiculous"! Revisions

[45] *See id.* at 613.
[46] *See* Cooter & Fikentscher, *supra* note 18, at 538.
[47] *Id.*
[48] *See* COMAROFF & ROBERTS, *supra* note 12, at 132–74.
[49] Woodman, *supra* note 33, at 87.
[50] Aseno v. Nkyidwuo, 1956 (1) W. AFR. L.R. 243.
[51] Akomea v. Biei, 1958 (1) W.A.L.R. 174, *reprinted in* N.A. OLLENNU, PRINCIPALS OF CUSTOMARY LAND LAW IN GHANA, at 186–92 (1962).

in human rights and new national constitutions have led to some changes in appellate review of native court decisions in some nations. For example, the new South African Constitution creates a right to non-Western cultural traditions that commentators predict will result in less emphasis upon marital registry and greater deference to native court findings.[52] In the United States, customary law determinations in Native American courts have long been given great deference under the notion of "full faith and credit" to judgments of another state.[53] If native court sovereignty is respected, "custom is the 'underground' law of the courts."[54] Therefore, native court sovereignty is a critical counter-force to the stifling effects that evidentiary standards in state or national courts have upon customary law.

B. Public Policy Limitations to the Recognition of Custom

Public policy limits on formal recognition of customary law may be one of the most widely discussed issues in the study of law and anthropology. Immediately, issues such as child marriage or polygamy come to mind. But there is a larger pattern of social definitions that surround each decision that one custom is "reasonable" to Western society while another is not.

First, the policy depends upon the public. In Western colonies abiding by ideals of Christian scripture, the validity of non-Western customary laws was tested by the extent to which each custom was "contrary not only to the scripture but to common sense and common humanity."[55] In a Victorian society steeped in ideals of technological and economic progress, public policy was defined in terms of "civilized" versus "uncivilized": civilized society was seen as doing the uncivilized a favor by pulling them from their traditional "barbaric" laws.[56]

The characterization of any marital custom as "repugnant" or contrary to public policy lies in the very definition of marriage. In early colonial contexts in which the term "marriage" was defined as a "Christian union between man and woman," the essence of marriage was its performance by

[52] *See* Attorney-Editors of Int'l Legal Materials for the Am. Soc'y of Int'l Law Reports and Other Documents, *International Law in Brief, Jan. 18–29, 1999: Developments in International Law*, http://www.asil.org/ilib18.htm (visited Feb. 1, 2000).

[53] Cooter & Fikentscher *supra* note 18, at 561. The authors note that native courts have created their own "tribal laws" for substantive matters such as what constitutes a valid marriage ceremony. Other laws of procedure and some other specific issues have been specifically legislated by the federal government and thus present a body of "Indian law." While federal courts do review and apply "Indian law," deference is given to the substantive findings of the native court in terms of "tribal law." *See id.* at 558–61.

[54] *Id.* at 563.

[55] Ormichund v. Barker, 125 Eng. Rep. 1310 (Ch. 1744).

[56] *See* Ross Russell, *Legal Pluralism in New Zealand over the Last One Hundred and Twenty Three Years*, 5 LAW & ANTHROPOLOGY 66, 67–68 (1990).

an ordained member of a Christian church.[57] This definition of marriage automatically precludes recognition of any union not solemnized in a Christian Church.[58] There have, however, been many alternative definitions of marriage throughout history. Some courts accept a "partnership theory of marriage" that looks to the shared relationship between spouses instead of a particular religious doctrine.[59] Indeed, it is this "partnership" concept of marriage—a trade of obligations and expectations between two people—that generally justifies common-law marriage in Western culture. The case of *Zimnat Insurance Company v. Chawanda*[60] aptly illustrates how social policies toward customary marriages mirror changes in the social definition of marriage.

In the Zimbabwean case of *Chawanda*, the court recognized an unregistered customary union in the face of precedent that defined marriage strictly in terms of proper licensing procedures. Older common-law and legislative authorities defined marriage strictly in terms of written licensing requirements for fear of unfettered liability in the context of marital disputes and lack of procedural efficiency. Moving away from formalistic notions of marriage as a written license, the *Chawanda* Court chose to redefine marriage as a series of partnership-like, familial obligations between man and woman.

This redefinition was likely a result of changing policies in South Africa (cultural rights and justice became more forceful policies). Moreover, redefining marriage allows the court to overwrite previous policies that demanded strict licensing and limited standing to sue. In fact, the court even recognizes customary marriages for purposes of recovery for wrongful death where the union was polygamous. The issue of polygamous marriage rears its head as a threat to public policy in terms of indeterminate liability and gender equality.[61] Polygamous marriages, which are a traditional custom of many African tribes, are of great judicial concern in Africa because of their potential to create indeterminate liability. But, the *Chawanda* court notes:

---

[57] *See, e.g., id.* (discussing the recognition of customary law in New Zealand and the effect of different definitions for legal terms on social policy in legislation).

[58] For example, colonial New Zealand laws actually contained a list of churches that a marriage ceremony had to be performed in to be valid. *Id.* at 80.

[59] Some U.S. courts have propounded a definition of marriage that emphasizes the sharing of rights and duties between two people of any gender. The definition of marriage is at the heart of the single-sex marriage debate in which courts and legislatures do not always agree upon one definition or which social policies should take priority in defining marriage. *See, e.g.*, Baehr v. Miike No. 91-1394, 1996 WL 694235 (Haw. Cir. Ct. 1996).

[60] 1991(2) SA 825 (claiming that widow's customary marriage to her husband was valid for purposes of recovering damages for his wrongful death).

[61] It is notable that the *Chawanda* court does not discuss polygamy as a policy concern for reasons of moral or social integrity.

> Damages for loss of support resulting from the death of the breadwinner, unlike instalment [sic] payments of maintenance which are subject to variation dependent upon any change in the circumstances of the parties, are awarded in a lump sum for past and future deprivation of support. This type of action would be confined within reasonable and manageable bounds and not fraught with what has been described as 'overwhelming potential liability'. [sic] There would not be a multitude of claims brought against one defendant, but a single claim in every instance [of a spouse's death]. If the deceased breadwinner had more than one customary law wife, the amount of the award would be divisible between them.[62]

In sum, by reinterpreting the definition of marriage the court is able to recognize a custom that was previously deemed contrary to public policy. This redefinition of marriage corresponds with a shift in priorities in public policy. Moreover, the court is able to open a "window" of recognition for polygamous marriages, which were previously considered contrary to public policies of finite liability.

But changes in public policy do not come rapidly and do not issue from thin air. The court finds interpretive room for valid customary marriages in legislative revisions to the law of wrongful death claims. The *Chawanda* court bases much of its seemingly expansive holding on the fact that the Workmens' Compensation laws had recently been amended to embrace broader notions of a valid marriage. There is no indication that narrower and more formalistic definitions of marriage may still be the law in other legal contexts.[63] In sum, customary marriage may be enforceable in some legal contexts, but not in others. For example, even though the claimant in *Chawanda* was given standing to recover wrongful death damages, this does not mean that the union would have been recognized as valid with regard to other questions of law.[64] Thus, there is a possibility that a claimant's marriage is "valid" for some legal claims, but not for others.

Customary law and communal rights often conflict with individual rights. For example, the *Chawanda* court discusses policies of gender equality (rights of the individual) in its assessment of potentially polygamous customary marriages (group rights). Angeline Shenje-Peyton uses the Zimbabwean example of *lobola*, or the gift of money to a wife's family before marriage, as an example of a cultural practice (to which some tribal members claim to have a right) that perpetuates female subordination (an individual right).[65] Many anthropologists argue that *lobola* is not really

---

[62] *Chawanda*, 1991(2) SA at 831.

[63] *Id.*

[64] *Id.* The statute in question was the South African Fatal Accidents Act 1976, as amended by § 3 of the Administration of Justice Act 1982.

[65] Angeline Shenje-Peyton, *Balancing Gender, Equality, and Cultural Identity: Marriage Payments in Post-Colonial Zimbabwe*, 9 HARV. HUM. RTS. J. 105, 105 (1996). Some commentators have also argued that customary law is "always" subordinating to women in that it is, by definition, traditional.

"wife purchase," but instead a means of creating family and community bonds by the exchange of duties and obligations between extended family members of a man and woman.[66] It is possible, however, that where the formal system has attempted to accommodate *lobola*, it has ironically destroyed these benign motives through misinterpretation and unintended imposition.[67] Recall, for example, that the application of traditional Western contract principles to customary law may cause some cultural practices to look like a "wife purchase" even though purchase transactions are entirely outside the original cultural meaning of the custom.[68]

In sum, the idea that public policy limitations are immutable, timeless, and clear is misleading. Public policy standards may contradict each other. In South Africa, for example, the newly adopted constitution guarantees both gender equality and rights of cultural traditions.[69] But, in the context of customary marriage, traditional practices like polygamy and *lobolo* pose a contradiction in policy that has not been entirely resolved.[70]

Often, the issue of whether a marriage is contrary to public policy may seem easy to Western courts. Criminal offenses involving "child marriage" or "marriage by kidnap" are often regarded as repugnant to policy without further inquiry into mens rea or validity of the customary practice.[71] Here, I have attempted to show that the nature of public policy toward customary unions is not always as clear cut as these headline criminal cases may seem to the westerner public.

III. EQUITABLE DOCTRINES AND POLICIES APPLIED TO CUSTOMARY MARRIAGES

In this Part, I discuss the treatment of marital customs under a variety of legal doctrines. Indigenous cultures usually have customary laws accommodated under broad federal or state statutes. As noted in Part II, however, the recognition of customary law is curtailed by evidentiary and policy standards within the formal system despite these protections. Where Western courts are asked to recognize the custom of non-Western

Many cases dealing with customary law, like *Chawanda*, however, are brought by women whose social standing and finances would be harmed if the marriage were found invalid; suggesting that very often it is the formal system's treatment of customary law, and not the customary law itself, that is subordinating.

[66] *See*, Shenje-Peyton, *supra* note 65, at 105–06.

[67] *See id.* at 105.

[68] *See* notes 18–22 and accompanying text.

[69] *See* S. AFR. CONST. of Feb. 7, 1997, §§ 9, 31.

[70] *See* Mail & Guardian, *Marriage Law Will Be Transformed*, http://www.mg.co.za/news/96oct1/04oct-marry1.htm (last visited Feb. 10, 2000).

[71] Deirdre Evans-Pritchard & Alison Dundes Renteln, *The Interpretation and Distortion of Culture: A Hmong "Marriage by Capture" Case in Fresno, California*, 4 S. CAL. INTERDISC. L.J. 1, 6 (1995).

immigrants, those evidentiary and policy limitations are much more stringent since courts are unfamiliar with and suspicious of foreign customs, and imported customary laws do not fall under protection of federal statutes like 25 U.S.C. § 348.[72] Consequently, when dealing with nondomestic customs, formal courts usually turn to common-law principles. Marriages (and divorces) imported from other nations are generally considered to be "valid where consummated" (this has been codified in some states). That is, if the marriage or divorce was valid in its country of origin, it is theoretically valid in the United States. Alternatively, there is an array of other equitable doctrines that may be invoked to "save" the validity of a customary marriage. These other equitable doctrines or policies include the common-law marriage, the putative marriage doctrine, and the "cultural defense" (regarding criminal mens rea). While most of these doctrines have the potential to bring cultural evidence into the legal system and better accommodate cultural minorities, we will see that the treatment of customary law under each of these doctrines obstructs cultural meaning, actually hindering the preservation of customary law and non-Western culture.

A. "VALID WHERE CONSUMMATED" AND ACCOMMODATION OF CUSTOMARY MARRIAGE

While the idea that a marriage valid in its country of origin is valid everywhere seems attractively clear and fair, the doctrine is not as bright lined as it appears, and the rule often subjects claimants to evidentiary double standards. "Valid-where-consummated," as a legal construct, is also applied inconsistently between different jurisdictions and within different legal matters in the same jurisdiction. For instance, a court in the United States is likely to require documentation that would not be required for a valid marriage in the claimant's country of origin. More critically, whether a marriage is valid in its country of origin is not always a "yes" or "no" question: a marriage can be valid for some purposes, but invalid for others (as discussed below, courts may turn to equitable doctrines to try and "save" the marriage). In general, the formal system forces the nonindigenous cultural minority to "westernize" customary laws and cultural practices by fitting them into a doctrine that is familiar to Western jurisprudence.

[72] 25 U.S.C. § 348 (2000) (demanding formal recognition of any marriage between Native Americans under Native American custom). *See also* Osborne v. Babbitt, 61 F.3d 810 (10th Cir. 1995).

1. *Valid-Where-Consummated and Evidentiary Limits to Recognizing Customary Marriage*

The evidentiary standards that an immigrant must meet to prove the validity of a customary marriage are more complex than the standards that must be met by an indigenous claimant. The case of *DaBaase v. INS*[73] aptly illustrates the evidentiary double standard. In *DaBaase*, the claimant sought recognition of his customary divorce completed in Ghana. The court claims to apply the rule of "valid where consummated": if DaBaase's divorce is valid in Ghana, then it is valid in the United States. Trends in many African nations toward recognition of unrecorded customary marriages and divorces will likely lead people from those countries to believe that their customary marriage or divorce will be recognized in the United States under the promise of "valid-where-consummated." Immigrant claimant, however, *actually* must meet a higher evidentiary standard than necessary in their country of origin. This is due to the fact that foreign customary laws lack federal statutory protection whereas Native American marital customs are often protected under federal statute. In *DaBaase* the U.S. court required documentation of Francis DaBaase's marital status as valid in Ghana. This documentation would not have been required in the case of a Native American customary marriage because, as discussed above, Native American customary law is explicitly protected by federal statute. Moreover, this documentation was not required by any law in DaBaase's home country, Ghana. Although DaBaase provides the court with affidavits from his ex-wife that "she had been divorced [from] her husband Francis A. DaBaase under the Ghanian Tribal Native Customs Divorce" and a letter from the Ghanaian Embassy asserting that "the Ghana government recognizes tribal marriage and divorce customs," these did not satisfy DaBaase's burden of proving that the divorce was a valid custom under Ghanaian law.

It seems that what the court really wanted DaBaase to supply was a certified government document that individually recorded DaBaase's divorce. This requirement poses several problems for the cultural minority seeking recognition of a customary marriage or divorce in the United States. First, Ghana does not require individual governmental recording of customary unions, and such certified documents are likely unavailable or even detrimental to the married couple.[74] More importantly, these

[73] 627 F.2d 117 (8th Cir. 1980).

[74] *See, e.g.*, Appomasu v. Bremawuo, [1980] G.L.R. 278 (ACCRA Ct. App. Ghana) (noting that a marriage ceremony that did not yield a certificate or license was, by definition, a valid customary union). The Ghanian law of marriage is similar to Zimbabwean marriage in that one may choose to marry in the Western fashion and subscribe to formal, Western laws, or, if a non-Western native, one may marry by tribal custom and subscribe primarily to customary law in all family matters with no written, procedural requirements. In fact, many couples may prefer to marry by custom since this entails

documents, especially the affidavit, would probably have met DaBaase's burden of proving the validity of his divorce in any Ghanaian court.[75] Therefore, it is quite possible that DaBaase's customary divorce *would* have been valid under Ghanaian law. How can one then say that customary marriages in the United States are valid-where-consummated? Inconsistent applications of the valid-where-consummated rule cause many practitioners to advise immigrant spouses to record their customary marriages in a U.S. formal proceeding: "In some cases it may be a good idea to re-marry if necessary to get a marriage certificate."[76] The problem with this advice is that, on a theoretical level, it destroys any sense of customary law. Secondly, a cultural minority may not know that a U.S. certificate is necessary unless they have access to legal advice. Lastly, there are often practical hurdles to formalizing a customary marriage in the United States, especially if the other spouse, or ex-spouse, is located in another country and the immigrant is unable to give another person power of attorney in that country.

Recall that many customary laws may be recognized as valid for some purposes, but held invalid for others.[77] This presents another problem for formal courts and the customary claimant: how is the court or the claimant to know if a customary marriage is valid under the laws of the original country if the custom is valid for some purposes and invalid for others? In uncertain cases, the courts in the United States decide against finding the ceremony to be valid. Thus, as seen in the *DaBaase* case, where the status of the marriage in its country of origin is of some question, or is invalid for any purpose, the court refuses to recognize the marriage.

United States courts interpret cases against the cultural minority for fear that "lenient" recognition of customary laws in other nations will lead to fraud in immigration and potential public policy violations. In cases of citizenship via marriage, courts are especially suspicious of fraud if the marriage was performed by custom or if a divorce in the claimant's previous country was performed by custom. In such cases, courts effectively forego the valid-where-consummated doctrine. For instance, in *Egan v. INS*,[78] the court was asked to recognize a customary divorce performed in the immigrant's home country of Nigeria. The court refused to even reach the question of whether the customary divorce was valid in

fewer procedural complications and also determines the choice of law ("formal" or "customary") under which the marriage will be treated.

[75] *See DaBaase*, 627 F.2d at 117.

[76] *See* Richard Madison, *A Brief Look at Marriage and Immigration*, http:www.lawcom.com/marriage.shtm (last modified Nov. 17, 1997).

[77] *See Zimnat Ins. Co. v. Chawanda*, 1991 (2) SA 825, 831 (determining that the customary union may not be completely valid, but is at least valid for the narrow purposes of new legislation in the Fatal Accidents Act 1976).

[78] 119 F.3d 106 (2d Cir. 1997).

Nigeria despite a confirmation of a tribal Nigerian court that the claimant was not married. The court's refusal to recognize the divorce was based on the court's finding that ambiguous circumstances made the credibility of the witness questionable and that a "foreign judgment may not be accepted by the courts where the proceedings underlying that judgment may have been conducive to fraud or collusion, even though the propriety of the judgment itself is not in question."[79] Thus, where a United States court senses a "taint of fraud," the court may refuse to recognize a marriage even if the marriage is clearly valid where consummated. The concurrence in *Egan* disparages:

> [A] Customary Court in Oyo, Nigeria has confirmed, apparently to the satisfaction of the Nigerian process requirements, that despite the husband's earlier (and fraudulent) representations to the contrary, he was never married before he left Nigeria. It is one thing for the INS to challenge his credibility, but quite another to disparage the official act of the Oyo Customary Court. . . .
>
> [T]he INS nonetheless sought to "tear asunder" an apparently long-standing, valid Connecticut marriage by deporting her husband.[80]

Other courts dealing with immigration issues have simply stated that, as a general rule, naturalization cases involve very high burdens of proving the validity of any foreign marriage or divorce. Furthermore, the INS is given great deference in its decision to not recognize a marriage whether or not the marriage is valid where consummated. In *Oddo v. Reno*, the court notes, "The Attorney General may revoke an approved visa petition at any time fo.r "good and sufficient cause."[81] It continues:

> This court may set aside the INS's action, findings, and conclusions if found to be "arbitrary, capricious, an abuse of discretion, or otherwise not in accordance with law." . . . This is a highly deferential standard and our review is limited. . . . The agency will stand if the record reveals a rational basis for the decision.[82]

2. *Valid-Where-Consummated and Public Policy Limits to Recognizing Customary Marriage*

Public policy trumps recognition of a custom, even where the valid-where-consummated doctrine applies. For example, in *People v. Ezeonu*, the court could disregard the valid-where-consummated rule if the marriage was against public policy: the court did find that the Nigerian man's marriage was valid under Nigerian law, but that it was "absolutely void

---

[79] *Id.* at 108 (quoting the Board of Immigration Appeals).
[80] *Id.* at 109.
[81] 175 F.3d 1015, 1999 WL 170173, **2 (4th Cir. 1999).
[82] *Id.*

even where it was legally consummated in Nigeria."[83] Public policy limits to the recognition of customary law have earned much criticism from scholars of law and anthropology since public policy limits almost never address the fact that the claimant has a bona fide belief in the validity of his marriage.[84] Overall, the invocation of public policy will overcome any request that a customary marriage is recognized.

In sum, we see that the rule of valid-where-consummated is limited on several grounds. Evidentiary standards in the United States may render a marriage that is valid in its country of origin invalid in the United States. While formalizing a marriage or divorce in the United States or obtaining a certificate from a customary court of the country of origin may be helpful, this option is not always available to the immigrant. Such certification also greatly undermines the significance and meaning of customary law to those trying to preserve their culture. A taint of fraud, even if there is only a rational basis for suspicion, may overcome any claim that the custom was valid in its country of origin. Naturalization cases also present a special problem to immigrants who must overcome judicial deference in favor of the INS. In sum, despite a first impression that valid-where-consummated is a clear rule, the doctrine is actually very limited, and often puts the immigrant claimant in a no-win situation.

B. COMMON-LAW MARRIAGE AND VALIDATION OF A CUSTOMARY MARRIAGE

When a court is unable to apply the valid-where-consummated doctrine to enforce a customary marriage, the cultural minority may invoke the doctrine of common-law marriage in those jurisdictions that recognize it. The common-law marriage doctrine is often treated very differently from one state to the next. Most U.S. states simply recognize or refuse recognition of common-law marriage entirely; some allow common-law marriages made within the state, but not elsewhere; and others allow common-law marriages if they are valid where consummated, but do not recognize marriages created through cohabitation in that state.[85]

Applications of the common-law marriage doctrine to customary marriages in the United States clearly present the important difference in treatment between indigenous claimants and nonindigenous claimants. Recall the case of *Osborne v. Babbitt*,[86] in which otherwise illegitimate

[83] 588 N.Y.S. 2d 116, 118 (Sup. Ct. 1992). *See* discussion *infra* Part III.D. for further discussion of the *Ezeonu* case.

[84] This has been most criticized in the criminal context where intent plays such an important role and specifically may be invoked in the context of the cultural defense. *See* discussion, *infra* Part II.D.

[85] *See* Madison, *supra* note 76.

[86] 61 F.3d 810 (10th Cir. 1995).

Native American children sought to inherit by intestacy from a decedent whose marriage was valid only under Pawnee custom. 25 U.S.C. § 371[87] allows for the recognition of Native American marriages through cohabitation even if the marriage would otherwise be invalid under state law. Thus, Native American customs that would otherwise be cognizable only under a common-law marriage doctrine are "saved" from state laws proscribing common-law marriage by the federal statute.

In the case of an immigrant to the United States, there is no federal protection for the customary practices of the claimant; if the claimant asks that a customary marriage be recognized under the common-law marriage doctrine, the outcome is usually dependent upon state law. *People v. Suarez*[88] exemplifies how and why immigrants would need to invoke legal constructs alternative to the valid-where-consummated doctrine. In *Suarez*, a Puerto Rican citizen claimed that he was married to his wife under a Puerto Rican custom. The claimant, however, did not offer sufficient evidence of the custom to prove that such a custom was valid in Puerto Rico according to the New York court. In the alternative, the claimant asserted that his marriage was valid as a common-law marriage in Ohio. The court accepted this alternative argument and thus allowed for the validation of Suarez's marriage in the trial court.[89] Thus, Suarez's customary marriage was "saved" under this legal construct.

From an anthropological perspective, the problem with the common-law marriage doctrine is that it does not recognize *customary law*—the doctrine does not even get cultural evidence into the courtroom at all. As a legal construct, common-law marriage is a way of validating a marriage without validating, or even acknowledging, the customary process. Indeed, the rationale behind proscribing common-law marriage in many states has been the fear that it will lead to recognition of customary laws, and that this in turn would "lead to varied, ad hoc determinations, and eventual discriminatory effects that would afford certain groups greater protection than others."[90] Recall also that for many westerners, common-law marriage implies the moral transgression of "living in sin." This makes cultural

[87] 25 U.S.C § 371 (1999) (validating the rights of heirs to a deceased Native American to be recognized even if the individual was married or born from a marriage that is only recognized in the Native American culture. *See also* 25 U.S.C. § 348 (2000).

[88] 560 N.Y.S.2d 68 (Sup. Ct. 1990) (defense claim of a valid marriage so the defendant could invoke evidentiary privileges for statements made between spouses).

[89] Of course, if Suarez's marriage had been consummated in New York, which has prohibited common-law marriage, the marriage could never be recognized as valid.

[90] *Suarez*, 560 N.Y.S.2d at 69. This rationale may be criticized for being ambiguous: why the effects of recognizing customary unions under common-law marriage doctrine would be "discriminatory" or why it would afford common-law spouses "greater protection" than non-common-law spouses is unclear.

minorities feel that their otherwise respectable and revered cultural practice has been assigned to a degraded or immoral category of formal law.[91]

Therefore, the application of the common-law marriage doctrine to customary marriages exemplifies apparently irresolvable problems between formal law and cultural preservation. For the formal court, customary unions must be recognized in a way that does not substantiate the custom, since the nearly infinite number of customs would lead to "ad hoc determinations," and because the potential for fraud is so high. For courts in jurisdictions that allow it, the common-law marriage is a good means of enforcing marital rights without dealing with a morass of unfamiliar customs and cultures. For the anthropologist and cultural minority, common-law marriage is an empty shell that creates marital rights recognized by the state, while failing to recognize religious or cultural meaning.

C. THE PUTATIVE MARRIAGE DOCTRINE AND ACCOMMODATION OF CUSTOMARY MARRIAGES.

While the valid-where-consummated and common-law marriage doctrines look only at "objective" manifestations of the marriage and ignore the customary law and cultural meanings by which the marriage was actually consummated, the putative marriage doctrine could *potentially* bring cultural evidence into court. The putative marriage doctrine renders an otherwise invalid marriage valid through the reasonable expectations of one spouse. Upon finding *a reasonable, good-faith belief,* by one or both parties, that a valid marriage was consummated, the court shall divide property between these "putative spouses" according to state law.[92] The putative marriage doctrine is often invoked in cases dealing with customary marriages because of its focus upon intent and belief: claimants wish to have the reasonableness of their beliefs judged in terms of their culture and customary law. Furthermore, the open-ended concept of "reasonableness" invites discussion of group and cultural rights in a multicultural society; an invitation that has generally been declined by courts. Despite its potential for bringing cultural evidence into United States courtrooms, the putative marriage doctrine is often limited by the simplistic notion that a belief in customary marriage may be "unreasonable" simply because the practice is different from state law or unrecognizable in traditional Western terms.

The case of *Vryonis v. Vryonis*[93] aptly illustrates this point. There, a woman named Fereshteh, an Iranian citizen and member of the Shiah Moslem Twelve Imams (Islam), claimed that she held a reasonable, good

[91] *See* Cooter & Fikentscher, *supra* note 18, at 538.
[92] *See, e.g., In re* Marriage of Monti, 185 Cal. Rptr. 72, 72 (Ct. App. 1982).
[93] 248 Cal. Rptr. 807 (Ct. App. 1988).

faith belief that a *Mut'a* marriage ceremony created a valid marriage. The ceremony was conducted in private, with no witnesses. It was agreed that both parties were fully informed about the customary significance of the ceremony. The "husband," Speros, did not contest that he assured petitioner that the marriage was valid in California.[94] Speros then chose to "break" the *Mut'a* and marry another woman. Upon learning that her marriage was unrecorded and thus void under regular California law, Fereshteh claimed quasi-marital property rights under the putative marriage doctrine. Nonetheless, the court found that even if Fereshteh's belief in the validity of the *Mut'a* was bona fide and true to Islamic custom, the belief was unreasonable.[95]

The trial court in this case found that Fereshteh had a good faith, reasonable belief in her marriage to Speros given the customary law of her culture. The appellate court, however, found that Fereshteh's belief was unreasonable *not because it was invalid according to her culture,* but because the *Mut'a* was so incompatible with California law that Fereshteh could not believe it to be valid in that state. Thus, the ability of this doctrine to "save" customary marriages is again measured against U.S. formal standards of compliance. If the appellate court had measured "reasonableness" by Fereshteh's belief in the customary law of her culture, her claim may have been successful: the *Mut'a* is indeed contracted in private, with no witnesses, and the terms of the marriage need only be agreed upon in advance, with both parties being *'aqil* (of sound mind).[96] In short, Fereshteh's ceremony may have been valid under Islamic law and the law of Iran.[97]

The appellate court in *Vryonis*, however, did not focus upon the reasonableness of Fereshteh's beliefs under Shi'ite Islamic law, but instead found that the facts of Fereshteh's customary marriage were "at odds with the formation and existence of a valid marriage pursuant to California law."[98] Thus, the less a custom "looks like" it complies with California law, the more "unreasonable" the belief in a valid marriage. The court's logic follows that since "no license was obtained and there was no authentication or recordation . . . Fereshteh could not believe reasonably a valid California

[94] *See id.* at 809.

[95] *Id.* at 812.

[96] *See* e-mail from Dr. Hossein Ziai, Chairman of Iranian Studies, University of California, Los Angeles to Lona Laymon (Mar. 3, 2000) (noting that it is likely that Fereshteh's *Mut'a* ceremony would have established a legal form of marriage in Iran where all legal principles are based upon Islamic religion) (on file with the author).

[97] *See Vryonis*, 248 Cal. Rptr. at 813. Fereshteh's financial claim may have been erroneous under Islamic law: the *Mut'a* is not typically subject to claims on inheritance or support. However, she may have had a rightful claim to money agreed to be exchanged according to the *Mut'a* verbal contract. Although such a mutually agreed upon "brideprice" is at the heart of the *Mut'a* contract, this court does not address the issue and fails to explicate the basis for Fereshteh's financial claims.

[98] *Id.*

marriage came into being,"[99] even though the court agrees that Fereshteh was unfamiliar with California law. Moreover, the court also fails to address the fact that this marriage contract may be lawfully valid in Iran.[100] Lastly, Speros' misleading assurances that the marriage was valid could not render Fereshteh's belief in the validity of the marriage reasonable.[101]

The overall effect of the *Vryonis* decision in California is the complete preclusion of unfamiliar customary laws from the putative marriage doctrine.[102] The doctrine is practically limited to cases in which the parties attempted to obtain marriage licenses that are technically deficient. The appellate court was concerned that accommodations of customary law in the putative marriage doctrine would allow parties to assert a binding marriage based on "ignorance of the law."[103] This general concern, however, is often misplaced in the equitable doctrine of putative marriage since most of the successful putative marriage claims also involve some degree of ignorance of the law. Furthermore, the putative marriage doctrine is primarily concerned with equity and the prevention of fraudulent assurances that the marriage is valid where one party knows that it is not. By neglecting to address customary law when considering the putative marriage doctrine, courts fall seriously short of these goals: the court's approach in *Vryonis* allowed Speros to take advantage of Fereshteh's "unreasonable" beliefs in a fraudulent manner (hardly an "equitable" outcome).

Since the putative marriage doctrine looks to reasonableness and bona fide belief in the validity of the marriage, it does have potential to bring customary evidence into the formal legal system and open up discussion of group and cultural rights. It seems unlikely that application of the putative marriage doctrine to customary marriages would lead to a "slippery slope" of cases allowing gross ignorance of law as an excuse. This is because the threshold requirement that the belief is bona fide and related to a genuine system of customary law should weed out cases of mere ignorance and "sham" claims of marriage. However, even under an approach that gives more weight to cultural evidence, judicial biases and ignorance about non-

[99] *Id.* at 812.

[100] The court notes that the belief in the marriage must be a belief in a statutorily valid California marriage which the court sees as separate from a marriage valid according to religion or customary law. *See Vryonis*, 248 Cal. Rptr. at 813. This fails to account for the fact that in Iran, the legal system is based upon religious beliefs of the parties. Fereshteh may thus have had good reason to believe that the religious laws of the parties would govern "marriage" in California.

[101] *Id.*

[102] Even a "customary law approach" to the *Vryonis* case may not have helped Fereshteh at the appellate level, since there were some doubts about the sincerity of Fereshteh's belief (e.g., she did not file a joint tax return). *Id.* It is also possible that Fereshteh's education as a UCLA professor was also read against her since the court may have believed that she was "too sophisticated" to sincerely believe in a valid marriage. *Id.*

[103] *Id.* at 813.

Western cultural systems will still put cultural minorities in the uncomfortable position of being told that their beliefs are "wild."[104] Thus, despite its promise to better ally customary and formal law, the putative marriage doctrine falls short of fostering real legal pluralism.

D. Criminal Cases and the Accommodation of Customary Marriages

Thus far, I have only examined the legal treatment of marital customs in the civil context. But are there any analogous doctrines of accommodation that may be invoked in a criminal case? The "cultural defense," which holds that the criminal behavior and mens rea of certain defendants should be judged with some consideration of their cultural context, does not actually *validate* any marriages. If a claimant in a civil case successfully invokes, for instance, the putative marriage doctrine, that claimant leaves court with enforceable marital rights; this is not true for the criminal defendant. The invocation of the cultural defense never achieves such a level of validation. The cultural defense requests judge and jury to excuse defendants to the extent that they reasonably believed they were acting in accordance with cultural practices. The emphasis is on the defendant's state of mind as an excuse for behavior and not on the actual validity or enforceability of the customary practice.

There are numerous reasons why the cultural defense does not lead to real marital rights. First, criminal cases almost always involve marriage practices that are considered to be repugnant to public policy. These are usually cases of child marriage, marriage by kidnap, marriage by money payment, or polygamy, all of which are categorically repugnant to public policy in the United States. Since public policy trumps the recognition of any custom, it logically follows that, as a practical matter, validation of customary marriages will not occur in the criminal context.

Second, the cultural defense is extremely limited in its application to criminal defendants as a result of both judicial interpretation and the level of intent required under the laws most subjected to cultural defense tactics. For instance, the cultural defense has often been employed in criminal cases dealing with customary marriage practices, especially rape cases: defendant is accused of raping a woman to whom he claims to be validly married under customary law. Or, a defendant may argue that "consent" is culturally specified. In *People v. Moua*,[105] a Hmong man claimed that he had a bona fide, reasonable belief that a Hmong woman, Seng Xiong, consented to sexual intercourse because her behavior perfectly fit the

[104] *Id.* at 812 (quoting language from Speros' brief which terms Fereshteh's beliefs as "wild").

[105] No. 315972-0 (Cal. Sup. Ct. 1985). *See also* Evans-Pritchard & Renteln, *supra* note 71, at 8.

behavior of a woman consenting to marriage under Hmong custom. Other defendants assert general lack of culpability and intent as a defense to charges of rape. In *Nebraska v. Al-Hussaini*,[106] the defendant claimed that he had a bona fide belief that his marriage was valid under Iranian Islamic laws, and that this should warrant a more lenient sentence given general principals of culpability. Courts critically limit the cultural defense in rape cases, whether it is invoked in connection with specific elements of rape, or invoked under general principals of intent or culpability. There are several reasons for this. First, rape tends to not be a specific intent crime and it may be a strict liability crime in some cases (e.g., statutory rape). Second, many courts interpret the cultural defense as a mistake of law and thus will not accommodate cultural defenses because "ignorance of the law is no excuse." [107] Finally, the use of the cultural defense almost inevitably leads to the balancing of victim's rights against defendant's culpability; a balancing test that usually falls in favor of the victim. In sum, while some courts concede that the non-Western defendant is "a victim of the laws which he has little, if any, familiarity and which are, according to him, vastly different from the customs and laws of his native country,"[108] very few courts have accepted the cultural defense as even a partial excuse, and no jurisdiction considers it to be a complete excuse.

This is not to say that the validity of the criminal defendant's marital customs will not be an issue in court. When dealing with the cultural defense, courts focus upon the defendant's state of mind, and not on the validity of the actual practice, but the practice must have enough validity to render the defendant's worldview reasonable to the court. Thus, the court may have to look into the cultural meaning and processes of the custom in its nation of origin. In some cases, the defendant may even attempt to receive complete exoneration by showing that the marriage was in fact valid-where-consummated and thus valid in the United States. This is, again, usually invoked in rape cases, where actual marriage to the victim provides a full or partial excuse to rape. While this does present an opportunity for the criminal court to determine the marriage to be valid and complete with at least some marital rights and obligations, this result is never reached as a practical matter. Again, the nature of the marital customs at issue in criminal cases precludes real validation. For example, in *People v. Ezeonu*,[109] the court found that a marriage was validly consummated under Nigerian law; however, because it was a polygamous union, it was against public policy in the United States. The court could thus not validate

[106] 579 N.W.2d 561 (Neb. Ct. App. 1998).
[107] For a criticism of this interpretation see Evans-Pritchard & Renteln, *supra* note 71, at 22–25.
[108] *Al-Hussaini*, 579 N.W.2d at 563.
[109] 588 N.Y.S.2d 116 (Sup. Ct. 1992).

the marriage for purposes of providing Dr. Ezeonu any marital defense to charges of rape.

I do not argue the extent to which the cultural defense or customary practices should or should not be considered an excuse in criminal cases involving marital customs; that topic is well beyond the scope of this Note.[110] I only wish to outline the fact that the cultural defense is critically limited, and it is not a full accommodation of customary marriages. After all, the cultural defense only seeks some level of exoneration for the criminal defendant as a proxy for state of mind; it is not designed to actually enforce the marriage or the custom at hand. Thus, in criminal cases, it is particularly true that "[t]he disadvantage of having a cultural defense as a complete and formal excuse is that if it were successful, cultural rights could take precedence over other human rights such as those of women and children."[111]

IV. CONCLUSIONS

For members of traditional communities, the law comes in several different layers. At the closest level, the customary law of one's community governs. At the next level, the formal legal system of one's nation governs. Finally, the formal legal system of the country where one expatriates governs.[112]

Although statutory laws and courts of most nations claim to recognize the customary laws of their indigenous populations, this formal recognition usually falls short of accommodating the cultural meaning embedded in indigenous customary laws. While formal legal systems purport to uphold the rights of insular, indigenous groups, they really only do so to the extent that the customary law can be fit into preexisting formal, Western constructs that emphasize verifiability and consistency. The same is true, but to a greater extent, of the valid-where-consummated construct. Therefore, the tension between customary and formal law is deeply rooted in the very nature of each system of law, and it parallels inherent tension between the goals of anthropology and the goals of the legal system. For the anthropologist, the accommodation of customary law means more than mere enforcement of a marriage in the formal system: it means preservation of customary law in a way that preserves cultural meaning and significance.

[110] For a more complete discussion of the cultural defense, see Alison Dundes Renteln, *A Justification of the Cultural Defense as Partial Excuse*, 2 S. CAL. REV. L. & WOMEN'S STUD. 437 (1993).

[111] Evans-Pritchard & Renteln, *supra* note 71, at 58.

[112] Of course, an immigrant may also be governed by the customary law of his cultural group if, when he relocates, there is already an immigrant population in that nation that has established its own insular group.

Anthropologists would view the accommodation of customary law as treatment of "custom on custom's terms," with emphasis on oral narration, cultural growth and change, the subjective significance of the custom, and its varied, community-based nature.[113] The aims of the legal system are often in stark opposition to these anthropological principles: written or "hard" evidence, consistency, objective fact-based tests, and emphasis upon national or state society rather than smaller, community units.

Doctrines like valid-where-consummated and common-law marriage validate customary marriage with no regard to the actual custom or intent of the parties, thus making the actual customary law irrelevant to the determination of its validity (e.g., cultural evidence is not admitted in court). Furthermore, at least amongst Native Americans, the legal system's treatment of customary law under legal labels like common-law marriage leads to embarrassment about customary practices, or a sense that those practices are morally inferior.[114] Thus, if the formal system imposed upon the customary law doesn't immediately change the nature of the customary system through codification and formalization, the cultural meaning and significance of the customary laws will slowly erode as formal courts validate marriage customs only where they fit into preestablished Western legal concepts.

For the nonindigenous claimant, the putative marriage and the cultural defense doctrines have more potential to incorporate anthropological principles, and may be more deferential to customary law and cultural meaning. This is because the putative marriage doctrine and the cultural defense purport to scrutinize the claimant's intent and beliefs. One would guess that these doctrines require courts to understand the worldview of the claimant and other community members in order to determine the reasonableness of the claimant's beliefs. The concept of reasonableness also invites courts to utilize rhetorics of group and cultural rights when analyzing the worldview of a claimant. Contrary to these expectations, however, both doctrines are severely limited by evidentiary standards that favor mere documentation of marriage, and judicial discretion about which cultural beliefs are reasonable (as opposed to which beliefs in a culture are

[113] For example, in a society whose marital customs are founded in the concept of a bond between two families, or even clans, an inquiry into the "validity" of a marriage in that culture would necessarily entail an inquiry into the relationship that has been established or intended between the family groups. The inquiry *would not* focus primarily on the "contract" created between the future spouses, as would be the treatment in the United States. Indeed, for such a group, the "contract" between individuals may not exist as a concept, since every change in the relations of individuals is seen as a change of relations of families and friends.

[114] Some scholars have pointed out that this result is also apparent in non-Western immigrant communities, in which the fear of the judicial system, or embarrassment about "non-American" cultural identity makes it difficult to procure witnesses from the group to testify. Interview with Professor Alison Renteln, Vice-Chair, Political Science Department, University of Southern California, in Los Angeles, Cal. (Mar. 4, 2000).

meaningful to that culture). Much judicial bias against customary law seems to stem from the idea that these matters are more "religious" than "legal," and thus are not within the realm of legal enforcement by the courts (even where "religious" claim would be enforceable in courts of the claimant's country). Finally, policy limitations are the trump card to any customary marriage claim.

Is there any way to, at least partially, bridge the gap between anthropological goals and goals of the legal system? A culturally relativistic approach in the formal system does not prove satisfying since this opens the door to customary laws that are generally viewed as harmful to greater society or to people within the cultural minority itself (e.g., child marriages, or marital customs that are harmful to women within the insular minority group). But, we saw that many customary marriages are not harmful or repugnant, especially where the marriage would be valid-where-consummated. When dealing with such nonrepugnant customary laws that engender an apparently bona fide, nonfraudulent belief in the claimant, courts may bridge the gap between customary law and formal law by *reassessing standards of reasonableness*. The scope of reasonableness applied in putative marriage cases is at the heart of the bias against cultural minorities.

The materials in this Note not only demonstrate the gap between formal judicial systems and the preservation of cultural identity, but also illustrate biases against communal rights perspectives in many formal courts. In the United States, the source of this bias derives from the "individualist perspective" inherent to the American legal tradition.[115] "The individualist perspective is hostile to the notion of group/ethnic rights because it posits that the individual is the only agent to which a right can attach."[116] Moreover, the idea that government need only be bound by "negative rights" continues to be very influential in many Western legal systems, and this hinders claims for the right to cultural identity through positive rights. Few accommodations of group or cultural rights originated in common law, and today most accommodations come from legislative bodies. Nations like South Africa and Namibia have constitutionalized indigenous group/ethnic rights while other nations have tried to accommodate cultural minorities through the use of statutory protections and tribal court systems. In Part II, we saw that, at least in the context of marriage, the formal system holds a myriad of problems for the claimant of cultural rights, despite legislative protection of indigenous, traditional marriage practices. But, these legislative protections rarely, if ever, reach immigrant groups. Thus, Part III explored possible routes of

[115] *See* Wing, *supra* note 1, at 298.
[116] *Id.*

accommodation for immigrant customary marriages in the United States. The common-law doctrines explored were often biased, inconsistently applied, and never engaged in a rhetoric of ethnic or group rights, even where the customary practice presented no threat to public policy of evidentiary standards.

There are some simple routes of judicial reform that may lead to fuller incorporation of group rights and cultural identity. First, courts should be encouraged to use nonlegal (e.g., anthropological) materials to supplement their analyses of reasonable beliefs; ideally, a court would have at its disposal "expert" witnesses or descriptions of cultural practices that come from within the cultural group. Cultural minorities seem to greatly increase their chances of successful claims where they provide expert witnesses from within their cultural group.

Second, courts should be encouraged to look toward progressive reforms within international law forums and within other nations. Both of these sources have explored progressive, nontraditional standards of public policy and evidentiary requirements. For instance, recall that in most African nations, a different standard of evidence—one that was more deferential to community norms and individual testimony—was applied to customary law cases. African nations have also approached public policy. Comparisons between the laws of different nations and the laws of the United States may better acquaint U.S. judges with a wider range of potential judicial responses to customary law. The comparative approach may also mend some misapplications of the valid-where-consummated doctrine.

Third, the legal education should incorporate more anthropological materials when students explore the problem of reasonableness standards: even the simple step of introducing the fact that not all cultures view "marriage" as a contract between two individuals would be a step in the right direction. Such a curriculum should also offer students the chance to compare the ways in which the United States, other nations, and international law deal with customary laws.

Fourth, if courts consider the fact that other cultures do not always conceive of a married-unmarried dichotomy, then a sliding scale of "marital status" and "rights" may develop to more equitably accommodate non-Western groups. This approach has been taken in some African nations where courts have recognized that although a couple may not meet the status of "completely" married, the relationship was enough of a union under tribal standards to require judicial enforcement of some rights and obligations.[117] Thus, while the union does not receive all the rights and

[117] *See, e.g.*, Owusu v. Nyarko, [1980] G.L.R. 428 (Sekondi High Ct. Ghana).

benefits of a "full" marriage, the court recognizes that some level of "marriage agreement" was achieved under customary law and that there should be an enforcement of rights reasonably expected by custom. This treatment of non-Western cultures better fits those cultures that lack the married-unmarried dichotomy. This approach also avoids forcing customary laws into legal concepts like common-law marriage, which may connote immorality or render the customary practice irrelevant. Both indigenous and immigrant cultural groups would benefit from this rights-based approach to customary marriage.

If legal doctrines, like the putative marriage doctrine, or valid-where-consummated doctrine, can more fully incorporate accurate cultural evidence, the legal system will be one step closer to true legal pluralism, with some rhetoric of group/ethnic rights. Forcing cultural practices into Western legal molds and defining customary marriages by reference to Western concepts (e.g., common-law marriage) allows accommodation of only those practices that are "moldable" to Western doctrines; any other system of customary law is seen as illegitimate. The legal system thus perpetuates Western concepts through the practices of other cultures that may be catalogued in "familiar" terms. This is not legal pluralism, and it is contrary to the preservation of cultural identity. Legal pluralism will be no more than an illusion unless courts can evaluate cultural practices in and of themselves and do so in a consistent way.

Part II
Children

[19]

CHILDREN BETWEEN CULTURES

JOHN EEKELAAR*

ABSTRACT

Research into issues of inter-cultural conflict has paid relatively little attention to the position of children who find themselves caught up in such circumstances. When courts have needed to make decisions about individual children in this context, they have found it difficult to adopt a consistent and principled approach. This article examines the kinds of contexts in which some problems have arisen, and puts forward a framework, rooted in liberal theory, according to which they may be resolved.

1. INTRODUCTION

In this article I wish to consider some problems which arise for the legal and social system related to the upbringing of children who belong to minority groups in a society. My focus is on family law, and the problems I will consider are those which arise when conflict has arisen about the upbringing of a child; perhaps between the child's own parents, or sometimes between those parents and others, whether the state or private persons. However, these private, individual, problems cannot be considered in isolation from larger, social, even political, issues. For the adults children turn out to be will be the result of their cultural experiences during their childhood, and tomorrow's adults will define the nature of tomorrow's society. We may think that our present decisions concerning our children are directed at our children's interests, but they may be just as strongly directed at designing a future society as we would like it to be. Such issues are of particular relevance when decisions are made concerning the upbringing of children of minority groups.

2. COMMUNITY INTERESTS AND CHILDREN'S INTERESTS

It is natural that adults should be deeply concerned about the cultural context in which their children grow up. They tend to see it as part of their own interests. For example, minority language groups may claim the right that their children be educated in that language. Religious communities characteristically claim the right to bring their children up in their faith as part of the fundamental right to religious freedom. In a different context, some Jews in the United States have advocated taking active steps to reduce the increasing extent to which American Jews resort to marriage with people of other faiths, which some see as threatening to the future of the Jewish community.[1] This is not only because deprivation of cultural expression has often been used as a means of oppression, but because it is often argued that many, perhaps all, people are only able to achieve their full potential, and realize their well-being, within a cultural context.[2] The protection of minorities is an important political goal, and in 1994 the Council of Europe adopted the Framework Convention for the Protection of National Minorities, which entered force on 1 February 1998. Its effects are regularly monitored by the Council. This seems to be limited to 'national' minorities, and would not cover, for example, immigrant communities.[3] Yet conferring positive rights on groups, especially minority ethnic groups, is fraught with difficulty. States fear social divisiveness at best, or actual dismemberment at worse. In any event, the call on resources could be prohibitive. For example, how far should the state go in making community provision for minority languages? Over 300 different languages are spoken in London.[4] Despite these difficulties, people frequently claim minority rights of this kind. One of the best known advocates of this position was Taylor (1992), who argued that communities are entitled to survive 'through indefinite future generations'.

There is, however, a severe objection to this position. For the individuals concerned are making the claim not only for themselves but also for their successors. By what right can they claim to do that? The point was picked up by Appiah (1992) in his comments on Taylor's piece, when he said: 'it seems to me not at all clear that this aim is one we can acknowledge while respecting the autonomy of future individuals'. Blake (2003) has identified the difficulties which privileging communal groups can cause for individuals (for example, those of bicultural descent or upbringing) who might be caught between them. What are we saying about the worth of such people if communities, by a necessary act of self-definition, exclude them? In itself, it seems that every child, taken as an individual, could have an equally good future if it spoke only the majority language, unless you took the view that such children would suffer some personal sense of loss in the eventual disappearance of the language of their forbears. The same might be said about minority religions. It could also be argued that the well-being of individuals requires that they are connected with a culture, and that they are therefore brought up within a cultural context. So much is uncontroversial, but this proposition does not specify *which* culture it should be. People can be very adaptable, as the biographies of many individual immigrants can show.[5] Of course a culture itself would decline by reason of persistent losses. That in itself may be a cause for regret, but the basis could lie only in some belief such as that humanity necessarily benefits by the presence of a variety of cultures: that is, that cultural variety is in itself a good.

That cultural diversity has value may be assumed, though it may be hard to prove; but as far as the well-being of individuals is concerned, a widely accepted analysis by Berry *et al* (1989) suggests that there are four models of interaction with a majority culture which may be followed by individuals in minority groups.

(i) Assimilation (where the individual abandons his/her cultural values in favour of those of the host community);
(ii) integration, or 'biculturalism' (where the individual retains his/her cultural values, but also places importance on relations with the host community);
(iii) marginalization (where the individual becomes distant from both sets of values;
(iv) separatism (where the individual identifies with only his/her community and values).

It appears that individuals who opt for separatism and marginalization suffer poorer psychological outcomes than the other groups (Ward, 2002), but it is harder to know whether assimilation or integration produces better outcomes for individuals.[6] This is important: while it seems that neither assimilation nor integration is characteristically harmful, it is uncertain which is better. On the other hand, isolating individuals from any culture (creating marginalization) or erecting barriers between the individual's culture and a wider culture (separatism) are both likely to be harmful. But, apart from that, a fundamental value is at stake, which is that of individual liberty, and the obligation of liberal states to treat all its members with respect. It is this that forms the basis for protecting cultural rights and practices, rather than some inherent right in the communities themselves. It includes respecting the interests of members of those groups to bring their children up in the beliefs and practices of the group.[7] But by the same token, this duty to respect individual rights imposes limits, because the state must also respect the interests of the children of the communities to determine their own futures. This article discusses one context in which there is interplay between both sets of interests.

3. CHILDREN OF MINORITIES

There is a widespread view that it is harmful for children of minority groups to be brought up otherwise than in their minority culture. A striking example occurred in England in 1996.[8] A white Afrikaans woman had, with the parents' consent, been bringing up a Zulu child in South Africa, from his babyhood. When he was six she brought him to London, where he was integrated into the English community. The parents made many efforts to have him returned and, when he was ten, the Court of Appeal ordered his return to South Africa, accepting the trial judge's view that the boy's development 'must be, in the last resort and profoundly, Zulu development and not Afrikaans or English development', so that he had a 'right' to be reunited with his parents. Despite the boy's objections he was returned to South Africa, but he was so desperately unhappy that he eventually came back to England. What lay behind the disastrous decision? Why the court thought his development 'must' be Zulu and not Afrikaans or English is not explained. Perhaps the idea is that a child is somehow 'attached' to the culture of his birth parents at his birth, and that failure to develop in that culture is some kind of loss. It may be that his colour played a part: the feeling that a black child could never properly integrate into white society, and could only find his true identity in a black one. This seems possible, because the case sits unhappily with a famous House of Lords decision in 1970, when the House refused to order the return to Spain of a ten-year-old Spanish child who had been brought up by English foster parents.[9]

But if it is true that the judges succumbed to a form of racism, it can be said that they were acting consistently with the views held, at least at some time by a number, perhaps even a predominant number, of black organizations. During the 1970s in the US the National Association of Black Social Workers criticized the placement of black children for adoption by white adoptive parents, and such criticisms became common in Britain during the 1980s. One reason for opposing such adoptions was that it amounted to 'stealing' black children, a form of genocide (Hayes, 1995). Such claims may or may not have merit. It is certainly true that the policy pursued until about the 1950s in Australia of removing mixed-parentage Australian aboriginal children from their families and placing them with white families was overtly pursued in order to diminish the numbers in the aboriginal community and hasten its disappearance (Buti, 2003). There are quite independent reasons to view a policy of deliberate annihilation of a racial group as being immoral. But much of the opposition was, and is, based on the ground that such placements were damaging to the children. This is thought to be true partly on the basis that only black parents can prepare black children to face a racist society. But the main reason is that it is thought that bringing up a black child in a white family will cause identity confusion; when adults, such children will be able to relate well neither to white nor to black society, and as a result they will be seriously damaged.

This argument, if true, would support the court's decision in the case of the Zulu boy. It would give weight to some practices of adoption agencies criticized by a judge in a different case which took a very different approach to the court in that case. In *re N*[10] a Nigerian child of four and a half years had lived with white foster parents since she was three-weeks-old. The father now wished to have her returned to him. Faced with much argument that the child would develop a 'black' identity only if brought up by black parents, the judge pointed to the extremes to which this argument was taken: for example, attempts would be made to find parents with the same 'mix' of colours as the child; or colour could be regarded as more important than culture, so that a Sikh child would be placed with a Muslim family simply because of the colour match. He refused to return the child. However, he did recognize that the child had 'cultural roots', and observed:

> the later harm that may arise in her teens when she wishes to seek out her cultural roots can best be dealt with by sympathetic understanding and education, upon which the (foster parents) have already embarked, and it can hopefully be met by the father continuing his interest ...

So what should be done in these types of case? In a recent examination of the relevant social scientific and psychological evidence, Tizard and Phoenix (2002: 73) have cautioned against seeing racial identity in essentialist terms. While the evidence suggests that it would be wrong to adopt a purely colour-blind approach, which ignores the existence and importance of racialized identities, it also indicates that the concept of 'black' identity (and, if this is so, this applies to any racial identity) is not static. 'The very notion of what it means to be black is dynamic, shifting with changes in political agenda and social theory.' The idea that an individual can experience self-esteem only by identification with clear-cut ethnic identity, is not supported by evidence. People can experience identities in a complex, fluid, way, so that black transracial adoptees can experience 'blackness' even though it may be of a different kind from that experienced by other black children; and everyone may experience multiple identities which override race, such as gender, class, and political affiliation. Indeed the evidence on outcomes for transracially adopted children stubbornly continues to show it to be generally favourable for the children.[11]

However, the main evidence relied on by Tizard and Phoenix (2002) is their own, and other, growing evidence about the position of children of mixed-race parentage, although it has to be said that there is a surprising lack of social scientific research on the influence of cultural conflicts on children.[12] Drawing on a sample of children of mixed white and Afro-Caribbean parentage interviewed in London in 1990–91, their findings contradicted the expectations of those from both white and black communities who applied a modern form of the ancient 'one-drop' rule,[13] according to which such children would see themselves as black, but then be confused by the presence of a white parent, or participation in white culture. On the contrary, the large majority of these children were completely comfortable with their identity, seeing themselves as neither white nor black, but 'brown' or 'mixed', with an ability to move between the white and black cultures according to circumstances. When asked to decide with whom they would side in the case of hypothetical conflict, 41 per cent chose the black, 13 per cent the white side, but 38 per cent refused to say. This might suggest divided loyalties among about half the children, but the authors strongly concluded that this did not indicate any sense of marginality or pain, for the great majority expressed pride in their mixed racial background.[14] As far as their wider allegiances were concerned, they felt themselves only weakly to be British (but more so than the nationality of their non-British parent). Their primary allegiance was to their region: they took pride in being 'Londoners'.

Root (2001: 154) reports that the evidence about mixed Asian-American children looks a little less positive, but also states that:

> all of the parents I interviewed realized that something was changing in racial identity politics. Whereas some black–white families raised their children to identify as black, not all the children did, which puzzled their parents and siblings. Some parents worried that a multiracial identity or insistence by a child that she was both black and white or Asian and black was an indication of self-loathing. But without public conversation on race and racial mixing, parents are not necessarily informed about how the young may be constructing their racial identities in ways that break the rules by which their parents were socialized.

It is of course true that children of mixed parentage are not in exactly the same position as children of a single ethnic origin who experience cultural influences in their upbringing which are different from those of their parents. Nevertheless, the evidence is important in indicating how young people are able to respond to their cultural environment and forge identities for themselves. Children of mixed parentage are in a particularly favourable position, however, because they usually come from homes where their parents are an example of inter-cultural collaboration. In reading about the experiences recounted by children brought up in mixed households, I am struck by the absence of descriptions of conflict between the parents as to how to bring up the child. The children often recount problems they encountered from their peers, but never from within their homes.[15] This does not of course mean that conflict does not occur, and I will consider this in due course; but it does indicate that inter-cultural collaboration is possible, often between individuals with backgrounds which seem at first sight poles apart; for example, an Irani Muslim and an American Mormon.[16] More importantly, the effect on children can be, and usually is, positive, provided the surrounding community is not hostile. Tizard and Phoenix (2002: 49) say that the only studies reporting serious problems in mixed-parentage children are clinical studies, which are confined to children who have been identified as troubled in the first instance, and not in studies involving children found in schools or community networks. The price paid for this new sense of identity is inevitably some diminution in the transmission of the culture of one or the other, or often both, of the parents. It may become assimilated into the wider, dominant, culture, or undergo some transformation in itself at the hands of the child. My point is that this would appear not to be to the detriment of the child. It may be to the detriment of the parents' cultures, but that is another matter.

The evidence then appears to show that children can forge a positive identity which incorporates features of two, or even more, cultures, without suffering harm. It is difficult to find a representative quotation from a set of diverse experiences recounted by 19 bi-racial and bi-cultural writers collected by O'Hearn, but the following gives a fair flavour:

> I, too, have come to reject the idea of a simple, dualized family heritage and the simple bicultural understanding of self internalized as a child. My cultural influences, in terms of my genetic heritage and my personal experience, look a lot more like a bush than a tree – maybe a tumbleweed is an even more fitting analogy, since it helps to capture the sense of movement, migration, and mixing that has characterized and shaped my life ... In the end, I am both African and African American – and therefore neither. I envy others their hometowns and unconflicted patriotism, but no longer would I exchange them for my freedom to seek multiple homes and nations and to forge my own.[17]

However, as that quotation also shows, the evidence also reveals a certain fluidity in the way people from mixed cultural parentage identify culturally. Events can tilt them to associate more with one culture than another, as was the case of one of Maxwell's interviewees, born to an Iraqi Muslim father and Irish Catholic mother, who began to identify with his Iraqi inheritance after the First Gulf War, whereas his sister identified as Irish since she disliked her father.[18]

There is, though, a very important qualification that must be made to this account. The wider environment in which the children are brought up might be very significant. Where children are rejected by both sides of their wider family, or by both sections of the community with which they have cultural affiliation, the consequences are of course much less positive. There would be risk of marginalization. It is interesting that there was relatively little evidence of this in Tizard and Phoenix's study, although it seemed that children related better to those communities when they went to schools in strongly multi-racial communities. They found that the few children who did seem to be constantly concerned about their identity, and therefore had a 'problematic racialized identity', all went to predominantly white schools; so, while this need not necessarily be a problem,[19] it would be less likely to be so if the child lived in a multi-racial social environment. Despite this, they found that:

> a substantial proportion of our sample, in both racially mixed and predominantly white schools, had no strong sense of black–white boundaries; that is, of black and white people having distinct characteristics and cultures. Only a quarter, for example, thought that black and white people have different tastes in such matters as music and fashion, the majority arguing that there is a good deal of overlap.[20]

Of course, it may be argued that there is, in fact, little difference between 'white' and 'black' cultures, and all that is happening here is a breakdown of perceptions based solely on colour: Tizard and Phoenix's children were from the mixed white and Afro-Caribbean group only, not some other cultural intermixture. On the other hand, that is the largest single group with mixed ethnic origins in Britain.[21] I do not know whether white people and black people in these mixed areas would take a similar view of the lack of difference between white and black cultures. It must be at least a possibility that they would not, or not to the same extent, and that the interrelationship between the cultures is largely a perception of these children, in the same way as the child of an American Mormon and Irani Muslim saw interrelationships between Mormonism and Islam which outsiders would be slow to grasp. The anecdotal evidence is that children have the ability to move, chameleon-like,[22] between cultures without suffering harm, and indeed adding to the quality of their lives. But more systematic research is required.

4. MAKING DECISONS

A. Dynamic Self-determinism

Some years ago I tried to suggest a way in which it might be possible to reconcile the use of the 'best interests' tests with a concept of children's rights when decision-makers were called upon to resolve conflicts about the care or upbringing of children (Eekelaar, 1994). I drew upon the psychological theory of E.H. Erikson regarding the establishment of self-identity of adolescents and Joseph Raz's philosophical account of well-being in arguing that an individual's self identity is established gradually, and that the process enables each individual to determine, to some extent at least, what outcomes instantiate his/her personal well-being. The only qualification to what I wrote earlier would perhaps be that I would now be less ready to accept Erikson's rather monolithic view of individual identity, and his notion that 'diffusion' of identity is some kind of deviation. If, as Tizard and Phoenix (2002: 5; 72–6; 221–2) claim, people can have several identities at the same time, and that racial identity is dynamic and fluid, this only reinforces the message of dynamic self-determinism: identity is, in some senses, perhaps never finally determined for any individual. All the more reason to be reticent about ascribing an identity to an individual too readily. The practical consequence was to suggest that in making decisions about children's upbringing, care should be taken to avoid imposing inflexible outcomes at an early stage in a child's development which unduly limit the child's capacity to fashion his/her own identity, and the context in which it flourishes best.

Of course, this was only a framework, and had to be subject to various qualifications, especially concerning the competence of the child, but it does seem to be entirely consistent with the evidence discussed above concerning the way children become socialized in different cultures. We can summarize the evidence as showing that, provided the children do not experience serious hostility from external sources, there is no reason why they cannot realize their well-being within a cultural context which they themselves substantially forge from diverse sources which surround them. The fact that, at an early age, they have access to divergent cultural resources makes them more open, in the years immediately following childhood, to empathy with those resources, and they may choose to identify closely with any of them. While some children find this unsettling, most see it as source of strength rather than of weakness.

It is important to remember the context in which I advocated dynamic self-determination. I was concerned with the way decisions were taken when it was necessary for decision-makers, usually courts, to resolve conflicts about the context in which a child or children should be brought up, and it was intended as a framework within which such decisions could be made. Of course it is based on a broad view of psychological development, and it must not be pressed to extremes. For example, it is not to be implied that children should *not* be brought up in only one culture, or that parents must make anxious efforts to expose their children to as many religious or cultural influences as possible. There can be nothing wrong, either, if a child is encouraged to develop a particular talent, even if this means less time is devoted to other pursuits; but even here the approach suggests a balance should be maintained. A child may well find life difficult if its talents are developed too exclusively in one direction.

B. Principles for Making Decisions

How, then, should all this affect the way decisions about children are made in the context of cultural dispute? The courts are, of course, generally required to decide what is best for the child. I have argued elsewhere that it should be legitimate to give independent weight to other interests, and weigh them against those of the children, though the children's interests should be 'privileged'; that is, while other factors might properly lead to a less than optimal result for children, it should never result in actual harms to them (Eekelaar, 2002). In the present context, this could mean weighing up the child's autonomy interest alongside the interest of the child's parents and perhaps even of the community. The difficulty is that it is so very difficult to know, now, what will turn out to be in the long-term interests of children. However, it does suggest a principled approach. In most cases we cannot say whether it is better for a child to be brought up in one culture rather than in another, or whether it is better to assimilate into one culture rather than to maintain links with more than one culture under the integration model. So the respect which we owe to present-day adults, and their communities, should allow them a wide remit as to which of these models they choose for their children. However, such a remit is not without limits. No solution should be adopted which visits real distress on children *now* in the hope that things will turn out well for the child much later. That would rule out acting in the way the Court of Appeal did in the case of the Zulu boy.

Similarly, where children are brought up in contexts where they come into contact with other cultures, either in wider society or in their own families, it could be harmful for them to be brought up in ignorance of, and antagonistic to, such other cultures. Separatism is the least favourable model to follow. To this must be added the premise of autonomy on which the principle of self-determinism is grounded. Thus in the case of the Zulu boy, it would have been important that he should be brought up with knowledge of Zulu culture, and the evidence also suggests that he might, at least to some extent, choose to identify with it later in life. This does not mean that the child must be *brought up* in both cultures – only that the gate must be left open for the child to choose later where on the spectrum between assimilation (and into which culture) and integration he wishes to lead his life.

Transracial adoption can be approached in the same way. The arguments that children should not be 'lost' to their culture of origin seem to be less strongly argued recently than formerly, and, except in some extreme circumstances where an entire culture might be threatened (as in the Australian aboriginal example), it is hard in most cases seriously to believe that transracial adoption normally threatens the future of entire cultures. In such a case other principles may well come into play. More usual is the argument that, despite generally favourable short-term psychological results, transracially adopted children lose or are at risk of losing, something important by being brought up in a culture different from their culture of birth. Maybe we cannot measure the effects of the loss, but it is a loss nevertheless.

My suggestion is that the concept of dynamic self-determinism is helpful in dealing with this issue. There is no reason to follow an approach under which the child's culture of origin *alone* determines what the adoption placement should be.[23] Thus the concrete benefits adoption might bring should not be seen to be threatened by the fact that the child might develop a biracial identity, or move to a new identity later. However this requires that the adoptive parents, if not of the culture of the child's birth, should not be 'culture-blind'. It is important that they should bring up the child with knowledge of its culture of origin, and to keep open channels of communication with that culture.[24] That, it is suggested, is how the direction in the Adoption and Children Act 2002 that 'in placing the child for adoption, the adoption agency must give due consideration to the child's religious persuasion, racial origin and cultural and linguistic background' should be understood. That is, these matters are not to be seen as mandating or even recommending racial or cultural matching, but as indicating that openness to biculturalism may need to be a necessary element in the upbringing of certain children.

5. THE RELIGIOUS CONFLICT CASES

Cases of religious conflict can be dealt with on the same principles. Cultural difference often involves religious difference. But difference does not necessarily imply conflict, and there are countless children who are successfully brought up in households where the parents are of different faiths, or of one faith and no faith. Decision-makers recognize this. The English Court of Appeal once said 'Thus a child who lives with an English Anglican mother may be enriched by learning from his father about his Muslim background and culture'.[25]

Yet conflicts over religious and cultural practices can occur even when the parties agree on many other matters. *Re J*[26] is a good example. The father was a non-practising Turkish Muslim, who had separated from the non-practising Christian English mother, but he wished his five-year-old son to be brought up according to some Muslim traditions. One was that he wanted the boy to be circumcized, and another that he should not eat pork. The mother was quite willing for the son to spend time with the father, and to become acquainted with Muslim traditions, but she opposed circumcision. The judge recommended that the mother should respect the father's views about diet, but declined to make an order to that effect, and also declined to order circumcision. He took the view that this would be contrary to the child's interests, since he would be brought up in an English context where circumcision was not the norm, it would upset the mother, and it was irreversible. In that case the court recognized the possibility that the child could be brought up in a bicultural environment. This necessitated compromise on both sides and on the whole this was forthcoming without the necessity of judicial intervention. No compromise was possible on the circumcision issue however. The judge resolved it on the basis of an assessment of what he felt were the child's immediate interests. This could be justified only on the basis that the immediate harm to the child was sufficiently serious that it outweighed speculative future benefits should he later identify as a Muslim.

A similar issue split the Supreme Court of Canada in *Young* v *Young*.[27] The parents separated when the father converted to the Jehovah's Witness faith. The issue was whether he should involve his children in his religious activities (which the children disliked) when they visited him. The trial judge had made orders restraining him from doing that, but the British Columbia Court of Appeal removed the restrictions on the ground that they interfered with the father's religious freedom protected under the Charter. That could be done, the court said, only if his activities were shown to be harming the children. The Supreme Court agreed, but L'Heureux-Dubé J gave a passionate dissent. In her view the only criterion for decision was what was best for the children, and not what might harm them. She argued that the children's best interests were served by allowing the parent with whom they were living the right to decide such issues. The problem here is that, by giving that parent the sole right, the state was thereby restricting the equivalent right of the other parent. Since any assessment as to which course of action was better for the children was very speculative (and neither seemed to be harmful) it is suggested that there were no grounds to restrict either parent. It should not be assumed that exposure to, or even upbringing in, two religious viewpoints would damage the children. This was the approach taken in the American case, *Zummo* v *Zummo*,[28] where the court stressed the constitutional right of *each* parent to instruct the children in their respective faiths (Judaism and Roman Catholicism). This should be departed from only if there was clear evidence of harm: mere speculation that it might be harmful was insufficient. The European Court of Human Rights followed the same principle in holding that the French courts had discriminated against a Jehovah's Witness mother by transferring her children to their father on the sole basis that her faith was harsh and intolerant, without seeking evidence of its actual effect on the children through the customary social inquiry report.[29] These cases do not abandon the welfare principle. Rather, they resist submerging important individual rights beneath speculation about children's future well-being.

6. CHILD PROTECTION

References to harm to children raise a separate issue with regard to children in multicultural societies. What if the dominant culture defines harm in a different way from that of the child's culture? This problem has arisen in the context of child protection practice in Britain. A recent highly publicized case involved the death of Victoria Climbié, a young girl from the Ivory Coast, who had been brought to the United Kingdom by relatives. The carers were imprisoned for their neglect, and a government inquiry made serious criticisms of social services. There was some evidence of a reluctance on the part of welfare services to intervene for fear of being accused of racism, and also suggestions that some observers overlooked warning signs of maltreatment in the belief they may have been cultural practices (such as the child standing to attention before her carers, or certain marks on her body). The report did not examine the issue in depth, being content with the observation that:

> Cultural heritage is important to many people, but it cannot take precedence over standards of child care embodied in the law... A child is a child regardless of his/her colour and he or she must be kept safe. Cultural issues must be considered, but the objective is the safety of the child.[30]

There is no doubt that some practices, widely considered harmful, are supported by people on cultural grounds: female circumcision, or forced marriage, would be examples. Yet one should be careful not to exaggerate the extent to which culture in itself erects a barrier to understanding. In a rare study of child protection cases which involve 'minority' children, Brophy *et al* (2003) found no evidence that practices thought by social agents to be harmful were defended on cultural grounds. When harm was perceived by social agents to be present, it was usually accompanied by a cluster of factors, and was not occasioned by cultural-specific practices alone. This is not to state that cultural difference is not important. For example, it might sometimes be denied that a specific harmful practice *could occur* within a culture. Or, certain practices which might be thought by the dominant culture to be inappropriate (for example, shouting at a child in public) might be considered a beneficial way of correcting a child in some cultures. The researchers certainly thought that more effort should be made to view the cases within their cultural context, and many problems (mostly linguistic) were detected in presenting the parents' views to courts. The dominant message from the research is that many basic values are shared between the cultures, at least insofar as they are openly acknowledged, but that modes of expressing them, and the meanings attributed to specific acts, may vary considerably. As is true about this whole area, however, a great deal more empirical work needs to be done.

6. CONCLUSIONS

The evidence which we have considered about the effects of cultural difference on children who are exposed to, or connected with, different cultures, indicates that it would be wrong to think that it is harmful to children to be exposed to a variety of cultures in their upbringing. Indeed, insulating them from such influences is more likely to be harmful. On the other hand, it is too speculative to try to predict whether it would be better in the longer term for such children to be brought up in one religious or cultural world view, or in more than one. It is like trying to judge whether a child is better brought up with a religion or with no religion at all. So the state or the courts should respect the right of each parent to pass on this religion or culture to their children, and not favour bringing up children in a religion or not in a religion, or mono-culturally or multiculturally. The state should, of course, intervene if the parents' actions would result in clear harm to the children,[31] as for example if differences between the parents engender serious conflict; or if one parent's attitudes would alienate the children from the other parent,[32] or from that parent's culture or religion; or if it would close the children's mind entirely to the community around them.[33] In cases of children with mixed racial or religious background, this requires parents to keep them sympathetically informed about the alternative culture or religion. This is a desperately difficult path for many religious parents to follow, but is the due they owe in return for the respect given to their religion, and the key to building a tolerant society.

Indeed it is an important condition for a successful multicultural upbringing that it occurs in a tolerant community. Thus the comfort of the child's movement between cultural experiences is secured in such a context, which is why some people argue that 'faith' education for children should best be carried out in a school environment in which a variety of faiths can flourish (Gundara, 2000: 76). Conversely, in an intolerant society, a child brought up to respect both sides might be damaged by rejection by each community and become an outcast from each. That has been the fate of some mixed race children. The bleakness of this (which seems to predict the perpetuation of intolerance, and proves the adage: intolerance breeds intolerance) is matched by the virtuous circle of mutual reinforcement in tolerant communities, for the presence of children who are able to move between cultures is in itself likely to promote tolerance. So both the interests of the wider community and those of children themselves are enhanced. What of the interests of the cultural communities themselves? Perhaps we should acknowledge that, at least normally (that is, outside cases of persecution), communities may have no specific interests *as communities*. Their individual members most certainly do, and this includes the interest in passing on their culture to their children. But that interest is limited, and it is limited first and foremost by the interests of the communities' own children.

NOTES

[1] This is very controversial among American Jews: for example, Berkofsky, J. 'Study finds positive trends along with rising intermarriage': www.JTA.org (visited 14 September 2003).

[2] See the arguments for this presented by Keller (1998). See also Kymlicka, (1995).

[3] Article 27 of the UN International Covenant on Civil and Political Rights seems to go wider. It states that members of 'ethnic, religious or linguistic minorities . . . shall not be denied the right to enjoy their own culture, to profess and practice their own religion, or to use their own language'. This is, however, expressed in negative terms. France has reserved against it.

[4] Gundara, (2000) at 66.

[5] See Snowman (2002) for an excellent account of how central Europeans (mostly Jews) adapted to, and, in turn, strongly influenced, British culture.

[6] For example, a study of Croatian and Polish immigrants in Italy found no significant difference between the individuals who adopted those strategies, while the marginalized and separated did worst (Kosic, 2002). Another study of Korean immigrants in the USA found that the assimilated did better, while also, puzzlingly, finding that loss of Korean culture also had negative effects (Oh *et al*, 2002).

[7] Thus the right to practice one's religion includes the right to impart the belief to one's children: *Wisconsin* v *Yoder* 406 US 205 (1972).

[8] *Re M (Child's Upbringing)* [1996] 2 FLR 441. These issues are well discussed by Freeman (2000).

[9] *J* v *C* [1970] AC 668. The Anglican foster parents were required to bring the child up as a Roman Catholic, his parents' religion.

[10] [1990] 1 FLR 58.

[11] Tizard and Phoenix (2002) at 65–6. See also Bagley (1993), Vroegh (1997) and Swize (2002) who also argue (boldly) that the obvious racial dissimilarity forces the adoptive parents to face up to the adopted status of the child and not to try to pass it off as their biological child.

[12] It is notable that the comprehensive overview of cultural studies Matsumoto (2002) has barely any references to children.

[13] This 'rule', deriving from the era of slavery, classified a child as black if there was any single drop of 'black blood' in its inheritance. This discriminatory and exclusionary rule was much later appropriated by the black consciousness movement as a matter of pride.

[14] See for example, Tizard and Phoenix (2002) at 113–15.

[15] I refer here to Maxwell (1998) ch 12 and O'Hearn (1998).

[16] See Roxane Famanfarmaian in O'Hearn (1998), who points out various similarities between the faiths.

[17] P. Wamba in O'Hearn (1998) at 168–69.

[18] See Maxwell (1998). See also Tizard and Phoenix (2002) at 233.

[19] Tizard and Phoenix (2002) at 110–11, 115.

[20] Tizard and Phoenix (2002) at 227.

[21] According to the 2001 Census, 15 per cent of the minority population (which is 7.9 per cent of the total) is mixed; of them, one-third are mixed white and Afro-Caribbean.

[22] The analogy with the chameleon appears quite frequently in the accounts of these children.

[23] This does seem to have been an approach used by a number of adoption agencies in the UK, and even by courts: see *re P (A Minor) (Adoption)* [1990] 1 FLR 58.

[24] As in *Re A (A Minor) (Cultural Background)* [1987] 2 FLR 429 (nine-year-old Nigeria child who had been brought up for over five years by English family allowed to remain: the judge noted that the child was brought up with extensive contact with Nigerian culture).

[25] *Al-Okaidi* v *Al-Okaidi* (1983, Court of Appeal, unreported: cited in Hamilton (1995) at 208. See also *In re Mentry* 192 Cal. App (3d) 260, 190 Cal. Rptr. 843 (1985).

[26] [1999] 2 FLR 678.

[27] (1994) 108 DLR (4th) 193.

[28] 394 Pa. Supr. 30, 574 A 2d 1130 (1990).

[29] *Affaire Palou-Martinez c. France*, Requête 64927/01, 16 December 2003.

[30] *Report of the Victoria Climbié Inquiry* (Chairman: Lord Laming, CM 5730, 2003), ch 16, especially paras. 16.11 and 12.

[31] Drobac (1998) dubs this the NOAH test, after the decision in *Osier* v *Osier* 410 A 2d 1027 (Me. 1980). She argues that courts should resolve such disputes in two stages: first, determine what the

arrangements should be without regard to any religious factors whatsoever; and only then allow religious factors to affect that provisional decision, provided that they would introduce clear harms to the children. In this way she claims that the risk of courts showing bias towards any specific religion is minimized, and proper respect is given to parents' constitutional rights.

[32] See *re R (A Minor) (Residence: Religion)* [1993] 2 FLR 163.

[33] Courts standardly proclaim their neutrality as to religions, but some (Ahdar, 1996; Mumford, 1998) have doubted whether this is always achieved.

REFERENCES

Ahdar, R. (1996) 'Religion as a factor in custody and access disputes', 10 *International. Journal of Law, Policy and the Family* 177–204.

Appiah. K. A. (1992) in A. Gutman (ed), *Multiculturalism and the Politics of Recognition* at 157.

Bagley, C. (1993) 'Transracial adoption in Britain–A follow-up study, with policy considerations' 72 *Child Welfare* 3, 285–99.

Berry, J.V., Kim, U., Power, S., Young, M. and Bujaki, M. (1989) 'Acculturation attitudes in plural Societies', *Applied Psychology: An International Review*, 38, 185–206.

Blake, M. (2003) 'Liberal multiculuralism and asymmetries in recognition', Paper given to the Analytical Leal Philosophy Conference, Oxford, 16 May.

Brophy, J., Jhutti-Johal, J., Owen, C. (2003) *Significant Harm: Child Protection Litigation in a Multi-Cultural Setting* (Lord Chancellor's Department, Research Series 1/03).

Buti, A. (2003) Australian Aboriginal Child Separations and Guardianship. PhD thesis, University of Oxford.

Drobac, J, (1998) 'For the sake of the children: Court consideration of religion in child custody cases', 50 *Stanford Law Review* 1609–70.

Eekelaar, J. (1994) 'The interests of the child and the child's wishes: The role of dynamic self-determinism' in P. Alston (ed), *The Best Interests of the Child: Reconciling Culture and Human Rights* ch 3, Oxford: Clarendon Press.

Eekelaar, J. (2002) 'Beyond the welfare principle', 14 *Child and Family Law Quarterly* 237–49.

Freeman, M. (2000) 'Disputing children' in S. N. Katz, J. Eekelaar and M. Maclean (ed), *Cross Currents: Family Law in the US and England* 264–8 Oxford University Press.

Gundara, J. S. (2000) *Interculturalism, Education and Inclusion*, London: Paul Chapman Publishing.

Hamilton, C. (1995) *Family, Law and Religion*, London: Sweet and Maxwell.

Hayes, P. (1995) 'The ideological attack on transracial adoption in the USA and Britain', 9 *International Journal of Law and the Family* 1, 14–16.

Keller, P. (1998) 'Re-thinking ethnic and cultural rights in Europe', 18 *Oxford Journal of Legal Studies* 29, 34–8.

Kosic, A. (2002) 'Acculturation attitudes, need for cognitive closure and adaptation of immigrants', 142 *Journal of Social Psychology* 2, 179–201.

Kymlicka, W. (1995) *Multicultural Citizenship*, Oxford University Press.

Matsumoto, D. (2002) (ed), *The Handbook of Cultural Psychology*, Oxford University Press.

Maxwell, A. (1998) 'Not all issues are black or white: Some views from the offspring of cross-cultural marriages' in R. Breger and R. Hill (ed) *Cross-Cultural Marriage: Identity and Choice* ch 12, Oxford: Berg.

Mumford, S. E. (1998) 'The Judicial Resolution of Disputes involving Children and Religion', 47 *International and Comparative Law Quarterly* 117–48.

Oh, Y., Koeske, G. and Sales, E. (2002) 'Acculturation, stress and depression symptoms among Korean immigrants in the US', 142 *Journal of Social Psychology* 4, 511–26.

O'Hearn, C.C. (1998) (ed), *Half and Half: Writers on Growing Up Biracial and Bicultural*, New York: Pantheon Books.

Root, M. P.P. (2001) *Love's Revolution: Interracial Marriage*, Philadelphia: Temple University Press.

Snowman, D. (2002) *The Hitler Emigrés*, London: Chatto and Windus.

Swize, J. (2002) 'Trans-racial adoption and the unblinkable difference: Racial dissimilarity serving the interests of adopted children', 88 *Virginia Law Review* 5, 1079.

Taylor, C. (1992) 'The Politics of Recognition' in A. Gutman (ed), *Multiculturalism and the Politics of Recognition*, Princeton: University of Princeton Press.

Tizard, B. and Phoenix, A. (2002) *Black, White or Mixed Race?* Routledge, revised edn 2002.

Vroegh, K. S. (1997) 'Transracial adoptees: Developmental status after 17 years', 67 *American Journal of Orthopsychiatry* 4, 568–75.

Ward, C. (2003) 'The A, B, Cs of acculturation' in D. Masumoto (ed), *The Handbook of Cultural Psychology*, Oxford University Press, 429, 432–3.

[20]

Complicating Culture in Child Placement Decisions

annie bunting

J'ai été frappée immédiatement par la façon dont l'étude de Marlee Kline sur les femmes autochtones, l'idéologie de la maternité et la protection des enfants au Canada demeure au premier plan de la recherche scientifique dans ce domaine. Bien qu'il y ait eu des études et des enquêtes des gouvernements provinciaux portant sur l'administration de la protection de la jeunesse et des peuples autochtones, l'étude de Marlee est dotée du cadre théorique le plus exhaustif et le plus politiquement engagé. De fait, je n'ai trouvé que peu d'articles à caractère scientifique traitant des aspects juridiques des familles autochtones et des décisions de placement d'enfants au Canada. Dans ce processus, j'avais l'impression d'une conversation avec l'étude de Marlee dans ce domaine. Cela dit, je traite du sujet avec une lentille différente et à partir d'une perspective différente. J'approfondis certaines questions au sujet de l'identité culturelle des enfants qui ne sont pas touchées dans son étude et je soutiens qu'il faut une compréhension anti-essentialiste du développement culturel. J'examine l'importance accordée au lien culturel dans l'application du critère du «meilleur intérêt de l'enfant» dans le droit de la garde des enfants aussi bien que dans les décisions de la protection de la jeunesse. Le présent article est le fruit d'une recherche sur l'importance de la culture, de la communauté et du racisme dans les décisions de placement des enfants au Canada.

The National Judicial Institute recently asked if I would be interested in developing a workshop on Aboriginal child welfare issues for Alberta judges. I was initially reluctant as my research on multicultural issues in family law focuses on child custody rather than child welfare and on religion and culture rather than Aboriginal heritage. These differences are not insignificant. I agreed to co-design a workshop when paired with Carol Carifelle Brzezicki of the Métis Nation of Alberta, who has extensive experience as a social worker and policy analyst with Aboriginal communities. I learned a great deal as we designed the workshop and as I prepared a short paper on child placement decisions.

I was immediately struck by how Marlee Kline's work on Aboriginal women, the ideology of motherhood, and child welfare in Canada remains the leading scholarly contribution in this area. While there have been provincial government studies and inquiries into the administration of child welfare and Aboriginal peoples, Marlee's work is the most deeply theorized and politically engaged. Indeed, I could find few scholarly articles on the legal dimensions of

Aboriginal families and child placement decisions in Canada. As I proceeded, I felt as though I was in conversation with Marlee's work in this area. That said, I approach the topic with a different lens and from a different perspective. I pursue some questions about children's cultural identity that are not explored in her work and argue in favour of anti-essentialist understandings of cultural formation. I examine the importance given to cultural connection in the best interests test in child custody law as well as child welfare determinations. This article is the product of research into the importance of culture, community, and racism in child placement decisions in Canada.

Introduction

Controversies over the removal of Aboriginal children from their homes and placement in non-Aboriginal foster and adoptive homes continue today as First Nations claim the repatriation of Aboriginal children raised outside of their cultural heritage[1] and Aboriginal peoples struggle to recover from the "Sixties sweep."[2] Controversies also abound about whether non-racialized parents have the skills and experience to teach mixed heritage children about racism. Child welfare agencies do not, of course, test most parents raising biologically related children about their "cultural competence" or anti-racist philosophies.[3] These issues do arise, however, when parents separate or when children are the subjects of custody, child protection, or adoption hearings. In these contexts, histories of racism and colonialism are mapped onto individual children's narratives, even when decisions are silent on history. While I will not fully excavate these histories, I will argue that we must be mindful that individual cases occur in particular historical and social contexts. I will examine child placement decisions that concern evaluating children's cultural background and identity in the context of the "best interests of the child" test. I will analyze both child custody and child

I wish to acknowledge the generous financial support of the Social Science and Humanities Research Council (SSHRC) and the Faculty of Arts at York University, which provided release time from my teaching and administrative responsibilities through a Faculty of Arts Research Fellowship. This article forms part of my SSHRC-funded project, "Cross-Cultural Conflicts in Canadian Family Law." I wish to thank the Special Issue editors, Susan Boyd and Margot Young, the anonymous reviewers, and Bruce Ryder for their excellent suggestions on how to improve this article.

1. See, for example, the recent case in Hamilton, Ontario, covered by Christie Blatchford, "In the Best Interests of the Little Girls? Not on Your Life," *Globe and Mail* (4 June 2004) at A12.
2. British Columbia, Aboriginal Committee Community Panel—Child Protection Legislation Review in British Columbia, *Liberating our Children, Liberating Our Nation* (British Columbia: Government of British Columbia, 1992) at 14–16 and Manitoba Community Services, *No Quiet Place: Interim Report of the Review Committee on Indian and Metis Adoptions and Placements* (Manitoba: Manitoba Community Services, 1983). See also Christine Davies, "Native Children and the Child Welfare System in Canada" (1992) 30 Alberta Law Review 1200; and Patricia A. Monture, "A Vicious Cycle: Child Welfare Law and the First Nations" (1989–90) 3 Canadian Journal of Women and the Law 1.
3. Randall Kennedy makes this point: Randall Kennedy, *Interracial Intimacies: Sex, Marriage, Identity, and Adoption* (New York: Pantheon, 2003) at 444–6.

welfare decision-making, with a primary focus on child custody, which has been examined less often in this context.[4] In particular, I will argue that any evaluation of children's cultural identities must avoid essentialist views of culture and community in the lives of children. Culture is a complicated process, not a product devoid of history.[5] Seeing culture as a negotiated, contested, and constitutive process challenges simplistic or biological approaches to identity. Further, as Ann Anagnost cautions, constructions of cultural identity for children may "produce race in a new form"[6]—"the discourse of multiculturalism sets up the paradox of absorbing 'difference' into the intimate space of the familial while also reinscribing it ... embracing diversity as a way of 'containing' difference."[7] This article attempts to enhance an understanding of how to value children's cultural heritage in child placement decisions in Canada without reiterating hierarchies of cultural difference.

Marlee Kline argued that in the case of Aboriginal women,[8] intersections of gender, race, and class must be appreciated when considering assessments of who is a "good" or appropriate mother. Similarly, when judges evaluate the importance of a child's heritage, culture must be seen as intersecting with other aspects of the child's identity, including gender, class, ability, and sexuality. As well, I will contend, building on Kline's arguments,[9] that for social and historical reasons, collectivist or community interests may often deserve more weight in the placement of Aboriginal children. Given the central role of child welfare practices—the removal of children from their homes—in assimilationist policies applied to Aboriginal peoples since the 1950s, "the material relations of colonialism and racial oppression within the child welfare system and more generally within society must be directly challenged and replaced."[10]

I will review the statutory context, leading cases, and academic commentary on race and culture as factors in assessing the best interests of the child. In particular, I will discuss later in this article two custody cases that reached the Supreme Court of Canada. The first involves an American-born boy named

4. With the exception of Emily Carasco's piece in Canada: "Race and Child Custody in Canada: Its Relevance and Role" (1999) 16 Canadian Journal of Family Law 11. In the American context, see Katharine T. Bartlett, "Comparing Race and Sex Discrimination in Custody Cases" (1999–2000) 28 Hofstra Law Review 877.
5. Manuela Carneiro De Cunha, "Children, Politics and Culture: The Case of Brazilian Indians," in Sharon Stephens, ed., *Children and the Politics of Culture* (Princeton, NJ: Princeton University Press, 1995) 282 at 282.
6. Ann Anagnost, "Scenes of Misrecognition: Maternal Citizenship in the Age of Transnational Adoption" (2000) 8(2) Positions: East Asian Cultures Critique 389 at 391.
7. *Ibid.* at 390–1.
8. Marlee Kline, "Complicating the Ideology of Motherhood: Child Welfare Law and First Nation Women" (1993) 18 Queen's Law Journal 306.
9. Marlee Kline, "Child Welfare Law, 'Best Interests of the Child' Ideology and First Nations" (1992) 30 Osgoode Hall Law Journal 375.
10. Kline, "Complicating," *supra* note 8 at 341.

Ishmael[11] and the second involves another four-year old boy named Elijah.[12] Both boys have mixed heritage, African-American fathers, and complicated stories. I will explore questions of children's identity in these cases and ask whether their best interests were abstracted from specific cultural considerations in what Kline refers to as the tendency to see the child as an abstract individual already "out of culture," already disconnected from his or her particular cultural and familial identity.[13] Yet first, I will argue that considerations of culture and community in the placement of children need to be informed by more fluid understandings of culture and identity than those provided in these decisions.[14] For example, the British Columbia Court of Appeal considered Ishmael to *be* "Aboriginal" while Elijah was seen *as* "black," whereas, in fact, both boys have mixed cultural heritage.

In Elijah's case, the Supreme Court of Canada offered a tentative approach to the importance of race and culture in the best interests test—one that resisted making race a determining factor in custody assessments. The Court's approach is consistent with my own suggestions regarding children's identity. Questions of cultural identity need to be taken seriously in custody and access cases, but judges ought to resist neat equations or formulae for assessing the weight to be given to these factors. No simple presumptions or tests can capture the complexity and fluidity of children's heritage as well as their families' and communities' interests. I would argue that a place to start in judgments concerning culture is with what Marilyn Strathern calls a "laying bare of assumptions."[15] With a spirit of openness and self-reflection, essentialist conceptions of identity can be avoided and the social contexts in which children's identities and needs are shaped more fully appreciated.[16]

---

11. *H.(D.)* v. *M.(H.),* [1999] S.C.R. 328 [hereinafter *H.(D.)* (S.C.C.)], (1998), 158 D.L.R. (4th) 548 (B.C.C.A.) [hereinafter *H.(D.)* (B.C.C.A.)], [1997] B.C.J. No. 2144 (B.C.S.C.) (QL) [hereinafter *H.(D.)* (B.C.S.C.)].
12. *Van de Perre* v. *Edwards* (2001), 204 D.L.R. (4th) 257 (S.C.C.), (2002) 184 D.L.R. (4th) 515 (B.C.C.A.) [hereinafter *Van de Perre,* cited to S.C.C.].
13. Kline, "Best Interests Ideology," *supra* note 9 at 395–6: "By constructing the child *conceptually* as separate from her culture, the *actual* removal of the child from it is made to seem unproblematic."
14. While I intend my observations to apply to both Aboriginal children and racialized children, I focus more on Aboriginal children and communities in this article in part due to Marlee Kline's focus on Aboriginal women and child welfare. Given their histories of oppression and contemporary racism, all racialized children and communities have a claim to particular attention to cultural considerations in child placement decisions. While the situation of Aboriginal communities is distinctive, African-Canadian and African-American communities also may claim collectivist interests in child placement determinations. Kim Forde-Mazuri critiques this argument in "Black Identity and Child Placement: The Best Interests of Black and Biracial Children" (1993–4) 92 Michigan Law Review 925 at 960–2.
15. Marilyn Strathern, *Gender of the Gift: Problems with Women and Problems with Society in Melanesia* (Berkeley: University of California Press, 1988) at 8.
16. Anne Fadiman's book, *The Spirit Catches You and You Fall Down: A Hmong Child, Her American Doctors and the Collision of Two Cultures* (New York: Farrar, Straus and Giroux, 1997), is an example of a rich study of one Hmong family's encounter with the medical and child

Culture and Racialization

It is widely accepted that culture matters to children. The United Nations *Convention on the Rights of the Child*[17] includes a child's right to her or his culture in various articles, including a right to cultural life, nationality, and indigenous or minority culture. In Article 23, the convention requires state parties to pay due regard "to the desirability of continuity in a child's upbringing and to the child's ethnic, religious, cultural and linguistic background" when placing a child outside her or his family. However, as Sharon Stephens argues on reviewing the preambular statement and these articles, "the culture to which the child has *primary* rights is the international culture of modernity, the unmarked, taken-for-granted background to more specialized cultural rights."[18] Further, in order to fully exercise a right to culture, more radical reforms than those contemplated by the rights document, including "resource development and environmental policies" for indigenous populations, would need to take place.[19] To paraphrase Barbara Yngvesson, the relations between nations and within the state that produce children who are "available" for international adoption are not addressed in these articles.[20] Kline might well have levelled the same criticisms at child welfare statutes in Canada.

Cultural identity is not important only when children are adopted transnationally or transculturally. Identity—whether ethnic, national, cultural, sexual, or racial—is a very personal and, at the same time, a very collective matter. Individuals often have deeply personal understandings of their identity, and these understandings may change depending on the context or their age. Identities that are ascribed to individuals may or may not conform to their own sense of self. On the other hand, communities have historically organized around identities, most recently in what many refer to as the identity politics of the last two decades. Further, different communities relate to mainstream society with more or less assimilation at different historical moments.[21] Aboriginal communities and First Nations in Canada, in particular, are self-governing in some respects and have authority over child and family services in some regions

welfare systems in California. Fadiman does not come to easy conclusions about cross-cultural treatment nor simple prescriptions for cross-cultural interactions.

17. *Convention on the Rights of the Child*, GA Res. 44/25, UN GAOR, 44th Sess., Supp. No. 49, UN Doc. A/44/25 (1989), [1992] Can.T.S. No. 3.
18. Sharon Stephens, "Introduction: Children and the Politics of Culture in 'Late Capitalism,'" in Stephens, ed., *supra* note 5 at 37 [emphasis in original].
19. *Ibid.* at 38.
20. Barbara Yngvesson, "Placing the 'Gift Child' in Transnational Adoption" (2002) 36(2) Law & Society Review 227 at 237: "The dual role of the state in producing a child [with rights] ... even as it produces the conditions for the abandonment of children and determines the terms of their adoptability by other states illuminates once again the tension between giving and selling in commodity thinking, and the significance of marking the divide between state and market in these transactions."
21. For a discussion of communal religious communities, see William Janzen, *Limits on Liberty: The Experience of Mennonite, Hutterite, and Doukhobor Communities in Canada* (Toronto: University of Toronto Press, 1990).

of the country.[22] While it is not my intention to weigh into the debates on identity politics in North America, it is useful to remember both the individual and community dimensions of these debates.

The situation is further complicated for children subject to custody decisions, since we tend to ascribe to them their parents' identity or an identity based on stereotypical assumptions about religion, culture, race, or ethnicity. For children who have a genetic connection to, and look like, their parents or one of their parents, it is assumed that identity is acquired in an unproblematic fashion. This biological approach to ethnic identity often does not provide a satisfying account, however, for children of first generation immigrants, children of mixed ethnic parentage,[23] or children with parents of different faiths. Moreover, such an approach does not capture personal negotiations of identity and can lead to essentialist understandings of culture, race, and gender. Why, for instance, are mixed-race children so often referred to as "black"?[24] Why and how do we value religious upbringing for children?[25] How often do we provide space for children to articulate a sense of a heritage that is not their parents'? To see identity as something that is acquired through genetics and maintained through symbolic rituals oversimplifies cultural identity. Indeed, simplistic understandings of gender, race, or culture are often grounded in ideas about essential differences between people on those bases—whether they are biologically or socially constructed essential differences.[26] With respect to race, for example, essentialist perspectives hold that there is an essence of blackness and, with regard to gender, that there are quintessentially female characteristics.

Essentialism in turn nurtures an approach to culture that obfuscates histories of oppression and colonialism because difference is presented as biological or natural or ahistorical. The role of the social relations of racism, sexism, and colonialism in constructing categories of difference may be masked in the process. Bringing social relations of unequal power to the fore, drawing them out of the

---

22. See discussion accompanying footnote 133.

23. I was surprised by the results of the Census 2001, which reported that only 3.1 per cent of the over seven million marriages that year were "intermarried" couples, either both spouses identifying as visible minority (0.4 per cent) or one visible minority and one non-visible minority (2.7 per cent). "What changed [since 1996], however, was the number of people reporting more than one ethnic ancestry. In 2001, 11.3 million people, or 38% of the population, reported multiple ethnic origins, up from 10.2 million, or 36%, in 1996. In 1991, 7.8 million people reported multiple ancestries, as did 7.0 million in 1986," available online at <http://www12.statcan.ca/english/census01/products/analytic/companion/etoimm/canada.cfm> (date accessed: 21 June 2004).

24. The answer is related to the erasure of whiteness as race and the underestimation of racism in Canada. See Sherene Razack, ed., *Race, Space, and the Law: Unmapping a White Settler Society* (Toronto: Between the Lines, 2002), and Sherene Razack, *Looking White People in the Eye: Gender, Race and Culture in Courtrooms and Classrooms* (Toronto: University of Toronto Press, 1998).

25. See Shauna Van Praagh, "Religion, Custody, and a Child's Identities" (1997) 35 Osgoode Hall Law Journal 309.

26. See Diana Fuss's work on the social construction/essentialism debate: Diana Fuss, *Essentially Speaking: Feminism, Nature and Difference* (New York and London: Routledge, 1989).

analytical shadows, was a major theme in Marlee Kline's work. Thus, for example, she pointed out that without historicizing contemporary legal treatments of Aboriginality, culture, and racial identity, legal decisions "naturalize and legitimate intersecting oppressive relations of race, gender, and class in particular contexts, such as that of child welfare law."[27] However, while Kline developed a strong critique of the deficient understanding of Aboriginal culture underlying judicial reasoning in child welfare cases, she did not subject her own understanding of culture to the same anti-essentialist critique.

The historical context for the removal of Aboriginal children from their families and communities in North America is linked to child welfare intervention in Aboriginal communities and policies of assimilation. The history includes "adopting children out" of Aboriginal communities, marked most significantly by the "60s sweep,"[28] residential schools,[29] and ongoing struggles for Aboriginal communities to regenerate. Joanne Crook reminds readers that "the Department [of Indian Affairs] and the churches rationalized their actions at the time of residential schools by determining that it was in the *best interests* of the children to become assimilated."[30] Bernd Walter, Janine Alison Isenegger, and Nicholas Bala review the Canadian history of child welfare in Aboriginal communities and conclude that "[c]hild welfare legislation, judicial decision making and casework practices, in failing to adequately address the distinct characteristics of aboriginal culture, have been termed 'cultural genocide.'"[31] As a result, some commentators, including Kline, argue that judges in Canada ought to pay particular attention to the cultural and psychological needs of Aboriginal children, the integrity of families, and the survival of communities.

The history of Aboriginal children being removed from, and sometimes adopted out of, their communities reveals that devastating effects can result for both children and communities.[32] Many Aboriginal children raised in non-Aboriginal homes experience a profound sense of loss.[33] Certainly, parents and

27. Kline, "Complicating," *supra* note 8 at 315–16. And see Razack, *Looking White People in the Eye*, *supra* note 24.
28. For in-depth discussions, see Kline, "Best Interests Ideology," *supra* note 9; Davies, *supra* note 2; and Monture, *supra* note 2.
29. "There are approximately 12,000 claims across Canada arising out of Indian Residential Schools": Justice Ronald S. Veale, "Residential School Litigation" (presentation to the National Judicial Institute, 23–5 January 2003) [unpublished, on file with author].
30. Joanne Crook, "The Best Interests of the First Nations Child" (1999) 24(2) Law Now 18 at 19 [emphasis added].
31. Bernd Walter, Janine Alison Isenegger, and Nicholas Bala, "Best Interests in Child Protection Proceedings: Implications and Alternatives" (1995) 12 Canadian Journal of Family Law 367 at 405. In the American context, the Association of Black Social Workers argued that the placement of black children with white families was cultural genocide. See Kennedy, *supra* note 3 at 34–5.
32. Canada, Royal Commission on Aboriginal Peoples, *Report of the Royal Commission on Aboriginal Peoples,* vol. 1 (Ottawa: Royal Commission on Aboriginal Peoples, 1993) at 333–409; Canada, Royal Commission on Aboriginal Peoples, *Choosing Life: Special Report on Suicide among Aboriginal People* (Ottawa: Royal Commission on Aboriginal Peoples, 1994) at 1–67.
33. Pauline Turner Strong, "To Forget Their Tongue, Their Name, and Their Whole Relation: Captivity, Extra-Tribal Adoption and the Indian Child Welfare Act," in Sarah Franklin and Susan

communities suffered immense loss as their children were taken from them.[34] An overwhelming majority of Aboriginal people in conflict with the law were raised out of their culture or off-reserve.[35] As Rita Simon and Howard Altstein write in the American context, "the case of Native American children is a special one. Native Americans have been subjected to a singularly tragic fate, and their children have been particularly vulnerable."[36] Thus, when exploring collective or community identity, the best interests of the child are layered with, and connected to, the best interests of the community.[37] It is trite to say that communities need children who feel integrated and "at home" in order to thrive and grow.

However, do children need to be connected socially to their communities marked by an apparently common racial heritage in order to thrive and grow? In thinking through this difficult question, it is important to bear in mind that the relationship between children's social experiences and their birth communities vary widely. For example, the review of the Office of the Children's Advocate in Alberta calls for a broad approach to Aboriginal culture, stating that Aboriginal children in contact with children's services in Alberta "are part of the *continuum* of Aboriginal culture." The full range of experiences needs to be considered and differences taken into account in decision-making:

> Some are comfortable with traditional ways and have spent much of their lives in First Nation or Métis communities. Others have spent their whole lives in urban environments with friends and neighbours who represent the full range of Canada's ethnic mix. And many Aboriginal children have experience in both Aboriginal and non-Aboriginal worlds. This review calls for approaches that recognize this continuum, and the different ways in which mainstream culture and traditional cultures may view the process of advocacy.[38]

McKinnon, eds., *Relative Values: Reconfiguring Kinship Studies* (Durham: Duke University Press, 2001) 468 at 486. See also Barbara Yngvesson, "Adoption, Loss of Bearings, and the Mythology of Roots" (2003) 21 Social Text 2.

34. Aboriginal children are over-represented in the child welfare system. For example, "Aboriginal children make up about 21 per cent of Manitoba's population under the age of fifteen, but they account for 78 per cent of children in care of the overall child and family services system": Manitoba, Aboriginal Justice Inquiry—Child Welfare Initiative, *Promise of Hope: Commitment to Change* (Manitoba: Aboriginal Justice Inquiry, 2001) at 8.
35. Personal communication with Jonathan Rudin, Aboriginal Legal Clinic of Toronto (23 January 2003). The history for Aboriginal children also includes institutional and foster care, multiple moves between homes, and complicated and often abusive foster experiences. See Canada, Royal Commission on Aboriginal Peoples, *Bridging the Cultural Divide: A Report on Aboriginal People and Criminal Justice in Canada* (Ottawa: Royal Commission on Aboriginal Peoples, 1995).
36. Rita J. Simon and Howard Altstein, *Adoption, Race and Identity: From Infancy to Young Adulthood,* 2nd ed. (New Brunswick, NJ: Transaction Publishers, 2002) at 18.
37. This argument is made by Philip Lynch, "Keeping Them Home: The Best Interests of Indigenous Children and Communities in Canada and Australia" (2001) 23 Sydney Law Review 501.
38. Chan Durrant Limited, "A Review of the Office of the Children's Advocate" (Calgary, Alberta: Minister of Children's Services, 2000) at 2–3.

Moreover, research indicates that children's racial and cultural identities are quite fluid. Although little research exists on multicultural families and custody in Canada, insights about children's cultural identity may be drawn from adoption literature. The empirical research on transracially adopted children offers some insight into the development of ethnic identities in multicultural families. While decision-makers often assume that there is a straightforward relationship between biologically related children and their heritage, they assume adopted children (who may not *look* like their parents) will have self-esteem and identity issues as teens and young adults. Yet the literature on trans-ethnic or trans-racial adoption suggests that identity for adoptees can shift and change during their lifetime and that such adoptees can develop a positive sense of self.[39] Cultural identity depends on the child's age, demographics, peer group, siblings, and exposure to cultural activities. Some studies of adoptees report strong self-esteem (similar to comparator groups).[40] Other research reveals weak racial identification, as in the case of black children adopted by white families.[41]

Simon and Altstein's multi-phase study of adoption followed families with adopted children over three decades. They found "no differences in self-esteem scores by race, nor did the adoptive status of the respondent affect their scores."[42] In regard to ethnic identity, "their findings did not offer any evidence that black children reared by white parents acquired a preference for black over white. They showed only that black children perceived themselves as black as accurately as white children perceived themselves as white."[43] Of course, one might ask of Simon and Alstein what an "accurate" self-perception entails. One research study of forty Korean children adopted into non-Korean families in the United States found that "[c]hildren who were high participators in Korean cultural activities scored higher on Korean identity ... Parental encouragement and co-participation

39. Kira Lieberman, *The Process of Racial and Ethnic Identity Development and Search for Self in Adult Korean Transracial Adoptees* (Psychology dissertation, Massachusetts School of Professional Psychology, 2001) [unpublished]: "The implications of Korean adoptees achieving a strong ethnic identity remain unclear. However, the results of this study support previous findings that racial and cultural identity is fluid, and that a reworking of one's identity may occur as one develops and encounters new experiences" (abstract).

40. See Leslie Doty Hollingsworth, "Effect of Transracial/ Transethnic Adoption on Children's Racial and Ethnic Identity and Self-Esteem: A Meta-Analytic Review" (1997) 25(1/2) Marriage & Family Review 99.

41. M. Devon Brooks, *A Study of the Experiences and Psychosocial Development Outcomes of African American Adult Transracial Adoptees* (Psychology dissertation, University of California, Berkeley, 2001) [unpublished]: "Findings revealed that the long-term psychosocial development of adult, transracial adoptees was positive overall. Neither transracial placement nor racial identity was a predictor of adoptees' psychosocial development. Yet, transracially adopted subjects did experience numerous challenges related to the unique nature of their adoption. In contrast to the current law, data from this study call for child welfare professionals to routinely assess the racial needs of children who may be adopted transracially, as well as the ability of adoptive families to raise a transracially adopted child" (abstract).

42. Simon and Altstein, *supra* note 36 at 163.

43. *Ibid.* at 140–1.

in cultural activities seemed critical to the process [of developing ethnic identification]."[44]

The laudable efforts of adoptive parents who assist their internationally adopted children to develop a sense of their birth identity do not, however, disrupt the systemic conditions that produce children available for adoption nor the global inequities that see predominantly white North American and European couples adopting Asian and Latin American girls.[45] The "practice of constructing a culture for a child adopted internationally appears to entail the insertion of the child into an economy of racialized difference that tends to contain or domesticate differences in discrete boxes or 'culture bites.'"[46] Further, Korean adoptions in North America take place in a particular historical context—the socio-political context is different again for Vietnamese or Chinese adoptions in the United States and Canada. As Anagnost and Yngvesson both insist, such "dehistorization"[47] can maintain racial hierarchies by ignoring Western complicity in creating or sustaining conditions of poverty in adoption-production countries.

The studies suggest that culture ought to be understood as a contested and dynamic process rather than as a static or abstract concept that is accessed rather than lived. Furthermore, when assessing the best interests of the child, the cultures of parents must also be seen from this dynamic perspective. This point is particularly important for Aboriginal and racialized women, as gendered racism affects the assessment of their legal claims: "Racial hierarchies come into existence through patriarchy and capitalism, each system of domination mutually constituting the other ... [R]ace, gender, and class hierarchies structure (rather than simply complicate) each other."[48] For example, Susan Boyd notes that Aboriginal mothers engaged in custody disputes with white fathers have not "benefited" from the "potentially simplistic, essentialist conclusion that only a visible minority parent is capable of engendering an appreciation of a child's racial and cultural identity."[49] In fact, as Kline's work documented, Aboriginal women are constructed as incompetent mothers who do not fit the ideal model of motherhood (selfless, responsible, stable, tidy, and middle class).[50] Given the legal history of devaluing Aboriginal culture, including the extended family, judges may continue

---

44. Nam Soon Huh and William J. Reid, "Intercountry, Transracial Adoption and Ethnic Identity: A Korean Example" (2000) 43 International Social Work 75 at 85. Again, I do not intend to weigh into the debates about transracial adoption. For my purposes, the empirical research is relevant in so far as it documents a fluid understanding of culture and cultural identity for children, youth, and adults. See "Special Issue on Nonbiological Parenting" (2002) 36 Law and Society Review.
45. Bernie D. Jones, "International and Transracial Adoptions: Toward a Global Critical Race Feminist Practice?" (2004) 10(1) Washington and Lee Race and Ethnic Ancestry Law Journal 43 at 44–5.
46. Anagnost, *supra* note 6 at 413.
47. *Ibid.* at 391.
48. Sherene Razack, "Introduction: When Place Becomes Race," in Razack, ed., *Race, Space, and the Law*, *supra* note 24 at 6 and 15.
49. Susan B. Boyd, *Child Custody, Law, and Women's Work* (Don Mills: Oxford University Press, 2003) at 14 and 180 .
50. Kline, "Complicating," *supra* note 8 at 319–29.

to find Aboriginal heritage to be dangerous or unhealthy for children and Aboriginal women to be "bad" mothers.

Another complication is that judges and Aboriginal communities may see a child with an Aboriginal mother *as* being Aboriginal (with a need for exposure to his or her Aboriginal heritage) for many different reasons, but the child's own sense of his or her Aboriginal heritage will rest somewhere on the continuum of cultural experience described earlier. Interrogating assumptions about cultural identity and children raises questions about simple formulae that would require that a child's placement correspond to the child having a particular racial identity or a certain mother tongue. A preferable approach to assessing the importance of children's heritage in the context of the best interests test is to identify the parents who are most willing to facilitate an open approach to culture—one that allows children to explore their cultural heritages and histories throughout their lives. "Attention to the child's heritage" ought, then, to be interpreted as attention to a fluid and changing identity as the child matures. Determining that a parent is capable of nurturing such an identity needs to be based on an assessment of their ability to meet the child's needs, rather than a superficial assessment of the parent's culture or racialized experience, which might occur in "race-matching."[51]

Another key point is that a mixed-race child with an African-American father, for example, may be seen by the world *as* black due to factors that include both racialization and racism.[52] Colour is still noticed in this society, and children experience racism based on the colour of their skin.[53] As a result, while race and racial difference may be fictions, racism is not.[54] Hawley Fogg-Davis makes a similar point in her argument on transracial adoption in a "race-conscious" world: "We can make choices within and against these categories, but we cannot escape them. For instance, a person ... may define herself as biracial, multiracial, or 'just a person.' But ... she must live in a social world built on census categories."[55] Narratives from people of colour in Canada confirm the persistence or tenacity of racism.[56] However, in the process of appreciating the impact of racism, one need not overlook the continuums of culture that exist. Racism is not the only

51. Elizabeth M. Vonk and Ruth Angaran, "A Pilot Study of Training Adoptive Parents for Cultural Competence" (2001) 4(4) Adoption Quarterly 5.
52. For an American history of the treatment of "mixed-race" children, see Kennedy, *supra* note 3 at introduction, 220–2, and 366–7.
53. "Some Aboriginal children felt that they were subject to racist attitudes at school and in the justice system, and were unfairly subject to police attention in urban areas, for example, if three or four of them gathered on a street": Chan Durrant Limited, *supra* note 38 at 21.
54. Howard Winant, "Race and Race Theory" (2000) 26 Annual Review of Sociology 169; Paul Gilroy, *Against Race: Imagining Political Culture beyond the Color Line* (Cambridge: Belknap, Harvard, 2000); and Francisco Valdes, Jerome McCristal Culp, and Angela P. Harris, eds., *Crossroads, Directions and a New Critical Race Theory* (Philadelphia: Temple University Press, 2002).
55. Hawley Fogg-Davis, *The Ethics of Transracial Adoption* (Ithaca: Cornell University Press, 2002) at 17–18.
56. For a collection of experiences growing up in Canada, see Carl E. James and Adrienne Shadd, eds., *Talking about Identity: Encounters in Race, Ethnicity, and Language* (Toronto: Between the Lines, 2001).

determinant of cultural identity or individual self-esteem, nor should we allow the awareness of racism to push us into embracing the essentialism upon which it relies. As medical anthropologist Janelle Taylor writes:

> "Culture" is not a "thing," somewhere "out there," that books are "about." It is a process of making meanings, making social relations, and making the world that we inhabit, in which all of us are engaged—when we read and teach, or when we diagnose and treat, no less than when we embroider *nyas* and conduct sacrifices.[57]

Once we accept that the formation of cultural identity is fluid and dynamic, and its relationship to self-esteem and perception complex, we must reject simplistic conceptions of children's best interests that insist on making their "true identities" match their "true communities." Yet it is not only the nature and importance of children's cultural identities that need to be interrogated. As Kline's work emphasizes, unspoken cultural norms and assumptions may be embedded in legal frameworks for analysis and decision-making. Legal decision-makers need to interrogate their own cultural attitudes and identities as well as those of the children whose lives they have the power to affect. Many sectors are involved, each with its own challenges, when working towards cultural competence: social workers, psychologists, evaluators/assessors,[58] lawyers,[59] mediators,[60] judges, academics, parents,[61] and children. While there is a distinction between striving for cultural sensitivity/competence and making culture a factor in the best interests of the child assessment, the two exercises are related. Only with a nuanced and open-minded assessment of the diversity of cultural experience and identity are we likely to achieve results that give children the best chance of having secure, fully realized lives.

Let us turn now to the statutory context that guides judges and others in their child placement determinations (custody, access, and child protection), as a prelude to the subsequent discussion of cases and in order to introduce the role of the "best interests" test in provincial and territorial statutes across the country. The child placement statutes also reveal that different approaches are taken to

---

57. Janelle S. Taylor, "The Story Catches You and You Fall Down: Tragedy, Ethnography, and 'Cultural Competence'" (2003) 17(2) Medical Anthropology Quarterly 159 at 179.
58. See Pratihba Reebye, "Child Custody-Access Evaluation: Cultural Perspectives," available online at <http://www.priory.com/psych/custody.htm> (date accessed: 21 June 2004) (written by a psychiatrist, this article concerns how cultural bias could occur in the evaluation process and explores "cultural profiles" of families. The author includes clinical examples).
59. See Susan Bryant, "The Five Habits: Building Cross-Cultural Competence in Lawyers" (2001) Clinical Law Review 33 (Bryant has developed extensive materials for teaching students and lawyers).
60. I explore the issue of culture and mediation in "Mediating Culture, Mediating Family Disputes in Toronto Muslim Communities" (updated version of this article presented at the *Reach of Law* conference of the Canadian Law and Society Association and the Law and Society Association, Vancouver, 30 May 2002) [unpublished].
61. Vonk and Angaran, *supra* note 51.

Vol. 16 *2004* *149*

children's cultural identity in custody and access decisions, as opposed to child protection and adoption cases.

Statutory Context

Custody and Access

Most provincial and territorial statutes do not explicitly direct judges to consider a child's cultural, racial, or religious heritage when making custody and access orders. The typical legislative approach is to implicitly allow, but not require, such factors to be considered as part of an assessment of the "best interests of the child."[62] For example, the Saskatchewan *Children's Law Act*[63] directs judges to make custody determinations in accordance with the best interests of the child. To that end, judges are required to consider a list of factors, including "the personality, character and emotional needs of the child" and "the physical, psychological, social and economic needs of the child."[64] While the provisions make no explicit mention of culture, the listed factors, in particular the social and psychological needs of the child, could be construed to include the cultural or racial heritage of the child before the court.

In three jurisdictions, the relevant legislation does direct judges to consider a child's cultural heritage. The New Brunswick *Family Services Act* requires that a child's best interests are to be determined, taking into account, among other factors, "the child's cultural and religious heritage."[65] In the Northwest Territories

62. The ten provincial and territorial statutes that direct courts to consider the "best interests of the child" but do not specify that culture, race, or religion are relevant factors are: *Domestic Relations Act*, R.S.A. 2000, c. D-14, s. 59 (2) (custody and access decisions to be made with regard to "the welfare of the minor"); *Family Relations Act,* R.S.B.C. 1996, c. 128, s. 24(1) (best interests of the child paramount; list of factors to be considered); *Family Maintenance Act,* C.C.S.M., c. F-20, s. 2 (best interests of the child paramount in section 39 custody and access determinations); *Children's Law Act*, R.S.N.L. 1990, c. C-13, s. 31 (custody and access to be determined on the basis of the best interests of the child; non-exhaustive list of factors to be considered); *Maintenance and Custody Act.* R.S.N.S. 1989, c. 160, s. 18(5) (welfare of the child paramount; no factors specified); *Children's Law Reform Act*, R.S.O. 1990, c. C-12, s. 24(2) (non-exhaustive list of factors to be considered in determining best interests of the child); *Custody Jurisdiction and Enforcement Act*, R.S.P.E.I. 1988, c. C-33, s. 15 (custody and access to be determined on the basis of the best interests of the child); *Civil Code of Québec*, S.Q. 1991, c. 64, s. 514 and s. 521.17 (custody determinations to be made in best interests of the child); *Children's Law Act*, S.S. 1997, c. C-8.2, section 8(a) (custody determinations to be made in the best interests of the child; list of factors to be considered); *Children's Act*, R.S.Y. 1986, c. 22, s. 30 (custody and access decisions to be made in accordance with the best interests of the child; courts directed to consider "all of the needs and circumstances" of the child, including list of specified factors).

63. *Children's Law Act,* S.S. 1997, c. C-8.2, s. 8(a).

64. *Ibid.*

65. *Family Services Act*, S.N.B. 1980, c. F-2.2. Section 129 directs courts to make custody and access orders based on the best interests of the child. Section 1 requires that a child's best

and Nunavut, the *Children's Law Act* provides that respect for cultural pluralism must infuse all custody and access decisions[66] and requires that judges consider all of the needs and circumstances of the child, including "the child's cultural, linguistic and spiritual or religious upbringing and ties."[67]

The federal *Divorce Act* currently takes an approach similar to the majority of provinces and does not identify culture or race as factors to be considered in custody determinations. Instead, the act gives direction to judges, in very general terms, to "take into consideration only the best interests of the child of the marriage as determined by reference to the condition, means, needs and other circumstances of the child."[68] Whether, and to what extent, the racial and cultural conditions or needs of a child are relevant to his or her best interests is left to judicial assessment.

The legislative proposal to amend the *Divorce Act,* Bill C-22, died on the order table in anticipation of the June 2004 election call and may or may not resurface under the new government.[69] The bill is nonetheless worth taking seriously since it is the most recent expression of legislative reform and consultation and because it proposed significant changes to the custody provisions of the *Divorce Act.* Custody and access orders would have been replaced by "parenting orders" and "contact orders."[70] The best interests of the child would have remained the guiding principle for the making of such orders.[71] However, in determining the best interests of the child, the bill would have provided that judges "shall consider all the needs and circumstances of the child" and would have set out a non-exhaustive list of twelve factors that must be considered. One of these factors was "the child's cultural, linguistic, religious and spiritual upbringing and heritage, including aboriginal upbringing or heritage."[72]

Bill C-22 marked a shift from the dominant approach embodied in the current *Divorce Act* and the majority of provincial/territorial statutes dealing with custody and access. It signalled an acceptance of the view that a consideration of a parent or other applicant's ability to preserve and promote a child's understanding of, and connection to, his or her cultural heritage is an important aspect of the child's

interests are to be determined taking into account, among other factors, "the child's cultural and religious heritage."

66. *Children's Law Act*, R.S.N.W.T. 1997, c. 14 (in force in Nunavut by the operation of section 29 of the *Nunavut Act*, S.C. 1993, c. 28). Section 17(1) provides that custody and access decisions are to be made in "accordance with the best interests of the child, with a recognition that differing cultural values and practices must be respected in that determination."
67. *Ibid.* at section 17(2).
68. *Divorce Act*, R.S.C. 1985, c. 3 (2nd supp.), s. 16(8).
69. Canada, Bill C-22, *An Act to Amend the Divorce Act, the Family Orders and Agreements Enforcement Assistance Act, the Garnishment, Attachment and Pension Diversion Act and the Judges Act and to Amend Other Acts in Consequence*, 2nd Session, 37th Parl. (second reading, 25 February 2003).
70. *Ibid.* at section 10, replacing section 16 of the *Divorce Act* with a new section 16 (parenting orders), section 16.1 (contact orders), and section 16.2 (best interests of the child). Contact orders applied only to non-spouses.
71. *Ibid.*, proposed new section 16.2(1).
72. *Ibid.*, proposed new section 16.2(2)(e).

welfare. Even in those provincial jurisdictions where culture is not specified as a factor to be considered, this approach is likely to become increasingly predominant. A common feature of the legislation across the country is that the best interests of the child are paramount, and any factors that affect a child's welfare are thus relevant.

Notably absent from Bill C-22, and all of the provincial/territorial statutes dealing with custody and access, is any express indication of the relevance of race, racialization, or racial heritage. One could interpret this absence in Bill C-22 as suggesting that race is relevant only insofar as it may relate to a child's "cultural, linguistic, religious or spiritual" heritage. However, race may be relevant to a child's welfare in other ways. For example, a parent's ability to educate a racialized child about racism, and to prepare him or her for a racist world, is obviously relevant to the child's welfare.[73] It is unfortunate that no Canadian statutes dealing with custody refer explicitly to racial heritage, but judges are not thereby prevented from giving weight to evidence of parents' ability to foster conscious and confident racial identities in children as part of their overall assessment of children's best interests in custody determinations. Indeed, as we will see in the discussion of Elijah's case later in this article, the case before the Supreme Court of Canada was framed in terms of racial identity or heritage as opposed to ethnic or cultural identity. As a result, this precedent in the area of custody and children's identity directs judicial attention to race.

Child Welfare

By contrast with the legislation governing custody and access orders, child welfare statutes in all provinces include references to a child's cultural, religious, or racial heritage.[74] In thirteen jurisdictions, the best interests of a child in need of protection includes the consideration of the child's cultural background and often includes explicit reference to the child's religious faith and language.[75] For

73. This position was argued by the interveners, the African Canadian Legal Clinic, the Association of Black Social Workers, and the Jamaican Canadian Association, in *Van de Perre, supra* note 12 (factum of the intervenors, File no. 27897, 22 May 2001).

74. In Prince Edward Island, for example, the preamble to the *Child Protection Act,* R.S.P.E.I. 2002, C-5.1., states that "the preservation of the cultural, racial, linguistic and religious heritage of a child promotes the healthy development of the child."

75. *Child Welfare Act*, R.S.A. 2000, c. C-12, s. 2(f)(i) ("any decision concerning the removal of a child from the child's family should take into account (i) the benefits to the child of maintaining, wherever possible, the child's familial, cultural, social and religious heritage."); *Child, Family and Community Service Act*, R.S.B.C. 1996, c. 46, s. 4(1)(e); *Child and Family Services*, C.C.S.M. c. C-80, s. 2(1)(h) ("the child's cultural, linguistic, racial and religious heritage" to be considered in best interests determination); *Family Services Act*, S.N.B., c. F-2.2, s. 1 (best interests of the child defined as including a consideration of "the child's cultural and religious heritage"); *Child, Youth and Family Services Act*, S.N.L. 1998, c. 12.1, s. 9(c) ("the child's cultural heritage" must be considered in determining the best interests of children in need of protection and/or placement); *Children and Family Services Act*, S.N.S. 1990, c. 5 (factors to be considered in determining the best interests include in section 3(2)(g) the child's cultural, racial and linguistic heritage and in section 3(2)(h) "the religious faith, if any, in which the child is

example, in British Columbia the *Child, Family and Community Service Act* refers to "the child's cultural, racial, linguistic and religious heritage" as an aspect of the best interests of the child for the purposes of child welfare decisions.[76] The Nova Scotia *Children and Family Services Act* includes culture, race, language, and religion as factors in the best interests determination.[77] The latter statute also balances the need to place children "within a reasonable time" with the need to respect children's heritage in the placement.[78]

The uniqueness of Aboriginal children's best interests and the importance of placing First Nations, Métis, and other Aboriginal children within their own communities are now emphasized in some provincial child welfare statutes. Section 57(5) of the Ontario *Child and Family Services Act* specifically directs the court to place an Aboriginal child with a member of the child's extended family, native community, or another native family.[79] Particular reference is made to Aboriginal children, and it is mandatory to consider their cultural identity according to child welfare legislation. In cases involving Aboriginal children, the BC statute directs the court as follows: a guiding principle in the interpretation and administration of the act is that "the cultural identity of aboriginal children should be preserved."[80] And in related sections, the act states:

---

being raised"); *Aboriginal Custom Adoption Recognition Act*, S.N.W.T. 1994, c. 26; *Child and Family Services,* R.S.O. 1990, c. C-11 s. 37(3) (best interests of a child in need of protection includes consideration of the "child's cultural background" and the "religious faith, if any, in which the child is being raised"); *Child Protection Act*, R.S.P.E.I. 2002, C-5.1. s. 2(2)(i) (the considerations relevant to the best interests of the child include "the cultural, racial, linguistic and religious heritage of the child"); *Youth Protection Act,* R.S.Q., c. P-34.1, s. 2.4(5)(b) and (c) (stipulates the need to take into consideration the characteristics of cultural communities and native communities); *Child and Family Services Act*, S.S. 1989–90, c. C-7.2, s. 4(c) (factors to be taken into account in determining best interests of the child include "the child's emotional, cultural, physical, psychological and spiritual needs"); *Children's Act*, S.Y. 1986, c. 22, s. 107 (the child's "own cultural background" and "lifestyle in his home community" be considered in adoption cases).

76. *Child, Family and Community Service Act*, R.S.B.C. *supra* note 75 at s. 4(1)(e).

77. *Children and Family Services Act*, S.N.S., *supra* note 75.

78. *Ibid.*, religion (section 47(4)): "Where practicable, a child who is the subject of an order for permanent care and custody shall be placed with a family of the child's own religious faith but, where such placement is not available within a reasonable time, the child may, with the approval of the Minister, be placed in the most suitable home available." Culture, race, or language (section 47(5)): "Where practicable, a child, who is the subject of an order for permanent care and custody, shall be placed with a family of the child's own culture, race or language but, if such placement is not available within a reasonable time, the child may be placed in the most suitable home available with the approval of the Minister."

79. Section 57 of the *Child and Family Services Act*, R.S.O. 1990, c. C-11. See also section 37(4) concerning the best interests of the Indian or native child.

80. *Child, Family and Community Service Act*, R.S.B.C., *supra* note 75 at section 2(f). See also section 3(b): "[A]boriginal people should be involved in the planning and delivery of services to aboriginal families and their children."

If the child is an aboriginal child, the importance of preserving the child's cultural identity must be considered in determining the child's best interests.[81]

The director must inform relevant Aboriginal organization of proceedings regarding child protection orders.[82]

The court's broad discretion in Alberta is found in the list of "matters to be considered" in relation to the best interests of the child in need of protective services.[83] Section 67 of the *Child Welfare Act* requires consultation with the band if the child being placed for adoption is an Indian child.[84]

The pattern that thus emerges is that attention to linguistic, religious, cultural, and, sometimes, racial heritage is mentioned in child protection, but not in custody and access, determinations.[85] However, as Kline's work documents,[86] even in child welfare cases, factors such as stability, bonding, and economics have tended to trump a child's connection to her or his cultural heritage: "[T]he retention and promotion of First Nations identity has seldom been recognized as an overriding, or even a substantially weighty, factor."[87] The most infamous case is that of *Racine* v. *Woods,*[88] where an Ojibway mother's claim for custody or access was lost to that of the non-Ojibway foster parents who adopted her daughter. In the child welfare cases that Kline studied, judges distinguished the individual child's best interests from "maintaining cultural connection" and constructed the child as already "abstracted out of her culture."[89]

81. *Ibid.* at section 4(2).
82. *Ibid.* at section 33.1(4). Similar provisions apply when a child is removed from a home (section 34(3)).
83. *Child Welfare Act*, R.S.A. *supra* note 75.
84. *Ibid.* As well, in section 107, the act requires adoptive parents to (1) take reasonable measures on behalf of the child necessary for the child to exercise any rights the child may have as an Indian, and (2) as soon as, in the opinion of that person, the child is capable of understanding the child's status as an Indian, inform the child of that status. It should be noted that these sections are restricted to Indian children.
85. Legislative attention to cultural heritage, especially Aboriginality, is also evident in the adoption context. See, for example, the British Columbia *Adoption Act,* R.S.B.C. 1996, c. 5, s. 3(2), and the Ontario *Child and Family Services Act*, *supra* note 75 at part VII, Adoption, ss. 136(2) and (3).
86. Kline, "Best Interests Ideology," *supra* note 9 at 397–401 and Kline, "Complicating," *supra* note 8 at 317–38.
87. Kline, "Best Interests Ideology," *supra* note 9 at 399.
88. *Racine* v. *Woods,* [1983] 2.S.C.R. 173 [hereinafter *Racine*]. *Racine* was cited with approval in 1993 in *Sawan* v. *Tearoe* (1993), 48 R.F.L. (3d) (B.C.C.A.), leave to appeal to the S.C.C. refused, [1993] S.C.C.A. No. 418 (Q.L.). See Tshepo L. Mosikatsana, "*Sawan v. Tearow*—Case Comment" (1994) 11 Canadian Family Law Quarterly 89.
89. Kline, "Best Interests Ideology," *supra* note 9 at 398 and 401.

The legislation, jurisprudence,[90] and academic commentary assume that there is a material difference between adoption (which often follows the removal of a child under a child welfare statute) and custody determinations because adoption may sever a child's future connection to his or her biological parents. While adoptions can be open in some jurisdictions, the majority of adoptions terminate the relationship between adopted children and their biological parents and, therefore, potentially the relationship between the children and their biologically related cultures or religions. However, I would argue that custody and adoption assessments should not be so neatly distinguished. As mentioned, adoptions can be open and custody decisions can, in effect, terminate relationships. The distinction that is typically drawn between adoption and custody also rests on the assumption that biological parents can meet the needs of their child's identity negotiation, which may sometimes be false.

Furthermore, the distinction between adoption and custody is based on a limiting view of culture and identity—that is, culture as a birthright rather than as a complicated negotiated process. A child may be "born Christian" but grow to be atheist;[91] be "born Canadian" but grow to be Québecois; or be "born Sikh" and choose to be Canadian[92] or a person may be *both* Sikh and Canadian. In the words of one Canadian writer, Lawrence Hill,

> I knew what I was, and I felt it tranquilly. I was both Black and white, and this was irrevocable, whether other people noticed my colours or not.
>
> Years have since passed, but I still feel that way. I'm a man of two races.[93]

The next section considers to what extent this fluid approach to culture and race is adopted in judicial decision-making.

Jurisprudence

Since the assessment of a child's best interests is tailored to the individual child before the court, it is often difficult to glean general principles from the

90. *Van de Perre*, *supra* note 12 at para. 40.
91. Or "born" straight and become "queer," as I saw on a (somewhat dated) postcard, "It takes two heterosexuals to make a homosexual."
92. Howard Ramos discusses an encounter when his father (originally from Ecuador) insisted on describing himself as "from Toronto" even when others tried to ascribe an otherness to him: "I was disappointed when my father decided not to identify with his country of origin, but instead with the country he had been living in for the last thirty years ... In thinking about time and the process of maintaining or perhaps more appropriately re-creating culture, I wondered why I had expected my father to hold onto his identity as a foreigner for so long. How long do people have to stay in Canada before they are Canadian?": James and Shadd, *supra* note 56 at 106 and 108.
93. Lawrence Hill, "Zebra: Growing up Black and White in Canada," in James and Shadd *supra* note 56 at 49–50.

jurisprudence. Nevertheless, the leading decisions provide some insight into the judicial assessment of culture, community, and racism in relation to the best interests test. The recent decision in *Van de Perre* v. *Edwards*[94] was the first time the Supreme Court of Canada discussed the importance of racial identity of a child in the context of a custody dispute between parents.[95] This case, involving a child called Elijah, will be discussed along with *D.H.* v. *H.M.*, a case from British Columbia concerning a child named Ishmael.[96] In the latter case, the Supreme Court of Canada did not issue reasons when it overturned the British Columbia Court of Appeal decision in 1999, but reasons did accompany the dismissal of a motion for a re-hearing.[97] While both cases are custody disputes (albeit between grandparents, not parents, in the case of *D.H.*), the Court's discussion of the importance of a child's heritage is also relevant in child welfare and adoption determinations. *Van de Perre* involved the weight to be given to Elijah's racial identity and heritage, whereas *D.H.* focused on the significance of Ishmael's Aboriginal heritage.

Ishmael's case is somewhat convoluted and very sad. Ishmael has dual citizenship between Canada and the United States and is the son of a Canadian-born Aboriginal mother and an African-American father. His mother, Melissa, was adopted and raised by a white couple in Connecticut. Melissa's story is a tragically familiar one for Aboriginal children in the 1970s. After being born into the Swan Lake First Nation in Manitoba, she "passed through a long list of foster homes in [her] infancy"[98] before being adopted along with her sister by the H's in Connecticut. It is clear from the information in the decisions that she had a difficult adolescence and struggled with drug addiction. While Melissa was not invisible in the judicial decisions, her life history was not put in its historical context and her choices with regard to her son were not ultimately valued. The role of the state in producing the conditions in which Aboriginal families live was thereby rendered invisible.[99] It is an example of judicial decision-making, as Kline remarked in her work, not "recognizing the roots of [Aboriginal women's] difficulties in the history and current structures of colonialism and racial oppression."[100]

The trial judge did state at the outset of Ishmael's case that "[i]ssues of blood ties and the preservation of Ishmael's aboriginal heritage figure in this difficult

---

94. *Van de Perre, supra* note 12.
95. *Racine, supra* note 88 predates *Van de Perre* by almost two decades. It was not a custody dispute between two parents, but rather between the child's Aboriginal mother and the prospective non-Aboriginal adoptive parents. Wilson J.'s comment in *Racine* that the significance of culture as opposed to bonding abates over time has been much criticized and, perhaps significantly, was not referred to by the Supreme Court of Canada in *Van de Perre*.
96. *H.(D.)* (B.C.C.A.), *supra* note 11.
97. *H.(D.)* (S.C.C.), *supra* note 11. Motion for rehearing dismissed, [1999] 1. S.C.R. 761 [hereinafter *H.(D.)* (motion for rehearing)].
98. *H.(D.)* (motion for rehearing), *supra* note 97 at para. 2.
99. Kline, "Best Interests Ideology," *supra* note 9 at 414.
100. Kline, "Complicating," *supra* note 8 at 318.

fact situation."[101] The mother, Melissa, did not consistently care for her son since she was having psychological problems and would disappear for two to three weeks at a time after his birth. When the baby was eight months old, however, Melissa took him to Vancouver and moved into the home of her biological father, H.M. The case was therefore a custody dispute between H.M., the Aboriginal grandfather to Ishmael, and D.H. and N.H., his adoptive (white) grandparents in Connecticut. Melissa was neither capable nor willing to parent Ishmael. In an *interim* order when Ishmael was one, sole custody was granted to H.M.[102] However, the trial judge concluded that custody should go to the Connecticut grandparents.

The trial judge heard arguments about the relative weight to be given to Ishmael's Aboriginal heritage: "Counsel for H.M. submit[ted] that the consideration of Ishmael's aboriginal heritage should be given great weight in these proceedings."[103] The trial judge found Ishmael's Aboriginal heritage to be important, but no more so than his "African-American background and American citizenship. That heritage is also of importance and it is *equally* deserving of preservation and nurturing.".[104] The trial judge weighed other considerations in the best interests of Ishmael including his ties of blood and adoption to the parties, the wishes of his mother (for him to remain in H.M.'s care), the status quo, bonding, and the parties' ability to provide for his needs. The fact that Ishmael had adjusted well to the many disruptions in his short life seemed to give licence to the judge to order yet another change in his custody (at age two and a half).[105]

The British Columbia Court of Appeal overturned the trial decision and ordered that custody be given to H.M., Ishmael's Aboriginal grandfather. In its decision, the Court of Appeal found that the trial judge had erred in weighing the evidence—the error had been an over-emphasis on economic matters and an under-emphasis on "ties of blood and culture that bind Ishmael to H.M. [and to the other members of his family unit]."[106] Further, the court took a negative view of disrupting Ishmael from the home he had known for over two years.[107] Finally, trans-cultural adoption of Aboriginal children was discussed:

101. *H.(D.)* (B.C.S.C.), *supra* note 11 at para. 5.

102. This interim order came about after the Connecticut grandparents, concerned about their daughter's ability to care for Ishmael, contacted the child welfare department in their state who in turn contacted British Columbia. Ishmael was apprehended by the Ministry of Children and Families in British Columbia and placed in foster care for four months (*Ibid.* at para. 19–20).

103. *H.(D.)* (B.C.S.C.), *supra* note 11 at para. 45.

104. *Ibid.* at para. 46 [emphasis added]. Ishmael's putative father had denied paternity and did not take part in the case.

105. *Ibid.* at para. 55: "I observe that he was taken from one set of primary caregivers—the petitioners—into foster care and then into the care of H.M. at what is generally acknowledged to be an important point in his development. This has occurred without any apparent detrimental effect on his development." In fact, Ishmael had not been in the sole custody of the H's. Rather, they had shared care with Melissa when she lived at home with Ishmael. The order was stayed pending the hearing of the appeal.

106. *H. (D.)* (B.C.C.A.), *supra* note 11 at para. 13.

107. *Ibid.*

> While there are doubtless many successful instances of cross-cultural adoption and custody situations involving children of aboriginal descent and non-aboriginals, there also exists a very considerable history of unsuccessful outcomes ... Perhaps because of this, Indian bands and governments in Canada are moving in directions exemplified by the above noted provisions of the Child, Family and Community Service Act. Whether success will be attained or enhanced by this sort of initiative, only future experience can demonstrate, but it seems to me that the courts ought to show due deference to the legislative initiatives in this area. This is a major factor in this case that influences me to differ from the conclusion of the trial judge concerning the custody of this young child.[108]

The Supreme Court of Canada disagreed with the approach of the British Columbia Court of Appeal and restored the trial decision. In later dismissing the motion to rehear the appeal, the Supreme Court of Canada stated: "We concluded that in fact the trial judge had given careful attention to the aboriginal ancestry of Ishmael, together with all the other factors relevant to Ishmael's best interests."[109] While this refusal to accord determinative weight to biological connection is consistent with the approach I have outlined, the British Columbia Supreme Court's consideration of the boy's Aboriginal heritage was superficial. It was sufficient, the Court wrote, that D.H, the adoptive grandfather, had "researched the Swan Lake First Nation on the Internet"[110] and that he and N.H. had "established contact with the Mohegan and the Pequot groups in New England and hope by this and other means to help young Ishmael to be made aware of his aboriginal culture."[111] In effect, by restoring the trial decision, the Supreme Court of Canada affirmed Ishmael's "connection to First Nations ancestry in the *abstract*"[112] rather than a connection to his particular First Nations heritage. Kline's thesis concerning the individualistic construction of the child and the abstraction of culture is demonstrated in Ishmael's case.

Furthermore, while the Connecticut grandparents' abilities to parent an Aboriginal child were not thrown into question by the problems experienced by Melissa and her sister, H.M.'s parenting skills and style were questioned in relation to another daughter's problems with the law.[113] While clearly not a "mother-blaming" manoeuvre, as in the cases involving Aboriginal mothers that Kline explored, similar dynamics emerge in the trial judge's assessment of H.M.'s parenting, poverty, unemployment, and uncertainties—many of the factors that

108. *Ibid.* at paras. 16–17 and see para. 20.
109. *H.(D.)* (motion for rehearing), *supra* note 97 at para. 5.
110. *H.(D.)* (B.C.S.C.), *supra* note 11 at para. 25.
111. *H.(D.)* (B.C.C.A.), *supra* note 11 at para. 3.
112. Kline, "Best Interests Ideology," *supra* note 9 at 410.
113. *H.(D.)* (B.C.S.C.), *supra* note 11 at paras. 35 and 49.

Kline identifies with the ideological construction of a "bad home" and "bad mother" in cases involving First Nations children.[114]

Elijah's case also involved parties of contrasting cultural and economic backgrounds. Elijah is the son of Kimberly Van de Perre and Theodore (Blue) Edwards. At the time of the litigation, Van de Perre, who is white, lived in Vancouver with Elijah. Edwards, who is African American, was married with ten-year-old twin girls and lived in North Carolina. He was a professional basketball player who had a brief relationship with Van de Perre in Vancouver. After a lengthy trial featuring many contested issues, the judge awarded custody to Van de Perre stating that, in part, he was worried about Edwards's marriage not surviving his sexual infidelities.

The British Columbia Court of Appeal reversed the trial decision, stating that the judge had not applied the best interests of the child test appropriately in relation to some important facts and evidentiary conclusions. For example, the trial judge had emphasized negative aspects of the father's personality without also emphasizing the mother's "narcissistic and histrionic" personality.[115] Indeed, the Court of Appeal's construction of Van de Perre as a poor, white, single-mother and basketball groupie was problematic in the decision. As a matter of evidence, the British Columbia Court of Appeal concluded that undue emphasis had been placed on the possible instability of the Edwards marriage.[116] Further, Justice of Appeal Newbury commented in relation to culture and heritage:

> On the question of E.(1)'s "needs," the [trial] Court observed that there was some evidence of E.(1)'s need to be exposed to his "heritage and culture" as the son of an African-American but "there is also the need of the child to be exposed to the heritage and culture as the son of a Caucasian Canadian." With respect, I am not sure there is a "Caucasian Canadian" culture, but I will return to the subject of ethnicity and race in due course.[117]

The British Columbia Court of Appeal also assessed the evidence of the experts presented at trial. One expert was clinical psychologist Dr. Korpach who, it was noted in the decision, had lived in North Carolina (but was not qualified to speak to racism in the United States and Canada).[118] She recommended that custody go to the mother unless Edwards's wife was to be considered a co-applicant for custody along with the father. In other words, not until Mrs. Edwards was considered to be the caregiver to Elijah when he was with the Edwards did the expert (and the court) shift her opinion in favour of Edwards. The British Columbia Court of Appeal awarded custody to the Edwards jointly. The court wrote:

114. Kline, "Complicating," *supra* note 8 at 319–26.
115. *K.V.* v. *T.E.*, [2000] B.C.J. 491 (B.C.C.A.) (QL) at paras. 26 and 42 [hereinafter *K.V.*]
116. *Ibid.* at para. 45.
117. *Ibid.* at para. 38.
118. *Ibid.* at para. 49.

> If it is correct that E.(1) will be seen by the world at large as "being black," it would obviously be in his interests to live with a parent or family who can nurture his identity as a person of colour and who can appreciate and understand the day-to-day realities that black people face in North American society—including discrimination and racism in various forms.[119]

The Supreme Court of Canada overturned the British Columbia Court of Appeal's decision and restored the trial decision, finding that the trial judge had not erred in assessing the personalities and parenting abilities of the parents, nor had he failed to consider the bonds between Elijah and his paternal family. As for "stereotypical views of Mr. Edwards as a black man or as a black basketball player [it is] important to stress that nothing stated by Warren J. indicated a bias against black people in general or black basketball players in particular."[120] The Supreme Court of Canada found the appellate court had erred in its scope of appellate review, and, in overturning the British Columbia Court of Appeal decision, it held:

> [R]acial identity is but one factor that may be considered in determining personal identity; the relevancy of this factor depends on the context ... All factors must be considered pragmatically. Different situations and different philosophies require an individual analysis on the basis of reliable evidence.[121]

In addition, Justice Michel Bastarache wrote for the Court:

> Race can be a factor in determining the best interests of the child because it is connected to the culture, identity and emotional well-being of the child ... The adoption and custody contexts may differ because the adopted child will generally cease to have contact with the biological parent while custody will generally favour contact with both parents. Nevertheless, it is generally understood that biracial children should be encouraged to positively identify with both racial heritages.[122]

It is not clear from the decisions whether the courts saw Elijah and Ishmael as having mixed racial identities that the custody determinations would positively foster. Paradoxically, while Elijah had always been in the primary care of his mother (with regular access visits to North Carolina with his father), Elijah

119. *Ibid.* at para. 50.
120. *Van de Perre*, *supra* note 12 at para 34.
121. *Ibid.* at para. 38. In *Van de Perre*, the status quo was on the mother's side.
122. *Ibid.* at para. 40. And in paragraphs 42–3, the Court notes that "there was absolutely no evidence adduced which indicates that race was an important consideration" and states that "without evidence, it is not possible for any court, and certainly not the Court of Appeal, to make a decision about the importance of race."

seemed more racialized in the court deliberations than Ishmael, who had lived with his Aboriginal grandfather for three of the four years leading up to the Supreme Court of Canada decision and also had an African-American father. While Elijah's racial identity was not a determining factor that trumped other considerations in the best interests test, it did not need to—Elijah was always seen as "black" by the courts. Elijah's white/Caucasion heritage faded to the background just as Ishmael's African-American heritage seemed to fade as his Aboriginal heritage became the politicized focus of the custody dispute.

Both Susan Boyd and Carol Rogerson describe the Supreme Court of Canada decision in *Van de Perre* as "cautious" and based primarily on the scope of appellate review.[123] The trial judges offered little in-depth analysis or "guidance." However, "the Court should be given credit for at least beginning to grapple with the serious issues at stake and for signalling both the importance and the complexity of the issues of racial identity for biracial children."[124] As James Carlisle and Elizabeth Ramsden point out, the "Supreme Court decision was in line with most lower courts ... judges mention the importance of race and cultural background, but these factors are almost always trumped by other considerations."[125] The other considerations may include stability, bonding to other siblings in the home, custodial parent's willingness to facilitate access, or the child's preferences.

Contrary to the decision of the Supreme Court of Canada that race "is but one factor," the interveners before the Court in Elijah's case (the African Canadian Legal Clinic, the Association of Black Social Workers, and the Jamaican Canadian Association) argued that "race is an important or major factor which must be given explicit consideration and considerable weight in custody and access disputes."[126] While the interveners recognized that each custody case has unique characteristics, they directed the Court's attention to the particular needs of biracial children and the particular abilities of racialized parents "to relay lived experiences of racism to their children, to have empathy based on experience and to relay oral community history."[127] They did not say that the non-racialized parent would be unable to meet the child's needs.

While it is clear that the interveners did not state that racialized parents will necessarily be better able to meet the racial and cultural identity needs of the child, there is a risk that judges might draw this simplistic conclusion. An example

123. Boyd, *supra* note 49 at 180, and Carol J. Rogerson, "Developments in Family Law: The 2001–2002 Term" (2002) 18 Supreme Court Law Review (2d) 335 at 335 and 351. Rogerson offers a more lengthy comment on *Van de Perre*. My own findings are consistent with Rogerson's findings at 350–1, note 26, that "*Van de Perre* is being read primarily as a case supporting the narrow scope of appellate review of fact-based and discretionary decisions."

124. Rogerson, *supra* note 123 at 360.

125. James Carlisle and Elizabeth Ramsden, "Other Considerations Usually Trump Race and Cultural Background," *Lawyers Weekly* (1 March 2002).

126. *Van de Perre, supra* note 12 (Factum of the Interveners, the African Canadian Legal Clinic, the Association of Black Social Workers, and the Jamaican Canadian Association, File no. 27897, 22 May 2001, at para. 3).

127. *Ibid.* at para. 91.

is the decision in *Kassel* v. *Louie,*[128] where the custody of a seven-year-old boy named Ashton was awarded to his Chinese-Canadian father despite the fact that Ashton had to that point lived exclusively with his Caucasian-Canadian mother, with generous access by his father. The mother wanted to move with her new spouse out of the province. The judge noted that Ashton looked like his father, shared a love of computers, and was the only male heir in his father's family. I would argue that this approach does not reflect or encourage a careful consideration of all of the factors in the child's life. Further, as suggested earlier, children have their own identities, which are different from both of their parents, and need to be encouraged to find and explore their own identities.

Although I am arguing for a complex approach to culture in custody and child welfare decisions, one has to wonder whether other factors will routinely overshadow a careful consideration of the child's cultural identity or undervalue its importance. As Marlee Kline argued, courts tend to see culture "in abstract terms," with the specificity of a given child's experience being lost:

> This tendency is, I suggest, partly the result of the abstract and individualistic character of best interests ideology. "Cultural connection" cannot be seen as directed to the maintenance of a tie between a child and her particular First Nation when the child has already been constructed as an individual abstracted out of her culture.[129]

This obscuring and abstracting did occur in the case of Ishmael and his mother, Melissa, discussed earlier.

In summary, I have argued that to take race as a critical factor, or one that is always predominant in the best interests analysis for a racialized child, may itself essentialize race and fail to encourage judges to see children as individuals with complex and multiple identities, including, but not limited to, their cultural or racial identity. The Supreme Court of Canada in *Van de Perre* said what makes intuitive, but perhaps not political, sense: because the persistence and history of racism in Canada is so often minimized, it is important to stress racism and racial identity for biracial children. To advocate as a matter of legal principle, however, that race is a critical factor in all custody assessments may perpetuate, not undermine, this history. Racial identity, like cultural identity more generally, is an important factor that should always be considered, and sometimes it may be a critical or determinative factor. However, it may often not point in any clear direction.

128. *Kassel* v. *Louie,* [2000] B.C.J. No. 1925 (B.C.S.C.) (QL). Ashton had lived exclusively with his mother and had generous access visits with his father. The three had never lived together as a family.

129. Kline, "Best Interests Ideology," *supra* note 9 at 401.

Special Case of Aboriginal Children

As noted earlier, in child welfare cases, judges make placement decisions based on many of the same factors considered in custody determinations, including the child's cultural, social, and religious heritage. Some commentators have, however, asked whether the interests of Aboriginal communities ought to be given greater consideration in these decisions, as is required by statutes in some jurisdictions. Indeed, rather then being just one factor to consider in the placement of children, Walter, Isenegger, and Bala argue the "best interests of the individual aboriginal child are often inseparable from the best interests of the wider aboriginal community."[130] To date, this collectivist perspective has not taken hold in child placement decisions: "For aboriginal children in out-of-culture placements, other factors associated with best interests ... have tended to outweigh considerations of cultural background."[131] Thus, despite the difference in statutory language, child welfare jurisprudence is more or less consistent with child custody decisions with respect to the weight effectively accorded to culture, race, and community.

In deciding the placement of an Aboriginal child who has resided in a non-native foster home for a significant period of time, a judge faces difficult and complex issues. While the courts have tended to favour "psychological parenting" bonds, continuity, and economic stability, they also recognize the importance of the child's Aboriginal heritage. The situation remains, however, that non-Aboriginal decision-makers in child welfare agencies and courts are deciding the fate of Aboriginal children and their future connection to their families and communities. Judicial discretion is exercised in the historical context of Aboriginal children being removed from their homes.[132] Studies also show that Aboriginal children are more likely to spend lengthy periods in foster care and frequently move between foster homes. The experiences of abuse and disruption contribute to severe "psychological, social, developmental and identity problems that such youth frequently encounter."[133]

Some of the concerns about decision-making in child placement may be addressed through delegated Aboriginal child welfare agencies. In Alberta, some First Nations possess delegated authority over child welfare services in their communities.[134] These agencies, however, deal primarily with families on reserve

---

130. Walter, Isenegger, and Bala, *supra* note 31 at 405.
131. *Ibid.* at 407.
132. Twila L. Perry, "Race and Child Placement: The Best Interests Test and the Cost of Discretion" (1990–1) 29(1) Journal of Family Law 51: "When race becomes a factor, child placement issues, which are already complex, difficult and painful, take on an added dimension. The problem of subjectivity for which the best interests rule has long been criticized is present and this is further complicated by constitutional considerations, political issues and the practical realities of our foster care and adoption systems."
133. Walter, Isenegger, and Bala, *supra* note 31 at 409.
134. See materials provided by Child and Family Services concerning the First Nations agencies with delegated child welfare authority in Alberta: Chris Welligan, "Agreements for on Reserve Delivery by Delegated First Nation Agencies" (24 January 2003) [unpublished]. Since 1972,

and not urban or off-reserve Aboriginal children. For the latter group of children, the issues of identity, community, and belonging are complex and need attention. And for the communities of their parents, whether directly involved in their lives or not, the issues of collective survival are no less urgent. In the case of urban "Indian" children, notice is to be given to the relevant First Nation,[135] and, as a matter of policy in Alberta, placements are to start with the immediate family, move out to the extended family, and then to the community. Nonetheless, Aboriginal children are still routinely placed in non-Aboriginal homes for foster care and then adoption in Alberta and elsewhere across the country. As we saw in Ishmael's case, despite similar legislative directives in British Columbia and a willing maternal grandparent, he was placed with his non-Aboriginal grandparents in Connecticut. Ishmael's best interests were abstracted from his specific cultural interests and the broader Aboriginal community interest.

Conclusions

Marlee Kline noted the tendency of decision-makers to separate "the analysis of best interests from concerns about maintaining cultural connection"[136] and to construct the child as an abstract individual who is already "out of culture." I have attempted to build on Kline's work on child welfare law and First Nations to push our analyses of culture in child placement decisions more generally. Informed by intersectionality in feminist theory, Kline was always attentive to the multiple dimensions of oppression affecting Aboriginal women and their children. While my analysis of the cases and statutes begins from the perspective of racialized children, I argue that we must be attentive to the fluid understandings of cultural identity and wary of essentialist constructions of these identities.

I have also suggested that Aboriginal communities have a two-fold claim in the area of child placement. First, the importance of Aboriginal community or collectivist claims in individual cases should be given greater weight. Preserving connections between children and their Aboriginal heritage may be crucial for communities whose traditions, languages, and survival can be at risk after years of removal of children from Aboriginal homes. Cultural connection can also be important for children as witnessed by the poor track record for individual Aboriginal children severed from their heritage. Second, given their histories of colonialism and racism, Aboriginal communities ought to be supported in their efforts to take over child welfare services in their communities. Kline argued that

> the only way to stop the problematic application of dominant legal and ideological processes, however, is to support First Nations communities

some seventeen First Nations agreements have been negotiated with the provincial government to take over child protection services in their communities, covering thirty-eight of forty-seven First Nations in Alberta.

135. *Child Welfare Act,* R.S.A., *supra* note 75 at section 67.

136. Kline, "Best Interests Ideology," *supra* note 9 at 398.

in working through these difficulties [in developing their own child welfare services]. This means First Nations communities—both urban and reserve-based—should be provided full financial, institutional, and legislative support to facilitate meeting this challenge.[137]

137. Kline, "Complicating," *supra* note 8 at 342.

[21]

Understanding Sending Country's Traditions and Policies In International Adoptions: Avoiding Legal and Cultural Pitfalls

*Jini L. Roby**

I. INTRODUCTION

The beautiful young woman[1] was wiping tears from her cheeks as she struggled to tell her story. She paused many times, often overcome with sorrow, and frequently searching for the right English words. I waited for her, knowing that attentive and empathic silence on my part was not uncomfortable for her in context of her culture. She looked to be in her early twenties, but she had already given birth to three children and relinquished the older two.

At her home in Majuro, Marshall Islands, a small Pacific country with a population of just over 50,000,[2] she had been solicited to bring her children to the United States (hereinafter U.S.) to place them with an adoptive family. When she and her husband divorced, she had been left without means to support the children. A local adoption 'facilitator' (child finder) had visited her, and urged adoption. To make things easier, she would travel to the U.S. with her children and relinquish them on U.S. soil; thus the adoptive family would avoid the complicated process of international adoptions and she would have a trip to the U.S.[3] She was promised on-going help and continuing contact with her children, which did not strike her as anything unusual.[4]

---

* Jini L. Roby is a member of the Utah Bar and an assistant professor in the School of Social Work, Brigham Young University, Provo, Utah where she researches and teaches social welfare and family policy, both domestic and international.

[1] Based on a real case. The facts were changed slightly and all identifying information is withheld. Her account, in her handwriting, is in the author's possession.

[2] Statistical Abstract 2001, Economic Policy, Planning, and Statistics Office, Republic of Marshall Islands (14th ed.) *available at* http://www.spc.int/prism/country/mh/stats/Publication/-2001_YB.pdf (last visited Mar. 23, 2004).

[3] Compact of Free Association, Pub. L. No. 99-239, 99 Stat. 1770 (1986)) (Marshallese citizens were allowed into the U.S. without a visa as long as it was not for permanent immigration.); *see also* Compact of Free Association Amendment Act of 2003, (Pub. L. No. 108-188, 117 Stat. 2720, 2799 (2003)) (this law was changed in late 2003 to provide procedural safeguards in adoptions. Under the newly amended Compact, a visa is required for Marshallese citizens traveling into the U.S. for purposes of adoption, made retroactive to March 1, 2003 . Whether this visa requirement applies to only the child already born in the Marshall Islands or also to the pregnant birthmother who travels into the U.S. and delivers the baby on U.S. soil is not sorted out by federal officials at this time); Letter from several U.S. Senators to Tom Ridge, Secretary of Homeland Security (Jan. 2004) (These Senators who participated in the Compact negotiation process indicating that their legislative intent was to include the birthmother who would travel to U.S. for purposes of relinquishing her unborn child.).

[4] *See* Julianne M. Walsh, *Adoption and Agency*: American Adoptions of Marshallese Children (unpublished manuscript) *at* http://www.yokwe.net/ydownloads/AdptionandAgency.doc (Presented at a conference sponsored by the Center for Pacific Island Studies, University of Ha-

Had she known that adoption meant something entirely different in the Western world from her own knowledge of adoption, she may not have considered it an option. In fact, the notion that a mother can sign away her relationship with her children had never been a concept in her culture. As further explained below, in the Marshallese culture adoption only bridged two families together to bring up children. She also did not know that it was morally and legally permissible for her to decline signing the papers at that moment. Not signing those papers would be a breach of a promise in her mind. In addition, she had been raised all her life to respect authority figures and to never challenge directives by someone in a higher social class than herself. Even though things felt strangely awry, she had signed the papers. Without understanding, she had "voluntarily" relinquished all her parental rights in her children.

Months went by, during which time she was told the family would meet her at certain times and places only to be disappointed. Her repeated calls went unanswered. She contacted others, in an attempt to understand what had happened to her children and to her, and that is how she came to be in my office, seeking understanding and perhaps help. She had been offered a one-way ticket back to the Marshall Islands by the adoption agency, but she could not return there without her children. That had never been her plan.

In their zeal for international adoption, American adoption agencies are often reluctant to acknowledge the foundational forces that are reflected in the sending jurisdictions' policies, often responding with hostility to anything they consider a hindrance to their desired goal. But an understanding of those factors is critically important in a mutually respectful and dignified adoption process and to avoid any legal or cultural pitfalls. In addition, other critically important factors include cultural traditions, religious beliefs, national family and child welfare policies, the capacity development of sending countries, and the history between the sending and receiving jurisdictions. In Part II, this paper provides perspective by reviewing the "foreign" nature of adoption laws among the states and between states and tribal jurisdictions, arguing that no less respect should be given to the laws of the foreign countries that send their children into the U.S. In Part III, this paper presents the factors influencing national policies regarding international adoptions. Finally in Part IV, I present the current international normative standards and agreements which seek to provide mutually acceptable parameters.

II. NOT-SO-FOREIGN IDEAS

International adoption is a multi-step legal process that culminates in the creation of a legally sanctioned parent-child relationship between the adopting parent and the adopted child; however the biological and adoptive parents are

waii a Manoa Oct. 22, 1999, Honolulu, Hawaii, entitled Out of Oceania: Diaspora, Community, and Identity.); *see also* Jini L. Roby & Stephanie Matsumura, *If I Give You My Child, Aren't We Family? A Study of Birthmothers Participating in Marshall Islands—U.S. Adoptions*, 5 ADOPTION QUARTERLY 4,7,10–11, 24–25 (2002).

citizens of two different countries. Thus, the laws of two countries are involved, as well as other applicable bi-lateral or international standards. Typically, there must be a proper termination of rights under the laws of the sending country, legal transfer of the child in transit, and finalization of the adoption in the receiving country. Depending on the applicable law and procedures, additional steps may be involved, as described in the laws of the jurisdiction. Failure to comply with any of the necessary steps may result in an invalid adoption, civil or criminal liability, or a risk to the child's legal status.

Common problems in international adoptions typically arise out of a lack of clear regulations, failure to enforce existing regulation, or attempts to shortcut or circumvent the process which at times can be arguably long and arduous. Some violations may occur out of a profit motive. However, it is not unusual for a well meaning professional to make mistakes also, because they do not understand the reasons behind a foreign country's laws and standards, which have their foundations in the nation's deeply rooted cultural values and traditions. Understanding these variations in culture, traditions and perceptions can aid in building mutually respectful and effective practice, and to avoid legal and cultural pitfalls.

A. *Interstate Adoptions within the United States*

Understanding and respecting the laws of a foreign jurisdiction in adoptions is not a novel idea in the patchwork legal scheme currently in place in the United States. Adoptions were rather informal and mostly accomplished out-of-court in colonial times, but adoption became a more formal legal process in the latter part of the nineteenth century.[5] Although interstate adoptions are a common occurrence, state law, not federal, controls much of the family law in the United States, including the laws of adoption. Hence, if more than one state is involved in an adoption, it requires compliance with the laws of both states, and compliance with any inter-state custody change requirements, such as the Interstate Compact on Placement of Children ("ICPC"),[6] thus respecting the "foreign" state's law. For example, in the famous Baby Jessica case, *In the Interest of B.G.C.*, 496 N.W.2d 239 (Iowa 1992), one of the issues raised was the validity of the birthmother's consent to the adoption because she had signed a consent form and waived her right to a hearing before seventy-two hours had expired after the birth.[7] In contrast, in Michigan, the state of the adoptive parents, there was no mandatory waiting period before valid relinquishments could be signed.[8] The court would not grant a revocation of the adoption based on her own fraudulent representations, but the case was ultimately decided on the issue of the birthfather's rights applying Iowa law where the birth father

[5] Alice Bussiere , *The Development of Adoption Law*, 1 ADOPTION QUARTERLY 3, 3,5 (1998).

[6] *See infra* note 14.

[7] *See id.* at 242.

[8] *See* Mich. Comp. Laws§ 710.29 (2003).

filed his petition.[9] The Iowa Supreme Court held that the birthfather had done everything reasonable to protect his parental rights as soon as he learned that he might be the birthfather.[10] The child's custody was given to the birthfather who, interestingly, had married the birthmother by this time. Had the laws of another state been applied,[11] the birthfather's rights could have easily been trumped by strict statutory requirements that provide little notice to the birthfather.[12] Therefore, compliance with the respective laws of the involved states is absolutely essential for the integrity of adoptions.

Due to these uneven expectations and results, uniform adoption acts were presented in 1969 and again in 1994. Their stated intention was to make the laws and processes more uniform across state lines, but the Uniform Adoption Act ("UAA") of 1994 was opposed by most leading child advocacy groups on the grounds that it unfairly favored the adoptive parents at the expense of birth parents and adoptees.[13] Thus, attempts to standardize adoptions across interstate lines have met with less than enthusiastic response, and so the patchwork approach continues. To minimize some of the impact of interstate placements of children, states utilize the Interstate Compact on Placement of Children ("ICPC") process[14] which requires communication between officials of two states if a child's custody changes from one set of parents or guardians to another; and the Uniform Child Custody Jurisdiction Act ("UCCJA")[15] provides guidance on which state has jurisdiction in cases of interstate custody change. The federal Parental Kidnapping Prevention Act ("PKPA")[16] provides further regulations for interstate movement of children. While interstate adoptions are

---

[9] *See* 496 N.W.2d at 246.

[10] *See Id.*

[11] *Compare* In re Adoption of Michael H., 898 P.2d 891, 900–01 (Cal. 1995) (Adoption contested by unwed father whose efforts to obtain custody of his son after birth were impressive but the adoption was finally approved, terminating the biological father's rights, because unwed fathers must assume significant parental responsibilities during pregnancy.).

[12] *E.g.*, in Utah, unmarried birth fathers are statutorily declared "on notice" by having sexual relations with a woman that such actions may result in pregnancy and adoption of that child, and has the duty to protect his own rights even though he may not learn of the actual pregnancy or adoption. UTAH CODE ANN.§ 78-30-4.13 (2003); *see also* Beltran v. Allan, 926 P.2d 892, 895 (Utah Ct. App. 1996).

[13] The Uniform Adoption Act of 1994 would have sealed adoption records for 99 years, criminalized searching, did not define identifying information to be entered in public records, and created inadequate system of notifying birthfathers. Symposium, *Uniform Adoption Act*, 30 FAMILY LAW QUARTERLY 2, 333–518 (1996).

[14] *See, e.g.*, UTAH CODE ANN. § 62A-4a-701(Repl. 2000) (The ICPC is typically administered through the central child welfare office of the state, such as the Division of Child and Family Services in Utah. For an example of a state's law providing ICPC); *see also* Assoc. of Admr's of the Interstate Compact on the Placement of Children, *at* http://icpc.aphsa.org/ (last visited Mar. 23, 2004) (provides more information on the ICPC and its administration).

[15] *See, e.g.*, UTAH CODE ANN. § 78-45(c)-101 *et. seq.* (repl. 2002) (The UCCJA has been adopted by every state with slight but insignificant variation.).

[16] *See* 28 U.S.C. § 1738A (The PKPA was passed by Congress in 1980 to clarify jurisdictional issues consistent with the UCCJA, and to specifically prohibit a parent's interstate movement to avoid child custody orders in the original state, if such movement constitutes child kidnapping or criminal flight.).

considered to be somewhat more complicated than in-state adoptions, for the most part practitioners acknowledge the laws and powers of both the sending and receiving jurisdictions. Professional ethics and competence require such knowledge and compliance; and the same principle applies to international adoptions, except that it can only be more complicated.

B. The Indian Child Welfare Act

In addition to state-by-state adoption laws, practitioners are aware of federal laws and treaties that require attention and competence. One example is the Indian Child Welfare Act ("ICWA"), which varies significantly from state laws. In order to understand and correctly follow the ICWA, it is essential to study the background of this legislation. At the time of the Senate hearings concerning the Indian Child Welfare Act in 1974, large numbers of Indian[17] children were being placed, either permanently or temporarily, in non-Indian homes.[18] In many states two-thirds of Indian child placements were in non-Indian homes and the risk for Indian children of being involuntarily separated from their parents was up to one thousand times greater than for non-Indian children.[19] The reasons for the removal of high numbers of Indian children were listed as high rates of alcoholism, poverty, perceived neglect or mistreatment of Indian children, and even religious zealotry to "save" these children from a dismal future.[20] All of these "reasons" were reported from a non-Indian perspective,[21] and translated into the Indian Adoption Project, which facilitated a national effort to place children out of their race and culture into adoptive homes.[22]

The ICWA recognizes a distinctly non-Western right: the right of a tribe, or community, to protect its children.[23] Specifically, the ICWA creates a legal right in American Indian tribes to intervene in adoptions, foster care placements and terminations of parental rights, in which case intervention may be asserted even if the biological parents choose not to intervene.[24] This recognition of tribal rights was necessary to preserve the Indian tribes because Congress expressly found that "an alarmingly high percentage of Indian families are broken up by the removal, often unwarranted, of their children from them

[17] Although "Native American" is considered the more politically correct terminology to refer to people of original descent in this country, the statute specifically uses the original term "Indian." Therefore this article will refer to them by the original language of the statute in this article.

[18] Joan Heifetz Hollinger, *Beyond the Best Interests of the Tribe: The Indian Child Welfare Act and the Adoption of Indian Children,* 66 U. DET. L. REV. 451, 454 (1989).

[19] *Id.*

[20] *See id.* at 455–56.

[21] *See id.* at 454.

[22] The Adoption History Project, *available at* http://darkwing.vieworegon.edu/~adoption/-topics/IAP.html (last visited Mar. 15, 2004).

[23] *See* 25 U.S.C. § 1901 (2003).

[24] *See* 25 U.S.C. § 1911(c).

by nontrivial public and private agencies"[25] and that "there is no resource that is more vital to the continued existence and integrity of Indian tribes than their children."[26]

Among the most pronounced differences between state laws and the ICWA, the ICWA provides strict jurisdictional guidelines on tribal court jurisdiction in all cases involving child custody of children who are enrolled members of recognized tribes or are eligible for such membership.[27] It also requires a minimum waiting period of ten days after the birth of a baby before a biological mother can sign a valid consent.[28] For involuntary termination of parental rights, it imposes the "beyond a reasonable doubt" standard of evidence[29] which must be presented by a qualified expert who has knowledge of the Indian culture.[30]

The concept that the child belongs not only to himself but to the larger community is not a foreign idea, but one which is difficult for many to accept.[31] The struggle to uphold the ICWA with its culturally laden structure often collides with the state courts' ideas of what is in the children's best interest. Case law demonstrates confusion and apparent resistance to the ICWA among the states. When jurisdiction has been exercised by state courts, some of them have applied the "Existing Indian Family" doctrine to avoid application of the ICWA standards.[32] Nine states have adopted this doctrine,[33] reasoning that the ICWA was not intended to force an Indian culture upon biologically Indian children who had been raised in a non-Indian culture and did not have any contact with their tribe.[34] To be sure, it is a challenge to reconcile the two seemingly disparate systems of state laws and the ICWA, but an examination of the background of the legislation and culture of the Native communities and their concerns help to ease this challenge.

III. FORCES SHAPING SENDING COUNTRIES' ADOPTION POLICIES

In order to understand and respect the traditions and laws of foreign jurisdictions, it is important to reverse the paradigm and recognize that many of the ideas held by Western societies seem rather "foreign" to other cultural norms. Americans and other Northern societies have been accused of being ethnocen-

---

[25] 25 U.S.C. § 1901(4).

[26] 25 U.S.C. § 1901(3).

[27] *See* 25 U.S.C. § 1901(5); 25 U.S.C. § 1913.

[28] *See* 25 U.S.C. § 1913(a).

[29] *See* 25 U.S.C. §1912(f).

[30] *Id.*

[31] *See* Madelyn Fruendlich, Window to the World; *Families Without Borders* 1, 36 U.N. CHRONICLE no. 2, 88–90.

[32] *See In the Interest of D.A.C., P.D.C., and S.D.C.*, 933 P.2d 993, 998 (Utah Ct. App. 1997).

[33] Alabama, Indiana, Kansas, Kentucky, Louisiana, Montana, Missouri, Oklahoma and Washington.

[34] *See supra note 32*; *In re Adoption of Baby Boy L.*, 643 P.2d 168, 176 (Kan. 1982).

tric, or judging the "rightness" of perspectives or standards by their own.[35] Before excusing any ideas different from the Euro-American norm as being "undeveloped" or "substandard," a careful re-examination of these ideas is essential to avoid cultural and legal pitfalls. This section presents some of these perspectives.

A. *Cultural Traditions Regarding Parent-Child Relationships*

In the summer of 2001, I taught a continuing education course on international adoptions at the College of Marshall Islands in Majuro, Marshall Islands. I had led the drafting of the nation's adoption code in 2000, and had been working to raise public awareness about the need to stop some of the grey and black market adoption practices. Most of the students in the class were experienced teachers, government officials, and other professionals. I explained rather perfunctorily that in a Western society adoption was comprised of two major legal steps: the rights of the biological parent and establishing a new parent-child relationship between the child and the adoptive parents. Sensing confusion, I diagramed these two steps on the blackboard. Still, I saw furrowed eyebrows and looks of disorientation. I invited questions and waited.

Slowly, people began shifting in their seats and then a hand went up. An insightful, intelligent member of class asked, "Do you mean that a law can *undo* something like a mother-child relationship?" Yes, I said, a parent can either give away all of his or her rights, or a judge can take them away if the parent has been abusive or neglectful. Sometimes this happens because a child needs a new family, and that requires cutting off the original parents and giving the child new parents. Slowly, as understanding dawned, a sense of great outrage filled the room. "How can a man say that the truth is no longer true?" "How can anyone have that much disrespect for a mother?" "How will the child know who he is?" They were collectively offended by the idea of creating a legal fiction that could erase something as unchangeable as a parent-child relationship. They were struggling to understand such an outrageous notion.

In the Marshallese culture, adoption was practiced within the extended family or in the tribe, and the child became the link between the birth and adoptive families. The child was free to go between the two families, and often returned to the birth families in the parents' old age. Termination of birth parents rights was never instituted as part of the culture or law. In fact, Marshallese law provides for an individual to inherit land rights through maternal lines of birth, regardless of adoption by another family.[36] Given this cultural context, I was easily able to empathize with their sense of confusion, outrage,

[35] Melone, Thomas, *Adoption and the crisis in the Third World: Thoughts on the future.* CHRONICLE, 28, 20–25 (1976).

[36] Marsh. Is. Revi.Code § 26-1-123. *But see* interview with H. Dee Johnson, former High Court Associate Judge (Feb. 11 2004)(stating, "practically, an adopted Marshallese who has been away from the Marshall Islands for a long period of time will not be acknowledged as having workable land rights in the islands. This is consistent with customary practices.")

and distrust of the Western legal process. To my Marshallese colleagues, the Western idea of adoption seemed an extremely illogical and offensive way to provide for the needs of a child.

The Marshallese are not alone in believing that a child will always belong to his bloodline regardless of later arrangements necessary to raise him or her to adulthood. Throughout the Pacific Islands, adoption practices have been fluid, encompassing, and linking rather than permanent, exclusive, and divisive.[37] Because of these cultural differences, a 2001 study revealed that 83% of the birthmothers who had relinquished their children for U.S. adoptions did not understand the full and permanent nature of adoption as a mechanism to terminate that parent-child relationship.[38] As a result of these cultural gaps, the Republic of Marshall Islands has found it necessary to protect its citizens from being misled about the consequences of adoptions and from being solicited by local facilitators who offer incentives and promises of future benefit to the birth families. Under the Adoption Act of 2002,[39] it is a crime to solicit birth families or facilitate their travel outside the nation to place children for adoption.[40] The Act also established a statutory central adoption authority which will monitor and facilitate all adoption-related activities, including the counseling of birth families to assure that they are assisted in seeking all options and if adoption is necessary that they understand the permanent legal implications of adoption.[41]

B. Traditions Regarding Full Family Membership

In some cultures, due to the dual-family membership system, adopted children can enjoy some rights both as a member of the birth family as well as in the adoptive family. For example, in the Pacific Islands, where land rights are typically inherited through matrilineal lines, a child who is adopted out of the family can still inherit land from the birth mother. On the other hand, in some other cultures, adoption is seen merely as a means of providing support for the child but not extending full family membership. For example, in some African regions, it is culturally acceptable to exclude adopted children from inheriting from the adoptive parents.[42] The impact of these traditions on international adoption is that many parents or government leaders are reluctant to send children for international adoptions, believing that they will not be treated as full

[37] Roby & Matsumura, *supra* note 4 at 24.

[38] *Id.*

[39] Rep of Marsh. Is. Pub.. Law 2002–64 ("RMI Adoption Act 2002") (effective on October 1, 2003). The Act was drafted as joint effort between the author of this article, the Republic of Marshall Islands Legislative Council, and a child advocate attorney from UNICEF.

[40] RMI Adoption Act 2002, Section 10.

[41] RMI Adoption Act 2002, Section 14.

[42] *See, e.g.*, J. Rutayuga, *Assistance to AIDS Orphans Within the Family/Kinship System and Local Institutions: A program for East Africa*. AIDS EDUCATION AND PREVENTION (Supp.), 57–68 (1992). In those African countries, children inherit through blood lines only, and adopted children are excluded from land inheritance.

members of the adoptive families. To address these concerns, the Convention on the Rights of the Child requires its signatories to "ensure that the child . . . enjoys safeguards and standards equivalent to those existing in the case of national adoptions" (Art. 21).[43] Further, the Hague Convention on Protection of Children and Cooperation in Respect of Intercountry Adoptions[44] demands that internationally adopted children enjoy the same rights as those who are adopted domestically.[45] These international conventions are discussed in greater detail later.

C. *Religious Beliefs*

In some cultures religious beliefs still restrict or prohibit adoptions. In countries with predominantly Islamic populations, it is believed that records of blood lines must be kept free of modifications by adoption. Muslims can therefore take in children and raise them, but the child's legal parentage cannot be modified. In addition, the child cannot inherit from adoptive parents, nor they from him or her. This belief and tradition of prohibiting legal adoptions is based on the declaration of the Prophet Muhammad,[46] who adopted a son and later saw the wisdom of keeping the records of bloodlines accurate. This declaration teaches that even when the child's biological paternity is not known, the child's parentage should not be substituted by the adoptive father's name.

My conversation in 2003 with government leaders from Afghanistan reiterated this strong belief. They reported that that at least one million children were orphaned and living on the streets. They lamented that there are not enough resources to care for them. They were saddened by daily reports of the demise of children. Just a week before our conversation, one of the northern villages had been invaded by child traffickers and at least a dozen children had been sold, they fear, into the international human organ market. A mother with four children, when she could no longer feed them, had thrown each child into a well and then jumped in herself, killing all of them. The father had gone off to fight and never returned. Such tragedies occur daily, they said sadly. However, when the topic of international adoption was cautiously brought up, the quick response was a decisive 'no.' It was better for children to remain and

[43] *See infra* note 78.

[44] The U.S. ratified the Hague Convention in 2000. As of submission time of this article, the U.S. has not deposited the Hague document, pending the final drafting of implementation regulations . The Intercountry Adoption Act of 2000, however, anticipates full implementation by 2005.

[45] *See* Hague Convention, *infra* note 78.

[46] The Prophet Muhammad declared "nor has He made those whom you assert to be your sons your real sons; these are the words of your mouths; and Allah speaks the truth and He guides to the way. Assert their relationship to their fathers, this is more equitable with Allah; but if you do not know their fathers, then they are your brethren in faith and your friends; and there is no blame on you concerning that in which you made a mistake, but [concerning] that which your hearts do purposely [blame may rest on you], and Allah is Forgiving, Merciful." (Surat ul Ahzab 33:4–5).

struggle in their culture than to be given to a strange culture with different religious beliefs, they explained.[47]

This Islamic prohibition against adoption is not strictly followed in every country in which there is a preponderance of Moslem population. For example, in Malaysia, it is possible for Muslim families to adopt a Muslim child. In those cases the prospective parents are often required to reside in Malaysia for a minimum of two years with the child, providing full support for the child. In contrast, non-Muslim children can be adopted by either Muslim or non-Muslim families, and they need only show having resided with and cared for the child for three months.[48] Therefore the dividing lines are along religious affiliation of both the child and the prospective parents.

The Islamic community in the U.S. has dealt with this issue in its desire to assist orphaned children of war-torn Afghanistan. Dr. Ali Suleiman Ali, the director of Muslim Family Services, states that some Muslims in the U.S. are providing "kafala" (adoption without inheritance) to Afghan children. While he recognizes that such an adoption is different from the Western concept of adoption, the care of orphaned children is highly praised in the culture.[49] They therefore encourage U.S.-based Muslims to follow the legal procedure outlined by the United States government, and such an adoption would be legally indistinguishable from any other international adoption except for the inheritance issue later on.[50]

D. Past History Between Sending and Receiving Countries

A lengthy explanation is not necessary to point out why most African countries are not keen on sending their children to the U.S. for adoption. Beginning in the early 1500's and lasting through the Emancipation Proclamation in 1865, the American slavery has been called one of the most tragic and disturbing episodes in the history of mankind.[51] The century following the emancipation saw rampant social discrimination against African Americans, in many ways embedded in the American social structure. The Civil Rights movement begun in the 1950's has led to significant improvements in government policies, but studies show that discrimination lingers in subtle ways in health care, higher education, employment, residence, and social status.[52] The painful past of slavery is kept alive by on-going slave trade within Africa. Al-

[47] Personal communication with leaders of Afghanistan in Salt Lake City, Utah, (April 30, 2003). Most of them introduced themselves as both government and religious leaders in Islam.

[48] *International Adoptions—Malaysia*(last modified on June 2001) < http://travel.state.-gov/adoption_malyasia.html; *see also* Malyasian Adoption Act of 1952 (Act 257).

[49] Personal correspondence from Dr. Ali (January 5 & 7, 2004).

[50] Kaleema Sumareh, *Adopting Foreign Orphan Children*, ISLAMIC FAMILY SERVICES 2ND QUARTER NEWSLETTER, 2002, *available at* http://www.reliefonline.org/mfs/NewsLetter2rd-Quart2002.htm.

[51] *See* DUNCAN CLARKE, SLAVES AND SLAVERY 6 (PRC Publishing Ltd. 1998).

[52] *See* ELIJAH ANDERSON, & DOUGLAS S. MASSEY, PROBLEM OF THE CENTURY: RACIAL STRATIFICATION IN THE UNITED STATES (Russell Sage Foundation 2001).

though slavery was officially banned in Africa in the 1880's, children continue to be sold into domestic, agricultural, and sex industries within Africa. Rumors that some African children may be sold for purposes of adoption heighten apprehension, although there are no documented cases of adoption trafficking into the U.S. from Africa.

The history and on-going concerns of slavery are major contributing factors to the African reluctance to explore international adoptions. Only a handful of African countries are participating in international adoptions into the U.S. The highest number by far from any country in Africa in 2002 was 105 in Ethiopia where the government has approved three U.S. agencies to conduct adoptions. Many African countries have lengthy processes that make it difficult to adopt, and some do not allow adoption at all.[53] This reservation has been increased by recent events in Liberia in which some children's status as orphans has been scrutinized and their visas delayed or denied by U.S. officials.[54]

Yet, the African response cannot be oversimplified. On my recent trip to an international orphan care conference in Kenya, some African government and private sector leaders expressed an interest in exploring international adoptions, along with strengthening their current efforts to shore up the existing approach. Concerned leaders inquired about the feasibility and desirability of such adoptions into the U.S. A social worker and teacher who struggles to operate a center for over 120 orphans wrote:

> We are hit by so much poverty, HIV/AIDS, and sometimes ignorance which we can't fight, and drought which makes it so difficult for our lives are cut short by lack of enough food and lack of human rights for especially women and orphaned children and widows. I will work with all my friends in the world to open more doors and create hope for all children. If adoption will be officially accepted [by my country], and get the right information and caring families who *love life*, I will be willing to help to make children [who are] orphaned and desperate have a family and get education and freedom to choose their rights. I was so blessed to hear you [discuss adoption], for I had very low feelings about adoption but now am changed and willing to facilitate.[55]

It would seem that at least for some African leaders, there is not necessarily a strong opposition to adoption but a lack of information and dialog.

[53] *See* Jini Roby, & S. Mosman, The African Orphan Crisis and International Adoption (unpublished manuscript under review, on file with author).

[54] http://ethicanet.org (last visited Mar. 20, 2004).

[55] Letter from D. Nzomo to Jini L. Roby (Sept, 2003) (on file with author) (emphasis in original).

E. National Child Welfare and Family Policies

National policies on international adoption are directly linked to policies regarding children and families. One of the darkest chapters in international adoptions had its genesis in the national child bearing policies in Romania. During Nicolae Ceausescu's regime as dictator of Romania, he required every married woman of child-bearing age to produce at least four children. Such a requirement was in the nation's interest, and any woman who shirked her duty would be considered a traitor to her country's cause.[56] As a result, many families found themselves with more children than they could care for, with little government support to do so. When the Ceausescu regime fell in 1989, the world was shocked to learn of hundreds of thousands of children who were abandoned or warehoused in large institutions with severely inadequate medical, nutritional, or human care. Individuals and entities rushed in, some with humanitarian and others with profit motives to facilitate international adoptions, resulting in gray and black market practices. As a result, the Romanian government declared a moratorium on all international adoptions and is currently in the process of redrafting its adoption laws as well as its monitoring structures.[57]

The nation of Georgia was vehemently opposed to international adoptions for reasons of national identity for the children. The first lady of Georgia, Mrs. Schevardnadze, has been a vocal opponent on such grounds. She personally advocated for the placement of orphaned Georgian children within the country.[58] More recently, however, the country has eased its policy and is redrafting its adoption laws. In May 2003, the U.S. Consulate in Tbilisi was allowed to process visa applications for children traveling to the U.S. for adoptions. At submission time of this article, the nation prohibits direct international adoptions between birth and adoptive parents, but the government may consider such adoptions after six months of its own efforts to place the child within the country.[59]

Another example of national family policy directly impacting international adoption is that of China. China is currently the leading "sending" coun-

[56] Bill Delaney, *Sewers Home to Romania's Forgotten Orphans*, at http://www.-cnn.com/WORLD/9707/23/romanian.orphans/; *see* ALEXANDRE ZOUEV, FROM GENERATION IN JEOPARDY 2–17(UNICEF 1999) (summary of the deplorable plight of children in Eastern European countries after the fall of communism).

[57] In late January 2004, the Romanian government released its final draft of the proposed adoption law, including provisions governing international adoptions. Pending final passage, this final draft can be viewed at http://www.ethicanet.org/item.php?recordid=romania. In the meantime, the moratorium continues as of mid-February, 2004.

[58] Allesandra Stanley, *Hands Off Our Babies, A Georgian Tells America,* N.Y TIMES, June 29, 1997, at E1

[59] The U.S. Consulate in Tablici, Georgia in January 2004 issued the following statement, regarding amendments signed by President Eduard Schevardnadze in September, 2003: "Those amendments . . . require all orphans to be registered on the MOE's central orphan database for at least six months before orphans can be considered for international adoption." *Available at* http://www.ethicanet.org/item.php?recordid=-romania (last visited Mar. 20, 2004).

try into the U.S. in terms of numbers of children, most of whom are girls.[60] Because of its *One Child Only* policy started in 1979, coupled with a strong cultural preference for male children, girls are much more likely to be abandoned than boys. Families who find that their first child is a girl may abandon them so that they do not have to register a child as being born to them,[61] and then try again for a boy. Boys born with disabilities are also frequently abandoned, in hopes of the next child being healthy. While the enforcement of the policy varies slightly from region to region, families may resort to selective gender-based abortion.[62]

At the same time, China's policy of promoting in-country adoptions seems to be having some positive effect.[63] Couples are allowed to adopt, even if the adopted child will push them over the limit of children allotted to them. This is based on the condition, however, that the child is abandoned. This policy allows the desire of families for more than the allotted number of children, and also eases the government's burden to care for abandoned children.[64] The adopting couple may face a fine for having more than the number allowed, but the fines tend to be nominal compared to the penalties to be paid for biologically producing and keeping an extra child. In a touching account of one family's experience with such an adoption, they wrote:

> It was autumn . . . we got up very early and went to the field after breakfast. We found the girl, who was still deeply sleeping, on our way to the field. There was a note and 50 *yuan* with the baby. It noted the date and place of the birth and her family of origin. The note indicated that the child was born by an unmarried mother who wrote that she could not keep the baby, and wished good-hearted people to bring the child up. After a glance at the girl, I could not let her remain there in [sic] abandoned. She was so lovely. She did not even cry after she woke up, and she stared at me with her big eyes. I was so moved. I thought it was my fate that I found this girl. Also we were not too poor to

[60] The number of children from China has grown steadily over the decade. In 2003 6,859 children were adopted from China into the U.S., compared to 206 in 1992. *See* United States Department of State, *Immigrant Visas issued to Orphans coming to U.S. available at* http://-travel.state.gov/orphan_numbers.html.

[61] Girls who are abandoned at orphanages may face a better fate than those who are aborted *in utero* or killed after birth. Although the numbers of children eliminated by such methods are difficult to ascertain, the ratio of boys to girls who are kept alive in China is 117 to 100 *at* http://www.genocide.org/case_infanticide.html (last visited Jan. 31, 2004).

[62]*See* Chu Junhong, *Prenatal Sex Determination and Sex-Selective Abortion in Rural Central China*, 27 Population and Dev. Rev. ,259(2001).

[63] Kay Johnson et al, *Infant Abandonment and Adoption in China*, 24 Population and Dev. Rev. 469(1998). (The authors report, based on a 1995-1996 study in central China that: (1) not only childless couples but biologically reproductive couples are also adopting; and (2) couples are adopting girls at an increasing rate.);*See also* Child Adoption in Contemporary Rural China (unpublished manuscript, on file with author).

[64] Wanbao Shanxi, *Fuliyuan Changqi Rubu Fuchu (Welfare Institutions Cannot Sustain Themselves), available at* http://www.riterdigest.com.cn/(last visited January 31, 2004).

> feed the baby, so we decided to keep her.
>
> On the same day that I took the baby home, the family-planning cadres came to me. They wanted to impose a penalty of 3000 *yuan* if I wanted to keep the baby. I refused to pay any money. I told them that this baby was not ours, and what was wrong in keeping a baby abandoned by her own parents? The officials said they had the policy with regard to adoption, and they would have to follow the policy. I later went to the township to reason with township officials. Finally the penalty was reduced to 1000 *yuan*.[65]

In an interesting twist to the impact of this policy, some couples choose to become sterilized in order to adopt a child of desired gender. In a 2001 study, it was shown that about half of the families had already been sterilized and then decided to adopt, while others strategize by having one child and then adopting the child of the other gender.[66] The *One Child Only* policy is difficult to measure; at this time, it is clearly influencing the in-country adoption of Chinese children and resulting in a disproportionate number of abandoned girls who become available for international adoptions.

F. Poverty and Political Crises in Sending Countries

There is unanimous agreement that poverty is the major determining factor in the sending country's policy determination regarding international adoptions. Through the ages child welfare practices have been shown to reflect the state of the economy. When survival is difficult, children tend to be devalued, and when there is economic surplus there is greater emphasis on children.[67] Some scholars view international adoptions as a form of economic exploitation by the people of rich countries committed against people in poverty-stricken countries.[68] This can, without regulations and oversight, result in the frightening prospect of baby selling and brokering by residents of poor nations on the international market.[69] Even with laws and regulations in place, a country's policy to allow international adoptions can be viewed as "marketing" their babies on the international market.[70]

---

[65] *See Child Adoption in Contemporary Rural China*, *supra* note 63, at 21 (Based on currency exchange rates on January 31, 2004, 1,000 yuan is roughly equivalent to $120 USD).

[66] *See* Johnson et.al., *supra* note 63 (Most Chinese families see the ideal family size as having one boy and one girl.).

[67] Genevieve De Hoyos et al., *Adoption differentials in Three Cultural Settings*, 57 INT'L CHILD REV.35 (1983).

[68] *See* Leslie D. Hollingsworth, *International Adoptions among Families in the United States: Considerations of Social Justice*. 48 SOC. WORK 209 (2003).

[69] *See* John Terrell & Judith Modell, *Anthropology and Adoption*, 96 AM. ANTHROPOLOGIST 155 (1994).

[70] *Id.*

A nation's inability to respond to children in need is often exacerbated by national crises such as civil war,[71] natural disasters, or political turmoil.[72] Such crises can influence a nation's adoption policies as shown by Japan after World War II,[73] Korea after the Korean conflict (1950-1953),[74] Viet Nam after the fall of Saigon,[75] and in former Soviet Union countries such as Romania[76] and Russia[77] after the fall of communism. Romania has been particularly highlighted in the global media, and has been the focus of much international criticism as well as humanitarian efforts. How Romania deals with the adoption issue is likely to set precedent and pace for many of the remaining Eastern European nations. Following intense international scrutiny, Romania is on the threshold of passing revised adoption laws as of February, 2004.

IV. INTERNATIONAL CONVENTIONS

Just as the risks of interstate adoptions are monitored by the ICPC, UCCJA and the PAKA, there are instruments in place that are designed to provide ethical and procedural parameters for international adoptions. This discussion will be limited to the two leading instruments that directly affect international adoptions: 1) the Convention on the Rights of the Child ("CRC"),[78] and 2) the Hague Convention on Protection of Children and Cooperation in Respect of Intercountry Adoptions ("Hague Convention").[79]

---

[71] Such as the Korean conflict and Viet Nam war.

[72] *E.g.* fall of communism with all of its social safety net programs.

[73] *See* Richard H. Weil, *International Adoption: The Quiet Migration*, 18 INT'L MIGRATION REV. 276, 280–81 (1984). (American families adopted approximately 3,000 children from Japan and 840 children from China between 1948 and 1962).

[74] *See* RITA J. SIMON, & HOWARD ALTSTEIN, *ADOPTION ACROSS BORDERS: SERVING THE CHILDREN IN TRANSRACIAL AND INTERCOUNTRY ADOPTIONS* 89–92 (Rowman & Littlefield) (2000) (In all, approximately 100,000 Korean children are estimated to have been adopted into the United States starting in 1950. Korean adoptees comprise the largest group of trans-racial adoptions in the U.S.).

[75] *See* Jorge L. Carro, *Regulation of Intercountry Adoption: Can the Abuses Come to an End?*, 9 AM. J. OF FAM. L., 135(1995).

[76] *See* MADELYN FRUENDLICH, ADOPTION AND ETHICS: *The Role of Race, Culture, and National Origin in Adoption* (Child Welfare League of America 2000) (The first wave of children came from Eastern Europe in 1989 with the fall of communism in Romania. However, adequate regulations were not in place and the government was forced to impose a moratorium while it established a regulatory scheme. Adoptions were resumed after the Romanian Adoption Committee was organized. However, the Romanian government again imposed a moratorium in 2001 and still remains under it.).

[77] *See Immigrant Visas Issued to Orphans Coming to the U.S.*, *supra* note 60 (Russia has been among the top five countries in numbers of children coming into the United States for international adoptions during the most recent five years for which reports are available. The numbers were: 4,348 in 1999, 4,269 in 2000, 4,279 in 2001, 4,939 in 2002; and 5,209 in 2003.).

[78] United Nations Convention on the Rights of the Child, G.A. res. 44/25, annex, 44 U.N. GAOR Supp. No. 49, at 167, U.N. Doc. A/44/49 (1989), *available at* http://www1.umn.edu/-humanrts/instree/k2crc.htm.

[79] *Convention on Protection of Children and Co-operation in Respect of Intercountry Adoption*, May 29, 1993, *available at* http://www.hcch.net/e/conventions/text33e.html.

A. Convention on the Rights of the Child

The United Nations Convention on the Rights of the Child was entered into force in 1990, and has been the leading global child welfare instrument. As of February 2004, 192 countries have ratified it, and only two countries—the United States and Somalia—have not ratified it. Although an analysis of the U.S. non-ratification is beyond the scope of this paper,[80] it is important to recognize that the CRC is almost universally accepted as *the* foundational standard regarding children's rights. This article assumes that the U.S. government and most practitioners have no apparent disagreement with the CRC's provisions dealing with adoptions.

Under the CRC, children have the right to grow up in a family environment in an atmosphere of happiness, love, and understanding.[81] To this end, parents, extended family, and the community have responsibilities to the child.[82] National governments have the responsibility to take all appropriate legislative and administrative measures to ensure such protection for children.[83] Whenever possible, the continuity of a child's upbringing and his or her ethnic, religious, cultural, and linguistic background should be carefully considered.[84] The countries comprising the international community are urged to cooperate with one another in improving the conditions of children in every country, particularly in the developing countries.[85] Specifically addressing international adoption, the CRC requires in broad terms that:

> 1. The child's best interest should be the paramount consideration in international adoptions; [86]
> 2. International adoption may be considered if the child cannot be placed in a foster or an adoptive family or cannot be cared for in a suitable manner in the child's country;[87]

---

[80] *See Convention on the Rights of the Child, Frequently Asked Questions, available at* http://www.unicef.org/crc/faq.htm#009; *See also* Gary B. Melton, *The Child's Right to a Family Environment: Why Children's Rights and Family Values are Compatible*, 51 AM. PSYCHOL. 1234 (1996); *but see* Alison D. Renteln, *United States Ratification of Human Rights Treaties*, 3 ILSA J INT'L & COMP L. 629 (1997).

[81] *See* CRC, *supra* note 78, at pmbl.

[82] *Id.* at art. 5.

[83] *Id.* at art 3.

[84] *Id.* at art. 20.

[85] *Id.* at pmbl.

[86] *Id.* at art. 21.

[87] *Id.* at art 21(b). (Prior to January 15, 2004, this phrase was interpreted by many to suggest that children should be raised in their birth countries, even if it required keeping them in institutions. However, in a landmark statement released on that date, UNICEF, the multinational monitoring body for CRC implementation, clarified that institutionalization was to be used only as a last resort and as a temporary measure until a family could be found); *available at* http://www.unicef.org/media/media_-15011.html. (For children who cannot be raised by their own families, an appropriate alternative family environment should be sought in preference to institutional care, which should be used only as a last resort and as a temporary measure. Intercountry adoption is one of a range of care options which may be open to children, and for indi-

3. Children adopted internationally should enjoy all the safeguards and standards equivalent to those existing in the case of national adoptions;[88]
4. Participating nations should ensure that there is no improper financial gain for those involved;[89]
5. Competent authorities or entities carry out adoption functions in both nations pursuant to bilateral or multilateral agreements;[90] and
6. The proper consent of all parties having rights to the child be obtained, on the basis of counseling if necessary.[91]

B. The Hague Convention

Following in the wake of the CRC, the international child welfare community adopted the Hague Convention.[92] The major purposes of the Hague Convention are "to take measures to ensure that intercountry adoptions are made in the best interest of the child . . . and to prevent the abduction, the sale of, or traffic in children."[93] To serve these ends, the Hague Convention provides substantive and procedural safeguards for international adoptions. The provisions apply whether the adoption takes place in the country of the child's origin or in the adoptive family's country.[94] It envisages a process in which the designated authorities ("Central Authorities" who must be not for profit) of the sending and receiving countries work together to provide the necessary safeguards and serve the best interest of the child. Under this scheme, the sending country has the responsibility to:

1. Ensure that the child is "adoptable" and that after possibilities of in-country placement has been given due consideration, international adoption has been determined to be in the child's best interest;[95] and

---

vidual children who cannot be placed in a permanent family setting in their countries of origin, it may indeed be the best solution).

[88] CRC, *supra* note 78, at art. 21(c).

[89] *Id.* at art. 21(d).

[90] *Id.* at art. 21(e).

[91] *Id.* at art. 21(a).

[92] *See Convention on Protection of Children, supra* note 79.

[93] *Convention on Protection of Children, supra* note 79 at pmbl. art. 4.

[94] *See id.* (Adoptions can be granted to foreign couples or individuals in the child's country of birth, if the country allows it. Many countries choose this option because it allows jurisdiction in their own courts and tighter control by them over the adoption process. Other countries, however, allow children to be taken out of the country in the custody of U.S. licensed adoption agency personnel who deliver the temporary physical custody of the child to the adoptive parents, who then must "finalize" the adoption in their state courts to gain permanent custody and full rights as parents. Depending on which process is used, the U.S. Department of Homeland Securities (DHS) and its Bureau of Citizenship and Immigration Services (BCIS) require similar but different documents.).

[95] *Id.* at art. 4.

> 2. Ensure that all due process rights have been extended and valid consents received, including the child's (depending on age and maturity), after proper counseling and having received no inducements;[96]

The authorities in the receiving country have the responsibility to:

> 1. Determine the suitability of the adopting parents (upon counseling if necessary); and
> 2. Ensure that the child will be able to enter and reside in the country.[97]

Procedurally, once the studies are completed on both sides, and consents obtained, both sides must agree to the adoption. Either side can delay or stop the adoption from going forward at any point. Typically the adoptive parents' "homestudy" is sent to the sending country who assigns a child that has been pre-approved, or will be approved. When all required steps have been taken, the child is to be transferred securely and appropriately, and if possible, in the company of the adoptive or prospective adoptive parents.[98] Once the child is in the adoptive home, the two sets of authorities are to maintain contact regarding the progress of the adoption if there is a probationary period,[99] and in the event of a disrupted adoption, the receiving country is responsible to arrange for alternative care for the child.[100] An adopted child is to enjoy a full parent-child relationship with the new adoptive parents; but interestingly, the Hague Convention recognizes that adoption may not always terminate pre-existing parent-child relationships with the child's birth parents if the sending country's policies do not provide for that termination.[101] In the alternative, the termination may be effected if valid consents were signed in the sending country and the laws of the receiving state permit such termination.[102]
The Hague Convention is explicit in addressing ethics involved in adoptions. It requires, *inter alia*, the following practices:

> 1. Prohibiting contact between birth and adoptive parents, unless the adoption is within the family or according to rules established by the sending country's authorities;[103]
> 2. Preserving the records concerning the child's origin;[104]

---

[96] *Id.*

[97] *Id.* at art. 5.

[98] *Id.* at art. 19.

[99] This would be the case in which the adoption was not finalized in the sending country.

[100] *See Convention on Protection of Children*, *supra* note 79, at art. 21 (Sending the child back to the country of origin is highly discouraged, but is allowed as a last resort if it is in his or her best interest.).

[101] *Id.* at art. 27.

[102] *Id.*

[103] *Id.* at art. 29.

[104] *Id.*, at art. 30.

3. Allowing only for the payment of costs and expenses and prohibiting improper financial gain (including remuneration to authorities);[105] and
4. Reporting to and handling of ethics violations to the central authorities.[106]

The Hague Convention had been ratified by 64 countries as of December, 2003.[107] The U.S. ratified it in October, 2000 but has not yet deposited the instrument, awaiting the completion of implementation regulations which are in the final draft stage. It is expected that by early 2005 the full Convention will be implemented. While the Hague Convention will not bring drastic changes to the practice of agency-based international adoptions, it will mean that bilateral agreements and central authorities will be the center components of international adoptions, virtually doing away with independently arranged adoptions.

V. CONCLUSION

The young mother went back home without the two children. State child welfare authorities determined that they could do nothing because no laws had been broken, since her country had no laws governing adoptions yet. Her entry into the United States had been legal, and under the laws of the state, the agency did not have a legal duty to provide the consent document in the client's own language or provide an interpreter. She had signed a well-drafted relinquishment document in front of an authorized agency director. There were no third party witnesses. She could have filed an action to set aside the adoption, but she decided in the end that her children were better off here after all, since they had attached to the adoptive family and she could not provide them with the education and opportunities that they could. If the adoption agency had understood her culture, they certainly had not respected it. Rather, they had exploited it. I am quite certain that the cultural traditions of continuing contact after adoption, the practice of exchanging gifts, the unquestioning trust in authority figures, the culture in which one cannot refuse something to someone who asks for it and gives another gift first, and the incentives offered may have deterred caution on her part.

Marshallese laws passed since that time safeguard against the recurrence of such a scenario. Now, all adoptions of resident Marshallese children must be completed in the High Court of the Marshall Islands, birth parents must receive counseling and the central authority must ensure that they understand the full impact of adoption. On the U.S. side, a visa is now required for anyone coming into the U.S. for purposes of adoption.

I often think of that young mother and wonder how many more victims

[105] *Id.* at art. 32.

[106] *Id.* at art. 33.

[107] *Hague Conference on Private International Law, Concise Status Report Convention #33, available at* http://www.hcch.net/e/members/members.html (last visited Mar. 20, 2004).

live with unhealed wounds caused by continued lack of understanding and respect for the sending country's culture and policy. There is comfort in knowing that for the most part their children are growing up in loving families with adoptive parents who most likely knew nothing about their agency's misconduct. Still, efforts should be continued to make the adoption process dignified and compassionate for all involved. Birth parents live with the pain of loss and grief already; we do not need to heap an extra layer of pain on top.

[22]

Placing the "Gift Child" in Transnational Adoption

Barbara Yngvesson

In this article I focus on discourses of freedom and exclusive belonging that structure the conventions of giving in transnational adoption, and I examine state practices for regulating the production and circulation of children in a global market economy. I argue that while the gift child, like the sold child, is a product of commodity thinking, experiences of giving a child, receiving a child, and of being a given child are in tension with market practices, producing the contradictions of adoptive kinship, the ambiguities of adoption law, and the creative potential in the construction of adoptive families.

gratuitous 1. Given or granted without return or recompense; unearned.
2. Given or received without cost or obligation; free; gratis (*American Heritage Dictionary of the English Language*).

What would be a gift that fulfills the condition of the gift, namely, that it not appear as gift, that it not be, exist, signify, want-to-say as gift? A gift without wanting, without wanting-to-say, an insignificant gift, a gift without intention to give? Why would we call that a gift?

—Jacques Derrida, *Given Time*, 1992

Even if reversibility is the objective truth of the discrete acts which ordinary experience knows in discrete form and calls gift exchanges, it is not the whole truth of a practice which could not exist if it were consciously perceived in accordance with the model. The temporal structure of gift exchange, which objectivism ignores, is what makes possible the existence of two opposing truths, which defines the full truth of the gift.

—Pierre Bourdieu, *The Logic of Practice*, 1977

Research on which this paper is based was supported by the National Science Foundation (grant no. SBR-9511 937) and by faculty development grants from Hampshire College. I am grateful to the individuals who agreed to be interviewed for this project, to staff of Stockholm's Adoption Centre, without whose support and assistance it would not have been possible, and to Susan Coutin and Bill Maurer, with whom I have been collaborating on a related project.

Address correspondence to Barbara Yngvesson, Hampshire College, Amherst, MA 01002 (e-mail: byngvesson@hampshire.edu).

Complex Truths

A front-page story in the October 25, 1998, edition of the *New York Times* describes an open adoption in which Kim Elniskey chose Yvette Weilacker and her husband to adopt her newborn son. The story, illustrated by a picture of the future adoptive mother reaching out to touch the child in the arms of his birth mother, quotes Elniskey as saying, "I want you to feel that this is your baby, your family" (Fein 1998:1). The only intimation of tension between giver and receiver, and the force this might have in shaping the landscape of adoption and the experience of the adopted child, is the comment, made almost in passing, that "loaded" phrases such as "real parent" and "natural parent" have been replaced in the current climate of transparency surrounding adoption. The birth parent gives, relinquishes, and chooses; the adoptive parent receives. Together, they become "part of a clan."[1]

The fascination this story evokes—its representation of a selfless mother who gives her child away in order to create a family for him—is an effect of its moral ambiguity for the educated, white, middle-class audiences to whom it is directed. A mother who gives away her child is unthinkable. She gives the child away because she loves it so much, the story and its accompanying image imply; but the unspoken subtext—If she really loved the child, how could she bear to part from it?—is no less powerful a message in a moral economy in which becoming a woman is inseparable from the work of motherhood and the assumptions about nurturance this implies (Ginsburg 1989). A birth mother I interviewed several years ago, who had placed her infant son in an open adoption in 1993, described the shocked admiration of friends who told her she was "so brave," followed immediately by the cautionary statement, "I could *never* give away my child." This woman is still haunted by the sense that her gesture of love and trust was morally wrong, whatever her aspirations for her son, and that he will eventually condemn her for it, possibly hate her (Yngvesson 1997:55–56).[2]

What is one to make of the "gift child"? How are we to place such a child in a cultural universe where being given away by a mother is tantamount to abandonment, the worst fate that can be imagined for *any* child? In "Abandonment: What Do We Tell Them?" social worker and adoptive parent Jane Brown argues

[1] Fein (1998:30), quoting Jim Gritter, director of Catholic Human Services in Traverse City, Michigan, who advocates adoption as a "collaborative experience."

[2] See Modell (1999) for a discussion of the rhetoric of giving in open adoptions.

that the "a-word" should be abandoned in favor of more neutral language—"making an adoption plan," "placing" a child for adoption—which depict the motives of a mother in a way that is less injurious to the feelings of the adoptee (Brown 2000). For similar reasons, the rhetoric of giving has been criticized in how-to books on adoption, which suggest that placing the child is more of a piece with the birth mother's increased visibility in contemporary (American) society. The visible birth mother makes "a voluntary decision and a positive plan" for her child, rather than giving her child away (Melina 1989:26–27; 1998:94–95). Similarly, the giving nation is positioned differently in contemporary adoption rhetoric, as vigilant over the loss of its most precious national resources—children—rather than as a country that has only children to give away (Carlson 1994:256; Yngvesson 2000:185; Stanley 1997:1).[3] The rhetoric of giving and the experience of loss go hand-in-hand in these representations, in which alienation (the split subject, the fragmented nation) is an inevitable consequence of "giving." By contrast, child "placement"—understood as planned, consensual, and regulated by the nation-state—is celebrated by adoption professionals and policymakers.

In spite of efforts to reconceptualize the physical movement of a child between persons or nations as placement rather than gift, the gift child remains a powerful and persistent image in adoption discourse. I suggest that the reason this is so is related in part to the ambiguity of the concept—the difficulty of interpreting what gifts signify about the relationship (or absence of a relationship) between donor and receiver, an ambiguity that resonates with the experience of the adoptee, the adoptive family, and, in some cases, the birth family. Ambiguity, in turn, is a function of the traces gifts bear of their passage in the world—their movement from and to some*one* and some*place*, however vague the identity of the donor may be. By contrast, "placement" conveys a sense of grounding and permanence that is at odds with the experience of *being adopted*, of *giving in adoption*, or of *adopting*, verbs that imply a transformation of belonging and identity. A woman who wrote in response to the *New York Times* article with which I began, commented on this disjunction between language and experience:

> As an adult adoptee who has been struggling with her own feelings, I'd like to remind birth and adoptive parents that the question "why did your real mother give you away?" will haunt the adopted child no matter how trained we all become in using the "language of adoption"—for example, the term "birth mother" as a substitute for "real mother" or "natural mother."

[3] Nanuli Shevardnadze told the *New York Times* in 1997 that she was "categorically against foreign adoption," adding that "our nation's gene pool is being depleted" (Stanley 1997:1).

> Though your Oct. 25 front-page article claims that open adoptions make the process an "infinitely more transparent experience," the anxiety to cover the painful feelings of all parties is still obvious in the concern with controlling language. (Duckham 1998:A28)

In what follows, I examine the concept of the adopted child as gift and explore the difficulties of an interpretation of such gifts as "freely given." Building on Marilyn Strathern's (1988) discussion of giving relationships as "enchaining" giver and receiver, rather than freeing them, and drawing on the experiences of agencies, orphanages, adoptive parents, birth parents, and adoptees, I argue that the enchainments of adoptive kinship open up our understandings of family and identity, and the ideas about exclusive belonging these understandings assume. Practices of adoptive kinship that seek to counter the alienation of the child and the divisions of the adoptive family by imagining placement to be a consequence of voluntarism by a birth mother or of "choice" by prospective adoptive parents obscure the dependencies and inequalities that compel some of us to give birth to and give up our children, while constituting others as "free" to adopt them.[4] By examining the ways in which the gift of a child always leaves a trace and implies the potential for a return, I suggest how an adoptee's lived experiences of being given away may transform our understandings of personhood, identity, and belonging in an adopted world. However freestanding the child is "made" by adoption law, he or she can *never* be free of the "implicate field of persons" in which he or she was constituted as legally adoptable.[5]

Commodity Thinking

The emphasis on freedom in forging the relations of adoptive kinship is deeply embedded in adoption law, both at national and international levels. Adoption lawyer Joan Hollinger noted some years ago in a discussion of U.S. adoption law that "birthparents are said to 'bestow' their children directly upon the adoptive parents or to 'surrender' them to child-placing agencies. . . . 'Solicitation' of children is deplored" (1993:49). In Massachusetts, the birth mother is required by law to "voluntarily and unconditionally surrender" her child to the guardianship of the state or of the future adoptive parents (Yngvesson 1997:34). In California, a social worker who obtains a birth mother's consent

4 Susan Wadia-Ells (1995) provides a moving account of her own coming to terms with the material reality confronting her adopted son's birth mother, and her sense of the "profound cultural arrogance" involved in the assumptions and practices surrounding what she had assumed to be the "incredible gift" of a child (1995:118–22).

5 The phrase is Marilyn Strathern's (1997:298), in a discussion of the relationship of sociality to the production of persons in Melanesia.

to relinquish her child is required to ascertain that she is not "taking any medications that might alter [her] reasoning" (Interview, RP 11/16/94)—that is, the social worker must ensure that there is nothing that might inhibit the freedom with which the birth mother gives her consent to the adoption. International conventions, such as the *Hague Convention on Protection of Children and Co-operation in Respect of Intercountry Adoption* (Hague Conference, 1993) also emphasize that "persons, institutions and authorities have given their consent freely, in the required legal form, and expressed or evidenced in writing." The consents must "not have been induced by payment or compensation of any kind" (1993, Article 4).

Concern regarding the freedom of a birth mother from inducements that might jeopardize the validity of her consent is matched by the conceptualization of the institutions and/or parents who receive the child as receiving him or her gratuitously. Any payment must be characterized as a payment for services or as an "act of charity" to an orphanage or other child welfare institution, not as payment for a child (Hollinger 1993:49). As Hollinger notes, "The notion that adoption is not contractual is so powerful that it obscures the extent to which bargaining is intrinsic to a transfer of a child by a birthparent in exchange for a promise by adoptive parents or an agency to support and care for the child and thereby relieve the birthparent of these legal duties" (1993:49).

The centrality of freedom in the discourse of giving and receiving children in adoption is linked to a second key feature of adoption law, its finality. The laws of most adopting nations, whether they typically "give" children or "receive" them, require or state a preference for "strong" adoptions. In strong adoptions, the decision of a woman to surrender her child is irrevocable, and the adoption that follows creates a permanent and exclusive relationship of adoptive kinship that cannot be "undone."[6] In the United States, where adoptions are both unconditional and irrevocable (Hollinger 1993), efforts by adoptees, adoptive parents, and many birth mothers to secure legislation that would make adoption records public have had only limited success (Wegar 1997; Carp 1998; Verhovek 2000; Yngvesson & Mahoney 2000). The only way for adopted adults and the birth parents who "placed" them to discover how the adoption "plan" was made, and what led to the decision to make such a plan, is to work around laws that define the adoptive family as the *only* family of an adopted child. In Chile, an official who oversaw thousands of surrenders of children by women who could not keep them and who hoped to find homes for them through adoptions to Sweden

---

[6] This term was used by a Swedish official commenting on a contested adoption involving a Colombian-born child (see p. 242).

and other nations in the 1970s and 1980s advised these women that "it will be like your child is dead to you" (Yngvesson 2003). International conventions urge "the termination of a pre-existing legal relationship between the child and his or her mother and father" (Hague Conference 1993, Art. 26) and suggest that receiving nations be permitted to "convert" an adoption that does not terminate such a relationship in the sending nation into an adoption that does so in the receiving nation (1993, Art. 27).

The combination of freedom to choose (to exit from a parenting relationship that is presumed to be natural and given) and closure (the new relationship is exclusive of other ties) are both dimensions of a global market economy in which commodity thinking defines the meaning of personhood. In commodity thinking, "persons are assumed to be proprietors of their persons (including their own will, their energies, and work in the general sense of directed activity)" (Strathern 1988:157). These "properties" of the person "belong" to them in a definitional sense and constitute the possessor "as a unitary social entity" (104). Moreover, "belonging" is understood as "an active proprietorship" (135). Persons "'are' what they 'have' or 'do.' Any interference with this one-to-one relationship is regarded as the intrusion of an 'other'" (158). Just as the individual is assumed to be the owner of his or her own person in commodity thinking, so too is society conceptualized as "owning" the properties (persons) that intrinsically constitute it. The transferal of a child from one "owner" to another unsettles this relationship of product to producer—of a nation to "its" citizens, a parent to "its" child, or a person to his or her "nature" (as Colombian or Korean, or as the "natural" child of a particular parent or parents). In commodity thinking, separation from this ground of belonging cannot help but produce an alienated (split) subject, which will always be pulled "back" to where it *really* belongs.

The idea of gratuitous bestowal of the child that is so central a feature of adoption law developed as a response to the perceived danger of producing an alienated subject. Baby-giving could be interpreted as "admirable altruism," because "we do not fear relinquishment of children unless it is accompanied by—understood in terms of, structured by—market rhetoric" (Radin 1996:139). But as Viviana Zelizer argues in her study of the sentimentalized or "priceless" child in America during the late-19th and early-20th centuries, baby-selling and baby-giving are part of the same system, a system in which licit markets depend on illicit ones to establish the value of "priceless" objects (1985:202–3). Indeed, a priceless (gift) child presents a legal quandary that is no less a cultural and social quandary: "How could value be assigned if price were absent?" (14). The adopted child embodies this quandary, in a world where the "fundamentally seductive idea of exchange" (Kopytoff 1986:72) leaves its trace on all entities, whether these are distinguished as "persons" or as "things." In her movement from one family (and one nation) to another in adoption, the child experiences (and symbolizes) the meaning of pricelessness "in the full possible sense of the term" (1986:75): "thrown away like a blade of grass" by her mother (to quote a 6-year-old girl adopted from China by American parents), she is embraced by someone who has "traveled to the ends of the earth" (Serrill 1991:41) to become her parent.

Price and Pricelessness

The interplay of value and the child's capacity to be thrown away is the central paradox of adoptability, one that is especially salient in the international arena. In India, for example, which together with Korea became one of the earliest nations to "give" children to the overdeveloped world in adoption, the value of physically abandoned, institutionalized children developed as part of an economy of desire in which heterosexual, Caucasian couples from Europe and North America sought to adopt them (Yngvesson 2000).

The desire to adopt children from Third World orphanages was not initially a function of infertility and the "scarcity" of healthy, white infants in Western nations, although this rapidly became a central consideration. Instead, this desire took shape as a dimension of development discourse (Escobar 1995) in a postcolonial world in which child adoption operated in conjunction with other forms of aid. In Sweden—which has the largest percentage of international adoptees per capita of any nation (approximately 40,000 in a nation of 39 million) and is widely regarded as a pioneer in the field—international adoption was regarded in the 1960s and early 1970s as a *responsibility* for socially conscious citizens.

Reaction to this sense of responsibility in what were to become "sending" or "giving" nations was mixed. As one woman who adopted her daughter from a Delhi orphanage in 1964 explained, "[W]e weren't exactly encouraged" by local officials. When she and her husband came to fetch their daughter at the orphanage, "they kept asking us, 'Why on earth are you doing anything like this?'"[7] At the same time, one of the earliest contact persons in India for Swedish adopters observed that "as an underdeveloped country, the only thing we [could] give away is children, you know?" (Yngvesson 2000:185).

As the numbers of children moving to the overdeveloped world in adoption increased steadily during the 1970s and a growing international movement to protect children's rights took shape (Therborn 1995), officials in sending nations began

[7] GA, interview, August 1999.

to voice concern about the potential for exploitation of children sent abroad in adoption.[8] These concerns provoked child welfare officials in India to hold a series of workshops, which continued into the late 1990s, with concerned adoption professionals from Western receiving nations. The workshops were sponsored by Sweden's Adoption Centre and the International Social Service Committee in Geneva, and were held at regional and international meetings of the International Council of Social Welfare. In 1981, workshop participants produced the "Bombay Guidelines," a document that defined the issues that were subsequently incorporated into a 1985 Indian Supreme Court Judgment, *Lakshmi Kant Pandey v. Union of India.* Justice Bhagwati, who presided over this landmark case, declared the Indian child to be a "supremely important national asset" on which the "physical and mental health of the nation is dependent" and which should be kept, whenever possible, in its nation of origin (*Lakshmi Kant Pandey* 1985:4–5). His judgment established a quota system for international adoptions, requiring that at least 50% of Indian children placed in adoption be placed domestically.

Justice Bhagwati's ruling was a key moment in the legal recognition of the value of internationally adoptable children as a national resource of the country that produced them (Carlson 1994:256), a moment that was contingent, however, on the experiences of Indian child welfare officials that destitute children had become "commodities [in] an export market."[9] By the early 1990s, when the Hague Conference on Protection of Children and Co-operation in Respect of Intercountry Adoption was convened with representatives of 66 sending and receiving nations, the most divisive issue separating senders from receivers was that of regulating an international market in adoptable children, while at the same time "placing" children in need of families in suitable homes.

The idea that legal adoption is a "market" is anathema to many adoptive parents, adoption agencies, and government officials in sending and receiving countries. But it is accepted as common (if sensational and often disturbing) sense by the public and many adoptees, some of whom comment ironically on their status as "Made in . . . Colombia [India, Korea, Nepal, Chile, and so forth]."[10] In a front page, three-part series featured in the *New*

[8] Adoptions from India to Sweden increased from 30 per year in the late 1960s to 300 to 400 annually between 1979 and 1985. For a discussion of trends during the growth period of international adoption, see Pilotti (1993).

[9] AD, interview, November 1995.

[10] In a performance by Swedish adoptees for adoptive parents at the biennial meeting of Stockholm's Adoption Centre in 1997, over 100 intercountry adoptees marched onto a stage wearing identical white shirts with a Swedish flag on the front, then turned to reveal the words "Made in Colombia" (and so forth) on the back of each shirt. This was an obvious reference to Swedish products that are made in the developing world but identified as uniquely Swedish by a small blue and yellow flag glued to the side or bottom.

York Times in the fall of 1998, one article titled "Market Puts Price Tags on Priceless" presents adoption as a baby bazaar in which the color, culture, and condition of a child are for sale and race determines fees (Mansnerus 1998:A14). While noting that the actual sale of children is illegal in the United States and internationally, the *Times* points out that many adoptions today maintain only the finest line between buying a child and buying adoption services that lead to a child. This view underscores Viviana Zelizer's argument that, in the United States (and, at the present time, internationally), adoption is a legal market in children, one that is entwined in complex ways with illegal markets to establish the value of an adoptable child (1985:202–3).

I suggest that what seems to be an irresolvable tension between the gift child and market practices that make her priceless is a function of the "double evocatory power" of gifts in commodity thinking (Strathern 1997:301). For an object to become a gift, it must be made freestanding: It must be broken free from a producer and constituted as "part of a[n anonymous] store on which others draw" (1997:302). Gifts, then, are alienable, like any other commodity. At the same time, once given, they become a means of building relationships; and relationships constituted through "giving" are interpreted as a function of love (1997:303). Gifts represent "the intimate altruism of transactions that typify personal relations outside the market . . . the wrapped present, the exhibited taste" (1997:301–2). This representation is only possible, however, if they are (imagined to be) "free" and "freely given." The compelled gift is an oxymoron, suggesting that the giver has been induced, seduced, or otherwise placed in a relationship of indebtedness to the receiver. Indebtedness enters time and history into what is envisioned as a timeless relation of love, a relation that endures in spite of all contingencies.[11]

Conceptualizing the relinquishment of a child for adoption as a gift constitutes the relations involved as family relations in an economy where family is imagined as "natural" and not contractual (Schneider 1968), the site of "love relations" (Coontz 1992:53), not of law. Indeed, the given child constitutes the adoptive family as "family," almost as though no adoption had taken place at all. It is precisely the complex identity of the adopted child as, on one hand, a "gift of love" that makes a family (complete), and, on the other, a "resource" that has been contractually alienated from one owner so that it can be attached to another, that produces the contradictions of adoptive kinship, the ambiguities of adoption law, and the creative tension in practices that surround the construction of adoptive families.

[11] See Hervé Varenne's (1977:188–9) discussion of the place of love in American kinship as a way of "relating to" people who are seen as fundamentally separate from the "self."

The Production of Adoptability

These considerations are central to placing the gift child in the context of transnational adoption, and especially to an explanation of the role of the state in these types of transactions. Documents such as the *Hague Convention* (Hague Conference 1993), the earlier *UN Declaration on Adoption and Foster Care* (1986), and the *Child's Right to Grow Up in a Family: Guidelines for Practice in National and Inter-country Adoption and Foster Care* (Adoption Centre 1997), as well as *Lakshmi Kant Pandey v. Union of India* (1985)—which established terms for the commodification of the child vis-à-vis the state—emphasize the rights of the child as a state resource and the state's obligation to protect this resource. In particular, these documents focus on "identity rights"—to a name, a nationality, and to be cared for by one's parents—that are essential in defining the resource status of the child: his or her ownership or belonging in or to a specific family or nation (Stephens 1995).

I suggest that while these rights are crucial protections in a global economy that promotes the circulation of children, to focus on them deflects attention from the role of the state in *producing* the physically abandoned child. Reconfigured as a "legal orphan" that is "available" for adoption, this child becomes a particular kind of "natural resource" for the state that has produced it. The role of the state in this form of production is both more subtle and more powerful than its role in producing identity rights. The transnational adoption of children cannot be explained without reference to state reproductive policies (Ceauşescu's pro-natalism, China's one-child policy, Korea's protection of patriarchal bloodlines), to the *violencia* of wars, kidnappings, and disappearances in which the state is a key player (in Colombia, Chile, Argentina, Honduras, and other Latin American nations, e.g.), and to the incentives for "giving" these children in adoption that are provided by conventions and agreements among cooperating states. Children's rights to an identity are constituted so that the mobility of certain children (who are defined as "adoptable" by the state) is facilitated (Hague Conference 1993, Art. 4), while the identities of all children are fixed so that they can *only* be thought in terms of a "State of origin" (1993:Preamble) and can only be defined in terms of exclusive "identity rights" that are authorized by the state.[12]

[12] A striking recent example of how state policy determines the mobility of children internationally is China's recent decision to change its adoption law, permitting domestic adoptions of children by families who already have one child (Johnson 2002 [herein]). Experience with India's regulation of international adoption in the mid-1980s suggests that such moves to encourage domestic adoption of "available" children transform the range of children considered adoptable abroad (and eventually, at home), in this way increasing the size and diversity of the pool of children available for adoption (see Yngvesson 2000 for an elaboration of this point).

The dual role of the state in producing a child whose right to "the full and harmonious development of his or her personality" entitles him or her "to grow up in a family environment, in an atmosphere of happiness, love and understanding" (1993:Preamble) even as it produces the conditions for the abandonment of children and determines the terms of their adoptability by other states illuminates once again the tension between giving and selling in commodity thinking, and the significance of marking the divide between state and market in these transactions. The adoptable child is not sold, but is given to other states in exchange for a donation of money, a transaction that creates an orderly (and hierarchical) relation of states to one another through the movement of valued resources (children) in adoption.

This orderly traffic is officially distinguished from a market in children (Hague Conference 1993, Art. 1), which is viewed as the source of alienation and loss for the adopted child. In the marketplace (of adoption), all that counts is money, and children become, in effect, *only* money, in this way losing "themselves."[13] The gift child, by contrast, does *not* lose him- or herself (according to national laws and international conventions), either because the move is erased (the child's belonging is transferred to a new family or country), or because the child's source of belonging (his or her national identity) moves with the child. The assumption that identity is inalienable and moves with the child is implicit in everyday depictions of adopted children as "Chinese," "Russian," "Colombian," and so forth. It can be seen as well in popular representations of adoption, such as the *New Yorker* cartoon that appeared a few years ago depicting two couples having dinner. One woman says to the other, "We're so excited. I'm hoping for a Chinese girl, but Peter's heart is set on a Native American boy" (7 July 1992). Here, the child moves, but "Chineseness," "American Indianness," "Koreanness," or "Colombianness" remains the same (or rather, these qualities are enhanced and constituted anew as immutable in this movement).

As this discussion suggests, it is the *circulation* of persons, as promoted or prevented by state policy, that establishes borders, belongings, and the right of a child to "an identity."[14] Indeed, studies of undocumented immigrants in the United States suggest that their mobility or immobility is constituted by agents of the state in ways that secure a traversal of boundaries (the official act of immigration or deportation) only when recognized by im-

[13] See Greenhouse et al. (1994:100) for a discussion of people with "dollar signs in their eyes"; and see Radin (1996:18–21, 136–48) for a discussion of children and market inalienability.

[14] See Elizabeth Grosz's discussion of this issue in *Space, Time and Perversion* (1995:131). Citing Massumi (1993:27–31), Grosz argues that "boundaries are only produced and set in the process of passage. Boundaries do not so much define the routes of passage: it is movement that defines and constitutes boundaries."

migration officials, regardless of when the immigrants physically entered or departed the country (Coutin 2000:29–34). Likewise, the idea that adoptees originate in one place or another and have or lack parents (they are legally abandoned or do not qualify as abandoned) is also constituted by state agents.[15] Mobility (and the traversal of boundaries this implies) is fundamental to modernity and the fixed identities this requires.[16]

If identity is grounded in movement rather than immobility, what does this suggest about the place of the gift child? If identity (and its associated rights) is contingent on the cut-offs mandated by adoption law, citizenship decrees (Coutin 2000), and other legal processes that establish rights by erasing pre-existing social and legal ties, how might "giving" a child in adoption refigure not only identities but the transactions in which identities take shape? To explore this question, I begin with a re-examination of the meaning of a gift.

Identity and Enchainment

The concept of "gratuitous transfer" of a child in adoption might be viewed as a legal and social fiction that "misrecognizes" the contractual nature of a process in which children are separated from one author and attached to another, in exchange for a promise to (exclusively) care for them. Marilyn Strathern, for example, argues that the alienability of gifts in a market economy is systemic—"[I]t is hardly admissible to decide that this particular transaction results in alienation, while that particular one does not" (1988:161). But as Pierre Bourdieu argues in *Outline of a Theory of Practice* (1977:3), this approach fails to take into account the limits of a standpoint that grasps practices "from outside, as a *fait accompli*," instead of situating itself "within the very movement of their accomplishment." In order to situate oneself within the movement of practices, attention must be directed to their temporal structure, a structure that differs depending on whether one is a participant or an observer. With regard to gift exchange, "[T]he observer's totalizing apprehension substitutes an objective structure fundamentally defined by its *reversibility* for an

15 See Coutin & Yngvesson (2002) for a discussion of the parallels between adoptees on roots trips and deportees who have been forced "back" to a country they no longer consider their "own." In both cases there is a "back" but what constitutes such a place (and the desires and fantasies associated with it) is dependent on the role of the nation-state in producing a place from which each form of expatriate is exiled.

16 Slavoj Zizek, in a reinterpretation of Marx's work on commodity fetishism, argues that the essential (unchanging) "nature" of an object is constituted in the act of exchange. Drawing on the work of Sohn-Rethel, Zizek argues that commodity exchange requires a fundamental "as if" ("*als ob*"): that the object exchanged is not subject to the uncertainties of time and the processes of generation and corruption that transform all objects in the world. Commodity exchange (and the transacting states that guarantee it) stamps the object exchanged with an unchanging essence, a kind of "immaterial corporality" that "endures all torments and survives with its beauty immaculate" (1989:18).

equally objective *irreversible* succession of gifts which are not mechanically linked to the gifts they respond to or insistently call for" (Bourdieu 1977:5). This suggests that the "full truth" of the gift of a child in adoption lies neither in the experienced truth of a cut-off from the past nor in the longing for reconnection, but in the capacity of such a gift to evoke "two opposing truths" (5) at the same moment:

1. The truth that identity is located in the inseparability of a child from an author, a concept of selfhood (or of nationhood) in which there is "an identity between owner and thing owned" and in which there is no place for the intervention of social others "except in the guise of supplanted authorship" (Strathern 1988:158). In this account of identity, legal adoption is a process that alienates a child from its "origins": the mother (nation) must give the baby *up* (Yngvesson 1997:53, quoting a birth mother), termination of parental rights is irrevocable, and legal adoptions cannot be "undone" (see case that follows). The finality of law in adoption—what Duncan (1993:51) describes as the principle of the "clean break"—reflects a specific cultural perspective on the child as property, but has come to dominate the practices of transnational adoption.
2. At the same time, and co-existing in painful tension with this finality, is a parallel truth that is both hard to hold onto and impossible to let go: that the identity of the adopted child is created in its exchange *among* partners (states, agencies, orphanages, and very occasionally, parents), neither of whom is the "author" of the child. This competing story about the gift child places the emphasis on *giving*, rather than on giving *away*, and requires that the connection between giver and receiver ("giving" nations and "receiving" nations) be kept open rather than shut down. Unlike commodity thinking—where the emphasis on single authorship means that the connection to "roots" is always in the foreground, constituting a pull on adopted children either to find their roots or replace them (but in any case to define only one set of roots as "real")—the given child cannot be alienated from roots, but can only "find" herself in the relationship *between* self and other, birth country and adopted country, birth parent and adopted parent. In this sense, the gift of a child in adoption enchains giver and receiver, even as it alienates a child from his or her "roots."

The concept of giving as enchainment creates forms of identity that are both more complex and inherently more divisible than the "in"dividuals created by the identity rights spelled out in the *Hague Convention*, the *UN Convention on the Rights of the Child*, and other legal instruments. Enchainment is a function of the link between persons and nations out of which the internationally adoptable child is born; it presumes a field that is not dissolved but strengthened with the passage of the child. This relational field connects rather than separates, and has implications for the confusions and ambiguities that surround the internationally adopted child's "identity." Adoptive identities, constituted in the "in-between" of nations, agencies, and orphanages, position the adoptee as simultaneously "placed and not stitched in place" (Hall 1997:50)—she "belongs" in Korea when she is in the United States or in Sweden, but is "American" or "Swedish" when she is in Korea (Trotzig 1996; von Melen 1998; Liem 2000). The simultaneity of fixity and non-fixity, and the placement in an in-between that this compels, forges identity for persons no less than for nations.

The adoption story below lays open the tension in the concept of a given child, elucidating the child's connection to market "forces" and to the longing for exclusive belongings these forces provoke. In this particular story, the tragedy that underpins so many adoptions is explicit. The story also makes plain both the fragility of connections which tie "identity" and belonging to one particular place and the power of the structures of feeling these connections incite, propelling people to challenge the law (even as they use it), to undo an adoption that cannot be undone and to create unexpected relationships across nations and across the more conventional family boundaries these nations seek to maintain.

Carlos Alberto/Omar Konrad[17]

On the night of December 9, 1992, Nancy Apraez Coral was kidnapped with her 11-month-old son, Carlos Alberto, from the home of her son's father in Popayan, a town in the district of Cauca in southern Colombia. The kidnappers were later identified as members of UNASE (Unidad Antiextorción y Secuestro), an anti-kidnapping unit connected with Colombian state security forces in Popayan. They were apparently searching for the father of Nancy's child, who himself was suspected of involvement in a recent kidnapping. When they did not find him, they took Nancy and her infant son instead.

Nancy was killed some time in the next 8 days. In the early morning of December 16, her baby boy was left, dressed warmly and with a bottle of milk, on a street in Pasto, a town about 300 miles south of Popayan, in the Andes near the Ecuadorian border. The child's cries were heard by Cecilia and Conrado España,

[17] The following discussion of this case appears as well in an earlier publication (Yngvesson 2000:173–8).

who took him in and later that morning notified the Colombian child welfare department, ICBF (Instituto Colombiano de Bienestar Familiar). According to a subsequent Colombian newspaper story, "[H]e was a precious child, swarthy [*trigueño*], robust, acceptably clothed and had a little white poncho" (Calvache 1995:12A). The child was picked up that evening by welfare officials, and subsequently placed in a foster home pending location of his family or a legal declaration of abandonment. The local newspaper, *Diario del Sur*, published his picture on its front page the following day, along with an account of his discovery by local residents (Calvache 1992:1).

Colombian law requires that efforts be made to locate a "lost" or "abandoned" child's family by placing a notice in the local or national mass media. If no family member appears to claim him, the child becomes available for domestic or international adoption. In this case, apart from the report in *Diario del Sur*, the effort to locate Carlos Alberto's family consisted of announcements on the local (Pasto) radio station on January 14, 15, and 18. When there was no response to these notices, he was declared legally abandoned on February 4, 1993, and was named Omar Conrado España, after the family who found him. Two months later, a Swedish couple was selected by ICBF as adoptive parents for the child, and on June 4, 1993, the adoption was completed in Colombia. The child left for Sweden with his new parents, and his adoption was officially recognized by the Swedish government on August 4, 1993. His new parents named him Omar Konrad Vernersson, retaining in his new legal identity the traces of the violent displacements that had shaped his brief life.

In September 1993, three months after the adoption of Omar Conrado and nine months after the kidnapping, the baby's maternal grandmother received an anonymous phone call telling her that her grandson had been abandoned at the town plaza in Pasto. When she arrived there and found no baby, she went from door to door with a picture of the child and eventually located the España family, who sent her to the ICBF. There she was told by the director of child welfare that her grandchild had been legally adopted, the adoption was final, and the record of the adoption was sealed, thus there was no possibility of locating the child (Calvache 1995:12a,1b).[18]

The grandmother hired a lawyer, who filed an appeal with the Pasto Superior Court to have the record opened, and the appeal was approved in February 1994. On June 9, 1995, the adoption was overturned by a Colombian court, which ordered the Colombian authorities (ICBF) and the adoptive family to return the child to his maternal grandparents. Sweden, however

[18] Colombian law requires that adoption documents be sealed (*reservados*, hidden or shut away) for 30 years (*Codigo del Menor*, Art. 114, 1990).

(representing the position of the Adoption Centre, which arranged for the adoption, and of NIA, the Swedish State Board for International Adoptions) did not recognize this action, arguing that since the child was now a Swedish citizen, a Colombian court decree could not affect his legal relationship to his Swedish adoptive parents. In Sweden, according to the Adoption Centre, "adoptions cannot be undone."

The child's grandmother visited Sweden in June 1995, with the assistance of Colombia's ASFADDES (Association of the Family Members of the Disappeared) and Norway's Council of Political Refugees. The Adoption Centre, under pressure because of widespread media publicity in both Colombia and Sweden, received the grandmother at its office in Stockholm, and facilitated a meeting between the grandmother, her grandson, and his adoptive parents. No agreement was reached, however, about the child's return, and the Colombian government said that it lacked the resources to pursue the case in Sweden.

In 1996, Amnesty International intervened on the grandmother's behalf by providing a lawyer for her, and she made a second trip to Sweden, where she visited her grandson and his adoptive parents at their home. During this visit, an unofficial agreement regarding visitation and the child's education was drawn up and eventually (in 1997) signed by the adoptive parents and the grandmother. The agreement specifies that the child is to remain with his adoptive parents, that his grandmother has visitation rights once a year, that the child is to take Spanish classes, and that when it is "suitable," the adoptive family will visit Colombia. These terms satisfied the Adoption Centre, which continued to affirm its position that it was in the best interest of the child (now six years old) to remain with his adoptive parents—"He has no other parents"—but conceded that "the biological maternal grandparents should continue to be the child's grandparents." This concession by adoption officials, together with the signed agreement between the parents and grandparents, blurs the concept of adoption as a "clean-break" process and tacitly contributes to the official endorsement of a model of family that is heterotopic (Foucault 1973), in that it suggests forms of belonging that disrupt the orders, divisions, and groupings of blood kinship and of exclusive national identities.[19]

This story illuminates the complications of any simple interpretation of parental "abandonment" of a child. It demonstrates the embeddedness of physical abandonment in the violence of the state and in the "pull" of international agreements and un-

[19] As Foucault argues, "*Heterotopias* are disturbing . . . because they make it impossible to name this *and* that, because they shatter or tangle common names, because they destroy 'syntax' in advance, and not only the syntax with which we construct sentences, but also the less apparent syntax which causes words and things to 'hold together'" (1973:xviii).

derstandings (such as those that underpin intercountry adoptions from Colombia to Sweden). Physical abandonment and the legal erasures that follow (and may provoke) this abandonment are central to the commodification of the adoptable child. While the routinization in processing that is implied by this story is not necessarily characteristic of other Colombian adoptions, it is nonetheless revealing of the erasures of belonging—the effacement of traces that would link the child to a specific social, cultural, and political surround—that have accompanied the emergence of adoption as a practice for creating families among infertile couples of the north and for managing a political or economic "excess" of children in the south.

These erasures of belonging—and the identities and histories they imply—have become a site of personal struggle for adoptees and their families, as well as an arena for ongoing policy negotiation between sending and receiving countries. This was particularly in evidence during the three years of the Hague Conference on Intercountry Adoption that culminated in the signing of the 1993 Convention. Negotiations at the Conference focused on reconciling the apparent "need" for the adoption of children transnationally with the reassertion of nationalisms, ethnicities, and identities grounded in a particular national soil—particularly with the proclamation of the key place of the child as a "natural" resource through which a claim to a "national" identity can be made.

In this sense, adoptions such as that of Carlos Alberto both challenge (and entrench ever more deeply) ideas of children's identity rights as tied to exclusive national belongings and as deeply rooted in the blood connections of one generation to another "through" time (Anderson 1983). The tenaciousness of Carlos Alberto's grandmother in pursuing her "right" to a relationship with her grandchild, and her skill in mobilizing both national and international groups in support of this right, together with the persistence of Sweden's Adoption Centre in affirming Omar Konrad's Swedish citizenship, the irrevocability of his adoption, and the applicability of Swedish, rather than Colombian law in this case, point to the complex ways in which identity rights may be deployed to secure a specific cultural embeddedness for a particular child.[20] At the same time, this case suggests the unexpected permutations of belonging that struggles over these contradictory rights may produce.

[20] The success of Carlos Alberto's grandmother in mobilizing international support for her right to a relationship with her daughter's son is surely connected, in part, to the publicity surrounding the efforts of the Mothers of the Plaza de Mayo in Argentina to establish their right to a relationship with grandchildren who had been "adopted" by agents of the state, following the murder of their parents. See Bouvard (1994) for a study of the Mothers.

Nevertheless, what is most interesting about this case is not its illumination of the contradictions of rights discourse, but the way it gestures toward a more complex adoption story than the familiar narrative of identity rights. In this more complex narrative, a child (and the parents/grandparents to whom he or she is connected and from whom he or she is separated) is at the same time alienated and enchained. The trace of enchainment is signaled in the implied continuity of mothering (or of parenting) that the terms "biological" grandmother and [adoptive] mother suggest, even as the distinction of the marked terms (*biological* grandmother, *adoptive* mother or parent) sets them apart from "real" mothering/parenting (Yngvesson 1997:73) and embeds in them the hierarchies and injustices of an economy in which the desire for a "real" family shapes the actions of both kinds of parents—the parents who adopted Carlos Alberto so they could have an "as if" real family, and his grandmother who fought for him so she could have a relationship with her "real" grandson (the biogenetic son of her biogenetic daughter). In this case, while the longing for conventional families is apparent, the "in practice" family has not been pinned down by law and is instead evolving over time in the relations among adoptive parents, birth grandparents, and adopted child.[21] This actual family is tacitly acknowledged in the unofficial agreement between grandparents and parents—one that defies the official clean-break policy that established this adoption as final (in accordance with both Swedish and Colombian adoption law)—and provides a blueprint for similar, more "open" relationships in the future.

As this example suggests, the "full truth" of the gift relation in adoption is in the simultaneity of closure and openness it represents, in its deferral of meaning, and in the play with time this deferral requires, as "the trace of something which still retains its roots in one meaning while it is, as it were, moving to another, encapsulating another" (Hall 1997:50). The tension between closure and openness in adoption can be found in legislation, such as the Hague Convention, that makes provisions both for cutting the adopted child off from his or her birth family and country (1993, Art. 26, 27) and for connecting the child to his or her "background" or "origin" (1993, Art. 16, 30). While the simultaneity of cutting off "the past" and of preserving it might be viewed as simply reflecting the power of commodity thinking and the alienability of identity it makes possible, it can also be seen as more than this. Indeed, it is the ambiguity of the gift in commodity thinking that gives the gift its power. It is all "a matter of style"—whether and how an exchange for the child is handled, whether the relations between nations and organizations is main-

[21] This is reminiscent of a birth mother in an open adoption who didn't want to "make a plan" for her relationship with the adoptive parents of her son, but felt they should "just basically leave it open."

tained, whether the records are open or sealed, whether the adoptee goes "back"—not only in relations between families but also in relations between nations, and in the ways adoptees experience the "pull" to return to the nations where they were born.

Inter/national Attachments

At the national level, the gift child of adoption and the donations the child provokes is one of the forms of exchange that creates an order of nations (see Malkki 1992), an order in which the child as gift is arguably a key symbolic resource. When we locate the child of one nation in the heart of another (in its middle-class families), we can forge the most intimate international ties (as in the adoption of Carlos Alberto). The repeated performance of these ties through continued adoptions, over time; their expansion in return visits by adoptees to their birth countries; and their formalization in policies that facilitate ongoing connections between adoptees and their birth countries (see discussion below), suggest strongly that adoption, both at the national and increasingly at the individual/familial level, is as much about enchainment and the multiple authorings and attachments this implies as it is about fixing a child to an identity.[22]

This enchainment is most apparent in the relations connecting representatives of Western adoption organizations with the officials of orphanages, child welfare organizations, and other institutions through which Third and Second World children are made adoptable to families in the North and West. These relations began as person-to-person connections and eventually developed as "a network of social workers, honorary secretaries of institutions, magistrates, doctors, and lawyers in various countries," which made possible "a cooperation built very much on personal trust and a shared belief that children fared better in families than in institutions" (Andersson 1991:7). These networks of cooperation are the operative mechanism that makes intercountry adoptions possible among established agencies and organizations approved by international conventions (the Adoption Centre in Stockholm, Holt in Eugene, WACAP in Seattle, Danadopt in Copenhagen, and so forth). Similar networks underpin the activities of so-called private operators and facilitators who negotiate for babies in the shadow areas cast by "Central Authorities" and by official adoption laws.

These networks and the transactions they make possible involve multiple reciprocities, dependencies, and commitments, including "donations" of several thousand dollars that are paid by First World agencies and parents to Third World orphanages and

22 Intercountry adoptees are referred to in some literature as "bridges" or as "little ambassadors" (Aronson 1997:103–4).

facilitators (but not to birth parents) in exchange for the gift of a child. Donations are explained in terms of the support they provide for the activities of the orphanage, and they are a key dimension of the reciprocity that defines southern orphanages and northern agencies as exchange partners. They are never defined as a per-child payment, or as "buying" a child. Indeed, some Colombian adoption homes are attempting to shift the terms of the donations so that they are paid on an annual basis, rather than on a per-child basis, so the appearance of impropriety is avoided. As the director of what is arguably the premier private adoption home in Colombia told a *Time Magazine* reporter in 1991, her organization "is not a business; it's total devotion to children" (Serrill 1991:46).

What never takes place in these exchange relations is a reversal of the flow of children in one direction and of donations in the other. In this sense, the enchainments of intercountry adoption, like those of other forms of gift exchange, function "*both* as relations of production *and* as ideologies . . . upon which mythologies are built" (Strathern 1988:146). Strathern (161) argues that "enchainment is a condition of all relations based on the gift." Legal adoption bears the traces of this condition, even as it is premised on the erasure of the mutual dependencies enchainment assumes.

The gift of a child in adoption bespeaks the potential for an enchainment that is unthinkable in commodity thinking but that exists as a kind of "shadow other" to commodity thought—it is the foreclosed relationship on which the exclusivity of commodity thought is contingent (see Butler 1993:8). Enchainment haunts the gift relationship of adoption with what sociologist Avery Gordon (1997:8) describes as a kind of "seething presence" that "act[s] on and often meddle[s] with taken-for-granted realities." Haunting, Gordon argues, "draws us affectively, sometimes against our will and always a bit magically, into the structure of feeling of a reality we come to experience, not as cold knowledge, but as a transformative recognition" (1997:8).[23]

What is transformative about the recognition of adoption as giving, and not simply as giving *up*, is the always unfinished quality of the exchange, its inherent incompleteness (in contrast to the inherent completeness of the identities of commodity thought), and the potential for a response that may exceed the alienation of the gift and the commodification of a child. This is so in spite of all the pressures—legal, social, political, bureaucratic, economic—for closure and for the reproduction of identical selves and national identities that this closure secures. From this perspective, the emphasis on identity rights in international agreements such as the 1989 *UN Convention on the Rights of the*

[23] See Mahoney & Yngvesson (1992) for a related approach to structures of feeling.

Child, the 1993 *Hague Convention*, and the 1997 *Guidelines for Practice on National and International Adoption and Foster Family Care* is as much about openings as it is about closures. It is not only about the right to an identity but about "the right to [a] . . . life story . . . which may be presented in many forms" (Adoption Centre 1997:2, 10), leaving open the possibility that a life story might connect the adoptee to *two* names, *two* nationalities (or more) and to multiple parents (as in the adoption of Carlos Alberto). A life story of this kind is less about "identity" than it is about "points of identification and attachment" (Hall 1996:5); and it is less about "wholeness" (Lifton 1994) than it is about doubleness, about splitting, and about holding the tension between identity and difference. The ways in which this tension manifests itself and the kinds of openings and closures that adoption stories entail are as diverse as the circumstances of physical abandonment that underpin the adoptability of a child.

Adoption is a hot topic these days, not so much because it transgresses familiar assumptions about what a family should be, but because it compels us to contemplate what commodity thinking produces, over and over again, as its most unsettling "frontier effect" (Hall 1996:3): not the alienation of self from author, but the possibility that there *is* no author, no "core" that owns the self (or to which the self belongs) other than the states of origin that produce (and then exchange) the adoptive child. The popular wisdom that adoptees will "find themselves" or "complete themselves" or become "whole" (Aronson 1997; Trotzig 1996; von Melen 1998; Lifton 1994) by returning "home" is one way in which the affirmation of "identity" takes place in this frontier zone. This is the flip side of Swedish adoptee Astrid Trotzig's observation that it is "annoying . . . to always be met with questions about me and my origins. [As though] it is not natural that I am here" (1996:62).

The idea that identification with a nation to which s/he belongs pulls the child "back" nicely captures the compelling quality of "the nation" as a root metaphor and the multiple ways the power of an "original" identity makes itself felt in the life of the adoptee.[24] For example, President Kim Dae Jung invited Korean adoptees from eight adoptive nations on an all-expense-paid visit to the Republic of South Korea in 1998. In a ceremony at the Blue House, held in their honor, the President apologized for South Korea's foreign adoptions (which until the mid-1990s regularly topped the lists of foreign adoptions to the United States, Sweden, and other receiving nations). He described South Korea as "filled with shame" over the practice; but he also pointed out that "no nation can live by itself" and urged adoptees to "nurture

[24] Liisa Malkki (1992:31) describes a similar "powerful sedentarism" in the lives of refugees. See also R. Radhakrishnan (1996).

[their] cultural roots" because "globalization is the trend of the times" (Kim 1998:16).

In a related move (one not directed specifically at adoptees, however), current government policy in India encourages close ties between India and its diaspora. For example, the Persons of Indian Origin Card, established in 1999, is intended to "make it easier for people of Indian descent sprinkled around the globe to travel to their familial homeland and invest in it" in ways that are "hassle-free" (Dugger 1999:4). The card is "part of a broader recognition by a growing number of countries that people who move abroad remain potentially valuable contributors in an economically interdependent world" (1999:4).

Doubling and the Politics of the "In-Between"

> "Because of my exterior, the foreigner, the unknown, is always with me."
> —Astrid Trotzig, *Blood Is Thicker Than Water*, 1996.

During the 1990s, as the push to open adoptions and search for roots mounted in intensity in countries of the overdeveloped world, and as the number of intercountry adoptions to the West from Asia, Eastern Europe, and Latin America continued to rise, intercountry adoptees who had arrived as infants or children in the 1950s, 1960s, and 1970s began to speak and write about their experiences of coming from one world and living in another. Their narratives reveal how complex their effort is to occupy the "in-between" constituted by the double evocatory power of a gift child (her capacity to evoke alienation and connection at the same time) and to resist pressures to resolve the opposing truths of gift exchange as a lived experience, into a single reality—what Jean-Luc Nancy (1991:76) describes as resolving "the play of the juncture" into "the substance . . . of a Whole."[25] The lived experience includes what R. Radhakrishnan (1996:175) describes as the "painful, incommensurable simultaneity" that accompanies efforts to inhabit a location where "the political reality of one's present home is to be surpassed only by the ontological unreality of one's place of origin."[26] In this concluding section, I draw on

[25] "By itself, articulation is only a juncture, or more exactly the play of the juncture: what takes place where different pieces touch each other without fusing together, where they slide, pivot, or tumble over one another, one at the limit of the other—exactly at its limit—where these singular and distinct pieces fold or stiffen, flex or tense themselves together and through one another, unto one another, without this mutual *play*—which remains, at the same time, a play *between* them—ever forming into the substance or the higher power of a Whole."

[26] Betty Jean Lifton (1994:57ff) also describes what she terms the "ghost kingdom" in which adoptees reside. Unlike Radhakrishnan's subtle exploration of the notion of a ghostly "location," however, Lifton regards this place as one that can be escaped, or come out of, by searching for and finding a birth parent. What Lifton misses is the constitution of this kingdom and its co-existence with one's "present home," by histories that cannot be erased by simply "finding" what seems to be lost. A search for a birth parent (or the

memoirs of adult adoptees in Sweden and the United States and on interviews conducted with adoptees in Sweden to explore what it means to inhabit this "ghostly" place.

Sara Nordin, who is now 34, was adopted from Ethiopia by Swedish parents in 1969, when she was one-and-a-half-years old. She recounts her experience of growing up black, in a special issue of the journal *SvartVitt* [*BlackWhite*] (1996:4-5) devoted to accounts by international adoptees. Nordin says that the meaning of the word "BLACK"

> has grown with each passing year, until I have finally understood that I am black. It is something big, personal and hard. It is a fact for me. The people who only see my color don't see all of me. The people who suggest that they can look beyond my color don't see all of me. When I try to gather together all the bits of myself, I easily lose myself. In colors and stories. In theories and dreams. When I walk by a mirror I see something exotic that I barely recognize from TV, newspapers and books. Sometimes it makes me happy, sometimes sad, and sometimes astonished. But most often the reflection in the mirror evokes questions that have no simple answers. I have tried to absorb [*ta till mig*] the "black" but then I have difficulty holding onto [*få med mig*] the Swedish. I have tried to absorb the "Swedish" but then I haven't understood what I see in the mirror [freely translated].

In an interview four years later, Nordin spoke of a particularly awkward situation (*en jobbig sits*) in which she found herself in the early 1980s when she was a teenager, a time when "I became almost an immigrant even though I felt myself to be extremely Swedish (*jättesvensk*). And the immigrants thought I was like them. And my Swedish friends thought I was like them. And I couldn't really decide where I belonged" (Interview, 8/22/99, freely translated).[27]

The ambiguities of identity and confusions of belonging experienced by Nordin in Sweden were intensified in the late 1990s when she returned to Addis Ababa. She explained in an interview that Addis "is not a place I would have chosen to live," apart from the fact that she was "from" there. "It wasn't terrible. It was poor, but the poverty wasn't catastrophic. And people were really nice." But she added that once she got back to Sweden, she had a diffi-

opening of adoption records) cannot undo the fundamental alienability of a unitary self that participation in a commodity economy assumes, and the unrealizable "wholeness" that such an economy always sets up as the heart's desire of those who "belong" to it.

[27] It might be argued that the centrality of race to Swedish identity is in inverse relation to official silence about race in that country. Thus, in Sweden, "[i]t is not fitting to describe immigrants in terms of race or ethnic minority groups. Even if there is a terminology for race (e.g., black or white skin color) and ethnic minority groups (e.g., Gypsies, Jews, Sami, etc.) in everyday language, no official concepts have been developed to register persons in such terms. It would be widely considered as discriminatory to ask a person about his or her 'race' in a survey or official questionnaire. The basic concepts used when officials classify immigrants' ethnic background are citizenship and country of birth" (Martens 1997:183).

cult (*jobbigt*) time. "It was hard there [in Ethiopia], but since I was alone I more or less shut off those feelings, just so I could manage. When I got home [to Sweden], it all caught up with me and everything seemed unfathomable. 'Why just me?' And all the children you see. 'What would have become of me if I had stayed there? Who was I while I was there?'" (Interview, 8/22/99, freely translated).

Amanda F., who is 29 and has visited her birth family in Ethiopia twice, describes what she experiences as a constant process of "doubling":

> I felt that a lot when we were there recently—that there is so much one has to relate to all the time. Here I have to relate to the fact that I look different and all that. And there I have to relate to the fact that I don't look different, but I *am* different. I don't know the language, I know almost nothing of what they are about or what they do. And so one has to relate to that also. There is a lot to keep track of. . . . It's hard, because when you are there everything is so real to you. As soon as you come here—after just a couple of weeks, Ethiopia feels so far away and they [her family] feel *really* far away. You have to struggle all the time to keep everything in mind and look at pictures. Although I have begun to feel clearer now, I mean I feel that they are my family and I love them. But we haven't lived together, so there are things that make it seem—I mean, we can't recover twenty years, it isn't possible, it has to start with now. (Interview, 8/22/99, freely translated.)[28]

Astrid Trotzig, adopted by Swedish parents in 1971, returned to South Korea when she was in her twenties, in hopes that she might find a place where it would feel "natural" to be. Instead, as with so many other intercountry adoptees who return to a homeland where they have never lived, what she encountered there was a powerful sense of loss. She found "no memories . . . which all of a sudden could well up from my subconscious, be remembered, be reborn here and now. . . . [N]othing [was] awakened other than melancholy" (Trotzig, 1996:214). Rather than finding a homeland, Trotzig found that "I have no home, nothing that constitutes both an outer and an inner homeland, a place where I belong [*hemvist*]. In Sweden I can never be fully integrated. My appearance is against me. In South Korea it's the opposite. I disappear in the crowd, people who see me think I am Korean, but inside I am in another place."

Experiences such as these reveal the impossibility of fully belonging in Sweden for these adoptees, whose names, skin color, facial configuration, or hair texture set them apart, tying them to a forgotten past that nonetheless infuses the present, separating adoptive parent from child, the Kingdom of Sweden from its "im-

[28] And see Amitav Gosh's (1988:194) description of people like his narrator's grandmother, who because "they have no home but in memory, learn to be very skilled in the art of recollection."

migrant" adoptees, and adoptees from the country of birth that made them "adoptable." This past will always haunt their present, dividing the identities of adoptees and challenging the unstable boundaries of nations that seek to absorb adoptees as citizens. At the same time, the constant presence of this "past" challenges the concept of identity as either divided or whole.

Deann Borshay Liem, whose autoethnographic film, *First Person Plural* (Liem 2000), has been aired to wide acclaim on U.S. television, was adopted from South Korea when she was eight years old. Liem's adoptive history was complicated by the fact that she was sent to her American parents with the false identity of another child. When she arrived, she attempted to explain that she already had a family in Korea and was not an orphan, but her new parents told her (and believed themselves) that this was a fantasy. Her adoption papers confirmed the deaths of her birthparents. Eventually, Liem recounts, she came to believe this story. She forgot Korea, forgot her home, forgot the path that led from her home to the orphanage, and lost her capacity to speak Korean. She became in most ways a typical American girl—prom queen, cheerleader, popular classmate, adored by her parents. After graduating from high school, however, Liem became increasingly depressed. Dreams of the orphanage, and the sudden appearance of her father's face "flying" into her car and around her kitchen, sent her back to the file of documents in her parents' house, where she found what had been previously overlooked: two pictures, one of Liem as a child with her name penciled on the back, the second of an unknown child. The second picture also bore her name.

Liem wrote to the orphanage in 1983, asking about the two pictures. Six weeks later, she received a letter from her brother confirming that she had a family in Korea and that her adoption had been a mistake. *First Person Plural* follows Liem and her adoptive parents on a journey to Korea, where they meet her birth family and she tries to come to terms with the significance of a "forgotten" past for her sense of belonging in the present. Especially traumatic for her is the realization over the course of this journey that although she has returned to her "real" mother in Korea, the only possibility of developing a relationship with this woman is to accept the fact that she is *not* her "real" mother. Indeed, Liem's film hints at the realization that the very question "Who is my real mother?" may be the wrong question. In spite of a past that lives in Liem's imagination, time is not reversible, the "gift" cannot be given back. There is no "return," only a new journey that embeds the implicate field of persons out of which Deanne Borshay Liem was born in new, inevitably painful, sometimes astonishing, ways.

Astrid Trotzig's sense that, as an adoptee, there is nothing that constitutes for her both an inner and an outer homeland, no "belonging" that is "beyond the reach of play" (Derrida 1978:279) is echoed in descriptions by other adoptees of an inner landscape that never quite fits with their lived experience but that becomes an enabling place, a site of "painful, incommensurable, simultaneity," through which they can make contact with a ghostly "past." This often vivid inner landscape, constituted from exclusions that construct the adoptee as "legally abandoned" by/in her homeland (family, nation), becomes a point of investment, a surface of desire, a site of temporary identification with a "past" that is a constant unknown presence.

An adoptee, now in his thirties and living in the United States, describes this "absent presence" as a life that has always run parallel to his everyday life but has never overlapped it. When he was asked by his adoptive mother if he would like to search for his birth parents, he answered that to do so would be like "removing an organ": he was so used to the doubled vision of an unknown interior life and a known life of the everyday that he couldn't imagine living without it.

This adoptee is "white," like his adoptive parents, and it is striking that, in the metaphor of doubling he uses, the unknown self is on the "inside," while his "outside" self is one that connects him to the familiar world he knows. For Korean, Ethiopian, Colombian, and other adoptees of color in contrast, the split is more likely to be experienced, as in Astrid Trotzig's case, as involving a familiar Swedish (American, Dutch, etc.) inside and an unknown exterior that connects them to a homeland that is not their home.

This kind of doubling and the doubled vision it bespeaks might be interpreted as simply a replication of the familiar story about alienation from roots and the split self this produces.[29] While the narratives of these adoptees speak about fragmentation and loss, they also seem to be pointing in the direction of what Stuart Hall describes as "not the so-called return to roots but a coming-to-terms with our 'routes'" (1996:4, quoting Paul Gilroy), a sometimes agonizing process that is captured in Sara Nordin's struggle to "absorb the 'black'" while holding onto the Swedish, and to absorb the Swedish while at the same time understanding "what I see in the mirror."

This process of holding onto points of identification that are contradictory builds on the exclusions of commodity thinking but produces a "constantly shifting frontier" (Balibar 1991:44) rather than an "identity." This shifting frontier emerges from the

[29] An anonymous reviewer of this article pointed to the relevance for my discussion here of Nahum Chandler's discussion of "double consciousness" in his essay on W. E. B. Dubois (1996:250). Chandler describes the sense of double consciousness as a "pivotal recognition" in Dubois' (1975) [1940] *Dusk of Dawn: An Essay Toward an Autobiography of a Race Concept*, one which was "self-consciously and strategically apprehended as a path of inquiry and understanding" (Chandler 1996:251).

adoptee's experience of not fully belonging anywhere and of being suspended between mutually exclusive places and conditions. "Roots trips," depending on how they are enacted, allow a kind of retracing of the "routes" through which the adoptee moved from one condition to the other, and may provide the material context (the enabling surfaces) for a desire that is not so much about a "return" to origins that cannot be found, but about the "mandate . . . to live 'within the hyphen' and yet be able to speak" (Radhakrishnan 1996:175–76). This hyphen, for many adoptees, is a space "between two humanities which seem incommensurable, namely the humanity of destitution and that of 'consumption,' the humanity of underdevelopment and that of overdevelopment" (Balibar 1991:44). Adoptees cannot serve as "bridges" between these incommensurable humanities (Aronson 1997:104–6), but may be able to bear witness to the tension between them.

References

Adoption Centre (1997) *The Child's Right to Grow up in a Family: Guidelines for Practice in National and Intercountry Adoption and Foster Family Care.* Bangalore, India: Adoption Centre.

Anderson, Benedict (1983) *Imagined Communities.* London: Verso.

Andersson, Gunilla (1991) "Intercountry Adoptions in Sweden: The Experience of 25 Years and 32,000 Placements." Sundbyberg, Sweden: Adoption Centre.

Aronson, Jaclyn C. (1997) *Not My Homeland: A Critique of the Current Culture of Korean International Adoption.* Unpublished senior thesis, Dept. of Social Science. Hampshire College, Amherst, MA.

Balibar, Etienne (1991) "Racism and Nationalism," in E. Balibar & I. Wallerstein, eds., *Race, Nation, Class: Ambiguous Identities.* New York: Verso.

Bogard, Howard E. (1991) "Who Are the Orphans? Defining Orphan Status and the Need for an International Convention on Intercountry Adoption," 5 *Emory International Law Rev.* 571–616.

Bourdieu, Pierre (1977) *Outline of a Theory of Practice.* Cambridge: Cambridge Univ. Press.

Bouvard, Marguerite Guzmán (1994) *Revolutionizing Motherhood: The Mothers of the Plaza de Mayo.* Wilmington, DE: Scholarly Resources.

Brown, Jane (2000) "Abandonment: What Do We Tell Them?" 2 *Adoption Today* 5:32–34.

Butler, Judith (1993) *Bodies That Matter: On the Discursive Limits of Sex.* New York: Routledge.

Calvache, Jaime Eliecer (1992) "Caso de un niño conmueve a habitantes del Javeriano," *Diario del Sur,* Pasto, Colombia, 17 Dec., p. 1.

——— (1995) "Abandonado en Pasto y hallado en Suecia," *Diario del Sur,* Pasto, Colombia, 1 Sept., p. 12a.

Carlson, Richard R. (1994) "The Emerging Law of Intercountry Adoptions: An Analysis of the Hague Conference on Intercountry Adoption," 30 *Tulsa Law J.* 243–304.

Carp, E. Wayne (1998) *Family Matters: Secrecy and Disclosure in the History of Adoption.* Cambridge: Harvard Univ. Press.

Chandler, Nahum D. (1996) "The Figure of the X: An Elaboration of the Duboisian Autobiographical Example," in S. Lavie & T. Swedenburg, eds.,

Displacement, Diaspora, and Geographies of Identity. Durham, NC: Duke Univ. Press.

Coontz, Stephanie (1992) *The Way We Never Were: American Families and the Nostalgia Trap.* New York: Basic Books.

Coutin, Susan (2000) *Legalizing Moves: Salvadoran Immigrants' Struggle for U.S. Residency.* Ann Arbor, MI: Univ. of Michigan Press.

Coutin, Susan, & Barbara Yngvesson (2002) "Roots, Trips, and Deportations: Reconfiguring Belonging, Place, and Return" (unpublished ms.).

Derrida, Jacques (1978) *Writing and Difference.* Chicago: Univ. of Chicago Press.

——— (1992) *Given Time: 1. Counterfeit Money.* Peggy Kamuf, trans. Chicago: Univ. of Chicago Press.

Du Bois, W. E. B. (1975) [1940] *Dusk at Dawn: An Essay Toward an Autobiography of a Race Concept.* CPW. H. Aptheker, ed. Millwood, NY: Kraus-Thomson.

Duckham, Janet (1998) "Letter to the editor," *New York Times,* 27 Oct., p. A28.

Dugger, Celia W. (1999) "India Offers Rights to Attract Its Offspring's Cash," *New York Times,* 4 Apr., p. 4.

Duncan, William (1993) "Regulating Intercountry Adoption: An International Perspective," in A. Bainham & D. S. Pearl, eds., *Frontiers of Family Law.* London: John Wiley & Sons.

Fein, Esther B. (1998) "Secrecy and Stigma No Longer Clouding Adoption," *New York Times,* 26 Oct., pp. 1, 30–31.

Foucault, Michel (1973) *The Order of Things.* New York: Vintage Books.

Ginsburg, Faye D. (1989) *Contested Lives: The Abortion Debate in an American Community.* Berkeley: Univ. of California Press.

Gordon, Avery F. (1997) *Ghostly Matters: Haunting and the Sociological Imagination.* Minneapolis: Univ. of Minnesota Press.

Gosh, Amitav (1988) *The Shadow Lines.* Delhi, India: Ravi Dayal.

Greenhouse, Carol J., Barbara Yngvesson, & David M. Engel (1994) *Law and Community in Three American Towns.* Ithaca: Cornell Univ. Press.

Grosz, Elizabeth (1995) *Space, Time, and Perversion.* New York: Routledge.

Hall, Stuart (1996) "Who Needs 'Identity'?," in S. Hall & P. du Gay, eds., *Questions of Cultural Identity.* London: Sage Publications.

——— (1997) "Old and New Identities, Old and New Ethnicities," in A. D. King, ed., *Culture, Globalization and the World System.* Minneapolis: Univ. of Minnesota Press.

Hollinger, Joan H. (1993) "Adoption Law," 3 *The Future of Children* 43–61.

Kim, Dae Jung (1998) "President Kim Dae Jung's Speech: October 23, 1998, at The Blue House," 1 *Chosen Child* 5:15–16.

Kopytoff, Igor (1986) "The Cultural Biography of Things: Commoditization as Process," in A. Appadurai, ed., *The Social Life of Things.* Cambridge: Harvard Univ. Press.

Liem, Deann Borshay (2000) *First Person Plural.* Ho-He-Kus, NJ: Mu Films.

Lifton, Betty Jean (1994) *Journey of the Adopted Self: A Quest for Wholeness.* New York: Basic Books.

Mahoney, Maureen A., & Barbara Yngvesson (1992) "The Construction of Subjectivity and the Paradox of Resistance: Reintegrating Feminist Anthropology and Psychology," 18 *Signs* 44–73.

Malkki, Lisa (1992) "National Geographic: The Rooting of Peoples and the Territorialization of Identity among Scholars and Refugees," 7 *Cultural Anthropology* 24–44.

Mansnerus, Laura (1998) "Market Puts Price Tags on Priceless," *New York Times,* 26 Oct., pp. 1, A16–17.

Martens, Peter (1997) "Immigrants, Crime, and Criminal Justice in Sweden," M. Tonry, ed., *Ethnicity, Crime, and Immigration: Comparative and Cross-National Perspectives.* Chicago: Univ. of Chicago Press.

Massumi, Brian (1993) "Everywhere You Want to Be. Introduction to Fear," in B. Massumi, ed., *The Politics of Everyday Fear.* Cambridge & London: MIT Press.

Melina, Lois R. (1989) *Making Sense of Adoption: A Parent's Guide.* New York: Harper & Row.

——— (1998) *Raising Adopted Children.* New York: HarperCollins.

Modell, Judith S. (1994) *Kinship with Strangers: Adoption and Interpretations of Kinship in American Culture.* Berkeley: Univ. of California Press.

——— (1999) "Freely Given: Open Adoption and the Rhetoric of the Gift," in L. L. Layne, ed., *Transformative Motherhood: On Giving and Getting in a Consumer Culture.* New York: New York Univ. Press.

Nancy, Jean-Luc (1991) *The Inoperative Community.* Minneapolis: Univ. of Minnesota Press.

Nordin, Sara (1996) "Mer eller mindre svart" [More or less black]; 1 *SvartVitt* 4–6 (Stockholm, Sweden).

Pilotti, Francisco (1993) "Intercountry Adoption: Trends, Issues, and Policy Implications for the 1990s," 1 *Childhood* 165–77.

Radhakrishnan, R. (1996) *Diasporic Mediations: Between Home and Location.* Minneapolis: Univ. of Minnesota Press.

Radin, Margaret Jane (1996) *Contested Commodities.* Cambridge: Harvard Univ. Press.

Schneider, David M. (1968) *American Kinship: A Cultural Account.* Chicago: Univ. of Chicago Press.

Serrill, Michael S. (1991) "Wrapping the Earth in Family Ties," *Time International,* 4 Nov., pp. 41–46.

Stanley, Alessandra (1997) "Hands Off Our Babies, a Georgian Tells America," *New York Times,* 29 June, pp. 1, 12.

Stephens, Sharon (1995) "Children and the Politics of Culture in 'Late Capitalism'," in S. Stephens, ed., *Children and the Politics of Culture.* Princeton: Princeton Univ. Press.

Strathern, Marilyn (1988) *The Gender of the Gift.* Berkeley: Univ. of California Press.

——— (1997) "Partners and Consumers," in Alan D. Schrift, ed., *The Logic of the Gift: Toward an Ethic of Generosity.* New York: Routledge.

Therborn, Göran (1996) "Child Politics: Dimensions and Perspectives." 3 *Childhood* 29–44.

Trotzig, Astrid (1996) *Blod är tjockare än vatten* [Blood is thicker than water]. Stockholm, Sweden: Bonniers Förlag.

Varenne, Hervé (1977) *Americans Together: Structured Diversity in an American Town.* New York: Teacher's College Press.

Verhovek, Sam H. (2000) "Debate on Adoptees' Rights Stirs Oregon," *New York Times,* 5 Apr., pp. A1, A14.

von Melen (1998) *Samtal med vuxna adopterade* [Conversations with adult adoptees]. Stockholm, Sweden: Raben Prisma.

Wadia-Ells, Susan (1995) "The Anil Journals," in S. Wadia-Ells, ed., *The Adoption Reader: Birth Mothers, Adoptive Mothers and Adoptive Daughters Tell their Stories.* Seattle, WA: Seal Press.

Wegar, Katarina (1997) *Adoption, Identity and Kinship: The Debate Over Sealed Birth Records.* New Haven: Yale Univ. Press.

Yngvesson, Barbara (1997) "Negotiating Motherhood: Identity and Difference in 'Open' Adoptions." 31 *Law & Society Rev.* 31–80.

——— (2000) "'UnNiño de Cualquier Color': Race and Nation in Intercountry Adoption," in J. Jenson & B. de Sousa Santos, eds., *Globalizing Institutions: Case Studies in Regulation and Innovation.* Aldershot, England: Ashgate.

——— (2003) "'Going Home': Adoption, Loss of Bearings, and the Mythology of Roots," *Social Text* 74, Special Issue on Transnational Kinship.

Yngvesson, Barbara & Maureen A. Mahoney (2000) "'As One Should, Ought, and Wants to Be': Belonging and Authenticity in Identity Narratives," 17 *Theory, Culture and Society* 77–110.

Zelizer, Viviana A. (1985) *Pricing the Priceless Child: The Changing Social Value of Children.* Princeton: Princeton Univ. Press.

Zizek, Slavoj (1989) *The Sublime Object of Ideology.* London: Verso.

Statutes Cited

Codigo del Menor, Decreto 1310 del 1990 (junio 20). Republica de Colombia. Santafe de Bogotá: Ecoe Ediciones.

Hague Conference on Private International Law, Final Act of the Seventeenth Session, May 29, 1993, 32 I.L.M. 1134.

Lakshmi Kant Pandey Vs. Union of India (Writ Petition Crl. No. 1171 of 1982. Decided on 27 Sept. 1985).

United Nations (1986) *Declaration on Social and Legal Principles Relating to the Protection and Welfare of Children, with Special Reference to Foster Placement and Adoption, Nationally and Internationally,* G.A. Res. 41/85, U.N. GAOR, 41st Sess., Annex at art. 5.

——— (1989) *Convention on the Rights of the Child,* G.A. Res. 44/25, U.N. GAOR, 61st plen. mtg., Annex at art. 21.

Part III
Multicultural Dispute Resolution

[23]

CROSS-CULTURAL DISPUTE RESOLUTION: THE CONSEQUENCES OF CONFLICTING INTERPRETATIONS OF NORMS

ALISON DUNDES RENTELN*

TABLE OF CONTENTS

I. INTRODUCTION

In many disputes involving a cultural clash, ethnic minorities ask that the dominant national legal system use customary law as the basis for the decision. In other conflicts a mode of behavior considered acceptable in the ethnic minority community is regarded as reprehensible by the larger society because the phenomenon in question is subject to multiple interpretations. When culture conflicts reach the legal system, there is often a technical question as to whether the cultural evidence is admissible in a court of law. In other cases, it is not simply a question of whether cultural information can be introduced, but whether such evidence can function to exonerate a defendant. Defendants prosecuted for following traditions accepted in their own communities often attempt to raise cultural defenses, arguing that they should not be held responsible or that they should be exempt from general policies because of their cultural upbringing. This essay is concerned with the circumstances under which the cultural background of litigants should be treated as germane to dispute resolution.

---

* Alison Dundes Renteln, Associate Professor of Political Science at the University of Southern California; J.D., Ph.D. in Jurisprudence and Social Policy. Her other works include: Alison Dundes Renteln, *Raising Cultural Defenses*, *in* CULTURAL ISSUES IN CRIMINAL DEFENSE 7-1–7-8 (James G. Connell, III & Rene L. Valladaras eds., 2000); ALISON DUNDES RENTELN, THE CULTURAL DEFENSE (Oxford University Press, forthcoming, 2003).

Research on the "cultural defense" focuses on the extent to which a national legal system allows for the consideration of traditional law, folkways, and beliefs. This type of research is a form of applied legal pluralism.[1] Legal pluralism scholarship generally addresses the interaction among and between varying normative systems. To elucidate some of the difficulties associated with multicultural jurisprudence, in this essay I investigate the implications of recognizing diverse standards in the context of several examples. These cases will demonstrate the extent to which misinterpretations can occur in cross-cultural dispute resolution, and furthermore, how these misunderstandings can result in the miscarriage of justice.

This essay not only examines empirical data revealing value conflicts between normative systems, but it also suggests that general principles of law and human rights law require that national legal systems take into account the standards of the ethnic minority group.[2] Such well established rights as equal protection, privacy, and religious liberty militate in favor of the recognition of folk law and other customs. The most important principle which serves to justify the consideration of culture in the courtroom is arguably the right to culture, which is itself a fundamental human rights norm.[3] As I have explained elsewhere, it is my view that the right to culture, insofar as it is an established part of international law, should be incorporated in domestic legal systems so as to ensure the consideration of the folkways of ethnic minority groups.[4]

---

1. *See, e.g.*, John Griffiths, *What is Legal Pluralism?*, 24 J. LEGAL PLURALISM 1 (1986) (developing the classic conceptual analysis of legal pluralism). See also NORBERT ROULAND, LEGAL ANTHROPOLOGY (Philippe G. Planel trans., The Athlone Press 1994); Masaji Chiba, *Other Phases of Legal Pluralism in the Contemporary World*, 11(3) RATIO JURIS 228-245 (1998); Anne Griffiths, *Legal Pluralism*, *in* AN INTRODUCTION TO LAW AND SOCIETY THEORY (R. Banaker & M. Travers eds., 2002); Martha-Marie Kleinhans & Roderick A. MacDonald, *What is a Critical Legal Pluralism*, 12 CAN. J.L. & SOC'Y 26 (1997); and LEGAL POLYCENTRICITY: CONSEQUENCES OF PLURALISM IN LAW (Hanne Peterson & Henrik Zahle eds., 1995).

2. Alison Dundes Renteln, *In Defense of Culture in the Courtroom*, *in* ENGAGING CULTURAL DIFFERENCES: THE MULTICULTURAL CHALLENGE IN LIBERAL DEMOCRACIES 194-215 (Rick Shweder, Martha Minow & Hazel Rose-Markus eds., 2002).

3. *See International Covenant on Civil and Political Rights*, Article 27 G.A. Res. 2200A(XXI), U.N. GAOR, 21st sess., Supp. No. 16, at 52, U.N. Doc. A/6316 (1966) (guaranteeing minorities the right to culture). Interestingly, it contains no restrictions clause and no state but one attempted to attach a reservation when ratifying the ICCPR.

4. Alison Dundes Renteln, *Cultural Rights and Culture Defense: Cultural Concerns*, in INTERNATIONAL ENCYCLOPEDIA OF THE SOCIAL AND BEHAVIORAL SCIENCES 3116-21 (Neil J. Smelser & Paul B. Baltes eds., Elsevier 2002).

II. CROSS-CULTURAL MISINTERPRETATION

Central to many disputes is a sharp difference in perceived facts. Parties simply have different versions of what occurred in a given case. When individuals come from different parts of the world, it is all the more likely that there will be cross-cultural misunderstandings. Sometimes members of the dominant culture are unable or unwilling to comprehend the explanations proffered by members of ethnic minority groups.

In some rather shocking cases adult males, immigrants from other countries, touch children in the genital area and then profess their innocence, saying this "fondling" is considered normal in their countries of origin.[5] The question confronting U.S. courts is whether this sort of touching is an innocent sign of parental affection or rather brazen child sexual abuse.

Consider, for instance, the case of *State v. Kargar*[6] which involved an Afghani refugee, Kargar, who kissed his eighteen-month-old son's penis in the presence of an American teenage babysitter. Evidently, the father was not ashamed of his behavior at all, as is clear from his touching of his son in front of others and from the presence of photographs of the conduct in the home. After being notified, the authorities arrested him and charged him with gross sexual misconduct.[7]

At Kargar's trial, testimony underscored the innocent nature of the act in the Afghani context; it was merely a showing of paternal love. For a father to kiss the part of the body that urinates allegedly shows the extent of his affection. Despite the attempt to contextualize the cultural meaning of the conduct, the jury convicted Kargar, and he was sentenced to several years in prison. During the several years it took to appeal the decision, he was required to live apart from his family.[8]

In most jurisdictions the cultural significance of his behavior would disprove the specific intent necessary to convict a defendant of child sex-

5. State v. Kargar, 679 A.2d 81 (Me. 1996), is a highly publicized case discussed below. *See also* Nancy A. Wanderer & Catherine R. Connors, *Culture and Crime: Kargar and the Existing Framework for a Cultural Defense*, 47 BUFF. L. REV. 829 (1999); and Farah Sultana Brelvi *'News of the Weird:' Specious Normativity and the Problem of the Cultural Defense*, 28 COLUM. HUM. RTS. L. REV. 657 (1997) (discussing an Albanian father in Texas accused of fondling his own daughter).

6. *Kargar*, 679 A.2d at 82.

7. *Id.* at 82-83. In Maine a "person is guilty of gross sexual assault if that person engages in a sexual act with another person and . . . [t]he other person has not in fact attained the age of 18 years and the actor is a parent." ME. REV. STAT. ANN. tit. 17-A, § 253(1)(H) (West 2001).

8. *Kargar*, 679 A.2d at 82-83.

ual abuse.[9] Maine, however, had modified its sexual abuse statute, so that it was essentially a strict liability standard;[10] if inappropriate touching occurred between adult and child, the crime occurred. The only way to avoid a conviction was under the *de minimis* clause, i.e., that the legislature did not envision the application of the statute to the conduct in question. Ultimately, in 1996 the Maine Supreme Court reversed Kargar's conviction on this ground.[11]

Success in overturning the conviction by no means signaled acceptance of the touching, however. A footnote toward the end of the decision explicitly mentions the need to socialize immigrants, so they know not to continue this manner of showing affection for children.[12] While one may concur that the behavior is to be discouraged to avoid ordeals for unwitting parents and to spare children caught between two cultures which have different interpretations of the touching, one must be clear that the decision, in the final analysis, still favors the forced assimilation of the newly arrived.

People v. Moua, a well-known "marriage by capture" case, dramatically illustrates the problem of disentangling the facts in cultural defense cases.[13] It demonstrates the tremendous challenges judges face in analyzing cultural traditions in their courtrooms.[14] Here the question was whether a Hmong man and woman had married in accordance with customary law in what was dubbed a "marriage by capture," or whether this was a rape and the defendant was invoking culture in an illegitimate attempt to avoid punishment.

A Hmong man, Kong Moua, and a Hmong woman, Xieng Xiong, had been courting, and twenty-one year-old Kong Moua carried off eighteen-year-old Xieng Xiong as part of a gravitational Hmong marriage ritual. According to tradition, the man proves his virility by abducting her in this fashion, and she demonstrates her modesty by not being too eager to go with him. Afterwards, the man is supposed to take the woman to his family's home to consummate the marriage.[15]

9. *Id.* at 81. Child sexual abuse is one of the few crimes in which the defendant's motive is an element of the crime. Self-defense is another.

10. *Id.* at 85 n.5.

11. *Id.* at 86.

12. *Id.* at 85 n.5.

13. *See* People v. Moua, No. 315872-0 (Cal. Super. Ct. Fresno County, Feb. 7, 1985).

14. For a more detailed account, see Deirdre Evans-Pritchard & Alison Dundes Renteln, *The Interpretation and Distortion of Culture: A Hmong Marriage by Capture Case in Fresno, California* 4 S. CAL. INTERDISC. L.J. 1, 1-48 (1994).

15. Alan Dershowitz, *'Marriage by Capture' Runs Into the Law of Rape*, L.A. TIMES, June 14, 1985, at II 5.

The first attempt at abducting his bride failed because her parents prevented her from leaving their home. Kong and two friends took her from the Fresno City College campus. When her American friends witnessed her being thrown into a station wagon screaming in protest, they called the authorities.

The police eventually arrived at Moua's relatives' home. When the couple opened the door, the police asked who the man was who stood beside her and whether she wanted to leave with them. She replied that Kong was her husband and that she wanted to stay with him. A few days later she and her parents called the police and filed kidnapping and rape charges against Kong Moua.

In this case, the judge had considerable difficulty simply determining what the facts were. He had to decide whether to admit evidence concerning Hmong marriage rituals, though it would have been virtually impossible to determine the course of events without having the benefit of this information. To his credit, the judge did permit the consideration of some extremely limited information about Hmong marriage customs. Subsequently, the judge dropped the kidnapping and rape charges, and Kong Moua agreed to plead guilty to false imprisonment, the lesser-included offense under kidnapping. Moua received ninety days, with credit for time served and was fined one thousand dollars.

The public defender ostensibly declined to go to trial because an American jury would have had difficulty comprehending the Hmong ritual in an American setting. Had the case gone to trial, the most appropriate defense, given the facts, would have been mistake of fact as to consent. Kong Moua would have argued that when he carried Xieng Xiong away, her protest was culturally expected, and therefore, did not signify a lack of consent. In short, he thought she was consenting to marry him. However, as the mistake of fact defense requires that the mistake be objectively reasonable, there was little likelihood of success. An American jury would simply not consider a woman thrown into a car shouting in protest to be consenting; hence, Kong Moua could not effectively avail himself of the defense.

Feminists have condemned the mistake of fact defense because it is often employed to the detriment of women. They have sought to educate the public, especially males, that "no" means "no" and not "yes." Consequently from this perspective, the mistake of fact defense, misused in sexual assault cases, should be abolished. In the mean time, however, if the defense remains a part of the criminal law in a given jurisdiction, it is highly problematic that it cannot be invoked by defendants who come from other cultures. The way it has been interpreted, namely to require an "objectively reasonable" mistake, leads to an equal protection violation inasmuch as cultural defendants, in reality, are unable to use it.

Journalists and legal scholars have erroneously referred to this case as a "marriage by capture" case and one which illustrates the principle that "ignorance of the law is no excuse." From Kong's point-of-view, it was a Hmong marriage and from Xieng Xiong's it was allegedly a kidnapping and rape. No one in the Hmong community apparently construed the event as a marriage by capture, and yet this misinterpretation was accepted in the non-Hmong community. Moreover, it is erroneous to classify this case as one involving the principle of ignorance of the law, which does not constitute an excuse. If one accepts Kong's version of the facts, his claim was there was a mistake of fact as to consent, which, if accepted does constitute an excuse. Overall, this case was misused as an example outside the Hmong community.

Many wonder how this case could have generated so much confusion. What actually happened? In reality, the couple originally wanted to marry, but the woman's parents, particularly her mother, objected to the match. Consequently, leaders of each of the two clans met to try to resolve the conflict, but failed to reach an agreement. Her clan wanted restitution because it would be difficult for the young woman to marry after the sequence of events which had transpired. His clan refused, saying that after all it was the woman's family which was calling off the marriage. Ultimately, her clan said that if his clan failed to pay restitution, her family would call the authorities to report the commission of a crime. An unfortunate consequence of this case was the reticence of police to intervene in future situations. Having been manipulated by the family of the Hmong woman, law enforcement did not want to be placed in that position again.

Another complicated cross-cultural dispute involved Nadia, a young woman born in Norway of Moroccan ancestry. The highly publicized case of arranged/forced marriage shows all too well the tragic circumstances of some of these conflicts. Nadia's parents were Moroccan immigrants, devout Muslims, living in Norway who were concerned about the identity of their daughter.[16] When she appeared to be rejecting the Muslim way of life, preferring instead the Scandinavian lifestyle, in October 1997 her parents apparently kidnapped her and took her to Mor-

16. Nadia and her parents were all Norwegian citizens.

occo to be married against her will.[17] Supposedly her parents drugged her, forced her into a van, and drove her from Europe to Morocco.[18]

While in Nador in her aunt's home, Nadia managed to call her employer in Oslo who immediately contacted the police.[19] This led to consultations between the police and the Foreign Ministry, and between the Ministry and the Norwegian Embassy. The ambassador spent three weeks trying to locate Nadia, but was unable to persuade local authorities to intervene. The difficulty was the difference in the legal age of adult between Norway and Morocco: Nadia was eighteen, technically an adult according to Norwegian law, but in Morocco a girl is a minor until the age of twenty.[20] As Unni Wikan put it: "And so Nadia, a Norwegian adult, became Nadia, a Moroccan child."[21] Various negotiations between the Norwegian ambassador in Morocco and Nadia's father and between the Norwegian foreign minister and his Moroccan counterpart produced no result. Although Nadia's parents promised several times to take her to the Embassy in Rabat, they failed to appear.[22] Her father only relented when threatened with losing his social welfare benefits in Norway.[23]

---

17. Unni Wikan, Parents' Rights, the Rights of the Child, and Citizenship: The Case of Nadia 1999 (unpublished paper, on file with author) [hereinafter Wikan, Parents' Rights]. Evidently, in Norway an expert may be called by the court and, similar to U.S. jury duty, under some circumstances cannot decline to serve, even if disinclined to do so. She says she was astonished that she was asked to be a special witness for the defense because she had publicly sided with Nadia on national television. *See also* Unni Wikan, *Citizenship on Trial: The Case of Nadia*, 129 DAEDALUS 55-76 (2000); Hans Wang, The Nadia Case 1999 (unpublished paper, on file with author). *See also* UNNI WIKAN, GENEROUS BETRAYAL (2002) [hereinafter Wikan, GENEROUS BETRAYAL].

18. Her mother awakened her telling her she needed to leave the house which was on fire. As Nadia left the house, she realized the house was not on fire. When she was unwilling to get into the van, her father beat her, handcuffed her and placed her in the back of the van. Wang, *supra* note 17, at 2.

19. *Id.* at 5. During the period of negotiations Nadia was reportedly held captive and physically punished for having brought shame on her family. Wikan, Parents' Rights, *supra* note 17, at 2.

20. Wang, *supra* note 17, at 4. In addition, Norway considered Nadia a Norwegian citizen because she was born there because it relied on the principle of *ius soli* for purposes of determining citizenship; Morocco also claimed Nadia was a citizen of Morocco because it based its citizenship policy on the principle of *ius sanguinis*, i.e., that her parents were Moroccan citizens.

21. Wikan, Parents' Rights, *supra* note 17, at 1-2. Wikan expresses concern about the "value of citizenship" if one country can "simply 'undo'" the citizenship of another country.

22. Wang, *supra* note 17, at 4.

23. Wikan, Parents' Rights, *supra* note 17, at 2; Wang, *supra* note 17, at 4. Wikan says the idea for the "ingenious strategy" came from the Norwegian police. Nadia's father received social security payments from the Norwegian Government of approximately $30,000 per year since becoming a Norwegian citizen, and Nadia's mother received approximately $3,000 per year.

Eventually Nadia returned to Norway where initially she retracted her story, denying her previous the allegations. She explained that she decided to travel to Morocco to see her sick grandmother. Although she claimed she concocted the abduction story when she thought she would have to stay longer in Morocco than she wanted to, she reverted to the original story shortly afterwards.[24]

At the direction of police, she phoned her parents. In the recorded phone conversation her father admitted that she was coerced to leave Oslo. The police recommended charging Nadia's parents and her younger brother with violations of sections 223 and 224 of the Norwegian Criminal Code.[25]

In the fall of 1998 the Norwegian state decided to prosecute her parents under the two sections, much to Nadia's dismay.[26] Nadia was so distraught during the trial that she asked that her parents leave the courtroom while she testified.[27] After a one-week trial, the parents were found guilty, and received sentences much lower than the usual minimum of a year in jail. The father received one year and three months and the mother one year, both as suspended sentences. In addition, Nadia's father had to pay court expenses of approximately $10,000.[28] The court's decision to mete out a light sentence was influenced by Nadia's plea for leniency.[29] Despite this, however, the court noted that "traditions cannot supersede Norwegian law," particularly if parents rely on violence and kidnapping as means for the transmission of folkways.[30]

The case shows how children can be caught between two traditions. While the children may prefer the worldview of the new country, they do not wish to have their parents punished for adhering to a traditional one. The Norwegian legal system in this case indicated that while it would

24. Wikan, Parents' Rights, *supra* note 17, at 2. Her parents subsequently denied the story of abduction and forced marriage, saying Nadia had made it up because she was homesick for Norway.

25. Wang, *supra* note 17, at 7. Wang explains that sections 223 and 224 both deal with holding persons against their will. Section 223 concerns the reason why the person is held; Section 224 does not take into account the reasons for doing so. *Id.* at 6.

26. *Id.* at 7. The charges against her brother were dropped. The Government did not have sufficient evidence to charge her parents with attempting to force her to marry someone from Morocco. *Id.* at 7.

27. *Id.* at 8. The trial was in the Oslo Byrett, the "entry level court" in Norway.

28. Both of her parents decided to exercise their right to appeal the judgment. The appeal means the case may be litigated again at the appeals stage.

29. Wang, *supra* note 17, at 8. It is also appears that Nadia's father was criticized in the Moroccan community for not accepting full responsibility and making sure his wife avoided having to serve any time in jail. The court's judgment accepts Nadia's version completely and her plea for leniency.

30. *Id.* at 9.

show compassion in a case of first instance, the right of children to become assimilated had to be vindicated. The court emphasized the need for the newly arrived to let their children become "Norwegian." Unni Wikan's interpretation of the case emphasizes this point:

> The verdict against Nadia's parents is an historic one in Norway. For the first time, the court declared that the law applies equally to all parents irrespective of ethnic background. Kidnapping is a crime even when it is done with the best of intentions — as to raise one's child in one's own traditions. The verdict went even further: it stated in plain language that when people choose to live in Norway, as Nadia's parents have, they must be prepared to let their children be influenced by their surroundings, that is, Norwegian society. To refuse children the right to be or become "Norwegian" in that respect, is not their right. In the case of Nadia's parents, it was even noted (in the several page long verdict declaration) that they have chosen to remain in Norway with their two young children; it must mean that they cherish the good that Norway has to offer over and above the benefits of Moroccan society: this entails a choice and the choice has consequences, some of which may be unwanted, but are unescapable by Norwegian law.[31]

The Moroccan community in Oslo expressed great displeasure with the verdict. They regarded the decision as sanctioning interference with parents' rights to bring up their children as they see fit. The actual concern was with the sexual freedom of women. When Nadia's mother was quoted as saying to the Norwegian ambassador: "All Norwegian women are whores, and I don't want my daughter to become one of them," this highlighted the worry of Muslim parents.[32]

The difficulty with cases like this one is that it can be hard to tell whether coercion has been used. Indeed, families may employ different types of pressure. In this case the Government did not have sufficient evidence to charge the parents with attempting to force Nadia into marriage with someone in Morocco, despite the father's remarks on the phone about protecting the honor of the family. Furthermore it is unclear whether the parents' actions would have been considered legitimate in Morocco. Evidently leaders of Muslim organizations in Norway throughout the trial claimed that such marriages were no longer accepted in

31. Unni Wikan, Parents' Rights, *supra* note 17. *See also* Wikan, GENEROUS BETRAYAL, *supra* note 17, at 1901-10.

32. Wang, *supra* note 17, at 9. The term "whore" apparently is a "usual non-dramatic swear word in Arabic and Berber" according to Wikan.

Morocco. Ironically, it is sometimes immigrant parents who adhere to traditions more strictly than those in the country of origin.[33]

Cross-cultural jurisprudence can at times involve quite bizarre facts. For example, in some cases the controversy centers on whether a dead body is a "person."[34] In a remarkable decision, *Onyeanusi v. Pan Am*, an Ibo man from Nigeria sued Pan Am for mishandling his mother's corpse while transporting it from the United States to Nigeria.[35] Olamma Onyeanusi died on October 1, 1986 during a visit to her son who resided in Philadelphia. Her son, Onyebuchim arranged to have her body flown from New York to Port Harcourt, Nigeria via Paris. Her body was scheduled to leave New York October 15th and arrive in Nigeria on the 17th. In the meantime, 20,000 members of the Ibo tribe gathered in the village of Uzuakoli waiting for the body to arrive, so that they could perform a traditional funeral. There was a nine-day delay, and when Mr. Onyea- nusi went to get the corpse from the airport in Port Harcourt, he received the remains of a stranger. When he finally received the correct body, it was in a burlap sack. This error caused special trauma to him and his people because her body arrived in a burlap sack, which meant to the Ibo that her death had been by suicide, and her body was face down, which meant to the Ibo that the death was under dishonorable circumstances.[36]

The legal question was whether or not the Warsaw Convention applied.[37] That depended on determining whether the mother's body was a "person[], baggage, or goods."[38] If her corpse fit one of the three categories, then the Convention applied. If the Convention applied, then the statute of limitations barred the son from bringing the lawsuit.[39] In the end the court[40] ruled that the dead body was "goods."

Of course, from the cultural viewpoint the human remains were still considered a "person," but making this argument would not have helped win the lawsuit. So, even if the cultural interpretation of the body as a "person" had been employed, it would not have changed the disposition

33. *See, e.g.*, Fons Strijbosch, *The Concept of Pela and Its Social Significance in The Community of Moluccan Immigrants in the Netherlands*, 23 J. LEGAL PLURALISM 177 (1985).

34. For a consideration of whether the law should protect the rights of the dead in their own right, see Alison Dundes Renteln, *The Rights of the Dead: Autopsies and Corpse Mismanagement in Multicultural Societies*, 100 (4) S. ATL. QUARTERLY 1005-27 (Fall 2001).

35. Onyeanusi v. Pan Am, 952 F.2d 788, 789 (3rd Cir. 1992).

36. *Id.* at 790.

37. *Id.*

38. *Id.*

39. *Id.*

40. *Id.* at 795.

of the case.[41] But the real point is that airlines can traumatize people in unforeseen ways if they negligently transport corpses. Even with the delay the airline could still have avoided putting the mother in a burlap sack and placing her face down.

III. ASCERTAINMENT OF FOLK LAW

Some cases center on practices whose authenticity is in question. Then one must determine who is the legitimate representative of the group. Who can attest to the "centrality" of the custom with respect to the group's way of life? When an expert speaks on behalf of the ethnic minority group, this is offensive to members of the group who often are capable of explaining the practice themselves. Even if the group acknowledges the necessity of bringing in an "expert" with credentials to persuade a jury composed of non-members of the group, some may, nonetheless, resent the legal system for not taking their word for the existence of the tradition and for its central importance to their way of life.

Cases also arise in which conflict exists within the group as to the proper way to perform a ritual. For example, in Cha'are Shalom Ve Tsedek ("CSVT") a branch of the Orthodox Jewish community in France objected to the decision by the French government to have a central Rabbinical committee (ACIP, Association Consistoriale Israelite de Paris) maintain exclusive control over the ritual slaughter of animals.[42] Unconvinced that the meat was sufficiently pure or "glatt," the organization filed a lawsuit. After CSVT lost in the French judicial system, it turned to the European human rights system.

After the European Commission on Human Rights concluded, by a vote of fourteen to three, that there had been a violation of Article 9 taken together with Article 14, France appealed to the European Court of Human Rights.[43] Although the European Court of Human Rights thought

41. The problem was that the son's attorney ought not to have waited so long to file the suit.

42. Cha'are Shalom Ve Tsedek v. France, App. No. 27417/95 2000-VII Eur. Ct. H.R. _____, http://www.echr.coe.int/eng/judgment.htm.

43. Article 9 provides:

> 1. Everyone has the right to freedom of thought, conscience, and religion; this right includes freedom to change his religion or belief and freedom, either alone or in community with others and in public or private, to manifest his religion or belief, in worship, teaching, practice and observance. 2. Freedom to manifest one's religion or beliefs shall be subject only to such limitations as are prescribed by law and are necessary in a democratic society in the interests of public safety, for the protection of public order, health or morals, or for the protection of the rights and freedoms of others.

ritual slaughter was protected under religious freedom, it accepted France's argument that there was a benefit in avoiding unregulated slaughter.[44] In the end, the Court found no violation of religious freedom largely because it was not impossible for ultra-Orthodox Jews to find "glatt" meat; it was available in some places in France and in Belgium.[45] The court also failed to see the significance of any difference in techniques used by the ACIP and the applicant: "[t]he only difference lies in the thoroughness of the examination of the slaughtered animals' lungs after death."[46]

The Court explicitly said that the great majority of Jews accept the ACIP kosher certification system. The implication is that the dominant part of the minority should speak for the rest of the minority, i.e., religious pluralism includes pluralism within a single religious tradition. This controversy exemplifies well the concern of those who worry about oversimplifying religious practices. Obviously, divergent practices exist within the same group. Despite the variation with the group, however, one can say that ritual slaughter is part of Jewish customary law. Per-

---

Europ. T.S. No. 005.

Article 14 provides, in pertinent part: "Enjoyment of the rights and freedoms set forth in this Convention shall be secured without discrimination on any ground such as religion." Europ. T.S. No. 005. Technically, the case was referred to the Grand Chamber of the European Court of Human Rights by the European Commission of Human Rights and the French Government.

44.

> The Court considers, like the Government, that it is in the general interest to avoid unregulated slaughter, carried out in conditions of doubtful hygiene, and that it is therefore preferable, if there is to be ritual slaughter, for it to be performed in slaughterhouses supervised by the public authorities. Accordingly, when in 1982 the State granted approval to the ACIP, an offshoot of the Central Con-sistory, which is the body most representative of the Jewish communities in France, it did not in any way infringe upon the freedom to manifest one's religion.

Cha'are Shalom Ve Tsedek, 2000-VII Eur. Ct. H.R. at para. 77.

The Court's ruling is consistent with its generally narrow interpretation of religious freedom. For an analysis of the doctrine, see T. Jeremy Gunn, *Adjudicating Rights of Conscience Under the European Convention of Human Rights*, *in* RELIGIOUS HUMAN RIGHTS IN GLOBAL PERSPECTIVES: LEGAL PERSPECTIVES 305, 305-30 (Johan D. van der Vyer & John Witte, Jr. eds., 1996).

45. The Court applied the margin of appreciation doctrine, which gives governments some leeway to interpret their own laws. The Court voted twelve to five that there had been no violation of Article 9, the religious freedom provision and ten to seven no violation of Article 9 taken together with 14. A joint dissent by seven judges noted that "public authorities must take... all necessary measures to ensure that the competing groups tolerate each other." Cha'are Shalom Ve Tsedek, 2000-VII Eur. Ct. H.R. at para. 1. They also thought that even if permission had been granted to one religious body, that did not "absolve" the government from considering claims by other religious bodies of the same religion. *Id.*

46. *Id.* at para. 79.

haps the real problem is that the dominant legal system decides which group to designate as the spokesperson for the minority group.

Although the group lost in the French courts as well as in the European Court of Human Rights, the case reveals conflict within the Orthodox Jewish community. The question of which individual or what group can speak on behalf of the entire minority group can be contentious.

IV. Conclusion

I turn now to the jurisprudence of culture conflict and ask what the implications of allowing folk law considerations are. When, if ever, is it desirable to empower courts to review evidence concerning the traditions of various ethnic minority groups?

At least three reasons exist for evaluating cultural evidence in the courtroom. First, insofar as the right to culture is part of international human rights law, an international obligation exists for all states party to the International Covenant on Civil and Political Rights, to treat cultural information as admissible in court. The right to culture should mean, at the very least, that such evidence is "relevant," irrespective of how much weight it carries and whether it ultimately affects the disposition of a case.

Second, by allowing culture in the courtroom there is a greater likelihood of a just outcome in cross-cultural cases. There is, of course, no guarantee of the accuracy of the information which is considered in court. Moreover, even if it is an accurate representation of the group's way of life, the jury will have to decide how much weight, if any, to give it. Nevertheless, despite the difficulties associated with the evaluation of cultural information, courts will be better equipped to render just decisions than they would in the absence of the information.

Finally, contrary to the usual presumption that accommodating minorities is "special" treatment, which violates equal protection and creates resentment among the majority, acknowledging cultural differences ensures that ethnic minorities feel included. More inclusive policies minimize the potential threat to political order posed by minorities who feel alienated by a culturally hegemonic political system. In the long run, courts that open their doors to cultural evidence will help promote greater cross-cultural understanding.

[24]

Constructing an Islamic Institute of Civil Justice that Encourages Women's Rights

I. INTRODUCTION

Many Canadians are voicing concerns over the proposed Islamic Institute for Civil Justice ("IICJ") that would allow Muslims to settle certain disputes in Ontario in accordance with their religious Sharia law.[1] Some fear that an approved IICJ invites unjust situations comparable to those experienced by Amina Lawal and Bariya Magazu.[2]

In 2002, a Nigerian Sharia court sentenced Amina Lawal to be stoned to death for having a child out of wedlock; in contrast, the man named as the father denied responsibility, and as a result, the court dropped charges against him.[3] In another case, teenager Bariya Magazu asserted that she was raped by three men and became pregnant as a result. Because she had sex outside of marriage, a Sharia court sentenced her to one hundred lashes, even though seven people corroborated her story.[4] The men accused of the rape received no punishment.[5]

---

1. The Sharia is Islamic law that provides a religious code of living. Susie Steiner, *Sharia Law*, GUARDIAN UNLIMITED, Aug. 20, 2002, *at* http://www.guardian.co.uk/theissues/article/0,6512,777972,00.html. Sharia, an Arabic word, has been translated differently into English in various forms. Some of the most common national and regional translations are Shari'ah, Sharia, Shari'a, Shariah and Shariat. Lindsey Blenkhorn, Note, *Islamic Marriage Contracts in American Courts: Interpreting Mahr Agreements as Prenuptials and Their Effect on Muslim Women*, 76 S. CAL. L. REV. 189, 234 n.15 (2002). Sharia is spelled the same way throughout this comment, unless embedded in a direct quote.

2. Evelyn Myrie, *Women's Equality Is at Risk; Sharia Law: Unjust*, THE HAMILTON SPECTATOR, Sept. 25, 2004, at F09; Chris Wallace, *Letter of the Day Column*, THE TORONTO SUN, June 10, 2004, at Editorial/Opinion 18.

3. AMNESTY INT'L, *Amina Lawal: Sentenced to Death for Adultery* (Sept. 25, 2003), *at* http://web.amnesty.org/pages/nga-010902-background-eng [hereinafter *Amina Lawal*].

4. Rhoda E. Howard-Hassmann, *The Flogging of Bariya Magazu: Nigerian Politics, Canadian Pressures, and Women's and Children's Rights, in Globalization Working Paper Series* (2003), *at* http://strange.mcmaster.ca/global/servlet/Xml2pdf?fn=x5.

5. *Id.*

The extreme bias against women is apparent in sentences of adultery or fornication under Sharia. A woman is convicted simply by becoming pregnant, but a man is not condemned unless four people can testify that they *witnessed* the normally private acts of adultery or fornication.[6] Countries such as Nigeria impose flogging, stoning, or severing off a hand as *hudood*, all of which are deterrent punishments for serious crimes mentioned in the Qur'an.[7] The Canadian IICJ, however, will only arbitrate certain civil disputes; no criminal matter is subject to arbitration.[8]

The IICJ, though its authority vested by the Arbitration Act of 1991, can arbitrate civil matters according to Islamic personal law; at this time Sharia is legal in Ontario, "as long as both parties agree to it and the arbitrators' decisions don't violate Canadian law."[9] This provides Canadian Muslims an opportunity to settle their personal disputes according to Canadian positive laws and their own beliefs. More importantly, this gives arbitrating parties "peace of mind and satisfaction that the Shariah law is obeyed and that the Ontario law is not flouted."[10] The IICJ is also beneficial because arbitration is conducted in an informal religious setting, is cost and time efficient, and provides more flexibility than the court system.

The Canadian province of Ontario should allow Muslims to arbitrate according to Sharia law in accordance with the 1991 Arbitration Act, because the advantages of a Sharia tribunal far outweigh the disadvantages. Due to the real probability that Sharia law could constrict women's equality, however, Ontario

---

6. Carina Tertsakian, *"Political Shari'a"? Human Rights and Islamic Law in Northern Nigeria, Discrimination Against Women*, 16 HUM. RTS WATCH (2004), *available at* http://www.hrw.org/reports/2004/nigeria0904/3.htm#_Toc82565158.

7. Abdullah Mohammed, *Lashing, Stoning, Mutilating: Islamic Law Is Barbaric and Outdated: Defend the Case of Islam*, *available at* http://www.jannah.org/moreArticles/4.html. The *hudood* offenses include "adultery, fornication, false imputation of being unchaste (*qadhf*), drunkenness, armed robbery, sedition and apostasy." *Id.* In addition, the Arbitration Act excludes disputes involving public status, like marriage and divorce, from arbitration. NATASHA BAKHT, NAT'L ASS'N OF WOMEN & LAW, FAMILY ARBITRATION USING SHARIA LAW: EXAMINING ONTARIO'S ARBITRATION ACT AND ITS IMPACT ON WOMEN, http://www.nawl.ca/brief-sharia.html#14.

8. BAKHT, *supra* note 7.

9. *See* Arbitration Act, S.O., ch. 17, § 32(1), at 121 (1991) (Can.); Kerry Gillespie, *Sharia Protest Gets Personal*, THE TORONTO STAR, Sept. 9, 2005, at A9.

10. SYED MUMTAZ ALI & AZIM HOSEIN, AN ESSENTIAL ISLAMIC SERVICE IN CANADA: MUSLIM MARRIAGE MEDIATION & ARBITRATION SERVICE, *at* http://muslim-canada.org/brochure.htm [hereinafter MEDIATION & ARBITRATION BROCHURE].

needs to implement stricter guidelines to guard against inequality of women in areas such as child custody, inheritance, and spousal support.

Part II of this comment examines Sharia, Canadian, and international laws, as well as the recommendations made by Marion Boyd, who was chosen to study and report her findings on how the IICJ would affect vulnerable people. Part III discusses the advantages and disadvantages of the IICJ, and offers solutions, such as providing independent legal advice and education, amending current laws, and keeping written records. Part IV analyzes the civil matters that are possible subjects to Islamic arbitration.

II. LEGAL FRAMEWORK

Currently, the following report and laws are not mandatory in the Islamic tribunal, but the addition of the recommendations made in Marion Boyd's report, the Canadian Charter of Rights and Freedoms, Divorce Act, Family Law Act, and CEDAW would strengthen women's rights.

A. The Sources of Sharia

Muslims view the Sharia as the "will of God and a guide by which to live," that governs "every aspect of Muslim private life, social transactions, piety, and rituals."[11] Today, Sharia influences and shapes laws across the world.[12] The Sharia is the Islamic code of law based on the Qur'an, Sunnah of the Prophet, *qiyas* and *imja*, all of which are mutually independent and listed by weight of authority.[13]

The principal source of Sharia is the Qur'an, the Islamic holy book. The Qur'an is a collection of revelations that the Prophet Muhammad received from God which Muslims believe to be the literal word of God.[14] Next in importance is the *Sunnah* of the Prophet Muhammad; the deeds, sayings and approvals of the

---

11. Religion A to Z, Canada and the World Backgrounder (Dec. 1999), *at* http://www.findarticles.com/p/articles/mi_qa3695/ is_199912/ai_n8868098.

12. Kristine Uhlman UmHani, *Overview of Shari'a and Prevalent Customs in Islamic Societies: Divorce and Child Custody* (Jan. 2004), *at* http://www.expertlaw.com/library/ attyArticles/islamic_custody.html [hereinafter *Divorce and Child Custody*].

13. JOHN L. ESPOSITO, WOMEN IN MUSLIM FAMILY LAW 3 (1982); *Divorce and Child Custody*, *supra* note 12.

14. FARLEX, INC., *Sharia*, *at* http://encyclopedia.thefreedictionary.com/Sharia.

Prophet Muhammad are translated into *hadith*, stories and anecdotes, to illustrate a concept.[15] Third is the *ijma*; specific personal or political issues that are solidified by Islamic scholars.[16] Of least importance is the *qiyas*, the legal precedent from former cases that a Sharia judge may use to decide a pending case.[17]

Critical to the development of Sharia was the division of Muslims into two groups, the Sunni and the Shia, after the death of the Prophet Muhammad. Each group subsequently developed different *madhhabs of fiqh*, also known as schools of law.[18] The different *madhhabs* agree on "certain fundamental legal issues, but their various interpretations and views of the sources of Shari'a have given rise to different rules on many points of law."[19] The Sunnis have four *madhhabs of fiqh* whereas the Shias have three.[20] Sharia has been codified in many countries with Muslim populations, to apply to both personal and family law issues, such as marriage, divorce, child custody, familial succession, and criminal law issues.[21]

B. Canadian Laws

1. Constitutional Act

Canada's main constitutional instrument, the Constitution Act of 1867, distributes legislative powers.[22] Section 91 of the Constitution Act lists areas with exclusive federal jurisdiction, including marriage and divorce, whereas Section 92 lays out areas of exclusive provincial jurisdiction, including the solemnization of marriage, property rights and civil rights in the province.[23]

---

15. *Id.*; Dennis J. Wiechman et al., *Islamic Law: Myths and Realities*, 12(3) CRIM. JUSTICE INT'L ONLINE 1, 3 (May-June 1996), *reprinted in* Office of Int'l Crim. Justice at the Univ. of Ill., *at* http://muslim-canada.orgIslam_myths.htm [hereinafter *Islamic Law: Myths and Realities*].

16. *Islamic Law: Myths and Realities, supra* note 15; *Divorce and Child Custody, supra* note 12.

17. *See Islamic Law: Myths and Realities, supra* note 15.

18. *Divorce and Child Custody, supra* note 12.

19. *Id.*

20. *Id.* The four Sunni *madhhabs of fiqh* are Hanafi, Shafi'i, Maliki and Hanbali. The three main Shia *madhhabs of fiqh* are Ithna-Ashari, Zaidi, and Ismaili. *Id.*

21. ESPOSITO, *supra* note 13, at 3. *See generally* Tertsakian, *supra* note 6, *at* http://www.hrw.org/reports/2004/nigeria0904/3.htm#_Toc82565158.

22. Claude Belanger, The Constitution Act, 1867, *at* http://www2.marianopolis.edu/quebechistory/federal/bna-act.htm (last modified Feb. 19, 2001).

23. *Id.*

2. Canadian Charter of Rights and Freedoms

The Constitution Act was amended in 1982 to include the Canadian Charter of Rights and Freedoms ("Charter").[24] The Charter guarantees everyone the fundamental freedom of conscience and religion; thought, belief, opinion, and expression; peaceful assembly; and association.[25] Most importantly, the Charter guarantees equality between the sexes.[26]

The Charter, however, applies only to state actions, not to private individuals. In Section 32, the Charter applies to "the Parliament and government of Canada," and to the "legislature and government of each province."[27] Thus, the Charter does not per se bind arbitrators in actions involving private individuals. Furthermore, it is "difficult to predict what impact [the Charter] will have on legislation that allows two parties with informed consent to agree to arbitration using any rules of law."[28]

3. Divorce Act & Family Law Act

The Divorce Act is a federal law in Canada. The Act holds jurisdiction over the divorce procedure itself and other issues inherent in a divorce, such as child custody, child support, and spousal support.[29] Canada's federal law, however, does not apply to couples who are not married, or who are separating. It is left to the provinces to legislate in these areas.[30]

Ontario's provincial laws, the Family Law Act and the Children's Law Reform Act, are much broader than the federal Divorce Act. These provincial laws are open to anyone, to both married couples seeking divorce as well as married and unmarried couples desiring legal separation.[31] Therefore, married couples who file for divorce may use either the federal or provincial laws to settle their particular disputes, whereas common law couples

24. *See generally* CAN. CONST. (Constitutional Act, 1982) pt. I (Canadian Charter of Rights and Freedoms), schedule B, *available at* http://laws.justice.gc.ca/en/const/annex_e.html.

25. *Id.* § 2(a).

26. *Id.* § 15, 28.

27. *Id.* § 32.

28. BAKHT, *supra* note 7.

29. *See generally* Divorce Act, R.S.C., ch. 3, §§ 2(1), 3(1), at 2, 3 (1986) (Can.).

30. *See id.*

31. *See generally* Family Law Act, R.S.O., ch. F.3 (1990) (Can.); Children's Law Reform Act, R.S.O., ch. C.12, pt. II, § 4, at 2 (1990) (Can.).

and married couples, who separate rather than divorce, *must* use the provincial laws.[32]

4. Arbitration Act of 1991

The Arbitration Act of 1991, adopted by Ontario in 1992, provides Ontarians an alternative forum to take their disputes, rather than taking their case into the judicial court system. Under this Act, arbitrating parties agree to let a third person resolve their dispute using the parties' choice of law, and the parties consent to abide by the third party's decision.[33] The main legal limitation, in contrast to the court system, is that the arbitration must be voluntary.[34] In addition, the arbitrator's decision is binding on the parties, unless the parties opt to appeal their decision to the courts.[35]

The drafters of the Arbitration Act originally intended that choice of law would mean parties could choose any provincial law.[36] The language of the Act, however, which states that "[i]n deciding a dispute, an arbitral tribunal shall apply the rules of law designated by the parties," allows religious groups to resolve civil family disputes within their faith, provided that the parties give their consent and the outcomes respect Canadian laws and human rights codes.[37] In practice, the Ontario government has accepted the plain language of the act rather than the drafter's intent; since the act passed, Christians, Jews, and Muslims arbitrate according to the precepts of their faith.[38]

Parties have the option to arbitrate disputes involving matters of child custody, inheritance, and spousal support. Parties may not, however, arbitrate matters prohibited by jurisdiction or statute, such as federal jurisdiction over criminal offenses or civil divorce.[39]

32. MARION BOYD, DISPUTE RESOLUTION IN FAMILY LAW: PROTECTING CHOICE, PROMOTING INCLUSION, 18 (2004), *available at* http://www.attorneygeneral.jus.gov.on.ca/english/about/pubs/boyd/fullreport.pdf (emphasis added) [hereinafter BOYD REPORT].

33. *See* Arbitration Act, S.O., ch. 17, §§ 1, 32(1), 34, 37 at 110, 121 (1991) (Can.).

34. BOYD REPORT, *supra* note 32, at 33.

35. Arbitration Act § 37, at 121.

36. BOYD REPORT, *supra* note 32, at 12.

37. Arbitration Act § 32(1), at 121; Tarannium Kamlani & Nicholas Keung, *Muslim Group Opposes Sharia Law*, THE TORONTO STAR, Aug. 28, 2004, at A2.

38. BOYD REPORT, *supra* note 32, at 4.

39. Arbitration Act § 2, at 110.

C. International Laws: Convention on the Elimination of All Forms of Discrimination Against Women

The United Nations General Assembly, in response to discrimination towards women throughout the world in the 1960s and the 1970s, and recognizing the need for a comprehensive human rights treaty to ensure women's equality, created the Convention on the Elimination of All Forms of Discrimination against Women ("CEDAW") in 1981.[40] As of October 2004, CEDAW has been ratified by Canada and 178 other state parties, over ninety percent of the UN member states.[41]

By ratifying CEDAW, these parties declared that they consented to be bound by the terms of the treaty.[42] Ratifying state parties have the option, before or after ratification, to make a reservation to the treaty, declaring that they are not bound by a certain provision or provisions within the treaty.[43] In accordance with the Vienna Convention on the Law of Treaties, a state can submit a reservation to any provision, as long as it is not incompatible with the object and purpose of the treaty.[44] A reservation is considered incompatible if it intends to derogate from the essential provisions of the treaty.[45] This principle is codified in Article 28 of CEDAW, which explains that a "reservation incompatible with the object and purpose of the

40. United Nations Division for the Advancement of Women, Dep't of Economics and Social Affairs, *Short History of CEDAW Convention*, *at* http://www.un.org/womenwatch/daw/cedaw/history.htm (last modified Oct. 4, 2004).

41. *Id.*

42. United Nations, Convention on the Elimination of All Forms of Discrimination Against Women, Signatures and Ratifications, Sept. 3, 1981, 1249 U.N.T.S 13, 80, *available at* http://untreaty.un.org/ENGLISH/bible/englishinternetbible/partI/chapterIV/treaty10.asp [hereinafter CEDAW, Signatures and Ratifications]; United Nations, *United Nations Treaty Collection, Treaty Reference Guide*, *at* http://untreaty.un.org/English/guide.asp [hereinafter *UN Treaty Guide*].

43. *UN Treaty Guide*, *supra* note 42.

44. Vienna Convention on the Law of Treaties, Jan. 27, 1980, art. 19(c), 1155 U.N.T.S. 331, *available at* http://www.un.org/law/ilc/texts/treaties.htm [hereinafter Vienna Convention]. In 1951, prior to the passage of the Vienna Convention, the International Court of Justice (ICJ) stated that reservations to treaties are allowed as long as they do not conflict with the object and purpose of the treaty. This principle was ultimately incorporated in the Vienna Convention on the Law of Treaties. William A. Schabas, *Invalid Reservations to the International Covenant on Civil and Political Rights: Is the United States Still a Party?*, 21 BROOKLYN J. INT'L L. 277, 318 (1995).

45. Convention on the Rights of the Child, Sept. 2, 1990, 1577 U.N.T.S. 3, n. 24, *available at* http://www.ohchr.org/english/countries/ratification/11.htm#reservations [hereinafter CRC].

present Convention shall not be permitted."[46]

The CEDAW committee, which monitors state parties' implementation of CEDAW, declared that Articles 2 and 16 are core provisions that relate to the "object and purpose" of the treaty.[47] Article 2 explains that states agree to eliminate discrimination against women by implementing equality between the sexes in their constitutions, legislation, and legal systems through proficient national tribunals and other public institutions, and by abolishing laws, regulations, customs, practices and penal provisions that discriminate against women.[48]

A reservation to these core provisions violates the object and purpose of CEDAW in two ways: first, a state may try to "invoke the provisions of its internal law as justification for its failure to perform a treaty," and second, a state fails to take affirmative steps to eliminate discrimination against women.[49] Article 2 lays out the nature of state parties' obligation to end such discrimination.[50] Article 16 directs states to eliminate discrimination against women in matters of marriage and family relations.[51] Specifically, women are granted equal rights: to enter marriage, within a marriage, at dissolution, as parents, to have children, to choose a profession, and in property.[52] The committee declares that because "[n]either traditional, religious or cultural practice nor incompatible domestic laws and policies can justify violations of the Convention," reservations to Article 16 are incompatible with CEDAW and thus impermissible.[53]

Significantly, twelve parties have made reservations to

---

46. Convention on the Elimination of All Forms of Discrimination against Women, Dec. 18, 1979, art. 28(2), 1249 U.N.T.S. 13, 19 I.L.M. 33, (entered into force Sept. 3, 1981), *reprinted in* DAVID WEISSBRODT ET AL., SELECTED INTERNATIONAL HUMAN RIGHTS INSTRUMENTS AND BIBLIOGRAPHY FOR RESEARCH ON INTERNATIONAL HUMAN RIGHTS LAW [68, 77] (3rd ed. 1999) [hereinafter CEDAW].

47. United Nations Division for the Advancement of Women, Dep't of Economics and Social Affairs, *Reservations to CEDAW*, *at* http://www.un.org/womenwatch/daw/cedaw/reservations.htm (last modified Oct. 04, 2004) [hereinafter *Reservations to CEDAW*]; AMNESTY INT'L, *Reservations to the Convention on the Elimination of All Forms of Discrimination Against Women -Weakening the Protection of Women from Violence in the Middle East and North Africa Region*, *at* http://web.amnesty.org/library/Index/ENGIOR510092004.

48. CEDAW, *supra* note 46, at 69.

49. *See* Vienna Convention, *supra* note 44, at art. 27.

50. *See Reservations to CEDAW*, *supra* note 47.

51. CEDAW, *supra* note 46, at art. 16.

52. *Id.*

53. *Reservations to CEDAW*, *supra* note 47.

CEDAW Article 2 and/or Article 16, explicitly asserting that these provisions are incompatible with Sharia.[54] Some Muslim states enter very broad reservations, such as making a reservation to any article in general which conflicts with religious law.[55] Others have entered narrowly tailored reservations, such as making a reservation to a particular article as to why it conflicts with Sharia.[56] But some Islamic party states, such as Nigeria, have ratified CEDAW without making any Sharia-based reservations. This makes Sharia-based CEDAW reservations perplexing because the precise requirements of Sharia are unknown and the future is unclear as Sharia is subject to evolving, and multiple interpretations and practices.[57]

There are multiple interpretations of Sharia because it derives from four sources, is divided into two distinct branches, and is further separated into different schools of law. Confusion also arises because there is no distinction between the sources of Sharia, "such as the Quran, which is sacred, and Islamic *fiqh* (jurisprudence), which is not."[58] For example, even though CEDAW Articles 2 and 16 do not conflict with the Qur'an, which guarantees women's rights, several states have taken reservations because it is sometimes unclear whether Sharia and CEDAW will actually conflict.[59] Because the interpretation of Sharia can vary from state to state and even among citizens within a state, states may make a reservation, "not because Islam [is] against the equality of women, but as a precautionary measure."[60]

It is unclear whether the arbitrational tribunal, IICJ, as constituted, would violate the core principles of Articles 2 and 16 as evidenced by the murky relationship between Sharia and CEDAW. Inconsistent explanations given on how Sharia will

---

54. *See generally UN Treaty Guide, supra* note 42.

55. *See generally id.*

56. *See generally id.*

57. *Reservations to the Convention on the Elimination of All Forms of Discrimination Against Women: Report by the Secretariat,* Comm. on Elimination of Discrimination Against Women:, U.N. GAOR. 16th Sess., Provisional Agenda Item 8, CEDAW/C/1997/4 (1996).

58. Mariz Tadros, *Women Debate Rights on Woman's Day*, AL-AHRAM WEEKLY ON-LINE, *at* http://weekly.abram.org.eg/1999/420/focus.htm (Mar. 11-17, 1999).

59. *Id.*

60. *See* Press Release, Committee on the Elimination of Discrimination against Women, Monitoring Body for Women's Anti-Discrimination Conventions Takes up Reports of Egypt, WOM/1250 (Jan. 19, 2001), *available at* http://www.un.org/News/Press/docs/2001/wom1250.doc.htm [hereinafter *Press Release on Egypt*].

apply in the IICJ elevates this confusion. Syed Mumtaz Ali, one of the founders of the Islamic Institute of Civil Justice, explains that the IICJ will apply "a watered-down Sharia, not 100 per cent Sharia. Only those provisions that agree with Canadian laws will be used. If there is a conflict between the two, Canadian law will prevail."[61] Previously, however, Mr. Ali stated that Sharia "cannot be customized for specific countries. These universal, divine laws are for all people of all countries for all times."[62] Thus, it is unclear what kind of Sharia Muslims will be subjecting themselves to when they take their cases to arbitration.[63] This is because the IICJ has yet to release any rules or guidelines explaining how the different schools of Muslim law will interact with family law matters in relation to women's rights.[64]

D. Marion Boyd's Recommendation

Marion Boyd, who previously served as both Attorney General and Women's Issues Minister of Ontario, was appointed to review Ontario's arbitration process and its impact on women.[65] She delivered her report to the Ontario government in December 2004 on whether Ontario should have an Islamic arbitration tribunal.[66] She advised that arbitration continue as an alternative dispute resolution in family and inheritance cases and that Canadians may continue to resolve disputes using religious law in the confines of the Arbitration Act, subject to the recommendations of her report.[67]

Her main recommendations are: (1) amend the Family Law Act and Arbitration Act to make the acts more interconnected; (2) require independent legal advice or an explicit waiver of such; (3) publicly educate the community regarding the Arbitration Act,

---

61. Lynda Hurst, *Ontario Sharia Tribunals Assailed*, THE TORONTO STAR, May 22, 2004, at A1.

62. *Id.*

63. MEDIATION & ARBITRATION BROCHURE, *supra* note 10.

64. *Id.*

65. News Release, Ministry of the Attorney General, Ontario Government Releases Report on Review of Arbitration Process (Dec. 20, 2004), *at* http://www.attorneygeneral.jus.gov.on.ca/english/news/2004/20041220-boyd.asp.

66. BOYD REPORT, *supra* note 32, at 1.

67. MARION BOYD, DISPUTE RESOLUTION IN FAMILY LAW: PROTECTING CHOICE, PROMOTING INCLUSION: EXECUTIVE SUMMARY, 3 (2004), *available at* http://www.attorneygeneral.jus.gov.on.ca/english/about/pubs/boyd/executivesummary.pdf [hereinafter BOYD SUMMARY].

family law and immigration law issues, alternative forms of dispute resolution and general rights and obligations under the law; (4) train and educate the arbitrators; and (5) add more checks and balances so the Ontario government can oversee and evaluate the arbitration process.[68]

III. The Inner Workings of the IICJ

The Islamic Institute for Civil Justice ("IICJ") is a tribunal that arbitrates disputes using Sharia law. Discussed below are the advantages and disadvantages to arbitrating according to religious principles as an alternative to the court system. In addition, possible solutions are laid out to rectify the disadvantages of the IICJ.

A. Advantages of the IICJ

Many people prefer settling their legal disputes in arbitration rather than through the court system because the arbitration process is more private, less expensive, and the arbitral award can be filed with a court and enforced as a court order.[69] In addition, courts may be willing, in the family law context, to interpret arbitral awards equitably because the Arbitration Act allows courts to intervene to prevent unfair treatment of parties to arbitration agreements.[70]

But what draws people to faith-based arbitration, and in particular Muslim arbitration, is the opportunity to resolve their disputes while following the tenants of their religion. Many people prefer this system because it allows them to comply with the teachings of their faith, and it can be specifically tailored to the school of Muslim law to which they subscribe. Furthermore, the Qur'an states that Muslims cannot call themselves Muslim unless they abide by the "guidelines, counsel, and principles related to them through the Qur'an and the Prophet Muhammad."[71] Thus, it is the duty of each Muslim to follow the Sharia, and the IICJ provides him or her with a forum to abide by their religious obligations.

68. *See generally id.*
69. BAKHT, *supra* note 7.
70. Arbitration Act, S.O., ch. 17, § 6, at 111-12 (1991) (Can.).
71. Interview by Rabia Mills with Syed Mumtaz Ali, President, Canadian Society of Muslims (Aug. 1995) *at* http://muslim-canada.org/pfl.htm.

B. *Disadvantages of the IICJ*

1. Coercion

Despite the advantages of the IICJ, many concerns still exist over the possible implementation of a Sharia tribunal. The first potential problem is that women, especially immigrants, might feel coerced into participating in a binding arbitration according to Muslim family law, rather than resolving disputes through the Canadian secular court system.

This fear exists because women who have recently emigrated from a Muslim county will have limited contact with society.[72] Since the women generally do not speak English and are accustomed to staying in their own communities, the only contact these women have is through their husbands and in-laws.[73] Therefore, these women will need more protection under the law, because their frame of legal reference is limited to what their community and husbands tell them.

Syed Mumtaz Ali, the founder of the IICJ, however, assures detractors that these women will not be coerced into settling matters at the IICJ, rather than through a secular court. He supports his assertion by citing two Qur'an verses: 2:256, "There is no compulsion in religion" and 4:35, which states that two arbitrators, one from his family and the other from hers, should be appointed in matters of divorce.[74] But, he adds "to be a good Muslim, one *must* go to a Muslim court rather than a secular court."[75] He states further that those "Muslims who would prefer to be governed by secular Canadian family law may do so. It would be preferable, however, for Muslims to choose governance by Muslim Personal Family Law for *reasons of conscience*."[76]

The Council on American-Islamic Relations Canada (a non-profit organization who seek to educate and empower Canadian Muslims) also approves a Muslim-based arbitration system, but it is concerned that "there are no safeguards to ensure all parties are

---

72. Clifford Krauss, *Canadian Tolerance Meets Islam's Sharia Law; Critics Say Openness Must Have Limits*, THE INT'L HERALD TRIB., Aug. 5, 2004, at News2.

73. *Id.*

74. Mirko Petricevic, *A Choice in Law; Legal Application of Sharia Divides Canada's Muslim Community*, THE REC., June 26, 2004, at Faith18.

75. *Id.* (emphasis added).

76. Interview with Syed Mumtaz Ali, *supra* note 71 (emphasis added).

acting voluntarily, especially the vulnerable; there are no mechanisms to ensure that parties are fully apprised of their rights under the act; and the act does not specify any standards for arbitrators."[77]

In addition, devout women will be pressured to consent to arbitration under Sharia law. Ali's previous statement is consistent with the views of many Muslims and applies to all Canadian Muslim women; they will all feel the pressure of being a "good Muslim" and might have their disputes arbitrated in a Sharia court simply out of religious obligation. Furthermore, their husbands or other community members may *remind them* that Muslims are bound to regulate their conduct, according to Islamic laws, wherever they may be.[78] Thus, the implementation of a Sharia tribunal will put all Canadian Muslim women at the risk of "coercion, condemnation and alienation within the Muslim community, should disputes arise and they fail to *voluntarily* opt for resolution through Sharia tribunal."[79]

The prospect of this happening has been presaged in Beis/Beit Din arbitration tribunals. Jews have arbitrated successfully in several Canadian provinces, according to Jewish law, *halacha*, to resolve business, commercial, and divorce disputes.[80] One rabbi from the Toronto Beit Din stated the tribunal is not coercive, but the "[h]alachah forbids Jews from taking each other to secular court," and secular court may only be used if everything else fails.[81] Another rabbi admitted they encourage Jews a little to arbitrate according to Jewish law, because using the Beis Din is a commandment from God, an obligation.[82] This type of subtle coercion is very likely to occur in a Sharia tribunal as well because Sharia is based upon the Qur'an, which is the literal word of God, and Muslims living in non-Muslim countries are called to "observe the Divine Laws just like all the

77. Riad Saloojee, *CAIR-CAN: Announcements*, at http://www.caircan.ca/ann_more.php?id=1162_0_9_0_C.

78. *See* MEDIATION & ARBITRATION BROCHURE, *supra* note 10 (citing As-Sarakhsy, '*Al-mubsut*' X,95).

79. Bonnie Collings, *Allowing Sharia Law a Threat to Women*, LONDON FREE PRESS, Sept. 3, 2004, at A8 (emphasis added).

80. Ron Csillag, *Jewish Input Sought in Review of Religious Courts*, THE CANADIAN JEWISH NEWS, Aug. 5, 2004.

81. *Id.*

82. BAKHT, *supra* note 7 (citing Letter from Ministry of Attorney General, Policy Branch, to Ms. Alia Hogben, Executive Director (Apr. 26, 2004)).

believers."[83]

Similarly, in cases where a woman agrees to settle a dispute in the IICJ, she has the option to take the arbitration settlement to a secular court if she believes the settlement was unfair. Unfortunately, many women may not exercise this right because of the "overwhelming pressure from her family and community."[84]

2. Premarital Agreement Coercion

Another type of coercion disadvantageous to women in an Islamic tribunal is premarital agreement coercion. Even though there is a defense of duress/coercion in holding premarital agreements invalid, the courts have set a high threshold for establishing this defense.[85] In *Hartshorne v. Hartshorne,* Mr. Hartshorne presented his new bride a marital agreement and a pen during the wedding reception.[86] In front of her husband and friend, Leslie Walton, the new bride, cried and proclaimed, "[y]ou're my witness, I am signing this under duress."[87] She testified that she had no choice but to sign the agreement because she had a toddler, was planning on having another child, and believed Mr. Hartshorne would not marry her unless she signed the agreement.[88]

The trial judge ruled that even though Mrs. Hartshorne was upset when she signed the agreement, "the evidence falls far short of establishing a basis for a finding that the agreement was unconscionable, or that it was entered into by the defendant under duress, coercion or undue influence."[89] On appeal, both the Court of Appeals and Supreme Court of Canada agreed with the trial judge's ruling.[90] Because it is difficult to establish premarital coercion in the court system, presumably it is as hard, if not harder, to establish this defense in an informal arbitration system.

---

83. MEDIATION & ARBITRATION BROCHURE, *supra* note 10 (citing Sahih Muslim: V. 139-140).

84. *Id.*

85. BAKHT, *supra* note 7.

86. Hartshone v. Hartshone, D110253, 1999 B.C.T.C. LEXIS 2016.

87. *Id.* para. 44.

88. *Id.* para. 43.

89. *See id.*

90. *See* Hartshorne v. Hartshorne, [2004] 236 D.L.R. (4th) 193, 196; *see Hartshorne v. Hartshorne*, [2002] 220 D.L.R. (4th) 655.

C. Solutions to the Disadvantages of the IICJ

There are a number of women who will freely agree and want to arbitrate in the IICJ. For those women who want to observe their religious faith but who are unaware of their legal options, it is possible to encourage them to make voluntary decisions through independent legal advice, education, by amending current laws and written records.

1. Independent Legal Advice

The majority of Canadians agree that the single most important mechanism for protecting vulnerable people is Independent Legal Advice ("ILA"), but currently ILA is not required in arbitration.[91] ILA usually helps parties achieve a clear understanding of the nature and consequences of the agreement, as required by the Family Law Act. The Family Law Act states that the court may set aside a domestic contract, *i.e.* a marriage contract, separation agreement, or cohabitation agreement, if one of the parties did not "understand the nature or consequences" of the contract.[92]

ILA would also help eliminate involuntariness by providing an independent legal counselor who can explain to women their rights under Canadian law.[93] The voluntary nature of arbitration can be supported by "insisting that both parties receive independent legal advice and be informed of their right to appeal the arbitration decision once rendered, and of their right to challenge the arbitrator's ruling under section 13 of the act."[94] To further assure that parties freely enter arbitration on their own volition, the independent legal counselor should have both parties sign a document stating they understand their legal rights and are voluntarily consenting to religious arbitration.

Despite the overwhelming advantage of mandating ILA, some believe that if enforced in actuality, ILA would be of little use in the IICJ because Ontario lawyers are trained to counsel their clients in the Canadian legal context, and are "unaware of [the] repercussions and consequences of a system of law" with

91. BOYD REPORT, *supra* note 32, at 119.
92. Family Law Act, R.S.O., ch. F.3, § 56(4), at 382 (1990) (Can.).
93. *See* Saloojee, *supra* note 77.
94. *Id.*

which they are not familiar.[95] A more pressing concern, however, is the financial constraints with arbitration. Those who decide to arbitrate are not eligible to receive any legal aid; parties must use their own resources to pay for the arbitrator, any independent legal advice, and all other costs associated with the case.[96]

Without financial assistance, it is unreasonable to mandate that each party seek independent legal advice before going to arbitration. Because it is in the court's best interest to encourage parties to use alternative dispute resolution, so as to alleviate the burdens on the court, legal aid should be extended to cover anyone seeking legal advice, whether it be for court, arbitration, mediation, or conciliation.

Arbitration is economically advantageous as well because even when ILA is required, it may be significantly cheaper than the secular court process.[97] For example, the court can set aside an agreement if there is no clear understanding of the nature and consequences of the agreement, as in *Dhanna v. Dhanna*.[98] In that case, Mrs. Dhanna, the wife, did not receive meaningful independent legal advice and the court set aside their marital agreement that released any claims to net family property, other property, and spousal support, on the grounds that Mrs. Dhanna did not understand the nature or consequences of the agreement.[99] Analyzing this situation, it is apparent that it would have been more efficient for the parties to spend a smaller amount of money at the start of the lawsuit to receive legal advice, rather than having to pay the court expenses for an entire trial and possibly an appeals process. Thus, the most efficient solution, taking into account women's equality and economic exigencies, is to mandate ILA and provide financial assistance.

2. Education

Independent legal advice will help minimize coercion, but, alone, it is insufficient. Many parties are unaware of the arbitration process and all their legal options. The public, especially

95. BAKHT, *supra* note 7 (citing Lynne Cohen, *Inside the Beis Din*, CANADIAN LAWYER 32, May 2000.

96. BOYD REPORT, *supra* note 32, at 104.

97. BOYD REPORT, *supra* note 32, at 10.

98. Dhanna v. Dhanna, 03-FA-11700FIS, 2004 CanLII 46660 (ON S.C. Dec. 10, 2004), *at* http://www.canlii.org/on/cas/onsc/2004/2004onsc12724.html.

99. *Id.*

immigrant and minority women, need to be educated about their rights and options in family-law disputes, through a proactive education campaign using culturally and linguistically accessible literature.[100] Such education can be achieved by expanding the system already in place.

At present, the Ministry of the Attorney General and the Department of Justice Canada provide a resource booklet, "What You Should Know About Family Law in Ontario."[101] This booklet, however, is only in English and French, is not distributed to all minority communities, and does not even *mention* arbitration.[102]

In India, which is twelve percent Muslim, the majority of the population speaks Hindi.[103] Sri Lanka has a Muslim population of seven percent with Sinhala as the main language.[104] Both India and Sri Lanka rank in the top five countries of recent immigrants to Canada, but this booklet is not understandable to the majority of Muslim immigrants.[105] Thus, a woman emigrating from either of these popular countries is at a disadvantage because she cannot comprehend this booklet.

But even for those women who can read French or English, the family law booklet will not help them understand Canada's arbitration system. Presumably, if the woman's husband were to take her to a religious arbitration proceeding, she would think the laws in force there were similar to those in her home country. In addition to distributing the booklet in various languages to accommodate Canada's immigrant population, the publishers of the booklet ought to update it to explain faith-based arbitration and the alternatives.

Besides the written word, the government can educate

---

100. Saloojee, *supra* note 77.

101. MINISTRY OF THE ATTORNEY GENERAL, WHAT YOU SHOULD KNOW ABOUT FAMILY LAW IN ONTARIO (1999), *available at* http://www.attorneygeneral.jus.gov.on.ca/english/family/familyla.pdf.

102. BOYD REPORT, *supra* note 32, at 128. (emphasis added).

103. CIA, WORLD FACTBOOK INDIA, *available at* http://www.cia.gov/cia/publications/factbook/geos/in.html (last modified Apr. 21, 2005).

104. CIA, WORLD FACTBOOK SRI LANKA, *available at* http://www.cia.gov/cia/publications/factbook/geos/ce.html (last modified Apr. 21, 2005).

105. Grant Schellenberg, Statistics Canada: Business and Labour Market Analysis Division, *Trends and Conditions in Census Metropolitan Areas: Immigrants in Canada's Census Metropolitan Areas* (Aug. 2004), *available at* http://www.statcan.ca/english/research/89-613-MIE/2004003/89-613-MIE2004003.pdf.

through other media resources, such as television and radio. This has the potential of reaching more people and is usually easier to understand. This may be as effective, or more effective, than the booklet.[106] Regardless of whether the government increases education through an improved booklet and/or the media, a more important effect is that the government has taken proactive steps towards educating immigrant and minority women.

In addition to the government's efforts, Muslim Canadian groups can provide help to these isolated women. This may be more effective because these groups tailor their message to the needs of Canadian Muslims, and thus, are better equipped and more knowledgeable on how to reach and educate women who may be unaware of all their legal options. Also, if fellow Muslims counsel these women, this will tend to promote equality in their religion and make it less likely for them to think that they are departing from the pillars of their faith, if they choose not to take their dispute to faith-based arbitration.

3. Amending Current Laws

The Canadian Charter does not currently apply to private arbitration, but many people believe that the Charter must apply to parties involved in faith-based arbitration.[107] Marion Boyd points out that the Charter does not prohibit the use of arbitration, but that "additional safeguards that recognize the values inherent in the *Charter of Rights and Freedoms*," need to be implemented.[108] Such implementation can be achieved by amending Section 32, which states to whom the Charter applies.[109] Therefore, the Charter can be amended to apply to private arbitrators in alternative dispute resolution settings, in addition to the legislature and government of each province, the government of Canada and the Parliament.[110]

4. Written Records

The 1991 Arbitration Act does not mandate that the

---

106. BOYD REPORT, *supra* note 32, at 132.

107. *See* Saloojee, *supra* note 77 ("significant efforts must also be made by the provincial government, in partnership with minority communities, to craft a regulatory scheme for the selection, education and training of qualified arbitrators.").

108. BOYD REPORT, *supra* note 32, at 77.

109. CAN. CONST., *supra* note 24, at § 32.

110. *See id.*

arbitration tribunals keep written records or transcripts. In fact, the arbitration agreement does not even need to be in writing; only the arbitration award becomes part of the legal record.[111] With no written evidence required to document the proceedings, the potential for illegal activity and unjust awards arises.[112] Compounding the problem, without written records of the decision, the appeals process becomes more difficult, because if an appeal were granted it would involve one person's word against another.

The solution to this quandary is simple: mandate that after a decision is rendered, arbitrators provide a written transcript of their decisions to a provincial created registry.[113] Marion Boyd further recommends encouraging arbitrators to keep a written record of the arbitration by amending the Arbitration Act or the Family Law Act, to state that if written records are not maintained, then a party may seek to have the arbitral award set aside.[114]

VI. Civil Matters That Can Be Arbitrated in the IICJ

The IICJ only arbitrates civil disputes. Some of the most controversial topics that may be arbitrated in the IICJ are discussed here: iddat, Mahr, child custody, and inheritance.

A. Iddat

In Bangladesh, and in many Muslim countries, laws are written in ways that favor men. For example, men can get a divorce much easier than women can, men get more money when they divorce, they pay minimal spousal support, and are awarded custody of the children.[115] At divorce, a Muslim husband only needs to pay maintenance; that is, he is required to pay spousal support to his ex-wife during the iddat, which is the mandatory waiting period for a woman that begins at the time of divorce and ends after her third menstrual cycle, after which a new marriage is

111. Arbitration Act, S.O., ch. 17, §§ 5(3), 38(1), at 111, 121 (1991) (Can.).

112. Bakht, *supra* note 7 (citing Letter from Ministry of Attorney General, Policy Branch to Ms. Alia Hogben, Executive Director, (April 26, 2004) Canadian Council of Muslim Women at 5).

113. *See* Saloojee, *supra* note 77.

114. Boyd Report, *supra* note 32, at 137.

115. *See* Danial Latifi & Anor v. Union of India and Other Petitions, [2002] 4 LRI 36.

permitted.[116]

Consequently, the ex-husband must give his former spouse maintenance in that time frame and provide for her in the future as well, in an amount that is "reasonable and fair."[117] But, after this three-month period expires, if the wife is inadequately compensated, her family must pay her maintenance.[118] If the family is unable to pay her expenses, then the burden falls on the State Wakf Board, a charitable Islamic organization that is regulated and overseen by the state.[119] Encouragingly, in a few recent Bangladeshi cases, the Bangladesh Supreme Court has extended a divorced woman's period of iddat until she remarries.[120]

In predominantly Muslim countries, organizations like the State Wakf Board will collect money to support women in divorce cases, who do not receive adequate maintenance from their ex-husbands. Canada, however, maintains a different standard. In *Moge v. Moge*, the court stated that the Divorce Act embraced the notion that the "primary burden of spousal support should fall on the family members, not the state."[121] Since then, courts in every province have adhered to this principle. The only exception occurred in one Ontario decision, in which the judge ruled that the primary burden of support should not rest "upon the shoulders of a . . . former spouse whose income is at the margin of self-support."[122] The judge in this case based the wife's support on two sources: the social welfare system, and the ex-husband in an

116. Majid Fakhry, An Interpretation of the Qur'an 40 (2004).

117. Danial Latifi v. Union of India, A.I.R. 2001 S.C. 3958, para. 37.

118. *Id.*

119. *Id.*

120. Consideration of Reports Submitted by States Parties under Article 18 of the Convention on the Elimination of all forms of Discrimination Against Women: Third and Fourth Periodic Reports of States Parties (Bangladesh), Committee on the Elimination of Discrimination Against Women, U.N. Doc. CEDAW/C/BGD/3-4 (1997), *available at* http://www.un.org/esa/gopher-data/ga/cedaw/17/country/Bangladesh/C-BGD3-4.EN [hereinafter Bangladesh Report]. The Bangladesh government, however, has continued to validate the inequity between men and women in their rights and responsibilities during both marriage and at divorce. *Id.*; CEDAW, *supra* note 46, at art. 16. Even though this inequality is beginning to be recognized, the Bangladesh government is not publicly discussing it for fear of offending the religious sentiments of the majority Muslim population in the country. *See* Sultana Kamal, Law for Muslim Women in Bangladesh, *in* Women Living Under Muslim Laws: Publications Dossier 4: Law for Muslim Women in Bangladesh (1988).

121. Moge v. Moge, [1992] 3 S.C.R. 813, 865.

122. Papaspirou v. Soussoudis, [1999] 90 A.C.W.S. (3d) 610.

amount he could reasonably afford.[123]

Sharia and Canadian laws have different methods for awarding spousal support. In order to reconcile the two so that the practice of iddat may continue, the iddat period should be lengthened. The iddat period could extend until the woman remarried, as in Bangladesh, or be lengthened for another period of time that the IICJ and the Ontario government deem reasonable, to ensure that a majority of women can financially support themselves.

B. Mahr

The second civil issue subject to arbitration is Mahr, a gift that the husband promises to give his wife if the marriage ends by divorce or death; without it, there can be no Muslim marriage.[124] Giving Mahr derives from the Qur'an, which states that a man must give Mahr to the woman at marriage as a free gift.[125] The purpose of the Mahr is to assist the wife at divorce, while simultaneously discouraging the husband from exercising his right, unilaterally in many countries, from ending the marriage.[126] The wife can only lose her entitlement to the Mahr if the husband or the wife dissolves the marriage before consummation.[127]

In *Kaddoura v. Hammoud*, the groom, his father and father-in-law negotiated a $35,000 Mahr, $5,000 to be paid before the wedding ceremony and $30,000 to be payable at death or divorce.[128] Eighteen months after the couple exchanged vows, they divorced.[129] The wife argued entitlement to the $30,000 Mahr, claiming that it constituted a marriage contract under Section 52(1) of the Family Law Act, which covers agreements by couples in "which they agree on their respective rights and obligations under the marriage or on separation, on the annulment or dissolution of the marriage or on death," including support

---

123. *Id.*

124. Abed Awad, Court Enforces Mahr Provision in Muslim Marriage Contract, at http://www.niqabiparalegal.com/awad.php; Kaddoura v. Hammoud, [1998] 168 D.L.R. (4th) 503, 507 (Ont. Gen. Div.).

125. MAJID FAKHRY, AN INTERPRETATION OF THE QUR'AN 81, 85 (2004).

126. Awad, *supra* note 124.

127. DAVID PEARL & WERNER MENSKI, MUSLIM FAMILY LAW 180 (Sweet & Maxwell eds.-3d ed. 1998).

128. *Kaddoura*, 168 D.L.R. (4th) at 508.

129. *Id.* at 505.

obligations and other matters in the settlement of their affairs.[130] The husband, on the other hand, argued that the Mahr contract is a question of religious obligation, and thus, not justiciable in the Ontario civil courts.[131]

Even though the court agreed that giving the Mahr is obligatory, the judge found in favor of the husband, agreeing that the Mahr contract should not be adjudicated in the civil courts. He stated that courts cannot safely and should not go through the "religious thicket," but that "only an Islamic religious authority could resolve such a dispute . . . [through] proper application of principles derived from the Holy Qur'an, the words of the Prophet and from the religious jurisprudence."[132] Most likely, the outcome of this case would have been different had the contract been civil; the judge stated that he "drew a boundary between a debt enforceable in civil law and the obligation of the Mahr."[133] Thus, the reason this contract was not justiciable was due to its religious nature; cases of Mahr today are not adjudicated.

In Britain, the Islamic Shari'a Council (ISC) provides conciliation services, similar to mediation, using Islamic law.[134] The ISC handles approximately fifty cases a year, the majority of which involve Mahr.[135] Muslims in Britain prefer this type of legal service; sixty-six percent of British Muslims would rather settle their dispute using Muslim law versus English law.[136]

If Ontario allows Muslims to arbitrate within the bounds of the Arbitration Act, this would provide Muslims an opportunity to collect on their Mahr in the IICJ. Since Mahr is not a court issue, women's contractual rights to Mahr are not being enforced. Therefore, allowing a Muslim arbitration system would further both justice and women rights.

C. Child Custody

In Islamic law, the mother has *hadana*, the right to custody of

130. Family Law Act, R.S.O., ch. F.3, § 52(1), at 380 (1990) (Can.).

131. *Kaddoura*, 168 D.L.R. (4th) at 510.

132. *Id.* at 511-512.

133. Kaddoura v. Hammoud, No. 53247/96, 1999 WL 33181569 (Ont. Gen. Div. Jan. 22, 1999).

134. BOYD REPORT, *supra* note 32, at 81.

135. *Id.*

136. *Id.*

a child, for the first part of the child's life.[137] At a certain time in a child's life, the mother's *hadana* ends and the father can then claim custody.[138] Typically, this time is when a male child reaches the age of seven and when a female child reaches puberty.[139] While these are the default rules, a divorcing couple can mutually consent to altering the *hadana* through a written agreement.[140] The agreement, however, neither affects the father's financial responsibility to provide maintenance and custody costs for the child, nor eliminates the possibility of the mother losing custody of her child if she remarries a person not related to her child.[141]

Tunisia and Bangladesh have been interpreting Sharia-based gender laws far more liberally than other countries with Sharia. In Bangladesh, the Bangladesh Supreme Court has been granting mothers custody of their children beyond the typical age limits, based on the best interests of the child.[142] Tunisia has interpreted *hadana* more liberally than Bangladesh; in Tunisia, *hadana* of every child belongs to the parents jointly. At divorce, the child can be awarded to either parent or a third party, taking into account the child's interest.[143] There is no age when the mother's custody is terminated.[144]

Canadian law is similar to Tunisian law; in child custody and access cases, the court must always determine what is in the best interest of the child.[145] The Family Law Act codifies this principle, stating that the court "may disregard any provision of a domestic contract . . . where, in the opinion of the court, to do so is in the best interests of the child," when determining the custody of or access to a child.[146]

Mr. Ali asserts that Islamic family law would not apply to child custody cases in Canada, because "Canadian law is very

137. TAHIR MAHMOOD, STATUTES OF PERSONAL LAW IN ISLAMIC COUNTRIES: HISTORY, TEXTS AND ANALYSIS 269 (2d ed. 1995).

138. *Id.* at 268-69.

139. *Id.* at 269. The different schools of Islamic law vary on when the mother's hadana ends, but only a few have extended the "mother's custody beyond seven years of a male child's age and beyond puberty or marriage of a female child." *Id.*

140. *Id.* at 270.

141. *Id.*

142. *Bangladesh Report*, *supra* note 120 at 2.15.8.

143. MAHMOOD, *supra* note 137, at 270.

144. *Id.*

145. Wiltshire v. Wiltshire, [2003] O.J. No. 3099 (ON.C., 2003).

146. Family Law Act, R.S.O., ch. F.3, § 56(1), at 382 (1990) (Can.).

sensitive to the interest of the child" and therefore only Canadian law can be used to decide custody.[147] Yet, the National Association of Women and the Law ("NAWL"), Canadian Council of Muslim Women ("CCMW"), and National Organization of Immigrant and Visible Minority Women of Canada ("NOIVMWC") all assert that there is no legal impediment to arbitrate child support, custody of or access to the child.[148]

Although the Family Law Act protects a mother's right to custody, in that the child will not be taken away from her simply because the child has reached a certain age, when couples arbitrate in the IICJ, they may choose *any* legal rules they want, even those that do not use the Family Law Act or Divorce Act.[149]

Marion Boyd suggested that both the Arbitration Act and the Family Law Act be amended, so that when a dispute is arbitrated in the IICJ, the Family Law Act must be followed.[150] Specifically, the Arbitration Act should be amended so that a court could not allow an arbitral award in a family or inheritance matter if the "award does not reflect the best interests of any children affected by it."[151] The best interest of the child will thus prevail above all else in custody cases.

D. Inheritance

The last civil matter that may be arbitrated in the IICJ is inheritance. According to Ontario law, if the net family property of the deceased spouse is greater than that of the surviving spouse, "the surviving spouse is entitled to one-half the difference between them," regardless of whether the person died testate (with a will) or intestate (without a will).[152] In addition, dependent children have an automatic first claim on their parent's estate.[153] Aside from these two regulations, an Ontarian may leave their assets to whomever they chose, as long as they leave a will.[154]

---

147. Marina Jimenez, *Islamic Law in Civil Disputes Raises Questions*, THE GLOBE AND MAIL, Dec. 11, 2003, at A1.
148. BAKHT, *supra* note 7.
149. *Id.* (emphasis added).
150. *See generally* BOYD REPORT, *supra* note 32.
151. BOYD SUMMARY, *supra* note 67, at 4.
152. Family Law Act, R.S.O., ch. F.3, § 5(2), at 354 (1990) (Can.).
153. *See* BOYD REPORT, *supra* note 32, at 27.
154. *Id.* at 26-27.

If the deceased dies intestate and there are no children, the spouse inherits everything.[155] If there is one child, the spouse receives a preferential share as prescribed by the Lieutenant Governor in Council and the remainder of the money is divided equally among the children.[156] If there is more than one child, the surviving spouse again receives his or her preferential share plus one-third of the inheritance, and the children equally divide the rest of the inheritance.[157]

Conversely, under Sharia law, men get the bulk of marital assets; the Qur'anic rule is a double share for the male, such that a widow's share is only half to that of the widower and a son inherits twice as much as a daughter.[158] Opponents of the IICJ thus argue that the tribunal may distribute unequal inheritance settlements for women.[159]

If the deceased dies testate, then Ontario law is not in conflict with Sharia law, as long as the deceased has acted in accordance with Ontario's rules regarding the surviving spouse and dependent children. However, Sharia law may conflict with Ontario law if the deceased assigns assets in a way that is not prescribed by the Qur'an.

If the deceased dies intestate, however, there is a conflict between both Sharia law and Ontario law. Ontario gives the spouse the largest proportion and then divides the remainder equally among surviving children, whereas Sharia law mandates that the deceased's male relatives receive fifty percent more of the share than the deceased's female relatives, independent of actual relationship. If the surviving parties decide to bring an inheritance dispute to the IICJ, all parties need to be clear on the implications of both Canadian and Sharia inheritance laws.

VII. CONCLUSION

Ontario could realize potential advantages in granting their Muslim citizens the opportunity to take their disputes to faith-based arbitration. The Canadian Charter of Rights and Freedoms, Divorce Act, Family Law Act, and CEDAW, although not

155. Succession Law Reform Act, R.S.O., ch. S.26, pt. 2, § 44, at 329 (1990) (Can.).

156. *Id.* § 46(1).

157. *Id.* § 46(2).

158. MAHMOOD, *supra* note 137, at 275.

159. AFP, *Some Canadians May Use Sharia Law,* AL JAZEERA ENGLISH EDITION, Dec. 26, 2003.

currently required in arbitration, should be implemented to protect women's rights. To further safeguard women's rights, rules or guidelines need to be prepared so that those subjecting themselves to arbitration know what kind of Muslim law they will be using.

Coercion without knowledge of other alternatives is the biggest impediment to women's equality and must be adequately addressed, along with keeping written records to increase the accuracy of the appeal process. Although coercion can never fully be eliminated, requiring independent legal advice, educating women, and amending current laws would protect Canadian Muslims who voluntarily decided to have their dispute resolved in faith-based arbitration. The benefit is that in the areas of iddat, Mahr, child custody, and inheritance, Muslims have the opportunity to arbitrate according to their belief systems, albeit with some restrictions, whereas they would not have the same alternatives in the secular court system. These benefits allow for the fundamental right of freedom of religion to be expressed.

Marie Egan Provins *

---

* J.D. Candidate, Loyola Law School, Los Angeles, 2006; B.S. Managerial Economics, with honors, University of California at Davis, 2002. I would like to thank my parents, Karen and Pat, and my husband, Jarrod, who have been my lifetime editors, for their creativity and precision in the editing process, and most importantly, for their love, support, and encouragement.

* The reader is advised to note that on September 11th, 2005, Ontario's Premier Dalton McGuinty declared that "[t]here will be no Sharia law in Ontario. There will be no religious arbitration in Ontario. There will be one law for all Ontarians." Prithi Yelaja and Robert Benzie, *McGuinty: No Sharia Law*, THE TORONTO STAR, Sept. 12, 2005, at A1. His ruling will ultimately eliminate the 1991 Arbitration Act and subsequently the Jewish, Christian and Muslim arbitration systems in Ontario. This decision follows the Quebec legislation's unanimous vote on May 26th, 2005 that "rejected the use of Islamic tribunals in the[ir] legal system." Les Perreaux, *Quebec Rejects Islamic Law*, THE TORONTO STAR, May. 27, 2005, at A8.

[25]

BUILDING A BRIDGE
Lessons Learned From Family Mediation Training for the Hmong Community of Minnesota

James R. Coben

This article examines how family mediation training was used to construct a bridge between cultural and legal norms in an attempt to help heal a community struggling with assimilation challenges.

"Should the shamans be mediators?" Not a routine question overheard by a family mediation trainer during a lunch break. But then, this was not the usual mediation training. For five days in mid-December 2001, a joint project of the Dispute Resolution Institute at Hamline University School of Law, the Mediation Center for Dispute Resolution, and Merit Translations, Inc. brought together twenty-eight elders from eighteen Hmong clans, mediation trainers, and several Ramsey County family court referees to explore how mediation might be used to help reconcile Hmong cultural traditions and Minnesota divorce law.

Even in America, which is known as a "melting pot" of diverse immigrant communities, it is difficult to conceive of a more radical transition than that experienced by the Hmong in their move from the mountains of Laos to the cities of the United States. Enlisted by the Central Intelligence Agency (CIA) to fight America's secret war in Laos during the Vietnam War era, the Hmong suffered mightily, ultimately becoming a community of refugees forced to seek new lands following the Pathet Lao communist takeover of Laos in May 1975.[1] In the intervening twenty-seven years, the Hmong have been forced to adapt from their centuries-old tradition of nomadic "slash-and-burn" agriculture; complete political autonomy; and tightly structured, patrilineal clan society to life in the heart of America's metropolitan areas—industrialized, high tech, heavily regulated (especially for refugees initially caught up in the welfare bureaucracy), and defined by individual rather than community achievement. The Hmong brought with them one of history's most astounding traditions of cultural independence and separateness.

Mediation trainings often end with participants and teachers sharing in a closing circle the insights and lessons learned. But few such events are as full of joyful tears, hope, and awareness of the challenges to come as the circle ending this unique training effort. In the words of training organizer Sia Lo, newly appointed deputy city attorney in Saint Paul,

> Here in America, Hmong culture is like a gold bracelet that has fallen onto the ground. It is dirty. Many in my generation don't want to wear it and don't believe the elders who have held it have anything to offer us. But the week together has taught me there is much wisdom in this room that makes me proud to inherit the jewelry. Our tears fall now to clean away the dirt. Our challenge is to fix the bracelet so it can be worn with pride in a new country, where we can thrive respecting both American law and Hmong cultural traditions.[2]

Like the trainees, Mr. Lo made his comments in the Hmong language; his words, and those of others throughout the training, were simultaneously interpreted for those of us involved who did not speak Hmong. Our comments in English were consecutively interpreted into Hmong for the benefit of all participants.[3]

At one level, the forty-hour training provided a state-mandated curriculum that family mediators must complete before they can join the roster of neutrals maintained by the Minnesota state supreme court;[4] roster listing makes one eligible to accept court referrals for mediation of divorce and child custody matters.[5] Framed narrowly, the training focused on how to conduct mediation, defined by Minnesota district court rule as "a forum in which a neutral third party facilitates communication between parties to promote settlement. A mediator may not impose his or her own judgment on the issues for that of the parties."[6]

But as the training week progressed, it became apparent we were doing something more; together, we were constructing a bridge between cultural and legal norms in an attempt to help heal a community struggling with assimilation challenges. Of course, the mediation process is itself a bridge—"a time, place, or means of connection or transition."[7] For the Hmong, given their incredibly tumultuous historical journey in the latter half of the twentieth century, a bridge is a particularly apt metaphor.

A BRIEF HISTORY

For at least five thousand years, the Hmong were a known minority and distinct cultural group indigenous to China. Theirs is a history marked by violence, rebellion, and two incompatible desires: the Hmong people's wish for independence and autonomy and the conflicting wish of the Chinese ruling dynasties for subjugation and control of resident populations.[8]

Hmong society is tightly structured into patrilineal clans; eighteen clans constitute the Hmong community now present in Minnesota.[9] According to Yang Dao, a world-renowned scholar and educator, "children are considered members of their father's clan and take its name. . . . A clan is considered a male ancestor, his sons and daughters, and the children of his sons."[10] Wives retain their maiden name but at the same time become members of the husband's clan.[11]

Within clans, leadership roles are assumed and power is exercised by implied consent rather than by formal election.[12] Power is revoked by noncompliance of family members.[13] Between clans, the relationship "follows the doctrine of laissez-faire, incorporating a practice similar to the doctrine of good faith and credit as found among the states in the United States."[14] Clans generally do not intervene in the internal affairs of another except on request; all will respect the finality of other clans' decisions on internal matters.[15] Disputes between clans are resolved through negotiation and mutual agreement, with nondisputing clan leaders sometimes playing the role of impartial parties.[16] Clan elders are accorded tremendous respect and power. A Hmong proverb ably makes the case: "they have eaten more rice, they have seen more things, and they have done more thinking."[17]

Clan solidarity has historically been the counterweight to the absence of official administration and involvement in government or social structures.[18] As a migrating, oft-persecuted, minority culture, "the main reason for the traditionalism of their aspirations is the self-defensive reflex of the group, which, in order to ensure its survival, must oppose any drain of resources or energies on the part of its members."[19] As noted by sociologist William Robert Geddes,

> the preservation by the Miao [Hmong] of their ethnic identity for such a long time despite their being split into many small groups surrounded by different alien people and scattered over a vast geographic area is an outstanding record paralleling in some ways that of the Jews but more remarkable because they lacked the unifying forces of literacy and a doctrinal religion and because the features they preserved seem to be more numerous.[20]

Migration and the resulting alienation and separateness is a constant theme in Hmong history. Their slash-and-burn agricultural methods necessitated leaving depleted fields. Their tight clan structure sometimes forced movement for social organization reasons, such as a minority clan feeling too isolated by a dominant clan or when imbalances in clan numbers made it increasingly difficult to find appropriate spouses from other clans. Epidemics and war posed additional reasons to migrate. In the early 1800s, ongoing attempts by Chinese authorities to control and tax led to a mass exodus from China to Laos of as many as five hundred thousand Hmong.[21]

In Laos, the Hmong settled in the mountains, steering clear of the Lao populations.[22] French colonial attempts to tax the Hmong at the end of the 19th century caused yet another Hmong rebellion.[23] In 1920, tired of an unwinnable battle, the French gave the Hmong a form of administrative independence.[24] Several decades of relative peace were to follow.[25]

Things changed in late 1949 when the communist Pathet Lao was formed and aligned with the Viet Minh in Vietnam.[26] The United States began covert operations in Laos as early as 1957 to fight this communist insurgency.[27] In the two decades to follow, the CIA effort in Laos would become the largest CIA operation in the world, fought virtually entirely by a Hmong proxy army recruited because of their reputation as ferocious fighters and their political independence.[28] The highlands occupied by the Hmong were especially critical for U.S. military strategists.[29] Through these highlands ran a Vietnamese supply line popularly known as the "Ho Chi Minh Trail," the lynchpin of communist logistics.[30]

The devastation inflicted on this region in the name of cutting a supply line is beyond comprehension. Moreover, at the time, it also was beyond the knowledge of anyone in the West but those few with top national security clearances.[31] According to historian Keith Quincy,

> on average, American aircraft dropped a bomb every eight minutes, twenty four hours a day, eventually delivering more than two million tons of explosives—fifteen hundred pounds for every man, woman, and child in the country, making Laos the most heavily bombed nation in history.[32]

More than 35,000 Hmong were killed in battle—a death rate equal to the United States losing 16.5 million soldiers (rather than the actual 57,000-plus who perished in Vietnam);[33] nearly one-third of the Hmong population perished from disease and starvation.[34] A community that took great pride in self-sufficiency and independence found many of its members reduced to being in-country refugees, dependent on U.S. Agency for International Development airdrops of rice to stave off starvation.[35]

In May 1975, the Pathet Lao backed by North Vietnamese troops occupied the major cities of Laos and seized control of the country.[36] Unlike the secrecy that had been the hallmark of the Hmong/CIA collaboration, the ensuing attack on the Hmong was not at all a clandestine affair. Quite to the contrary, "on May 9, the KHAO XANE PATHET LAO, the newspaper of the Lao People's Party, announced: 'the Meo [Hmong] must be exterminated down to the root of the tribe.' "[37] While some Hmong began a guerilla resistance that continues to this day, many were forced into "reeducation" camps.[38] Within ten years, half of all Hmong had fled the country; by 1988, 130,000 had crossed into Thailand.[39]

A hand-woven story cloth in my office tells this phase of the history with graphic simplicity: in the upper right, Pathet Lao soldiers and airplanes destroy Hmong villages; at upper left, a Pathet Lao helicopter spreads poison on Hmong crops; in the center, villagers take only what they can carry on their back during a perilous, month-long walk to the Mekong River, where they then swim, raft, or (if really fortunate) boat to the relative safety of refugee camps in Thailand. At bottom left, they board buses at the beginning of a journey to a new country. Of course, the reality of this monumental trek is a much harsher narrative, far beyond the scope of this short article.

With a history of rebellion by its own indigenous sixty-thousand Hmong, Thai authorities were not enthusiastic supporters of the refugee effort.[40] Only by significant American pressure was an initial CIA airlift of approximately twenty-four thousand Hmong permitted.[41] Hmong who later reached the Thai border on foot were turned away at gunpoint until additional agreements brokered by the United Nations High Commissioner of Refugees in July 1975 led to the creation of twenty-one temporary camps.[42]

The resettlement of refugees to the United States began slowly. In May 1975, immediately following the communist takeover of Laos, General Vang Pao, the Hmong military leader, had come directly to the United States, together with a small group of approximately 500.[43] A year later, 5,000 refugees were permitted entry;[44] in 1980, 25,000 gained entry.[45] All told, it is estimated that 130,000 Hmong have now resettled in the United States.[46] Today, St. Paul, Minnesota, the location of our mediation training, has more Hmong than any other U.S. city—24,400 according to 2000 census figures, with an official statewide Hmong population of 41,800.[47]

Resettlement of these mountain farmers in a flat city like St. Paul, with its harsh winter, is one of history's most bizarre ironies. Of course, Immigration and Naturalization Service (INS) bureaucrats, not known for sensitivity to irony, were merely following a well-established refugee policy known as "dispersal"—which posits that no single American community should be overtaxed by the arrival of too many refugees.[48] It was logical, therefore, from the INS perspective, to scatter the Hmong to fifty-three cities in twenty-five different states.[49]

Not surprisingly, the Hmong refugee community has seen tremendously high rates of migration and population concentration[50] after the initial "dispersal" resettlement. One driving force is the dynamics of Hmong family law.

HMONG FAMILY LAW BASICS

In Hmong culture, "what counts is most often the group—the family, the clan—rather than the individual, whose sojourn on earth is a brief one."[51] Marriage is not only critical in the balance of relationships between clans, it is itself a relationship of clans rather than simply a contracted relationship between an individual husband and wife.[52]

In Laos, early marriages (ages eighteen to twenty for boys, fourteen to sixteen for girls) and high birth rates were an economic necessity given the agricultural and nomadic lifestyles.[53] While the economic motivation for these traditions are absent in the United States, cultural momentum still supports the notion that married people with children are considered most worthy of respect and status. Underage, culturally brokered marriages are still quite common, reflecting a Hmong cultural norm that "girls are pressured to marry at the mere suspicion of a sexual relationship or else bring shame to the family."[54] Likewise, the Hmong birthrate in the United States continues to be among the highest in the world.[55]

Although monogamy is the rule, polygamy has always been part of Hmong culture, especially for clan leaders, as has the tradition of *levirate*—the practice of a younger brother marrying a widowed sister-in-law.[56] Both polygamy and levirate were on the decline prior to the war years, but the grim combination of thousands of dead soldiers and large numbers of widows by necessity revived both traditions.[57]

Marriage traditionally occurs in a number of ways but most commonly by negotiations between families brokered by intermediaries known as *Mej Koob* (pronounced *may kong*).[58] Even today, a vast majority of all Hmong in Minnesota marry in this manner.[59] The percentage of the community that goes on to legally solemnize and record a marriage is unknown.[60] Failure to do so, of course, leaves Hmong vulnerable to complex legal disputes about marital status in connection with family law, insurance, social security, and pension matters.[61]

Underage marriage is tolerated, in part because competency of the contracting individual parties is not the fundamental issue it is under American family law; in Hmong culture, it is the clan elders and parents who contract the marriage, just as much or more so than the individual spouses.[62] However, consistent with contemporary American family law, cultural prohibitions limit marriages between brothers and sisters and, for that matter, between any members of the same clan.[63]

Marriage negotiations typically begin after an informal proposal between a prospective husband and wife.[64] However, elopement also occurs in Hmong society, especially in those cases where the children suspect or know that parental consent to the marriage is unlikely.[65] There also is a practice known as "marriage by capture," which thankfully occurs relatively rarely in the United States, given the Hmong community's growing awareness that it is prohibited by kidnapping and sexual assault statutes.[66]

If an informal marriage proposal is accepted, the prospective husband then seeks consent of his parents, who in turn will arrange for the Mej Koob to take a formal marriage proposal to the wife's parents.[67] Mej Koob are then also chosen by the wife's family; together, the selected intermediaries negotiate terms of the marriage.[68]

Chief among the issues to be decided is a "bride price"—a payment from the husband's family to the wife's family.[69] The payment represents two things: "a symbolic recognition of the hardship of raising the girl, and . . . a consideration for a promise of love."[70] According to the elders, it is not uncommon for bride prices to approach $10,000, though most are for lesser amounts.[71] Marriage negotiations also discuss consequences for breach of the mutual promises made in marriage and may formalize in advance dissolution remedies.[72] Typically, should a husband breach his promise to love and care for his wife, for example by committing adultery or domestic violence, the money would be forfeited upon divorce.[73] Conversely, should a wife commit adultery or some other grave offense against the marriage, her clan may have to return the bride price in full or in part.[74]

Once married, a wife becomes a member of the husband's clan.[75] As noted by Yang Dao, "because of the practice of clan exogamy, the same rule that cements the unity of the group also leads to its partial dissolution when its daughters marry."[76] Traditionally, all of the property that each spouse brings to the marriage is considered marital; while a wife shares a joint interest in all marital property, she cannot transfer her interest without her husband's consent.[77]

Like marriage, divorce also is a negotiated process with decision making dominated by clan elders, not the individual spouses.[78] Until the disruption caused by the war in Laos, divorce was quite uncommon.[79] A failed marriage was seen not only as a failure of the spouses (particularly the wives) but of their wider families and the clans themselves.[80] Moreover, since Hmong divorce is fault-based, there was tremendous incentive to reconcile marriages as a way to avoid the inevitable discord between clans that a fault-finding process would necessitate.[81] Until the dislocation of war, these social pressures were sufficient by themselves to keep the divorce rate low.[82]

Disposition of property at dissolution, in particular status of the "bride price" contracted at the time of marriage, turn on fault determinations.[83] Custody decisions, although also subject to fault concepts, are dominated by a single central value: how identity—clan lineage—of the children can best be preserved.[84] Given the patrilineal structure of Hmong society, this means an inevitable preference for paternal custody, especially of male children. Visitation by a noncustodial parent would be unusual; likewise, it would be unheard of for a noncustodial parent to have a support obligation.[85]

To say the least, these centuries-old traditions of marriage and divorce, with clan rather than individual decision making at their heart, do not mesh neatly with principles of contemporary Minnesota family law. That body of law, which had evolved relatively slowly over several decades to finally provide at least some measure of gender equity, was superimposed on a culture as patriarchal as they come, with no time for adjustment or acclimatization. As the second millennium reached its end, the Hmong in Minnesota were a community in crisis.

ORIGINS OF THE MEDIATION PROJECT

Beginning in the late 1990s, a series of highly publicized crimes of violence rocked the Hmong community.[86] In September 1998, a Hmong woman deeply traumatized by domestic violence killed her six children and attempted suicide.[87] In 2000, there were multiple shootings in which Hmong men killed themselves, four women were fatally shot, and twenty-five children were left without one or both parents.[88] The year ended with a contract killing over a child support dispute and a murder suicide.[89]

At uncharacteristic rates, the Hmong are divorcing.[90] Hmong children are disproportionately represented in juvenile court.[91] Underage marriage is leading to Hmong men being prosecuted for criminal sexual conduct and risking deportation.[92] Domestic violence also is alarmingly prevalent, exacerbated but certainly not in any way excused by the stresses of assimilation, language barriers, lack of education, and inability to find work.[93]

Luckily, these profoundly disturbing trends are matched by some achievements worth celebrating, giving reason for hope. First, a new generation of highly successful and highly educated Hmong professional men and women are taking leadership roles throughout the community. On February 4, 2002, Hmong woman Mee Moua was sworn in as the first Hmong state senator in the United States, representing St. Paul's diverse east side in the Minnesota legislature.[94] A month earlier, the first public act of the incoming St. Paul city attorney was to appoint Hmong man Sia Lo as deputy city attorney, with oversight of the criminal division.[95] Second, Hmong entrepreneurs are leading an economic revitalization of key parts of the city. Third, the Hmong United International Council, one of the leading Hmong nonprofit mutual assistance organizations, recently reorganized.[96] The agency is governed by a board representative of each of the eighteen clans that make up the Minnesota Hmong community, including men and women Hmong leaders. Finally, a core group of Ramsey County district court judges and family court referees have reached out to the community, making real an oft-pronounced, but rarely acted upon, quest for cultural literacy and understanding.[97]

The time was ripe for some constructive dialogue. Unfortunately, past invitations to engage have not always been warmly extended. Take, for example, this harsh editorial in the *St. Paul Pioneer Press* from 1998:

> If these tragedies are to stop, change must come from within the Hmong community and it must begin soon. Wise clan leaders whose directives carry weight in the Hmong culture could convey urgent messages that domestic abuse is not permitted here, that bigamy is not permitted here, that girls 12 or 13 years of age should not get married. It comes as no surprise that youngsters born and raised in the United States rebel against a centuries-old Laotian tradition that demands they become breeding vehicles at the age of 12 and produce numerous children in order to extend their husband's clan.[98]

By 2001, the elders were indeed ready to deliver these messages. The Hmong United International Council of Minnesota decided that one way to do so was through family mediation training.[99]

BUILDING THE BRIDGE

In January, 2001, Sia Lo and Ong Lo, the two Hmong interpreters mentioned at the beginning of this article, attended a forty-hour family mediation training presented by the Mediation Center for Dispute Resolution. They then worked with Center Director Aimee Gourlay and with me to adapt the training schedule, course content, and training simulations to be relevant for Hmong families. Knowing that language barriers would be profound, we decided to do much of the mediation practice in large group rather than in the more intimate three-person role-play groupings often used in family mediation training. We purposely provided opportunity for dialogue on those areas where Hmong tradition and contemporary family law diverge.

At the same time, we built into the process presentations by the judiciary and law professors to emphasize that some subjects were not open to cultural relativity. Specifically, four themes were repeatedly emphasized: domestic violence cannot be tolerated or negotiated, "self-help" to seize property or enforce judicial decisions is prohibited, bigamy is illegal, and underage marriages are voidable.

For a few participants, the week-long training was the first school of any kind they had attended. For many others, it was a first exposure to American law. Of course, by design, the education and learning went in two directions. Trainers offered up a model of facilitative mediation and an introduction to the basics of Minnesota family law. Trainees offered an introduction to Hmong traditions and explained the painful challenges of assimilation.

Six main themes emerged. First, no-fault divorce is a very difficult concept to overlay on a centuries-old fault tradition. No surprises here. Indeed, one of the first spans in the construction of our "bridge" was confirming that most Minnesotans going through divorce (not just members of the Hmong community) have trouble with this concept! It was reassuring for the elders to hear that mediators frequently assist couples to address fault, both as the emotional prerequisite to effective problem solving and because many couples are eager to create their own "norms" for deciding fairness in ending their marriage. In short, mediation provides a forum to discuss fault and, with mutual agreement, structure settlements that reflect it.

Second, the elders repeatedly emphasized that marriage and divorce are clan, not simply individual, issues. Since the clans negotiated the marriage in the first place, they argued, they should be meaningful participants in the divorce. As it is now, the elders may spend hours and hours negotiating divorces only to find that the brokered deal is rejected by the "cultural" loser who then seeks redress in the family court system.

Several significant points emerged from this discussion. The elders were able to share their frustration over the alienation of Hmong youth from their past. As the younger generation lives more independently, there is less incentive to heed the clan and less consequence for failing to be bound by its rulings or recommendations.

At the same time, like all mediation trainees, the Hmong elders grappled mightily with the distinction between arbitration and mediation. By midweek, many were expressing their realization that culturally brokered deals were "falling apart" because they were imposed as arbitral decisions. Facilitative mediation, at least theoretically, provides a vehicle for getting input from elders and increasing understanding of cultural norms to help inform, but not necessarily dictate, divorce settlements. Moreover, mediation can be structured to formally include a role for extended family, participation that often is foreclosed in court, other than for offering up polarizing testimony.

Third, we explored how divorcing couples from all communities may experience a tension between their "court-ordered future" and their "actual future."[100] Couples dissatisfied with court rulings often create their own rules (sometimes by agreement and sometimes not), suggesting that court-ordered finality in the chaos of postdivorce family dynamics is a myth. For Hmong families, this tension may be especially profound because of the possibility of dramatic differences in the terms of their cultural and legal divorces.

Fourth, there was considerable discussion about the mixed roles elders are called on to perform. Above all else, they are a voice for reconciliation. Another span in our bridge was sharing that all players in the family court system—lawyers, judges, social workers, guardians, mediators—encourage reconciliation. But we also conveyed a message that once the decision is made by a couple to divorce, the task of these court professionals is to assist in the decision making necessary to secure the divorce, not to lobby to save the marriage. By the end of the week, it was fascinating to hear trainees describing their own version of a multidoor courthouse—one where the Hmong Council provides neutral services in a way that keeps reconciliation, arbitration, and mediation functions distinct.

Fifth, we explored how mediation provides a forum to consider a host of issues that would not be addressed at law. For example, a parent who wants his or her spouse to pay for a child's college education cannot obtain a court order compelling payment as part of a divorce. In Minnesota, there is no statutory or common-law authority for the judge to so rule. But parties are free to seek agreement on such issues in mediation and have their agreements entered as an order of the court. Thus, the wide range of issues that are part of Hmong divorce but not recognized at law can certainly be discussed and resolved in mediation, including such things as payment obligations between clans (including "bride price" disposition), responsibility for burial of parents, or financial obligations for cultural celebrations.

Finally, we began but certainly did not finish a conversation addressing some of the value conflicts emerging out of a comparison of cultural and legal norms. For example, the disinclination of Minnesota judges to award split custody is inconsistent with Hmong cultural preference to sometimes split custody along gender lines. The IV-D child support system, which mechanically applies child support guidelines based on an obligor's net income to set the presumptively correct support amount, fails utterly to account for a cultural tradition that would assign a custodial parent full responsibility to support a child. For a community that continues to be highly mobile (especially on divorce), the presumption favoring a move out of state by a custodial parent exacerbates the disconnect between Minnesota's multifactor "best interests" approach to custody adjudication and the Hmong unidimensional cultural emphasis on clan identity.

In the end, we are left on the horns of a classic dilemma. There is no way to escape the reality that mandating acknowledgment and incorporation of Hmong cultural norms into divorce would inevitably "favor" fathers and husbands. At the same time, simply ignoring cultural norms and traditions altogether means continued generational alienation and dislocation. The Hmong mother and wife who successfully asserts the full panoply of rights in the American legal system also continues as a member of a larger Hmong community. The collective hope is that through mediation, cultural norms can be considered in a way that makes the journey of divorce a little easier for everyone involved.

This hope is tempered by concern for gender equity, well captured in the following e-mail I received from a former law student who had read publicity about the training in the local papers:

> I was very interested to read about the recent certification of a group of Hmong elders as family law mediators. I continue to devote my pro bono hours exclusively to the representation of Hmong women in family law matters. Clan meetings regarding the marriages have never really been fruitful, and sadly enough my clients have experienced lots of pressure to return to bad situations. I'm really hopeful about this new tool . . . do you know where I can get a complete list of the recently trained mediators/addresses/phones etc.?[101]

Of course, the strength of this bridge will be measured as it ages. As a result of the training, twenty-eight Hmong elders are now on the roster of neutrals maintained by the Minnesota State Supreme Court.[102] Several Ramsey County family court referees already are referring cases to these newly trained mediators. Planning is under way for additional training and technical assistance as the Hmong Council of Minnesota moves forward to create a viable multidoor private courthouse, one in which mediation will be used to complement the traditional arbitral and reconciliation functions of clan elders. I am humbled enough from my initial week of training to know that I cannot anticipate what all the questions will be as we move forward, let alone know all the answers.

Speaking of answers, the trainees during their lunch break concluded after a spirited (no pun intended) discussion that shamans should not be mediators. The interpreter's summary of the group consensus went something like this:

> Shamans' schedules are wildly unpredictable. Without advance notice and with great urgency, they can be called upon at any time to perform needed spirit ceremonies. They might not return for hours. This will make it impossible to efficiently schedule mediations and manage a caseload. It just wouldn't be fair to mediation consumers.[103]

In retrospect, I might have guessed the right answer. I never would have guessed the rationale. And, that in a nutshell, is why building a bridge, and working together to maintain it, is so important.

NOTES

1. A number of recently published books detail this political history, including Jane Hamilton-Merritt, Tragic Mountains: The Hmong, the Americans, and the Secret Wars for Laos, 1942-1992 (Indiana University Press, 1999); and Keith Quincy, Harvesting Pa Chay's Wheat: The Hmong and America's Secret War in Laos

(Eastern Washington University Press, 2000). For a wonderful but heart-breaking narrative describing the profound disconnect between Hmong and American medical traditions, *see* ANNE FADIMAN, THE SPIRIT CATCHES YOU AND YOU FALL DOWN: A HMONG CHILD, HER AMERICAN DOCTORS, AND THE COLLISION OF TWO CULTURES (Farrar, Straus and Giroux, 1997).

2. Statement of Deputy City Attorney Sia Lo in closing circle on the last of five days of mediation training, 21 December 2001.

3. The training would have been impossible without the tireless efforts of Mr. Lo and his sister Ong Lo, two of the most acclaimed Hmong/English legal interpreters in Minnesota. The quote attributed here to Mr. Lo, and others cited later in this article, are based solely on my notes of the event. Unfortunately, my reconstruction fails to convey my perception throughout the training that the elders, as well as Mr. Lo and Ms. Lo, spoke poetically, which to my amazement was captured even in the simultaneous translation into English.

4. Minn. Gen. Prac. Rule 114.13(c) (2001).

5. Minn. Gen. Prac. Rule 114.05(b) (2001) (requiring judges to appoint only those mediators listed on the court-maintained roster of neutrals).

6. Minn. Gen. Prac. Rule 114.02(a)(7) (2001).

7. WEBSTER'S NINTH NEW COLLEGIATE DICTIONARY (1983).

8. See generally Fadiman, *supra* note 1, at 13-19; and Quincy, *supra* note 1, at 23-29.

9. Consensus of the Hmong elders at the mediation training, 17-21 December 2001 (hereafter, Consensus of Hmong Elders). See also Todd Nelson, *Hmong Marriage Legislation Comes Undone*, ST. PAUL PIONEER PRESS 1A (March 3, 2002).

10. YANG DAO, HMONG AT THE TURNING POINT 23 (WorldBridge Associates, 1993).

11. *Id.*

12. Christopher T. Thao, *Hmong Customs on Marriage, Divorce and the Rights of Married Women*, THE HMONG WORLD, VOL. 1, 76 (Yale Center for International and Area Studies, 1986).

13. *Id.*

14. *Id.*

15. *Id.*

16. *Id.*

17. Dao, *supra* note 10, at 24.

18. *Id.*, at 82.

19. *Id.*

20. WILLIAM ROBERT GEDDES, MIGRANTS OF THE MOUNTAINS: THE CULTURAL ECOLOGY OF THE BLUE MIAO (HMONG NJUA) OF THAILAND (Clarendon, 1976), at 10.

21. Dao, *supra* note 10, at xiv; Fadiman, *supra* note 1, at 16-17.

22. *Id.*

23. Fadiman, *supra* note 1, at 16.

24. *Id.*, at 17.

25. *Id.*

26. Hamilton-Meritt, *supra* note 1, at 49.

27. Quincy, *supra* note 1, at 3.

28. *Id.*, at 3-5.

29. *Id.*, at 1-2.

30. *Id.*, at 3.

31. Fadiman, *supra* note 1, at 126; Quincy, *supra* note 1, at 3-5.

32. *Id.*

33. *Id.*, at 5.

34. *Id.*

35. Dao, *supra* note 10, at 80-81 (caption on photo).

36. Quincy, *supra* note 1, at 6.

37. Fadiman, *supra* note 1, at 138.

38. *Id.*, at 158-59; Quincy, *supra* note 1, at 6.

39. *Id.*

40. *Id.*, at 459.

41. *Id.*

42. *Id.*

43. *Id.*, at 446.

44. *Id.*

45. Fadiman, *supra* note 1, at 167.

46. Quincy, *supra* note 1, at 6.

47. Todd Nelson, *Hmong Elders Now Official Mediators: Courts Can Refer Marriage Disputes to Them*, ST. PAUL PIONEER PRESS B1 (27 January 2002). Precensus estimates had put the statewide count at sixty to eighty thousand, suggesting a census undercount. See Todd Nelson, *Hmong Seeks to End Plague of Domestic Violence: Answers Sought in Summits with Elders, within Traditions, in Western-Style Counseling*, ST. PAUL PIONEER PRESS 1A (10 December 2000) (noting population estimate of seventy thousand); and Joy Powell, *Help Is Nearby, Hmong Leaders Advise Turning to Elders, and Kin Can Prevent Domestic Disputes from Escalating into Violence*, STAR TRIBUNE 1B (7 December 2000) (noting population estimate of sixty to eighty thousand).

48. Fadiman, *supra* note 1, at 185.

49. *Id.*

50. According to the 2000 census, there are currently only eighteen counties with Hmong populations greater than one thousand.

51. Dao, *supra* note 10, at 22.

52. Consensus of Hmong Elders, *supra* note 9; Thao, *supra* note 12, at 75-76.

53. Dao, *supra* note 10, at 22.

54. Matt Peiken, *A Generation Lost? Five Hmong in the Pioneer Press Class of 2000 Are Caught between Cultures and Are Entering Adulthood without Clear Directions or Identities*, ST. PAUL PIONEER PRESS 1A (9 April 2000).

55. According to Fadiman, *supra* note 1, at 72, "in the mid-eighties, the fertility rate of Hmong women in America was 9.5 children, which, according to one study, was 'at the upper limits of human reproductive capacity,' second only to the Hutterites."

56. Consensus of Hmong Elders, *supra* note 9; Fadiman, *supra* note 1, at 135; Dao, *supra* note 10, at 22-23.

57. *Id.*

58. Consensus of Hmong Elders, *supra* note 9; see also Nelson, *supra* note 9.

59. *Id.*

60. See Nelson, *supra* note 9, detailing the recent demise of legislation introduced this year in both the Minnesota House (H.F. 2826) and Senate (S.F. 3368) that would have amended Minn. Stat. § 517.18 to recognize marriages solemnized by Hmong Mej Koob.

61. Indeed, a Wisconsin appeals court recently certified the following appeal question to the state's supreme court:

> Under Wis. Stat. § 895.04, when the father survives, may the children of an ethnic Hmong couple bring a wrongful death claim for the death of their mother by asserting that their parents' marriage, performed according to traditional Hmong ceremonial rites in Laos in 1975, is not valid? (*Xiong v. Xiong*, no. 01-0844, 2002 WL 207523 [Wis. Ct. App., 12 February 2002]).

62. Consensus of Hmong Elders, *supra* note 9.

63. *Id.*

64. *Id.*

65. *Id.*

66. Choua Ly, *The Conflict between Law and Culture: The Case of the Hmong in America*, WISCONSIN LAW REVIEW 478-81 (2001).

67. Consensus of Hmong Elders, *supra* note 9; Thao, *supra* note 12, at 78.

68. *Id.*

69. Consensus of Hmong Elders, *supra* note 9.

70. Thao, *supra* note 12, at 79-80.

71. Consensus of Hmong Elders, *supra* note 9; see also Interview with Deputy City Attorney Sia Lo, 17 April 2002 (notes on file with author).

72. *Id.*; see also Thao, *supra* note 12, at 78-80.

73. *Id.*

74. *Id.*

75. Dao, *supra* note 10, at 23.

76. *Id.*

77. Thao, *supra* note 12, at 85.

78. Consensus of Hmong Elders, *supra* note 9.

79. *Id.*

80. *Id.*

81. *Id.*

82. *Id.*

83. *Id.*; Thao, *supra* note 12, at 83.

84. Thao, *supra* note 12, at 96.

85. Consensus of Hmong Elders, *supra* note 9.

86. Nelson (10 December 2000), *supra* note 47.

87. *Id.*

88. *Id.*

89. *Id.*

90. Consensus of Hmong Elders, *supra* note 9.

91. Speech by newly appointed St. Paul City Attorney Manuel Cervantes made at the training on 18 December 2001 (notes on file with author).

92. *Id.*

93. *Id.*; see also Nelson (10 December 2000), *supra* note 47.

94. Bill Salisbury, *Mee Moua: "We Really Belong Here': Moua's Swearing-In a National First*, St. Paul Pioneer Press A1 (5 February 2002).

95. Paul Gustafson, *St. Paul's Kelly Makes Two More Key Appointments; Don Luna Is Named City Clerk; Sia Lo Will Be Lead Prosecutor*, St. Paul Pioneer Press 9B (29 December 2001).

96. Sia Lo interview, *supra* note 71.

97. Consensus of Hmong Elders, *supra* note 9; see also Paul Gustafson, *Lawrence Cohen: A Positive Force on the Bench; the Former St. Paul Mayor Has Avoided Cynicism As Ramsey County's Chief Judge*, Star Tribune 1B (2 January 2002).

98. Editorial, St. Paul Pioneer Press 6A (29 September 1998).

99. Sia Lo interview, *supra* note 71.

100. See Nina Meierding, *Religion, Rituals, and Mediation*, Family Mediation News, 6 (Fall 2001).

101. E-mail received on 29 January 2002 from one of my former law students, now a practicing attorney in Minneapolis (copy on file with author).

102. Sia Lo interview, *supra* note 71. Neutral roster applications were completed by all participants on the last day of the training.

103. Summary of group consensus translated to author by interpreter Ong Lo during lunch break in the training on 19 December 2001.

James R. Coben is a clinical professor and director of the Dispute Resolution Institute at Hamline University School of Law in St. Paul, Minnesota.

Name Index

Ollscoil na hÉireann, Gaillimh
3 1111 40183 6166